FEMINIST JUDGMENTS

Reproductive justice (RJ) is a pivotal movement that supplants the language and limitations of reproductive rights. RJ's tenets are that women have the human rights to decide if or when they'll become pregnant, whether to carry a pregnancy to term, and to parent the children they have in safe and healthy environments. Recognizing the importance of the rights at stake when the law addresses parenting and procreation, the authors in this book re-imagine judicial opinions that address the law's treatment of pregnancy and parenting. The cases cover topics such as forced sterilization, pregnancy discrimination, criminal penalties for women who take illegal drugs while pregnant, and state funding for abortion. Though some of the re-imagined cases come to the same conclusions as the originals, each rewritten opinion analyzes how these cases impact the most vulnerable populations, including people with disabilities, poor women, and women of color.

KIMBERLY M. MUTCHERSON is Dean and Professor of Law at Rutgers Law School in Camden. She is an expert in reproductive justice and the law and the 2013 recipient of a Center for Reproductive Rights Innovation in Scholarship Award. She received her B.A. from the University of Pennsylvania and her J.D. from Columbia Law School.

Feminist Judgments Series Editors

Bridget J. Crawford
Elisabeth Haub School of Law at Pace University

Kathryn M. Stanchi
University of Nevada Law Vegas William S. Boyd School of Law

Linda L. Berger
University of Nevada, Las Vegas William S. Boyd School of Law

Advisory Panel for Feminist Judgments Series

Feminist Judgments: Reproductive Justice Rewritten

Edited by

KIMBERLY M. MUTCHERSON

Rutgers Law School

CAMBRIDGE
UNIVERSITY PRESS

University Printing House, Cambridge CB2 8BS, United Kingdom

One Liberty Plaza, 20th Floor, New York, NY 10006, USA

477 Williamstown Road, Port Melbourne, VIC 3207, Australia

314–321, 3rd Floor, Plot 3, Splendor Forum, Jasola District Centre, New Delhi – 110025, India

79 Anson Road, #06–04/06, Singapore 079906

Cambridge University Press is part of the University of Cambridge.

It furthers the University's mission by disseminating knowledge in the pursuit of education, learning, and research at the highest international levels of excellence.

www.cambridge.org
Information on this title: www.cambridge.org/9781108425438
DOI: 10.1017/9781108348409

First published 2020

Printed in the United Kingdom by TJ International Ltd., Padstow, Cornwall

A catalogue record for this publication is available from the British Library.

Library of Congress Cataloging-in-Publication Data
NAMES: Mutcherson, Kimberly M., 1972– editor.
TITLE: Feminist judgments : reproductive justice rewritten / edited by Kimberly M. Mutcherson, Rutgers University, New Jersey.
OTHER TITLES: Feminist judgments (Reproductive justice) Description: Cambridge, United Kingdom ; New York, NY, USA : Cambridge University Press, 2020. | Series: Feminist judgment series | Includes bibliographical references and index.
IDENTIFIERS: LCCN 2019042485 (print) | LCCN 2019042486 (ebook) | ISBN 9781108425438 (hardback) | ISBN 9781108442350 (paperback) | ISBN 9781108348409 (epub)
SUBJECTS: LCSH: Human reproduction–Law and legislation–United States–Cases. | Abortion–Law and legislation–United States–Cases. | Parent and child (Law)–United States–Cases. | Feminist jurisprudence–United States.
CLASSIFICATION: LCC KF3760 .F46 2020 (print) | LCC KF3760 (ebook) | DDC 342.7308/4–DC23
LC record available at https://lccn.loc.gov/2019042485
LC ebook record available at https://lccn.loc.gov/2019042486

ISBN 978-1-108-42543-8 Hardback
ISBN 978-1-108-44235-0 Paperback

I write for those women who do not speak, for those who do not have a voice because they were so terrified, because we are taught to respect fear more than ourselves. We've been taught that silence would save us, but it won't.

Audre Lorde

The thing about reproduction is that, more than anything else, it tells you how a society values people.

Dorothy Roberts

Contents

Advisory Panel

Jill E. Adams, Executive Director, If/When/How

Khiara M. Bridges, Professor of Law UC Berkeley School of Law

Judith Daar, Dean & Professor of Law, Northern Kentucky University Chase College of Law

Michele Goodwin, Chancellor's Professor of Law, Director, Center for Biotechnology and Global Health Policy, University of California, Irvine School of Law

Lisa Ikemoto, Martin Luther King Jr. Professor of Law, University of California, Davis, School of Law

Maya Manian, Visiting Professor, Howard University School of Law

Dorothy Roberts, George A. Weiss University Professor of Law and Sociology and the Raymond Pace and Sadie Tanner Mossell Alexander Professor of Civil Rights, University of Pennsylvania

Priscilla Smith, Clinical Lecturer in Law, Associate Research Scholar in Law, and Senior Fellow, Program for the Study of Reproductive Justice, Information Society Project, Yale Law School

Advisory Panel

Notes on Contributors

Aziza Ahmed is a Professor at Northeastern University School of Law and an expert in health law, criminal law, and human rights. Her scholarship has appeared in the *American Journal of Law and Medicine, University of Denver Law Review, Harvard Journal of Law and Gender,* and *Boston University Law Review* (online). Prior to joining Northeastern, Professor Ahmed was a Women's Law and Public Policy Fellow with the International Community of Women Living with HIV/AIDS. She has consulted with United Nations agencies and international and domestic non-governmental organizations.

Ann Cammett is the Senior Associate Dean of Academic Affairs and Professor of Law at CUNY School of Law. Before becoming Academic Dean, Professor Cammett directed the Family Law Practice Clinic. She is a recognized expert on the policy implications of incarcerated parents with child support arrears and other collateral consequences of criminal convictions. Prior to entering academia, Professor Cammett was a Skadden Fellow; served as the Reentry Policy Analyst for the New Jersey Institute for Social Justice; a Clinical Teaching Fellow in the Georgetown University Law Center's Domestic Violence Clinic; and a Women's Law and Public Policy Fellow.

Ederlina Co is a Professor at University of the Pacific McGeorge School of Law and teaches Reproductive Rights and Justice in the Prisoner Civil Rights Mediation Clinic and the Global Lawyering Skills program. She spent nearly a decade clerking for the Honorable Dale A. Drozd at the United States District Court for the Eastern District of California where she worked on prisoner civil rights cases. Prior to clerking, Professor Co was Counsel at NARAL Pro-Choice America where she spearheaded the Prevention First initiative and led NARAL's proactive policy efforts to reduce racial and ethnic disparities in reproductive health care.

David S. Cohen is a Professor of Law at the Drexel University Thomas R. Kline School of Law where he teaches courses in Constitutional Law, Reproductive

Rights and Justice, and Sex, Gender, and the Law. He is the coauthor of *Obstacle Course: The Everyday Struggle to Get an Abortion in America* (California 2020) and *Living in the Crosshairs: The Untold Stories of Anti-abortion Terrorism* (Oxford University Press 2015). He also writes about masculinity and sex segregation. David graduated from Columbia Law School and Dartmouth College.

Lisa A. Crooms-Robinson teaches Constitutional Law, Gender and the Law, and International Human Rights Law at the Howard University School of Law in Washington, D.C. Since 2012, she has also served as the Associate Dean of Academic Affairs. Crooms-Robinson serves on the board of the Center for Constitutional Rights and the U.S. Human Rights Network. She was a Fulbright Scholar at the Norman Manley Law School – University of the West Indies, as well as a visiting scholar at the Feminist Legal Theory Project at Emory University Law School.

Farah Diaz-Tello is a human rights attorney dedicated to the pursuit of reproductive justice, focusing on pregnancy and the full spectrum of pregnancy outcomes. She is Senior Counsel for the SIA Legal Team, where she uses litigation and policy strategies to ensure that people can make reproductive decisions with dignity and without punishment. Previously, Farah developed and directed programming in human rights and Birth Justice at National Advocates for Pregnant Women. Her writing for scholarly and popular press includes publications about obstetric violence and economic coercion during birth, criminalization of pregnancy, and mass media representation of reproductive justice issues.

Nancy E. Dowd is Professor and David Levin Chair in Family Law at the University of Florida Fredric Levin College of Law, and Emeritus Director of the Center on Children and Family. Her scholarship focuses on issues of children, family, race, gender, and inequality, and has delved into subjects including single parent families, fathers and fatherhood, juvenile justice, masculinities, and inequalities among children. Her most recent book is *Reimagining Equality: A New Deal for Children of Color* (2018).

Michele Gilman is the Venable Professor of Law and Director of Clinical Education at the University of Baltimore School of Law. She teaches in the Civil Advocacy Clinic, and also teaches Evidence and Administrative Law. Professor Gilman's scholarship on social welfare issues has appeared in journals including the *California Law Review*, the *Vanderbilt Law Review*, and the *Washington University Law Review*. She is a codirector of the Center on Applied Feminism, which works to apply feminist legal theory to legal practice and policy. She received her B.A. from Duke University and her J.D. from the University of Michigan Law School.

Michele Goodwin is a Chancellor's Professor at the University of California, Irvine and founder of the Center for Biotechnology & Global Health Policy. Her op-eds and commentary have appeared in the *New York Times, Los Angeles Times,*

Washington Post, *Politico*, and *Forbes*, among others. Her work has been highlighted on NPR, HBO's Vice, and in documentaries. She has published five books and dozens of articles, book chapters, and commentaries on law's regulation of the human body. Her scholarship is published in the *Yale Law Journal*, *Harvard Law Review*, *NYU Law Review*, *Cornell Law Review*, and *Georgetown Law Journal*, among others.

Meredith Johnson Harbach is Professor of Law at the University of Richmond School of Law, where she teaches courses in Family Law, Children & the Law, and Reproductive Justice. Her recent scholarship has analyzed and critiqued the state's relationship to families and children through the lens of America's childcare law and policy. She also writes on reproductive justice and state politics. She recently completed a three-year, gubernatorial appointment to the Virginia Council on Women, where she served as Chair of the Women's Healthcare Initiative.

Jasmine E. Harris is Professor of Law at the University of California–Davis School of Law and Martin Luther King, Jr. Hall Research Scholar. Her research lies at the intersection of disability rights and antidiscrimination law. Professor Harris is particularly concerned with the ways in which rules and procedures can change social norms in the context of disability. Her publications have or will appear in the *Columbia Law Review*, *New York University Law Review*, and *American University Law Review*, among others. Professor Harris received a J.D. from Yale Law School and A.B. from Dartmouth College.

Melanie B. Jacobs is the Senior Associate Dean and Professor of Law at Michigan State University College of Law. Her scholarship advocates for legal recognition of non-traditional families and changes to the traditional establishment of parent–child relationships due to the increased use of assisted reproduction. Her work has been featured in the *Buffalo Law Review*, *Arizona State Law Journal*, and *Yale Journal of Law & Feminism*. She is the 2018 recipient of the Donald F. Campbell Outstanding Teaching Award and was awarded an MSU Lilly Teaching Fellowship. She is a graduate of Boston University School of Law and Columbia University.

Margo Kaplan is a Professor of Law at Rutgers Law School, where she teaches courses on criminal law, health law and policy, and sex crimes. Her research explores legal limitations on intimate decisions, particularly the impact of criminal law in issues of sex and health. Professor Kaplan's publications have examined topics such as sex-positive law, sexual assault, pedophilia, HIV-exposure criminalization, and reproductive rights. Professor Kaplan has also explored these issues in op-eds and interviews for publications such as the *New York Times* and the *Washington Post*.

Suzanne A. Kim is Professor of Law and Judge Denny Chin Scholar at Rutgers Law School. Her research and teaching focus on family, procedure, constitutional law, antidiscrimination, critical theory, and socio-legal studies. Her interdisciplinary scholarship examines relationships between law, critical theory, and social sciences in relation to the regulation of intimacies, gender, family, discrimination, and resilience. Professor Kim is a past winner of the Association of American Law Schools Women in Legal Education New Voices in Gender Studies Paper Competition. Her current book project, tentatively titled *Marriage Equalities*, is under contract with NYU Press.

Anthony Michael Kreis is a visiting assistant professor of law at Chicago-Kent College of Law. Professor Kreis specializes in employment law and family law, with a focus on the law of sexuality, religious liberty, and social movements. He earned a Ph.D. from the University of Georgia, a J.D. from Washington and Lee, and a B.A. from the University of North Carolina at Chapel Hill.

Myrisha Lewis is an Assistant Professor of Law at the William and Mary Law School where she teaches Health Law, Bioethics, and Property. Professor Lewis earned a law degree from Columbia Law School and an A.B. in Government from Harvard College. Her work has been published in the *American Journal of Law and Medicine, Utah Law Review, Cardozo Law Review, William and Mary Journal of Women and the Law, Nevada Law Journal, Charleston Law Review*, and *Wisconsin Journal of Law, Gender and Society*.

Kevin Maillard is Professor of Law at Syracuse University and a contributor to the *New York Times*. He specializes in Family Law, Constitutional Law, and Popular Culture. His legal scholarship has been published in the *Fordham Law Review, Cardozo Law Review, Michigan State Law Review*, and the *SMU Law*, among others. He is the coeditor of *Loving v. Virginia in a Post-Racial World* (with Rose Villazor, Cambridge University Press 2012). An enrolled member of the Seminole Nation of Oklahoma, he splits time between Upstate New York and Manhattan.

Solangel Maldonado is the Eleanor Bontecou Professor of Law at Seton Hall Law. She has also taught at Columbia Law School, where she was a visiting scholar in the Center for the Study of Law and Culture. Her research and teaching interests include family law, estates and trusts, torts, gender and the law, and race and the law. She is an Associate Reporter of the Restatement of the Law, Children and the Law (in progress) and coeditor of *Family Law: Cases and Materials* (Foundation Press, 7th ed. 2019) and *Family Law in the World Community* (Carolina Academic Press, 3rd ed. 2015).

Maya Manian is a Visiting Professor at Howard University School of Law. Professor Manian received her B.A. from the University of Michigan and her J.D. from Harvard Law School. Her research investigates the relationship between constitutional law, family law, and health care law, with a focus on access to reproductive health care. Her articles have appeared in the *Washington and Lee Law Review*, the *Ohio State Law Journal*, and the *Duke Journal of Gender Law & Policy*, among others. She thanks Amy Wright for outstanding assistance as research librarian and Kimberly M. Mutcherson for helpful comments.

Melissa Murray is Frederick I. and Grace Stokes Professor of Law at New York University School of Law, and an expert in constitutional law, family law, and reproductive rights and justice. Before NYU, Murray taught at the University of California, Berkeley, where she received the Rutter Award for Teaching Distinction, the Association of American Law School's Derrick A. Bell Award, and served as interim dean. She coauthored *Cases on Reproductive Rights and Justice* (Foundation Press 2014) and *Reproductive Rights and Justice Stories* (Foundation Press 2019). She graduated from Yale Law School and clerked for Sonia Sotomayor, on the Court of Appeals for the Second Circuit, and Stefan Underhill of the District Court for the District of Connecticut.

Kimberly M. Mutcherson is Co-dean and Professor of Law at Rutgers Law School in Camden. She writes and teaches about topics in family law, health law, and bioethics, and focuses on reproductive justice, assisted reproduction, and abortion. She has been a visiting scholar at the Center for Bioethics at the University of Pennsylvania and a Sabbatical Visitor at the Center for Gender and Sexuality Law at Columbia Law School. She is a recipient of the Center for Reproductive Rights Innovation in Scholarship Award. She received her B.A. from the University of Pennsylvania and her J.D. from Columbia Law School.

Priscilla Ocen is a Professor of Law at Loyola Law School. Her work examines the relationship between race, gender, and systems of punishment, particularly how criminalization and incarceration are used to police the reproductive choices of poor women of color. Her work has appeared in the *California Law Review*, the *UCLA Law Review*, and popular media outlets such as the *Los Angeles Daily Journal*, *Ebony*, and *Al Jazeera*. Ocen received the inaugural PEN America Writing for Justice Literary Fellowship and a Fulbright Fellowship to study women's incarceration in Uganda. Ocen also coauthored the influential policy report, *Black Girls Matter: Pushed Out, Overpoliced and Underprotected*.

Kim Hai Pearson is an Associate Professor of Law and Associate Dean of Academic Affairs and Program Innovation at Gonzaga University School of Law. Prior to joining Gonzaga Law in 2010, Pearson held a Law Teaching Fellowship at the Williams Institute housed at UCLA Law School, where she taught Law and Sexuality, Legal Scholarship, and Family Law. Her current research and writing projects focus on identity and children in international trafficking streams. In her earlier work, Pearson's scholarship focused on the impact of identity classification for domestic family law purposes, including unfair outcomes for racial, religious, and sexual minority families.

Nancy Polikoff is Professor Emerita of Law at American University Washington College of Law. For more than forty years, she has been writing about, teaching about, and working on litigation and legislation about LGBT families. Her book, *Beyond (Straight and Gay) Marriage: Valuing All Families under the Law* (Beacon Press) was published in 2008. Before academia, Professor Polikoff cofounded the Washington, DC Feminist Law Collective and supervised family law programs at the Women's Legal Defense Fund (now the National Partnership on Women and Families). Professor Polikoff is a recipient of the Dan Bradley award from the National LGBT Bar Association, the organization's highest honor.

Dara E. Purvis is an Associate Professor and the Associate Dean for Diversity and Inclusion at Penn State Law. Prior to joining Penn State Law, Professor Purvis was a visiting assistant professor at the University of Illinois College of Law and a visiting fellow at the University of Kent Research Centre for Law, Gender, and Sexuality. A former editor-in-chief of the *Yale Law Journal*, she clerked for the Hon. Gerard E. Lynch, U.S. Court of Appeals for the Second Circuit and the Hon. Raymond C. Fisher, U.S. Court of Appeals for the Ninth Circuit.

Radhika Rao is a Professor of Law and Harry & Lillian Hastings Research Chair at the University of California, Hastings College of Law. After graduating from Harvard Law School, she clerked for Justices Harry Blackmun and Thurgood Marshall at the Supreme Court. Professor Rao teaches and writes in the areas of biolaw, constitutional law, comparative constitutional law, and property. As a Fulbright Distinguished Professor, she held the Trento Chair in Law at the University of Trento, Italy. She was a member of the California Advisory Committee on Human Cloning and serves on the California Human Stem Cell Research Advisory Committee.

Catherine Sakimura is the Deputy Director and Family Law Director at the National Center for Lesbian Rights. Cathy also founded and oversees NCLR's Family Protection Project, which improves access to family law services for low-income LGBT parents and their children, with a focus on families of color. She received her J.D. from UC Hastings College of the Law and her B.A. from Stanford University. In 2012, she was named one of the Best LGBT Lawyers under forty by the National LGBT Bar Association. She is a coauthor of the book *Lesbian, Gay, Bisexual, and Transgender Family Law* (2019).

Cynthia Soohoo is Professor of Law and Co-Director of the Human Rights and Gender Justice Clinic at CUNY Law School. She is in expert on women's human rights, the human rights of youth in conflict with the law, and human rights advocacy in the United States. Her scholarly work emphasizes intersectional identities and barriers to reproductive health and abortion services, including cost, regulatory burdens, and criminalization of pregnant women. She has authored submissions to the U.S. Supreme Court, appellate courts and international forums on access to abortion, forced sterilization, and criminalization of women for reproductive choices and pregnancy outcomes.

Rose Cuison Villazor is Professor of Law and Chancellor's Social Justice Scholar at Rutgers University School of Law. She is the Director of the Center for Immigration Law, Policy and Social Justice. Professor Villazor teaches, researches, and writes in the areas of immigration and citizenship law, property law, critical race theory, Asian Americans and the law, and equal protection law. Her books include *The Immigration and Nationality Act of 1965: Legislating a New America* (2015) (with Gabriel "Jack" Chin) and *Loving v. Virginia in a Post-Racial World: Rethinking Race, Sex, and Marriage* (2012) (with Kevin Maillard).

Thomas Wilson Williams, JD, MBE, is a Senior Lecturing Fellow and Supervising Attorney in the Duke Law School Start-Up Ventures Clinic, and a lecturing fellow in the Masters in Bioethics and Science Policy program. His scholarship focuses on the intersection between property rights and bodily integrity, and research ethics.

Mary Ziegler is the Stearns Weaver Miller Professor at Florida State University College of Law. She is the author of *Beyond Abortion: Roe v. Wade and the Fight for Privacy* (Harvard, 2018) and *After Roe: The Lost History of the Abortion Debate* (Harvard, 2015), the winner of the 2014 Harvard University Press Thomas J. Wilson Memorial Prize. Her latest project, *Abortion in America*, was published by Cambridge University Press in 2020. She has served as a commentator in leading mass media outlets, including *The Atlantic*, Fox News, MSNBC, the *New Republic*, the *New York Times*, NPR, and *The Washington Post*.

Preface

During her U.S. Supreme Court confirmation hearing, Senators called on now Justice Sonia Sotomayor to explain her belief that, when it comes to judging, "[A] wise Latina woman with the richness of her experiences would more often than not reach a better conclusion than a white male who hasn't lived that life." The premise of Justice Sotomayor's quote underlies much of the writing in this volume and in the Feminist Judgments series. Few of the judicial opinions from U.S. Courts that deeply impact procreative decision making have been made by people who are capable of pregnancy. This is not to say that only women, or people capable of pregnancy, can think critically about the role of law in protecting access to reproduction and the avoidance of reproduction. It is to say, however, that those who intimately understand and have lived the complex relationship between femaleness and procreative autonomy bring a different perspective to cases that impact this relationship. Identity matters in these cases, especially given that much of the U.S. history of procreative abuse has impacted poor women, women of color, especially but not only Black women, and other women who live at the margins of societal acceptance.

This volume brings together an array of scholars with unique perspectives who are steeped in feminist theory or reproductive justice theory or both. Their task was to reimagine seminal cases in reproductive rights and justice and ponder how those cases might have been decided or analyzed differently if put in the hands of a wise feminist (of color) who brought the richness of her (or his) life experience to the case. The opinions in this volume deal with assisted reproduction, abortion, forced sterilization, welfare caps, court ordered cesarean section, and more. The facts and legal theories that animate these cases vary but what unites them is the impact of subjectivity on the law. Too often, professed objectivity and neutrality mask and reinforce dominant norms that serve the privileged and disserve the marginalized. In a country whose founding documents enshrined chattel slavery and the broad disenfranchisement of women, while extolling the virtues of liberty and equality for all men, the idea that the reach of the law falls equally on all belies our past and present and will mar our future if we are unwilling to understand law as a tool of domination.

We can build that better future only by being intentional in recognizing that law, as written and as interpreted, is subject to the vagaries of the life experiences, values, and belief systems of those who wield power in our judicial system. And, for a very long time, white men have dominated our courts and legislatures at most levels. Bringing a critical eye to the law and to judging gives us the opportunity to make law different and, if we are doing it right, more just.

I hope that reading these cases will be enlightening and inspiring to the next generation of lawyers, lawmakers, and judges who will be called to shape the laws of tomorrow, which they will build on the laws of today. If we are lucky, that generation will be committed to law in service of the greater good. I look forward to the day when the world in which we live catches up to the world created by the judges and commentators in these pages. The art of judging should never ignore historical realities and lived experiences that lead to a case winding its way through the judicial system. When judges bring a wide array of experiences to the bench, the law benefits, as do those whose lives the law most impacts.

Acknowledgments

When I began this process, I had no idea how long it would last but I am grateful to have started, and finally ended, this journey. My deepest thanks go to Kathy Stanchi, Linda Berger, and Bridget Crawford, who entrusted me with this volume and gave me the space and time to produce a work of which all of us could be proud. Kathy, in particular, was a patient steward of this volume, and I am very much in her debt.

I am also enormously lucky to have access to a community of amazing scholars, activists, and practitioners who were kind enough to act as an advisory board for this project and scale down my original unwieldy list of cases to the fifteen that appear in this volume. I thank them for their time, their wisdom, their friendship, and their mentorship.

The opinion writers and commentators in this volume were a stalwart bunch who remained committed to the vision of this volume, despite changing timelines for publication. I thank them for their patience, for their willingness to endure my copious edits, and for lending their wise voices to this project. Reading and editing their words has made me a better writer.

As the volume came together, Julianna Koster and Courtnie Bolden provided research assistance to bring together some lingering missing links, and I am very appreciative of their contribution to helping me cross the finish line.

Table of Cases

PART I

Introduction and Overview

Kimberly M. Mutcherson

INTRODUCTION

American history is replete with examples of people with privilege controlling reproduction to assert power and domination over others. During chattel slavery in the United States, slaveowners denied black women and men the most basic forms of dignity – subjecting enslaved black women to sexual abuse and rape at the whim of people who believed that they could own human beings as property. When pregnancies resulted from rape by slave owners or consensual relationships among slaves, enslaved women frequently watched their children taken from them and sold for profit. Control of fertility and parenting decisions too often meant self-induced abortion or infanticide because other tools were out of reach.

Post-emancipation, and well into the present day, the experiences of black women and other women of color, as well as poor women and women living with disabilities, are a reminder that procreation remains a space of power and constraint. The eugenics movement in the United States led to thousands of unconsented sterilization procedures, largely on women. Today, parents seek to consent to sterilization on behalf of their adult children living with disabilities. The myth of the welfare queen, always depicted as a poor black woman with too many children, allowed states to create welfare caps that harm poor children by withholding needed financial resources from their families. States treat pregnant women and new mothers who are living with substance use disorder as criminals who need punishment, rather than sufferers who need a public health response. The federal government makes access to safe and legal abortion more difficult for poor women who are forbidden in almost all instances from using federal Medicaid dollars to pay for pregnancy terminations. It is fitting, then, that this entry into the Feminist Judgments canon focuses on procreation and parenting as sites of oppression and discrimination.

REPRODUCTIVE JUSTICE REWRITTEN creates greater context for and extends the reach of the original volume (FEMINIST JUDGMENTS: REWRITTEN OPINIONS OF THE UNITED STATES SUPREME COURT) by introducing readers to reproductive justice (RJ). While many people have at least passing familiarity with the term reproductive rights, fewer are familiar with the concept of RJ, which began as a movement and has expanded into a framework for scholarly inquiry.

The Reproductive Justice Framework

Black women started the RJ movement in 1994 because they refused to accept being second class citizens in a women's rights movement led largely by middle class white women. The traditional reproductive rights movement and its rhetoric and issues failed to capture the complexities of the lived experiences of women who lacked class, race, or sexual orientation privilege.[1] RJ rejected the mainstream women's reproductive health movement's myopic focus on abortion, and the resulting exclusion or downplaying of other issues that were significant in the lives of poor black women, including sterilization abuse, educational disparities, and inadequate access to reproductive healthcare. Further, the justice frame allowed RJ to move beyond the rhetoric of rights and embrace a broader social justice paradigm.

RJ rests on three pillars of equal importance: the human rights to have a child, to not have a child, and to parent one's child or children in safe and sustainable communities.[2] Thus, RJ is about procreation but it is also about environmental justice, criminal justice reform, immigration reform, birth justice, education equality, the end of police brutality, and more.

This expansive set of ideas rests on several tenets that separate RJ from the narrower movement that it moved beyond. For instance, it thoroughly discards the idea that liberation comes from choices, because the ability to make choices and effectuate those choices is directly tied to privilege. In her call to move from reproductive rights to reproductive justice, Dorothy Roberts explains that:

> For too long, the rhetoric of "choice" has privileged predominantly white middle-class women who have the ability to choose from reproductive options that are unavailable to poor and low-income women, especially women of color. The mainstream movement for reproductive rights has narrowed its concerns to advocate almost exclusively for the legal right to abortion, further distancing its agenda from the interests of women who have been targets of sterilization abuse because of the devaluation of their right to bear children.[3]

---

[1] For more information about the RJ movement, see http://strongfamiliesmovement.org/what-is-reproductive-justice and www.sistersong.net/index.php?option=com_content&view=article&id=141&Itemid=81.

[2] What Is Reproductive Justice?, www.sistersong.net/reproductive-justice.

[3] Dorothy Roberts, *Reproductive Justice, Not Just Rights*, DISSENT 79–82, 79 (Fall 2015).

Choices without economic or social resources cease to be choices at all. Thus, legal abortion creates access to abortion for those who can afford it but the Hyde Amendment's[4] ban on using federal Medicaid dollars to fund abortions for poor women means that the rhetoric of choice is not enough to lead to justice. Further, as Dorothy Roberts describes, organizing around choice has been ineffective in attempts to claim "public resources that most women need in order to maintain control over their bodies and lives."[5] Even more pernicious, arguing for choice has made it harder to garner support for movements to expand state support for women who need it. This is because policymakers declare that these women have made bad choices with which they should be forced to live and for which the state, and by extension taxpayers, should not have to bear the cost.[6] Thus, the rallying cry of choice fails to encompass the needs of a broad swath of women.

Importantly, and in keeping with Roberts' critique of reproductive rights, RJ is explicitly intersectional. Kimberlé Crenshaw coined the term intersectionality in her 1989 article, *Demarginalizing the Intersection of Race and Sex: A Black Feminist Critique of Antidiscrimination Doctrine, Feminist Theory and Antiracist Politics*.[7] Intersectionality is a guiding principle of RJ. Since Crenshaw offered up the name for a phenomenon long understood by black women and other women of color, the term intersectionality has been deployed all over the world within a range of disciplines and movements. Unfortunately, not all of those who use it do so in a way that is commensurate with the letter or spirit of its original meaning. Therefore, it is critical in this book to reclaim its origins to avoid distortions that have seeped into the framing over the decades.

In *Demarginalizing the Intersection of Race and Sex*, Crenshaw explored how discourses of feminist theory and antiracism erase black women because "both are predicated on a discrete set of experiences that often does not accurately reflect the interaction of race and gender."[8] Using the example of employment discrimination cases, Crenshaw deftly exposed how black women's discrimination claims slip between the cracks in a legal system that measures discrimination based on the experiences of white women or black men. She explained:

> Black women can experience discrimination in ways that are both similar to and different from those experienced by white women and Black men. Black women sometimes experience discrimination in ways similar to white women's experiences; sometimes they share very similar experiences with Black men. Yet often they experience double-discrimination – the combined effects of practices which

---

[4] Hyde Amendment, 1 U.S.C. chapter 4, Sec. 301–2.
[5] Roberts, *supra* note 3, at 80.
[6] *Id.*
[7] Kimberlé W. Crenshaw, *Demarginalizing the Intersection of Race and Sex: A Black Feminist Critique of Antidiscrimination Doctrine, Feminist Theory and Antiracist Politics*, 1 U. CHI. LEGAL F. 139 (1989).
[8] *Id.* at 140.

discriminate on the basis of race, and on the basis of sex. And sometimes, they experience discrimination as Black women – not the sum of race and sex discrimination, but as Black women.[9]

Crenshaw concluded that politics of black liberation and the tenets of feminist theory could not ignore the intersectional experience of black women if they sought to be successful in their liberation work. Black liberation must take account of gender and patriarchy, and feminist theorists must take account of how race impacts the experience of being female. Crenshaw called for a re-centering of discrimination discourse "at the intersection."[10]

In 1993, Crenshaw explored intersectionality again in her article, *Mapping the Margins: Intersectionality, Identity Politics, and Violence against Women of Color.*[11] Here, she turned the intersectional lens on the issues of violence against women and rape and again revealed how failure to see and credit the impact of intersecting identities meant that black women who were survivors of battering or rape were placed in the unenviable position of choosing a single identity, black or woman, in order to be seen and provided the services that they needed to be safe or heal.[12]

The commitment to intersectionality means that RJ organizes around the ways that interlocking identities impact women's lived experiences. Thus, RJ is never just about a single identity standing separated from an individual's whole self. An RJ analysis takes account of race, class, sexual orientation, gender identity, immigration status, and beyond to highlight how treatment based on overlapping identities affects women's lives.

Equally as important as the commitment to intersectionality is RJ's commitment to being a bottom up, rather than top down movement. This means that the movement centers on the lived experiences of those who are most at risk to be the targets of reproductive oppression. In the RJ context, the category of woman, which in feminist theory often translated into white, middle-class women, starts with women on the margins, especially black women and poor women.

Finally, the RJ frame is steeped in human rights, rather than constitutional rights. This creates a structure that is not bound by U.S. Supreme Court cases and state statutes. Instead, RJ recognizes that governments do not grant the rights surrounding procreation and parenting in the first instance, and these rights do not depend on where and how one is born or in which country one has citizenship. The rights inherent in RJ are global and far-reaching, and the narrow confines of any particular societal or governmental structure do not cabin its reach.

RJ began as a movement, not a theory, so it is also defined by a focus on community level action. Within the world of academia, this often translates into

---

[9] *Id.* at 149.
[10] *Id.* at 167.
[11] Kimberlé W. Crenshaw, *Mapping the Margins: Intersectionality, Identity Politics, and Violence against Women of Color*, 43 STANFORD L. REV. 1241 (1991).
[12] *Id.* at 1242.

work that is academic activism or scholarship that is deeply and unabashedly publicly engaged. The language of RJ has slowly but inexorably made its way into the realm of scholarship, producing books with titles such as REPRODUCTIVE JUSTICE: A GLOBAL CONCERN,[13] REPRODUCTIVE JUSTICE: AN INTRODUCTION,[14] and UNDIVIDED RIGHTS: WOMEN OF COLOR ORGANIZING FOR REPRODUCTIVE JUSTICE.[15] Even so, there are few law books that take up the project of RJ as a scholarly concern and a framework for analyzing issues related to pregnancy, parenting, and childbirth. An exception is CASES ON REPRODUCTIVE RIGHTS AND JUSTICE[16] by Melissa Murray and Kristin Luker. This is not to say that no legal scholars infuse their work with RJ principles but there is much room for growth. This book helps to further that necessary growth through a re-imagining of important cases about procreation and parenting through an RJ lens.

In keeping with the tradition of the original Feminist Judgments volume, the opinion authors were bound by the precedent and surrounding facts upon which the original decisions are based. The writers, however, transformed the opinions, sometimes in drastic ways, by bringing an RJ perspective to the facts and the law. In so doing, the fifteen opinions in this volume, which cover topics as varied as the regulation of abortion, welfare caps, forced sterilization, pregnancy discrimination, and adoptions under the Indian Child Welfare Act, highlight not only how parenting and procreation continue to be sites for discrimination and oppression but how the experiences of marginalized women, and marginalized communities in general, too often go unexplored in feminist discourse. Framing the book around RJ, rather than the narrower concept of reproductive rights, allows for a more far-reaching and impactful discussion of how the law shapes the lives of the people it touches, especially those with minimal power to change the systems that make their lives more challenging.

With the assistance of a stellar advisory board, I chose the cases for this book based on their potential for robust RJ analysis that did not exist in the original cases. While I did not want to exclude cases related to abortion, it was critical that the volume cover a range of issues that touched on the three-pronged vision offered by RJ – the right to have a child (assisted reproduction, forced sterilizations, court-ordered c-sections, punishing pregnant women with substance use disorders, pregnancy discrimination), the right to not have a child (abortion access and contraception coverage), and the right to parent a child in safe and healthy environments (adoption procedures and welfare caps). I deliberately chose an abundance of cases

[13] JOAN C. CHRISLER, ed, REPRODUCTIVE JUSTICE: A GLOBAL CONCERN (Praeger 2012)

[14] LORETTA J. ROSS & RICKIE SOLINGER, REPRODUCTIVE JUSTICE: AN INTRODUCTION (University of California Press 2017).

[15] JAEL SILLIMAN, MARLENE GERBER FRIED, LORETTA ROSS, & ELENA GUTIERREZ, UNDIVIDED RIGHTS: WOMEN OF COLOR ORGANIZING FOR REPRODUCTIVE JUSTICE (Haymark Books 2004).

[16] KRISTIN LUKER & MELISSA MURRAY, CASES ON REPRODUCTIVE RIGHTS AND JUSTICE (Foundation Press 2015).

that reflect in some way on the right to have a child to highlight how the state has impeded access to childbearing, especially for black women considered to be overly fertile. At the same time, I included cases about assisted reproduction in part because the fertility industry raises such thorny questions about to what use women can put their own bodies but also because of the questions of maternity, parentage, and family in these cases that force discussion about how outsider families struggle for legal protection and recognition.

Cases on abortion and contraception were a natural fit for the issue of the right not to have a child but I did have to cut out some cases related to the right to parent in safe and heathy environments that I would have liked to include to showcase the breadth of issues that RJ covers. For instance, I considered including *District of Columbia v. Heller*,[17] in which the U.S. Supreme Court struck down parts of a D.C. law intended to reduce gun violence in the city by making it more difficult to own a handgun for personal use. The link to RJ may not be immediately obvious but gun control is a critical issue for those who wish to reduce gun violence, especially in low-income communities of color. RJ encompasses efforts to make all neighborhoods places where parents need not fear that a stray bullet will callously end a child's life far too early. In the same vein, I could have included cases about environmental justice, perhaps the class action litigation related to the water crisis in Flint Michigan, or cases that strike at the overincarceration of black women and men. Though I had to draw a line somewhere, the fact that cases of this nature could have been in the book is a testament to the movement-straddling nature of RJ.

USING RJ TO REWRITE JUSTICE

Many of the authors in this volume would not explicitly describe their work as being reflective of RJ, though I think most, if not all of them, would accept that their work traffics in various feminist principles. As an editor, I worked hard to ensure that the collective work in this book reflects the tenets of RJ as a practice and as a theory. This meant that black women had to be well reflected in the volume as a whole even if not in every case; that authors needed to embrace the complicated analysis required by considering intersectional identities; that the stories of the central characters in each of these cases needed to be at the core of the legal analysis, rather than an afterthought; and that the cases needed to be understood within the larger framework of RJ and reproductive oppression. The work that the opinion authors and commentators did to achieve those goals make this volume a timely entry into the canon of RJ theory in the legal academy.

Multiple themes find expression in the opinions in the book, such as the reality that choice is always exercised within constraints; that justice in the procreative realm requires resources as well as rights; that intersectional analysis is the best way

---

[17] *District of Columbia v. Heller*, 554 U.S. 570 (2008).

to capture the complex nature of reproductive oppression and this includes taking a bottom-up approach to problem solving; that people live in complicated circumstances that are relevant to their interactions with the law and that they deserve to have their full stories told; that movements overlap and intertwine and we should be mindful of how gains for some could be setbacks for others; and, finally, that law should not exist devoid from an understanding of its real-world impact on marginalized people.

THE ART OF STORYTELLING

From the beginning, the first two rewritten cases in the volume set the tone for what follows. *Buck v. Bell*[8] and *Skinner v. Oklahoma*[19] are seminal cases in the world of law and procreation. *Buck* represents the shameful history of eugenic sterilizations in the United States.[20] Carrie Buck was one of approximately 8,000 people sterilized in Virginia under the auspices of the eugenic sterilization law that the Supreme Court endorsed and found constitutional in its 1927 decision.[21] That 1924 law, as described by the Supreme Court:

> [R]ecites that the health of the patient and the welfare of society may be promoted in certain cases by the sterilization of mental defectives, under careful safeguard, &c.; that the sterilization may be effected in males by vasectomy and in females by salpingectomy, without serious pain or substantial danger to life; that the Commonwealth is supporting in various institutions many defective persons who if now discharged would become a menace but if incapable of procreating might be discharged with safety and become self-supporting with benefit to themselves and to society; and that experience has shown that heredity plays an important part in the transmission of insanity, imbecility, &c.[22]

The language of the time and the justification offered for a barbaric practice do and should appall the modern reader.

In the actual court opinion, Justice Oliver Wendell Holmes describes Carrie Buck as a "feeble-minded woman" who is the product of a "feeble minded" mother and who has given birth to an "illegitimate feeble minded child."[23] In Kim Hai Pearson's rewritten opinion, however, facts from the trial record give a fuller and more accurate depiction of Carrie's history to explain how she came to be pregnant

---

[18] 274 U.S. 200 (1927).

[19] 316 U.S. 535 (1942).

[20] PAUL LOMBARDO, THREE GENERATIONS, NO IMBECILES: EUGENICS, THE SUPREME COURT, AND BUCK V. BELL (John Hopkins University Press 2010).

[21] In 2002, then Virginia Governor, Mark Warner, issued a formal apology for the state's past eugenic practices, which lasted from 1927–1979. William Branigin, *VA. Apologizes to the Victims of Sterilizations*, WASH. POST (May 3, 2002).

[22] *Buck, supra* note 18, at 205–6.

[23] *Id.* at 205.

and have a child as an unmarried woman and how the state failed her and her family over the course of her lifetime. Thus, Pearson makes clear that the State's culpability in the pain it brought to Carrie Buck's life started well before her case made it to the U.S. Supreme Court.

In *Skinner v. Oklahoma*, decided 15 years after *Buck*, the Supreme Court faced a law that functioned as a three strikes and you get sterilized statute. The plaintiff, Jack Skinner, challenged the Oklahoma statute that would have allowed the state to sterilize him upon conviction for his third felony. Without overruling *Buck*, the *Skinner* Court decided that the statute could not stand because it violated equal protection. In his concurrence in this volume, Thomas Williams uses details of Skinner's life and the reality of the economic and social aftermath of the Great Depression to place Skinner's acts in a context, rather than view him as an isolated bad actor.

The theme of placing actors in context flows through many of the opinions in this volume, including Nancy Dowd's bold and illuminating re-telling of the facts that led to a challenge to the spirit, if not the fact, of the Indian Child Welfare Act in *Adoptive Couple v. Baby Girl*.[24] Dowd transforms a father who the Supreme Court describes as absent and unconcerned about his infant daughter into a man who was kept from his child after a mistake led him to consent to an adoption that he did not want.

And Margo Kaplan, in her opinion in *Ferguson v. City of Charleston*,[25] does not allow the ten plaintiffs in that case to be a faceless monolith. Instead, each name and story get a telling in her opinion, and she relays the horror of arresting women the day after they give birth or shackling pregnant women during labor and delivery – a practice that remains in place today in some jurisdictions.[26]

In the re-telling of these stories from the perspective of the people who were living them or with greater depth than happened in the opinions issued by courts, these authors allow the people at the center of controversial cases involving deeply questionable state actions to exist within the complex reality of their own lives, rather than in the flat pages of a legal opinion.

FEMINISTS, FEMINIST THEORY, AND RACE

There is nothing new or radical about asserting that feminism has a race problem. Sojourner Truth's declaration that she, too, was a woman despite the deep differ-ences that separated her from the white women with whom she was agitating for

---

[24] *Adoptive Couple v. Baby Girl*, 570 U.S. 637 (2013).
[25] *Crystal M. Ferguson v. City of Charleston*, 532 U.S. 67 (2001).
[26] Ginette Ferszt, Michelle Palmer, and Christine McGrane, *Where Does Your State Stand on the Shackling of Pregnant Incarcerated Women?* 22 NURSING FOR WOMEN'S HEALTH 17–23 (Feb. 2018) (noting that only twenty-two states and the District of Columbia had legislation that outlawed the shackling of pregnant women).

women's suffrage still resonates.[27] The opinions and commentaries in this book take seriously the RJ call to be intersectional in their analysis and espouse a feminism that takes account of race and racism. This is not a book in which all the women are white, and all the black people are men.

In her opening sentence, Priscilla Ocen makes clear that her rewritten majority opinion in *Wyman v. James*[28] will integrate the race, class, and gender implications of the political and legal discussion of welfare caps – laws that reduce access to public benefits when a family already receiving such benefits adds another child. In his majority opinion in the actual case, Justice Blackmun ignores race. Ocen begins her opinion by noting that Barbara James is not just a woman and a mother who receives Aid to Families with Dependent Children benefits – she is a black woman who receives those benefits. This framing immediately signals that Ocen's opinion will reflect ways in which race, class, and gender shape the welfare discussion in the United States. As a jurist, she takes seriously the intersectional implications of the totality of the experience of poor Black women who receive AFDC. It is the combination of being black, a woman, and poor that allows the state to justify a requirement that these women sacrifice privacy in their own homes and submit to state inspections as a requirement for continued state aid.

Similar to the Ocen opinion in *Wyman*, in *Sojourner A. v. N.J. Dep't of Human Servs.*[29] Cynthia Soohoo takes the state of New Jersey to task for its welfare cap that harkens back to coercive population control or eugenic efforts that targeted poor women of color. That she does so by reference to international human rights law brings her into territory that the U.S. Supreme Court studiously avoids.

In *Whole Woman's Health v. Hellerstedt*,[30] David Cohen adds a much needed perspective to the discussion of abortion by foregrounding the pernicious impact that laws that over-regulate abortion have on poor women of color. He focuses on black women who access abortion at higher rates than other women and who are more likely to be uninsured than other woman, thus increasing the likelihood that they will get their reproductive health services from the clinics that restrictive abortion laws target. He further highlights the Latina population in Texas—the state from which from which the Supreme Court case grew. This population faces the same burdens as black woman plus the burden of clinic closures for women living in rural areas. Under the law successfully challenged in Whole Woman's Health, These women would have found their ability to access reproductive health-care, including abortion care, stymied by long travel times, if they could even find transportation to make a 500 mile or more trip for healthcare.

In *Maher v. Roe*,[31] Michele Goodwin painfully highlights the bankrupt nature of choice in a world in which a state deprives poor women of the economic means to

---

[27] Sojourner Truth, AIN'T I A WOMAN? (1851).

[28] *Wyman v. James*, 400 U.S. 309 (1971).

[29] *Sojourner A. v. N.J. Dep't of Human Servs.*, 134 S. Ct. 2751 (2014).

[30] *Whole Woman's Health v. Hellerstedt*, 136 S. Ct. 2292 (2016).

[31] *Maher v. Roe*, 432 U.S. 464 (1977).

end a pregnancy. And in *In re Madyun*,[32] Maya Manian rewrites a case in which a judge issued an order giving physicians the right to perform a c-section on a nineteen-year-old married Muslim woman delivering her baby in a public hospital over the objection of the woman and her husband. A choice to get pregnant that leads to a court ordering submission to major surgery belies any notion of justice or autonomy.

Mainstay feminist principles of autonomy, bodily integrity, and choice are relevant in the cases described above but those principles only go so far as the examples in the above paragraphs illustrate. Justice demands taking notice of the fact that a young Muslim woman giving birth or receiving prenatal care in a public hospital may find her healthcare team more dismissive of her wants and demands as a patient than they might a white woman in a private hospital. Similarly, In a world in which poor black women get labeled as incapable of making good choices about reproduction, the right to privacy that protects abortion access may not seem broad enough to protect the right to use Medicaid funds to access a desired pregnancy termination. And, finally, courts may be deeply dismissive of a black woman's assertion of privacy in her home if she pays for that home through funds provided by the government.

THE RELATIONSHIP BETWEEN RIGHTS AND JUSTICE

Some of the cases in this volume read as much more conventional court opinions than others but a reader can discern their radical nature in the subtleties. In *Young v. UPS*,[33] Meredith Johnson Harbach takes pains to note that pregnancy discrimination in paid work has long been an issue for women of color, immigrants, and low-income women who have had high levels of work force participation, even when white women did not. Further, women who are low wage workers have less power to protect themselves against workplace harassment and discrimination than those who are more economically privileged. In this arena, removing barriers that keep and kept women from certain types of work, creating more choices, is a small step in a much larger process. Justice, as Harbach argues, sometimes demands that the law and employers treat people differently in order to give them the same access to paid work.

A case about assisted reproduction, *Johnson v. Calvert*,[34] raises profoundly difficult questions about rights and justice. In *Johnson*, Melanie Jacobs uses her opinion to explicitly extend the right to procreate to encompass a right to use assisted reproduction – a leap that the U.S. Supreme Court has yet to make. She then reckons with that expansive right to procreate as measured against the real risks of the exploitation of poor women who sell their reproductive services in fertility markets, including women who contract as gestational carriers known more colloquially as surrogate mothers. Especially where intended parents are white or even just non-black and the

---

[32] *In re Madyun*, 114 Daily Wash. L. Rptr. 2233 (D.C. Super Ct. July 2, 1986).
[33] *Young v. UPS*, 135 S. Ct. 1338 (2015).
[34] *Johnson v. Calvert*, 5 Cal. 4th 84 (1993).

surrogate mother is a black woman, the spectre of the decades in which black women, as enslaved people and later as low paid domestic workers, raised white children demands that markets for reproductive labor be especially attuned to the risk that our past becomes prologue.

Finally, *Burwell v. Hobby Lobby*, a case in which the Supreme Court allowed a business to assert religious objection to providing health benefits that included contraception to their female employees,[35] seems to be a straightforward case about religious liberty. But the flipped holding by Anthony Kreis would not only protect female employees from having their employers limit their contraceptive choices, it would have far-reaching implications for religious liberty claims seeking to justify discrimination against LGBT people and against women in the workplace.

INTERTWINING IDENTITIES AND MOVEMENTS

Unsurprisingly, the ramifications of the decisions in some of these cases may seem to pit allies against each other or may benefit one group while unwittingly causing harm to another. In her opinion in *Reber v. Reis*,[36] Dara Purvis weighs the competing rights to procreate or not procreate in the context of an embryo dispute between formerly married partners. In *K.M. v. E.G.*,[37] Melissa Murray determines parentage in a case involving two women who are no longer romantic partners, where one woman gestated and another provided her ova, for children they planned to raise together. In both cases, the authors came to their conclusions only after puzzling through the ways in which a decision could traffic in stereotypes that could have long-term negative implications for a range of different women. Purvis shies away from using tropes of natural maternal instinct to justify giving embryos to the woman who wanted to gestate them over the objection of her ex-husband. In so doing, though, she runs the risk of placing some women at the mercy of ex-partners who will use the woman's desire to use embryos to extract other concessions from her in a divorce proceeding. In trying to avoid a stereotype about women and mothering, Purvis' position potentially lays waste to the desire for genetic parenthood of a woman who endured physical and emotional trauma in the hope of one day bearing a child who would share her genes.

In *K.M.*, Murray balks at a rationale for finding parenthood in both women that is rooted in conservative notions of family, including the disdain for single parenthood and the desire to privatize dependence that undergirds much of family law and, to a large extent, public assistance policy. But, to protect this family, she endorses a statute that in later years would allow a sperm donor to thwart a woman's plans to become a single mother.[38] Thus, Murray's opinion could hurt the very families she sought to protect.

---

[35] *Burwell v. Hobby Lobby Stores, Inc.*, 134 S. Ct. 2751 (2014).
[36] *Reber v. Reiss*, 42 A.3d 1131 (2012).
[37] *K.M. v. E.G.*, 37 Cal. 4th 130 (2005).
[38] *Jason P. v. Danielle S.*, 9 Cal. App. 5th 1000 (2017).

CONCLUSION

Ferguson was precipitated by a public hospital's policy of partnering with local police and prosecutors to test pregnant women for cocaine and follow-up with arrest and incarceration if the women failed to engage in drug rehabilitation. Arresting women for cocaine use immediately after they give birth impacts the woman, her child, her family, and perhaps whole communities. Capping welfare benefits to discourage childbearing among people already receiving state benefits, as the state of New Jersey did, precipitating *Sojourner A.*, makes it harder for poor families to sustain themselves; thus punishing the entire family. Allowing companies to exempt themselves from birth control mandates, as the Supreme Court did in its decision in *Burwell*, makes it harder for women to access contraceptives and avoid unplanned or unwanted pregnancy.

Being able to control when, if, and how one becomes a parent is vital to the ability to build a sustainable life. Furthermore, having access to social supports to raise healthy and safe children is a vital part of parenting once a person achieves that status. The opinions in this volume show that the state plays a role, sometimes outsized, in how people, especially those who are low income and/or people of color, organize their reproductive lives. Only some of the cases rewritten in this book were decided by the U.S. Supreme Court but, even though lower courts decided other cases, the legacy they leave in terms of allowing or disallowing various forms of reproductive control is far reaching.

Judges matter. Lawmakers matter. Prosecutors and public defenders matter. If there are no or few people committed to RJ who play these roles, we will continue to see cases where rights and choices displace discussions of what is right and what is just. The rewritten opinions in this volume give us a path forward and a way to fundamentally shift beliefs in what the law can or should do to create more opportunities for flourishing for more people. REPRODUCTIVE JUSTICE REWRITTEN gives a glimpse into a possible future but not one that is preordained. If this is the future we want, then achieving it will require difficult conversations, our sustained advocacy, and constant vigilance in order to become our reality.

PART II

The Feminist Judgments

1

Buck v. Bell, 274 U.S. 200 (1927)

Commentary by Jasmine E. Harris

INTRODUCTION

Buck v. Bell has garnered much attention from legal historians and scholars across several areas including reproductive rights and disability law. Retrospective accounts profess collective enlightenment and vehemently reject the possibility of such overt inhumanity today. Yet *Buck*'s viability is not limited to a cautionary tale. In less than 1,000 words, Justice Oliver Wendell Holmes sent seismic ripples across the law of reproductive rights. Although the case remains on the books, it is rarely cited as legal precedent except to distinguish cases before courts. Rather, the power of *Buck* lies in its commentary on how the bodies of disfavored populations remain subject to state regulation and its implications for modern permutations of eugenic principles. Accordingly, *Buck v. Bell* was "never about mental deficiency; it was always a matter of sexual morality and social deviance."[1]

This Commentary contextualizes the feminist judgment rewritten by Kim Hai Pearson and highlights the ways in which Pearson's rewrite lays the foundation for the development of alternative rhetoric and doctrine in the area of reproductive justice. The original *Buck* decision is best understood within a broader political structure because *Buck* is part of a deeper history of intersectional discrimination based on race, ethnicity, class, gender, disability, and sexual identity. An explicit goal of this contribution is to lessen the distance between the rhetoric and practices in *Buck* and modern law and policy in the area of reproductive justice and disability law. In this sense, this project is descriptive in service of the normative mission of injecting public debates with critical feminist and disability rights perspectives.

---

[1] Stephen Jay Gould, *Carrie Buck's Daughter*, 2 CONST. COMMENT. 331, 336 (1985).

BUCK V. BELL (1927)

In one of the U.S. Supreme Court's shortest opinions, eight of the most respected federal jurists upheld the constitutionality of a Virginia compulsory sterilization law authorizing the state to police sexuality and procreation in the name of the public's good.[2] What surprises most people who engage in discussion about *Buck v. Bell* is not just the coarse language and sentiment expressed in the opinion, nor the consequential forced sterilization of Carrie Buck. What shocks the collective conscience is the calculated deceit that produced this infamous decision and the ways in which public institutions contributed to and maintained the legal and factual fictions at the heart of the case.

THE DECISION IN *BUCK V. BELL*

The case concerned the constitutionality of Virginia's Eugenical Sterilization Act of 1924 (the "ESA" or "Act"). The Act allowed state institutions to petition the state to perform compulsory sterilizations – by salpingectomy[3] or vasectomy – on individuals medically determined to be "mentally unfit." Procedural safeguards included notice and an opportunity to oppose the petition for sterilization.

The key question before the Court was whether the Virginia statute violated the due process and equal protection clauses of the Fourteenth Amendment of the U.S. Constitution. Carrie Buck appealed an order for sterilization from the Board of Directors of the Colony for the Feebleminded and Epileptics. The Supreme Court of the United States held in an 8-1 decision[4] written by Justice Oliver Wendell Holmes that the ESA did not offend due process or equal protection under the Fourteenth Amendment. Holmes' due process analysis occupies three-quarters of his opinion and details the "very careful provisions by which the Act protects patients from possible abuse,"[5] including notice of intent to sterilize to the individual, and, if a minor, to the parent; appointment of a guardian if the person does not already have one; presentation of evidence; decision and reasoning in writing; and appellate possibilities up to the state's highest court with de novo review. Reviewing the procedures available as a general matter and those of which Carrie Buck availed herself in the case before the Court, Holmes concluded "there can be no doubt as far as procedure is concerned, the rights of the patient are most carefully considered,

---

[2] Justice Oliver Wendell Holmes authored the majority opinion. Chief Justice and former United States President, William Howard Taft, joined Holmes' majority opinion, as did Justices Louis Brandeis – the first Jewish-American jurist on the Court – and Harlan Fiske Stone.

[3] A salpingectomy, or tubal ligation, is the surgical removal of one or both fallopian tubes which lead from the ovaries to the uterus.

[4] Justice Pierce Butler, without issuing an opinion, was the lone dissenter on the right side of history. *See generally* Ashley K. Fernandes, *The Power of Dissent: Pierce Butler and Buck v. Bell*, 12 J. PEACE & JUST. STUD. 115 (2002) (discussing Justice Butler's religious and class upbringing and its potential effect on his dissent in *Buck v. Bell*).

[5] *Buck v. Bell*, 274 U.S. 200, 206 (1927).

and as every step in this case was taken in scrupulous compliance with the statute and after months of observation, there is no doubt that . . . the plaintiff in error has had due process of law."[6]

Holmes briefly addressed whether sterilization is per se impermissible or as applied in the case before the court. He summarily recites the lower court's factual findings that Carrie Buck was the child of "socially inadequate offspring," is herself an "imbecile," and has an infant daughter found to also be an "imbecile."[7] According to the ESA, the state could, in the public's interest, compel individuals determined to be "imbeciles" by heredity to undergo "relatively painless" sterilization procedures. Holmes analogized the civic duty of such individuals to undergo sterilization to that of individuals serving in the military who sacrificed their lives for the greater public good. Such sterilization would allow individuals committed to state custody (such as Carrie Buck) to leave institutionalized settings, make space for others, and return to community living and employment. The social benefits, according to Holmes, included the elimination of the public costs of funding Carrie's residence in a state-funded institution and making it possible for her to move from a recipient of welfare support to a productive member of society.

Holmes rejected the proposition that the facts of this case violate equal protection under the Fourteenth Amendment. He relied almost exclusively on a 1905 case, *Jacobson v. Massachusetts*, for the proposition that the state has a similar interest in and legal authority to pursue compulsory vaccinations in the public interest – "vaccination extends to fallopian tubes" – to analogize the prevention of smallpox with the prevention of "feeblemindedness." Holmes, accepting the state's conclusory assertions that Carrie Buck, her mother, and her infant daughter were individuals with intellectual disabilities, infamously professed that "three generations of imbeciles are enough."[8] History has laid bare the dearth of evidence and deep conflicts of interest driving this opinion, most often discussed, the fact that neither Carrie nor her daughter, Vivian, had an intellectual or developmental disability.[9] Holmes states that while broad sterilization as an exercise of police power might offend equal protection, the Virginia statute was sufficiently cabined to "the small number" of those in institutional settings classified as "feebleminded," "imbeciles," "idiots," or "morons."

CONTEXTUALIZING *BUCK V. BELL*

Missing from the Supreme Court opinion in *Buck* is meaningful engagement with the social-political context surrounding the case, namely the eugenics movement and immigration.

---

[6] *Id.* at 207.

[7] *Id.*

[8] *Id.*

[9] *See, e.g.,* Paul A. Lombardo, *Three Generations, No Imbeciles: New Light on Buck v. Bell,* 60 N.Y.U. L. Rev. 30, 61 (1985) (discussing the "wrongly accused").

Eugenics

In 1883, Sir Francis Galton found himself in "want [of] a brief word to express the science of improving stock."[10] He settled on eugenics, from the Greek roots eu ("well" or "good") and gen(es) ("that which produces") – i.e., well-produced, or well-born.[11] Galton's "science," which advocated for improvement of the human race by curtailing the reproduction of the lower classes, attracted a number of prominent followers. In the United States, the eugenics movement was visibly expressed in policy at the highest levels of government, for example, the Immigration Restriction Act of 1924. At the state-level, too, eugenic thought was highly influential. Many states passed restrictive marriage laws intended to avoid comingling inferior genes with those of "superior" (meaning white) people. Some states moved from "soft" normative rejections of interracial marriage to hard guarantees. Virginia's Racial Integrity Act of 1924, for instance, paved the way for thousands of eugenics-based forcible sterilizations across the country. The law also served as the basis for the ESA, the Virginia legislation at issue in *Buck*.

Evidence suggests that *Buck* was a product of meticulous legal and social engineering rather than a historic inevitability. When *Buck v. Bell* reached the Supreme Court in 1927, the eugenics movement had lost much of its steam. In 1914, only nine states had sterilization laws on the books[12] and, in most states, these laws were challenged and rarely enforced.[13] Empirical evidence also indicates that *Buck* itself may have been responsible for the increase in legislation post-1927.[14] Despite contentions that legislation across the United States reflected Virginia's law, a full seventeen states never enacted a sterilization law. Indeed, in states where such laws did exist, the actual performance of sterilization procedures was negligible – at least until well after the Court decided *Buck*.

Immigration

Immigration law was a product of and a further catalyst for eugenics. Rhetorical claims of biological differences and inherent inferiority drove legislative

---

[10] FRANCIS GALTON, INQUIRIES INTO HUMAN FACULTY AND ITS DEVELOPMENT 24–25 n.1 (1883) (concluding "[t]he word *eugenics* would sufficiently express the idea" because it is "neater" and "more generalized" than *viriculture*).

[11] *Eugenic*, DICTIONARY.COM UNABRIDGED (accessed Oct. 28, 2017).

[12] Edward Manson, *Eugenics and Legislation*, 13 J. SOC. COMP. LEGIS. 123, 129 (1914) (listing Indiana, New York, Connecticut, California, Iowa, Utah, Nevada, New Jersey, and Washington). *See also* EDWARD J. LAWSON, SEX, RACE, AND SCIENCE: EUGENICS IN THE DEEP SOUTH at 124 (John Hopkins University Press 1995) (number reached thirty-two states at its peak).

[13] Gould, *supra* note 1, at 332.

[14] Only four of the sixteen Southern states (Alabama, Delaware, Mississippi, and Virginia) had sterilization laws on the books prior to *Buck v. Bell*.

responses.[15] The Immigration Quota Act of 1921, followed by the Immigration Act of 1924, represented landmarks of eugenic achievement. Eugenic preferences were so powerful that they supplanted the "goal of preserving family unity," which had, until that point, been the prevailing aim of immigration law and policy.[16] Collectively, the Acts sought to limit the number of immigrants entering the United States and regulate the perceived quality of those seeking entry. To those ends, the 1924 Act implemented a literacy test, a two percent quota restriction (based upon the total number of people of each nationality in the U.S. as of the 1890 census), and a wholesale prohibition against immigrants from Asia. According to the U.S. State Department, "the most basic purpose of the 1924 Immigration Act was to preserve the ideal of U.S. homogeneity."[17]

In the first decades of the twentieth century, homogeneity was a goal pursued via diverse mechanisms. H. H. Goddard – one of the alleged "pioneers of hereditarian-ism in America"[18] – advocated vociferously (and successfully) for intelligence quotient tests as taxonomic tools. As the director of the research lab at the Vineland Training School for Feeble-Minded Boys and Girls and the man responsible for importing Alfred Binet's IQ scale to America, Goddard was an eugenics convert. In 1920, he wrote, "If both parents are feeble-minded all the children will be feeble-minded. It is obvious that matings should not be allowed."[19] Armed with this conclusion – and an assessment tool – Goddard visited Ellis Island in 1912. There, he encouraged the selection of feeble-minded individuals by sight[20] and, applying

---

[15] An article by Vice President Calvin Coolidge in *Good Housekeeping* in 1921 is an especially apt example:

> ... [S]ince we are confronted by the clamor of multitudes who desire the opportunity offered by American life, we must face the situation unflinchingly ... It is a self-evident truth that in a healthy community there is no place for the vicious, the weak of body, the shiftless, or the improvident. ... *Biological laws tell us that certain divergent people will not mix or blend.* ... *Quality of mind and body suggests that observance of ethnic law is as great a necessity to a nation as immigration law.*
>
> Calvin Coolidge, Whose Country Is This?, 72 GOOD HOUSEKEEPING 13, 13–14 (1921) (emphasis added)

[16] Rachel Silber, *Eugenics, Family and Immigration Law in the 1920's*, 11 GEO. IMMIGR. L.J. 859, 878 (1997).

[17] *Milestones – The Immigration Act of 1924 (The Johnson-Reed Act)*, OFFICE OF THE HISTORIAN, BUREAU OF PUBLIC AFFAIRS, U.S. DEP'T OF STATE https://history.state.gov/milestones/1921-1936/immigration-act (last visited Nov. 5, 2017).

[18] STEPHEN JAY GOULD, THE MISMEASURE OF MAN 187 (1996).

[19] HENRY HERBERT GODDARD, FEEBLE-MINDEDNESS: ITS CAUSES AND CONSEQUENCES 561 (1920).

[20] Goddard described his method at Ellis Island as intuitive. "After a person has had considerable experience in this work," he wrote, "he almost gets a sense of what a feeble-minded person is so that he can tell one afar off." GOULD, *supra* note 18, at 195 (citation omitted). *See also* Jasmine E. Harris, *The Aesthetics of Disability*, 119 COLUM. L. REV. 895 (2019) (coining the term "aesthetics of disability" and developing a theory of disability rights law based on normative constructions of disability and functional capacity) [on file with author].

the Binet-Simon test, reached the general conclusion that the "average immigrant" had "below normal" intelligence.[21] His results ultimately claimed that eighty-three percent of Jews, eighty percent of Hungarians, seventy-nine percent of Italians, and eighty-seven percent of Russians were feeble-minded.[22] Though Goddard later admitted he had distorted application of the Binet test (i.e., had set the upper limit for feeble-minded classification too high), he never retreated from his eugenic theories that served as the foundational justifications for the 1924 Immigration Restriction Act.

COMMENTARY ON *BUCK V. BELL* REWRITTEN

Pearson's revised feminist judgment gives voice to Carrie Buck as the central figure in the case and adds to our understanding of three core issues that Holmes fails to address: (1) bodily integrity and the development of privacy jurisprudence as it relates to a broader state interest in public welfare, (2) failure to carry out the judicial role as evidentiary gatekeeper, and (3) a fundamental right to establish and raise a family that had emerged in the Court's jurisprudence at the time of the original decision.

In terms of voice, Pearson's re-write, unlike the majority opinion in *Buck*, offers details of Carrie's life that have been unearthed by historians and others who have written about *Buck*. Scholars have uncovered several factual inaccuracies that challenge the validity of the holding in *Buck*. All of the evidence indicates Carrie Buck's sterilization was based more on disfavored social traits than biological ones.[23] For example, the claim that Carrie had an intellectual or developmental disability based on her IQ test conflicted with evidence of her school records which demonstrated a neuro-typically developing student; similarly, the claim that Carrie's mental disabilities were inherited by her daughter, Vivian, conflicts with evidence of Vivian's later performance as a typically developing student.[24] Perhaps most troubling, the *Buck* narratives developed through litigation failed to acknowledge that Carrie Buck was a survivor of sexual assault by her employer's nephew. Her institutional commitment and sterilization were motivated, in part, by her employers' desire to eliminate a constant, tangible reminder of sexual violence at their hands.

---

[21] Henry Herbert Goddard, *Mental Tests and the Immigrant*, 2 THE JOURNAL OF DELINQUENCY 244 (1917).

[22] GOULD, *supra* note 18, at 196.

[23] Janet Simmonds, *Coercion in California: Eugenics Reconstituted in Welfare Reform, the Contracting of Reproductive Capacity, and Terms of Probation*, 17 HASTINGS WOMEN'S L.J. 269, 274 & n.45 (2006) ("Buck was of normal intelligence. The real reason she was sent to an institution was to have a baby out of wedlock[.]"); Gould, *supra* note 1, at 338 ("There were no imbeciles, not a one, among the three generations of Bucks").

[24] The Court did not have access to these records at the time; Vivian was an infant during the legal proceedings.

Thus, Pearson's rewrite helps situate *Buck* as both a case of reproductive justice and a case of disability rights. While *Buck* is frequently cited for its reproductive justice implications, the opinion has shaped disability rights law in important ways. The opinion reflects and depends on the inhumanity and disgust with which society approaches people with disabilities. The expressive value of the opinion – that people with disabilities are public charges with no right to live in the world – justified state-sponsored segregation of people with intellectual and developmental disabilities in state institutions that warehoused disabled people with minimal access to clothing, food, medical care, and education.[25] Medical researchers, in violation of ethical and licensing rules, used residents with disabilities as medical test subjects without their consent. Former Senator Robert Kennedy once described the Willowbrook State School, at the time the largest state institution for people with developmental disabilities, as a "snake pit" where residents were "living in filth and dirt, their clothing in rags, in rooms less comfortable and cheerful than the cages in which we put animals in a zoo."[26]

Additionally, *Buck* distinguished between legitimate state regulation of a "socially inadequate" person with a disability from illegitimate regulation of non-disabled persons' sexual decisions. What if the Bucks were indeed three generations of people with intellectual disabilities? Would *Buck v. Bell* have such a detested place in legal history? During the trial, a medical expert for the state defined a "socially inadequate" person broadly to include anyone who "is unable to maintain themselves according to the accepted rules of society." The majority opinion frames sterilization as a legitimate means of birth control for the benefit of society and to Carrie Buck as an individual with a disability who, without the burden of pregnancy, can become a productive, integrated member of society. This argument appears today in the debates around voluntary sterilization of people with disabilities, particularly minors. For example, some parents and legal guardians have argued that sterilization allows the individual with a mental disability to enjoy greater freedom and integration into society without the burdens and dangers of parenting a child s/he cannot care for.[27] Pearson's opinion strongly asserts that parenting, procreation, and family creation should not be denied to those who are living with disabilities, including intellectual disabilities.

With respect to three core issues omitted by Holmes's decision, first, Pearson's dissent challenges the majority's framing of the state's interest in sexual regulation as

---

[25] *See, e.g., New York State Assoc. for Retarded Children, Inc. v. Rockefeller*, 357 F. Supp. 752, 755 (1973).

[26] The Minnesota Governor's Council on Developmental Disabilities, *The ADA Legacy Project, Willowbrook Leads to New Protections of Rights*, Moments in Disability History 9, 2013, available at https://mn.gov/web/prod/static/mnddc/live/ada-legacy/ada-legacy-moment9.html.

[27] *See, e.g.*, Eva Feder Kittay, *Forever Small: The Strange Case of Ashley X*, 26 HYPATIA 610, 610–11 (2011) (discussing a case about the voluntary sterilization and reproductive management of a six-year-old girl with cognitive disabilities by her parents).

advancing a public interest. While recognizing the state's legitimate interests in executing particular policy preferences enumerated in legislation, as well as its parens patriae authority to protect vulnerable persons, the dissent argues that the majority fails to recognize that such authority is limited by an individual's right to self-determination, bodily integrity, and control. By justifying compulsory sterilization on the grounds of public charge, *Buck* opened the door to broader state regulation of sexual agency and compulsory sterilization for others deemed undesirable such as "unwed" mothers, sex workers, and juvenile and adult offenders.

Similarly, even if the Virginia statute reflected a legitimate state interest in preventing future generations of "public charges" in the public's best interest, a question remains whether sterilization was narrowly tailored to achieve those goals. Proponents of eugenics advanced their agenda through formal and informal avenues – e.g., prohibitions on interracial marriage, immigration law, public shaming, adoption and parental termination laws. Sterilization was the most direct method of population control but certainly not the only choice available or employed by eugenicists. Framing the issue as a need for balancing the individual interests in self-determination against the state's interests may have created an early doctrinal hook for the development of substantive due process under the Fourteenth Amendment, most notably, a right to privacy. This lens would have permitted the Court to more readily engage with the sexual violence that precipitated this case and the lack of protection afforded Carrie Buck – and women similarly vulnerable to sexual exploitation because of class, race, ethnicity, disability, or sexuality – from sexual assault.[28] Accordingly, any construction of the harm should have considered state action as an attack on Carrie Buck's agency, bodily integrity, and human dignity.

Second, Pearson takes issue with the lower court's cursory review and development of the facts in the case, some of which are discussed above. One major assumption highlighted by the dissent is an uncritical acceptance of the science of eugenics as reliable. At the time of *Buck*, courts employed a form of federal common law known as the *Frye* standard of "general acceptance" to determine the admissibility of expert evidence.[29] This evidentiary standard required a judge to defer to experts who employed methods and advanced theories that were "generally accepted" in the respective discipline. By the time the Court heard *Buck*, the reliability of eugenics had been publicly questioned sufficiently for the lower courts to at least raise its evidentiary validity. For example, the applicability of the peapod genetics tests to humans presented at least a viable evidentiary question of preliminary admissibility under *Frye*. This uncritical reliance on medical diagnoses to define

---

[28] The rate of sexual assault for women with disabilities is exponentially greater than the rate for non-disabled women which itself is quite high. *See, e.g.*, Jasmine E. Harris, *Sexual Consent and Disability*, 93 N.Y.U. L. Rev. 480, 491 n. 39 (2018) (noting the rate of sexual assaults committed against people with intellectual and developmental disabilities is seven times the rate of nondisabled people).

[29] *Frye v. United States*, 293 F. 1013 (D.C. Cir. 1923).

disability, impairment, and consequential limitations later constrains the reach of antidiscrimination laws such as the Americans with Disabilities Act.

Third, Pearson's dissent takes aim at the majority's reliance on a single precedent to analogize sterilization to compulsory vaccinations. Pearson challenges this claim on factual and legal grounds. She opines that the Court's opinion in *Jacobson* is not "broad enough" to cover sterilizations which are unlike vaccinations in the bodily and emotional harm experienced by the person. She also elevates the stakes of sterilization by noting that vaccination prevents disease, while sterilization removes the possibility of pregnancy and parenting altogether. Reframed as a right to parent, the Court could have relied on its emerging jurisprudence on the right to establish and raise a family.

CONCLUSION

Buck v. Bell is a dark moment in US history. When placed within a broader historical context – the evolution of the eugenics movement in the United States and its reciprocal relationship with federal immigration law – *Buck*'s significance moves beyond a cautionary tale to an example of a problematic approach to reproductive justice and disability rights whose underlying eugenic justifications continue today. Moreover, the result, as Pearson's dissent illustrates, was not inevitable.

Pearson's feminist rewriting of *Buck* offers a novel perspective on how the Court could have approached the questions presented as well as alternative doctrinal and policy justifications. Using feminist and reproductive justice lenses, Pearson relies on existing precedent in 1927 to show how the Court's emerging jurisprudence on the right to a family could have animated the equal protection claims. In addition, her opinion lays the groundwork for the development of equal protection jurisprudence and substantive due process protections in the next four decades.

Finally, *Buck v. Bell* demonstrates a lost opportunity to challenge the ways in which the state regulates women's bodies, particularly women with disabilities. A rewritten opinion in *Buck* could have championed reproductive injustice directly, with ripple effects in other areas of law such as informed consent, access to meaningful health care, and reproductive choices. Pearson highlights interpretive possibilities and reminds us of the critical role courts do and can play in shaping reproductive justice.

Buck v. Bell, 274 U.S. 200 (1927)

Justice Kim Hai Pearson, dissenting

The Virginia law in question authorizes the State to sterilize persons it deems mentally or physically incompetent. The State's reason for sterilizing incompetent persons is to promote the interest of said persons' health and the welfare of society.

In upholding the challenged law, the majority condones the State's dehumanization of persons with disabilities, harming Carrie Buck beyond repair. The State employs a guise of public interest to justify its sterilization scheme but the State's true purpose is to eliminate its obligation to care for people with disabilities by preventing Carrie Buck and others similarly deemed by the State to be "manifestly unfit" for procreation from exercising their constitutionally protected right to establish and raise families.

For the foregoing reasons, I respectfully dissent.

I CARRIE BUCK AND HER FAMILY

The majority describes Carrie Buck as a "feeble-minded white woman," "the daughter of a feeble-minded mother," and "the mother of an illegitimate feeble-minded child." Ante at 205. Virginia state law allows the state to sterilize "mental defectives," and the feeble-minded including "any patient afflicted with hereditary forms of insanity, imbecility, etc." via vasectomy for men and salpingectomy for women. *Id.* at 206. These forced sterilization procedures, according to the state, promote the "health of the patient and the welfare of society," *id*, because the state claims that "experience has shown that heredity plays an important part in the transmission of insanity, imbecility." *Id.* at 205. Once sterilized "mental defectives" would no longer be a "menace" with the ability to reproduce. *Id.* at 205–6. Thus, the state, which is currently supporting people in institutions, could release these individuals from their confinement and they could ostensibly become self-supporting citizens without the risk of transmitting their disability to any offspring. *Id.* The majority supports the state's interests, noting "that the Commonwealth is supporting in various institutions many defective persons who, if now discharged, would become a menace, but, if incapable of procreating, might be discharged with safety and become self-supporting with benefit to themselves and to society, and that experience has shown that heredity plays an important part in the transmission of insanity, imbecility." *Id.* at 205.

According to the majority, Virginia's sterilization law includes "careful safeguards" and "careful provisions" that "protect [...] the patients from possible abuse" *Id.* These protections include the requirement of a petition supported by affidavit by the superintendent of the State Colony, notice to the impacted party, a hearing to determine a patient's fitness for sterilization, and appointment of a guardian for the patient, if necessary. *Id.* The majority determines that the petition, notice, and hearing conducted on Carrie's behalf satisfied the law's procedural safeguards and cites *Jacobson v. Massachusetts*, 197 U.S. 11 (1905), a case about required vaccinations to support its decision. *Id.* at 207. To additionally support its views about the state's role in acting on behalf of "mental defectives," Justice Holmes declares that "[t]hree generations of imbeciles are enough" – a reference to Carrie, her mother, Emma Buck, and Carrie's infant daughter. *Id.* Carrie and her family do not deserve such dismissive treatment by this Court, nor should the majority ignore this family's circumstances. A careful review of those circumstances reveals that the procedure employed here failed Carrie in significant ways and that the statute strips those it impacts of their right to bodily integrity without proper justification from the State.

Carrie's mother, Emma, was admitted to the State Colony for Epileptics and Feebleminded ("State Colony") when Carrie was a young child of only "three or four" years old. Tr. of Trial at 22. She was placed with J.T. and Alice Dobbs. *Id.* In exchange for domestic service, Carrie lived under the Dobbs' supervision. She attended school until the sixth grade, working continuously throughout her stay with the Dobbs family. Tr. of Trial at 15. Carrie's half-sister, Doris Buck, was also removed from Emma's care and placed with "some people in the country." Tr. of Trial at 45.

While in the Dobbs' care, someone, perhaps a relative or close acquaintance of the Dobbs, had sexual intercourse with and impregnated Carrie, a minor child. Tr. of Trial at 59. At this time, the identity of the father of Carrie's child remains unknown to the Court but the fact that she was providing domestic labor and no longer attending school suggests that the Dobbs family was not sufficiently protective of Carrie. On learning of her pregnancy, the Dobbs did not continue to provide a work or home situation for Carrie, sending her instead to live at the State Colony, where she resided with her mother, Emma. Tr. of Trial at 9. At the time of her appeal to the Supreme Court of Appeals of Virginia, Carrie was eighteen years of age and her eight-month old infant was in the care of the Dobbs family. Tr. of Trial at 58. The State hints that the Dobbs may continue their domestic service arrangement with Carrie, provided she become sterilized before returning. Brief for Appellee at 2. There is no evidence of such an arrangement in the affidavit provided by the Dobbs family. Tr. of Trial at 22–23. Nor is there evidence that Carrie might ever have her child returned to her.

Since Carrie's birth, neither Carrie nor her family have been free of state or private institutions' interference in their lives. Researchers from the Carnegie Eugenics Institute studied Carrie's family, seeking evidence of hereditary links to mental and physical disabilities. Br. for Appellee at 6. The researchers traced family relationships with her immediate and extended family and tracked patterns of behavior in family groups with similar characteristics to Carrie's family, concluding that certain family groups were more likely to produce "socially inadequate offspring." Br. for Appellee at 5, 9. Emma's test results from the Binet-Simon standardized intelligence test reportedly determined that she had the mental age of seven years and eleven months at fifty-two chronological years of age. Tr. of Trial at 32. Using the same test, researchers concluded that Carrie's mental age was that of a nine-year-old child. *Id.* There was also a claim that Carrie's infant daughter was a "supposed . . . mental defective" at a mere six months of age but there is no evidence in the record that anyone conducted further testing of the child. *Id.*

The majority states that the state actors met the procedural safeguards outlined by Virginia law in this case. Dr. A.S. Priddy, Superintendent of the State Colony, petitioned for Carrie to be sterilized in an earlier action. Tr. of Trial at 2. Dr. Priddy died, and in his place, Dr. J.H. Bell as Superintendent of the State Colony took his place in the appeal to the Supreme Court of Appeals of Virginia. Tr. of Trial at 3. The court assigned a guardian, R.G. Shelton, to speak for Carrie's interests. Tr. of Trial at 24. R.G. Shelton was remunerated at the rate of $5.00 per day, not to exceed $15.00 for representing Carrie's interests in the proceeding to determine whether she would be sterilized. *Id.* For the lower court proceedings, Carrie's attorney was I. P. Whitehead. Brief for Appellant at 5.

II BODILY INTEGRITY

Appellant is a citizen who enjoys the same liberties guaranteed to all citizens, including the right to bodily integrity and the right to establish a family but the majority opinion in this case fails to extend these rights to Carrie Buck. Instead, the majority claims that the principle in *Jacobson v. Massachusetts*, 197 U.S. 11 (1905), is "broad enough" to authorize compulsory sterilization of incompetent citizens. In *Jacobson*, the Court upheld a state's right to require compulsory vaccination of its citizens against disease, thus infringing an individual's right to bodily integrity, defined as the right "to care for his own body and health in such a way as to him seems best." *Jacobson*, 197 U.S. at 26. The *Jacobson* Court explained that the benefit to society from requiring vaccination of most citizens was greater than the minor inconvenience of an injection. *Id.* at 26–28. *Jacobson*, therefore, stands for the principle that a person's constitutionally protected liberty interest is not an absolute right; rather, the state may infringe on this right with "restraints and burdens in order to secure the general comfort, health, and prosperity of the state." *Id.* at 26.

In the context of forced sterilization, the justifications for limiting bodily integrity that the Court elucidated in *Jacobson* are unpersuasive because, here, the State's reasons for compulsory sterilization are not sufficiently important to justify the invasion of Carrie's right to bodily integrity. The state claims "that the Commonwealth is supporting in various institutions many defective persons who, if now discharged, would become a menace, but, if incapable of procreating, might be discharged with safety and become self-supporting with benefit to themselves and to society, and that experience has shown that heredity plays an important part in the transmission of insanity, imbecility." Even if one accepts the State's rationale for the statute as valid, *Ante at 205–206.* the majority disingenuously equates an injection to prevent transmissible disease with an invasive surgery to prevent the reproduction of people who may or may not become insane or imbeciles. The minor infraction against a person's bodily integrity of an injection to prevent the spread of a known transmissible disease should not equal to an invasive medical procedure that permanently changes a person's body to prevent physical or mental conditions not reliably known to be transmissible. when prevention requires an invasive surgical procedure that will leave the individual sterile.

Furthermore, the right of bodily integrity is not contingent on one's ability to care for one's body without assistance. The majority implicitly draws an impermissible connection between Carrie's ability to care for her own body without state assistance and permissiveness for the state to violate her bodily integrity. The right to care for one's own body and health without interference from the state, as articulated in *Jacobson*, exists lest state action become "nothing short of an assault upon his person," which is a more apt description of the invasive, assaultive sterilization process against Carrie than it is of an injection to prevent smallpox. *Jacobson*, 197 U.S. at 26.

The majority describes Virginia's forced sterilization of "mental defectives" as a procedure that "may be effected in males by vasectomy and in females by salpingectomy, without serious pain or substantial danger to life." Ante at 205. Without further elucidation about the impact of an invasive surgical procedure, the majority presents a reductive interpretation of the substantive rights at stake when a state is authorized to sterilize its citizens. Unlike a vaccination, which is a simple procedure, sterilization requires a medical procedure that fundamentally and permanently changes the functioning of that person's body. Beyond the obvious difference in scale when it comes to comparing an injection to a surgery that requires anesthesia, sterilization surgery requires cutting through skin, muscle, and tissues to sever and irreversibly change the function of reproductive organs. In addition to the physical pain associated with the healing process, the majority never accounts for the pain that some patients will inevitably experience when discovering that they may never have children and establish a family of their choice.

Moreover, unlike vaccinations that benefit communities by stopping or slowing the spread of sometimes deadly diseases, sterilization does not bring beneficial effects for society and incompetent persons. It makes sense to stop the spread of serious sicknesses like smallpox. As demonstrated in *Jacobson*, a right to bodily integrity does not include a right to spread contagious diseases. Even if one were to rely on the evidence presented by the Carnegie Research Institute and several witnesses that testified about inheritable conditions, there is no evidence that Carrie would spread mental disability as one infected with smallpox would.

Even if the process of sterilization could be accomplished with a single injection, sterilizing a person has an impact entirely different from an inoculation. Compulsory sterilization violates Carrie's right to reproduce and irreparably harms her body, taking away her ability to make her own reproductive health decisions. That Carrie is she is dependent on the state for assistance does not make this rights violation less egregious. The majority conflates the public health concern of diseases that can be prevented through vaccination with a societal concern about the birth of children with unwelcome mental disorders. One has only to consider the majority's prediction that Appellant's offspring would be like a disease that would "sap the strength of the State" and overwhelm society "with incompetence" to see that the majority improperly fails to view Appellant as a citizen entitled to seek and enjoy legal protection of her rights to procreate and form a family.

Even if the majority simply meant to convey that the state's right to utilize the police powers extends to sterilization in times of great societal need just as it does to other medical procedures that are minor and not terribly invasive, the majority is wrong. Not only is the factual basis for comparing sterilization to minor medical procedures incorrect, the legal precedent used to lengthen the reach of the police powers is incorrectly applied. It may be true that the financial support of citizens with disabilities is a burden on the state; however, that is not a sufficient reason to support sterilization. There are many other burdens that the state must bear but the response by the state is not to shed itself of all populations and causes that benefit from the state's care. The principle in *Jacobson* is not broad enough to cover sterilization as it is specific to a non-invasive, beneficial procedure, not a life-changing surgery with questionable or negative effects both for society and the individual. *See Jacobson*, 197 U.S. 11. More importantly, the majority failed to apply the balancing test in *Jacobson* properly.

Jacobson set limitations on the burdens that a state may place upon its citizens, including establishing that the state's interest must meet a threshold of importance in order to justify infringement on a person's individual rights. *Id*. This Court held that if the state's demands are "reasonable conditions as may be deemed by the governing authority of the country essential to the safety, health, peace, good order, and morals of the community" (*Id*. at 26), then a court may deem those demands against an individual a constitutional exercise of the state's power. *Jacobson*, 197 U.S. at 26.

The Virginia law is unreasonable because its goal to reduce expenses by sterilizing members of society deemed unfit to produce children and thereby render them capable of living independent of state care is nonsensical. The sterilization of institutionalized populations is not "essential" to accomplishing the state's goals of releasing patients from state colonies to become self-sufficient workers who no longer pose a threat of being a "menace" to society as they reproduce "hereditary" conditions like insanity, imbecility, etc. Allowing the state to sterilize Appellant and others like her would condone the use of an "arbitrary and unreasonable" measure that is "beyond the necessities of the case." *Id*. citing *Bowman v. Va. St. Entomologist*, 105 S.E. 141, 147 (1920). If the state's interest is to benefit Carrie and society by allowing her to freely live and work outside of a state institution because she will no longer be at risk of becoming pregnant, as they claim, it is curious that the state's law aims at Carrie as Carrie seems to be the vulnerable party. If Carrie is at ongoing risk of becoming pregnant while working outside the asylum, then the state's concern should be ensuring that Carrie is not subject to exploitation, sexual or otherwise, whether she is in or outside of an institution. Protecting vulnerable people from exploitation is a complex problem that cannot be fixed by sterilizing Carrie, as sterilization terminates the risk of pregnancy but does not keep Carrie safe from sexual assault by those providing her care.

If the state is in need of space and funding to keep its population safe from the reproduction of feeble-minded and incompetent persons, it would make more sense to legislate for better funding and supervision for asylums. Even if Carrie were to be sterilized in furtherance of the state's goal to grant her freedom to work and support herself financially, the law goes above and beyond what is necessary to accomplish better supervision of those in state care. The law is unreasonable because it shifts the burden of care for its population to the population itself while allowing rank abuses to continue. The majority is not asking Carrie to make a heroic sacrifice for the well-being of the state; it is a disingenuous ploy to cover the state's refusal to properly care for its charges. It is arbitrary and unreasonable for a state to seek sterilization of its dependent population in lieu providing proper care and safety for this class of potentially vulnerable citizens.

III FUNDAMENTAL RIGHT TO ESTABLISH AND RAISE A FAMILY

In recent cases heard by this Court, the fundamental liberties enjoyed under the Fourteenth Amendment include establishing a home and raising one's children. In *Meyer v. Nebraska*, 262 U.S. 390 (1923), this Court described liberties protected by the Fourteenth Amendment as:

> not merely freedom from bodily restraint but also the right of the individual to contract, to engage in any of the common occupations of life, to acquire useful knowledge, to marry, establish a home and bring up children, to worship God according to the dictates of his own conscience, and generally to enjoy those privileges long recognized at common law as essential to the orderly pursuit of happiness by free men. *Id.* at 399.

These liberties are so important that the State must meet a high standard before those rights may be derogated. The Court has held that "this liberty may not be interfered with, under the guise of protecting the public interest, by legislative action which is arbitrary or without reasonable relation to some purpose within the competency of the state to effect. Determination by the Legislature of what constitutes proper exercise of police power is not final or conclusive but is subject to supervision by the courts." *Id.* at 399–400. In *Pierce v. Society of Sisters*, 268 U.S. 510 (1925) the Court identified the right that a parent has to establish a home and raise her child. Both *Meyer* and *Pierce* focus the right to reproduce around establishing a home and raising children. The right includes more than an individual's right to have a family but also includes the right to establish a home and enjoy the benefits of raising children.

In this case, the State denied Carrie her right to establish a home and to exercise her right to raise future children. Just as this Court protected the parents in *Meyer* and *Pierce* from state intervention in how they raised their families, so too should

Carrie have her right to have children and to raise her family protected, particularly since she will not be able to have children to raise should the state sterilize her. *Meyer* and *Pierce* indicate that disfavored family groups receive protection from state interference under the Fourteenth Amendment while they are raising their minor children. In *Meyer*, the Court permitted families to raise their children speaking German. In *Pierce*, the Court permitted families to educate their children in Catholic parochial schools.[30] There is ample evidence in the record for this case that the state and society disfavor Carrie, her family group, and those similarly situated to Carrie. Br. for Appellee at 5–9. The disfavor that society and the State have for Carrie's family group is rooted in its impermissible view that the state police power is broad enough to keep such families from being created in the first instance.

Whereas the families in *Meyer* and *Pierce* sought protection for activities that are benign yet disliked, the family in the present case could be characterized as disliked and detrimental to society. Raising children to speak German or be educated in religious schools does not threaten to financially burden the state. In contrast, the state characterizes the Buck family as a burden and threat to the state's finances and civil order. I reject this view of Carrie and her family. That a person is dependent on the state need not mean that the person or her family are detriments to society. Rather than heap approbation on Carrie and her family, the State has an obligation to care for those of its citizens who cannot care for themselves. Carrie should enjoy the protection and care of the state of Virginia, not its disdain or dire prediction that she might produce someone who commits a crime or has a disability. Raising a family without state support or supervision is not an express condition of enjoying the fundamental right to be a parent. Because the right to parent already exists, the state should not be permitted to burden the right to have a child for any specific population without just cause.

Even without any counterevidence, the majority's reasoning is flawed. Simply because individuals have a limitation on their right to marry, that does not naturally lead to a presumptive limitation on the right to procreate. Br. for Appellee at 30. Virginia state law makes it a misdemeanor to "knowingly marry any person lawfully adjudge to be insane, epileptic or feeble-minded." Br. for Appellee at 30 (citing Acts 1922, p. 470; Michie's Code, Sec 5088b). However, there is no language in that statute about procreation; it is only the Appellee who extrapolates, "Carrie Buck, is under the foregoing statutes already by law prohibited from procreation." Br. for Appellee at 30. Further, the state of Virginia does not require any other individuals to demonstrate their fitness to reproduce and raise children; nor must any other individual prove that future children will not commit crimes or become impoverished to continue exercising their rights to have or raise children. For this reason, the

---

[30] Oregon law mandated attendance at public schools for minor children. The *Pierce* Court determined that states could not interfere with parents' rights to "make basic educational decisions."

majority should have considered Carrie's case in light of *Meyer* and *Pierce*, and not only *Jacobson*.

Sterilizing Carrie is not essential to the state's stated interest in eradicating feeblemindedness, criminal activity, and poverty in its citizenry. The state has other laws and methods available for addressing incompetence, poverty, and criminality that do not necessitate intervening in an individuals' reproductive life. That is especially true where the state intervenes without due consideration of the magnitude of the right at stake nor the creativity to structure other, less invasive solutions for providing care and supervision to those in its care. There is no guarantee or even a likelihood that sterilizing a large number of persons with disabilities will eradicate undesirable qualities in society as a whole, and it is repugnant for a state to experiment on its wards.

The state's refusal to act in a protective capacity toward Carrie's fundamental rights is further evidence that its purpose is outside its competency to achieve; it is not competent to be simultaneously protective of Carrie and promote a societal goal that is diametrically opposed to Carrie's interest in having children. When the state presents its interest in society's welfare, it employs a "guise of public interest." *Meyer*, 262 U.S. at 400. The majority minimizes the significance of sterilization surgeries and oversells the state's ability to benefit society by eradicating disfavored family groups through sterilization. While it is costly to house, feed, and protect Carrie and similarly situated people from those who would take advantage of their situation, it is not necessary for the state to sterilize Carrie to further societal benefits that could be realized through less drastic measures. The state's purpose is to eliminate Carrie and others "manifestly unfit from continuing their kind." The pursuit of this purpose cannot be reconciled with the overarching legal duty the state has to care for Carrie. Indeed, it is an improper social goal for a state to attempt to lighten its burden of care for its citizens with a scheme to eradicate those who could be in its care. The majority is wrong to lend its support to the State's use of law to express disfavor for certain family groups that are characterized as a burden for society and thus less deserving of their rights.

IV PARENS PATRIAE AND DUE PROCESS

The state has an obligation to act as a parent to Carrie under the doctrine of parens patriae. By law and tradition, when acting under the authority of parens patriae, the state is a guardian over "persons under disability." *In re Turner*, 145 P. 871, 871 (1915) (citing to the principle that kings have sovereign power over their subjects), requiring states to "provide protection of the person and property of persons non sui juris, such as minors, insane and incompetent persons." *McIntosh v. Dill*, 205 P. 917, 921 (1922). To extend the metaphor, consider how the law defines a parent's role as a combination of rights and duties: "The child is not the mere creature of the state; those who nurture him and direct his destiny have the right, coupled

with the high duty, to recognize and prepare him for additional obligations."
Pierce, U.S. at 535–36).

The state may argue that it is authorized by the doctrine of parens patriae to act for
Carrie in a way that the state deems is in Carrie's and society's interest. Under this
theory, the state abridges Carrie's rights because she is incompetent to decide for
herself and requires the state to act as a parent for her. No doubt, at times the state
must act on behalf of those who are incapable of acting in their own interest or to
protect incompetent people from those who would do them harm. In so doing, the
state may abridge individual rights. However, the limitations and procedural safeguards against the state's exercise of its power should be commensurate with the
nature of the right being infringed upon. It is unreasonable for the state to seek
widespread sterilization of those in its care. The state has a duty of care for those in
its care, just as a parent has for a child. Carrie's identity as a person deemed
incompetent should not exclude her from enjoying her fundamental rights. Instead,
her identity should draw her under the state's protective wing in making decisions
on her behalf that are in her interest.

The state's duty to "recognize and prepare" persons deemed incompetent for
"future obligations" may include sterilization but the state in the instant case failed
to act as it should under parens patriae doctrine. The majority overlooks the state's
duty to act in a parental capacity to nurture and protect Carrie. In so doing, the
majority condones the state's failure to recognize the rights Carrie has to establish a
home and raise a family. The majority's language is unnecessarily cruel and wrong
about the Buck family's three generations of imbeciles. Relying on negative portray-
als of Carrie and her family to support the assertion that preventing her from having
more children is a logical, socially good choice is poorly reasoned. There is no
discussion about Carrie's suffering after being separated from her mother, her sister,
and her infant daughter. Much like the legal protection from state interference that
families in *Pierce* and *Meyer* enjoy, the state should have extended Carrie the same
non-interference in establishing a family.

The state has confused the duty to provide care with the right to dictate how
persons in receipt of care may exercise their individual rights. The rights to have
children and raise them includes the right to physically reproduce, as well as to
reproduce culture, morals, and traditions. There has been too much focus on
Carrie's mental and physical condition and too little on the benign and possibly
beneficial characteristics that she has a right to share with her family. There has
been no evidence about the nature of Carrie's ongoing relationships with those in
her family; they may continue to enjoy filial ties and have an emotional life that the
majority overlooks when it only focuses on the ease of a surgical procedure and the
benefit of having fewer of Carrie's family on the state's welfare rolls. There is no
discussion about Carrie's emotional pain suffered when she was taken advantage of
as a minor and no sense of whether she understood not only the circumstances of
her pregnancy but also the implications of sterilization. The state focuses on Carrie's

freedom to continue as a domestic worker but there is no evidence that the state entertained the possibility that Carrie's capacity for domestic work could be expanded to include training to care for her existing and future family members.

The evidence to support sterilization is insufficient and the process by which the state made its decision failed to meet the requirements of the Constitution. Nearly all of the evidence provided by the State about Carrie and her family group was derived from experts who embrace a social theory that is unsupported by law or tradition. *See* Br. for Appellee at 4–9. The social theory of eugenics or "purging the race" includes the practice of tracing patterns of inherited conditions and traits in family groups that are inferior to those of the general populace. Based on determinations of inferior genetic traits, the social theory justifies targeting these populations for sterilization as a method of slowing and ending the growth of disfavored traits. *See* Br. for Appellee at 39. Additionally, much of the record built against Carrie is based on family groups that are either not related to Carrie or are part of her extended family group, some of whom had never met Carrie and were in no position to testify as to her mental fitness. *See* Tr. of Trial at 69–80. The state's disfavor for Carrie is clear when it relies on evidence that Carrie was part of the "shiftless, ignorant, and worthless class of anti-social whites of the South" whose children threaten to become "debits to the future population of the State." Tr. of Trial at 34. The majority makes much of the possibility that Carrie's condition is hereditary and the possibility that her offspring will have the same characteristics. Br. of Appellee at 4–12.

There was no contrary evidence presented by experts whose work could provide a counter view of the social theories, such as "Purging the Race," expounded and supported by the state, Br. for Appellee at 39. Instead, Carrie's counsel deferred to the State in exercising its police powers in "what is best and proper for its citizens" in carrying out its policy goals. Reply Brief for Appellant at 5. It is unclear whether her attorney conceded that Carrie was mentally defective and/or that the state's methods for determining a person to be mentally defective were sound. There was no further investigation into Carrie's ability to provide care for herself, to maintain gainful work, and look after members of her family. If Carrie was capable of domestic service with supervision, there should have been an inquiry into the possibility that she is capable of caring for her own child and future children with supervision.

Carrie had a right to a full inquiry, not a pretext of due process with meaningless forms and sham hearings, into the question of whether she should be subject to sterilization without consent. The state's interest in lessening its financial and social burden of providing care is not a strong enough interest to counterbalance its infringement of Carrie's fundamental right to have children. The majority was wrong to rely so wholeheartedly and with little counter-evidence on the assumption that Carrie's condition is inherently detrimental to society as there was no credible evidence that she is incapable of being a contributing member of society.

In part, the poor funding that Carrie had for her case explains the dearth of evidence that might provide a fuller view of Carrie's circumstances. Her appointed guardian had a severely limited amount of money for her representation. Tr. of Trial at 24. Her counsel did not assemble affidavits from experts who could ably speak about whether Carrie's condition could be ameliorated with education and supervision, whether experiments with pea varieties should be directly analogized to the heritability of human traits, Br. for Appellee at 5, or the moral, cultural, and scientific implications for the social theory embraced by the majority.

Finally, the State's interests are in irreparable conflict with its obligations to protect its wards. Given that the state's interests are opposed to Carrie's, the majority should have delved into the State's motives in making a case that sterilization is truly in Carrie's interest and not just the State's fiscal interests. According to the State's brief, Carrie and others similarly situated to her could remain in the State's care at the cost of $200.00 per year for thirty years to achieve the same result that may be achieved with the one-time cost to the State of sterilization. The State does not answer the question of whether it is the proper body for making decisions on behalf of Carrie or whether the procedural safeguards in place for making decisions on Carrie's behalf are sufficient. Instead the State posits that because it will free inmates from the State Colony to make themselves productive members of society in exchange for sterilization, it should give consent for Carrie because the choice of freedom is unquestionably better. Br. for Appellee at 31–32. The lure of being able to reduce the number of persons in state colonies throughout the region and the possibility of eradicating entire family groups that persistently experience poverty might be tempting enough for a state to act without due care in petitioning for sterilization. It might induce a state to provide a minimal amount of resources to those appointed as guardians for its wards. Or, it might induce the state to select those who support state sterilization goals to provide expert testimony or hear petitions.

For Carrie's due process rights to be fully protected, her counsel at trial and her appointed guardian must not be entangled in any way with the State Colony or the supporters of the State's goals. At this stage in a proceeding, the record below could have been staged so that Carrie's counsel worked hand in glove with the State Colony to push forward its own social agenda. There is no way of discovering if due process was satisfactory because the majority focused on compliance with the minimum requirements for the administrative process without addressing any of the underlying concerns that necessitate having procedural safeguards at all.

The record hints at abuses suffered by individuals while in the State's care. Carrie was removed from her family as a young child, only to be placed in a home where she was vulnerable to being impregnated while still a minor. This was not an extraordinary occurrence but a pattern of poorly executed state programs for individuals with disabilities. A doctor for the state provided testimony that several young female wards sent out for domestic service returned impregnated, such that he was required to end the program. Br. for Appellee at 92. There was no sense that the State had a responsibility for providing better care and supervision of its wards.

In situations where the state wields outsized power over vulnerable people and, where the rights at stake are critically important to all citizens, it is disingenuous to imagine that a mere gesture of compliance to administrative requirements satisfies the promise of due process under the Fourteenth Amendment.

V CONCLUSION

There is no doubt that the majority has contempt for Carrie and the rights of those dependent on the state's care. The state of Virginia has grossly and inhumanely violated Carrie's due process and fundamental rights. The majority has cavalierly pushed aside important rights central to the human family in pursuit of mundane state budget goals and suspect social theories. I shudder to think of the dangerous precedent that my fellow Justices set with this decision. I can only hope that future generations will not fail to recognize the humanity in all of our brethren and sisters, regardless of their abilities and family connections.

2

Skinner v. Oklahoma, 316 U.S. 535 (1942)

Commentary by Radhika Rao

INTRODUCTION

No volume on reproductive justice could be complete without addressing the seminal case of *Skinner v. Oklahoma*.[1] *Skinner* is the first Supreme Court decision to subject a law limiting reproduction to stringent scrutiny, and it achieves this result by entwining constitutional protection of reproductive liberty with equality. Unlike the reproductive rights framework, which focuses upon the individual's right to make reproductive choices free from government regulation, reproductive justice emphasizes the political context within which race, gender, class, and other identities intersect to result in reproductive oppression. Skinner foreshadows this broader analysis, by striking down a state sterilization statute not because it interfered with individual liberty but based upon the recognition that governmental power to draw lines regarding who could reproduce and who could not posed the threat of "invidious discriminations ... against groups or types of individuals" in violation of the constitutional guarantee of equality.

Skinner makes an important gesture towards reproductive justice by grounding its holding in reproductive equality instead of autonomy but it falls short in its promise of a reproductive justice perspective. The original opinion fails to delve into the actual facts of the case, as well as the social and political context. And even though the Court recognized the risk in granting the government power to regulate reproduction, it confined its ruling to situations where the sterilization law was blatantly discriminatory, without confronting government's authority to experiment with eugenics in other contexts. As a consequence, poor people, women, and minorities continued to be targets of coercive sterilization laws and other forms of reproductive oppression long after the Supreme Court's decision in *Skinner*. A different opinion

[1] 316 U.S. 535 (1942).

cognizant of the manifold ways in which compulsory sterilization inflicts reproductive injustice could have had profound consequences for the future. In his concurring opinion, Thomas Williams applies a reproductive justice approach to remedy many of these shortcomings.

THE PATH TO *SKINNER*

In 1935, Oklahoma enacted a Habitual Criminal Sterilization Act, authorizing sterilization of those convicted of three felonies involving "moral turpitude." The law encompassed robbery and even such relatively petty crimes as chicken-stealing but explicitly exempted embezzlement, political offenses, and other white-collar crimes. Only a decade earlier, in *Buck v. Bell*,[2] the Supreme Court sustained a similar Virginia statute that authorized the sterilization of "feeble-minded" persons housed in state institutions. Writing for the Court, Justice Oliver Wendell Holmes concluded: "the principle that sustains compulsory vaccination is broad enough to cover cutting the Fallopian tubes."[3] Ironically, Holmes viewed eugenic sterilization as a compassionate policy that was less cruel, and thus preferable, to the alternatives, explaining: "It is better for all the world, if instead of waiting to execute degenerate offspring for crime, or to let them starve for their imbecility, society can prevent those who are manifestly unfit from continuing their kind."[4] Hence his infamous declaration that "three generations of imbeciles are enough."[5] Repugnant as it may appear today, eugenic sterilization was embraced at the time as a progressive policy to deal with crime and other social problems. According to legal historian Lawrence Friedman, "To Holmes, and so many of his contemporaries, the decision [in *Buck v. Bell*] was progressive."[6] Indeed, in a letter written around the same time, Holmes confessed: "I wrote and delivered a decision upholding the constitutionality of a state law for sterilizing imbeciles the other day – and felt that I was getting near to the first principle of real reform."[7]

By the time the Supreme Court decided *Skinner v. Oklahoma* in 1942, the United States was waging war against racial supremacy abroad, so that the racial connotations of such sterilization laws and their resemblance to Nazi eugenics had become too obvious to ignore. In the aftermath of the Great Depression, it was also clear that Oklahoma was authorizing the sterilization of those who had been convicted of crimes of desperation associated with their dire poverty, such as the theft of 23

---

[2]   274 U.S. 200 (1927).
[3]   *Id.* at 207.
[4]   *Id.*
[5]   *Id.*
[6]   Victoria F. Nourse, In Reckless Hands: Skinner v. Oklahoma and the Near Triumph of American Eugenics at 31 (W.W. Norton 2008), quoting Lawrence Friedman, American Law in the Twentieth Century at 110 (2002).
[7]   Oliver Wendell Holmes *Letter to Harold Laski of May 12, 1927*, 2 Holmes-Laski Letters 942 (Mark DeWolfe Howe ed. 1953).

chickens. But the blatant class-discriminatory nature of the lines drawn by the Oklahoma law raised an inference that it was intended to license other, even more invidious types of discrimination. All of these factors may have led the Supreme Court to see the discrimination that it had failed to recognize 15 years before in *Buck v. Bell*, and to conclude: "Sterilization of those who have thrice committed grand larceny with immunity for those who are embezzlers is a clear, pointed, unmistakable discrimination. ... When the law lays an unequal hand on those who have committed intrinsically the same quality of offense and sterilizes one and not the other, it has made as an invidious a discrimination as if it had selected a particular race or nationality for oppressive treatment."[8]

REWRITING SKINNER

Williams rectifies the factual and contextual omissions in the original *Skinner* opinion by vividly depicting "the rising tide of poverty" and "economic despair" following the stock market crash of 1929. Against this historical backdrop, he supplies the tragic details of Jack Skinner's conviction for the theft of 23 chickens at the tender age of 19, the loss of his leg, and his subsequent conviction for armed robbery of $17 from a gas station. He declares that "[j]udges have a responsibility to consider the realities of the times," as they may have played a part in Jack Skinner's life and choices. Williams deploys these facts to suggest that Skinner's dire economic circumstances, coupled with the loss of his limb and the lack of other options, may have driven him to desperate measures in order to feed his family. Williams ponders "how we treat those with the least amongst us in society" and ends by posing the question: "Shall we, as the highest court in the land, issue a statement that every impoverished American who turns to petty crime in an effort to feed their family might find themselves subject to sterilization?" In so doing, he intimates that Oklahoma's imposition of sterilization as a penalty for such crimes of desperation amounts to irrevocable punishment for the mere status of being poor.

The original *Skinner* opinion invoked equal protection but failed to consider the myriad other ways in which compulsory sterilization may violate the Constitution. Although the Supreme Court alluded to several different sections of the Constitution, suggesting that it could have struck down the Oklahoma law pursuant to the Fourteenth Amendment's Due Process Clause or the Eighth Amendment's prohibition of Cruel and Unusual Punishment, it did not rest its decision upon any of these provisions. Instead, the Court chose to invalidate the law based upon the Fourteenth Amendment's Equal Protection Clause, grounding its protection of reproductive liberty in the principle of equality. The Court observed that "the claim that state legislation violates the equal protection clause of the Fourteenth

---

[8] 316 U.S. at 541.

Amendment" is often denigrated as "the usual last resort of constitutional arguments."[9] But *Skinner* demonstrates the strength of the equality argument. Justice Douglas, writing for the Court, declared:

> We are dealing here with legislation which involves one of the basic civil rights of man. Marriage and procreation are fundamental to the very existence and survival of the race. The power to sterilize, if exercised, may have subtle, far-reaching and devastating effects. In evil or reckless hands it can cause races or types which are inimical to the dominant group to wither and disappear. There is no redemption for the individual whom the law touches. Any experiment which the State conducts is to his irreparable injury. He is forever deprived of a basic liberty.[10]

Despite the suggestion that marriage and procreation are fundamental rights, the Supreme Court did not rely upon the fact that compulsory sterilization is a gross invasion of individual liberty. *Skinner* is a seminal opinion because the Supreme Court explicitly rooted its defense of the right to reproduce in the systemic dangers of discriminatory government regulation. The Court refused to grant government indiscriminate power to draw lines between those who could reproduce and those who could not, explaining that "strict scrutiny of the classification which a State makes in a sterilization law is essential, lest unwittingly or otherwise invidious discriminations are made against groups or types of individuals in violation of the constitutional guaranty of just and equal laws."[11]

In his concurrence, Williams not only elaborates upon the majority's equal protection rationale, he extends it to point out other inequalities implicit in the law. Williams agrees that it is problematic for Oklahoma to sterilize chicken thieves but not embezzlers and other white-collar criminals but he goes further to argue that it is unconstitutional for the legislature to punish even the same crimes equally if they are motivated by different purposes that render them more or less culpable, such as crimes that are driven by economic necessity as opposed to the desire for power or pleasure. Williams also points out the inequality in the sterilization procedure, as it operates upon the bodies of women and men, declaring: "[t]his dichotomy creates issues of equal protection as salient as those created by the clumsy drafting of the law itself." He contends that sterilization statutes that purport to apply equally to men and women should also be deemed unconstitutional when they have a disparate impact due to biological differences in anatomy.

Williams articulates additional objections to the Oklahoma statute based upon the Due Process Clause of the Fourteenth Amendment and the Cruel and Unusual Punishments Clause of the Eighth Amendment. He criticizes the vagueness inherent in the Oklahoma law, which encompasses crimes of "moral turpitude,"

[9]   316 U.S. at 539.
[10] 316 U.S. at 541.
[11] *Id.*

contending that the judgment as to what constitutes moral turpitude rests in the eye of the beholder. He also questions the scientific validity of laws premised upon the hereditability of criminal traits, characterizing the science of genetics as "new, unclear, and fraught with ambiguity." And he emphasizes the dangers of genetic determinism and laws that impute fault to bad genes, suggesting that they "shift[] . . . responsibility from society to the germ-plasm." Williams concludes with a prescient warning: "We should collectively shudder to consider application of such science on a grand scale, only to look back once new scientific knowledge has come to light and see ourselves as monsters."

The problems with the Oklahoma statute suggest that it denies due process of law but Williams also argues that the statute inflicts cruel and unusual punishment by depriving individuals of the right to have children, which is a punishment almost as severe as deprivation of the right to life itself. Williams comes very close to holding that there is a fundamental right to have children but he could have gone one step further to call for the Court to explicitly overrule *Buck v. Bell* and confirm that compulsory sterilization is unconstitutional, even if administered in an evenhanded fashion. Nevertheless, by eloquently articulating the manifold ways in which sterilization laws amount to the "stripping of rights from an underclass," Williams rewrites *Skinner* to expose its profound implications for reproductive justice.

THE WORLD POST-*SKINNER*

Skinner is notable because it marked the first time that the Supreme Court applied strict scrutiny to strike down a law limiting reproduction, and because the constitutional protection of reproductive liberty was premised upon the ideal of equality. Yet the actual consequences of *Skinner* are less laudable. Despite its lofty language, *Skinner* failed to repudiate the despicable decision in *Buck v. Bell*. Moreover, the Court's resort to equal protection rather than due process may have been intended merely to restrict the scope of its ruling to situations where the sterilization law was flagrantly discriminatory, without challenging government's ability to experiment with eugenics in other contexts. As a result, women, minorities, and the poor continued to experience coercive sterilization and other forms of reproductive oppression long after the ruling in *Skinner*.

In spite of the Supreme Court's formal recognition that state-sponsored eugenics poses a serious risk of reproductive injustice, in the last century, "more than 60,000 people deemed unfit to reproduce were sterilized, many against their will or without their knowledge," as part of a "public health strategy embraced by 32 states under eugenics laws that advocated 'better breeding'."[12] States have only recently begun to grapple with this ugly history. California did not officially abolish its sterilization law

---

[12] Samantha Young, *California Lawmakers Seek Reparations for People Sterilized by the State*, WASHINGTON POST (Apr. 25, 2018).

until 1979 but, in the meantime, more than 20,000 Californians were sterilized pursuant to the state's eugenic policies, primarily poor people, persons with disabilities, and racial minorities. Records reveal that Latinas in California were fifty-nine percent more likely to be sterilized than non-Latinas: "They were young girls and women who probably didn't speak English well and ranked low on IQ tests," explains University of Michigan Professor Alexandra Minna Stern, who discovered the state's sterilization records in a file cabinet at the Department of Mental Health in Sacramento.[13]

Different forms of discrimination apparently prevailed in different geographical regions: African Americans were singled out for sterilization in Southern states, whereas in mid-Western states, it was often the poor. According to Stern, "[b]eing Hispanic, black or poor was characterized as a disability in those days. . . . The way these laws played out, they impacted racial minorities, but it was through the disability lens, which makes it more insidious."[14] Even quite recently, physicians are alleged to have sterilized 148 women in California prisons from 2006 to 2010.[15] Thus, in 2003, California issued an official apology, and in 2018, the California legislature contemplated a bill, sponsored by a state Senator aptly-named Nancy Skinner, that would have provided compensation to all the living victims of state-sponsored sterilization from 1909 to 1979.[16] Although this California bill was not enacted into law, similar laws have been approved in several other states. North Carolina, for example, allocated $10 million in reparations in 2013, and in 2015, Virginia authorized the payment of $25,000 to each of that state's victims of compulsory sterilization.

SKINNER'S CONTESTED CONSTITUTIONAL SIGNIFICANCE

Skinner is significant not just because it provides critical lessons regarding our constitutional past but because it stands at the crossroads of competing constitutional philosophies that may have profound consequences for the future. *Skinner* has engendered considerable controversy because it is indeterminate and may be read in several different ways. Some scholars have criticized the Supreme Court's reasoning in *Skinner* and several other cases for confusing reproductive liberty with equality, and have argued for "untangling the strands of the Fourteenth Amendment" and separating the rights to reproductive liberty and equality.[17] They imply that *Skinner* is actually a due process, fundamental rights case masquerading in equal protection, anti-discrimination garb. Others read *Skinner* as a precursor to the

---

[13] *See id.*
[14] *Id.*
[15] *See id.*
[16] *See id.*
[17] *See* Ira Lupu, *Untangling the Strands of the Fourteenth Amendment*, 77 MICH. L. REV. 981 (1979).

privacy cases defending a fundamental right not to procreate by means of contraception or abortion, and they have used *Skinner* to assert the existence of a countervailing fundamental constitutional right to procreative liberty.[18] Indeed, the battle over the doctrinal basis for *Skinner* dates back to the original decision, in which Chief Justice Stone concurred in the result but questioned the majority's reliance upon equal protection, stating: "If Oklahoma may resort generally to the sterilization of criminals on the assumption that their propensities are transmissible to future generations by inheritance, I seriously doubt that the equal protection clause requires it to apply the measure to all criminals in the first instance." He argued that the real basis for the decision was due process: "I think the real question we have to consider is not one of equal protection, but whether the wholesale condemnation of a class to such an invasion of personal liberty, without opportunity to any individual to show that his is not the type of case which would justify resort to it, satisfies the demands of due process." And Justice Jackson wrote yet another concurring opinion that invoked both due process and equal protection.

Yet untangling the strands of the Fourteenth Amendment would be a mistake, for constitutional rights should not be isolated and interpreted in a vacuum. *Skinner*'s intermingling of reproductive liberty and equality reflects deep historical wisdom,[19] and it is also remarkably modern in its recognition of more subtle forms of reproductive injustice. This is because government rarely abridges fundamental liberties across the board for everyone; instead, it typically targets selective groups, depriving them of their liberty in a discriminatory fashion. Hence, due process and equal protection often work in tandem: vindication of a right to reproductive liberty ensures equality for members of minority groups, while equality demands that fundamental rights be distributed in an evenhanded fashion. *Skinner* demonstrates that our understanding of reproductive liberty is informed and enhanced by recognition of its intimate relationship to equality. And if this juxtaposition of reproductive liberty with equality is emphasized, *Skinner*'s heirs are not *Griswold v. Connecticut* [right to contraception] and *Roe v. Wade* [right to abortion] but *Loving v. Virginia* [right to marry inter-racially] and *Obergefell v. Hodges* [right to marry a person of the same sex], which meld due process and equal protection to extend the fundamental right to marry to disempowered minorities. The same reasoning suggests that *Skinner* should not be read to protect an aggressive right to reproductive autonomy that would insulate those with power and privilege from regulation designed to protect vulnerable victims. *Skinner* stands for the proposition that government cannot single out vulnerable groups and deprive them of their right

---

[18] *See, e.g.,* JOHN ROBERTSON, CHILDREN OF CHOICE (1996).

[19] *See* Radhika Rao, *Equal Liberty: Assisted Reproductive Technology and Reproductive Equality,* 76 GEO. WASH. L. REV. 1457, 1466–67 (2008) (arguing that "[a]lmost all of the privacy cases may be reconsidered from the perspective of equality because they all involved selective or unequal deprivations of fundamental liberties").

to procreate in a discriminatory fashion, thus it represents a more judicious right to "equal liberty" or reproductive equality. There is wisdom in the marriage of reproductive liberty and equality, thus *Skinner* should be read to protect a more nuanced right to reproductive liberty that is tethered to its origins in inequality.

Williams' concurring opinion adds yet another dimension to this debate by demonstrating that constitutional law is not an abstract exercise in arid logic but a real-world practice that affects the lives of flesh and blood people. He offers a holistic approach to constitutional law by embedding the Oklahoma statute in a concrete context and examining its impact upon the lives of real people, who experience myriad forms of reproductive oppression. Williams' concurrence makes clear that compulsory sterilization is unconstitutional when it strips an underclass of a panoply of rights, simultaneously depriving them of due process and equal protection, while also inflicting an indelible punishment. By reading constitutional rights together and interpreting them with an awareness of the facts and the social and political context, Williams illustrates the dramatic disparity between the reproductive rights and reproductive justice frameworks.

These distinctions have practical consequences for contemporary controversies. A holding that the Oklahoma law violated a fundamental right to procreative liberty might threaten a variety of government regulations that have been proposed or enacted, including laws limiting commercial surrogacy, forbidding human cloning, or regulating in vitro fertilization and the genetic selection of offspring. But if *Skinner* represents a more limited principle of reproductive equality, it could authorize evenhanded regulation of reproduction. Many modern laws pit liberty against equality, thus the divergence between the libertarian and egalitarian readings of *Skinner* could result in dramatically different outcomes for constitutional challenges to laws that limit reproductive liberty in order to enhance equality.

Indeed, many of the modern justifications for regulation of assisted reproductive technologies – a topic that was decades away from being an issue in *Skinner* – involve equality. For example, some feminists contend that commercial surrogacy aggravates rather than alleviates inequality by reinforcing women's primary role as child-bearer, reducing women to their wombs and perpetuating patriarchy.[20] Although assisted reproductive technologies benefit some people by permitting them to have biological children, they may harm others by commodifying their bodies or exploiting their reproductive capacity. Other scholars argue that assisted reproductive technologies unduly emphasize biology and genetics, which poses an insidious threat to equality because it is often accompanied by – and may even

---

[20] *See, e.g.*, JANICE G. RAYMOND, WOMEN AS WOMBS (1993) (arguing that technological and contractual reproduction result in the reproductive exploitation of women); BARBARA KATZ ROTHMAN, RECREATING MOTHERHOOD: IDEOLOGY AND TECHNOLOGY IN A PATRIARCHAL SOCIETY (1989); SUSAN SHERWIN, NO LONGER PATIENT: FEMINIST ETHICS AND HEALTH CARE (1992).

reinforce – racist,[21] sexist, or other invidious stereotypes.[22] These concerns are further exacerbated by the advent of gene-editing technologies, such as CRISPR/ cas 9. Some scholars maintain that technologies that enable the genetic selection of offspring traits may fundamentally alter our concept of "normal" and disadvantage those who deviate from society's ideal, raising the specter of new genetic hierarchies.[23] Indeed, such fears came to the fore in November 2018, in response to claims that a Chinese scientist used CRISPR to create the first genetically-altered babies.[24] Many progressive policymakers immediately condemned his actions and called for a moratorium on the use of such technology, with enforceable policies to prevent further steps towards an era of free-market eugenics.[25] In light of these concerns, *Skinner*'s recognition of the systemic risks of unbridled power to select genetic traits seems remarkably prescient. *Skinner* applied strict scrutiny to strike down a statute that embodied state-sponsored eugenics, thus it would be incredibly ironic to interpret *Skinner* as granting individuals a license to engage in private eugenics.

CONCLUSION

Reproductive rights shield individual liberty, whereas reproductive justice seeks societal fairness and evenhanded administration of law without regard to social status. *Skinner* may be the most important case in the pantheon of Supreme Court decisions regarding a right to reproduce because it embodies both values, intertwining protection of reproductive liberty with equality. Williams' concurrence adds a critical dimension to *Skinner* by reading these constitutional rights together and embedding them in a concrete social and political context. His opinion illustrates a more nuanced reading of reproductive liberty, one that is sensitive to the systemic consequences of regulation upon the social status of disempowered groups. Such a reading of *Skinner* distinguishes between different forms of government action and

---

[21] *See, e.g.,* Dorothy E. Roberts, *Race and the New Reproduction,* 47 HAST. L.J. 935, 937–44 (1996); Dorothy E. Roberts, *The Genetic Tie,* 62 U. CHI. L. REV. 209, 209–14 (1995). *See also* PATRICIA WILLIAMS, THE ALCHEMY OF RACE AND RIGHTS: DIARY OF A LAW PROFESSOR (1991).

[22] *See* Lisa C. Ikemoto, *The In/Fertile, the Too Fertile, and the Dysfertile,* 47 HAST. L.J. 1017 (1996) (exploring ways in which infertility discourse construct boundaries that divide women into different categories and oppress women of color, poor women, and lesbians in different ways).

[23] *See, e.g.,* Adrienne Asch, *Disability Equality and Prenatal Testing: Contradictory or Compatible?,* 30 FLA. STATE UNIV. L. REV. 315 (2003).

[24] Gina Kolata, Sui-Lee Wee, and Pam Belluck, *Chinese Scientist Claims to Use Crispr to Make First Genetically-Edited Babies,* N.Y. TIMES (Nov. 26, 2018).

[25] Civil Society Calls for "International Summit on Human Genome-Editing" to Condemn Gene-Edited Baby Claims and Experiments, Press Statement by Center for Genetics and Society and Human Genetics Alert, Nov. 29, 2018. *See also* Denis Normille, *Organizers of Gene-Editing Meeting Blast Chinese Study but Call for 'Pathway' to Human Trials,* SCIENCE MAGAZINE (Nov. 29, 2018). www.sciencemag.org/news/2018/11/organizers-gene-editing-meeting-blast-chinese-study-call-pathway-human-trials

might permit government regulation of reproductive liberty in order to redress pervasive inequalities in our society.

Skinner v. Oklahoma, 316 U.S. 535 (1942)

Justice Thomas Williams, concurring

I concur in the result but am not persuaded that we are limited to reaching it by recourse to the equal protection clause alone. I respectfully raise a number of issues the majority relegates but that I believe are critical to the disposition, some of which I raise sua sponte.

The context of the decision is not in the ether but immediately before us. Acknowledging this context – a rising tide of poverty and disillusionment in both the American imagination and in its reality – is critical to interpreting the law at hand. Little more than half a decade ago, the country found itself in what has gone on to become a perpetual state of worry following the stock market crash of 1929. What began on that day has stretched itself into years of instability, even for men who were once of means. Now we call it the Great Depression and no person is untouched by its footprint. The American west was handed the additional blow of the Dust Bowl, decimating crops and livelihoods. Oklahoma is one of the states hit hardest by these concerted events. I believe it is no coincidence that this Court finds itself considering a set of events, if not orchestrated by this confluence, easily and directly connected to it. Many, if not most, Americans know someone facing the commonality of economic despair in these times.

That this played some part in the life and choices of Jack Skinner, and has for many, is surprisingly absent from the majority opinion, though it deserves consideration. The Depression has likely turned many an honest laborer to crime, hunger having led them to steal to feed themselves and their families.

This Court's responsibility is to interpret the law, and appropriately limit the actions of well-meaning governments and more problematic ones when they overstep their bounds. Doing so requires contextual exploration of the emergence of such laws, including where and how they function. Stated plainly, the circumstances in which they emerge matter. Justices and judges are called upon to take up this task. They must weigh the interests and protections our Constitution was crafted to embolden – a free-thinking citizenry to take up opposition against the powers provided to government. In this situation, the state legislature of Oklahoma is that government power. If courts always defer to the legislatures, they will cease to perform their legitimizing function, and, more importantly, leave the common person with no avenue to pursue justice when the government violates their most basic and closely held rights.

Judges have a responsibility to consider the realities of the times, and to embed that consideration into our opinions. Such realities should have a strong connection

to the structure of the law and its impact on, and limitations of, individual action –
especially when it displaces fundamental rights. Despite the lack of consideration
granted to realities of the time by the majority opinion, failures of the statute make
its constitutionality questionable on multiple grounds. That the majority reached
the same decision should not limit our analysis of its deficiencies to the narrow
equal protection analysis of their decision.

The story of Jack Skinner is not an easy one. The defendant came of age just prior
to the stock market crash and the Great Depression. He committed his first offense
in 1926, at nineteen. That crime would begin the dominoes of justice, perhaps
undercutting his access to a truly just result given economic realities. This has led to
the threat of his sterilization by the Oklahoma government under the Act.

Skinner stands in the place of every poor American subjected to a legislature's
failure to consider individual realities and individual rights. Because of this, the
question before the Court becomes bound not only to Skinner's indiscretions and
punishment but how we treat those with the least amongst us in society. Normally,
this is a question that the legislature address and which the courts defer to but the
circumstances at hand suggest Oklahoma has failed its citizenry in its responsibility
to honor the least among them. Such circumstances shout for Oklahoma's legislature to engage in an exercise revisiting the problems that its statute presents.

The reach of our criminal laws is limited, and for good reason. The instant case is
one in which I fear that the state of Oklahoma has moved beyond the pale in its
efforts to protect the public – curtailing individual rights, perhaps engaging in cruel
and unusual punishment, and robbing individuals of the right to beget children. We
should be especially circumspect of laws and regimes which strip citizens of their
most fundamental rights, and especially when public opinion tends towards the
stripping of rights of an underclass.

It would be a failure here to not note the role that poverty plays in the administration of justice insofar as the application of this statute applies. In their attempts to
differentiate between crimes, the state of Oklahoma has placed an unreasonably
heavy burden on the poorest in the state. The statute prohibits application of the Act
to "revenue acts, embezzlement, and political offenses" (Petition for Writ of Certiorari at 3), which is problematic in light of differential treatment of the destitute,
which the majority opinion fails to shed the light of day upon in its limited
consideration of unequal treatment under the law. The structure of the law and
its application make it clear that this was meant to protect the wealthy and powerful
class charged with the construction of a law and their benefactors.

The drafting of such a bill stinks of the moral turpitude the legislature claims to
protect society from. They protect themselves from sterilization even if they habitually engage in political offenses, including theft of public coffers, and men who
steal money from banks and business where they hold positions of power but claim
that the poor man stealing chickens must answer to a higher moral authority for the
good of the public. While the farmer is no doubt upset by the theft of his chickens,

can we not agree that the white-collar criminals protected from the reach of this statute owe a higher legal duty: one to the public that installs them in office or who place their hard-earned dollars in the bank to protect? Can we not agree that a legislature taking such action actively protecting the wealthy is a greater threat to the public good than is a lowly chicken thief when men can barely eat?

Oklahoma threatens many with sterilization under this statute, based in large part on a belief that their children will prove a detriment to society. Similar claims underlie our decision in the case of Carrie Buck. The validity of the claim that inmates at McAlaster State Prison, the Oklahoma correctional facility housing Skinner, will unquestionably pass along their criminal tendencies to their offspring should give the court pause. Without certainty on this point, the law is but the culmination of a fool's errand and an opiate of the people. This begs the court to consider, if not answer with authority, a threshold question that the majority looks past: what level of scientific authority must the state rely on to consider in good conscience permanent and uncorrectable sterilization of individuals in furtherance of an abstract public good?

This first appropriate inquiry in the conundrum before us I am not qualified to answer, unlike the more familiar questions the Act places before this Court. Limits on the power of a state legislature's action are old fare. If the scientific basis can be proven true, can my fellow justices and I be mandated to engage in procreative projects on the basis of obtaining a highest and best generation to follow? Can Skinner himself, or any individual, be proven "genetically undesirable" warranting sterilization based on commission of some unspecified crimes? Here, the state has a heavy burden – it must link its law in a direct and substantial way with proof of this as scientific fact but also ensure that it aligns with the ideas of liberty that govern the way that we endeavor to form our families whether it comes in the form of a positive or negative mandate.

The state of Oklahoma has provided no evidence of scientific agreement on these matters and fails to acknowledge it as a threshold question for enactment of the statute. Within science, as in other matters, there is acknowledged disagreement among scholars, despite what may be widespread public sentiment. While Mendel proved himself apt at understanding the genetic predisposition of peas, men are not so simple, and even for those men who would seem to be as simple as one in their thoughts and actions, it remains unclear as to whether such a fate is sealed for their children.

Courts, including our own, struggle to understand the predilections, dispositions, and intent of the individuals coming before them, let alone how those elements might be linked to the behavior and disposition of their children or their parents before them. Indeed, many parents find themselves befuddled for a lifetime while trying to understand how their own children's behavior and thoughts are linked to their own. Proof of such a scientifically infallible connection would fundamentally upend many tenets of our jurisprudence if confirmed.

Many a man who has been born to an alcoholic father went on to be a success, and the opposite continuum has also proven itself true. The science also seemingly fails to acknowledge the contributions of the second, and equally important parent in each case, making the solution posed by sterilization all the more dubious. Perhaps on this basis, the American Neurological Association is "wholly opposed to sterilization, believing it . . . a dodging of the issues and a shifting of responsibility from society to the germ-plasm."[26]

This connection between parental behavior and determination of the character and behavior of children is critical. As the majority contends, individuals hold a God given, sacred, and fundamental right in choosing when and whether to beget children. The right is as sacred as the right to choose whom and when to marry. A government's interest in curtailing any right as fundamental as these must always be viewed with circumspection, requiring a salient, immediate, and pressing need to limit it, and any such limitation must be crafted in the narrowest way possible. Certainly, a permanent limitation raises the bar even further, to a point at which a state should find it almost impossible to impose such a restriction or punishment

In addition to not addressing the threshold issue, the statute limits sterilization to individuals who have committed habitual crimes of "moral turpitude" but fails to elucidate how we might classify a crime as one of morality versus one of need, or some other basis. Even within the statute at question, reference to the crimes punishable is sometimes connected to moral turpitude and at other times not. Its language is inconsistent at best. The defendant, Jack Skinner, was initially convicted of the theft of twenty-three chickens. While the realization of this loss was no doubt troubling for the chicken farmer, how does that fact alone lead us to believe that moral turpitude was present in the petitioner's behavior? The intent of such a law, using such nebulous language, seems most certainly to be a subjective one. Each judge might determine for themselves what the measure of moral turpitude should be, and which crimes fit within it. All the statute does to guide us is to limit application of the law's enforcement to certain crimes.

There are many ways to steal a chicken, just as there are many ways to rob someone with a gun. Perpetrators are not only guided by what we assume is the underlying goal. That goal fits into a larger context of their lives. Would it be shocking to assume that criminals fall into disparate classes? One class of criminals is driven to crime by need. This first class of criminals do not wish to engage in criminal activity; they find no pleasure in taking from others or in the possibility of causing injury to another but are driven by life force. They want only to sustain themselves in periods during which their most basic needs fail to be met – to do so they take food and money or whatever else is required to make it to the next day. I do not believe that we would speak of these individuals as morally undesirable or

---

[26] Eugenic Sterilization, Report of the Committee of the American Neurological Association (1936).

violating the norms of circumstance. These individuals we could classify as moral criminals. Another class of criminals might be those who enjoy the power that comes with his engagement in criminal enterprises – perhaps he wants to control the chicken market. Each of his criminal actions is orchestrated to result in a larger share of some market which they trade, be it legal or otherwise. This class of criminals is the equivalent of the modern businessman but living outside the grasp of the law. This class of criminal likely has his basic needs met. He may threaten members of the general public in seeking to control his criminal marketplace. We may choose to call their behavior power-based criminality.

We can go on to list many other classes of individual criminals but the point is this – the same crimes can carry wildly different rationales for their commission. It seems likely that we venture closer to the "moral turpitude" the law attempts to encompass when we speak of the power-based criminality. In speaking of turpitude in the legal context, while we are given no direction, the legislature likely intended to refer to violation of our collective norms. Attempting to feed oneself through stealing a few dollars when the remaining option is starvation cannot be characterized as carrying the same moral problem in kind or degree as that which is done for pleasure, or for power, or for revenge. In addition, when we speak of moral reprehensibility, thoughts turn to the most heinous of crimes. Not simple theft.

The morally reprehensible criminal is the one who rapes, who commits homicide, who leaves the community in very real fear for their lives and for those around them. It is unclear whether Jack Skinner fits this mold, and equally unclear what the legislature was referring to when they used language of morality. Moral norms are, by their very nature, flexible and variant. Law, however, requires that prospective defendants be aware of the possible punishments which may come with the commission of their crimes.

Skinner faced a far greater loss than the rightfully upset chicken farmer during this period, which is unaccounted for in his crimes. He lost his own leg in an accident with an automobile as a young man. In thinking about the nature of his crimes this is contextually important because the incident served to narrow his access to economic freedom in a time where there was little such freedom available to anyone, especially those living in Oklahoma. A man without use of all of his physical abilities and no recognizable special skills or training starts the race far from the start of his competitors. Perhaps his economic circumstances are the reason that Skinner's crimes continued to mount. It is unclear in a review of the record but seems as though it is a matter requiring some inquiry by the courts when they determine it is appropriate to permanently rob an individual of the right to procreative choice in the future. Skinner committed two armed robberies, a serious crime, which puts lives at stake. The last time he robbed a gas station of seventeen dollars. It is unclear what motivated Skinner to partake in these crimes but many Americans might find themselves in financial straits, should we not endeavor to create a legal regime that requires us to at least ask the question: what moral failing attaches to this crime? In doing so, we can aim to create systems and processes in which we answer crime with the most well calibrated and least invasive punishment available and appropriate. Each of them might find themselves turning to untoward means of feeding their families where no other options exist.

This is not to say that Skinner and others like him should not be held accountable for their crimes. The argument I make here is not one that exonerates the poor who engage in criminal behavior because of the economic status. It is narrowly proscribed to a valid consideration of the context of the instant case. Criminal laws have always provided such accountability, both before and after the passage of the Act.

That a punishment should somehow connect to the severity of the crime is a longstanding accepted norm within our justice system. Men are not put to death for the theft of a pen. In many states they are not put to death for far more injurious crimes against others in society. While life is our most fundamental right through which we are able to express all the others accorded to us in this society, the right to bear children nips at its heels in the hierarchy of importance. The family is the center of private life. Barring an individual from the creation of that unit as a legal punishment must be almost as narrowly proscribed as the sentence of death. Jack Skinner has not murdered. He has not maimed a man. He has stolen chickens and robbed at gunpoint. He should serve a sentence – at the time of bringing this case he was serving sentences for each of these crimes. Those prison sentences, and the stigma that comes with them, seem more than enough to provide redress for the crimes committed.

These failures are the beginning, and not the most problematic. The court also fails to address the Eighth and Fourteenth Amendments claims of cruel and unusual punishment, choosing to "pass on these points without intimating an opinion on them" by condemning the law on other grounds. But these claims bear consideration and it is shortsighted and ill-informed to dismiss them. I will simply point to the decision of the D.C. Circuit Court in *Davis v. Berry*, in which it struck down a similar law concerning vasectomy on Eighth Amendment grounds. That court wrote:

> When Blackstone wrote his commentaries, he did not mention castration as one of the cruelest punishments quite likely for the reason that, with the advance of civilization, the operation was looked upon as too cruel, and was no longer performed. But each operation is to destroy the power of procreation. It is, of course, to follow the man during the balance of his life. The physical suffering may not be so great, but that is not the only test of cruel punishment; the humiliation, the degradation, the mental suffering are always present and known by all the public and will follow him wheresoever he may go. This belongs to the Dark Ages. *Davis v. Berry*, 216 F. 413 (S.D. Iowa 1914)

The same reasoning is applicable here and should be a standard the Court defers to when appropriate as a matter of course.

In *Buck v. Bell*, 274 U.S. 200 (1927), this Court stepped outside these boundaries, and also failed to engage on the fundamental threshold questions raised previously in a meaningful way. In doing so, it validated a science that none of the Justices can claim to be well trained in, and that is new, unclear, and fraught with ambiguity. Scientists themselves cannot easily prove or disprove the theories associated with it, and yet penalties have been situated atop a theory with eugenics as a foundation. We should collectively shudder to consider application of such science on a grand scale, only to look back once new scientific knowledge has come to light and see ourselves as monsters.

Carrie Buck, it should be noted, underwent a procedure far more physically onerous and mired with possible complications than vasectomy. I note this distinction because the statute in question was to be applied to men and women. The differences between vasectomy and salpingectomy matter in considering the law. The latter procedure is the surgical removal of a part of the internal female anatomy, the fallopian tube. It requires a far deeper incision, a laporectomy, and the opening of a large portion of the abdominal wall in order to access the part of the anatomy required to be removed to complete the procedure. By contrast, a vasectomy requires the severing of the vas deferens, necessitating a far shorter recovery period, and significantly less general risk to the person undergoing the procedure.

In the most well-known cases to date, sterilization's burden was placed upon the bodies of women. In that way, Skinner lies outside of the norm, though the rationale for his punishment is the same – eugenic improvement of society, which sits on tenuous scientific, and that being their basis, policy grounds. The majority's failure to acknowledge this is an important oversight with respect to due process and equal protection concerns.

This dichotomy creates issues of equal protection as salient as those created by the clumsy drafting of the law itself. Men and women subject to the same law seeking similar outcomes face radically different processes to achieve the law's ends, with altogether different risk for similarly situated individuals. This is as nefariously haphazard as the way in which the statute itself excludes certain crimes from consideration.

This argument is a logical endpoint of the rationalization that the majority utilizes in constructing its opinion. Justice Douglas argues that theft and embezzlement are the same in practice and one cannot be punished in a drastically different manner than the other, due to equal protection considerations. The same logic must be applied with respect to the application of a physically invasive punishment that carries vastly different pragmatic risks for men and women. A court must, in that case, yield to reason. This is as problematic as the difference in the treatment of the petty thief versus that of the embezzler. Here, I simply argue that the same logic must also be applied with respect to the application of punishments to all crimes with respect to the sex of perpetrator. When a criminal punishment itself though identical in language carries vastly different pragmatic risks the courts must there too yield to such reason. This as problematic as the difference in the treatment of the petty thief versus that of the embezzler.

Put another way, why should a woman's biology place her in the vice grip of a criminal sanction that itself already carries the stripping from her of her most fundamental autonomous right – that of choice to become a mother – but also require her to sustain greater actual physical harm and suffering than a male criminal found guilty of an identical crime? A female criminal in such a position deserves the same equal protection under the law, as does the chicken thief here.

Finally, we must deal with the issues of vagueness this law presents. While it both protects the crimes connected to wealth, and legitimizes cruel and unusual punishments, it fails to provide a proper rubric through which to evaluate one's own behavior. In *Connally v. General Construction Co.*, 269 U.S. 385, 391 (1926), this Court held that "[T]he terms of a penal statute [...] must be sufficiently explicit to inform those who are subject to it what conduct on their part will render them liable to its penalties . . . and a statute which either forbids or requires the doing of an act in terms so vague that men of common intelligence must necessarily guess at its meaning and differ as to its application violates the first essential of due process of law."

Oklahoma's statute fails to meet this standard. What is moral turpitude? It would seem to be the purview of the beholder. Many men of common intelligence would refer to crimes of murder, rape and kidnapping – but it is doubtful that chicken theft would meet the standard and questionable whether armed robbery, while violent, meets with such a definition.

Application and promulgation of laws like this one is myopic at best and nefarious at worst. Shall we, as the highest court in the land, issue a statement that every impoverished American who turns to petty crime in an effort to feed his family might find himself subject to sterilization? No. In a country founded by those who left the shores of their home countries to seek opportunities prohibited by their governments, we have a duty to protect fundamental rights, including that of individual procreative choice.

3

Wyman v. James, 400 U.S. 309 (1971)

Commentary by Michele Gilman

In *Wyman v. James*, the Supreme Court in 1971 upheld the constitutionality of home visits by social service caseworkers to verify the eligibility of welfare recipients. The case was a bitter blow to the welfare rights movement of the era and cemented a divide in privacy rights between the poor and the rich. The Supreme Court's decision rested on distrust of the motives and morality of low-income mothers, particularly women of color, and it fueled the harmful "welfare queen" trope that continues to bedevil American social welfare policy. It also failed to restrain increasing forms of surveillance that impact not only poor people but all Americans. By contrast, Priscilla Ocen's rewritten opinion contains a robust vision of privacy that does not discriminate based on race, gender, or income.

THE DECISION

The plaintiff in *Wyman*, Barbara James, received benefits under the Aid to Families with Dependent Children (AFDC) program, which provided cash assistance to low-income, single-parent families. As part of the welfare certification process, the Department of Social Services (DSS) advised Ms. James that she had to submit to a home visit. In response, Ms. James offered to provide documentation to the DSS but refused to permit a caseworker into her home. As a result, the DSS terminated her benefits. She, along with a class of similarly situated women receiving AFDC benefits, challenged the home visit policy, arguing that it was an unconstitutional search in violation of the Fourth Amendment. Although they won their case before a three-judge panel of the Southern District of New York, they lost before the Supreme Court in a 6-3 opinion.

Justice Harry Blackmun, who would later write the majority opinion in *Roe v. Wade*, authored *Wyman*'s majority opinion; it happened to be his first published opinion on the Court.[1] The Court began by proclaiming the sanctity of the home and acknowledging the Fourth Amendment's protections against warrantless government searches. However, it held those foundational principles did not apply to welfare recipients. Rather, the Justices reasoned, because AFDC recipients consented to a welfare home visit, the Constitution did not protect against the search. Moreover, the Court determined that even if home visits were searches, they were reasonable in light of the lack of criminal consequences that flowed from the searches, and given the state's interests in, among other things, deterring fraud, protecting the public fisc, and safeguarding the children of women receiving welfare.

BACKGROUND

American policy and rhetoric categorize the poor as either deserving, meaning they cannot be blamed for their poverty, such as children, widows, and the disabled; or undeserving, meaning they should be self-sufficient, such as non-disabled adults.[2] The deserving poor are worthy of support; the undeserving poor are not.[3] The undeserving poor are also stripped of privacy rights. Throughout history, the poor have had less privacy in their homes, as well as over their bodies and decision-making, than their more affluent counterparts. For instance, in colonial America, most towns had an "overseer of the poor," whose job was to chase poor people out of town or to conscript them for free labor.[4] When poorhouses became the dominant form of poor relief in the 1800s, the poor lived and labored in squalid conditions under the eye of the "keeper."[5] The late 1800s saw the rise of the Scientific Charity movement, which was more benevolent than prior approaches but subjected the poor to moral chastisement by "friendly visitors."[6] State surveillance was, and remains, the norm.

"Given the challenges husbandless mothers pose to the rules of both capitalism and patriarchy,"[7] single mothers occupy a shifting and uneasy space between the poles of deserving and undeserving.[8] In the early twentieth century, progressive

---

[1] In *Roe* and *Wyman*, Blackmun exhibited extreme deference to professionals – the doctors in *Roe* and social workers in *Wyman*, respectively. As discussed *infra*, he demonstrated far less respect or deference to the actual women impacted by these decisions.

[2] See JOEL F. HANDLER & YEHESKEL HASENFELD, BLAME WELFARE, IGNORE POVERTY AND INEQUALITY at 71 (2007); KHIARA M. BRIDGES, THE POVERTY OF PRIVACY RIGHTS at 48–51 (2017).

[3] *Id.*

[4] See JOHN GILLIOM, OVERSEERS OF THE POOR: SURVEILLANCE, RESISTANCE, AND THE LIMITS OF PRIVACY 22 (2001).

[5] *Id.* at 24.

[6] *Id.* at 24–25.

[7] MIMI ABRAMOVITZ, REGULATING THE LIVES OF WOMEN 313 (1992).

[8] See LINDA GORDON, PITIED BUT NOT ENTITLED: SINGLE MOTHERS AND THE HISTORY OF WELFARE 1890–1935 24–35 (1994); ABRAMOVITZ, *supra* note 7, at 318; HANDLER & HASENFELD, *supra* note 2, at 150.

reformers convinced states to adopt mother's pensions programs, which provided aid to "suitable" single women, mostly white widows, so that they could raise their children at home.[9] The New Deal program called Aid to Dependent Children (later renamed AFDC) federalized these early programs and presaged the controversy in the *Wyman* case. AFDC provided a measure of economic freedom to some women but only in their role as mothers.[10] Moreover, it was part of a New Deal dichotomy that reinforced the deserving versus undeserving paradigm by treating relief for white men differently than relief for minorities and women.[11] White working men benefited from programs such as old-age social security and unemployment insurance (UI) that have carried no stigma, provided more generous benefits pursuant to objective criteria, and been federally administered.[12] To appease Southern Congressmen who wanted to ensure availability of a low-wage workforce and white dominance, the social security program excluded agricultural and domestic workers, thereby barring most African American workers, who were concentrated in those workforces.[13] Meanwhile, cash assistance programs for single mothers, primarily AFDC, became stingy, stigmatized, state-administered, and discretionary.[14] Indeed, throughout the ensuing decades, states adopted a variety of discretionary policies, including man-in-the-house rules (cutting benefits to any woman found living with a man), midnight raids (surprise visits to enforce standards), and "suitable home" requirements (enforcing an unwritten moral code) that mostly operated to disqualify women of color from welfare, thereby making them available for low-wage jobs.[15] As Kaaryn Gustafson explains, "The unstated but underlying goals of the rules were to police and punish the sexuality of single mothers, to close off the indirect access to government support of able-bodied men, to winnow the welfare rolls, and to reinforce the idea that families receiving aid were entitled to no more than near-desperate living standards."[16]

Nevertheless, from the 1950s to the 1970s, AFDC rolls grew rapidly as family structures changed across society and economic dislocations disproportionately

---

[9] See Abramovitz, *supra* note 7, at 199.

[10] Gordon, *supra* note 8, at 291.

[11] *Id.* at 5.

[12] *Id.* at 293.

[13] See Juan F. Perea, *The Echoes of Slavery: Recognizing the Racist Origins of the Agricultural and Domestic Worker Exclusion from the National Labor Relations Act*, 72 Ohio State L.J. 95, 97 (2011); Jill Quadagno, The Color of Welfare: How Racism Undermined the War on Poverty 21 (1994).

[14] See Gordon, *supra* note 8, at 293–94. Even today, social security disability and retirement benefits and UI benefits carry less stigma because of their ties to work. Further, the benefit amounts for men are typically higher than those for women because benefits amounts are tied to earnings. Men generally earn higher wages than women and are in the workforce longer due to fewer family responsibilities. See Abramovitz, *supra* note 7, at 259–60; 292–300.

[15] See Abramovitz, *supra* note 7, at 323; Handler & Hasenfeld, *supra* note 2, at 157.

[16] Kaaryn Gustafson, Cheating Welfare: Public Assistance and the Criminalization of Poverty 21 (2011).

impacted African Americans.[17] In addition, a vibrant welfare rights movement flourished in which poor black women, building upon the civil rights and feminist struggles, asserted their political and economic rights.[18] Through organizing, political protests, and litigation, this movement achieved many of its goals. Its litigation victories included objective eligibility criteria rather than discretionary morals tests (*King v. Smith*, 1968), fair hearing rights to appeal adverse welfare decisions (*Goldberg v. Kelly*, 1970), and elimination of restrictive residency laws (*Shapiro v. Thompson*, 1969). The movement challenged the two-parent family as the norm and highlighted the economic and social value provided by domestic work, thus embodying feminist insights. Most importantly, the movement empowered poor women, such as Barbara James, to demand rights. In turn, these successes spurred a public backlash that blamed the behavior of poor, black women for the growing welfare rolls, rather than the structural changes in society and the economy. *Wyman* arose during this time of heightened conflict.

OCEN'S DECISION

Ocen makes five major feminist theoretical moves in her opinion that diverge from Blackmun's majority opinion. From the first line of the opinion, Ocen applies an intersectional perspective, recognizing that the government violated welfare mothers' privacy due to the combination of race, class, and gender. In his first sentence, Justice Blackmun calls Ms. James a "beneficiary." By contrast, Ocen describes Ms. James as a "poor black woman." This frames the remainder of her opinion – Ocen explains throughout how women receiving welfare are particularly vulnerable to governmental surveillance and suspicion in ways that do not impact other Americans. For instance, she brings a critique of the original opinion's dissenters to the foreground, highlighting that "no other recipient of government subsidies is subject to the indignities experienced by AFDC recipients."[19] As she notes, farmers, corporations, homeowners, and others receive billions of dollars in social welfare (usually masked in the form of tax subsidies) but government agents do not rummage through their cupboards to verify eligibility. Surveillance is more than an annoyance; indeed, welfare mothers report that "the hassle and degradation caused by surveillance ... hinder[s] their ability to meet the needs of their families."[20]

---

[17] See ABRAMOVITZ, *supra* note 7, at 319–20; GUSTAFSON, *supra* note 16, at 21.
[18] On the welfare rights movement, see PREMILLA NADASEN, WELFARE WARRIORS: THE WELFARE RIGHTS MOVEMENT IN THE UNITED STATES (2005) and FELICIA KORNBLUH, THE BATTLE FOR WELFARE RIGHTS: POLITICS AND POVERTY IN MODERN AMERICA (2007).
[19] Ocen in this volume at 66.
[20] GILLIOM, *supra* note 4, at 6.

Second, Ocen acknowledges the importance of privacy for women. She starts her analysis where Justice Blackmun does, with the sanctity of the home.[21] However, Ocen extends that sanctity to poor, single mothers. To be sure, privacy in the home has long been fraught territory for feminists. Second-wave feminists argued against the historical demarcation between the public sphere – where men pursued work and engaged in government and civil society – and the private sphere – the home where women raised children under the thumb of men. Feminists such as Catherine MacKinnon argued that men used the public/private divide to oppress women.[22] A home might be a man's castle but, behind the castle walls, men were free to abuse women. This view, however, arguably excludes the varying perspectives of women of color. It also oversimplifies the harms of privacy. As Anita Allen writes, "Privacy is often important, but there can be too much as well as too little privacy; subordinating as well as equalizing forms of privacy ..."[23]

By contrast, in stressing the sanctity of the home, Ocen avoids the oppressive potential of privacy by stressing the benefits of privacy for poor women, and poor black women in particular. Long subject to government surveillance, poor women need privacy to ensure the norms of dignity and autonomy that undergird the Fourth Amendment. Ocen's willingness to stress home privacy reflects her animating, intersectional perspective. Throughout American history, the public/private divide operated differently for single women, and particularly women of color. From the time African American women were brought to this country, they labored outside the home, first as enslaved people and later as domestics and agricultural workers.[24] In addition, the state coerced black women into sterilization or sanctioned the performance of unconsented sterilization procedures, and continues to disproportionately remove black children from their homes, and criminally prosecute black women who use illicit drugs during their pregnancies.[25] For these women, the home could serve as a sanctuary against a harsh public domain. Thus, in Ocen's decision, the home protects men but also the women who long toiled within its walls. Simply put, the Fourth Amendment protects all homes, regardless of the financial wherewithal of their occupants.

Third, Ocen applies a feminist understanding of consent that recognizes power differentials between the parties, rather than assuming the traditional "liberal" view that all individuals share equal agency. For his part, Justice Blackmun concluded

---

[21] Blackmun noted "[t]he [Fourth Amendment] right of the people to be secure in their persons, houses, papers, and effects," which the Court had long characterized as "basic to a free society." 400 U.S. at 316 (citations omitted).

[22] CATHERINE A. MacKINNON, TOWARD A FEMINIST THEORY OF THE STATE 194 (1989).

[23] Anita Allen, Gender and Privacy in Cyberspace, 52 STANFORD L. REV. 1175, 1200 (2000).

[24] See ABRAMOVITZ, supra note 7, at 110.

[25] See Dorothy E. Roberts, Punishing Drug Addicts Who Have Babies: Women of Color, Equality, and the Right to Privacy, 104 HARV. L. REV. 1419, 1437–40 (1991).

that a needy mother who did not want to abide by AFDC rules could simply decline benefits.[26] By contrast, Ocen recognizes that, for an indigent woman, consent is a myth due to the "disparities in power" between her and the state. Looking at the totality of the circumstances to determine whether Ms. James' consent is "freely and voluntarily" given (as precedent demanded in 1972), Justice Ocen points to Justice Brennan's decision in *Goldberg v. Kelly*, in which he explained that welfare recipients have a "brutal need" for financial support that makes welfare a necessity rather than charity. In turn, this "brutal need" to feed and house one's children makes consent illusory.

Fourth, Ocen shares an insight of feminist economists, such as Marilyn Waring, that caregiving is a form of unpaid labor that benefits society at-large.[27] In so doing, Ocen rejects the *Wyman* majority's framing of welfare as charity. This framing reflects an ongoing societal bias that praises white stay-at-home mothers, while denigrating poor black mothers and pushing them into the workforce. Highlighting the discriminatory working conditions faced by poor women of color, Dorothy Roberts has argued that they should have the same options to work or stay home with their children as middle-class women.[28] Similarly, Ocen evades the welfare-as-charity construct. She instead points to the central insight of *Goldberg v. Kelly* that welfare benefits are statutory entitlements. Ocen makes clear that welfare is payment for the work mothers perform on behalf of "their families, communities, and by extension, our nation."[29] She builds on existing precedent recognizing the constitutionally protected choice to have and raise children. To recognize this right, it is imperative to provide financial support for women who engage in this vital societal task. Ocen's argument foreshadows Martha Fineman's conception of the responsive state; that is, a society that recognizes and supports our mutual and inevitable dependencies.[30]

Fifth, Ocen rejects the deserving versus undeserving distinction that underlies so much of American anti-poverty policies. Khiara Bridges explains that the state deprives poor mothers of privacy rights because "they are presumed to be ethically and/or behaviorally flawed."[31] *Wyman* exemplifies her thesis; Blackmun remarks on Ms. James' "attitude," "evasiveness," and "belligerency" – all of which arose from her entirely reasonable belief that the state could verify her eligibility without a home visit.[32] The majority opinion also refers to Ms. James' social services case file (which was never introduced at trial or made part of the record), finding that

---

[26] 400 U.S. at 324.

[27] MARILYN WARING, IF WOMEN COUNTED, A NEW FEMINIST ECONOMICS (1988).

[28] Dorothy E. Roberts, *Welfare Reform and Economic Freedom: Low-Income Mothers' Decisions about Work at Home and in the Market*, 44 SANTA CLARA L. REV. 1029, 1039-40 (2004).

[29] Ocen this volume at 69.

[30] Martha Albertson Fineman, *The Vulnerable Subject: Anchoring Equality in the Human Condition*, 20 YALE J.L. & FEMINISM 1, 8-9 (2008).

[31] BRIDGES, *supra* note 2, at 34.

[32] 400 U.S. at 322 n.9.

Ms. James's son had been physically abused and bitten by rats. For the majority, "[t]he picture is a sad and unhappy one."[33] The Court also made short shrift of the twelve affidavits submitted by Ms. James's coplaintiffs, describing their discomfort and embarrassment at caseworker home visits. The Court's assumption was that Ms. James and her fellow mothers receiving welfare warranted suspicion and distrust. The Court silenced their narratives.

Ocen hears these women and refuses to reinforce a two-tiered system of privacy under American law. In doing so, she affirms the dignity and autonomy of poor women. To be sure, this is a difficult task because the Court has never read the Equal Protection Clause to provide heightened scrutiny of laws discriminating against the poor, nor has it found any substantive Constitutional right to basic subsistence support. Accordingly, Ocen instead emphasizes existing rights at the time – the right to be secure in one's home; the right to freely and voluntarily give consent; and the right to parent – and refuses to carve out a poverty exception to these foundational attributes of American citizenship.

IMPACTS

Wyman today remains good law. In 1996, a new welfare reform law discarded AFDC and created the Temporary Assistance for Needy Families (TANF) program, which made major changes to cash assistance for the poor. Under TANF, welfare recipients are required to work; no one can receive welfare benefits for more than five years in a lifetime; and states can impose behavior modification requirements, such as denying benefits to mothers who do not identify the paternity of their children and cutting benefits to families with truant children.[34] In addition, some jurisdictions still require home visits. When he signed the law creating TANF, President Clinton predicted that the work requirements would eliminate the stigma against welfare. He was wrong. The media, politicians, and the public continue to vilify women who receive welfare.

In fact, the stigma against mothers who receive welfare remains potent. President Reagan famously attacked women such as Ms. James as "welfare queens."[35] In this rhetoric, the welfare queen is a lazy, black woman living off the public dole while having too many children.[36] This rhetoric is effective. Martin Gilens explains that most Americans oppose welfare due to media-reinforced stereotypes of black people

---

[33] *Id.*

[34] 42 U.S.C. 601(b) (abolishing entitlement); 42 U.S.C. 608(a)(7) (lifetime limits); 42 U.S.C. 602 (a)(1)(A)(ii) (work within two years of receipt of benefits); 42 U.S.C. 607 (work requirements); 42 U.S.C. 604 (school attendance and diploma); 42 U.S.C. 608(a)(2) (paternity and cooperation with child support).

[35] *See* Michele Gilman, *The Return of the Welfare Queen*, 22 J. GENDER, Soc. POL'Y L. 247, 259–60 (2014).

[36] HANDLER & HASENFELD, *supra* note 2, at 163–64.

as lazy.[37] Welfare queen ideology blames individuals for their economic plight and distracts from structural, economic factors that shape the low-wage market and create inequality.[38] Yet, the welfare queen stereotype is a myth. Most TANF recipients are not African American; they stay in the program for short-term spells; they marry at the same rates as other women; and they have long worked to meet basic expenses.[39] The welfare queen rhetoric is harmful because it blames the poor for their plight, thus relieving society of obligations for their support. By contrast, throughout her opinion, Ocen views poor women as deserving of support, financial and otherwise, in a capitalist system that does not always provide jobs or living wages for those that need them and discounts the value of caregiving.

Hopes that *Wyman* would be overturned were dashed in a challenge to home visits that went to the Ninth Circuit in 2006. In *Sanchez v. City of San Diego*, the court refused to recognize differences between AFDC and TANF or to apply post-*Wyman* jurisprudence significantly limiting suspicionless searches.[40] Instead, the Court expressly lumped women receiving welfare with convicted criminals on probation and concluded that neither group has a reasonable expectation of privacy. In a bitter dissent from a denial of a petition for rehearing en banc, seven Ninth Circuit judges called the case "nothing less than an attack on the poor."[41] As the dissenters stated, most government benefits do not flow to the poor, "yet this is the group we require to sacrifice their dignity and their right to privacy."[42] They concluded, "This situation is shameful."[43] The Supreme Court denied certiorari.

Post-*Wyman*, our nation's fragmented and sectoral privacy law remains animated by middle-class norms and expectations, while the poor experience expanding forms of surveillance.[44] Low-income Americans are still subject to stigmatizing practices as a condition of receiving public assistance, such as home visits, drug tests, fingerprinting, and intrusive questioning and verification requirements.[45] At the same time, emerging technology is exposing them to a variety of newer privacy intrusions and harms that are harder to spot. For instance, some states monitor how recipients spend cash assistance and food stamps, and states share public benefits data with law enforcement and vice

---

[37] MARTIN GILENS, WHY AMERICANS HATE WELFARE: RACE, MEDIA, AND THE POLITICS OF ANTIPOVERTY POLICY at 5, 172–73, 205 (1999). Khiara Bridges notes that as more black women received welfare, public support for welfare plummeted. Khiara Bridges, *The Deserving Poor, The Undeserving Poor, and Class-Based Affirmative Action*, 66 EMORY L.J. 1049, 1095 (2017).

[38] HANDLER & HASENFELD, *supra* note 2, at 3. BRIDGES, *supra* note 2, at 44–45.

[39] *See* Gilman, *supra* note 36, at 263–64.

[40] 464 F.3d 916 (9th Cir. 2006), r'hrg en banc den., 483 F.3d 965 (2007).

[41] Sanchez v. San Diego, 483 F.3d 965, 969 (9th Cir. 2007), r'hrg en banc den., (Pregerson, J., dissenting).

[42] *Id.*

[43] *Id.*

[44] *See* Michele Estrin Gilman, *The Class Differential in Privacy Law*, 77 BROOK. L. REV. 1389, 1394 (2012).

[45] Kaaryn Gustafson, *The Criminalization of Poverty*, 99 J. CRIM. L. & CRIMINOLOGY 643, 645 (2009).

versa, thus making the welfare system an arm of the criminal justice system, which in turn devastates poor and minority families and communities.[46]

In addition, although data brokers are harvesting and selling the personal information of all Americans, low-income people are particularly vulnerable to discrimination that results from "collection and aggregation of big data and the application of predictive analytics."[47] Despite their seeming neutrality, the algorithms that fuel predictive analytics can contain inaccurate data, reflect systemic biases about minority groups, and confuse correlations with causation. Virginia Eubanks writes about this new "digital poorhouse," in which "[a]utomated eligibility systems, ranking algorithms, and predictive risk models control which neighborhoods get policed, which families attain needed resources, who is short-listed for employment, and who is investigated for fraud."[48] Current law offers scant accountability for discriminatory, illegitimate, or erroneous use of this data. If Ocen's opinion was the law of the land, it would have laid the groundwork for greater constitutional protections against government surveillance and led to stronger privacy norms that would benefit not only the poor but all Americans.

Wyman v. James, 400 U.S. 309 (1971)

Ms. Justice Priscilla Ocen delivered the opinion of the Court

Barbara James is a poor black woman who relies on Aid to Families with Dependent Children ("AFDC"), a federal cash assistance program for the indigent, to provide for herself and her two-year old son, Maurice. The city and state of New York, where she resides, require Ms. James to submit to an intrusive home visit by social workers in order to maintain her AFDC benefits. Evidence gathered by social workers during such visits is used to verify eligibility for benefits. In addition, observations during visits can uncover fraud and child abuse, both of which are felonies. Failure to submit to home visits results in the termination of benefits.

Ms. James, on behalf of herself and others similarly situated, asserts that because the City and State conduct the visits without a warrant, the home visit scheme violates the Fourth Amendment. A three-judge panel of the Southern District of New York agreed, finding that New York Department of Services may not "deny, reduce or terminate AFDC benefits to otherwise eligible persons who refuse to allow caseworkers to enter their homes without a warrant, issued upon probable cause." *James v. Goldberg*, 303 F. Supp. 935, 939 (1969).

The state of New York appeals, arguing that the home search policy is lawful because the visits are consensual and protect vulnerable children. In essence, the

---

[46] *Id.* at 667.

[47] *See* Mary Madden, Michele Gilman, Karen Levy, & Alice Marwick, *Privacy, Poverty, and Big Data: A Matrix of Vulnerabilities for Poor Americans*, 95 Wash. U.L. Rev. 53, 53 (2017).

[48] Virginia Eubanks, Automating Inequality (2017).

state of New York asks us to enact a dual system for privacy rights in the home: one for the rich and one for the poor. This we cannot do. For the reasons described below, we AFFIRM the judgment of the District Court and find that New York's home search policy constitutes an unreasonable search in violation of the Fourth Amendment.

I A (BRIEF) HISTORY OF THE AID TO FAMILIES WITH DEPENDENT CHILDREN PROGRAM

Since its founding, the United States has stigmatized the poor, often policing their decisions and requiring the forfeiture of individual rights to privacy, autonomy, and dignity. Influenced by English Poor Laws, the early colonies routinely appointed what were termed "overseers of the poor" to identify, monitor, and occasionally lease out non-disabled but unemployed adults. Such adults were cast as morally bankrupt because of their poverty and therefore in need of the discipline and guidance provided by religiously-affiliated private charities. Those who could not work because of age or infirmity, however, were often spared from moral condemnation and instead provided aid or placed in almshouses. Moreover, in the late nineteenth and early twentieth centuries, private charities created Mother's Pensions to aid poor, largely white, single mothers who could demonstrate that they met certain moral "suitability" criteria. These pensions were provided based on the notion that mothers were necessary for the inculcation of moral values and the promotion of the social good.

In the wake of the Great Depression, the federal government supplanted these private forms of charity to the poor, assuming primary responsibility for aid to the indigent with the passage of the Social Security Act of 1935 ("The Act"). With regard to single mothers, the Act consolidated Mother's Pension programs into a federally-funded, locally administered Aid to Dependent Children (later renamed Aid to Families with Dependent Children or "AFDC") public assistance program. According to a 1934 report on Social Security in America, "[t]he purpose of legislation for aid to dependent children has been to prevent the disruption of families on the ground of poverty alone and to enable the mother to stay at home and devote herself to housekeeping and the care of her children, releasing her from the inadequacies of the old type of poor relief and the uncertainties of private charity." CMTE. ON ECONOMIC SECURITY, SOCIAL SECURITY IN AMERICA, AID TO DEPENDENT CHILDREN (1934).

Although the aims of the Act and the corresponding AFDC program were benevolent, in practice, it reinforced the dual benefit structure of the private charities that the Act sought to replace. H. LEYENDECKER, PROBLEMS AND POLICY IN PUBLIC ASSISTANCE 45–57 (1955); J. M. Wedemeyer & Percy Moore, *The American Welfare System*, 54 Calif. L. Rev. 326, 327–28 (1966). Indeed, the Act created a generous, non-discretionary system of social insurance that benefited aged, disabled, and unemployed workers while simultaneously enacting a stingy, degrading, discriminatory system of public assistance for single mothers. For example, as we previously noted in *King v. Smith*, Congress authorized states participating in AFDC "to impose eligibility requirements relating to the 'moral character' of applicants." *King v. Smith*, 392 U.S. 309, 321 (1968). The government did not impose such an eligibility requirement on social insurance applicants. Thus, while individuals eligible for social insurance programs reliably received benefits upon applying,[49] women who sought assistance under AFDC were often subjected to intrusive investigations. Moreover, black women were disproportionately rejected because they were deemed to have "unsuitable homes," casting them as immoral, promiscuous, incompetent mothers. As a result of this discriminatory and degrading treatment, in the initial years following the enactment of AFDC, the majority of recipients were white widows.

States, particularly those in the South, also utilized welfare rules to police the sexual behavior and reproductive choices of welfare recipients. States routinely denied aid to women who had children out of wedlock, *see* W. BELL, AID TO DEPENDENT CHILDREN 3–19 (1965), as were women who cohabited with a man under "substitute father" rules. Under such rules, states terminated benefits upon a showing that "a mother who 'cohabits' in or outside her home with an able-bodied man, a 'substitute father' being considered a non-absent parent within the federal statute." *King v. Smith*, 392 U.S. 309, 312 (1968). Jurisdictions frequently engaged in midnight raids to detect substitute fathers, violating the privacy rights of AFDC recipients. In *King v. Smith*, this Court struck down substitute father rules as inconsistent with prevailing statutory regulations governing the provision of AFDC benefits. Although this Court resolved *King* on statutory rather than constitutional grounds, the privacy, dignitary, and equality rights of AFDC recipients were a central concern to the Court. Now this Court must directly address the scope of the constitutional right to privacy enjoyed by individuals who rely on government subsidies to meet their most basic needs.

II AFDC AND HOME SEARCHES IN NEW YORK STATE

In 1967, shortly before the birth of her son, Barbara James applied for benefits under the AFDC program. The federal government allocates AFDC funds to states to administer. Each state (and county government) that administers the federal AFDC program is tasked with promulgating rules that govern the eligibility for and distribution of the federal aid program. As such, the New York Code of Rules and Regulations requires that "[d]etermination of initial eligibility shall include contact

---

[49] This is not, however, to say that all workers were covered by social insurance programs. Agricultural and domestic workers were excluded from Social Security and Unemployment Benefits, which had a disproportionate impact on black workers.

with the applicant and at least one home visit ..." 28 N.Y.C.R.R. § 351.10. Once eligibility has been established and aid has been provided to the applicant, state law requires periodic assessments of the financial status and well-being of the AFDC recipient. In particular, state law provides that "mandatory home visits must be made in accordance with law that requires that persons be visited at least once every three months if they are receiving Home Relief, Veteran's Assistance of Aid to Dependent Children ...." *Id.*

Consistent with these policies, Ms. James was subject to an initial home visit by New York City Department of Social Services ("DSS") social workers to verify her eligibility for AFDC benefits. DSS approved her application. On May 8, 1969, a DSS caseworker sent a letter notifying Ms. James that a periodic home visit would take place on May 14, 1969. In response, Ms. James telephoned the caseworker and objected to the visit, asserting that these home visits were intrusive and violative of her constitutional right to privacy. While she would not permit a home visit, Ms. James indicated that she was willing to meet outside of her home and provide the information necessary to maintain her eligibility for the AFDC program. The caseworker rejected her offer.

Instead, on May 13, 1969, DSS notified Ms. James that the agency would terminate her benefits because she refused to allow social workers to conduct a home visit. Consistent with our opinion in *Goldberg v. Kelly*, 397 U.S. 254 (1970), the notice informed Ms. James of her right to a hearing, which she requested, and which was scheduled for May 27, 1969. At her termination hearing, James, through counsel, repeated her offer to provide relevant information to her caseworker outside of her home. DSS, again, rejected her offer. On June 2, 1969, James received notice that the termination was affirmed; her failure to consent to a warrantless home visit resulted in the termination of her AFDC benefits.

In response, Ms. James filed the instant action on behalf of herself and others similarly situated, alleging, inter alia, that the home visit policy violated her right to be free of unreasonable searches and seizures as guaranteed by the Fourth Amendment. Ms. James sought injunctive and declaratory relief. A three-judge panel of the Southern District of New York was convened, granting her requested relief. *James v. Goldberg*, 303 F. Supp. 935 (1969). The state of New York appealed, and this Court granted certiorari. The central question presented in this matter is whether warrantless "home visits," conducted by welfare officials under the threat of termination or reduction of benefits of eligible persons who refuse to allow entry, is consistent with the strictures of the Fourth Amendment.

III THE HOME VISITS CONSTITUTE SEARCHES GOVERNED BY THE FOURTH AMENDMENT'S WARRANT REQUIREMENT

The Fourth Amendment to the Constitution protects the "right of the people to be secure in their persons, houses, papers, and effects, against unreasonable searches and seizures." The gravamen of this Amendment is the protection of individual privacy, dignity, and security from arbitrary and unwarranted intrusions by the government. *Camara v. Municipal Court of the City & County of San Francisco*, 387 U.S. 523, 528 (1967). The right to be free from government intrusion has been understood as "basic to a free society." *Wolf v. Colorado*, 338 U.S. 25, 27 (1949).

The framers of the Fourth Amendment were particularly concerned about protecting the privacy of the individual in her or his own home. Indeed, the home – the place where we reside, rest, raise children, build families, and sustain intimate relationships – enjoys heightened protections against government intrusion. The conception of the home and the protections afforded to it under law are "indispensable ultimate essentials of our concept of civilization." *Boyd v. United States*, 116 U.S. 616, 626–30 (1886). In line with exceptional status afforded to homes and dwellings in our jurisprudence, this Court has consistently protected the privacy of the dwelling in ways that are too numerous for citation.

The framers of the Fourth Amendment understood that privacy and security in the home were essential not only to the individual but to a functional democracy. Indeed, the Fourth Amendment was enacted, in part, to prohibit the use of general warrants, which were deployed by the powerful in Britain and the early colonies to search the homes of their political opponents without any evidence of criminal wrongdoing. As such, the Fourth Amendment serves as a bulwark against abuse of power, preventing harassment and surveillance by the state, which is a particular concern for the marginalized and disempowered. Indeed, the protections of the Fourth Amendment are particularly important to the poor and for women, who have been stigmatized and routinely targeted for government regulation of their intimate lives. For example, individuals must disclose all sources of income, submit bank statements, tax returns, birth certificates, their children's school records, and more as part of an application for AFDC benefits. Because of the significant intrusions already accompanied by the receipt of government aid, protection of the home becomes more, not less, important for poor, subsidy reliant women.

That the home and its attendant functions are protected against state intervention is reflected not only in the Court's Fourth Amendment jurisprudence but the text of the Constitution itself. Indeed, the Third Amendment prohibits the use of private homes to house troops without the consent of the owner. This provision of the bill of rights reflects the framers' view that the home is a sacred space where individuals must be free of an intrusive government, even in times of national crisis. Further, the right to privacy extends to the accompaniments of the home, including marital and family life. In *Griswold v. Connecticut*, 381 U.S. 479 (1965), this Court struck down prohibitions against the use of contraception by married couples, affirming the sanctity of the home against governmental interference. There, we noted that "the principles laid down in this opinion ... affect the very essence of Constitutional liberty and security ... it is not the breaking of his doors, and the rummaging of his drawers that constitute the offense, but it is the invasion of his indefensible right of personal security." *Griswold*, 381 U.S. at 484 (quoting *Boyd v. United States*, 116 U.S. 616, 630 (1886)). Because of the significant privacy interests embodied by the home, "except in certain carefully defined classes of cases, a search of a private dwelling without a warrant or proper consent is presumptively unreasonable." *Katz v. United States*, 389 U.S. 347, 357 (1967).

Although this Court has been steadfast in its insistence that intrusions to the home are presumptively unreasonable unless justified by a warrant, the State of New York contends that its home search protocol is exempt from this basic requirement. Instead, the state argues that, because social workers conduct the home visits within the context of an eligibility verification for a civil welfare program, the Fourth Amendment's warrant requirement is inapplicable.

We reject the notion that AFDC recipients are subject to lesser protections in the home merely because they are indigent and reliant on government support. We refuse to create an exception to the warrant requirement that rests on a presumption that the poor have a lesser expectation of privacy in their homes than do the affluent, that they should uniquely suffer the indignity of a stranger rummaging through their bedrooms, closets, and drawers. The privacy that lies at the core of the Fourth Amendment is designed to protect the dignity and autonomy of all individuals and the spaces in which they reside. Welfare recipients, like everyone else, should reasonably expect their privacy to be respected and to be free from the prying eyes of the state. Welfare recipients, like everyone else, should reasonably expect that their intimate lives will not be upended by the arbitrary exercises of governmental power. There are no distinctions between those who are "deserving" or "undeserving" of privacy when it comes to the protections of the Fourth Amendment. Thus, absent a warrant backed by specific and credible allegations of wrongdoing, welfare recipients maintain a reasonable expectation of privacy in their homes and therefore enjoy heightened Fourth Amendment protections when a social worker or welfare official seeks admittance to their homes under the guise of an administrative review.

We note, incidentally, that no other recipient of government subsidies is subject to the indignities experienced by AFDC recipients. Indeed, federal, state, and local governments spend approximately 130 billion dollars per year on social welfare programs. Recipients include farmers, corporations, college students, homeowners, parents, military personnel, and others. In each of these areas, need may be exaggerated, and funds may be spent on areas beyond the scope of the governmental program. Yet, none of the beneficiaries of these programs is subject to warrantless home visits to ensure continued eligibility. For example, we do not require an individual seeking to claim a child on his or her income taxes to submit to a home verification visit by representatives of the Internal Revenue Service. Nor should we. Such warrantless visits offend our basic notions of propriety and violate our constitutional norms grounded in the protection of individual privacy.

Moreover, we are unconvinced that the civil nature of the AFDC program transforms what would otherwise be an unconstitutional search into a permissible visit. As we have noted repeatedly, the "indefensible right of personal security" in the home is universal. As such, protections against unwarranted government intrusions into private, intimate spaces such as the home apply in the context of criminal as well as civil searches. Indeed, over the last three decades, the administrative state has expanded dramatically. Federal, state, and local governments have established entities that regulate all aspects of our lives, including public health, child protection, education, employment, and housing. Our decision in *Camara v. Municipal Court*, 387 U.S. 523 (1967) reflects this Court's concern about the rapid growth of the administrative state and the scope of the Fourth Amendment. In *Camara*, we held that the Fourth Amendment prohibited an administrative search of a private dwelling without a warrant. In reaching this conclusion, we noted that civil or administrative intrusions may impose significant burdens on the individual, burdens that are often as onerous as criminal investigations.

Concerns regarding the burdens imposed by civil regulations are especially acute in the welfare context, where individuals must disclose the intimate details of their lives in order to obtain benefits and maintain eligibility. They must provide information regarding their income (or lack thereof), their children, current or former romantic partners, and their housing arrangements. Welfare recipients are required to routinely check in with caseworkers, to notify them if there is any change in their earnings or the number of individuals in their household. Given the myriad forms of privacy intrusions that often accompany welfare receipt, this Court must remain vigilant in ensuring that the state does not run roughshod over boundaries established by the Fourth Amendment, particularly in the home.

Moreover, the line between the criminal and civil arms of the state is not as stark as the state of New York would have us believe. Rather, the evidence gathered as part of a civil search may result in a loss of benefits, instigate a child welfare inquiry, or, in some cases, prompt a criminal investigation. Thus, drawing a distinction between civil and criminal searches would undermine the basic purpose of the Fourth Amendment as "even the most law-abiding citizen has a very tangible interest in limiting the circumstances under which the sanctity of his home may be broken by official authority, for the possibility of criminal entry under the guise of official sanction is a serious threat to personal and family security." *Camara*, 387 U. S. at 531.

Lastly, New York claims that the home visits cannot be considered a search within the meaning of the Fourth Amendment because the home visits serve a therapeutic purpose, as social workers seek to help the recipient and to protect children from abuse or neglect. What New York fails to appreciate, however, is that the intent of governmental actors is immaterial, particularly when it comes to the home. As we have observed elsewhere, "[i]t is the individual's interest in privacy which the Amendment protects, and that would not appear to fluctuate with the 'intent' of the invading officers." *Abel v. United States*, 362 U.S. 217, 255 (1960). Resting Fourth Amendment protections on the intent of the governmental actor would undermine the basic prohibition against unreasonable searches and seizures as law enforcement agents are often motivated by goals beyond immediate crime detection. In sum, the government's purportedly benevolent purpose in conducting the home visit does not negate the fundamental intrusion by the state. Rather, "the Constitution protects the privacy of the home against all unreasonable intrusion of whatever character ... it applies to all invasions on the part of the government and its employees of the sanctity of a man's [or woman's] home." *Poe v. Ullman*, 367 U.S. 497, 550–51 (1961) (dissenting opinion).

IV THE HOME VISITS ARE UNREASONABLE SEARCHES IN VIOLATION OF THE FOURTH AMENDMENT

This Court has long held that "the most basic constitutional rule in this area is that searches conducted outside the judicial process, without prior approval by judge or magistrate, are per se unreasonable under the Fourth Amendment – subject only to a few specially established and well-delineated exceptions." *Katz v. United States*, 389 U.S. 347, 357 (1967). The home visits in this case are flatly searches within the meaning of the Fourth Amendment and are conducted without a warrant. As such, the searches are presumptively unreasonable. In an attempt to rebut this presumption, the state of New York advances two arguments: First, they argue that the warrantless searches are reasonable because they advance the compelling state interest in the safety of children and the appropriate use of public funds. Second, they assert that the searches fall within an exception to the warrant requirement, as AFDC recipients consent to the searches of their homes or otherwise waive their Fourth Amendment protections. For the reasons described below, we reject these contentions.

To be sure, AFDC is intended to assist poor single women with children, who would otherwise be unable to provide for food, clothing, or shelter. As such, the needs of children are the paramount concern of the program. Indeed, one 1940 poster published by the Social Security Board reflected this focus on child welfare, noting "[s]o that dependent children can grow up in their own families, the federal government and states provide cash allowances. More children will thus have a chance to live normal, wholesome lives in their own homes." Certainly, the protection of indigent children is a compelling interest that may, in the appropriate circumstances, justify the abrogation of a constitutional right. The government may not, however, utilize a mere assertion of concern for children to circumvent the constraints of the Constitution. The state may not presume that AFDC recipients are more likely to abuse their children than other groups as a basis for broad, suspicionless searches. Instead, the government must have some degree of individualized suspicion of child abuse or neglect prior to conducting a home search.

Moreover, the state of New York argues that the home visits are reasonable because welfare constitutes "charity" and thus the government has the right to engage in warrantless home visits to ensure that recipients properly spend the funds.

This posture toward welfare recipients flatly contradicts our prior precedent. In contrast to New York's characterization of welfare programs, this Court has described AFDC as a "statutory entitlement" and a means to "help bring within the reach of the poor the same opportunities that are available to others to participate meaningfully in the life of the community." *Goldberg v. Kelly*, 397 U.S. 254, 256 (1970).

Indeed, the extension of aid to poor single mothers is not charity, it is a recognition of the valuable contribution such women make to their families, communities, and, by extension, our nation. Poor single mothers engage in unpaid labor – such as cooking, cleaning, reading to children, ensuring they attend school, and instilling critical values that will enable children to develop into healthy adults. These mundane, yet extraordinary, tasks are priceless and contribute to the collective good. As such, social welfare programs such as AFDC "foster the dignity and wellbeing" of poor families and allow poor mothers to raise their children with the means necessary for thriving. If the substantive right to procreate and parent means anything, if the constitutionally protected choice to "bear or beget children" is to have any force, then those who choose to procreate must be afforded the minimum necessaries to provide for themselves and their children. Given that indigent mothers are entitled to aid if they meet established eligibility requirements, the government may not use the choice to draw upon welfare benefits as a basis for the abrogation of the protections provided by the Fourth Amendment.

Nor may the government assume, without any evidence, that welfare recipients are more likely to misuse government funds and are undeserving of the public trust. Rather, the Court emphasized that the poor are not to blame for their poverty nor is it an indication of moral failure. *Goldberg v. Kelly*, 397 U.S. 254, 265 (1970). To be poor does not predispose one to dishonesty. Thus, the government may not rely on such baseless caricatures of the poor to justify its circumvention of fundamental constitutional privacy protections. The government may, however, take steps to advance its important interest in protecting public funds from misuse by any number of means. Nevertheless, if it seeks to vindicate its interest in protecting public funds by searching the homes of AFDC recipients, it must be justified by individual suspicion and a warrant issued by a magistrate.

V AFDC RECIPIENTS DO NOT FREELY AND VOLUNTARILY CONSENT TO WARRANTLESS HOME VISITS

The Fourth Amendment is not absolute. As we recognized in *Katz v. United States*, a search authorized by consent is a valid exception to the warrant requirement. In this case, the state of New York argues that AFDC recipients consent to the home visits by social workers as a condition for receipt of government aid, thus rendering the search lawful. When a state seeks to vindicate a search by relying on consent as a justification for the search, it bears the burden of proving that the consent was "freely and voluntarily given." *Bumper v. North Carolina*, 391 U.S. 543, 548 (1968). The state of New York has failed to meet this burden.

We determine whether consent to a warrantless search was freely and voluntarily given based on the totality of the circumstances. Disparities in power between the parties and the manner in which the state seeks entry into a home weigh heavily in this calculus. In weighing the totality of the circumstances, we must be convinced that there was "an intentional waiver of a constitutional right" without coercion by state agents. For example, in *Amos v. United States*, 255 U.S. 313 (1921) we found no waiver of the Fourth Amendment where officials from the Internal Revenue Service gained entry to a home without a warrant by telling the co-occupant of a home that they were there to "search the premises for violations of the revenue law." Under those circumstances, we found that "no [Fourth Amendment] waiver was intended or effected." Instead, we found that the entry to the home came as a result "implied coercion" given the power disparity between the resident and law enforcement agents.

The considerations that guided our analysis of the totality of the circumstances in *Jones* and *Amos* apply with equal force with respect to the purported waiver of Fourth Amendment rights by AFDC recipients. As noted in *Kelly v. Wyman*, 294 F.Supp. 893, 899, 900 (1968), welfare recipients are, by definition, "without funds or assets" and as such they face a "brutal need" for the support provided by entitlement programs like AFDC. Should they refuse the home visit, recipients risk the loss of benefits they so desperately need to survive. As such, the social workers who "request" to visit their homes wield immense power over the lives of poor, single mothers who are disproportionately black or Latino. Thus, the state's request to visit the homes of welfare recipients is not a real request; instead, it is inherently coercive because it carries with it an implicit risk of termination from a program that enables beneficiaries to pay for food, clothing and shelter. Quite literally, the livelihood of beneficiaries is on the line should they "choose" to decline a home visit. Under these circumstances, we find that ADFC recipients do not freely and voluntarily consent to a search of their homes.

Having failed to meet its burden to prove that AFDC recipients freely and voluntarily consent to home searches, the state of New York argues, in the alternative, that receipt of welfare assistance requires beneficiaries to waive their Fourth Amendment right to be free of unreasonable searches. We disagree. Our precedents establish that if the government is prohibited from directly burdening a constitutional right, they may not limit the right indirectly through the placement of conditions on a benefit or privilege. The government may not, for example, require that applicants forego their First Amendment right to the free exercise of religion in order to obtain unemployment benefits. As we observed in *Goldberg v. Kelly*, the prohibition against unconstitutional conditions on government aid applies with equal force in the welfare context: "Relevant constitutional restraints apply as much to the withdrawal of public assistance benefits as to disqualification for unemployment compensation ... denial of a tax exemption ... or ... discharge from public employment." *Goldberg v. Kelly*, 397 U.S. 254, 262 (1970). As such, the government may not require an indigent welfare recipient to waive Fourth Amendment rights in order to obtain the "very means by which to live." *Goldberg* at 264. Contrary to New York's contention, it is irrelevant whether one views welfare as a "right" or a "privilege;" as no unconstitutional conditions may be placed on its receipt under either view. Indeed, "[i]t is too late in the day to doubt that the liberties of [privacy] may be infringed by the denial of or placing of conditions upon a benefit or privilege." *American Communications Assn. v. Douds*, 339 U.S. 382, 390 (1950).

VI NEW YORK STATE LACKS SUFFICIENT JUSTIFICATION FOR AN EXCEPTION TO THE WARRANT REQUIREMENT IN THE WELFARE CONTEXT

The home visits conducted by New York as administrators of the AFDC program are conducted without a warrant and without the consent of the AFDC recipient. This means that the home visits are presumptively unreasonable and violate the Fourth Amendment. New York attempts to resist this conclusion, instead arguing that obtaining a warrant would be impractical, thus undermining the aims of the program. As a result, New York asks this Court to recognize a new exception to the warrant requirement in cases involving home searches by civil welfare authorities.

This Court has recognized that exceptions to the Fourth Amendment's warrant requirement are "jealously and carefully drawn." *Jones v. United States*, 357 U.S. 493, 499 (1958). Upon examination of the record, we find no need to create an exception to the warrant requirement in this context as "[n]o reason is offered for not obtaining a search warrant except the inconvenience to the officers and some slight delay necessary to prepare papers and present the evidence to a magistrate. These are never very convincing reasons and, in these circumstances, certainly are not enough to bypass the constitutional requirement." *Johnson v. United States* 333 U.S. 10,15 (1948). New York has not demonstrated that it would be difficult to obtain information about AFDC recipients outside of the home. Indeed, Ms. James offered to furnish housing, education, financial and health records to her case worker. If that information reveals irregularities, New York may seek a warrant from a magistrate authorizing a search of the recipient's home. There has been no showing that evidence of wrongdoing will be destroyed or that the recipient will flee.

For these reasons, this Court refuses to carve out a "poverty exception" to the Fourth Amendment, which demands that a warrant is issued prior to the search of a private dwelling. We AFFIRM the judgment of the District Court and remand for proceedings consistent with this opinion.

4

Maher v. Roe, 432 U.S. 464 (1977)

Commentary by Ederlina Co

INTRODUCTION

In *Maher v. Roe,* the United States Supreme Court upheld a state's regulation withholding public funding for abortion from poor women.[1] Although the Court insisted that its decision signaled no retreat from *Roe v. Wade, Maher*'s devastating consequences for women who relied on public funding for reproductive health care and its curtailing effect on abortion rights jurisprudence tell another story.

In Michele Goodwin's rewritten opinion of *Maher,* she strikes down the public funding regulation as a violation of the right to privacy and the right to equal protection, and as an improper penalty on poor women. In so doing, Goodwin crafts an opinion that bridges the gap between a woman's theoretical right to abortion under law and a woman's ability to exercise that right.

While *Maher* exemplifies the limitations of law, the *Maher* feminist judgment illustrates its possibilities. *Maher* cements the abortion right as a negative one based on the flawed assumption that all women have the resources and autonomy to exercise the abortion right. *Maher* also pretends that the state's interference with that right is isolated to the regulation at issue before the Court. In contrast, the *Maher* feminist judgment acknowledges that the abortion right is elusive for poor women unless it is a positive right with government support. It also recognizes that the state has played a cumulative role in oppressing the reproductive lives of the women who rely on public funding. What emerges from the juxtaposition of *Maher* and the *Maher* feminist judgment then, is that only when law acknowledges and responds to the disparities that exist between women along race and class lines, disparities the

---

[1] 432 U.S. 464 (1977).

state has contributed to, can law ensure equal access to, and meaningful protection of, the abortion right.[2]

ABORTION AFTER *ROE V. WADE*

The mortality rate associated with illegal abortion in the United States vastly declined after *Roe v. Wade*.[3] Even after the landmark decision, however, women of color experienced difficulty accessing abortion care.[4] In the year following *Roe*, women of color were disproportionately represented (eighty percent) among the women who died from illegal and unsafe abortions.[5]

The *Maher* Court had before it one study that detailed the case of a twenty-one year old African American woman whose physician told her that she was fourteen weeks pregnant.[6] She wanted an abortion but no local facilities would provide her with a second-trimester abortion.[7] After she weighed the expense and inconvenience of obtaining an abortion at an out-of-state hospital, she reportedly decided to continue the pregnancy and start prenatal care.[8] Six days later, she arrived at the local hospital emergency room in shock after two hours of severe vaginal hemorrhage.[9] Although doctors performed a series of surgical procedures on her to control the hemorrhage, she went into shock again and died of cardiac arrest. The pathology report showed her cervix and uterus had extensive deep lacerations indicative of an attempted illegal or possibly self-induced abortion.[10]

When the Supreme Court decided *Maher* several years later, women of color had the most to lose.[11] At the time, women of color obtained abortions at nearly twice the

---

[2] *See generally* LORETTA J. ROSS & RICKIE SOLINGER, REPRODUCTIVE JUSTICE: AN INTRODUCTION (2017); Zakiya Luna & Kristin Luker, *Reproductive Justice*, 9 ANN. REV. L. & SOC. SCI. 327 (2013).

[3] Willard Cates, Jr. & Roger Rochat, *Illegal Abortions in the United States: 1972–1974*, 8 FAM. PLAN. PERSP. 86, 87 (Mar.–Apr. 1976).

[4] *Id.* at 87–92.

[5] *Id.* at 88 (Table 1).

[6] Brief of Amici Curiae of American Public Health Association, Planned Parenthood Federation of America, Inc., the National Organization for Women and Certain Medical School Deans, Professors and Individual Physicians 27, *Maher v. Roe*, 432 U.S. 464 (1977) [hereinafter Brief of Amici Curiae] (citing Cates & Rochat, *supra* note 3, at 87, 88).

[7] Cates & Rochat, *supra* note 3, at 88.

[8] *Id.*

[9] *Id.* at 88, 91.

[10] *Id.* at 91.

[11] Lower courts had almost universally agreed that regulations similar to Section 275 were invalid on statutory grounds or under the Fourteenth Amendment Due Process Clause or Equal Protection Clause. *See* Alan J. Shefler, *Indigent Women and Abortion: Limitation of the Right of Privacy in Maher v. Roe*, 13 TULSA L. REV. 287 nn. 64–68 (1977); Frank Susman, *Roe v. Wade and Doe v. Bolton Revisited in 1976 and 1977 – Reviewed?; Revived?; Revested?; Reversed? Or Revoked?*, 22 ST. LOUIS U. L.J. 583 & nn. 15–16 (1978).

rate of white women.[12] In addition, almost forty percent of women of color (five times the proportion of white women) depended on Medicaid.[13]

MAHER V. ROE

In *Maher*, the Supreme Court considered the constitutionality of a Connecticut regulation ("Section 275"), which withheld state Medicaid funds for abortion, unless a physician certified that the abortion was "medically necessary."[14] In relevant part, the regulation stated:

275 Abortion Services
The Department makes payment for abortion services under the Medical Assistance (Title XIX) Program when the following conditions are met:
1. In the opinion of the attending physician the abortion is medically necessary. The term "Medically Necessary" includes psychiatric necessity.
2. The abortion is to be performed in an accredited hospital or licensed clinic . . .
3. The written request for the abortion is submitted by the patient, and in the case of a minor, from the parent or guardian.
4. Prior authorization for the abortion is secured from the Chief of Medical Services . . .[15]

Plaintiffs Susan Roe and Mary Poe both received Aid to Families with Dependent Children ("AFDC")[16] and challenged Section 275 in the United States District Court for the District of Connecticut.[17] Roe was a twenty-six-year-old mother of three children, ages nine, seven, and six months old. Her six-month old suffered from a lung defect and required close supervision and care. At the time of the suit, Roe had not obtained an abortion because she did not have the money to pay for it, and her doctor did not believe it was medically necessary.[18] Plaintiff Poe was a

[12] *Beal v. Doe*, 432 U.S. 454, 459 (1977) (Marshall, J., dissenting). Women of color experienced unintended pregnancy at a rate more than twice that of white women. Stanley K. Henshaw & Kevin O'Reilly, *Characteristics of Abortion Patients in the United States, 1979 and 1980*, 15 FAM. PLAN. PERSP. 5, 7 (table 3) (Jan.–Feb. 1983). There is no simple way to determine why this was the case but lack of access to or effective use of contraceptives were likely contributors.Willard Cates, Jr., *Legal Abortion: Are American Black Women Healthier Because of It?*, 38 PHYLON 267, 271 (1977).

[13] *Beal*, 432 U.S. at 459–60 (J. Marshall, dissenting). Medicaid is a health insurance program funded jointly by federal and state governments for low-income people.

[14] 432 U.S. 464. The Supreme Court considered two other abortion funding cases that term. In *Beal v. Doe*, the Court held that the Medicaid statute, Title XIX, did not require states to publicly fund elective abortion. 432 U.S. 438. In *Poelker v. Doe*, the Court held that a public hospital could provide services for childbirth but not services for elective abortion under the Fourteenth Amendment Equal Protection Clause. 432 U.S. 519 (1977).

[15] Brief of Appellees app. at 7, *Maher v. Roe*, 432 U.S. 464 (1977) [hereinafter Brief of Appellees].

[16] AFDC was a federal program that provided financial assistance to children of no or low-income families.

[17] *Maher*, 432 U.S. at 466–67.

[18] *Id.* n.3; Brief of Appellees, *supra* note 15, app. at 20–21.

sixteen-year-old excellent high school student. At the time of the suit, Poe had obtained an abortion but the state refused to reimburse the hospital for the cost because her doctor could not state that it was medically necessary. Poe's mother therefore owed the hospital $244.20.[19] Plaintiffs argued, inter alia, that Section 275 violated their constitutional rights under the Fourteenth Amendment.[20]

The United States Supreme Court held that the Connecticut regulation did not violate the Fourteenth Amendment Equal Protection Clause and made clear that states did not need to pay for the cost of abortions if they were not medically necessary, even if they paid for the cost of childbirth.[21] Questions arising under the Equal Protection Clause require the Court to analyze whether the law at issue disadvantages a suspect class or impinges on a fundamental right that the Constitution explicitly or implicitly protects.[22]

The Court quickly dispensed of any notion that *Maher* involved discrimination against a suspect class.[23] The Court has never recognized indigency as a suspect classification.[24] The Court then held that the regulation did not impinge on a woman's fundamental right to terminate a pregnancy.[25] The Court emphasized that *Roe v. Wade* did not declare that a woman has an unqualified constitutional right to an abortion.[26] Rather, the right protects her from "unduly burdensome interference with her freedom to decide whether to terminate her pregnancy."[27] The right did not limit the state from making a value judgment in favor of childbirth over abortion or limit the state from implementing its judgment with its allocation of public funds.[28] The Court distinguished Section 275 from the criminal statute it struck down in *Roe v. Wade* and the spousal consent requirement it held unconstitutional in *Planned Parenthood of Central Missouri v. Danforth*, 428 U.S. 52 (1976).[29] The Court explained:

> The Connecticut regulation places no obstacles absolute or otherwise in the pregnant woman's path to an abortion. An indigent woman who desires an abortion suffers no disadvantage as a consequence of Connecticut's decision to fund childbirth; she continues as before to be dependent on private sources for the service she desires. The State may have made childbirth a more attractive alternative, thereby influencing the woman's decision, but it has imposed no restriction on access to abortions that was not already there. The indigency that may make it difficult and in

---

[19] *Maher*, 432 U.S. at n.3; Brief of Appellees, *supra* note 15, app. at 24–25.
[20] *Maher*, 432 U.S. at 467.
[21] *Id.* at 474.
[22] *Id.* at 470.
[23] *Id.*
[24] *Id.* at 471.
[25] *Id.* at 474.
[26] *Id.* at 473.
[27] *Id.* at 473–74.
[28] *Id.* at 474.
[29] *Id.* at 472–74.

some cases, perhaps, impossible for some women to have abortions is neither created nor in any way affected by the Connecticut regulation.[30]

The Court maintained that its decision signaled no retreat from *Roe v. Wade* and explained that there is a "basic difference" between a state's direct interference with a fundamental right and a state's encouragement of an alternative activity that is consistent with legislative policy.[31]

In the absence of a suspect class or impingement of a fundamental right, the remaining question before the Court was whether Section 275 was rationally related to a constitutionally permissible purpose.[32] The Court held that Section 275 satisfied the rational basis test because subsidizing childbirth costs was a rational means of encouraging childbirth.[33] The Court granted states wide latitude in choosing how to allocate their public funds and noted that *Roe v. Wade* itself recognized the state's strong interest in protecting potential life.[34] In a democracy, the Court declared, the legislature is the appropriate forum to resolve policy issues as sensitive as public funding for abortion.[35]

Justice Brennan, joined by Justice Marshall and Justice Blackmun, dissented in the case, noting "a distressing insensitivity to the plight of impoverished pregnant women" in the Court's decision.[36] Justice Brennan emphasized that many indigent women would feel as though they had no choice but to continue their pregnancies because the state would pay for childbirth expenses, even if they would have chosen an abortion if the state had also provided such funds, or if the state did not provide funds for either procedure. Justice Brennan believed that the Court's decision coerced poor pregnant women to bear children that they would not otherwise opt to have and noted that no one could take seriously the Court's assurance that the decision did not signal a retreat from *Roe v. Wade*.[37]

Justice Blackmun also wrote a separate dissent, which Justice Brennan and Justice Marshall joined.[38] He remarked how the Court had allowed states to accomplish indirectly what it said they could not do directly in *Roe v. Wade* and *Doe v. Bolton*. He noted that the Court's decision, which suggested indigent women could simply go elsewhere for funds to help pay for an abortion, was disingenuous and alarming and almost reminiscent of the phrase "Let them eat cake."[39] He concluded, "This is a sad day for those who regard the Constitution as

---

[30] *Id.* at 474.
[31] *Id.* at 475.
[32] *Id.* at 478.
[33] *Id.* at 478–79.
[34] *Id.*
[35] *Id.* at 479.
[36] *Id.* at 483 (Brennan, J., dissenting).
[37] *Id.*
[38] 432 U.S. 454, 462 (Blackmun, J., dissenting).
[39] *Id.*

a force that would serve justice to all even-handedly and, in so doing, would better the lot of the poorest among us."[40]

Finally, Justice Marshall wrote a separate dissent and emphasized that, from the viewpoint of poor women, there is no real distinction between a prohibition on abortion and a restriction that "merely" makes exercising the constitutional right more difficult.[41] He also explained that, insofar as the state had any interest in potential life before viability, it did not outweigh the constitutional rights of poor and minority women.[42] Justice Marshall maintained that the Court's prior abortion decisions were sound law and good policy and that the Court had a duty to enforce the Constitution for the poor and powerless.[43]

Maher *Rewritten*

At the outset of Goodwin's rewritten opinion of *Maher*, she reaffirms *Roe v. Wade* and rejects Section 275 as a violation of a woman's fundamental right to decide whether to terminate a pregnancy under the Fourteenth Amendment right to privacy. If the Court allowed Section 275 to stand, she reasons, the state rather than a poor pregnant woman would choose whether that woman would become a mother. By reaffirming that the right to privacy protects a woman's right to abortion, Goodwin preserves the abortion decision alongside other fundamental rights including marriage, procreation, and contraception, all of which trigger strict scrutiny of restrictions impinging on those rights.

Goodwin's opinion in this regard addresses one of the most heavily-leveled criticisms of *Maher*, namely that it is inconsistent with *Roe* and *Doe*, and *Carey v. Population Services International*.[44] In *Roe*, the Court established a trimester framework for analyzing the constitutionality of restrictions on abortion.[45] Under that framework, the state's interest in restricting abortion did not become compelling until viability.[46] In *Maher*, however, the Court sanctioned the state's discouragement of abortion in the first trimester with no showing of the compelling state

---

[40] *Id.* at 463.

[41] 432 U.S. 454, 457 (Marshall, J., dissenting).

[42] *Id.* at 461.

[43] *Id.* at 462.

[44] *See generally* C. K. Barber, *Constitutional Law – Denial of State Medicaid Funds for Abortions Not "Medically Necessary" Does Not Violate the Equal Protection Clause* Maher v. Roe, 21 Howard L.J. 937 (1978); Andrea Bayer Felder, *Medicaid Funding for Abortions: The Medicaid Statute and the Equal Protection Clause,* 6 Hofstra L. Rev. 421 (1978); Constance Leistiko, *State Funding of Nontherapeutic Abortions – Medicaid Plans – Equal Protection – Right to Choose an Abortion,* 11 Akron L. Rev. 345 (1977); Michael J. Perry, *The Abortion Funding Cases: A Comment on the Supreme Court's Role in American Government,* 66 Geo. L.J. 1191 (1978); James S. Ryan, *A Right without Access? Payment for Elective Abortions after* Maher v. Roe, 7 Cap. U.L. Rev. 483 (1978); Shefler, *supra* note 11; Gary J. Simson, *Abortion, Poverty and the Equal Protection of the Laws,* 13 Ga. L. Rev. 505 (1979).

[45] 410 U.S. 113, 163–65 (1973).

[46] *Id.*

interest strict scrutiny demands. In *Doe*, the Court struck down as unconstitutional technical requirements involving hospital accreditation, committee approval, two-doctor concurrence, and state residence.[47] The public funding restriction upheld in *Maher* is as direct an obstacle and more prohibitive than the requirements struck down in *Doe*. Finally, in *Carey*, decided less than two weeks before *Maher*, the Court made clear that strict scrutiny applied to any regulation burdening the decision whether to bear or beget a child.[48] The Court rejected the distinction announced in *Maher* between laws that result in direct interference and those that purport to encourage alternative activity.[49]

By reaffirming a woman's fundamental right to decide whether to terminate a pregnancy under the Fourteenth Amendment right to privacy, Goodwin's opinion closely tracks *Roe*, *Doe*, and *Carey*, and demands continued strict scrutiny of restrictions that interfere with the abortion decision.

Next, Goodwin strikes down Section 275 as a violation of the Fourteenth Amendment right to equal protection because it impinges on a woman's right to terminate a pregnancy by refusing to fund elective abortions while agreeing to fund prenatal and postnatal care. Goodwin demands that the state proffer a compelling interest to justify its discrimination against a woman who chooses abortion over childbirth. She rejects the *Maher* Court's distinction between a state's direct interference and a state's encouragement of an alternative as misplaced in the welfare setting because an indigent woman could hardly decide to terminate a pregnancy without public funds.

Goodwin's equal protection analysis highlights the absurdity of deferring to the legislative branch in abortion funding cases. Restrictions on public funding were not designed to protect the public fisc or scarce resources. The average cost of a first-trimester abortion was $150; the cost of a normal delivery paid by Medicaid was $556.[50] As amici curiae argued in *Maher*, "never before has there been a case in which poor people have asked that they be afforded a less costly benefit, and the state has insisted that they may only have a more costly one."[51]

Goodwin's opinion also recognizes that the cost of abortion would put the abortion decision out of reach for many indigent women. Indeed, between 1975 and 1979, lack of public funding for abortion played a significant role in six of the seventeen deaths following illegal abortions reported to the Centers for Disease Control.[52] In one instance, a twenty-two-year-old African American woman with one child became pregnant and told a friend that she could not financially or

---

[47] 410 U.S. 179 (1973).
[48] 431 U.S. 678, 688 (1977).
[49] *Id.*
[50] Brief of Amici Curiae, *supra* note 6, at 15.
[51] *Id.* at 11.
[52] Nancy Binkin, Julian Gold, & William Cates, Jr., *Illegal-Abortion Deaths in the United States: Why Are They Still Occurring?*, 14 FAM. PLAN. PERSP. 163 (May–Jun. 1982).

emotionally afford to have another child. She consulted the only abortion provider in the area and learned that the procedure would cost $180, which she did not have. She then turned to someone living thirty miles away who purportedly could perform the abortion for $50. She died of septic complications two weeks later despite vigorous medical intervention on her behalf.[53] All six of the women who sought an illegal abortion because of financial hardships and died because of substandard care were African American or Latina.[54]

Indigent women who actually managed to obtain an abortion experienced two- to three-week delays, increasing the risk and cost of the procedure, usually because they needed time to come up with the money to pay for it.[55] Although the *Maher* Court suggested that indigent women could use "private sources" for funding, the truth was that adequate private sources did not exist. Instead, indigent women diverted funds intended for rent, utility bills, food, or clothing for them and their existing families.[56] By then, an abortion cost from $160 (clinic) to $460 (hospital); an average family received $238 per month under the AFDC program.[57]

By holding that Section 275 impinges on a woman's fundamental right to decide to terminate a pregnancy, Goodwin gives teeth to the well-established equal protection doctrine that when a state decides to provide benefits to the indigent, the way it provides them is subject to constitutional limitations.

Finally, Goodwin makes clear that a state cannot penalize a woman for exercising her right to terminate a pregnancy. To condition public benefits on forfeiture of that right would be an unconstitutional condition. Goodwin rejects the state's narrow interpretation of Title XIX as providing coverage of abortion only when necessary to save the life of an indigent pregnant woman. Title XIX neither favors nor disfavors abortion but rather authorizes provision of medically necessary services. All pregnancies require medically necessary services. The type of services, prenatal and postnatal care or an abortion is a woman's private right to decide.

By applying the unconstitutional conditions doctrine to public funding regulations, and by interpreting Title XIX to allow coverage of elective abortion, Goodwin provides indigent women with additional legal support of their right to decide whether to terminate a pregnancy.

---

[53] *Id.* at 165.

[54] *Id.* at 166. Restrictions on public funding for abortion also resulted in substantial human suffering. In Ohio, for example, a young mother shot herself in the stomach after a public hospital told her that she could not obtain an abortion unless she paid $600 for it. James Trussell, Jane Menken, Barbara L. Lindheim, & Barbara Vaughn, *The Impact of Restricting Medicaid Financing for Abortion*, 12 FAM. PLAN. PERSP. 120, 129 (May–June 1980).

[55] Stanley K. Henshaw & Lynn S. Wallisch, *The Medicaid Cutoff and Abortion Services for the Poor*, 16 FAM. PLAN. PERSP. 170 (1984).

[56] *Id.* at 179.

[57] Richard Lincoln, Brigitte Doring-Bradley, Barbara L. Lindheim, & Maureen A. Cotterill, *The Court, the Congress and the President: Turning Back the Clock on the Pregnant Poor*, 9 FAM. PLAN. PERSP. 207, 211 (table 3) (Sept.–Oct. 1977).

The Hyde Amendment and the Curtailing of Abortion
Rights Jurisprudence

Goodwin's rewritten opinion of *Maher* would have controlled future abortion
funding decisions. Just before the Court decided *Maher*, Congress passed the Hyde
Amendment, which prohibited the use of federal funds for abortions unless the
woman's life was endangered. Three years after *Maher*, the Court upheld the Hyde
Amendment in *Harris v. McRae*.[58] It explained, "The Hyde Amendment, like the
Connecticut welfare regulation at issue in *Maher*, places no governmental obstacle
in the path of a woman who chooses to terminate her pregnancy but rather, by
means of unequal subsidization of abortion and other medical services, encourages
alternative activity deemed in the public interest."[59] Under Goodwin's rewritten
opinion, indigent women in *Harris* could have found legal refuge in privacy and
equal protection principles, and under the unconstitutional conditions doctrine.

Goodwin's rewritten opinion also could have stemmed the erosion of abortion
rights in future non-funding decisions. The Court's distinction in *Maher* between
state action and inaction and inquiry about whether there was "unduly burdensome
interference" with a woman's decision to terminate a pregnancy seemed limited to
abortion funding decisions. Subsequent Courts, however, seized on the unduly
burdensome language to further narrow the interpretation of *Roe* and the strict
scrutiny requirement under the trimester framework. In *Bellotti v. Baird*, the Court
examined a parental involvement law in terms of whether it unduly burdened a
young woman's right to seek an abortion.[60] Justice Sandra Day O'Connor also
invoked the unduly burdensome language in her examination of abortion regulations.[61] Finally, in *Planned Parenthood of Southeastern Pennsylvania v. Casey*, the
Court abandoned *Roe*'s trimester framework altogether and adopted the undue
burden standard, inviting states to impose restrictions on abortion throughout
pregnancy.[62] Goodwin's rewritten opinion, which shores up the fundamental right
status of the abortion decision, could have diverted the Court's march toward this far
less rigorous standard of review.

CONCLUSION

The Supreme Court maintained that *Maher* did not signal a retreat from *Roe
v. Wade*. In fact, the decision proved disastrous for indigent women and marked a

---

[58] 448 U.S. 297 (1980).

[59] *Id.* at 315.

[60] 443 U.S. 622 (1979).

[61] *Akron v. Akron Reproductive Health, Inc.*, 462 U.S. 416, 453 (1983) (O'Connor, J., dissenting);
Thornburgh v. American College of Obstetricians & Gynecologists, 476 U.S. 747, 828 (1986)
(O'Connor, J., dissenting); *Webster v. Reproductive Health Services*, 492 U.S. 490, 530 (1989)
(O'Connor, J., concurring in part, concurring in the judgment).

[62] 505 U.S. 833, 873–79 (1992).

restrictive turning point in abortion rights jurisprudence. In contrast, in Goodwin's feminist judgment, she recognizes that not all women are socioeconomically empowered to make decisions purportedly guaranteed by law. While adhering to the precedent of the time, she crafts an opinion that avoids splintering a woman's fundamental right to abortion into one enjoyed by economically privileged women and one out of reach for many indigent women.

Maher, Commissioner of Social Services of Connecticut v. Roe, 432 U.S. 464 (1977)

Ms. Justice Michele Goodwin delivered the opinion of the Court

In this case, the Court has before it the question whether Connecticut may deny nontherapeutic abortion services to Medicaid recipients under its state welfare program even while it pays for childbirth and therapeutic abortions. The U.S. District Court for the District of Connecticut struck down the Connecticut law in question, declaring it unconstitutional, and enjoined enforcement of the law. *Roe v. Norton*, 408 F. Supp. 660, 665 (D. Conn. 1975). It ruled, "once a state chooses to establish a program for reimbursing the medical expenses of the indigent, and adopts as part of that program a provision that requires state funding for medical expenses arising from pregnancy, a serious equal protection issue arises if the state refuses to reimburse expenses incurred in procuring an abortion." *Id.* at 663.

Affirmed.

I BACKGROUND

A regulation of the Connecticut Department of Social Services[63] prohibits the use of Medicaid and state medical assistance for elective, nontherapeutic abortions. Connecticut law mandates that a poor woman who relies on Medicaid or state assistance may receive an abortion under those programs only when the procedure is "medically necessary."

Appellees Roe and Poe are two indigent women who qualify for Medicaid services and Aid to Dependent Children in the state of Connecticut. However both were unable to access abortion services due to their poverty and Connecticut's restrictions on abortion services through its Medicaid program. They challenge the constitutionality of the Connecticut regulation and bring this case against Edward W. Maher, the Commissioner of Social Services of Connecticut.

Appellee Mary Poe is a 16-year-old high school student who received an elective abortion at a Bridgeport, Connecticut hospital. The state of Connecticut refused

---

[63] Conn. State Dept. of Social Services, Medical Assistance Program Manual, Vol. 3, chapter III, § 275.

to reimburse the hospital because Miss Poe did not obtain necessary certification under Connecticut law. Ms. Susan Roe is a 26-year-old, unmarried mother of three young children. Both women sought abortions in their first trimesters of pregnancy.

Roe "desired an abortion to avoid further family burdens and complications." *Roe v. Norton*, 522 F.2d 928, 930 (2d Cir. 1975). Roe's physician did not believe the abortion was medically necessary within the definition of Connecticut's law, such as to prevent death or spare her from psychological trauma. However, because her physician believed an abortion would be medically appropriate for Ms. Roe, he was willing to perform the procedure. As a result, Ms. Roe could not obtain the necessary certification required under Connecticut law in order to have the costs of her abortion reimbursed under Medicaid. Unable to pay for the abortion, she sued on behalf of herself and other similarly situated women who, although eligible for Medicaid assistance from the state of Connecticut, were denied access to the program because they sought nontherapeutic abortion services.

Appellees argue that the state's certification process, which mandates that physicians certify the medical necessity of a woman's abortion, violates their constitutional rights, including the Fourteenth Amendment's guarantees of equal protection and due process. They argue that contrary to Connecticut law, Title XIX of the Social Security Act 79 Stat. 343, as amended, 42 U. S. C. § 1396 et seq. (1970 ed. and Supp. V) does not limit Medicaid reimbursements under state programs to instances where an abortion may be necessary to preserve the health and life of a pregnant woman. Rather, they claim Title XIX includes funding for elective abortions in consultation with physicians. Further, they argue that Title XIX prohibits states from denying Medicaid payment for elective abortions.

Connecticut officials originally defended its law, claiming that Title XIX prohibits reimbursement for nontherapeutic abortions. In fact, "[t]hey insist ... that the Section 275 restrictions on coverage of abortions are mandated by Title XIX." *Roe v. Norton*, 522 F.2d at 930. Connecticut officials claim that Medicaid requires it to restrict reimbursements of elective abortions.

Connecticut requires that a woman who qualifies for state assistance due to her poverty must submit a written request to the Department of Social Services asking that the state approve her request to terminate a pregnancy through this program. In addition, the woman's medical provider and the hospital or clinic where the procedure will be performed must obtain approval in advance of providing abortion services by submitting the Request for Authorization for Professional Services Form W-601, and Form W-217, confirming medical necessity. That is, the law requires the latter form "include a statement indicating the medical need for the abortion."[64]

---

[64] *Id.*

According to the law, "[T]he request will be reviewed by competent medical authority in the Division of Health Services in Central Office, and the hospital or clinic will be notified of the Department's decision by returning two (2) copies of Form W-601 to the hospital, maintaining one (1) copy for its own files."[65] The state of Connecticut singles out only abortion for such requirements. See Forms W-217 and W-217a. In the case of abortion, Connecticut law mandates that "payment for abortion will be made only when this prior authorization is obtained from the Chief of Medical Services, Division of Health Services, Department of Social Services." Appellees Brief at 3.

No other medical services are subjected to such scrutiny and intervention by the state. For example, Connecticut does not require certification of medical necessity approved by the Chief of Services and the patient's medical provider for any other medical service or treatment. Answer to Pl.'s Interrog. 9B. Abortions are the only medical services under this funding rubric in Connecticut for which stringent informed consent processes and validation attach. In no other instances except abortions are physicians required to provide advance certification of the patient's consent to treatment. As well, abortion is the only medical procedure whereby a medical facility's chief of staff must certify the hospital admitting privileges of the attending physician.

Further, if an abortion is provided for an indigent woman without prior authorization from the relevant Connecticut government agency, the hospital or clinic may not be reimbursed. The state will only compensate medical providers for abortions the state preauthorizes or deems "medically or psychiatrically necessary," such as to save the woman's life or to prevent psychological harm.

For Medicaid-eligible services, hospitals and clinics are reimbursed by the government after qualified providers perform the eligible medical procedures. Connecticut claims that Title XIX of the Federal Social Security Act, 42 U.S.C. § 1396 et seq., otherwise known as Medicaid, bars payment for nontherapeutic abortions. Connecticut cannot defend this assertion based on any language in the legislation, as the law says no such thing. To the contrary, the Act is neutral regarding payments for abortion services.

> On appeal, the Second Circuit, 522 F.2d 928 (2d Cir. 1975), held that the Social Security Act was entirely neutral as to abortion payments, neither requiring the states to pay for any abortion services at all, nor forbidding the states from reimbursing welfare recipients for the expense of an elective abortion. *Roe v. Norton*, 408 F. Supp. at 662

Connecticut offers no any medical justification for its prohibition of Medicaid funded elective abortions. Nor does the state provide any cogent and coherent medical distinction between when the procedure is performed for medical

---

[65] *Id.*

necessity and when it is not. The State fails to articulate a realistic distinction between a "medically necessary" abortion and one that is not, given that all pregnancies require medically necessary health services, whether treatment is administered to maintain a healthy pregnancy and delivery or to end the pregnancy, which this Court ruled in *Roe v. Wade* was the constitutional prerogative of the pregnant woman. *Roe v. Wade*, 410 U.S. 113, 153 (1973). There is no discernible, compelling reason to justify the State's interference with a clearly articulated fundamental right.

Indeed, the State fails to even attempt to articulate a compelling justification for the intrusions it now places on a pregnant woman's medical care and her right to terminate a pregnancy. In *Roe v. Wade*, the Court explained, the "right of privacy, whether it be founded in the Fourteenth Amendment's concept of personal liberty and restrictions upon state action, as we feel it is, or, as the District Court determined, in the Ninth Amendment's reservation of rights to the people, is broad enough to encompass a woman's decision whether or not to terminate her pregnancy." *Id.* We also take special note that the financial hurdles imposed by the state will introduce significant disincentives and burdens on clinics, hospitals, and doctors that would otherwise desire to provide reproductive health services, such as abortions, to indigent women.

II FUNDAMENTAL RIGHT TO AN ABORTION

Connecticut's argument that the statute in question does not unconstitutionally burden indigent women's fundamental right to an abortion does not merit extended, elaborate response. The fundamental privacy right established in *Roe* is not open to question. Nor is it vulnerable to the machinations and coercions of state laws such as those challenged in *Doe* or in the present case. The state of Connecticut may not deny nontherapeutic abortion services to Medicaid recipients under its state welfare program while it pays for childbirth and therapeutic abortions. To rule otherwise would enforce the State's unconstitutional impingement on the fundamental right to terminate a pregnancy. Currently, the State places a substantial economic obstacle in the path of an indigent pregnant woman's right to choose an abortion because it denies her the necessary financial support to carry out this medical decision.

The nature of the fundamental privacy right established in *Roe v. Wade* unequivocally reaches this case. In *Roe*, the Court concluded that "the right of personal privacy includes the abortion decision." *Id.* at 154. The right of personal privacy has been affirmed time and again by the Court in a robust line of decisions, dating back to *Union Pacific R. Co. v. Botsford*, 141 U.S. 250 (1891) and *Boyd v. United States*, 116 U.S. 616 (1886). Whether rooted in the First Amendment, *Stanley v. Georgia*, 394 U.S. 557, 564 (1969); the Fourth and Fifth

Amendments, *Katz v. U.S.*, 389 U.S. 347, 350 (1967); *Tehan v. United States* ex rel. Shott, 382 U.S. 406, 416 (1966); the penumbras, *Griswold v. Connecticut*, 381 U.S. 479, 484–85 (1965); or the Fourteenth Amendment, *Meyer v. Nebraska*, 262 U. S. 390, 399 (1923). This right of privacy is fundamental and can only be infringed on for compelling cause. We see no compelling interest articulated by Connecticut in this case.

In *Meyer v. Nebraska*, 262 U. S. 390, 399 (1923), the Court wrote:

> Without doubt, [liberty] denotes not merely freedom from bodily restraint, but also the right of the individual to contract, to engage in any of the common occupations of life, to acquire useful knowledge, to marry, establish a home and bring up children, to worship God according to the dictates of his own conscience, and generally to enjoy those privileges long recognized at common law as essential to the orderly pursuit of happiness by free men.

The Connecticut statute "is at war with the clear message of these cases – that a woman is free to make the basic decision whether to bear an unwanted child." *Doe v. Bolton*, 410 U.S. 179, 214 (1973). We need not repeat the rigorous analysis of the personal privacy right undertaken by the Court in *Roe*. It suffices to articulate the Court's recognition of the fundamental right of privacy established not only in *Roe v. Wade* related to abortion but also in other areas of intimacy such as procreation, *Skinner v. Oklahoma*, 316 U.S. 535, 541–42 (1942); contraception,- *Eisenstadt v. Baird*, 405 U.S. 438, 453–54, 460, 463–65 (1972); marriage, *Loving v. Virginia*, 388 U.S. 1, 12 (1967) and abortion, *Roe v. Wade*, 410 U.S. at 152 and *Doe v. Bolton*, 410 U.S. at 212. As this Court found in *Doe v. Bolton*, accreditation or certification requirements may be so overbroad as to infringe on fundamental privacy rights.

Doe v. Bolton is particularly instructive considering the Connecticut law in question. In that case, the Court struck down a Georgia law that made it a "crime for a physician to perform an abortion except when, as § 26-1202(a) [of the Georgia law] reads, it is "based upon his best clinical judgment that an abortion is necessary" as in instances of severe fetal abnormality, rape, or grave endangerment of the pregnant woman, such as death. *Id.* at 183, 191. The case was brought by a 22-year-old indigent pregnant woman who had three children – two were in foster care because she could not afford to care for them. The youngest was placed for adoption for similar reasons. Mrs. Doe was married but abandoned by her husband and living with her impoverished parents and their eight children. She could not afford to support and care for a child.

Georgia provided a narrow exemption where an abortion could be "authorized or performed as a noncriminal procedure," however additional strict criteria and certifications had to be met such as "written concurrence" of the doctor's judgment by "at least two other Georgia-licensed physicians." *Id.* at 183.

In addition, Georgia required "performance of the abortion in a hospital licensed by the State Board of Health and also accredited by the Joint Commission on Accreditation of Hospitals ..." and "advance approval by an abortion committee of not less than three members of the hospital's staff ... [and] certifications in a rape situation." *Id.*

In a 7–2 decision, this Court struck down the Georgia law, holding that the Joint Accreditation of Hospitals ("JCAH Accreditation") standard imposed by the state of Georgia did not "withstand constitutional scrutiny." *Id.* at 193. We held, "that the JCAH-accredited hospital provision and the requirements as to approval by the hospital abortion committee, as to confirmation by two independent physicians, and as to residence in Georgia are all violative of the Fourteenth Amendment." *Id.* at 201. We find similarities in the intrusiveness of the Georgia and Connecticut laws, as both single out abortion for added unconstitutional state intervention in a woman's fundamental right to end a pregnancy.

In *Roe* we explained, "where certain 'fundamental rights' are involved, ... regulation limiting these rights may be justified only by a 'compelling state interest'." *Roe v. Wade*, 410 U.S. at 155; see also *Sherbert v. Verner*, 374 U.S. 398, 406 (1963); *Kramer v. Union Free School District*, 395 U.S. 621–27 (1969). We further held "that legislative enactments must be narrowly drawn to express only the legitimate state interests at stake." *Roe v. Wade*, 410 U.S. at 155; see also *Griswold v. Connecticut*, 381 U.S. at 485; *Cantwell v. Connecticut*, 310 U.S. 296, 307–8 (1940). Similarly, in *Bellotti v. Baird*, 428 U.S. 132, 147 (1976), we held, that state laws that "unduly burden" the right to seek an abortion are unconstitutional.

This case is before the Court because Connecticut refuses to fund abortions that are not "medically necessary," thereby denying indigent women the right to terminate their pregnancies even while it underwrites the expenses of poor women to continue their pregnancies. In this vein, Connecticut, rather than the poor pregnant woman, chooses whether a woman should become a mother. In doing so, Connecticut now makes the fundamental privacy right carved out in *Roe* and *Doe* more illusory than real for the poor.

As this Court ruled in *Roe*, "the detriment the State would impose upon the pregnant woman by denying this choice altogether is apparent." *Roe v. Wade*, 410 U.S. at 153. Specific and direct harms no less than death and deadly depression may result from forcing a poor woman into pregnancy and motherhood as Connecticut now does. Legal abortions are very safe, minor medical procedures, that "under ideal circumstances ... can be done with very little vital risk." John McKelvey, 50 Minn. Med. 119, 124 (1967). Nevertheless, as Dr. John McKelvey, the former chief of the Department of Obstetrics and Gynecology at the University of Minnesota explains, "the procedures which are open to the poor" otherwise referred to as "back alley abortions," "on the contrary can be very risky not only to the life of the individual but to her future health." *Id.*

As Appellants articulated in *Doe* (and we cited), "a statute that requires a woman to carry an unwanted pregnancy to term infringes not only on a fundamental right of privacy, but on the right to life itself." *Doe v. Bolton*, 410 U.S. at 190; Appellants' Brief at 27.

For example, there is no debate on this subject: a woman is more likely to die during pregnancy and childbirth than by undergoing a legal abortion, which is a vastly safer medical procedure. Christopher Tietze, *United States: Therapeutic Abortions, 1963–1968*, 59 STUDIES IN FAMILY PLANNING 5, 7 (1970). Connecticut claims that its law has a safety valve – if the life of the mother is at risk, the state will fund such an abortion. Yet, this provision is a mere fig leaf that papers over the State's unconstitutional abortion restriction, because a woman's life may be threatened by pregnancy even when she and her physicians are not aware.

Indeed, maternal mortality is particularly acute for nonwhite women and poor women – the very class of pregnant women the state now targets for unconstitutional treatment. The Centers for Disease Control data shows that "for nonwhite women," the rate of maternal mortality is "almost four times the rate for white women." U.S. DEPARTMENT OF HEALTH, EDUCATION, AND WELFARE, VITAL STATISTICS OF THE UNITED STATES, Vol. II–Mortality, Part A, 1–17 (1963). Sadly, the state of Connecticut shows indifference to the rights and lives of these pregnant women, because it would choose to constrain their abortion rights and access while confining them to childbirth, which literally risks their lives.

At the same time, the state ignores the safety of abortions and singles it out for various certification and extraneous consent processes when it does not do the same for other operations that are far riskier to a woman's health, such as appendectomies and cholecystectomies. An abortion is "38.8 times safer than appendectomy, and 155 times safer than cholecystectomy, all other factors being equal." *Doe v. Bolton*, Appellants' Brief, at 31–32 (citing Appendectomy Profile, 1968, 7 PAS REPORTER No. 16, at 1–4 (Dec. 22, 1969) and Cholecystectomy Mortality, 8 PAS REPORTER No. 8, at 1 (Apr. 20, 1970)). Data on elective, induced abortions mortality compared to childbirth mortality exposes the fallibility of the state's certification regime.

Studies vary with regard to the safety of legal abortions. One study shows Hungary's induced abortion mortality rate is 1.2 per 100,000 and in New York the mortality rate for elective induced abortions from 1970 to 71 was 5.3 per 100,000 procedures. *Doe v. Bolton*, Appellants' Brief at 33–34. Yet all studies presented to the Court show a dramatic differential in the safety of legal abortions compared to childbirth. The rate of mortality for childbirth in the U.S. is 28 per 100,000. Sabrina Tavernise, *Maternal Mortality Rate in U.S. Rises, Defying Global Trend, Study Finds*, N.Y. TIMES, September 21, 2016. Thus, whether a woman is five times or twenty-eight times more likely to die in childbirth versus abortion, it is clear that

Connecticut's Medicaid rule has little to do with promoting patient safety, safe-guarding pregnant women's health, and informed consent. If the Connecticut law were a legitimate health and safety measure, it would not differentiate between a patient's choice to seek an abortion versus to pursue a pregnancy.

Connecticut's argument that the state does not infringe on indigent women's reproductive privacy rights hardly merits this Court's response. It is unnecessary for the Court to further elaborate on the many ways that motherhood may tether an indigent woman to grave hardship, poverty, a detrimental lifestyle, and a dishearten-ing future further exacerbated by shame, stigma, and the social realities of unequal opportunities in virtually all aspects of life, including education, employment, and social recognition.

As we similarly concluded in striking down Georgia's abortion statute in 1973, rejected applicants of Connecticut's certification legislation are forced to endure the "pain, higher mortality rate, and after-effects of childbirth; to abandon educational plans; to sustain loss of income; to forgo the satisfactions of careers; to tax further mental and physical health in providing child care; and, in some cases, to bear the lifelong stigma of unwed motherhood, a badge which may haunt, if not deter, later legitimate family relationships." *Doe v. Bolton*, 410 U.S. 179 at 215.

III EQUAL PROTECTION

Connecticut singles out poor, pregnant women for disfavored treatment. The state's Medicaid provision serves as an unconstitutional proxy for discriminating against indigent pregnant women, a class of disfavored persons. Sadly, we have seen before where the state has disfavored poor pregnant women. The nation's history with eugenics bears this out. Model laws adopted in various states urged the compulsory sterilization of indigent girls and women. These laws hardly applied to wealthy women. Such laws are not the subject of today's ruling. Suffice to say that this Court urges a revisiting of those cases, including its own decision in *Buck v. Bell*, 274 U.S. 200 (1927) to correct this shameful history. Nevertheless, we take historic note of the pernicious ways a state may impermissibly seek to single out indigent women for unequal treatment under the law and the shameful complicity and ignorance of Courts – including our own – that sanctioned such treatment.

In short, the Connecticut regulation claims neutrality. However, it stings only indigent women who seemingly make the state's disfavored choice to seek an abortion. It subjects this class of women to arbitrary and medically unnecessary paperwork, bureaucratic procedures, and invasions of privacy. Indigent pregnant women who make the state's favored choice are spared invasions of privacy and shielded from invasive, arbitrary certifications that do not further their health nor achieve any other state purpose save burdening and discouraging the choice of an abortion. By its very nature, such jockeying and roulette-playing with a fundamental constitutional right is impermissible.

Connecticut bullies indigent pregnant women to choose the life that the state would deem appropriate for them, such as motherhood. For example, "Defendants answers to interrogatories admit that no other form of obstetrical care requires prior authorization or proof of medical necessity." Appellees' Brief at 16. Further, indigent pregnant women in Connecticut "are required to undergo the burdensome and time-consuming procedure of obtaining prior approval of a service authorized by their physicians." *Id.* We note that this process is not required for any other hospital procedure, nor for any comparable physician's care. *Id.* The state manipulates public monies and welfare to carry out this unconstitutional agenda.

We agree with the lower court:

> The Constitution does not require the state to pay for any medical services at all. Nevertheless once a state chooses to establish a program for reimbursing the medical expenses of the indigent, and adopts as part of that program a provision that requires state funding for medical expenses arising from pregnancy, a serious equal protection issue arises if the state refuses to reimburse expenses incurred in procuring an abortion. *Roe v. Norton,* 408 F. Supp. at 663

By the very design of its legislation, Connecticut unlawfully and coercively forces healthy indigent women into the unintended and unwanted status of motherhood, because the state will pay to keep poor women tethered to unwelcome motherhood but deny them access to abortion. Connecticut shows a grave perversity and distressing insensitivity to indigent women in its state. When it could lawfully grant women their fundamental right to reproductive freedom and privacy for so little expense, the state prefers to pay extravagantly more to bind indigent women to motherhood, which too frequently conveys a second-class citizenship in our society.

The state foists this upon indigent women even as doing so will inevitably cost the state more money, because providing medical support for pregnancies (prenatal, delivery, and postnatal care) costs far more than allowing a woman who desires an abortion to receive that service. Moreover, not only are the medical expenses associated with pregnancy and child birthing far greater than those associated with an abortion, the state also commits itself to the expenses of rearing indigent offspring, including food, clothing, health, and housing.

The District Court held:

> When Connecticut refuses to fund elective abortions while funding therapeutic abortions and prenatal and postnatal care, it weights the choice of the pregnant mother against choosing to exercise her constitutionally protected right to an elective abortion. . . . Her choice is affected not simply by the absence of payment for the abortion, but by the availability of public funds for childbirth if she chooses not to have the abortion. When the state thus infringes upon a fundamental interest, it must assert a compelling state interest. *Id.* at 663–64.

This Court is acutely aware of the devastating harms states would impose on indigent pregnant women if abortion rights were conditioned on wealth. In effect, Connecticut's law constructs a tiered abortion right structure and subjects all indigent women in its state to this system. That is, for wealthy women in Connecticut (and elsewhere), the fundamental right to end a pregnancy remains intact under state law because their wealth does not hinder abortion access.

However, Connecticut, through its welfare program, has established rules that effectively condition abortion access so that only poor women who are deathly ill, physically or mentally, may exercise this fundamental constitutional right.

As a result, it subjects poor women to a hierarchy of fundamental rights, which this Court cannot let stand. The Court is particularly attuned to unconstitutional money hurdles imposed by legislation, which infringe on fundamental rights. The wisdom of Justice Frankfurter prevails today.

> To sanction such a ruthless consequence, inevitably resulting from a money hurdle erected by the State, would justify a latter-day Anatole France to add one more item to his ironic comments on the "majestic equality" of the law. "The law, in its majestic equality, forbids the rich as well as the poor to sleep under bridges, to beg in the streets, and to steal bread." *Griffin v. Illinois*, 351 U. S. 12, 23 (1956) (Frankfurter, J., concurring)

The indisputable reality for most indigent pregnant women is that the expense of abortion, while less than childbirth, will simply be out of reach. Connecticut's law reduces this fundamental right to a mere paper right. Poor women who desire to end their pregnancies will feel coerced into motherhood. Quite literally, under Connecticut law, they will not have the option to choose an abortion, because the state refuses to provide funds for the procedure. The result is the state's impermissible circumvention and interdiction of the abortion right.

In *Singleton v. Wulff*, 428 U.S. 106, 122, 128 (1976), the Court stated, "for a doctor who cannot afford to work for nothing, and a woman who cannot afford to pay him, the State's refusal to fund an abortion is as effective an 'interdiction' of it as would ever be necessary." We further explained that "since the right . . . is not simply the right to have an abortion, but the right to have abortions nondiscriminatorily funded, the denial of such funding is as complete an 'interdiction' of the exercise of the right as could ever exist." *Id*. at 118, n 7.

Connecticut chooses to impose an economic barrier in its funding of reproductive healthcare, creating stark disparities to an alarming and coercive degree. The state clearly designates its funding in a manner to steer indigent women toward motherhood. However, the state conscribes this life only to poor women who happen to be healthy enough to endure its coercion. Poor women who can demonstrate grave health are spared the cruelty of this statute.

Finally, we cannot equate abortion and childbirth as two equal solutions. Abortions are far safer than pregnancy and childbirth. Pregnancies and childbirth in the United States can be matters of life and death, particularly for indigent women of color. Pregnancies have been shown to be far more threatening to a woman's health and a serious burden on her future opportunities, independence, capacities to earn a living, achieve meaningful education, and equality and opportunity in society. An intelligible understanding of the health, economic, and social status concerns at stake in pregnancy underscore the primacy of the privacy right for pregnant women.

IV TITLE XIX

Title XIX permits Medicaid coverage of elective abortions. As established under the Social Security Act, Medicaid, "provides a comprehensive scheme of federal financial assistance to enable states electing to participate to furnish medical assistance to indigent families with dependent children and aged, blind and disabled persons." *Roe v. Norton*, 522 F.2d at 932 (citation omitted). The state plan must simply include "reasonable standards." Connecticut attempts to distort the meaning and purpose of Medicaid's provisions articulated under Social Security Act, 42 U.S.C.A. §§ 1396 et seq., 1396d, 1901 et seq., 1905.

Connecticut's law demands that the Court address whether a public benefit program can be used to penalize indigent women who seek to exercise their fundamental right to terminate a pregnancy. The state cannot condition a fundamental right on the economic status of the right's bearer. The state can no more impose such conditions on a pregnant woman who desires an abortion than it can on an indigent man who seeks to vote. The impermissibility of such an action is patently apparent and addressed by this Court in *Sherbert v. Verner*, 374 U.S. 398 (1963), where the Court ruled that South Carolina impermissibly denied unemployment compensation to a Seventh Day Adventist:

> Here not only is it apparent that appellant's declared ineligibility for benefits derives solely from the practice of her religion, but the pressure upon her to forego that practice is unmistakable. The ruling forces her to choose between following the precepts of her religion and forfeiting benefits, on the one hand, and abandoning one of the precepts of her religion in order to accept work, on the other hand. Governmental imposition of such a choice puts the same kind of burden upon the free exercise of religion as would a fine imposed against appellant for her Saturday worship. *Id.* at 404.

Connecticut misreads Medicaid and shows elementary understanding of pregnancy. The state frames the question in this case as one that examines whether Title XIX authorizes public moneys for unnecessary medical services. The state's presumption is that abortions are unnecessary medical services. And, therefore, its answer to the question is simply that Medicaid bars elective abortion services. The state errs in its reductive framing of pregnancy, abortion, and childbirth.

Indisputably, all pregnancies are physical conditions that require medical attention. The very nature of medical care provided to a woman in the instance of her pregnancy, whether continuing to childbirth or abortion, will be medically necessary. Simply put, pregnancy requires medical care. A woman's decision as to how she directs that medically necessary care is her private right, regardless of her economic status or circumstances. The latter point, which is the crux of this case, Connecticut mistakenly fails to acknowledge. Connecticut cannot sensibly nor credibly argue that the only medically necessary care in pregnancy is childbirth. Yet, the state's chief argument relies upon this thin and fragile logic.

As the lower court stated:

Nowhere in this long and complicated statute do we find any limitation on Medicaid payments for abortions. Indeed, the statute is devoid of any reference at all to abortions or abortion services. In our view, payments for all abortion services, whether the abortion be therapeutic or elective, are well within the definition of medical assistance which the states are authorized to furnish, as spelled out in Section 1396d(a). *Roe v. Norton*, 522 F.2d, at 933

The state misreads the Social Security Act and urges the Court to adopt its reasoning that only therapeutic abortions, to save the life of an indigent woman, are medically necessary. If the risk of death were the only trigger for Medicaid services, many indigent people would be denied care and suffer serious illnesses.

Statutes that establish the Medicaid program neither favor nor disfavor abortion. The law does not distinguish between categories of abortion. Therapeutic, elective, and emergency abortions are all necessary medical treatments in relation to a pregnancy. In other words, pregnancy is the medical condition, for which the range of necessary medical treatments may include termination or advancement to childbirth.

The Social Security Act does not exclude or disfavor state Medicaid coverage for elective abortions or favor Medicaid-funded pregnancy over pregnancy termination. Social Security Act, 42 U.S.C.A. §§ 1396 et seq, 1901 et seq. Rather, Medicaid statutes establish that "medically necessary" services will be provided to indigent individuals as a matter between the physician and patient. An elective abortion, thus, is medically necessary so long as it is the outcome of a decision made between the indigent patient and her physician. Social Security Act, 42 U.S.C.A. §§ 1396 et seq., 1396d, 1901 et seq., 1905.

Finally, we cannot take seriously Connecticut's implicit and explicit financial justifications for imposing such hardship on indigent women such as to render the abortion right meaningless and elusive for them. Connecticut argues that its needs "to control the amount of its limited public funds which will be allocated to its public welfare budget." Appellants' Brief at 22. However, as the District Court sagely ruled that the State's, "assertion that it saves money when it declines to pay the cost of a welfare mother's abortion is simply contrary to undisputed facts." *Roe v. Norton,* 408 F. Supp., at 664.

V CONCLUSION

We affirm the lower court ruling and hold that Title XIX of the Social Security Act does not prohibit state regulations denying Medicaid coverage for elective abortions, and that Section 275 of the Connecticut regulations is not invalid as in conflict with Title XIX. We reverse the holding of the court below to the contrary.

Concurring and dissenting opinions omitted.

5

In Re Madyun, 114 Daily Wash. Law. Rptr. 2233 (D.C. Super. Ct., 1986)

Commentary by Farah Diaz-Tello

Stare decisis dictates that some injustices endure in our jurisprudence, waiting for a moment when they might be dusted off and properly discarded. *Buck v. Bell*[1] and the forced sterilization of people with disabilities, *Korematsu v. United States*[2] and the detention of people of foreign descent, and *Geduldig v. Aiello*[3] and discrimination against pregnant people;[4] even though we have made progress slowly (and, in some cases, legislatively), each of these decisions stands as a threat to the communities they marginalize and to just and equitable rule of law. *In re Madyun* is such a case, representing a line of thinking that accords with neither medical ethics[5] nor law but which courts periodically cite as they grasp for justification for overriding a pregnant patient's decisions. This case and others like it persist as thorns in the side of advocates for Birth Justice and the elimination of obstetric violence.

Since the events recorded in the *Madyun* case, the jurisprudence on consent in birth has advanced, and the majority of courts that have examined hospitals' requests for nonconsensual medical intervention with the benefit of a full hearing and record have sided with the pregnant individual.[6] Nevertheless, the *Madyun* Court opened a

---

[1] 274 U.S. 200 (1927).

[2] 323 U. S. 214 (1944). The *Korematsu* decision was finally officially repudiated by the court during the writing of this commentary. *See Trump v. Hawaii*, 138 S. Ct. 2392 (2018) ("*Korematsu* was gravely wrong the day it was decided, has been overruled in the court of history, and – to be clear – 'has no place in law under the Constitution.'") (citations omitted).

[3] 417 U.S. 484 (1974).

[4] The discrimination described in this commentary is based on how bodies are gendered by others, not the gender identity of the individual. It can therefore apply to anyone with a uterus, including transgender men and some nonbinary persons.

[5] ACOG Comm. on Ethics, Opinion No. 664, *Refusal of Medically Recommended Treatment during Pregnancy* (Jun. 2016) ("Pregnancy does not lessen or limit the requirement to obtain informed consent or to honor a pregnant woman's refusal of recommended treatment").

[6] *See* Julie Kantor, *Court-Ordered Care – A Complication of Pregnancy to Avoid*, 366 NEW ENGL. J. MED. 2237 (Jun. 14, 2012).

door that has never been fully closed, even by the en banc DC Court of Appeals in *In re A.C.*, one of the most full-throated articulations of the right of pregnant patients to make their own decisions.

Fortunately, Maya Manian's feminist reconsideration of the *Madyun* decision demonstrates that a different world is possible. Most of the distinctions can be distilled to one point: the reconceived decision treats Ms. Madyun as a person with a full complement of human rights.

FACING THE FACTS

No line in the *Madyun* decision is more telling than this: "All that stood between the Madyun fetus and its independent existence, separate from its mother, was, put simply, a doctor's scalpel." The woman rendered invisible by this rhetorical flourish was Ayesha Madyun, a 19-year-old black, Muslim college student. By the time she arrived at George Washington Hospital with her husband in the early hours of July 25, 1986, she had been laboring for 36 hours. She had started at Greater Southeast Community Hospital but was eventually turned away for lack of insurance.[7]

Over the course of that day, Mrs. Madyun labored with limited progress. According to the record, physicians recommended that she undergo a surgical delivery, and she refused, desiring a vaginal delivery. When the doctors explained the potential risks, Mrs. Madyun informed staff that, in the Muslim faith, a woman may decide whether to risk her own life to save her pregnancy.

The hospital sought a court order authorizing it to perform a cesarean surgery over Mrs. Madyun's objections. A hearing was convened at 10:30 pm, and the court granted the hospital's petition. Mrs. Madyun appealed but, within hours, the appellate court had ruled against her in a telephonic hearing. The medical personnel performed the surgery against her will.

The clipped account of the facts in the decision – by contrast to Manian's opinion, which acknowledges Mrs. Madyun's marginalization as well as her strength of conviction even during a protracted labor – does not reach the devastation Mrs. Madyun experienced. After the ordeal, she told the Washington Post, "I felt like I was being raped."[8] Manian acknowledges the bodily and psychic violence done to a person forced to undergo unwanted medical treatment. Beyond the physical pain of scalpels and sutures and possible complications, the record of cases of court-ordered obstetrics is littered with horrifying indignities: women – disproportionately

---

[7] This is an occurrence that would now most likely be unlawful under the Emergency Medical Treatment and Active Labor Act (EMTALA), which was passed the same year amid concerns of "patient dumping" such as that experienced by Mrs. Madyun. 42 U.S.C. § 1395dd (2012).

[8] See, e.g., Cynthia Gorney, *Whose Body Is It, Anyway? The Legal Maelstrom That Rages When the Rights of the Mother and Fetus Collide*, WASHINGTON POST, Dec. 13, 1988. Manian's opinion draws facts from this account and Kenneth Jost, *Mother Versus Child*, 75(4) AM. BAR ASS'N J. 84 (Apr. 1989).

women of color[9] – shouted at, tied down, and forcibly sedated to carry out the recommendations of people charged with caring for them. Some flee, others acquiesce in fear. Manian's discussion of this violence, drawn from accounts of physicians who witnessed it firsthand, makes one wonder how any court could have ever approved such an order.

RE-CENTERING EQUALITY

To understand how a court could come to the decision that it had the authority to force medical personnel to cut through the body of an unconsenting woman where it would never permit such an intrusion on a man, it is important to understand that the *Madyun* case arose at an unfortunate moment in doctrine about decision-making during pregnancy. Nevertheless, Manian's thoughtful consideration of the case makes infuriatingly clear just how much the court had at its disposal, and how much it disregarded, to come to its decision. This is especially so with respect to the utter lack of an equality analysis.

Both statutory and case law on the common law right to be free from unwanted touching (where Manian begins her analysis) had been in existence for decades, if not longer,[10] and the U.S. Supreme Court had balked at the notion that a surgical removal of a bullet from a criminal suspect was a "reasonable" search under the Fourth Amendment.[11] However, a decision clearly articulating the constitutional dimensions of this right based in the Fourteenth Amendment substantive due process guarantee – the source of most jurisprudence protecting the dignity of marginalized individuals – would not arrive until *Cruzan* in 1990.[12] Furthermore, the jurisprudence on religiously-based refusal of unwanted medical care was still undeveloped, and would see significant improvement in the years to come due to litigation on the part of Jehovah's Witnesses who faced court orders because of their refusal to accept blood products.[13] Lacking these pillars, the court turned to other

---

[9] *See* Veronika E. B. Kolder, Janet Gallagher, & Michael T. Parsons, *Court-Ordered Obstetrical Interventions*, 316 N.E.J.M 1192 (1987) (reviewing 21 cases of court-mandated treatment during pregnancy, 81 percent were women of color, 24 percent were not native English speakers, all lived in poverty); *see also* Lisa Ikemoto, *Furthering the Inquiry: Race, Class, and Culture in the Forced Medical Treatment of Pregnant Women*, 59 TENN. L. REV. 487 (1992).

[10] *Schloendorff v. Socy. of N.Y. Hosp.*, 211 NY 125, 129-30 (1914) ("Every human being of adult years and sound mind has a right to determine what shall be done with [their] own body"); *See also Union Pac. Ry. Co. v. Botsford*, 141 U.S. 250, 251 (1891) ("No right is held more sacred, or is more carefully guarded by the common law, than the right of every individual to the possession and control of his own person, free from all restraint or interference of others, unless by clear and unquestionable authority of law").

[11] *Winston v. Lee*, 470 U.S. 753 (1985).

[12] *Cruzan v. Dir., Mo. Dep't of Health*, 497 U.S. 261 (1990) (denying that the Constitution protects a "right to die," but reiterating that the right to bodily integrity includes the right to refuse medical treatment, even lifesaving treatment.)

[13] *See, e.g., People v. Brown*, 689 N.E.2d 397 (1997); *In re Dubreuil*, 629 So. 2d 819, 823 (Fla. 1993) ("Patients do not lose their right to make decisions affecting their lives simply by entering a

substantive due process lines of cases to yield an idiosyncratic hybrid of case law regarding the care and control of children and a stunted reading of *Roe v. Wade*.[14]

Manian's approach instead begins with a soft-focus on gender equality. By leading the analysis with a discussion of the common law right to refuse unwanted medical care, and the closely related right to bodily integrity, the decision begins with a presumption that pregnant individuals have the same closely guarded rights as all other people.

Manian delves more deeply into this question by applying an Equal Protection analysis – a basis not yet addressed by any court with this issue before it. Because no court has analyzed the Equal Protection dimensions of a forced cesarean, there is no blueprint for how a court would handle the "*Geduldig* problem": the notion that pregnancy discrimination is not sex discrimination. The distinction Manian makes between qualifying for benefits and protecting fundamental rights – particularly when paired with a discussion of the sweeping control over pregnant individuals that permitting unconsented care would allow – elegantly reaches the heart of Equal Protection doctrine.

RIGHTING THE RELATIONSHIP TO MEDICAL AUTHORITY

Manian's careful consideration of the Equal Protection dimensions of decision-making in birth rectifies a persistent problem embedded in reproductive rights jurisprudence: balancing tests and battles of experts often obscure the pregnant individual's humanity.

Although it could be said that the rights protected by *Roe v. Wade* were at their apogee, not yet having been whittled down by subsequent case law, *Roe* did little for Mrs. Madyun. The court generally limited its examination of Roe to finding a compelling state interest in protecting "the potentiality of human life" at the point of viability.[15] By failing to distinguish between an individual's decision to end a pregnancy and a decision that might incrementally increase a risk to a fetus, the court flattens all of a person's interests with respect to pregnancy into the question of whether to carry to term, suggesting that they all may be extinguished in the third trimester.[16] Indeed, Mrs. Madyun ended up with all of the burdens and none of the benefits of *Roe*.

---

health care facility"), *Fosmire v. Nicoleau*, 75 N.Y.2d 218, 551 N.Y.S.2d 876, 551 N.E.2d 77 (1990); *Harrell v. St. Mary's Hosp.*, 678 So. 2d 455 (Fla. Dist. Ct. App. 1996).

[14] *Roe v. Wade*, 410 U.S. 113 (1973).

[15] *In re Madyun*, 114 Daily Wash.L. Rptr. 2233 (D.C.Super.Ct. July 26, 1986), *citing Roe v. Wade*, 410 U.S. at 162.

[16] *Id.*, *cited in* In re A.C., 573 A.2d 1235, 1255 (D.C. 1990) ("By the third trimester the state's intent 'become[s] sufficiently compelling to justify unduly burdensome state interference with the woman's constitutionally protected privacy interest'") (citing *Beal v. Doe*, permitting the state to prohibit Medicaid funding for non-therapeutic abortions and, perhaps ironically, finding an unquestionably strong and legitimate interest in encouraging "normal childbirth").

One such burden is *Roe*'s deference to medical authority. *Roe* can be understood as an interprofessional conversation between two power-holding (and at the time, almost exclusively white and male) groups: lawyers and physicians.[17] *Roe* certainly acknowledges the liberty interests of the pregnant person, holding that "the right of privacy . . . is broad enough to encompass a woman's decision whether or not to terminate her pregnancy."[18] But it also emphasizes that "the attending physician, in consultation with his patient, is free to determine without regulation by the state, that in his medical judgement, the patient's pregnancy should be terminated."[19]

The focus on the medical and public health dimension of abortion led to a decision in *Roe* informed by medical opinion but unclear on what should happen in the event of differing opinions between patient and doctor, obscuring the locus of the right to decide to end the pregnancy. That is, while the holding relied on concepts of privacy, the reasoning relied on concepts of safety as determined by medical professionals. The Supreme Court had, just months prior to the *Madyun* ruling, clarified in *Thornburgh v. American College of Obstetricians & Gynecologists*[20] that the fundamental rights at stake in the decision to end a pregnancy belong to the pregnant individual,[21] noting "the undesirability of any 'trade-off' between the woman's health and additional percentage points of fetal survival."[22] But the *Madyun* court did not consider *Thornburgh*, and the decision predated the significant evolution of the concept of privacy laid out in subsequent cases.[23]

RECONSIDERING THE EVIDENCE

Instead of engaging in a thorough consideration of Mrs. Madyun's constitutional rights, the court focused on medical evidence, deferring entirely to the medical opinions of a fourth-year resident in obstetrics and gynecology, Dr. Cummings.

---

[17] See, generally, Linda Greenhouse, *How the Supreme Court Talks about Abortion: The Implications of a Shifting Discourse*, 42 SUFFOLK U. L. REV. 41 (2008–2009). The considerable deference given to the healthcare providers may be unsurprising because the majority opinion's author, Justice Blackmun, previously served as counsel for the Mayo Clinic and was comfortable in the realm of professionalized medicine. *See* LINDA GREENHOUSE, BECOMING JUSTICE BLACKMUN (2005).

[18] *Roe*, 401 U.S. at 153.

[19] *Id.* at 163.

[20] *Thornburgh*, 476 U.S. 747 (1986).

[21] *Id.* at 772. ("A woman's right to [decide to end a pregnancy] freely is fundamental. Any other result, in our view, would protect inadequately a central part of the sphere of liberty that our law guarantees equally to all").

[22] *Id.* at 769.

[23] *See, e.g., Planned Parenthood v. Casey*, 505 U.S. 833, 851 (1992) (The right to make decisions about pregnancy allows people to define their "own concept of existence, of meaning, of the universe, and of the mystery of human life").

The court did not seek, or allow Mrs. Madyun to seek, medical testimony that would contradict the hospital's perspective. And while Dr. Cummings' opinions were given great evidentiary deference, Mrs. Madyun and her husband (however sincere the court found them in their religious convictions) had mere "preferences" for non-medical interventions to hasten delivery, "views" on whether the hospital had been sufficiently supportive, and "desires" to be "indulged." As the re-envisioned opinion alludes, Mr. Madyun's testimony featured heavily in the opinion of the court. He was supportive of his wife's decision-making and corroborated her description of her faith's perspective on assuming risks during pregnancy but his testimony's outsized role raises questions of how the court would have handled the case if the couple had disagreed and suggests that they had tried to induce him to override her refusal. The court notes the obvious – that neither Mrs. nor Mr. Madyun were trained physicians – to justify ignoring their concerns, claiming it could not ignore those of a "skilled and trained physician."

Just as the imbalance of power between the parties is evident from the court's turn of phrase, so too is the court's orientation toward regarding medical recommendations as authoritative commands. For instance, the court notes: "Normal obstetrical procedures with a term pregnancy call for delivery of a baby within 24 hours of the membrane's rupture. Failure to adhere to this procedure increases the risk [...]." This suggests an assumption on the part of the court that the process of parturition is one properly characterized as a "procedure," to which one might fail to "adhere." Either the individual giving birth is an object upon which physicians carry out procedures on a specific timetable, or they are subject to the standards created by the medical profession and "fail" when they deviate from them. The court refers to the possibility of sepsis as "one of the most insidious dangers in the situation presented by Mrs. Madyun," placing on her the blame not only for potential increased risk of sepsis but for the entire situation.

In contrast, in her rewritten opinion, Manian has performed more research into the potential risk of surgical delivery than any other judge to opine on the matter.[24] Her opinion lays bare the court's pretense of medical balancing: while Dr. Cummings describes specific risks and mechanisms of harm to the fetus (sepsis caused by bacteria introduced into the amniotic fluid), Mrs. Madyun is merely said to have a "risk" of a quarter of a percent. No explanation is given as to what that singular risk might be.[25] As Manian points out, though cesareans are common, they pose a

---

[24] Presented with an expert who opined that the risk of severe complication during an attempted vaginal delivery after cesarean was significantly lower than what the hospital's physician had indicated, one court disregarded medical opinion with a flippant analogy to airplane passengers and rates of crashes. *Pemberton v. Tallahassee Mem'l Reg'l Med. Ctr., Inc.*, 66 F. Supp. 2d 1247, 1253 (N.D. Fla. 1999).

[25] *See* Gorney, *supra* note 8(quoting attorney Lynn Paltrow, "Why is it okay for the court to make a decision that results in a tragedy, but not okay for the woman on whom the surgery is going to be forced to make a decision that may result in tragedy?").

number of serious risks: at the moment they are performed, in the recovery process, and in subsequent pregnancies. Accordingly, experts in obstetrics and maternal fetal medicine recommend avoiding surgery unless necessary.[26] Even the idea cited by Dr. Cummings that cervical dilation should occur on a relatively predictable timetable has been discredited.[27] Had the court requested even a modicum of medical evidence in Mrs. Madyun's favor, it would have found concern and controversy over the overuse of medical interventions and surgeries.

LEGAL STATUS OF THE FETUS

A critical feature of *Roe* that the *Madyun* Court sidestepped in its entirety was the notion that a fetus is not a juridical entity.[28] Contrary to the court's skewed interpretation, *Roe*'s grant of authority to circumscribe the personal autonomy of pregnant individuals is not unlimited: the state may "go so far as to" prohibit abortion after the point of viability, except when the life or health of the pregnant individual is at stake.[29] Rather than address this limitation, the court exercised the most intrusive jurisdictional power available to it: parens patriae, which permits the state to take custody of a child and override parental decisions. Under the *Madyun* Court's interpretation, the state is the ultimate parent of all children, even those yet to be born.

Unfortunately, this was not the only court to undertake such a logical leap, with other courts citing *Roe* to find that "[a] viable unborn child has the right under the U.S. Constitution to the protection of the State," granting custody of the fetus to child welfare authorities,[30] and holding that "the fetus can be regarded as a human being, to whom the court stands in parens patriae, and whom the court has an obligation to protect."[31] The latter standard, devised in an emergency hearing at the bedside of a Jehovah's Witness in critical condition in

---

[26] See ACOG & Soc'y Maternal Fetal Med, *Consensus No 1: Safe Prevention of the Primary Cesarean Delivery*, 123 OBSTETRICS & GYNECOLOGY 693 (2014).

[27] E.g., Olufemi T. Oladapo et al., *Progression of the First Stage of Spontaneous Labour: A Prospective Cohort Study in Two Sub-Saharan African Countries*, 15(1) PLoS MED e1002492 (Jan. 16, 2018), https://doi.org/10.1371/journal.pmed.1002492 (discouraging the use of "averaged lines or curves," emphasizing personalized, patient-centered care).

[28] *Roe*, 410 U.S. at 158 ("[T]he word 'person,' as used in the Fourteenth Amendment, does not include the unborn").

[29] *Id.* at 163–64.

[30] *Jefferson v. Griffin Spalding Cty. Hosp. Auth.*, 274 S.E.2d 457, 458 (1981). In this case, the court was not only wrong as a matter of law, it was wrong as a matter of fact: despite the hospital's insistence that there was a ninety-nine percent chance the infant would not survive, a fifty percent chance Mrs. Jefferson would die, and an "almost 100 percent chance" of survival for both with a cesarean (a claim that would surely make a malpractice defense attorney cringe), Mrs. Jefferson eventually gave birth to a healthy baby without a c-section. *See* Berg, *Georgia Supreme Court Orders Cesarean Section – Mother Nature Reverses on Appeal*, 70 J. MED. ASS'N GA. 451 (1981).

[31] *In re Jamaica Hospital*, 491 N.Y.S.2d 898 (N.Y. Sup.Ct. 1985).

the second trimester of pregnancy, has never been recognized before or since, though that case has been relied upon in a number of decisions authorizing forced procedures.[32]

RE-IMAGINING *MADYUN*'S LEGACY

Manian's dignity-affirming opinion shows how fortunate pregnant people are that the original decision made little impact at the time and was only published in the local law reporter. Yet the lack of attention the case garnered raises the alarming reality that cases deciding a right as fundamental as the ability to refuse an incursion into one's physical person might go unremarked and unexamined. In fact, similar cases suggest that – even now – many more such proceedings occur with little fanfare, creating no trace in the appellate record.[33]

The decision is only as well-preserved as it is because it was republished in full in *In re A.C. In re A.C.* garnered significant national media attention because high-profile advocacy groups organized an extensive amicus curiae brief strategy on behalf of Angela Carder, the woman at the center of the case, including briefs from groups such as the American Medical Association and the National Organization for Women.[34]

Other factors might further explain the disparities in attention to the two cases. While the A.C. opinion gives little insight into Mrs. Carder's socioeconomic status, she was a white woman who had long been receiving highly specialized health care and was being treated at a university hospital by a medical team familiar with her and her wishes. Mrs. Madyun was uninsured, seeking care from a public hospital where she was unknown, and presenting with religious beliefs outside the probable mainstream.

Even with a relatively low-profile, a troubling downstream effect of the case has been courts' seeming unwillingness to overturn even the most egregious cases. Given the option to follow *Madyun*, the A.C. court demurred, unwilling to tolerate the gruesome reality of how an order for forced surgery would have to be carried out. And yet it emphasized that the decision should not be read as "either approving or

---

[32] *See also Raleigh Fitkin-Paul Morgan Mem. Hosp. v. Anderson*, 201 A.2d 537 (1964) (court noted, perfunctorily, that it was "satisfied that the unborn child is entitled to the law's protection" in authorizing a blood transfusion).

[33] *See, e.g., Pemberton*, 66 F. Supp. 2d at 1249 (N.D. Fla. 1999) (hospital had "a procedure devised several years earlier (and used once previously) to deal with patients who refuse to consent to medically necessary treatment"). *See also*, Molly Redden, *New York Hospital's Secret Policy Led to Woman Being Given C-section against Her Will*, THE GUARDIAN (Oct. 5, 2017), http://bit.ly/2NTxU6Q (discussing a policy a New York City hospital created to override pregnant patients' refusal of medical treatment, which was used against a patient in 2011).

[34] *See, e.g.*, Gorney, *supra* note 8.

disapproving" the prior holding due to factual differences.[35] This is a pattern that persists to this day,[36] making getting a clear rule of law a challenge.

Most important, Manian's opinion shows the importance of a reproductive justice approach of centering the most marginalized. The D.C. Superior Court was unwilling to permit Mrs. Madyun to "gamble" with the life of her fetus but willing to gamble with hers. Judge Manian's opinion dignifies Mrs. Madyun by refusing to reduce her to a set of risks and rights – an approach judges would do well to heed. Rather than reasoning from the perspective that Ms. Madyun represented a deviation from the "normal" case, requiring a separate rule of law, it yields a reasoned approach that has the potential to create a just outcome for any patient.

In Re Madyun, Superior Court of the District of Columbia Civil Division

114 Daily Wash. Law. Rptr. 2233 (D.C. Super. Ct., 1986)
Associate Judge Maya Manian

This case presents the question of whether a court of law can authorize medical professionals to forcibly perform invasive medical interventions on nonconsenting pregnant women. Due to advances in medical technology, instances in which hospitals seek court orders to compel pregnant women to undergo obstetrical procedures have risen in the past decade. While these cases are often emotionally challenging, the legal principles are clear – the common law and constitutional rights to informed consent, privacy, bodily integrity, and equal protection of the law require that medical providers respect the right of all competent patients to refuse medical treatment. In almost all cases, competent patients have the right to refuse treatment even if the refusal will result in the patient's death. Similarly, a competent pregnant woman's right to refuse medical intervention must be unqualified. Even if the pregnant woman is at full-term and even if the treatment would assuredly protect her own life or health, the law cannot compel medical intervention upon the woman for her own benefit or for that of her fetus.

The issue presented is of great importance yet, given the time sensitive nature of these medical decisions, courts often have little time to gather the necessary expert testimony and issue carefully analyzed opinions, as illustrated by the facts of this case. This Court convened a hearing at the D.C. General Hospital ("Hospital") at 10:30 p.m. on July 25, 1986, upon the oral petition of the Hospital for an order authorizing it to forcibly perform a Cesarean section upon Ayesha Madyun to deliver her fetus. With less than an hour to prepare, Diane Weinroth, Esq. accepted

---

[35] *In re A.C.*, 573 A.2d 1235, 1252 n.23 (D.C. 1990).

[36] *Burton v. State*, 49 So.3d 263 (Fla. Dist. Ct. App. 2010) (reversing an order forcing a pregnant patient onto bed rest; leaving open the possibility that other fact scenarios might lead to court-mandated treatment).

appointment by the Court to represent the patient, Mrs. Madyun. Richard S. Love, Assistant Corporation Counsel for the Hospital, represented the Hospital's position.

Due to the emergency nature of the proceedings, the Court took oral testimony at the Hospital from the patient, Mrs. Madyun, and her husband, Mr. Mustafaa Madyun. Dr. John Cummings, Chief Resident on the Georgetown University Obstetrical/Gynecological service, provided testimony on behalf of the Hospital. After hearing testimony and arguments of counsel, the Court orally denied the Hospital's petition at 1:05 a.m., on July 26, 1986, and then denied the Hospital's motion for a stay. The appeals court heard a telephonic appeal and reversed this Court's decision at 2:08 a.m. on July 26, 1986.[37]

FINDINGS OF FACT

Mrs. Madyun is 19 years old and pregnant with her first child. She testified that she is a college student at George Washington University. Her waters broke during one of her classes and her husband came to take her to the hospital. Staff from Greater Southeast Community Hospital turned her and her husband away for lack of insurance. They went home, although the Greater Southeast staff had advised them to go by ambulance to D.C. General Hospital (a public hospital). Mrs. Madyun lay at home in bed until her labor pains began. Eventually, Mrs. Madyun checked in at D.C. General Hospital on July 25, 1986, at approximately 1:45 a.m. Upon admission to the hospital, the healthcare providers determined that she was at term. Mrs. Madyun testified that her membrane had ruptured at noon on July 23, 1986. She informed the hospital staff that her water broke some forty-eight hours prior to coming to the Hospital. Mrs. Madyun indicated throughout the entire time at the Hospital that she wanted a natural (vaginal) delivery.

By 11:00 a.m. on July 25, Mrs. Madyun was seven centimeters dilated. When this Court convened a hearing at the Hospital almost twelve hours later, Mrs. Madyun was still dilated at seven centimeters. By the time of the hearing, her contractions were coming at intervals approximately five minutes apart. Mr. and Mrs. Madyun had met with the medical staff at approximately 4:00 p.m. and again at 8:00 p.m. on July 25 to discuss available options. When no progress towards completing a natural delivery was evidenced by 8:00 p.m., the Hospital recommended that Mrs. Madyun consent to undergo a Cesarean section. Mrs. Madyun refused to consent to surgery.

Dr. Cummings presented the medical basis for the Hospital's emergency oral petition to this Court. After receiving his medical degree at George Washington

---

[37] The Court prepared interim findings of fact and conclusions of law on July 26, 1986, which were read to the appeals court telephonically. This Memorandum Opinion and Order provides a more detailed explication of the basis for the Court's decision in accordance with the testimony adduced at the hearing, issued for purposes of publication.

University, Dr. Cummings took a two-year general surgery program at Emory University followed by a four-year period as a physician in the U.S. Navy Medical Corps. He is now in the final year of a four-year obstetrical/gynecological program at Georgetown and is Chief Resident of the Georgetown Service at the Hospital.

On July 25, 1986, Dr. Cummings had taken over the evening shift at the Hospital. According to Dr. Cummings, normal labor for an uncomplicated first pregnancy is ten to fifteen hours. For a woman in her first pregnancy to remain dilated at seven centimeters for twelve hours was, in his opinion, abnormal. He stated that normal obstetrical procedures with a term pregnancy call for delivery of a baby within twenty-four hours of the membrane's rupture. Dr. Cummings testified that failure to adhere to this procedure increases the risk of chorioamnionitis (inflammation of the fetal placental membranes) which can lead to fetal sepsis (infection). Sepsis can result in the death of the fetus or brain damage and can start at any time from twenty-four hours after rupture of the membrane. Dr. Cummings testified that the likelihood of infection to the fetus increases greatly in proportion to the length of time between rupture of the membrane and delivery. It was Dr. Cummings' opinion that each passing hour increased the risk of fetal sepsis.

Furthermore, Dr. Cummings testified that one of the most insidious dangers in the situation presented by Mrs. Madyun was that sepsis could begin without detection and potentially cause the death of the fetus with little, or possibly no, warning because it is difficult to determine the commencement of fetal sepsis prior to birth. While there are certain symptoms, including elevated maternal temperature, foul smelling discharge, and changes in fetal heartbeat, Dr. Cummings stated that evidence of these symptoms may not become apparent until the fetus is already septic. The only symptom in this case was a slightly elevated maternal temperature. The number of examinations also increases the risk of introducing infection into the body. Excluding any examinations at Greater Southeast, Mrs. Madyun had experienced ten vaginal exams since admission to the Hospital. In addition, Dr. Cummings believed that a labor inducer was not appropriate in Mrs. Madyun's circumstances. Given that Mrs. Madyun's membrane had ruptured between sixty to seventy hours earlier, Dr. Cummings believed the risk of fetal sepsis in this case was fifty to seventy-five percent. Dr. Cummings characterized the risk to Mrs. Madyun undergoing a Cesarean section as a quarter of a percent. It is unclear if this risk to Mrs. Madyun represented a risk of death, risk to her health, or whether it accounted for future childbirth risks after undergoing a Cesarean.

Dr. Cummings further testified that the hospital staff tried to persuade Mrs. Madyun to agree to what they saw as the medically indicated and low-risk course of action – a Cesarean section. Dr. Cummings stated that the Hospital endeavors to follow the wishes of patients but, if the patient is doing something he feels is medically inappropriate, the Hospital has a responsibility to resolve the situation. Dr. Cummings expressed disdain for the Madyuns' opposition to the Cesarean section, despite the sincerity of their beliefs.

Counsel for Mrs. Madyun presented no contrary expert testimony on the medical situation, though, in fairness, counsel had insufficient time to rouse a medical expert on Mrs. Madyun's behalf at the late hour of the hearing. The Hospital did not make clear to this Court how it would force surgery upon Mrs. Madyun if the Court authorized surgery against her consent (e.g., would the Hospital use physical restraints upon the patient if she continued to refuse?).

Mrs. Madyun testified on her own behalf. When questioned during the hearing some four hours after the 8:00 p.m. conference with her physicians, Mrs. Madyun reiterated her preference for a natural delivery and expressed her belief that a Cesarean section was not necessary. She understood the risks of infection to the fetus resulting from continuing labor without delivery but sought to explain her decision to decline a Cesarean section by reference to her religious beliefs. Mrs. Madyun testified that a Muslim woman has the right to decide whether or not to risk her own health to eliminate a possible risk to the life of her undelivered fetus. At no time did the Court or counsel question Mrs. Madyun's competence to make this decision.

Mrs. Madyun further testified that she disagreed with Dr. Cummings' risk assessment in part because, as she explained, she had read a good deal about pregnancy and natural childbirth. While at the Hospital, the staff attached an external fetal monitor to Mrs. Madyun's abdomen that showed no serious signs of distress in the unborn baby.[38] Mrs. Madyun was convinced that if the hospital would leave her alone, she would deliver naturally, and therefore refused to consent to surgery. Mrs. Madyun emphasized her belief that the situation involved her baby and her body, and that her religion teaches that the decision must be hers. She believes a woman has the right to make this medical decision, even though the woman's decision may not result in the best outcome for the woman or baby. She felt the Hospital was trying to overpower her and dominate her. She testified that the experience of being forced into Cesarean surgery felt akin to rape.

For the purpose of obtaining informed consent to medical care from a competent adult patient, generally the only relevant consent must be taken from the patient herself, not her spouse. Nevertheless, this Court took testimony from the patient's husband to better understand the circumstances surrounding the dispute between patient and physician. Mr. Madyun has three children from a previous marriage, one delivered by Cesarean section. Mr. Madyun testified that he and his wife had a preference for natural childbirth, although they were not entirely opposed to a Cesarean if it became necessary. Mr. Madyun explained that he and his wife were aware that hospitals and doctors have been criticized in recent years for performing

---

[38] This Court uses the term "fetus" and "unborn baby" interchangeably. Although these terms are politically charged, as explained further below even if a viable fetus is considered a person, individuals generally do not have an obligation to sacrifice their health or bodily integrity to protect the life of another person.

Cesareans so readily and so often but they were not unalterably opposed to the idea. He stated that had they seen what they thought was any convincing evidence that the baby was in danger, they would have agreed instantly to the surgery, even though they eventually wanted a large family. He noted that Mrs. Madyun was afraid that the uterine scarring and occasional medical complications of a Cesarean might limit the number of children she could safely deliver in the future.

Mr. Madyun believed there was no demonstrable danger at that point to either Mrs. Madyun or the baby. He testified that although the hospital insisted that his wife and fetus faced a serious risk of infection, his wife's temperature had never climbed above ninety-nine degrees. Further, it was his belief that there had been insufficient opportunity for his wife to deliver vaginally. He explained that the hospital staff would not allow his wife to walk around or even sit up to help her labor along because of the fetal monitor. He testified that at one point the oxygen mask was gagging her, so he advised her to remove it so she could breathe. One of the residents told Mr. Madyun that if he advised his wife to remove the mask again, the resident would call security to remove Mr. Madyun from the hospital.

Mr. Madyun further testified that the Muslim religion gives the woman the final decision over what will and will not be done to her body and her fetus. He shared his wife's belief that this decision about the method of childbirth was Mrs. Madyun's alone to make, even if it resulted in a worse outcome for the fetus. Mr. Madyun understood the risks of infection and possible death to the fetus in the absence of a Cesarean section. He explained, similarly to his wife, his belief that a Muslim woman, confronted with a life or death situation, had the right to decide whether to risk her health or life to save an unborn fetus.

This Court denied the Hospital's motion to compel a Cesarean section and motion for a stay. The appeals court reversed this decision and authorized surgery upon Mrs. Madyun, although she still refused consent. On July 26, at 3:32 a.m., Mrs. Madyun delivered a six and a half pound baby boy by Cesarean section. The baby had no sign of infection.

I CONCLUSIONS OF LAW

It is by now well-established in the common law doctrine of informed consent that a competent adult may decline even life-saving medical treatment on religious or other grounds. *See, e.g., John F. Kennedy Mem. Hospital v. Heston*, 279 A.2d 670, 674 (N.J. 1971); *In re Osborne*, 294 A.2d 372, 374 (D.C. 1972); *In the Matter of B.B.H.*, 111 Wash.L.Rep. 1929, 1934 (D.C. Super. Ct., Oct. 6, 1983) (Schwelb, J.); *In the Matter of Bentley*, 102 Wash.L.Rep. 1221, 1225 (D.C. Super. Ct., June 17, 1974) (Burka, J.). The right to refuse medical treatment has constitutional dimensions as well. Several state and federal courts across the country have concluded that the constitutional rights to privacy and bodily integrity protect individuals against forced medical treatment by the state, even in life or death circumstances. *See, e.g., Bee v. Greaves*, 744 F.2d 1387, 1392–93 (10th Cir. 1984); *Tune v. Walter Reed Army Medical Hospital*, 602 F. Supp. 1452, 1456 (D.D.C. 1985). In the case of forced intervention into pregnancy and childbirth, the issue raises questions not only of constitutional liberty but also equal protection of the law along lines of sex and race. Each of these legal grounds for the right to refuse forcible Cesarean surgery is discussed further below.

I.I *Common Law Right Of Informed Consent*

The doctrine of informed consent is now well-established in our common law. In *Schloendorff v. Society of New York Hospitals*, 105 N.E. 92, 93 (1914), Justice Cardozo issued the first definitive pronouncement requiring informed consent to medical treatment: "Every human being of adult years and sound mind has a right to determine what shall be done with his own body; and a surgeon who performs an operation without his patient's consent commits assault." The subsequent development of informed consent doctrine has largely reflected the *Schloendorff* Court's concern with a patient's right to bodily integrity and self-determination in medical treatment. In *Canterbury v. Spence*, 64 F.2d 772, 781 (D.C. Cir. 1972) one of the leading cases articulating the parameters of informed consent law, the court explored the first principles of the doctrine in detail and placed great emphasis on respect for patient decision-making capacity. *Canterbury* notably declared: "To the physician, whose training enables a self-satisfying evaluation, the answer may seem clear but it is the prerogative of the patient, not the physician, to determine for himself the direction in which his interests seem to lie." *Id.* at 784.

A corollary to the right of informed consent is the patient's right to refuse medical treatment. In fact, the term informed "consent" is a bit misleading, because patients have the right not only to make the ultimate decision whether to accept treatment (consent) but also to refuse treatment entirely. *Natanson v. Kline*, 350 P.2d 1093, 1104 (Kan. 1960) discussed the importance of the right to informed refusal of treatment: "Anglo-American law starts with the premise of thorough-going self determination. It follows that each man is considered to be master of his own body, and he may, if he be of sound mind, expressly prohibit the performance of lifesaving surgery, or other medical treatment." Under the common law, the right to refuse medical treatment grew out of the doctrines of trespass and battery, which courts applied to unauthorized contact by a physician. *See Mills v. Rogers*, 457 U.S. 291, 294 n.4 (1982). Thus, courts applied a claim of battery where physicians failed to obtain consent to a procedure, performed a different procedure than the one to which the patient consented, or forced medical treatment on an unwilling patient.

Courts have recognized a claim of battery for forced medical treatment even in cases where the patient refused life-saving medical treatment. As one court stated, "[there is] a well-established rule of general law ... that it is the patient, not the physician, who ultimately decides if treatment – any treatment – is to be given at all … The rule has never been qualified in its application by either the nature or purpose of the treatment, or the gravity of the consequences of acceding to or foregoing it." *Tune v. Walter Reed Army Medical Hosp.*, 602 F. Supp. 1452, 1455 (D.D.C. 1985); *see also Downer v. Veilleux*, 322 A.2d 82, 91 (Me. 1974) ("The rationale of this rule lies in the fact that every competent adult has the right to forego treatment, or even cure, if it entails what for him are intolerable consequences or risks, however unwise his sense of values may be to others"). Numerous courts have concluded that the Constitution similarly protects the right to refuse medical treatment. *See, e.g., Rennie v. Klein*, 653 F.2d 836 (3d Cir. 1981), vacated on other grounds, 458 U.S. 1119 (1982), on remand, 720 F.2d 266 (3d Cir. 1983) (right to refuse medical treatment derives from the constitutional right to liberty, and is not extinguished if an individual is involuntarily committed to a mental institution); *Lane v. Candura*, 376 N.E.2d 1232 (1978) (irrationality of patient's refusal of amputation does not justify the conclusion of incompetence and surgery performed against the patient's consent violates the right to privacy); *In re Melideo*, 390 N.Y.S.2d 523 (Sup. Ct. 1976) (Jehovah's Witness' refusal of blood transfusion must be respected even though possibly necessary to save her life); *In re Quinlan*, 70 N.J. 10, 355 A.2d 647, *cert. denied*, 429 U.S. 922 (1976) (constitutional right to privacy includes right to refuse life-saving treatment).

Despite a long line of precedents protecting a patient's right to refuse even life-saving medical treatment, several courts have ordered forced obstetrical procedures upon pregnant women. Only one appeals court has authorized court-ordered Cesarean surgery. *See Jefferson v. Griffin Spalding County Hospital Authority*, 274 S.E.2d 457 (Ga. 1981). Several courts have compelled blood transfusions upon pregnant women against their wishes. *See In re Jamaica Hospital*, 491 N.Y.S.2d 898 (Sup.Ct. 1985); *Raleigh Fitkin-Paul Morgan Memorial Hospital v. Anderson*, 42 N.J. 421, 201 A.2d 537 (per curiam), cert. denied, 377 U.S. 985 (1964). These courts relied on the state's compelling interest in the life of the fetus to justify overriding the patient's right to refuse medical treatment. This Court respectfully disagrees with the decisions in these cases, as explained further below.

I.II *Constitutional Right to Privacy*

The Hospital argues that *Prince v. Massachusetts*, 321 U.S. 158 (1944) supports its claim that the Court may override a pregnant woman's right to refuse medical treatment. *Prince* allows the State to restrict parents' fundamental right to control over their children where it has a compelling interest to do so. *See id*. The Hospital emphasizes that it is a fundamental principle in child neglect law that parents cannot deny life-saving medical care to their children, and notes that many courts have ordered medical treatment of children over parental objections. Accordingly, the Hospital asserts that courts may order treatment for pregnant women, especially at full term, in order to protect the infant about to be born. Yet, *Prince* is readily distinguishable from the case at hand.

Unlike the case of parent and child, the fetus cannot be treated without invading the body of the mother. There is an "enormous conceptual and practical gulf between ordering treatment for a child and compelling a woman to submit to surgery for the benefit of a fetus, even where the fetus is on the threshold of independent life." Nancy K. Rhoden, *The Judge in the Delivery Room: The Emergence of Court-Ordered Cesareans*, 74 CAL. L. REV. 1951, 1952 (1986). *Prince* does not authorize violating the parent's bodily integrity in order to protect the health of the child.

In order to support its claim that the Court can invade Mrs. Madyun's bodily integrity to protect the fetus, the Hospital also relies on *Roe v. Wade*. 410 U.S. 113 (1973). The Hospital argues that *Roe* permits overriding the pregnant woman's consent, at least where the pregnancy is past the point of "viability."[39] *Roe*, 410 U.S. at 160. Because *Roe* held that the State's interest in the life of the fetus after viability is compelling enough to permit a ban on abortion, the Hospital asserts that the government interest in protecting the life of the fetus is also compelling enough to allow forced Cesarean surgery.

Yet, no principle articulated in *Roe v. Wade* and its progeny authorizes judges to favor the life or health of the fetus over the pregnant woman's life or health. To the contrary, the most recent Supreme Court ruling on abortion makes clear that the state's compelling interest in the life of a viable fetus must always be subordinated to the health of the pregnant woman. See *Thornburgh v. American College of Obstetricians and Gynecologists*, 106 S. Ct. 2169, 2183 (1986) (holding abortion statute facially unconstitutional where it required pregnant woman to bear increased medical risk to save her viable fetus); *see also Colautti v. Franklin*, 439 U.S. 379, 400 (1979) (holding that a statute requiring certain methods of performing a post-viability abortion must be struck down because it did not "clearly specify . . . that the woman's life and health must always prevail over the fetus' life and health when they conflict"); *Roe*, 410 U.S. at 162–63 (holding that government may not prohibit abortion even after viability if the abortion is necessary to preserve the life or health of the woman). Thus, a fundamental principle of abortion law is that the government cannot require a trade-off between the woman's health and the fetus' well-being. As explained further below, Cesarean surgery presents increased risks to the health of the woman, not only for the instant birth but for all her future childbearing. Compelling Cesarean surgery on a nonconsenting woman imposes greater health risks on the woman for the sake of preventing risks to the fetus, contrary to *Roe*'s mandate.

---

[39] Viability means the point at which the fetus is "potentially able to live outside the mother's womb, albeit with artificial aid . . . ." *Roe*, 410 U.S. at 160 (footnote omitted). *Roe* drew the line for when the state's compelling interest in the fetus outweighs the mother's liberty to seek abortion care at viability. See *Id.* at 160–65.

The Hospital asserts that once a woman decides to continue a pregnancy to term, as opposed to seeking abortion care, she waives her right to object to government intervention designed to protect the fetus. Some commentators support this proposition. *See, e.g.*, John A. Robertson, *Procreative Liberty and the Control of Conception, Pregnancy, and Childbirth*, 69 VA. L. REV. 405, 437 (1983) ("Once she decides to forgo abortion and the state chooses to protect the fetus, the woman loses the liberty to act in ways that would adversely affect the fetus"); *but see* Lawrence J. Nelson, Brian P. Buggy, and Carol J. Weil, *Forced Medical Treatment of Pregnant Women: "Compelling Each to Live as Seems Good to the Rest,"* 37 HASTINGS L.J. 703 (1986) (arguing that pregnant women should not be forced to alter their behavior to reduce risk to their fetuses). This argument does not follow from *Roe*.

First, as discussed above, *Roe* and its progeny make clear that women retain the right to protect their own health throughout pregnancy. Second, even if the compelled medical intervention would protect the health of the woman as well as the fetus,[40] *Roe* does not authorize forcible medical intervention. In the abortion context, the government's purpose is to preserve the life of the fetus against the pregnant woman's desire to terminate the pregnancy. In the medical treatment context, the state seeks to prescribe the woman's medical decisions during her pregnancy according to the state's own risk preferences. To move from a principle that the state can forbid abortion post-viability to a principle that the State can forcibly cut a woman's body open is a quantum conceptual leap. The viability line drawn in *Roe* does not restrict women's right to refuse obstetric intervention post-viability – it only restricts women's ability to terminate the pregnancy. The state's ability to prohibit abortion post-viability does not contain within it the additional requirement that women sacrifice their right to be free from physical invasion by the state. To the contrary, the right to refuse medical intervention is particularly important post-viability because typically a petition to compel Cesarean surgery arises late in pregnancy or during the process of childbirth.

By substituting its own judgment in place of the woman's, the state would deprive women of their right to make decisions related to reproduction and childbirth in contravention of the broad right of privacy described in *Roe* that protects the right to choose abortion and the right to procreate. *See Skinner v. Oklahoma ex rel. Williamson*, 316 U.S. 535 (1942). A rule of law providing that women who choose to bear a child rather than abort thereby waive their liberty interests in medical decision-making and bodily integrity penalizes women – and only women – for exercising their right to reproduce. Such a state-created penalty unconstitutionally impinges on women's right to bear children. *See* Dawn Johnsen, *The Creation of Fetal Rights: Conflicts with Women's Constitutional Rights to Liberty, Privacy, and Equal Protection*, 95 Yale L.J. 599, 618 (1986).

---

[40] In some circumstances, such as cases of *placenta previa* where the placenta blocks the cervix, physicians recommend a Cesarean section to protect the woman's life as well as the fetus' life.

I.III *Constitutional Right to Bodily Integrity*

The Hospital's argument not only misreads the right to privacy protected by *Roe* and *Skinner* but also fails to take the right to bodily integrity seriously. Regardless of how one perceives the status of a fetus or unborn child, the pivotal legal question turns on whether the state can usurp one individual's physical integrity to advance what it perceives to be the interests of another individual. Trumping the woman's consent in order to protect the fetus treats the woman as a mere incubator whose body the state owns and controls. Even if the woman is at full-term and in labor, a court cannot order invasion of one person's body to protect the life of another person – born or unborn. Such a court order is profoundly at odds with our legal tradition protecting bodily integrity.

The U.S. Supreme Court has implicitly recognized a right to bodily integrity in several decisions. The right to be free from government control over one's body has been variously described as a right to "personal privacy and dignity," *Schmerber v. California*, 384 U.S. 757, 767 (1966), "personal security," *Ingraham v. Wright*, 430 U.S. 651, 673 (1977), and "personal privacy and bodily integrity," *Winston v. Lee*, 470 U.S. 753, 761 (1985). The Court has repeatedly emphasized, in both civil and criminal cases, that government intervention involving physical intrusion into an individual's body is highly suspect: "No right is held more sacred, or is more carefully guarded . . . than the right of every individual to the possession and control of his own person." *Union Pac. R. Co. v. Botsford*, 141 U.S. 250, 251 (1891) (holding that under common law principles, the court has no power to require plaintiff in tort action to submit to surgical examination to verify injuries).

In *Winston v. Lee*, 470 U.S. 753 (1985), the Court held that surgical removal of a bullet from a suspect's body contrary to his wishes for use as evidence against him violates the Fourth Amendment. The Court weighed the community's need for evidence in a criminal case against the suspect's privacy interests, concluding that "compelled surgical intrusion into an individual's body for evidence . . . implicates expectations of privacy and security of such magnitude that the intrusion may be 'unreasonable' even if likely to produce evidence of a crime." *Id.* at 759. The Court found the proposed surgery to be an unconstitutional intrusion even though the risks of general anesthesia were minimal, noting that "whether the surgery is to be characterized in medical terms as 'major' or 'minor' is not controlling." *Id.* at 764 n.8.

Similarly, in *Rochin v. California*, 342 U.S. 165, 172 (1952), the Court held that forcible pumping of a criminal suspect's stomach violates the Fourteenth Amendment's substantive due process protections and was "conduct that shocks the conscience." The Court reached this conclusion even though police officers witnessed the suspect swallow two pills, which they believed to be narcotics, in an effort to hide criminal evidence from the officers. *See id.* at 166. Although the Court stressed that it must review criminal convictions from state courts with "due humility," it emphasized that forcible bodily invasion by the state "is too close to the rack and the screw" for the constitution to tolerate. *Id.* at 168, 172; *see also Schmerber v. California*, 384 U.S. 757, 772 (1966) ("The integrity of an individual's person is a cherished value of our society").

Given that our constitutional jurisprudence highly values the right to bodily integrity, lower courts have widely accepted that a person cannot be forced to have surgery for another person's benefit. *See, e.g., McFall v. Shimp*, 10 Pa.D. & C.3d 90 (Allegheny County Ct. 1978). In *McFall*, a Pennsylvania court was asked to force a man into donating bone marrow that could save his cousin's life. Testing found that the man was the only family member with potentially compatible bone marrow; nevertheless, he refused to undergo further testing or procedures. *See id.* at 90–91. The court concluded that, although it found the man's refusal morally repugnant, the law could not compel medical intervention. The court emphasized that to require such a Samaritan act "would change every concept and principle upon which our society is founded." *Id.* at 91. The Court further explained why it must permit a decision that would result in a man's death:

> For a society which respects the rights of one individual, to sink its teeth into the jugular vein or neck of one of its members and suck from it sustenance for another member, is revolting to our hard-wrought concepts of jurisprudence. *Id.* at 92 (emphasis in original).

In *In re Application of George*, 630 S.W.2d 614 (Mo. Ct. App. 1982) another tragic case of a dying man seeking a bone marrow donor, the court similarly refused to compel one individual – the dying man's father – to save the life of another. In that case, a thirty-three-year-old adoptee dying of leukemia sought a court order to open his adoption records to locate family members with compatible bone marrow. The man's birth mother was found and tested but was not a compatible donor. The trial judge then contacted the man's alleged birth father, whose name was listed in the adoption records. The alleged father denied paternity and refused to be tested for compatibility. The dying man still sought the identity of his birth father in order to seek the opportunity to convince his half-siblings to be tested for compatibility. The trial judge determined he could not open the adoption records to give the dying man his alleged birth father's name and the appeals court upheld the decision. *See id.* at 618–22.

The Hospital argues that some courts have ordered organ donations by one individual to save the life of another, analogizing the situation to a pregnant woman being ordered to undergo obstetric intervention to save the life of her fetus. *See Hart v. Brown*, 289 A.2d 386 (Conn. Super. Ct. 1972); *Strunk v. Strunk*, 445 S.W.2d 145 (Ky. 1969). However, courts decided these cases on entirely different grounds. In both cases, the court permitted organ transplants based on the concept of substituted judgment. In *Hart v. Brown*, the court approved the parents' consent to have one twin donate a kidney to her twin sibling, in part because the donation would also benefit the donor twin by keeping her sibling alive. *See Hart*, 289 A.2d at 376–78. In *Strunk*, the adult kidney donor was incompetent but the court concluded that the kidney donation to the donor's brother would also benefit the donor. The court emphasized that the donor was greatly emotionally dependent on his brother and that "his well-being would be jeopardized more severely by the loss of his brother than by the removal of a kidney." *Strunk*, 445 S.W.2d at 146. These courts essentially concluded that the donors themselves – who were not competent individuals – would have consented to the transplant had they been competent to do so. The substituted judgment doctrine makes no claim to override the consent of the individual but rather seeks to ascertain what their consent might be in order to respect their autonomy. Thus, these cases do not undermine the principle that courts cannot compel medical invasions upon a competent, nonconsenting person in order to protect the life of another person. *See also* Donald H. Regan, *Rewriting Roe v. Wade*, 77 MICH. L. REV. 1569 (1979) (analyzing Samaritan Law and concluding that one person cannot be forced to submit to physical invasion to save the life of another person).

I.IV *Heightened Scrutiny Applies to Infringements of Rights to Privacy and Bodily Integrity*

Considering the well-established constitutional rights to privacy and bodily integrity discussed above, even if the State has a compelling interest in protecting the life of the fetus post-viability, it does not follow that infringement of the pregnant woman's right to refuse medical treatment is constitutionally justified. *See Taft v. Taft*, 446 N.E.2d 395 (Mass. 1983) (refusing to order surgery on a pregnant woman at risk of losing her pregnancy); *Mercy Hospital, Inc. v. Jackson*, 510 A.2d 562 (Md. App. 1986) (trial court refused to issue order compelling blood transfusion for pregnant woman; case declared moot on appeal since woman had given birth safely without transfusion). When fundamental rights are at stake, the burden is on the government to satisfy heightened scrutiny in order to justify its intervention. Therefore, the proper line of inquiry does not begin with the course of action the physician recommends and compel the woman to justify choosing a different course of action. Rather, when a nonconsensual physical invasion is involved, the burden is on the state to justify overriding the competent individual's refusal. *See San Antonio Indep. School Dist. v. Rodriguez*, 411 U.S. 1, 16 (1973) (describing a strict scrutiny test for infringements upon fundamental rights, including that the government bears the burden of proving that the means selected are narrowly tailored to be the least intrusive available); *see also Winston v. Lee*, 470 U.S. 753 (1985) (applying balancing test to violation of bodily integrity, weighing the state's need for criminal evidence against risk to the defendant's health and degree of invasion of his privacy).

Forced medical intervention in childbirth, and the violation of women's bodily integrity it entails, is not a sufficiently well-tailored means to serve the government's end goal of protecting fetal life to satisfy any heightened level of scrutiny. Only one appellate court has authorized a forced Cesarean section, and the results in that case illustrate serious deficiencies with court-ordered obstetric interventions. In *Jefferson v. Griffin-Spalding County Hospital Authority*, 274 S.E.2d 457 (Ga. 1981), the patient's doctors informed the court that a forced Cesarean should be authorized because the woman's placenta was blocking the birth canal, a condition the physicians told the court kills ninety-nine percent of babies in natural childbirth and fifty percent of women. After the court issued its order authorizing the forced surgery, the woman fled the hospital and later delivered her baby vaginally. Her placenta had shifted, and her baby was born healthy. *See* George J. Annas, *Forced Cesareans: The Unkindest Cut of All*, 12(3) THE HASTINGS CENTER REPORT 16–17, 45 (June 1982); *see also* Robert N. Berg, *Georgia Supreme Court Orders Cesarean – Mother Nature Reverses on Appeal*, 70 JOURNAL OF THE MEDICAL ASSOCIATION OF GEORGIA 451–53 (1981). The *Jefferson* case illustrates two critical concerns with court-ordered Cesareans – the problem of medical uncertainty and the threat of driving pregnant women away from the health care system entirely.

First, some amount of medical uncertainty in decision-making during childbirth is inevitable. There are no guarantees that a court-ordered obstetrical intervention will be necessary to save the life or health of a fetus in any given case. This Court does not question the competence and expertise of Dr. Cummings. Yet, medical judgment is not infallible, even with advanced technology. *See, e.g.*, Ruth Hubbard, *Legal and Policy Implications of Recent Advances in Prenatal Diagnosis and Fetal Therapy*, 7 WOMEN'S RTS. L. REP. 201 (1982) (describing a long history of medical misjudgments in obstetrics and risks of unnecessary medicalization of childbirth); Watson A. Bowes & Brad Selgestad, *Fetal Versus Maternal Rights: Medical and Legal Perspectives*, 58 AMERICAN JOURNAL OF OBSTETRICS AND GYNECOLOGY 209–14 (Aug. 1981) (describing a case of court-ordered Cesarean surgery where the outcome was not as poor as expected, and stating that the case "simply underscores the limitations of continuous fetal heart monitoring as a means of predicting neonatal outcome"). This inevitable medical uncertainty is clear from several cases where physicians sought a court order to force Cesarean surgery upon a woman but the woman delivered a healthy baby naturally before the operation could be performed. *See* Rhoden, *supra*, at 1959–60 (describing cases where physicians predicted dire consequences from refusal of Cesarean surgery but women nevertheless delivered healthy babies vaginally). Given the evidence that a significant percentage of Cesareans in the United States may be unnecessary, Mrs. Madyun's skepticism about the need for surgery in her case is not irrational.[41] *See, e.g.*, Norbert

[41] Mrs. Madyun's refusal rested not only on her skepticism about the need for a Cesarean at that point in time but also on her religious beliefs. If the patient's refusal rests on religious belief, the right to free exercise of religion also comes into play. The analysis for a Free Exercise claim is like this Court's conclusions with respect to the rights of privacy and bodily integrity – the State is not justified in overriding the right without satisfying a strict scrutiny analysis. *See Sherbert v. Verner*, 374 U.S. 398 (1963) (holding that government bears the burden of showing that impingements on religious freedom are narrowly tailored to achieve a compelling state interest). This opinion focuses on the rights of privacy, bodily integrity, and equal protection as those must be protected even if the patient's refusal is not grounded in religious belief.

Gleicher, *Cesarean Section Rates in the United States: The Short-Term Failure of the National Consensus Development Conference in 1980*, 252 JOURNAL OF THE AMERICAN MEDICAL ASSOCIATION 3273–76 (1984) (discussing continued criticism of alarmingly high rates of Cesarean surgery in the United States); Charles Wolfson, *Midwives and Home Birth: Social, Medical, and Legal Perspectives*, 37 HASTINGS L.J. 909, 909–22 (1986) (describing growing critiques of the medicalization of childbirth).

In any other medical context, the law demands that a competent patient be permitted to decide the balance of risks for herself. It is irrelevant that the patient is not a trained physician – the law protects her right to refuse her physician's expert medical advice. *See In re KKB*, 609 P.2d 747, 749 (Ok. 1980) ("[L]iberty includes the freedom to decide about one's own health. This principle need not give way to medical judgment"). Of course, the patient's skepticism about the need for medical intervention in her case could be misplaced and tragedy could result from failure to timely proceed with Cesarean surgery. Yet, there is also a risk of tragedy if a court orders forcible surgery.

Cesarean surgery presents serious health risks to the woman, including the risk of death. *See* Gleicher, *supra*, at 3274 (stating that the mortality rate for cesarean delivery is two- to four-times higher than for vaginal delivery). For example, if Mrs. Madyun developed a severe allergic reaction to anesthetic, she could die from the surgery. Furthermore, the health risks to the woman from Cesarean surgery are present not only for the instant childbirth but also for all her future childbearing. *See id.* (noting that the rule in the majority of hospitals mandates that a prior cesarean delivery requires all future deliveries be accomplished by cesarean); *see also* Rhoden, *supra*, at 1958–59 (describing increased risks of Cesarean surgery compared to vaginal birth including significantly greater risk of potentially deadly placenta previa in a subsequent pregnancy). Other risks of Cesarean surgery include postoperative infection, trauma to organs such as the uterus, bladder, or bowel, pulmonary embolus, delayed wound healing, hernia, bowel obstruction, and hemorrhage. *See* National Institute of Health, U.S. Department of Health and Human Services, Pub. No. 82-2067, CESAREAN CHILDBIRTH: REPORT OF A CONSENSUS DEVELOPMENT CONFERENCE at 260–68 (1981) (describing various risks of cesarean surgery). Thus, a court ordering a forced surgery gambles with nature – its order could result in tragedy for the woman's life, just as the woman risks a tragic result with a mistaken medical decision. The court's gamble is worse. When the decision is left to the patient, any potential loss of life is limited to her case. In contrast, when a court issues a mistaken order, it communicates to all women that they cannot trust their doctors to respect their informed treatment decisions.

Court-ordered medical intervention thus raises a second, broader public health concern. The threat of compelled treatment may send women into hiding and deter a much larger swath of women from seeking prenatal care if they fear being forced into unwanted medical intervention. *See* Annas, *supra*, at 45 (noting that threat of forced surgery may lead to women avoiding hospital birth); Brian Flanigan, *Mom Follows Brief, Gives Birth in Hiding*, DETROIT FREE PRESS at A3 (June 16, 1982) (describing the case of a Mrs. Jeffries who went into hiding and gave birth vaginally after the court attempted to compel a Cesarean). As distressing as an emergency hospital petition for a laboring woman might be, courts must consider the larger public health consequences of legal precedents ordering forced medical intervention. Turning courts into medical decision-makers for competent adult patients – and doctors into coercive arms of the State – is not an effective means to deliver healthy babies into the world when one considers the wider collateral consequences of frightening pregnant women away from the health care system entirely. Women's right to refuse medical intervention, even during labor, must be preserved both to protect women's equal liberty and to protect public health. Ensuring that the law does not undermine the doctor–patient relationship of trust and respect for patient consent – as enshrined in the common law doctrine of informed consent – is essential to securing the public health benefits of prenatal care and medical assistance during childbirth.[42]

Finally, this Court must note what court-ordered Cesarean surgery – or any compelled medical intervention – looks like in practice. Courts under severe time constraints are likely to be swayed by the fear that an infant so close to birth will die seemingly unnecessarily due to religious tenets or personal beliefs that are unfamiliar to many mainstream medical and legal professionals. Lawyers for the patient have little time to prepare or to call for middle of the night expert testimony to counter the hospital's medical experts – as illustrated in this case where Mrs. Madyun's attorney had less than an hour to ready her case. On the other hand, the hospital is likely to employ lawyers who already have experience with technical medical litigation and with preparing their own physicians to testify. Emergency hearings in hospitals are bound to be inherently unfair and arbitrary. Given one-sided expert testimony arguing that the life of a pregnant woman and the infant are in the balance, it is not surprising that some courts have resorted to forced medical intervention rather than face the risk of the woman and fetus dying in childbirth.

Yet, the real-world application of a court order mandating medical treatment on an unwilling patient is equally horrifying. In a recent case, a woman expecting triplets was hospitalized for the final stretch of her pregnancy. The woman refused Cesarean surgery, despite her doctors' belief that the surgery was necessary for a safe multiple birth. A court granted the hospital administrator

---

[42] Thus, this Court also disagrees with decisions authorizing forced blood transfusions on pregnant women. *See, e.g., In re Jamaica Hospital*, 491 N.Y.S.2d 898 (Sup.Ct. 1985); *Raleigh Fitkin-Paul Morgan Memorial Hospital v. Anderson*, 42 N.J. 421, 201 A.2d 537 (per curiam), cert. denied, 377 U.S. 985 (1964).

temporary custody of the unborn triplets and authorized a Cesarean section as soon as the woman went into labor. The plan was known to the hospital staff but not to the woman, who was not given the opportunity to seek care elsewhere. When finally confronted with the hospital's intentions, the woman and her husband became irate. Her husband was forcibly removed from the hospital by seven security officers. The woman was placed in full leathers – leather wrist and ankle cuffs attached to the four corners of a bed to prevent her from moving. Despite these restraints, she continued to scream for help and bit through her intravenous tubing in her attempt to get free. The hospital later published a photograph of the woman and her three children without mentioning the violence attending the birth. *See* Veronika E.B. Kolder, Women's Health Law: A Feminist Perspective, 1–2 (Aug. 1985); *see also* Bowes & Selgestad, *supra*, at 211 (describing a Colorado court-ordered Cesarean case on an obese woman and cautioning that if "the patient steadfastly refused it might not have been either safe or possible to administer anesthesia to a struggling, resistant woman who weighed in excess of 157.5 kg"). Physicians and judges may have a strong impulse to act quickly to potentially save an unborn baby but any legal system that values liberty must not tolerate such shocking violations of bodily integrity, even when life is at stake. Otherwise, "to sanction the brutal conduct ... would be to afford brutality the cloak of law... [and] [n]othing would be more calculated to discredit law and thereby to brutalize the temper of a society." *Rochin v. California*, 342 U.S. at 173–74.

This Court is sympathetic to physicians facing the Scylla and Charybdis of respecting their patient's wishes despite the potential loss of life, versus violating their patient's bodily integrity to avoid what physicians' extensive training teaches is a preventable death. Nevertheless, forcing potentially life-threatening surgery on a competent adult patient who has denied consent does not comport with existing law. Physicians certainly may make every effort to convince the patient otherwise if they believe her decision is too risky but courts must not sanction resort to force or coercion. Instead, the state can seek less physically intrusive means to encourage women to choose the course of action it prefers.

For example, the state can provide resources to ensure that all pregnant women are able to obtain prenatal care, good nutrition, and safe housing. On a societal scale, these measures would be a much more effective and efficient way to decrease perinatal mortality and morbidity than compelling invasive medical treatment in individual cases. *See* Hubbard, *supra*, at 217–18 (noting program cutbacks and the irony of mandating expensive medical intervention in individual cases while failing to provide basic care for many); Sara Rosenbaum, *The Prevention of Infant Mortality: The Unfulfilled Promise of Federal Health Programs for the Poor*, 17 Clearinghouse Rev. 701, 703–4 (1983) (summarizing cutbacks in Medicaid and other programs resulting in a lack of access to prenatal care for many women).

I.V Constitutional Right to Equal Protection

As described above, in other medical situations, the law protects a competent individual's liberty to decide the balance of medical risks for herself and to protect her own bodily integrity even at the expense of another person's life. Equal protection of the law requires the same respect for women's medical treatment decisions regarding childbirth. The law does not require that parents risk their health or undergo medical procedures for their children's benefit. Although society may properly deem that parents are morally obligated to do so, there is no corresponding legal obligation. If the law does not require fathers to submit to even more minimal medical intrusions such as donating bone marrow to protect the life of a born child, it cannot compel mothers to submit to much greater bodily invasions for an infant not yet born.

Under our equal protection jurisprudence, the law must grant the same rights to men and women and must not reinforce gender stereotypes. *See Mississippi University for Women v. Hogan*, 458 U.S. 718 (1982) (invalidating the policy of a state-supported university that limited admission to its nursing school to women on the grounds that it reinforced traditional stereotypes); *Califano v. Goldfarb*, 430 U.S. 199 (1977) (invalidating the section of the Social Security Act that permitted survivors' benefits for widowers only if they were receiving half of their support from their wives); *Orr v. Orr*, 440 U.S. 268 (1979) (invalidating a state statute that imposed alimony obligations on husbands but not wives); *Caban v. Mohammed*, 441 U.S. 380 (1979) (invalidating a state statute that required the consent of the mother but not the father, to permit the adoption of a child born to unmarried parents); *Craig v. Boren*, 429 U.S. 190 (1976) (holding that gender based classifications are subject to intermediate scrutiny under the Equal Protection Clause, and thus must serve important governmental objectives and be substantially related to the achievement of those objectives). Court-ordered obstetrical interventions reinforce the gender stereotype that women are irrational and lack the capacity to make sound medical and moral decisions, particularly when it comes to decisions about reproduction and childbirth. Johnsen, *supra*, at 623–25. Furthermore, compelled intervention into pregnancy and childbirth rests on stereotypical notions about women's natural role as mothers and mothers as ultimately self-sacrificing. *See* Hubbard, *supra*, at 217 ("The expanded repertory of prenatal technologies may enable obstetricians to enforce society's contradictory beliefs that women's reproductive functions are (1) our natural and principal calling, and (2) suffused with pathology"). Requiring only mothers to sacrifice their bodily integrity for their children, while fathers can preserve their autonomy, renders women unequal citizens and perpetuates a system of sex discrimination.

The Hospital argues that Equal Protection principles do not apply to this case, because *Geduldig v. Aiello* held that discriminating against pregnant women does not amount to sex discrimination deserving of heightened scrutiny. *See Geduldig v. Aiello*, 417 U.S. 484 (1974). However, *Geduldig* is not apt here, where women's fundamental rights to protect their privacy and bodily integrity are at stake. *Geduldig* dealt with the State of California's decision to exclude pregnancy-related benefits from an employee benefits plan. *See Geduldig*, 417 U.S. at 486–96. *Geduldig* addressed only whether a state must include pregnancy benefits in insurance plans – it did not hold that pregnancy-related discrimination could never constitute sex discrimination. *See id.* at 496–97 & n.20. *Geduldig* stated: "While it is true that only women can become pregnant it does not follow that every legislative classification concerning pregnancy is a sex-based classification ..." *Geduldig*, 417 U.S. at 496 n.20 (emphasis added). This statement leaves open the possibility that some types of government regulation of pregnant women will constitute a sex-based classification. Given the Court's Equal Protection jurisprudence, those restrictions that reflect or reinforce sex-role stereotypes do constitute sex discrimination in violation of equal protection principles.

In contrast to *Geduldig*, with regard to compelled medical treatment, the question is whether women are entitled to the same fundamental constitutional rights of privacy and bodily integrity, not whether they are entitled to additional benefits from the state when pregnant. As discussed, requiring only women to sacrifice their bodily integrity for the sake of their children reinforces gender stereotypes. Furthermore, such a rule of law could impact all women in a wide range of activities. If pregnant women can be forced to submit to invasive medical intervention by the courts in order to protect the fetus, the state could also bar women from drinking alcohol, smoking, or engaging in unhealthy but otherwise legal behaviors. Courts could detain women against their will to control their behavior. *See In re Steven S.*, 178 Cal. Rptr. 525 (Ct. App. 1981) (disapproving use of juvenile court proceedings to order hospital detention of a woman during the final months of her pregnancy in order to protect the fetus). Courts could bar women from undertaking other activities the state deems too risky, such as working in toxic environments. *See, e.g.*, Wendy W. Williams, *Firing the Woman to Protect the Fetus: The Reconciliation of Fetal Protection with Equal Opportunity Goals under Title VII*, 69 GEO. L.J. 641 (1981); Pregnancy Discrimination Act, Pub. L. No. 95-555, §1, 92 Stat. 2076 (1978) (codified at 42 U.S.C. §2000e) (providing that pregnancy-related discrimination in employment constitutes sex discrimination in violation of federal law). Judges would eventually become arbiters of the entire scope of women's conduct, ranging from monitoring women's diet, to work, to sex life, despite medical uncertainty as to what constitutes a potential danger to a pregnancy. *See* David Westfall, *Beyond Abortion: The Potential Reach of a Human Life Amendment*, 8 AM. J.L. & MED. 97, 97–111 (1982) (arguing that all women, including "potentially pregnant" women, could be restricted in otherwise lawful activities on the basis of the state's compelling interest in the fetus). There would be no logical limit to the state's control over women. This slippery slope would result in treating women as second-class citizens, denied the human dignity that the rights to privacy and bodily integrity serve to protect.

Even more pernicious, this invasion of women's autonomy appears far more likely to occur for women whose race, religion, or class marks them as outsiders from the mainstream medical and legal community. Mrs. Madyun's case itself raises this concern, as she is a racial and religious minority seeking care at a public hospital. Other cases also indicate that women subject to court-ordered obstetrical intervention tend to be racial and religious minorities. *See, e.g.,* Rhoden, *supra,* at 2024.[43] Efforts to seek court orders to compel obstetrical interventions also seem to occur against those women with the least financial means, as many of these cases, like the present case, arise from public hospital settings. The cases on compelled medical treatment of pregnant women thus far indicate real reason for concern about race- and class-based disparate impact. This court takes judicial notice of the fact that vulnerability to forced medical treatment can arise from having limited venues for care due to economic circumstances. If court-ordered obstetrical interventions become more common at public hospitals, the public image of these hospitals and trust between these doctors and their patients may be eroded. The groups most in need of prenatal care may be driven away from the only care they can access.[44]

I.VI Conclusion

In sum, this Court declines to follow the few other court decisions that have authorized medical professionals to compel medical treatment on nonconsenting pregnant women. These cases present emotionally charged questions about the balance of risks between the pregnant woman and her fetus and, ultimately, the question of who should decide which risks are worth taking. Hospitals are likely to prefer erring on the side of caution and, therefore, seek court orders to immunize themselves from liability either if there is harm resulting to the infant or to the

---

[43] For example, Rhoden describes the case of an African woman who refused Cesarean surgery because she planned to return to Africa where there would be no facilities for a repeat Cesarean, and thus a Cesarean birth in the U.S. would risk her health in future childbearing. A judge was contacted and indicated his willingness to order a Cesarean but the woman delivered a healthy infant vaginally before the order could be issued. *See* Rhoden, *supra,* at 2024.

[44] At this point, even if there is sufficient evidence of discriminatory impact along lines of race, this Court does not have evidence that courts have acted with a discriminatory purpose in issuing court-ordered obstetrical interventions. *See Personnel Administrator of Massachusetts v. Feeney,* 442 U.S. 256 (1979). However, if further evidence indicates that women who are racial minorities are targeted for forced medical intervention, there may also be a claim for race-based discrimination. Heightened rational basis scrutiny under the Equal Protection Clause may also apply due to the confluence of gender, race, and class discrimination and the importance of the right to bodily integrity. *Cf. Plyler v. Doe,* 457 U.S. 202 (1982) (applying heightened rational basis scrutiny to Texas statute denying public education to children of illegal immigrants).

woman if they proceed with nonconsensual treatment. Courts face a difficult dilemma in these rushed proceedings. Particularly in cases where the woman is at term and in labor, courts feel an understandable pressure to intervene. However, judges must not act impulsively, without greater reflection on existing legal precedents and consideration of the future impact of their decisions.

A court wielding the doctor's scalpel to cut open a woman's body against her will is not a low risk, simple solution without collateral consequences to the woman's or the public's health. Pregnant women, even during childbirth, are not mere containers for fetuses whom the state can slice through when it disagrees with the woman's risk assessment or religious beliefs. Court orders compelling medical interventions on nonconsenting pregnant women violate the core principles of informed consent law and constitutional rights to reproductive liberty and bodily integrity. These principles must apply equally to all patients regardless of sex, race, religion, or class.

II ORDER

Accordingly, the Hospital's petition for an order authorizing it to forcibly perform a Cesarean section upon Ayesha Madyun is DENIED.

6

Johnson v. Calvert, 5 Cal. 4th 84 (1993)

Commentary by Catherine Sakimura

Johnson v. Calvert is one of the most significant cases in the development of surrogacy law. Its reasoning shaped not only the laws addressing surrogacy but how the industry of commercial surrogacy developed. The re-written opinion by Professor Melanie Jacobs centers how race, class, and gender affect commercial surrogacy agreements in contrast to published opinions addressing surrogacy that provide little insight into how these issues intertwine. The re-written opinion also addresses key issues left unresolved by the original opinion that would likely have significantly changed the evolution of laws addressing surrogacy and the practice of commercial surrogacy.

Although informal and uncompensated surrogacy has been practiced since at least biblical times, commercial surrogacy only began in the United States in the 1980s.[1] Since its inception, commercial surrogacy has been legally, politically, and socially controversial. Surrogacy requires a person to become pregnant with the intention that someone else will parent the child, thus implicating a number of potentially competing interests, especially the rights of women[2] to control their bodies during pregnancy, including whether to obtain an abortion. However, many argue that banning surrogacy denies the agency of these same women to choose to help other families have children and receive compensation for their labor, as well as the procreative freedom of intended parents.[3] Surrogacy also raises concerns related to class and economic inequality, racism, and globalism, as most intended parents are wealthy and white. Although most surrogates in the United States are

---

[1] Pamela Laufer-Ukeles, *Mothering for Money: Regulating Commercial Intimacy*, 88 IND. L.J. 1223, n.1 (2013).

[2] While it is possible for transgender men to serve as surrogates, this is very uncommon.

[3] Christine L. Kerian, *Surrogacy: A Last Resort Alternative for Infertile Women or a Commodification of Women's Bodies and Children?*, 12 WIS. WOMEN'S L.J. 113, 163 (1997).

middle-class white women, outside of the U.S. surrogates are mostly poor women of color.[4] On the other hand, assisted reproductive technology (ART), including surrogacy, provides reproductive justice to many parents who have historically been denied the ability to have children, including LGBTQ parents.[5] Finally, commercial surrogacy in the United States exists within a market economy that provides little or no health insurance coverage for any fertility services.[6]

Johnson v. Calvert[7] was the first published decision in the United States recognizing a compensated surrogacy arrangement. When the California Supreme Court issued its opinion in 1993, the few published opinions that had squarely addressed the issue held that compensated surrogacy arrangements were unenforceable and against public policy.[8] Only a few states legislatively addressed surrogacy at that time, and most of those laws prohibited or even criminalized compensated surrogacy arrangements based on fears of exploitation of women and the specter of baby selling.[9]

In *Johnson v. Calvert*, Mark and Crispina Calvert sought to have a child through surrogacy who was genetically-related to both of them – Crispina had no uterus but did have functioning ovaries.[10] Anna Johnson, a single mother and one of Crispina's coworkers, heard that they were interested in surrogacy and approached them with an offer to be their surrogate.[11] Anna and the Calverts entered a written agreement providing that Anna would become pregnant using an embryo created from Mark's sperm and Crispina's egg, that the Calverts would be the child's only parents, that Anna would earn $10,000 in installments ending six weeks after birth, and that the Calverts would purchase a life insurance policy for Anna to protect Anna's daughter in the event of Anna's death.[12] Anna became pregnant shortly thereafter.[13]

The relationship between the Calverts and Anna deteriorated during the pregnancy, and Anna sent a letter demanding early payment and threatening not to give

---

[4] Yehezkel Margalit, *From Baby M to Baby m(Anji): Regulating International Surrogacy Agreements*, 24 J.L. & POL'Y 41, 51–53 (2015).

[5] *See* Judy Keen, *Surrogate Relishes Unique Role: And Science Has a Place in the Family, Too*, USA TODAY (Jan. 23, 2007), at 2007 WLNR 1297188; Kevin Sack, *Fathers in the Making*, L.A. TIMES 1 (Oct. 29, 2006), at 2006 WLNR 18761565.

[6] *See* Deborah Zalesne, *The Intersection of Contract Law, Reproductive Technology, and the Market: Families in the Age of ART*, 51 U. RICH. L. REV. 419, 429 (2017).

[7] 851 P.2d 776 (Cal. 1993).

[8] *See, e.g., In re Baby M.*, 537 A.2d 1227, 1246–50 (N.J. 1988).

[9] *Compare, e.g.*, ARK. CODE ANN. § 9-10-201(c)(2) (allowing surrogacy); NEV. REV. STAT. ANN. § 127.287(5) (same) *to* ARIZ. REV. STAT. § 25-218 (1993 version) (prohibiting surrogacy); IND. STAT. 31-8-2-2 § (1993 version) (same); LA. STAT. ANN. § 9:2713 (1993 version) (same); MICH. STAT. § 722.855 (same); N.Y. DOM. REL. § 122 (same); VA. CODE ANN. §§ 20-156 to 20-165 (prohibiting compensated surrogacy).

[10] *Johnson*, 851 P.2d at 778–89, n.4.

[11] *Id.* at 778 & n.4, 789.

[12] *Id.* at 778.

[13] *Id.*

the child to the Calverts.[14] The Calverts and Anna filed competing actions seeking legal parentage, and blood tests proved that Mark and Crispina were the child's genetic parents.[15] After Christopher's birth, the court provided temporary custody to the Calverts with visitation by Anna. About a month after issuing this temporary order, the trial court issued its final order declaring that the Calverts were Christopher's legal parents and Anna was not.[16]

On appeal, the California Supreme Court upheld the trial court's order applying California's general parentage statutes. The Court explained that Anna had a claim to parentage based on giving birth, and Crispina had a claim based on being a genetic parent.[17] California statutes provided that a woman who gives birth is a parent and that a man could establish paternity based on blood tests.[18] The court explained the blood test statute applied to Crispina because another provision of California law provided that paternity provisions apply to questions of maternity.[19] The Court then turned to the question of whether Crispina or Anna's claim should prevail,[20] and explained that the intent of the parties was a significant consideration in determining parentage.[21] "But for" Mark and Crispina's decision to have a child and their actions to effectuate that decision, Anna would not have given birth to Christopher.[22]

The Court also held that surrogacy agreements are not against public policy.[23] First, it explained that they do not violate the prohibition on paying a birth mother in exchange for consenting to an adoption.[24] The Court reasoned that in this case the parties entered the agreement before conception, Anna was not genetically-related to the child, and the Calverts paid for her labor in pregnancy and birth, not for giving up her parental rights.[25] The Court also rejected arguments that surrogacy exploits women or turns children into commodities, explaining that there was no evidence of these effects and noting that such arguments echo the paternalistic reasoning of many past laws denying women economic rights.[26] The Court declined to address, however, the enforceability of other provisions of the agreement, including whether the agreement could allow the Calverts to decide whether Anna should have an abortion.[27]

---

[14] *Id.*

[15] *Id.*

[16] *Id.*

[17] *Id.* at 781.

[18] *Id.* at 780.

[19] *Id.*

[20] The opinion noted that amicus for the ACLU argued that all three parties should be parents but the Court declined to do so because the Calverts intended to be parents and recognizing Anna would diminish their rights. *Id.* at 781, n.8.

[21] *Id.* at 782.

[22] *Id.*

[23] *Id.* at 784.

[24] *Id.*

[25] *Id.*

[26] *Id.* at 784–85.

[27] *Id.* at 784.

Finally, the Court determined that the decision did not violate Anna's constitutional rights. The Court explained that Anna's substantive due process arguments assumed that she was a parent whose rights were terminated, while Anna was simply not a legal parent under California law.[28] The Court also held that finding that Anna had a liberty interest in the child would infringe on Mark and Crispina's liberty interests and procreative choices as intended parents.[29]

THE EFFECT OF THE OPINION

Johnson v. Calvert paved the way for legislation[30] and case law[31] allowing enforcement of compensated surrogacy agreements and, thus, allowed commercial surrogacy to expand. Consequently, the number of parents using gestational surrogacy has continued to rise dramatically over the decades.[32]

The fact that Anna Johnson was not genetically related to Christopher was significant both to the outcome of the case and its impact. Early commercial surrogacy was traditional or genetic surrogacy, where the surrogate carrier becomes pregnant through insemination with sperm from a donor or an intended parent and the child is genetically related to the surrogate.[33] Gestational surrogacy requires the use of in vitro fertilization (IVF) – where ova are surgically removed from a person's body and then fertilized in a lab to create an embryo that is transferred into a person's uterus.[34] IVF technology was only in its early stages when commercial surrogacy began in the early 1980s.[35] As a result, early arrangements tended to involve traditional surrogacy, and gestational surrogacy did not begin until the late 1980s.[36] Today, commercial surrogacy is almost exclusively gestational surrogacy,[37]

---

[28] *Id.* at 785–86.

[29] *Id.* at 786.

[30] *See, e.g.,* DEL. CODE ANN. tit. 13, § 8-102 et seq.; 750 ILL. COMP. STAT. ANN. 47/1 to 47/75; NEV. REV. STAT. § 126.500 et seq.; N.H. REV. STAT. ANN. §§ 168-B:1 to 168-B:22; TEX. FAM. CODE § 160.751 to 160.763; UTAH CODE ANN. §§ 78B-15-801 to 78B-15-809.

[31] *See, e.g., Hodas v. Morin,* 814 N.E.2d 320 (Mass. 2004); *J.F. v. D.B.,* 879 N.E.2d 740 (Ohio 2007); *Raftopol v. Ramey,* 12 A.3d 783 (Conn. 2011); *Nolan v. LaBree,* 2012 ME 61, 52 A.3d 923 (Me. 2012); *P.M. v. T.B.,* 907 N.E.2d 522 (Iowa 2018); *In re Baby S.,* 128 A.3d 296 (Pa. Super. Ct. 2015), *appeal denied,* 132 A.3d 456 (Pa. 2016).

[32] *See, e.g.,* K. M. Perkins, Sheree L. Boulet, Denise J. Jamieson, & Dmitry M. Kissin, *Trends and Outcomes of Gestational Surrogacy in the United States,* 106 FERTILITY & STERILITY 435, 435–42 (2016).

[33] Carol Sanger, *Developing Markets in Baby-Making: In the Matter of Baby M,* 30 HARV. J. L. & GENDER 67, 94, n. 52 (2007); *In re Roberto D.B.,* 923 A.2d 115, 117 (Md. 2007).

[34] In re Roberto D.B., 923 A.2d at 117.

[35] Alan C. Milstein, *The Brave New World of Assisted Reproductive Technology,* N.J. LAW. 42 (Aug. 2017).

[36] *See* Christine L. Kerian, *Surrogacy: A Last Resort Alternative for Infertile Women or a Commodification of Women's Bodies and Children?,* 12 WIS. WOMEN'S L.J. 113, 119 (1997).

[37] Noa Ben-Asher, *The Curing Law: On the Evolution of Baby-Making Markets,* 30 CARDOZO L. REV. 1885, 1918–19 (2009).

largely due to the decision in *Johnson v. Calvert* and the most famous early surrogacy case, *In re Baby M.*[38]

Baby M., decided five years before *Johnson v. Calvert*, involved a traditional surrogacy agreement. The New Jersey Supreme Court held such agreements unenforceable and found that providing compensation to surrogates constituted illegal "baby-selling."[39] In *Baby M.*, William and Elizabeth Stern sought to have a child through surrogacy due to Mrs. Stern's concerns about her health, and they were connected to Marybeth Whitehead through a surrogacy agency.[40] They agreed to have Mrs. Whitehead inseminated with Mr. Stern's sperm, to have her parental rights terminated, and for the Sterns to pay her $10,000.[41] At some point during her pregnancy, however, Mrs. Whitehead indicated that she was unsure that she could give up the baby and, after birth, she became suicidal and insisted that the Sterns allow her to see the baby.[42] She and her family fled the state with the baby and hid from the authorities until they were apprehended.[43] After extended court proceedings, the New Jersey Supreme Court found the surrogacy contract unenforceable based on a determination that the arrangement was an irrevocable agreement to adopt in exchange for payment.[44] However, the Court upheld the grant of sole custody to Mr. Stern.[45]

Unlike *Baby M.*, *Johnson v. Calvert* involved gestational surrogacy, so Anna Johnson was not genetically related to the child, a fact that the California Supreme Court viewed as significant in its discussion of the public policy implications.[46] The *Johnson v. Calvert* opinion did not explicitly address whether a traditional surrogacy agreement would be enforceable but its focus on Crispina's genetic connection to the child and Anna's lack of genetic connection made direct application of the decision to traditional surrogacy unlikely. Indeed, only a year later, a California Court of Appeal held that traditional surrogacy arrangements were unenforceable in *In re Marriage of Moschetta*.[47]

After *Baby M.*, commercial surrogacy arrangements moved away from traditional surrogacy,[48] and the decision in *Johnson v. Calvert* solidified this shift with significant implications for the health of the women involved in surrogacy. Gestational surrogacy exacts a much greater toll on the health and bodies of women.[49]

---

[38] 537 A.2d 1227 (N.J. 1988).

[39] *Id.* at 1242.

[40] *Id.* at 1235.

[41] *Id.*

[42] *Id.* at 1236–37.

[43] *Id.* at 1237.

[44] *Id.* at 1238–40.

[45] *Id.* at 1259, 1261.

[46] *Johnson*, 851 P.2d at 784.

[47] 25 Cal. App. 4th 1218 (1994).

[48] Sanger, *supra* note 33, at 94.

[49] Pamela Laufer-Ukeles, *Mothering for Money: Regulating Commercial Intimacy*, 88 IND. L.J. 1223, 1260 (2013).

It requires an egg donor or intended parent to induce a super ovulation through injectable drugs and have surgery, both of which have serious risks.[50] The surrogate must also take drugs not required for traditional surrogacy, and accept the greater risks of a pregnancy through IVF.[51] Gestational surrogacy is also at a much higher cost, creating an even greater financial and class divide between surrogates and intended parents.

Despite the greater health risks involved in gestational surrogacy, *Baby M.* and *Johnson v. Calvert* fueled a political and legal perspective that traditional surrogacy is more problematic than gestational surrogacy. This view, however, roots in the same paternalistic concern that motivates general opposition to surrogacy. For many, discomfort with traditional surrogacy is largely based on the assumption that a woman will be too bonded to a child who is genetically related to her, and, as such, she should not be able to agree in advance that she will have no parental rights. Additionally, this opposition assumes that the bond between genetic parents and their children is stronger than that between parents and children that are not genetically related. This view seems to ignore and diminish the strong bonds that thousands of nongenetic parents have with their children. Another critique is that surrogacy is tantamount to "baby selling." However, surrogacy, like egg donation, involves an agreement to conceive a child to be raised by intended parents, not a pregnant woman's agreement to adopt for pay. Recently, the tide has begun to shift. After decades of focus on legalizing only gestational surrogacy, there is new interest in pressing for the legal recognition of traditional surrogacy to allow a lower-cost option with fewer health impacts for women who work as surrogates and egg donors.[52]

THE RE-WRITTEN OPINION

Key issues left unaddressed by the original opinion in *Johnson v. Calvert* also shaped the development of commercial surrogacy by their absence. The re-written opinion addresses many of these unexamined issues, centering the role of race, class, and gender oppression in surrogacy. It does so in part by providing a much fuller recitation of facts than the original opinion, which fails to provide information

---

[50] *Id.*

[51] *Id.*; American College of Obstetricians and Gynecologists, Committee Opinion No. 671: Perinatal Risks associated with Assisted Reproductive Technology at 2–4 (2016).

[52] *See, e.g., In re Baby*, 447 S.W.3d 807 (Tenn. 2014); *Rosecky v. Schissel*, 833 N.W.2d 634 (Wisc. 2013); D.C. Code §§ 16–401 et seq. (2017); VT. H.B. 562 §§ 801–9, 2017 Leg. (effective Jan. 1, 2019); S.S.B. 6037 §§ 701–18 (Wash. 2018) (effective Jan. 1., 2019); *see also*, Unif. Parentage Act Article 8 (2017). This recent legislation requires the same safeguards for gestational surrogacy, including independent legal counsel for all parties but provides that a surrogate may revoke the agreement up to 72 hours after the child's birth, mirroring one of the key requirements in adoption laws regarding consent of the birth mother.

about the parties' race, employment, wealth, or details about how they came to this arrangement. In her re-write, Jacobs explains that Anna Johnson is black, Mark Calvert is white, and Crispina Calvert is Filipina. The Calverts considered surrogacy but could not afford an arrangement brokered by an agency. Anna and Crispina were both nurses at the same hospital, and Anna approached Crispina after hearing about her desire to use surrogacy. Anna told Crispina that she had been approved as a surrogate by another agency, a fact that turned out to be false. In their conversations, Anna discussed the *Baby M.* case and explained her view that this situation would be different because she would not be genetically related to the child.

The Jacobs opinion explains that the arrangement between the parties implicated structural racism, acknowledging the history of black women who were denied the opportunity to raise their own children while being forced to raise the children of white parents, either as enslaved people or underpaid domestic workers. However, it concludes that compensated surrogacy is not analogous to forced or underpaid caregiving, and notes that indeed most surrogates in the United States are white, middle class women. Since 1993, however, the growing industry of international surrogacy in developing countries relying mostly on poor women of color with little safeguards for their health or agency has changed the impact of racism on commercial surrogacy.[53] Accordingly, a vital issue in the international commercial surrogacy market is how to protect women in developing nations from exploitation at the hands of reproductive travelers and unscrupulous agents.

The role played by classism or income inequality in commercial surrogacy is nuanced and complex, as outlined in the Jacobs opinion. Anna had a middle-class job – indeed, the same job as Crispina – and most United States surrogates are middle-class, white women. Anna, unlike some surrogates, was well-educated and well-informed, as the parties' discussion of the *Baby M.* case demonstrated. Although the Calverts must have had more money than Anna, they were unable to afford the higher cost of utilizing a surrogacy agency. There is often a significant income disparity between surrogates and intended parents due to the very high cost of surrogacy but the facts provided in the re-written opinion demonstrate that this inequality is not necessarily inherent, and the reality is more complex. In any case, however, given the high cost of surrogacy, the lack of insurance coverage for nearly all kinds of ART in the United States, and the deeply-felt need of many intended parents to conceive a child, a lucrative surrogacy industry has developed within a capitalist system that markets surrogacy to wealthy prospective parents while limiting and channeling the ability of surrogates to negotiate the terms of the agreements.

The original opinion also did not address the significant question of the constitutional right of surrogates to control their own bodies during pregnancy.[54] The desire of intended parents to make decisions about the pregnancy, which can

---

[53] Margalit, *supra* note 4, at 51–53.
[54] *Johnson*, 851 P.2d at 784.

include prenatal care decisions, diet, exercise, and even whether to have an abortion, implicates the bodily autonomy and reproductive freedom of women. It took over a decade after *Johnson v. Calvert* before legislation specifically addressed the rights of surrogates to make these decisions, and two decades before some states enacted more comprehensive safeguards for surrogates.[55] The re-written opinion holds that a surrogate maintains her full procreative privacy and bodily autonomy during pregnancy, including decisions about her reproductive health and whether or not to have an abortion, and, had it replaced the original opinion, may have encouraged the earlier enactment of protective laws.

Both the original and re-written opinion hold that enforcing a surrogacy agreement does not violate the procreative freedom of the surrogate and the original opinion notes that intended parents have a substantive due process right to determine how they conceive children. The re-written opinion, however, delves more deeply into the latter issue and holds that procreative freedom includes the right to conceive children through surrogacy, providing an explicit constitutional protection for intended parents. This ruling would prevent the legislature from banning or criminalizing surrogacy. It also implies a constitutional right for intended parents who use other types of ART. Such a constitutional right would protect many LGBTQ parents, who continue to be denied recognition as legal parents because many states lack comprehensive, non-discriminatory ART statutes.[56] Because LGBTQ parents have historically been excluded from the right to have children or even continue to raise their children after their identities were discovered,[57] their ability to have children through ART is a reproductive justice issue.

In addition to directly addressing concerns of race, class, and gender, the re-written opinion deals with significant legal questions left open by the original opinion. First, unlike the original opinion, the re-written opinion appears to approve of compensated traditional surrogacy agreements. In so holding, the re-written opinion explicitly disapproves of *Baby M.* on legal grounds. In contrast, the original opinion merely distinguished the case factually. Had the original opinion rejected *Baby M.*'s legal reasoning, *Marriage of Moschetta* likely would have come to the opposite conclusion in 1994. Had California explicitly enforced compensated traditional surrogacy agreements it would have likely changed the industry in the state, allowing less wealthy intended parents to access surrogacy and allowing surrogates an option with fewer health risks. And because California is and has been a leader in providing these services, it likely would have impacted the industry well beyond its borders.

---

[55] *See, e.g.*, TEX. FAM. CODE §§ 160.751 to 160.763 (enacted in 2003); NEV. REV. STAT. § 126.500 et seq. (enacted in 2013); D.C. CODE § 16-401 et seq. (enacted 2017).

[56] *See* Courtney G. Joslin, *Nurturing Parenthood through the UPA (2017)*, 127 YALE L.J. FORUM 589, 591 (2018).

[57] *See, e.g.*, *Bottoms v. Bottoms*, 457 S.E.2d 102 (Va. 1995); *Pulliam v. Smith*, 501 S.E.2d 898 (N.C. 1998); *Morris v. Morris*, 783 So. 2d 681 (Miss. 2001); *L.A.M. v. B.M.*, 906 So. 2d 942 (Ala. Civ. App. 2004).

Second, the re-written opinion addresses two additional issues of particular significance to LGBTQ parents. The original opinion left the question of whether gestational surrogacy is permissible only where two intended parents are both genetically related to the child. Such a limitation would mean that same-sex couples and single parents would be largely excluded from its use. Several years after *Johnson v. Calvert*, a California Court of Appeal held that surrogacy agreements involving donor ova are equally enforceable,[58] but some states have chosen to limit surrogacy to different-sex, married parents who are both genetic parents, intentionally excluding same-sex, single, and unmarried intended parents from the ability to conceive through surrogacy.[59] The re-written opinion provides in dicta that a genetic relationship between each intended parent and the child would not be required to establish parentage.

The re-written opinion also eliminates language in the original opinion that there can be "only one" legally-recognized mother, which was previously relied on to reject arguments that a child can have same-sex parents under California law and was not rejected by the California Supreme Court until 2005.[60] The elimination of this language in the re-written opinion may have hastened the decision to allow same-sex parents to be legally recognized as parents of their children under California law.

CONCLUSION

As the re-written opinion recognizes, although surrogacy implicates potentially conflicting oppressions, banning the practice is not necessarily a best solution. The danger that surrogacy agreements will oppress poor women of color exists because of institutional and structural sexism, racism, classism, and capitalism, not the inherent nature of surrogacy itself. The ultimate solution is to work to dismantle the systems of oppression that create this danger. For example, universal insurance coverage that includes ART and surrogacy costs would significantly reduce the wealth and class inequality between surrogates and intended parents and the pressure to use international surrogacy. And a society in which no one experienced poverty and everyone's basic needs were met would eliminate the fear that surrogates agree to these arrangements because of a need for money. As we work toward these long-term visions, however, the best solution is to regulate surrogacy to safeguard the bargaining power of surrogates and their autonomy over their bodies during pregnancy, clearly recognize the parentage of all intended parents, and require industry oversight.

[58] *In re Marriage of Buzzanca*, 61 Cal.App.4th 1410 (1998).
[59] *See, e.g.*, LA. STAT. ANN.§ 9:2718.1(6) (2016).
[60] *Elisa B. v. Superior Court*, 117 P.3d 660, 665 (Cal. 2005).

Johnson v. Calvert, 5 Cal. 4th 84 (1993)

Ms. Justice Melanie Jacobs delivered the opinion

I INTRODUCTION

Like Solomon,[61] we are tasked with the difficult question of declaring which of two women is a child's legal mother. We must determine the enforceability of a surrogacy contract and, further, determine how to define legal motherhood in a situation in which one woman gave birth to a child but the child is the genetic offspring of another woman.

A range of assisted reproductive technologies ("ART") help infertile couples achieve a pregnancy. Certain ART procedures disaggregate genetic parenthood from gestational parenthood and, therefore, legal parenthood. The use of ART is still relatively new, and ART was not in mind when the legislature enacted our existing parentage laws. Commonly, the fact of giving birth raises a presumption of legal and genetic motherhood. Gestational surrogacy complicates what has been an ordinary task. Determining motherhood is no longer straightforward when motherhood could be assigned either to the birth mother, the genetic mother, or, possibly, a third woman who is neither the birth nor genetic mother but the woman who intends to mother and parent the child.

To determine this child's legal mother, we must consider the bounds of procreative privacy and respect the rights of each woman involved. This case is largely a matter of first impression, and we take seriously our obligation to decide it fairly. The facts are complicated, and our decision is not easy; we endeavor to reach an appropriate result guided by our laws and public policy, although our laws do not specifically address such a situation. Reproductive technologies are relatively new and, while they provide great benefit to infertile couples, the law has not caught up to the technology. As such, we also consider the wisdom of scholars and amicus curiae whose work helps fill the gaps in our current law and policy.

Gestational surrogacy provides those who desire to parent but who are medically infertile[62] an additional means by which to have children to whom they are genetically related. Gestational surrogacy first requires in vitro fertilization (IVF), which is a procedure by which a sperm fertilizes an ovum in a petri dish. John A. Robertson, *Embryos, Families, and Procreative Liberty: The Legal Structure of the New Reproduction*, 59 S. CAL. L. REV. 942, 948 (1986). To extract the ova for fertilization, a woman takes a series of drugs to stimulate ovarian follicle

---

[61] 1 *Kings* 3:16–28 (King James).

[62] "'Infertility' refers to a relative inability to achieve a pregnancy. The exact incidence of infertility is difficult to discern, but it is estimated that some degree of infertility affects 8.5 percent of the nation's population in its childbearing years." Lori Andrews, *Alternative Reproduction*, 65 S. CAL. L. REV. 623, 626 (1991).

development and growth; the ova are then retrieved surgically while the woman is under general anesthesia. *Id.* The embryo may contain the genetic material of one or more members of the couple who has contracted with the surrogate; it is also possible that the contracting couple may use donor gametes. If successful fertilization occurs, a doctor transfers the resulting embryo to the genetic mother's uterus or a gestational surrogate's uterus. In gestational surrogacy, the egg donor (possibly the intended mother) takes additional drugs to synchronize her menstrual cycle with the surrogate's. Brief for Respondent at 8. If the embryo implants successfully, the surrogate becomes pregnant and, barring any complications, she carries the baby to term.

We believe that procreative privacy is a sufficiently expansive concept to include pregnancy not only through sexual intercourse but through the use of ART too. "Our law affords constitutional protection to personal decisions relating to marriage, procreation, contraception, family relationships, child rearing, and education ... These matters, involving the most intimate and personal choices a person may make in a lifetime, choices central to personal dignity and autonomy, are central to the privacy protected by the Fourteenth Amendment ... ." *Planned Parenthood of Southeastern Pennsylvania v. Casey*, 505 U.S. 833, 851 (1992). As technology advances so, too, must the law. Our existing parentage laws – while not crafted with ART in mind – can and should apply to parentage determinations in which ART is used.

We recognize that surrogacy is a significant commitment for the surrogate and intended parents. We know, too, that each side bears risk but there is particular societal concern that a surrogate bears a greater risk of exploitation and harm than aspiring parents. For instance, Michigan has enacted a statute that makes all paid surrogacy contracts void and unenforceable and, further, subjects the parties involved to criminal penalties. Surrogate Parenting Act, Mich. Comp. Laws § 722.851 (1988). We believe those concerns can be adequately mitigated. In matters as personal as procreation, individuals have a broad realm of privacy into which the state should not ordinarily intrude. We further conclude that surrogacy does not represent a form of adoption; we reject the analogy to adoption, and we decline to apply adoption laws to the question of a surrogacy contract's enforceability. We affirm the judgment of the Appeals court and hold that this gestational surrogacy agreement may be enforced as detailed below.

I.I *Facts*

On September 19, 1990, Anna Johnson gave birth to Christopher, the genetic son of Mark and Crispina Calvert. Eight months earlier, on January 15, 1990, Mark and Crispina signed a surrogacy contract with Anna and a successful embryo transfer and implantation followed on January 19th. Shortly thereafter, the pregnancy was confirmed. Unfortunately, relations between the parties deteriorated – so much so that, nearly three years after Christopher's birth, the parties are still litigating to determine who is Christopher's legal mother.

Mark and Crispina are a married couple; he is white, and she is Filipina. For two years, they tried to have children. During this time, Crispina had several surgeries to remove uterine tumors. Ultimately, in 1984, Crispina required a hysterectomy which prevents her from gestating a child. Her ovaries remain intact, though, and Mark and Crispina investigated surrogacy as a means of having their own genetic child. After initial consultations with the Surrogacy Center, Mark and Crispina did not pursue surrogacy for financial reasons.

Anna Johnson, a black, single mother, is a nurse who works at the same hospital as Crispina Calvert. Anna told another coworker that the Center for Surrogate Parenting (a different agency from the one Mark and Crispina had consulted) had accepted her as a surrogate; the coworker told Anna of Crispina's and Mark's infertility difficulties and suggested she talk with Crispina. Anna approached Crispina and told her that she, Anna, had been accepted as a surrogate and further offered to serve as a surrogate for Crispina. Shortly thereafter, the Calverts had a lunch meeting with Anna and with her daughter. Anna again stated that she had been accepted by the Center for Surrogate Parenting. During the lunch, the parties discussed the New Jersey Supreme Court case, *In re Baby M*, 537 A.2d 1227 (N.J. 1988). Anna commented that because in this instance (unlike the surrogate in *Baby M*) she would have no genetic connection with the baby, she would not bond with nor want to keep the child; rather, she would be like an "incubator."

The parties discussed the need for a surrogacy contract during their lunch meeting but, prior to executing a contract, the women met with an infertility specialist who started them on a program to synchronize their menstrual cycles, which took about two months and required near daily appointments. Crispina picked Anna up for the appointments and then they often had breakfast. Sometime prior to January 5, 1990, Mark requested that an employee of the Surrogacy Center (the agency Mark and Crispina had initially consulted) prepare a standard surrogacy contract. Mark and Crispina received the contract between January 5 and 10, 1990 and provided Anna with a copy shortly thereafter. Prior to executing the contract, Anna consulted with an attorney to review the contract. The parties disagree about the extent to which Anna benefitted from independent counsel, although all parties agree that Anna had the opportunity to consult with an attorney and ask questions prior to executing the contract.

The surrogacy agreement provided that any child born to Anna would be the child of Mark and Crispina and would go their home "as their child." Further, Anna agreed to relinquish "all parental rights." In return, the Calverts would pay Anna $10,000 in a series of installments with the final installment due six weeks after the baby's birth. The Calverts also agreed to pay for a $200,000 insurance policy on Anna's life; Anna wanted to ensure some protection for her daughter if she died as a consequence of the pregnancy.

Although Anna claimed she was approved by the Center for Surrogate Parenting to serve as a surrogate, that was not so; the Center has no record of any contact by Anna. In fact, Mark learned shortly after Anna's pregnancy was confirmed that Anna had previously suffered several stillbirths and miscarriages – which would have made her ineligible to serve as a surrogate through either agency's program. Further, Anna told colleagues at work that she was carrying the Calverts' child; that they were going to take care of Anna for life; and that she was going to move in with the Calverts. The Calverts became increasingly uncomfortable after learning more about Anna's pregnancy history, her comments at work, and that she had been untruthful about her screening to serve as a surrogate. The relationship between the parties started to break down.

Anna was also growing frustrated. From her perspective, the Calverts were not supportive emotionally or financially during her pregnancy. As a single mother, Anna was particularly concerned about having a life insurance policy to benefit her daughter in case anything happened to her during her pregnancy or as a consequence of childbirth. Anna believed the Calverts did not do enough to secure that policy. More than that, she felt emotionally abandoned and was upset that the Calverts did not accompany her to prenatal appointments and did not assist her during several hospital visits related to pregnancy complications.

In July 1990, Anna became particularly upset and sent a letter to the Calverts demanding the balance of the payments due her or else she would refuse to give up the baby. The letter, dated July 23, 1990, provides, in part:

Dear Chris & Mark,

I am writing you this letter to inquire if an early payment can be made of what is left to be paid of me . . .. The lady that owns the house in which I reside in [is] selling it . . . Since I am to be hospitalized for three weeks due to [pregnancy complications] I need to find another place to live prior to this! . . .

I'm imploring nicely and trying not to be an ogre about this. But you must admit, you have not been very supportive mentally the entire pregnancy & you've showed a lack of interest unless it came to an ultrasound . . . There's only two months left & once this baby is born, my hands are free of this deal. But see, this situation can go two ways. One, you can pay me the entire sum early so I won't have to live in the streets, or two you can forget about helping me but, calling it a breach of contract & not get the baby! . . . [Y]ou'd want some help too, if you had no where to go & have to worry about not only yourself but your own child & the child of someone else!!! . . . This is the only letter you will get from me. The next letter you will receive will be from my lawyers . . .

Letter from Anna Johnson to Mark and Crispina Calvert (July 23, 1990)

Mark and Crispina were distraught upon receiving Anna's letter. They attempted to contact her by phone and by letter but were unsuccessful. The distrust between the parties grew. Despite Anna's claim that she needed to find new housing, her roommate later testified that the house was not being sold.

While Anna claims that the Calverts did not provide her with an insurance policy nor consistent support emotionally and otherwise during her pregnancy, the Calverts testified that Anna did not provide them with copies of bills necessary for reimbursement nor did she meet with their insurance agent so that they could secure the life insurance policy. Anna also continued to cash checks from the Calverts even after she wrote to them and said she planned to keep the child. At trial, witnesses further testified that Anna commented that she would be "famous" and earn millions from a book deal. During this time, Anna gave an interview to an *L.A. Times* reporter. In her interview, Anna stated that the baby was not hers; that she did not have a bond with the baby; and that she was the surrogate for the baby, not the child's mother.

A few weeks after Anna sent the letter to Mark and Crispina in which she threatened to keep the baby, they filed a lawsuit seeking a declaration of their parentage of the unborn child. Anna filed her own action seeking a declaration of her maternity, alleging the surrogacy contract is invalid and unenforceable, and that her constitutional parental rights are violated if Crispina is determined to be Christopher's mother and Anna has no parental status. The two cases were eventually consolidated.

Following Christopher's birth, the parties agreed to an order that Christopher would remain with Mark and Crispina but that Anna would have visitation rights. At one point, the trial judge suggested placing Christopher with a foster family but Anna agreed the Calverts' could maintain physical custody of Christopher if she could have visitation. In fact, as part of Anna's visitation, she nursed Christopher and thus maintained a bond with him. In support of her maternity claim, Anna relies heavily on the gestational bond she developed with Christopher as well as the post-partum bond she maintained by regularly nursing Christopher for several weeks following his birth. The trial court ruled that Mark and Crispina are Christopher's "genetic, biological, and natural" father and mother and that Anna has no parental rights. The trial court further found the surrogacy contract valid and enforceable and terminated Anna's visitation rights. Anna appealed the trial court's ruling, which was affirmed by the appellate court. We then granted review.

II DISCUSSION

Legal parenthood is an important concept because it requires the adult to assume significant responsibilities for the child, such as providing food, shelter, health care, education, and the many necessaries of life. Concomitantly, a legal parent can reap the benefits of the parent–child relationship and enjoy the care, custody, and companionship of her or his child. As such, the determination of parentage carries great legal and emotional meaning.

The parties stipulate that Mark is Christopher's genetic father and has the status of a legal parent. They disagree, however, on which woman is Christopher's legal mother. Anna avers that she is Christopher's legal mother because she is his birth mother. Crispina argues that as Christopher's genetic mother, she is his legal mother. As discussed below, both women have a cognizable legal basis upon which to state a claim of maternity. We are persuaded, though, that Crispina's claim is stronger and find that she is Christopher's legal mother. For reasons we will discuss, we do not believe that such a finding infringes on Anna's constitutional parental rights because we have determined that she is not Christopher's legal mother. We further hold that the surrogacy contract is valid and enforceable and does not violate California public policy.

II.I *Determining Maternity under the Uniform Parentage Act*

While ART has been referred to as the "new frontier," our existing parentage laws are relevant for situations beyond parentage through sexual intercourse and provide valuable guidance to answer the question of maternity. Our legislature has enacted the Uniform Parentage Act ("the Act"), which provides a fairly comprehensive statutory scheme for parentage determinations. The Act defines the "parent and child relationship" as "the legal relationship existing between a child and his natural or adoptive parents incident to which the law confers or imposes rights, privileges, duties, and obligations. It includes the mother and child relationship and the father and child relationship." Civ. Code § 7001. While the Act was enacted to help establish paternity for children born to unmarried parents – and corresponding child support orders – the Act provides that the provisions applying to paternity also apply to determinations of maternity. Civ. Code § 7015.

II.A The Act's Plain Language Provides a Basis for Determining Maternity When More than One Woman Can Claim Maternity

At the outset of our statutory analysis, we recognize that both Anna and Crispina have a basis upon which to assert legal maternity under the Act. Although determining maternity in this particular factual context differs from many paternity cases, the Act provides guidance for us to determine whose claim is stronger. The Civil Code provides that "any interested party" may bring an action to determine "the existence of a mother and child relationship." Civ. Code § 7015. Civil Code § 7003 further provides that the mother and child relationship "may be established by proof of her having given birth to the child, or under [the Act]." The Act's plain language anticipates that it is possible to establish maternity by a means other than having given birth to the child. The Act further provides that the provisions that apply to establishment of the father and child relationship apply also to the existence of the mother and child relationship. Civ. Code § 7015. Thus, Anna can claim maternity by having given birth but Crispina can also claim maternity based on other language in the Act.

Concerning Crispina's claim of maternity we look to Fed. R. Evid. 892 which allows for blood testing when paternity is a disputed fact. Relying again on Civil Code § 7015, which directs us to apply the text of the Act to maternity determinations as we do for paternity determinations, we find that the blood testing proves that Crispina is Christopher's genetic mother.

We are left, then, with two competing bases of motherhood: Anna is the birth mother of Christopher but not his genetic mother; Crispina is Christopher's genetic mother but not his birth mother. Both the status of birth mother and genetic mother can result in a legal determination of the mother and child relationship. Amicus ACLU has encouraged us to find that Christopher has two mothers, since both women are able to prove their maternity under the Act. We decline, in this case, to do so. As we explain below, we believe that in this case policy and logic dictate that this court find that only one woman – Crispina – is Christopher's legal mother.

II.B Crispina Demonstrated Her Intent to Parent

Both Crispina and Anna have demonstrated a claim for maternity under the Act. Crispina demonstrates something further: her intent to be Christopher's mother. Mark and Crispina wanted to have a child. Due to Crispina's hysterectomy, she could not gestate a child and the couple used a surrogate. But it was their intention that caused Christopher to be born. Several legal commentators provide a helpful lens by which to view intentional parenthood. Professor Marjorie Shultz has argued that within the sphere of ART, "intentions that are voluntarily chosen, deliberate, express and bargained-for ought presumptively to determine legal parenthood." Marjorie Shultz, *Reproductive Technology and Intent-Based Parenthood: An Opportunity for Gender Neutrality*, 1990 WIS. L. REV. 297, 323 (1990). Similarly, Professor John Hill has written, "[w]hat is essential to parenthood is not the biological tie between the parent and child but the preconception *intention* to have a child, accompanied by undertaking whatever action is necessary to bring a child into the world." John Lawrence Hill, *What Does it Mean to be a "Parent?" The Claims of Biology as the Basis for Parental Rights*, 66 N.Y.U. L. REV. 353, 414 (1991) (emphasis in original).

When parties use ART, a court should consider their intent in parentage determinations. By its very nature, ART requires the parties to engage in deliberate, intentional actions to cause a pregnancy and resulting baby. Especially when couples use IVF and gestational surrogacy, intent should play a primary role in parentage determination. We agree with Hill that preconception intent should guide our decision when ART is used. Given the emotional, financial, and time commitment involved for a successful pregnancy when IVF and gestational surrogacy are used, preconception intent is the fairest metric we can use to protect all of the parties involved: the intended parents, surrogate, and child. Here, preconception intent protects the parental rights of the intended parents. But it also protects the rights of a gestational surrogate if intended parents change their mind during a surrogate's pregnancy and no longer want to take the child. Relying on preconception intent means that the intended parents have a responsibility to the child at birth and that burden is not unfairly shifted to the surrogate.

Without Mark and Crispina's intent in the first instance, there would have been no pregnancy – and no Christopher. Mark and Crispina's intent to have a child set in motion Christopher's birth. In fact, even if Crispina were not Christopher's genetic mother, we would find that she is his legal mother because of her intent. Using intent as our metric for determining maternity in ART cases, we find persuasive Anna's intent, too. Anna signed a contract – after reviewing it with legal counsel – and agreed to provide her services to assist Mark and Crispina in having a child. In the letter that she sent to Mark and Crispina – even though she felt angry and frustrated – Anna repeatedly stated that the baby was not hers; that she did not feel a maternal bond with the baby; and that the baby was, in fact, Mark and Crispina's baby. Anna repeated similar statements in media interviews. In her July 23, 1990 letter, Anna specifically referred to the baby as "someone else's baby." Anna's intention to become pregnant was not motivated by her intent to parent but her intention to serve as a surrogate.

Anna asks us to focus on her biological connection to Christopher based on her gestation. She suggests that the maternal bond formed in the womb is of greater import in establishing the parent–child relationship than the fact of genetics. We agree that Anna's role as a surrogate is important and meaningful to Christopher's creation. We do not mean to minimize her physical and emotional efforts. But we believe that argument is misleading. In our view, the use of ART requires greater inquiry into the parties' intent – specifically, their preconception intent – rather than their status.

The parties' intentions at the time of conception are much clearer when ART is used than in coital reproduction. A woman is not accidentally inseminated with sperm; a surrogate does not have an embryo accidentally transferred to her womb. All of the parties are making intentional choices – including the intended parents, the gametic providers, and the surrogate. To eschew focusing on intent in making parentage determinations after ART would be inconsistent with the use of ART itself.

Building on those analogies, though, we recognize that the implementation of intentional parenthood could result in only one parent or more than two parents, particularly when parentage is not predicated on biology or gestation. It is possible that more than two individuals would decide to coparent a child and would undertake a pregnancy with the understanding that more than two adults would parent. With the increase in divorce and remarriage, many children have more than two adults who coparent them, formally or informally. Recognizing legal parentage in more than two adults for one child may make sense for some families, as argued by Amicus ACLU. Or, using intentional parentage doctrine, a court may recognize parentage for a child only in a single mother who used donor sperm. Since Anna did not manifest a preconception intent to parent and because the Calverts and Anna had no preconception intent that the three parties coparent, we do not believe that more than two parents makes sense for this family and child.

III *Constitutional Protection of the Parent–Child Relationship*

Anna argues that a finding that Crispina is Christopher's legal mother infringes on her constitutional parental rights. The U.S. Supreme Court has long venerated the rights of parents to the care, custody, and control of their children as a fundamental Constitutional protection. *See, e.g., Wisconsin v. Yoder,* 406 U.S. 205 (1972); *Meyer v. Nebraska,* 262 U.S. 390 (1923). Anna looks to the Supreme Court to support her contention that protection of the parent–child relationship is relative; that not all parent–child relationships are treated equally under the law; and that her maternal claim – as a birth mother – deserves greater protection than Crispina's – a genetic mother through IVF. Specifically, Anna argues that the Supreme Court's decisions in several cases concerning the rights of unwed fathers provides her a constitutional right to maternity and custody. She asserts that a biological connection alone does not automatically confer constitutional protection of the parental right and, therefore, argues that Crispina's rights as Christopher's genetic mother are not necessarily deserving of protection compared with her own as his birth mother.

In a series of opinions, the Supreme Court evaluated the due process and equal protection claims of unwed birth fathers who were denied rights that are conferred automatically on birth mothers. In *Stanley v. Illinois,* an unwed father challenged an Illinois statute that presumed nonmarital fathers are unfit to care for their children and had no standing to request a parental fitness hearing prior to the removal of children to foster care. *Stanley v. Illinois,* 405 U.S. 645 (1972). The Court held that the statute violated Stanley's due process and equal protection rights because the statute precluded Stanley from access to a hearing to determine his fitness – after he had lived with and raised the children for many years. *Id.* at 658. The Court's emphasis was largely on the effect the statute had in "the dismemberment of [Stanley's] family." *Id.*

In three subsequent cases, the Court addressed whether statutes that allowed a child born to unmarried parents to be adopted without his birth father's consent violated an unwed father's constitutional rights. The relationship that the father had with the child largely framed the Court's decisions. In *Quilloin v. Walcott,* 434 U.S. 246 (1978), the Court upheld a statute that required only the mother's consent to adoption and denied birth fathers a voice in the process. *Id.* at 256. The Court found that the father's rights were not violated because he had never sought custody of his son and that the adoption would support recognition of an intact family unit. *Id.* at 255.

Conversely, in *Caban v. Mohammed,* 441 U.S. 380 (1979), the Court found that a N.Y. adoption statute that granted a birth mother the right to preclude an adoption of her child by withholding her consent whereas the unwed father had no similar right did violate an unwed father's rights. *Id*. at 386–87. Rather, an unwed father could prevent an adoption only if he could prove the adoption was not in the child's best interests. *Id*. at 387. In this case, the children lived with their father for several years and, even after they had moved, he continued to visit with them and provide support. *Id*. at 382. Caban's relationship with his children was relevant to the Court's conclusion that the statute violated equal protection. *Id*. at 394.

Several years later, the Court again heard a case in which an unmarried father challenged a statute that did not require unwed fathers to receive notice and an opportunity to be heard before the child's adoption. *Lehr v. Robertson*, 463 U.S. 248 (1983). The Court emphasized that the father had not seen the child in the two years since her birth. Distinguishing *Stanley* and *Caban* from this case and *Quilloin*, the Court wrote that mere biological connection does not merit constitutional protection. Rather, the Court wrote, the biological link is significant because it offers the father "an opportunity that no other male possesses to develop a relationship with his offspring." *Id*. at 262. If he does not grasp the opportunity, "the Federal Constitution will not automatically compel a State to listen to his opinion of where the child's best interests lie." *Id*.

The final case in this group upon which Anna places reliance is *Michael H. v. Gerald D.*, 491 U.S. 110 (1989). In *Michael H.*, the child's genetic father, Michael, sought to establish his paternity of Victoria, a child born to Carol while she was legally married to Gerald. *Id*. at 113–14. Although Carol and Victoria lived with Michael for eight months and Carol initially agreed to rebut Gerald's presumption of paternity and help establish Michael's paternity, she then decided to reunite with Gerald. *Id*. at 114–15. Gerald then sought to enforce his parental rights and the marital presumption. The Court upheld the presumption of paternity. A plurality of the Supreme Court found that Michael had no constitutionally protected interest in establishing paternity. *Id*. at 126. Relying heavily on history and tradition, the plurality emphasized the preservation of family integrity and further emphasized that the constitution has not historically protected non-nuclear families. *Id*. at 124. The dissent, recognizing that families are changing and do not all neatly fit into the traditional nuclear family model, would have permitted Michael to challenge the marital presumption and to establish a right to visitation. *Id*. at 142–47.

We agree with Anna that *Michael H*. – and *Lehr*, *Caban*, and *Stanley* – do not stand for the proposition that biology will always dictate the determination of a legal parent–child relationship. We disagree, though, that this series of cases provides support for Anna's maternity claim. As Professor Janet Dolgin has observed, the unwed father cases demonstrate that constitutional protection of fathers' rights requires not only a biological connection to the child but a social relationship to the child and a relationship with the child's mother. Janet L. Dolgin, *Judicial Assumptions about Parenthood*, 40 U.C.L.A. L. REV. 637, 671 (1993). Protecting a family unit is a critical element of the Court's analysis.

Applying the biology-plus rationale, we do not agree these cases support Anna's maternal claim more than Crispina's. In this case, we have determined that both Anna and Crispina were able to exercise standing to claim their maternity of Christopher. But as we explained, Crispina is Christopher's legal mother because of her preconception intent to be his parent. Crispina's and Mark's actions to undergo IVF and use a gestational surrogate to achieve a pregnancy and child demonstrate more than a "mere biological connection" to Christopher. While we do not wish to endorse the constrained view of family that the *Michael H.* plurality describes, we certainly believe that the series of cases provides greater constitutional protection to a genetic mother with preconception intent to parent and who set in motion the pregnancy and surrogacy rather than to a surrogate.

IV *Enforceability of the Surrogacy Contract*

Surrogacy has supporters and critics. For couples like Mark and Crispina, surrogacy provides a means by which they can have a genetically related baby. Anna argues that the surrogacy contract is unenforceable because it violates her right to parent a child to whom she gave birth. California, unlike other states, has no laws concerning surrogacy. Cf. Surrogate Parentage Act, MI. Gen. Laws 722.851 (making paid surrogacy contracts void and unenforceable and setting forth criminal penalties for all parties to a paid surrogacy contract). Specifically, Anna alleges that surrogacy is unconstitutional; violates public policy; and violates statutes relating to baby selling and adoption. Anna and her counsel cite the New Jersey Supreme Court's *In re Baby M* opinion in support of those arguments. *In re Baby M*, 537 A.2d 1227 (N.J. 1988). Unlike our sister court, we uphold the validity of a surrogacy contract in which the intended parents pay the surrogate for her services.

In *Baby M*, the New Jersey Supreme Court held that a paid surrogacy contract was invalid. Like this case, a married couple, the Sterns, contracted with a surrogate to have a child. Unlike this case, the surrogate was both the genetic and gestational mother. We find the reasoning of the *Baby M* court unpersuasive for several reasons – not just because of the factual difference. The *Baby M* court found the surrogacy contract unenforceable because, in their view, enforcing a paid surrogacy contract is contrary to laws governing adoption, constitutes baby selling [*Baby M.* at 1240], and violates public policy [*Id.* at 1246]. We disagree that surrogacy implicates adoption and baby selling statutes or that it violates the public policy of our state. Surrogacy, in our view, is an extension of procreative privacy, as we discuss below.

Individuals have a broad right of procreative privacy. That privacy includes the ability to use surrogacy to achieve a pregnancy – even if the intended parent pays the surrogate for her services. We recognize that there are significant public policy concerns related to surrogacy that we discuss below; but we do not agree that those concerns require a ban on all paid surrogacy contracts. Moreover, we do not see surrogacy as baby selling and consider the analogy of surrogacy with baby selling to be inapt. Parents do not purchase their own babies. We recognize that the intended parents of a baby born through surrogacy are the child's legal parents at birth; it follows that the parents are not paying for the baby but rather paying the surrogate for her services. The adoption analogy is similarly inapt: adoption is a statutory scheme whereby an adult may adopt a child who had a previous legal parent. Parents do not adopt their own child. Requiring intended parents to adopt their child because the child is born to a surrogate suggests that the intended parents are not actually the child's parents at birth. For the reasons we discussed above, however, we believe that the intended parents are, in fact, the child's parents at birth, and they should be so noted on the child's birth certificate.

IV.A Procreative Privacy Includes Surrogacy

At the most general level, procreative privacy is the freedom either to have children or to avoid having them. Procreative privacy is a protected fundamental right under the United States and California Constitutions. Although most of the Supreme Court's jurisprudence concerning procreative privacy focuses on the right not to get pregnant or stay pregnant, those discussions inherently rely on the importance of the procreative right.

The Supreme Court has explicitly addressed the right to procreate only once, in *Skinner v. Oklahoma*, 316 U.S. 535 (1942). In that case, the Court held unconstitutional a law providing for the involuntary sterilization of a particular class of criminal offenders. *Id.* at 541. In holding that Oklahoma's Habitual Sterilization Act was unconstitutional, the Court wrote that "procreation [is] fundamental to the very existence and survival of the race." *Id.* Although the Court decided the case on equal protection grounds, the Court has incorporated the case into its substantive due process privacy analysis. Left unanswered by *Skinner* and its progeny is the breadth of procreative privacy. Particularly in the context of surrogacy, we must determine whether the intended parents' procreative privacy right extends to the use of a surrogate. Hill, *supra*, at 367–68.

As we wrote at the outset of our opinion, we are persuaded that procreative privacy encompasses the intention to create and raise a child – it is not linked solely to genetic parentage or giving birth to a child. *Id.* at 385. California's Constitution, unlike the U.S. Constitution, explicitly includes a right of "privacy," and we have noted in previous opinions that federal precedent is narrower than California's explicit constitutional protection. *Committee to Defend Reproductive Rights v. Myers*, 625 P.2d 779, 784 (1981) (holding that a California Act that restricted abortion funding for indigent women was unconstitutional under the California Constitution). Professor John Robertson has argued:

> if bearing, begetting, or parenting children is protected as part of marital privacy or privacy, those experiences are no less important when they are achieved noncoitally with the assistance of physicians, donors of gametes and embryos, or even

surrogates … The result is that coitally infertile married couples (and others accorded a right of coital reproduction) should have the same privacy to choose noncoital means of reproduction that they would have to reproduce coitally if they were fertile. JOHN A. ROBERTSON, *Procreative Liberty and the State's Burden of Proof in Regulating Noncoital Reproduction*, in SURROGATE MOTHERHOOD: POLITICS AND PRIVACY, at 26 (Larry Gostin, ed., 1988).

We find Robertson's argument particularly persuasive given California's explicit privacy right.

Procreative privacy of the intended parents does not trump a surrogate's procreative privacy. She should not be forced or coerced into surrogacy, and we consider best practices for an enforceable surrogacy contract below. A surrogate must fully retain her privacy and procreative privacy rights during the entire length of a surrogacy arrangement. A surrogate is choosing to become pregnant for someone else. As such, she is assuming the medical risks of pregnancy. A surrogate may not be required to abort a fetus at the intended parents' request, nor can a surrogate be prevented from having an abortion should she decide to terminate the pregnancy. For instance, a provision in a surrogacy contract that requires a surrogate to abort a fetus if genetic testing reveals a genetic or congenital defect would be invalid. Similarly, a surrogate could not be required to reduce a multifetal pregnancy. *See Roe v. Wade*, 410 U.S. 113 (1973) (confirming a woman's right to abortion in the stage before viability); *Planned Parenthood of Southeastern Pennsylvania v. Casey*, 505 U.S. 833 (1992) (reaffirming *Roe*'s central holding, the right of a woman to have an abortion pre-viability). The Court has held that the right to terminate a pregnancy belongs only to the pregnant woman. See e.g., *Planned Parenthood of Central Missouri v. Danforth*, 428 U.S. 52, 68–76 (1976) (holding unconstitutional statutory provisions that required the written consent of a married woman's husband and the written consent of at least one parent of a minor who seek an abortion).

Ensuring that the surrogate retains her constitutional rights to make decisions that affect her reproductive health is necessary for surrogacy to work. Concerns about surrogate exploitation would be more justified were a surrogate to lose her reproductive autonomy during the process. Although we expansively interpret the intended parents' procreative rights, we would not do so at the expense of the surrogate's procreative rights during the pregnancy.

IV.B Surrogacy Does Not Violate Public Policy

For surrogacy opponents, surrogacy is unnatural: it contravenes the moral order of parenthood. LISA SOWLE CAHILL, *The Ethics of Surrogate Motherhood: Biology, Freedom, and Moral Obligation*, in SURROGATE MOTHERHOOD: POLITICS AND PRIVACY, at 163 (Larry Gostin ed., 1988). "Motherhood" is often idealized and is seen as an essential part of womanhood. Martha L. Fineman, *Images of Mothers in*

Poverty Discourses, 1991 DUKE L.J. 274, 276 (1991). Arguably, a woman who cannot gestate her own child suffers from not meeting the idealized vision of woman and mother and, conversely, a woman who relinquishes a child for money is seen as debasing motherhood.

Critics of paid surrogacy argue that surrogacy exploits vulnerable women. In fact, some critics oppose use of the term "surrogate;" as Professor George Annas puts it, surrogacy is a fairy tale for intended parents who want to have genetic children and using the term "surrogate" falsely suggests that the woman bearing the child is something other than "mother." GEORGE J. ANNAS, *Fairy Tales Surrogate Mothers Tell*, in SURROGATE MOTHERHOOD: POLITICS AND PRIVACY, at 45–46 (Larry Gostin ed., 1988). Annas argues that children must be protected, "from the vicious exploitation that treating them as commodities would bring, exploitation of the poor by the rich, and the demeaning of pregnant women by treating them as breeders indentured to their 'employers'." *Id.* See also, LORI B. ANDREWS, *Surrogate Motherhood: An Ethical Analysis*, in SURROGATE MOTHERHOOD: POLITICS AND PRIVACY, at 170 (Larry Gostin ed., 1988) (detailing that opponents of surrogacy have used terms such as reproductive slavery, reproductive prostitution, incubatory servitude, and womb rental to describe the process).

Professor Ruth Macklin addresses the concern that surrogates will be treated as "baby factories" or wombs for hire. RUTH MACKLIN, *Is There Anything Wrong with Surrogate Motherhood?: An Ethical Analysis*, in SURROGATE MOTHERHOOD: POLITICS AND PRIVACY, 141 (Larry Gostin ed., 1988). As she writes, "[t]he charge of 'exploitation' contradicts the moral stance that women have the ability and the right to control their own bodies." Macklin concludes that if women – properly – have the right to other reproductive freedoms, they should have the right to voluntarily serve as a surrogate. *Id.*[63]

Opponents of surrogacy suggest that women cannot truly provide informed consent to a surrogacy contract because they cannot predict the psychological consequences of relinquishing the child after birth. This argument is often made by suggesting that the hormonal changes that accompany pregnancy make it impossible for her to predict the consequences of allowing the intended parents to take the baby after its birth. Yet, these arguments reify the notion that women are incapable of making informed decisions and knowing their own minds – and could potentially be used to deny women the right to make other decisions. LORI B. ANDREWS, *Surrogate Motherhood: The Challenge for Feminists*, in SURROGATE MOTHERHOOD: POLITICS AND PRIVACY, at 173 (Larry Gostin ed., 1988).

---

[63] We are not so naïve as to believe that all women are equally positioned to "volunteer" their services as a surrogate. We recognize that for poorer women, surrogacy – with all of its inherent risks – may seem a better option to earn money than for women of greater means. As we discuss below, we believe those concerns are mitigated through greater structure to the surrogacy process rather than by prohibiting paid surrogacy.

Surrogacy opponents observe that surrogacy arrangements involve mostly wealthy, white married couples seeking the services of women who have less income and, often, less education.[64] As Robertson observes, the

> notion of gestational surrogates [is offensive] since it views women as wombs to be rented and then discarded for the greater glory of middle- and upper-class couples. While surrogacy frees some women of gestational burdens and thus places them on a reproductive par with men, it transfers the burden to women who cannot resist the offer to bear the children of the rich. John Robertson, *The New Reproduction*, 59 S. Cal. L. Rev. 1028 (1986).

However, separating genetic and gestational motherhood provides a greater range of reproductive choice for individuals who may be unable to reproduce through coital reproduction.

Another concern is that white couples will seek the services of women of color to help them have white babies. Indeed, this case raises concerns of class and race. Anna has fewer financial resources than the Calverts; her need for additional income motivated her decision to offer her services. Moreover, we are mindful that Anna is a single mother and a black woman. The optics of this case – a black, single mother serving as a surrogate for a white man and his Filipina wife – help foster the exploitation narrative. In fact, though, studies of surrogates suggest that surrogates are ordinarily employed, married, and often white and middle-class. *See* Lori B. Andrews, *Alternative Reproduction*, 65 S. Cal. L. Rev. 623, 673–74 (1991). In this case, Anna and Crispina are both nurses and have similar education and vocational training. Crispina and Mark did not solicit Anna to serve as a surrogate; rather, she reached out to Crispina and asked to serve as a surrogate. Anna not only willingly entered into the surrogacy arrangement, she initiated it.

Although most surrogates have a sound educational background, are in stable relationships, and are in middle income brackets, paid surrogacy generates significant criticism. Inherent in this criticism of paid surrogacy, we believe, are two distinct concerns: first, there is a concern that poorer women are being treated as cheap labor and baby machines. Second, there is a concern that is perhaps even more sinister: that poorer women and/or women of color may be paid to perpetuate the breeding of upper middle-class white babies. While infertility affects women of color even more than white women, white couples are more likely to use IVF and surrogacy services. This notion of rich, white couples using poor and/or women of color to have babies is a legitimate concern. Our laws denied generations of black enslaved women the right to nurture and parent their own children so that they

---

[64] "The couples who most often seek out a surrogate motherhood arrangement are white, professional married couples in their thirties. ... The expense to the contracting couple may reach $25,000 or more, a factor that limits this reproductive option to the well-to-do." Andrews, *supra* note 62, at 673.

could do work required of their white owners.[65] We take judicial notice of generations of southern black women who raised white children as nannies and housekeepers, yet still were not allowed to use the same restroom as their young charges nor eat at the same table.[66] As one scholar and researcher has observed, black domestic laborers were seen as "symbolic and surrogate mothers to whites;" in her research, she documented that the women were troubled that "to support their own children, they had to mother other women's children."[67] We understand and credit the fear that paid surrogacy can exploit black women for the benefit of white women who want a child who resembles them. But we view paid surrogacy differently than the underpaid caregiver relationships in which millions of women had little (if any) choice in their work and the law denied them a full range of equal protections. As we discuss below, we approve of paid surrogacy arrangements when surrogates freely and knowingly enter into the arrangement, can meaningfully confer with legal counsel, and are appropriately compensated for their efforts.

Exploitation concerns largely emanate from the payment to the surrogate. Separate from the concern about baby selling is the concern that intended parents exploit the surrogate through their payment. Altruistic surrogacy has not met with as much criticism; a surrogate who serves to help a family member or friend is seen as noble.[68] Conversely, paying a surrogate is seen as exploitative. Commentators raise concerns that only poor women who have few options for gainful employment will serve as surrogates. We cannot pretend that a motivation to earn money may not induce some women to serve as surrogates. But this critique seemingly removes all agency from women who freely and knowingly agree to provide surrogacy services. We are not naïve: we recognize that women who have fewer financial resources will offer surrogacy services more often than women with significant financial means. Although, as we noted above, many surrogates do have middle class incomes. But we are loathe to agree that all women who willingly take on the role of paid surrogate are being commodified and preyed upon. For instance, in this case, Anna initiated the surrogacy arrangement. As we discuss below, we believe that various precautions can be employed to protect the rights of surrogates while also protecting the procreative privacy of intended parents.

---

[65] See Thelma Jennings, "Us Colored Women Had to go through a Plenty": Sexual Exploitation of African-American Slave Women, 1 J. WOMEN'S HIST. 45 (1990).

[66] For a good account of black domestic laborers as surrogate mothers, see Susan Tucker, A Complex Bond: Southern Black Domestic Workers and Their White Employers, 9(3) WOMEN IN THE AMERICAN SOUTH, J. WOMEN'S STUDIES 8–9 (1987).

[67] Id. at 9.

[68] As one scholar notes, however, "unpaid surrogacy may involve greater coercion than paid surrogacy. If payment is banned, the infertile woman is forced to pressure a friend or relative into acting as an unpaid surrogate. The pressure in a relationship – entwined by past guilts, rivalries, and other emotional minefields – may be more coercive than the dynamics of an arms-length commercial surrogacy arrangement with a stranger." Andrews, supra note 62, at 672–73.

IV.C Surrogacy Is Not Baby Selling Or a Form of Adoption

Relying on the New Jersey's Supreme Court's *Baby M* opinion, Anna alleges that the surrogacy contract cannot be enforced because surrogacy amounts to baby selling. Additionally, she argues that laws governing the voluntary termination of parental rights in conjunction with placing a child for adoption allow the mother time after the child's birth to surrender her parental rights and the surrogacy contract does not include such protection. See Civ. Code § 8700.

We begin by addressing Anna's baby selling claim. We disagree with the *Baby M* court that surrogacy is tantamount to baby selling. In holding that the surrogacy contract was unenforceable because it violates NJ statutes prohibiting baby selling, the Court presupposes that the Sterns were not both Baby Melissa's parents. Mr. Stern was Melissa's genetic father but Mary Beth Whitehead was her genetic mother, which differs from our facts. In part because of Whitehead's genetic connection to the baby, the court viewed the surrogacy contract as Whitehead's sale of her own child. We view the issue differently. As we explained earlier, we value the parties' intentions in determining parentage. Applying intentional parenthood theory, the Sterns are Melissa's parents by virtue of their intent to parent her. But for the Sterns actions, Whitehead would not have become pregnant nor given birth to Melissa. Mary Beth Whitehead did not sell her baby to the Sterns; she provided a means by which the Sterns could exercise their procreative privacy right and have a baby of their own. Here, Mark and Crispina used their own gametic material to create an embryo. Crispina was unable to gestate the pregnancy because she had a hysterectomy. So, the couple used the services of a surrogate and paid her to compensate for the work of gestation. Anna would not have become pregnant but for Crispina and Mark's embryo and their desire to have a child of their own. Crispina and Mark did not pay Anna for her baby; they paid her to help them have their own baby.

Further, we do not agree that adoption is the appropriate lens by which to determine parentage of a child born through surrogacy. A parent should not have to adopt her or his own child. An expansive view of procreative privacy includes surrogacy and intended parents should be the legal parents of the child at birth.

Adoption is a formal process to screen potential parents for a child who was born to other parents. The process is lengthy and deliberate because at the point at which the child is voluntarily relinquished for adoption or if the state terminates parental rights of parents, the state has a parens patriae duty to protect the child and her/his best interests. That comparison is inapt in a surrogacy case: a child born through surrogacy exists only because her or his intended parents caused her to be born.

Those who become parents through intercourse need not prove their fitness to parent nor that they will act in the child's best interest; rather, the parent's fitness is presumed, much as the law presumes the parent will act in the child's best interests. If a parent abuses or neglects her child, a court may determine she is unfit and, ultimately, may terminate her parental rights. Arguably, a person who becomes a parent through ART has greater interest in becoming a parent than a young woman in her teens who becomes pregnant through unprotected sex or the boy who gets her pregnant. We do not presume parental unfitness of a teenage mother or father. Regardless of the circumstances, rare is the case that a State implements a parental fitness test for those who become parents through intercourse. We would not impose such a test for individuals who use ART.

Relatedly, we disagree with Justice Kennard that this court should use the best interests of the child to evaluate the claims of Anna and Crispina. As with the baby selling and adoption analogies, an inquiry into the best interests of Christopher presupposes that both women have parental rights. The law presumes that children born to their parents through more traditional means are with parents who foster their best interests. The best interests of the child test is used in custody and visitation disputes as well as involuntary termination of parental rights. But, in this case, only Mark and Crispina are Christopher's parents: Anna is not Christopher's legal parent and has no parental standing.

V Conclusion

We recognize the validity of this gestational surrogacy contract and hold that its provisions should be enforced. Anna initiated the surrogacy arrangement and made repeated statements that she did not consider herself the baby's mother – until the time she felt she was not being adequately compensated nor being given adequate attention by the Calverts. While we think laws governing the validity of surrogacy contracts are more properly the domain of the Legislature, we must render a decision in this case so that all the parties in the case – especially the child – have their rights and relationships settled.

Although we understand that Anna feels wronged by this process, we believe enforcing the surrogacy contract and acknowledging Crispina's maternal rights is the best decision we can make on these facts. As noted, Anna initiated the surrogacy arrangement by telling Crispina that she had been accepted as a surrogate at the Center for Surrogate Parenting, thereby implying she had been vetted by the agency to serve as a surrogate. We think such a screening[69] is prudent to ensure that all parties understand the significant commitment they are undertaking to the other parties. In this case, litigation may have been avoided if the parties had availed themselves of a robust screening process.

[69] This case demonstrates the benefits of screening potential surrogates; had Anna undergone a thorough psychological screening, she may not have been approved to serve as a surrogate or Mark and Crispina might have chosen a different surrogate who did not have a history of miscarriages and stillbirths. We can envision, too, the benefits of psychological screening for the intended parents but believe any requirements related to screening of the parties is the purview of the Legislature.

Although Anna claimed she had been approved as a surrogate, she had not undergone an agency screening. A psychological and medical evaluation would have revealed that Anna had two stillbirths and two miscarriages prior to serving as a surrogate for Crispina and Mark. While she may not have been rejected as a surrogate, she might have been offered counseling or Mark and Crispina might have decided that she was not the best surrogate for them. A psychological and medical evaluation do not infringe on the surrogate's nor intended parents' procreative rights: the process does not deny anyone the ability to participate in the process but ensures much greater communication and the ability for the parties to make a more fully informed decision. While we think screening would be prudent, we do not find the lack of screening fatal to enforcement of the parties' contract. Unfortunately, Anna was untruthful about having been screened and the Calverts did not take steps to ensure that Anna had been screened by the agency. But bad facts should not make bad law.

Anna signed the surrogacy contract prior to the embryo transfer procedure and after consultation with an attorney. We are mindful of Anna's testimony that she felt constricted in her choice of counsel and we are hopeful that the legislature will act to enumerate best practices concerning surrogacy contracts. But we are not persuaded that Anna did not understand the nature of the contract and what surrogacy entailed.[70] In fact, Anna and Crispina had been visiting the fertility specialist and spent two months synchronizing their cycles before the contract was drafted. Anna repeatedly told others that she was carrying the Calverts' baby. She made a point of distinguishing her role from that of MaryBeth Whitehead in the *Baby M* case. She also accepted and cashed all the payments the Calverts made. Only when she was not receiving financial remuneration in an amount and as quickly as she wanted did she say she wanted to keep the baby. Anna's words and conduct belie her alleged ignorance of the process.

We hold that the surrogacy contract between Anna Johnson and the Calverts is enforceable.

III CONCLUSION

ART will continue to be used so that couples and individuals can have children. As we have stated, we believe that California's broad procreative privacy right includes the right to use ART. Greater use of ART, though, will likely lead to more cases in which this Court is asked to resolve parenting questions. We have embraced the doctrine of intentional parenthood in the context of ART and believe it provides a

---

[70] In this case, Anna had already successfully given birth to a daughter, and we believe she had an understanding of the commitment she was making. We offer no opinion whether having given birth previously is necessary for a valid surrogacy contract. We think it more appropriate for the Legislature to provide that guidance.

useful means to determine parentage in such cases. We are hopeful that the Legislature will enact greater guidance concerning paid surrogacy contracts to help families and reduce litigation. We believe paid surrogacy contracts are consistent with California law and public policy.

Regardless of not having had a surrogacy statute to review, California law provided necessary guidance to establish maternity between two women who both had a claim. Even though Anna is Christopher's birth mother, Crispina is his genetic and legal mother. Anna initiated the surrogacy arrangement and deceived Crispina and Mark into believing she had already been screened by the surrogacy center. She repeatedly stated that she was a surrogate with no maternal attachment to Christopher – until she felt that she was not being sufficiently remunerated. While she may have simply changed her mind and truly wished to assert her maternal rights, we believe that the parties' preconception intent must govern in surrogacy disputes – both to protect the intended parents and the surrogate. We hold that the surrogacy contract is enforceable and that Crispina is Christopher's legal mother. Affirmed.

7

Ferguson v. City of Charleston, 532 U.S. 67 (2001)

Commentary by Lisa Crooms-Robinson

The Fourth Amendment recognizes "the right of the people to be secure in their persons ... against unreasonable searches." A reasonable search requires a warrant supported by probable cause, "special needs" unrelated to law enforcement, or consent.[1] These requirements frame the dispute in *Ferguson v. City of Charleston* about the constitutionality of a policy under which healthcare providers reported obstetrical patients who tested positive for cocaine use to law enforcement officials who were empowered to arrest and detain them. The central question raised by the case was whether the Medical University of South Carolina (MUSC), a public hospital in Charleston, subjected its patients to reasonable searches within the meaning of the Fourth Amendment.

THE GENESIS OF POLICY M-7: COCAINE MOTHERS ARE KILLING THEIR BABIES[2]

Early in 1989, Nurse Shirley Brown headed the MUSC team that designed Policy M-7. Under the policy, obstetrical patients who tested positive for cocaine were arrested and charged with child abuse under South Carolina law. Brown and her team had seen their pregnant patients struggle with substance abuse and deliver babies with cocaine in their systems. The news was replete with stories of crack

---

[1] In addition to a warrant, "special needs," and consent, a reasonable search may involve items that are in "plain view," may be conducted incident to an arrest, or may involve exigent circumstances such as concerns about a fleeing suspect or destruction of evidence. This case involves the first three types of searches only.

[2] Barry Siegel, *In the Name of the Children: Get Treatment or Go to Jail*, L.A. TIMES MAGAZINE (Aug. 7, 1994) (quoting Charleston, South Carolina police chief Reuben Greenberg). http://articles.latimes.com/1994-08-07/magazine/tm-24470_1_south-carolina-hospital

babies born to women thought to be too selfish and irresponsible to be mothers.[3] "I have two patients, mother and unborn child," Brown said. "One patient can talk. One can't, and people on drugs don't always make the best decision for themselves. Sometimes you've got to choose between your two patients. We took the stance that you've got to choose for the unborn patient."[4]

In April 1989, Nurse Brown and her team implemented Policy M-7. The policy identified nine criteria, any one of which triggered a drug test.[5] Hospital personnel reported a positive drug test to the police who arrested and detained the women in the interest of protecting their unborn children. Crystal Ferguson, Lori Griffin, Sandra Powell, Ellen Knight, Laverne Singleton, Pamela Pear, Paula Hale, Theresa Joseph, Patricia Williams, and Darlene Nicholson were women whose substance abuse, race, and poverty made it more likely than not they would be tested. Like self-fulfilling prophecies, the positive drug tests combined with pregnancy made the women's medical information the basis for criminal charges.

THE LITIGATION

Crystal, Lori, Sandra, Ellen, Laverne, Pamela, Paula, Theresa, Patricia, and Darlene filed a suit in the United States District Court for the District of South

---

[3] E.g. Sandra Blakeslee, *Crack's Toll among Babies: A Joyless View, Even of Toys*, N.Y. TIMES (Sept. 18, 1989), www.nytimes.com/1989/09/17/us/crack-s-toll-among-babies-a-joyless-view-even-of-toys.html (reporting about a National Institute of Drug Abuse "follow-up stud[y] of babies born to mothers using crack … show[ing] that in early childhood they have serious difficulty relating to their world, making friends, playing like normal children and feeling love for their mothers or primary caretakers").Ira Chasnoff, Dan R. Griffith, & Scott MacGregor, *Temporal Patterns of Cocaine Use in Pregnancy: Perinatal Outcomes*, 261(12) JAMA 1741–44 (1989), https://jamanetwork.com/journals/jama/article-abstract/376771. Much of the concern about the "crack baby epidemic" turned out to be unwarranted. Liz Cox Barrett, *"The Epidemic That Wasn't" (Even If We Said It Was)*, COLUM. JOURNALISM REV. (Jan. 27, 2009), https:// archives.cjr.org/the_kicker/the_epidemic_that_wasnt_even_i.php. Prenatal exposure to cocaine does not appear to cause short- or long-term negative effects for children that are significantly more damaging than prenatal exposure to other drugs (including prescription drugs), nicotine, alcohol, or other substances. E.g. Barbara L. Thompson, Pat Levill, & Gregg D. Stanwood, *Prenatal Exposure to Drugs: Effects on Brain Development and Implications for Policy and Education*, 10(4) NAT. REV. NEUROSC. 303–12 (2009).

[4] Siegel, *supra* note 2 (quoting Nurse Shirley Brown). This choice is consistent with what appears to be a state interest in protecting unborn children. For example, South Carolina law defines a viable fetus as a person, and, in 1995, the South Carolina Supreme Court held that the ingestion of cocaine during the third trimester of pregnancy constitutes criminal child neglect. *Whitner v. State*, 328 S.C. 1 (1997), *cert. denied*, 523 U.S. 1145 (1998). *See also*, *State v. McKnight*, 352 S.C. 635 (2003), *cert. denied*, 540 U.S. 819 (2003) (Regina McKnight delivered a stillborn baby and admitted to using cocaine during her pregnancy. She was subsequently convicted of homicide by child abuse under South Carolina law).

[5] The nine criteria were: (1) "[n]o prenatal care"; (2) "[l]ate prenatal care after 24 weeks gestation"; (3) "[i]ncomplete prenatal care"; (4) "Abruptio placentae"; (5) "[i]ntrauterine fetal death"; (6) "[p]reterm labor 'of no obvious cause'"; (7) "IUGR [intrauterine growth retardation] 'of no obvious cause'"; (8) "[p]reviously known drug or alcohol abuse"; and (9) "[u]nexplained congenital anomalies." *Ferguson v. City of Charleston*, 532 U.S. 67, 71 (2001).

Carolina claiming MUSC's policy violated rights, including their constitutional rights to be free from unreasonable searches and seizures and racial discrimination.[6] They claimed that the "warrantless and non-consensual drug tests conducted for criminal investigatory purposes were unconstitutional searches."[7] In addition, Policy M-7 had a racially discriminatory impact that violated Title VI of the Civil Rights Act of 1964.[8]

The City of Charleston, the public hospital, Nurse Brown, the state solicitor, and the state police claimed Policy M-7 violated no one's constitutional rights for three reasons. First, the women consented to the searches when they signed general consent forms to receive medical care at MUSC's Charleston facility. Second, the searches conducted under Policy M-7 were designed to further public health interests unrelated to law enforcement and, as such, they fell within the Fourth Amendment's "special needs" exception. Therefore, the drug tests required neither consent nor a warrant. Third, the policy's racially disparate impact was incidental rather than intentional. Therefore, it was not evidence of impermissible racial discrimination under Title VI.

Chief Judge C. Weston Houck entered a judgment in favor of MUSC and those charged with implementing the policy based on the jury's conclusion that the ten women consented to medical treatment which included drug testing. Chief Judge Houck disagreed with the defendants' claim that the searches fell within the special needs exception to the Fourth Amendment's warrant requirement "because the searches ... 'were not done by the medical university for independent purposes'."[9] Instead, "there was an agreement reached that the positive screens would be shared with the police."[10] This was enough to turn Policy M-7 into a tool of law enforcement rather than public health.

The women appealed, and the Circuit Court of Appeals for the Fourth Circuit affirmed the District Court judgment. It did so, however, on the grounds District Court Chief Judge Houck rejected. Two of the three Circuit Court judges "held that the searches were reasonable as a matter of law under [the] line of cases recognizing that 'special needs' may, in certain exceptional circumstances, justify a search policy deigned to serve non-law-enforcement ends."[11] The majority was persuaded "that MUSC personnel conducted the urine drug screens for medical

---

[6] The women's claims also included a privacy violation stemming from the disclosure of medical information to law enforcement personnel and state-law tort of abuse of process in administering the policy. The privacy claim was addressed as part of the Fourth Amendment assessment of the reasonableness of the searches under the "special needs" exception. *See infra* discussion of *Chandler v. Miller*, 520 U.S. 305 (1997) and balancing test.

[7] *Ferguson*, 532 U.S. at 73.

[8] 42 U.S.C. §2000d *et seq.* (prohibiting discrimination based on race, color, and national origin in programs and activities receiving federal funds).

[9] *Ferguson*, 532 U.S. at 73.

[10] *Id.* at 73–74.

[11] *Id.* at 74.

purposes wholly independent of an intent to aid law enforcement efforts."[12] The persuasive medical purpose, to avoid the complications and subsequent medical costs that accompanied cocaine use during pregnancy, was sufficiently unrelated to law-enforcement to trigger the lower standard used in special needs cases.[13] This interest also "outweighed" what the Court of Appeals called "a minimal intrusion on the privacy of the patients."[14] Therefore, Policy M-7's drug tests were reasonable searches within the meaning of the Fourth Amendment.

The women appealed to the United States Supreme Court, and the Court granted certiorari to review the question of whether the MUSC drug tests fell within the special needs exception to the Fourth Amendment.[15] The opinion rests on the assumption "that the searches were conducted without the informed consent of the patients."[16]

The Supreme Court, by a 6-3 vote, reversed the Circuit Court's judgment. The Court held that the drug tests were searches within the meaning of the Fourth Amendment. Absent the women's consent, both testing and reporting the test results to law enforcement officers were unreasonable because MUSC failed to articulate a legitimate, non-law-enforcement justification for the policy.

"SPECIAL NEEDS," WARRANTLESS SEARCHES, AND INTERESTS UNRELATED TO LAW ENFORCEMENT

Writing for the majority, Justice Stevens concluded that MUSC's "interest in using the threat of criminal sanctions to deter pregnant women from using cocaine [did not] justify a departure from the general rule that an official nonconsensual search is unconstitutional if not authorized by a valid warrant."[17] Stevens' opinion rejected MUSC's claim that Policy M-7's "ultimate purpose" is to "protect the health of both mother and child . . ."[18] Instead, he determined that no meaningful distinction existed between the policy and regular attempts to curb crime.[19] To Stevens, the record showed "an initial and continuing focus . . . on the arrest and prosecution of drug-abusing mothers . . ."[20] The singular focus on law enforcement is illuminated by the absence of any protocols for "different courses of medical treatment for either mother

---

[12] *Id.* at 75.
[13] *Id.*
[14] *Id.*
[15] *Id.* at 76.
[16] *Id.*
[17] *Ferguson,* 532 U.S. at 70.
[18] *Id.* at 81.
[19] *Id.*
[20] *Id.* at 82 and 84. According to the majority, "the immediate objective of the searches was to generate evidence for law enforcement purposes to achieve what was purportedly "the ultimate goal of the program," that is "to get the women in question into substance abuse treatment and off of drugs." *Id.* at 84.

or infant, aside from treatment for the mother's addiction."[21] The policy's immediate focus on criminal punishment rather than medical treatment proved to be its fatal flaw.

Steven's original opinion and Margo Kaplan's rewrite agree that Policy M-7's mandatory drug tests are "nonconsensual, warrantless, and suspicionless searches" against which the Fourth Amendment protects the women who initiated the suit.[22] Both opinions conclude Policy M-7 is a law enforcement policy masquerading as medical care. Stephens finds the degree of cooperation between MUSC's medical professionals and Charleston's law enforcement enough to make it a law enforcement policy. Kaplan notes that virtually all medical professionals outside of MUSC agree that programs such as Policy M-7 do more harm than good.[23] Rather than improve obstetrical care for a group of women whose pregnancies might be characterized as "high risk," Policy M-7 is a disincentive for those who are among the women most in need of obstetrical care and prenatal support. Nurse Brown and her team apparently failed to appreciate the perversity of the incentive the policy created to avoid rather than to seek out prenatal care. In at least one case, the policy made a high-risk pregnancy riskier by jailing a pregnant woman who was shackled during labor and delivery.[24] Policy M-7 was part of the War on Drugs, which turned the public health epidemic of substance abuse into a criminal crusade.[25]

---

[21] *Id.* at 82. "Tellingly, the document codifying the policy incorporates the police's operational guidelines. It devotes its attention to the chain of custody, the range of possible criminal charges, and the logistics of police notification and arrests." *Id.*

[22] *But see Ferguson*, 532 U.S. at 92 (Scalia, dissenting – concluding that the case did not involve unconsented searches but, if there was no consent, then the Fourth Amendment was not violated because the searches fell within the special needs exception/doctrine).

[23] As one commentator warns, "[h]ealth care professionals who act on behalf of the state rather than for their patients breach the ethical duties of the patient-physician relationship." Kristin Pulatie, *The Legality of Drug-Testing Procedures for Pregnant Women*, 10(1) AMA J. OF ETHICS 41–44 (Jan. 2008).

[24] According to the Center for Reproductive Rights, "[w]ith the hospital's assistance, police arrested women days or even hours after delivery, removing them from their hospital beds in handcuffs and in shackles. Some women were taken to jail while still bleeding from giving birth. Others were arrested and jailed while they were pregnant, even though the prison could not provide prenatal care or drug treatment. When the incarcerated women went into labor, they were returned to the hospital in shackles. One woman was handcuffed to her bed throughout her delivery." Center for Reproductive Rights – *Ferguson v. City of Charleston* (www.reproductiverights.org/case/ferguson-v-city-of-charleston).

[25] In 1988 then Baltimore Mayor Kurt L. Schmoke advocated for a public health approach to crack addiction because he was convinced that criminal options were largely ineffective. *Baltimore Mayor Supports Legalization of Illicit Drugs*, N.Y. TIMES (Sept. 30, 1988). Rep. Charles Rangel (D-NY) dubbed Schmoke "The Most Dangerous Man in America," for advocating for the decriminalization of drugs such as marijuana and cocaine and the need for more effective treatment options. Kurt L. Schmoke, *Guest Editorial: Dark Cloud over Education: A Personal Perspective on the Drug War*, 76(2) J. NEG. ED. 93–102 (Sept. 2007). In 2014, Maryland's Republican Governor, Larry Hogan, advanced the same position championed by Schmoke almost 30 years earlier. This time, however, the racial makeup of those ravaged by the opioid epidemic has made the position much more palatable. *Schmoke's Vindication*, THE BALTIMORE SUN (Apr. 17, 2015).

DISSEMINATING MEDICAL INFORMATION OR TESTING
PREGNANT WOMEN FOR DRUGS WITHOUT
THEIR CONSENT

Both Stevens and Kaplan assess how, if the special needs exception is applied, the Court should balance the women's privacy rights against MUSC's asserted non-law-enforcement objectives. Stephens and Kaplan, however, part company in terms of how they frame the privacy at issue in the case.

For Stephens, "the unauthorized dissemination of test results to third parties"[26] violates the women's privacy interest. He considers privacy in terms of the reasonable expectations of the pregnant women whose medical information is shared with non-medical third parties who have nothing to do with the obstetrical care they receive. Stephens concludes that the women's privacy interests are not outweighed by MUSC's legitimate interests in stemming the tide of crack use among its pregnant patients and improving the birth outcomes for children exposed to cocaine in utero.

Kaplan frames the privacy issue in terms of non-consensual drug testing and finds that the lower court paid insufficient attention to the importance of the privacy interest inherent in diagnostic testing in a medical setting. She focuses on the breach of bodily integrity and autonomy that each woman experiences when healthcare providers at MUSC take their blood, test that blood for illicit drugs, and share that sensitive medical information with law enforcement personnel. The women's rights are violated when they are subjected to nonconsensual medical treatment.[27] She concludes that the state's asserted interests in this case are "comparably weak" as weighed against the women's interests. Kaplan's opinion puts the women, as well as their bodily integrity and consent, squarely at the center of her opinion. This shift foregrounds the perspective of the women being tested. Her opinion clarifies that the *Ferguson* case involves rights at the core of the essential personhood and humanity of pregnant black women and their children in Charleston, South Carolina.

A POSTSCRIPT ON PARTICULARITY: RACE, SEX, AND CLASS
IN SOUTH CAROLINA

The particularity of Charleston, South Carolina as the place in which MUSC pursued its policy further underscores the deeply entrenched narrative about black women's bodies, procreation, and children in South Carolina. The policy's racism is best understood as measured by this narrative. This "particularity of place" is

---

[26] *Ferguson*, 532 U.S. at 78.

[27] *See e.g. In re* A.C., 573 A.2d 1235 (*en banc*) (D.C. Court of Appeals, 1990) (requiring healthcare providers to secure a pregnant woman's consent to medical treatment and clear and convincing evidence of her prior consent if she is no longer capable of expressing her wishes.

different from the particularity the Fourth Amendment requires for warrants. Here, the particularity of Charleston is related to the city's history as a major port in a slaveholding state. According to one report, approximately 40 percent of enslaved Africans brought to the United States passed through Charleston.[28] This human chattel was bought, sold, branded, traded, bred, hired out, worked, raped, whipped, violated, and exploited. The integrity of their bodies and their families was subject to the whims and fortunes of those who the law allowed to own them as property.

After 1808, when Congress ended the legal importation of Africans into the United States for the purposes of enslavement, the continued sustainability of the plantation economy required enslaved Africans be bred – like horses, cows, pigs, and chickens. This increased the real and perceived threat to the bodily integrity and familial liberty of both enslaved Africans and free blacks.[29] Although slave owners controlled enslaved women's bodily integrity, reproduction, and familial choices, this control became more important to the sustainability of the plantation economy and slave labor after 1808. At that time, U.S. slave owners had to rely on reproduction among the extant enslaved population to meet the labor needs of slave owners. Each owner was permitted to determine how to manage the productive and reproductive labor of the black bodies the owners held as property. Some opted to encourage enslaved men and women to marry and within the confines of those marriages procreate. Still others sought to force enslaved women to name who fathered their children to force the women to marry the men. Others treated enslaved men and women as breeders with no familial bonds who merely added to the owners' property holdings.[30]

At the beginning of the decade in which the Thirteenth Amendment abolished slavery, approximately 400,000 or 10 percent of the four million enslaved people in the United States lived in South Carolina. The 1860 census found that 57 percent of those enumerated in Charleston were black, both free and enslaved.[31] Blacks

---

[28] Brian Hicks, *Slavery in Charleston: A Chronicle of Human Bondage in the Holy City*, THE POST & COURIER (Apr. 9, 2011).

[29] Free blacks found themselves in a precarious position. Their blackness carried a presumption of enslavement that could be difficult to rebut. The key to rebutting the presumption was the type of evidence that could be proffered and the extent to which blacks had whites willing to testify to support their claims regarding their free status. Following Denmark Vesey's thwarted uprising, South Carolina became more oppressive and restricted the movement of all blacks and sought either to exclude or to drive free blacks from South Carolina. There were similar efforts in other cities such as Baltimore. See MARTHA S. JONES, BIRTHRIGHT CITIZENS: A HISTORY OF RACE AND RIGHTS IN ANTEBELLUM AMERICA (Cambridge University Press 2018).

[30] *See generally*, Federal Writers' Project: Slave Narrative Project, Volume 14 – South Carolina, Parts 1–4 (1936–1938). www.loc.gov/item/mesn144/.

[31] In 1860, the population of Charleston County, South Carolina was comprised of the following: 29,136 whites, 3,622 free blacks, and 37,290 enslaved blacks. While there were roughly equal numbers of white men and women (14,737 and 14,399, respectively), black women outnumbered black men regardless of their status (17,957 enslaved black men versus 19,333 enslaved black women; 1,455 free black men versus 2,167 free black women). [www2.census.gov]

outnumbered whites. The white minority had to control the black majority and did so by way of both law and practice.[32]

Interest in policing the procreation of black women, generally, and poor black women, particularly, did not end with slavery. The State continued to control and interfere with black women's reproductive choices, bodily integrity, and decisional autonomy. For fifty years, for example, South Carolina had a forced sterilization law on the books. During thirty of those fifty years, "South Carolina forcibly sterilized more than 250 people to prevent them from giving birth to 'unfit' children ..."[33] These sterilizations were largely limited to people institutionalized in schools, hospitals, and prisons. While "females and [B]lack people were sterilized more than any other groups ... nearly all operations between 1945 and the 1960s were performed on [B]lack people."[34]

Sterilization fell into disfavor as birth control became more widely available. Other, less extreme and impermanent options to control births among a population whose procreation had always been a concern of either their owners or the state. Indeed, during the same time period in which the *Ferguson* case arose, changes to public assistance programs allowed states like South Carolina to impose family caps and to pay public assistance recipients to agree to use birth control devices such as Norplant.[35] The state pursued these policies either because of or in spite of the racial makeup of those who would be targeted, tested, and arrested. While none of the *Ferguson* courts found this disparity constituted racial discrimination, Justice Kaplan's rewrite makes discrimination part of the context in which the severity of the privacy violation is best understood. Policy M-7 was South Carolina's most recent attempt to control black women's bodies and reproductive choices. The racist tropes on which the policy relied cast black women as not only undeserving of decisional privacy but also unbelievable as competent decisionmakers. The privacy violation caused by the drug testing, combined with the race, class, and pregnancy of the ten women who challenged the policy, placed this case squarely within the history of women for whom reproduction is a matter of state control and intervention rather than privacy, individual rights, and justice.

---

[32] For example, the status of the children born to enslaved women followed the mother's status rather than the father's status. This special rule applied only to enslaved mothers and their children.

[33] Kathryn Winiarski, *At Least 259 Sterilized under South Carolina's "Purging" Law*, Go Upstate. com (Feb. 25, 2001).

[34] *Id.*

[35] According to the South Carolina Department of Social Services, "[a] family cap child born ... 10 or months after the family begins to receive ... cash benefits ... will not result in an increase in the ... cash benefit" to which the otherwise eligible family is entitled. South Carolina Department of Social Services, Family Independence Policy Manual. Vol 041-093015 (effective 10/01/15).

Ferguson v. City of Charleston 532 U.S. 67 (2001)

Justice Margo Kaplan delivered the opinion of the Court

I

In April 1989, staff members of the Medical University of South Carolina (MUSC), a public hospital in Charleston, began ordering drug screens on urine samples of pregnant patients suspected of using cocaine. MUSC staff referred patients who tested positive to the county substance abuse commission for counseling and treatment. Screening and referrals did not appear successful, however, in reducing the incidence of positive tests among MUSC patients.

The following autumn, a task force consisting of MUSC nurse Shirley Brown, the Ninth Circuit Solicitor (chief prosecuting attorney), the Chief of the Charleston County Police Department (CCPD), and physicians from various departments involved in prenatal care at MUSC created a policy requiring the hospital to test pregnant women suspected of cocaine use and report the test results to law enforcement officials under certain circumstances. The policy required the hospital to test a MUSC maternity patient's urine if any of the following chosen indicia of cocaine use were present: (1) separation of the placenta from the uterine wall; (2) intrauterine fetal death; (3) no prenatal care; (4) late prenatal care (beginning after 24 weeks); (5) incomplete prenatal care (fewer than five visits); (6) preterm labor without an obvious cause; (7) a history of cocaine use; (8) unexplained birth defects; or (9) intrauterine growth retardation without an obvious cause.

Positive tests resulted in arrest or the threat thereof. Initially, the policy called for the hospital to report a positive test result to the CCPD, which would arrest the patient for distribution of cocaine to a minor. The hospital soon amended this policy such that a patient who tested positive was given a choice between arrest and drug treatment. The threat of arrest "provid[ed] the necessary 'leverage' to make the [p]olicy effective" – that is, to induce women to enter treatment and remain there. Brief for Respondents 8. The hospital did not provide the CCPD the test results of a patient who chose drug treatment. If, however, the patient tested positive for cocaine a second time or failed to comply with treatment obligations, the hospital would notify the CCPD, which would arrest the patient.

MUSC tested Petitioners for cocaine use when they were obstetrical patients, and the CCPD arrested Petitioners when their tests yielded positive results. The CCPD arrested four of the Petitioners during the initial phase of the policy; MUSC therefore offered them no opportunity for treatment in lieu of arrest. The remaining six either failed to comply with the terms of the treatment program or tested positive for a second time.

The stories of the petitioners and their relationship with MUSC vary – most sought prenatal care, while at least one sought care for unrelated reasons or arrived at MUSC while in labor. Despite these differences, all Petitioners, save two, are African American women; Ms. Joseph, who is now deceased, was multi-racial (although her CCPD report described her as "black") and Ms. Nicholson is white. *See Ferguson*, 186 F.3d, 485 & n.3.

Lori Griffin sought prenatal care at MUSC, which tested her urine for cocaine. She denied that MUSC informed her, however, that her urine tested positive. She sought care again for premature labor, and MUSC again tested her urine for cocaine, with positive results. The CCPD arrested her just as she was released from the hospital. Griffin was incarcerated for three weeks, until she returned to MUSC, still shackled, for the duration of her labor and delivery. *See Ferguson v. City of Charleston*, 186 F.3d 469, 485 (1999) (Blake, J., dissenting); Dorothy Roberts, *Unshackling Black Motherhood*, 95 MICH. L. REV. 938, 943 (1997).

Sandra Powell initially sought prenatal care from a different physician but began seeking care at MUSC due to high blood pressure. She regularly attended prenatal care until Hurricane Hugo struck the area in September. When she went into labor in October, her urine and her infant's urine were tested for cocaine and she was arrested the next day because of her positive test result. *See Ferguson*, 186 F.3d at 485 (Blake, J., dissenting).

Ellen Knight received prenatal care and underwent labor and delivery at MUSC. She was arrested not based on her own urine test but because of the positive test result of her infant after delivery. *See id.*

Laverne Singleton delivered a child in the ambulance en route to MUSC. MUSC tested her urine only after delivery, when she arrived at the hospital, and she was subsequently arrested. *Id.*

Pamela Pear came to MUSC because of concerns about her risk for preterm labor. MUSC tested her for cocaine during her visit and, when she tested positive, referred her to counseling. When she came to the hospital the next month in preterm labor, she again tested positive for cocaine. The CCPD arrested her as soon as she was discharged. *See id.*

Paula Hale tested positive for cocaine when she arrived at MUSC in labor. She was referred to substance abuse counseling and was arrested a few months later for failure to comply with her treatment program. *See id.*

Crystal Ferguson tested positive for cocaine during a prenatal visit to MUSC and agreed to attend substance abuse counseling. Ferguson requested an outpatient referral because she had two sons. *See* Barry Siegel, *In the Name of the Children: Get Treatment or Go to Jail, One South Carolina Hospital Tells Drug-Abusing Pregnant Woman*, L.A. TIMES (Aug. 7, 1994), Magazine, at 14. Nurse Brown denied her request and ordered her to enter a two-week residential drug rehabilitation program. The residential program could not provide child care, and Ferguson could not find child care for her children for two weeks. Ferguson recalled "I saw the situation my kids were in. There was no one to take care of them. Someone had stolen our food stamps and my unemployment check while I was in the hospital.

There was no way I was going to leave my children for two weeks, knowing the environment they were in." *See id*. When she tested positive upon the delivery of her child, she was arrested for failing to comply with the drug treatment program. *Ferguson*, 186 F.3d at 485 (Blake, J., dissenting).

Theresa Joseph did not seek pregnancy related care; she went to MUSC for an unrelated medical matter but her urine was nonetheless tested for cocaine, which tested positive, and she was referred to the obstetrical clinic. *See id*. She returned for the same non-pregnancy-related matter; MUSC tested her urine again, which tested positive, and referred her to substance abuse counseling. She came into MUSC once more, MUSC tested her again, and she tested positive. When she arrived in labor and tested positive for cocaine, she was arrested at the hospital. *See id*.

Patricia Williams sought prenatal care from MUSC several times. The first time MUSC tested her urine, she tested positive for cocaine. MUSC referred her to a drug treatment program. Williams returned for prenatal care three subsequent times; MUSC tested her urine each time, with positive results. When she arrived in labor and delivered her child, MUSC tested her urine again and law enforcement arrested her at the hospital. *See id*.

Darlene Nicholson was also a regular prenatal patient at MUSC. When her urine tested positive for cocaine at a prenatal visit, MUSC staff informed her that she must voluntarily admit herself to the MUSC psychiatric unit for substance abuse treatment or face arrest. She was admitted to the psychiatric unit and remained there for thirty days. *See id*.

Petitioners brought this action claiming infringement of their constitutional right to privacy, violation of their Fourth Amendment right to be free of unreasonable searches and seizures, disparate impact discrimination because of race, and commission of the state law-tort of abuse of process. Respondents include MUSC, the City of Charleston, and law enforcement officials who helped develop and enforce the policy.

The district court granted judgment as a matter of law to Respondents on the claims of commission of abuse of process and violation of right to privacy. The jury found in favor of the Respondents on the Fourth Amendment claim. The district court ruled in favor of the Respondents on the Title VI claim of disparate impact discrimination at a post-trial hearing. The Court of Appeals for the Fourth Circuit affirmed.

With regard to the right to privacy, the Court of Appeals considered whether the disclosure of the patients' medical information to law enforcement violated their constitutional right to privacy and concluded that even if such a privacy right protected medical records, the state's compelling interest in identifying law breakers and deterring future misconduct outweighed the privacy right. *See Ferguson v. City of Charleston*, 186 F.3d 469, 483 (1999). The court held that the Petitioners' Fourth Amendment rights were similarly not infringed. Using a line of cases recognizing that non-law enforcement ends may justify searches in circumstances where there are "special needs," the Court of Appeals applied the balancing test set forth in *Chandler v. Miller*, 520 U.S. 305 (1997) and similar cases to determine whether the search was reasonable. It concluded that the interest in improving birth outcomes and maternal health and reducing medical costs associated with maternal cocaine use outweighed what the Court of Appeals considered a "minimal" intrusion on the Petitioners. *Ferguson*, 186 F.3d at 479.

Petitioners also appealed the jury's finding that Petitioners had consented to the diagnostic testing that constituted the search. *See id.* at 476. The Court of Appeals did not reach this issue. *See id.*

We granted certiorari, 528 U.S. 1187 (2000), to consider whether the search was reasonable under the special needs line of cases. We also consider the Petitioners' argument that the Respondents violated their right to privacy. Rather than focus on the disclosure of their medical information, however, we examine the act of medical treatment without patient consent. We reverse judgment on both issues and remand the case for a decision on the consent issue and for further proceedings consistent with this decision.

II

As a state hospital, MUSC and its employees are governmental actors and subject to the constraints of the Fourth Amendment. *See New Jersey v. T.L.O.* 469 U.S. 325, 335–37 (1985). The Fourth Amendment protects "[t]he right of the people to be secure in their persons . . . against unreasonable searches and seizures." U.S. Const. amend. IV. Searches ordinarily require a warrant in order to be reasonable; exceptions to this requirement are narrowly defined. *See Schneckloth v. Bustamonte*, 412 U.S. 218, 219 (1973); *Coolidge v. New Hampshire*, 403 U.S. 443, 454–55 (1971).

As the Court of Appeals noted, when "special needs" are alleged other than crime detection, state actors can conduct searches without a warrant or probable cause. We have established a line of cases determining whether drug tests fall within a limited category of permissible suspicionless searches. *See Chandler v. Miller*, 520 U.S. 305, 309 (1997). These cases balance the individual's interest in privacy against the state's interests in the given circumstances. *Id.* at 314. This context-specific inquiry examines the legitimacy of the government interest, how effective the intrusion is likely to be in furthering the interest, and the significance of the intrusion, both subjectively and objectively. *See Michigan Dep't of State Police v. Sitz*, 496 U.S. 444, 451-55 (1990).

Using this inquiry, we allowed drug testing of high school students participating in interscholastic sports, railway employees involved in train accidents, and government employees seeking sensitive employment positions. *Vernonia School Dist. 47J v. Acton*, 515 U.S. 646 (1995); *Skinner v. Railways Labor Executives' Assn.*, 489 U.S. 602 (1989); *Nat'l Treasury Employees Union v. Von Raab*, 489 U.S. 656 (1989). We struck down drug testing for designated state offices. *Chandler*, 520 U.S. at 305.

We are unconvinced that this case falls within the "special needs" category as distinct from ordinary law enforcement searches. A representative from MUSC initially contacted the chief prosecuting attorney after hearing a news broadcast about the arrest of pregnant women for cocaine use on the theory that such use harmed the fetus and was therefore child abuse. The task force initially formed to facilitate the arrest of pregnant women for cocaine use and then to coerce patients into substance abuse treatment using law enforcement and the threat of arrest. Law enforcement is essential to its core goals and functions. We agree with Judge Blake when she wrote in her dissent that the record reflects that "an initial and continuing focus of the policy was on the arrest and prosecution of drug-abusing mothers." *Ferguson v. City of Charleston*, 186 F.3d 469, 484 (1999) (Blake, J., dissenting).

That the Respondents' special need is truly health-based is a dubious claim at best. Respondents showed little evidence that the program furthered the health interests of the patient, prevented pregnancy complications, or led to better child health outcomes. Other than describing substance abuse treatment, the policy makes no mention of any change in prenatal care, nor does it prescribe any special treatment for newborns. The task force performed little research to ensure that the policy used evidence-based strategies to improve health outcomes. On the contrary, the one prominent health expert the task force consulted disagreed with the policy's strategy. *See* Brief for the Am. Pub. Health Ass'n *et al.* as Amici Curiae Supporting Petitioners at 15. In addition, MUSC's resident bioethicist's review of the policy later concluded that "no evidence suggests that this particular policy promoted healthy pregnancies or reduced costs ..." Mary Faith Marshall, Philip H. Jos, & Martin Perlmutter, *Letters to the Editor*, 23 J. OF LAW, MED. & ETHICS 299–300 (1995); *see also* Brief for the Am. Pub. Health Ass'n *et al.*, *supra*, at 16–25.

Women who decline treatment or test positive twice are sent to prison, and the policy seems to give little consideration as to what this means for their prenatal and labor and delivery outcomes; there is certainly no evidence that this benefits their health outcomes. The American Academy of Pediatrics has found that punitive measures such as prosecution and incarceration have no proven benefits for infant health. *See* Am. Academy of Pediatrics, Committee on Substance Abuse, *Drug-Exposed Infants*, 86 PEDIATRICS 639, 641 (1990). Petitioner Lori Griffin, for example, was jailed during her pregnancy, transported weekly to the hospital in handcuffs and leg shackles for prenatal care, and shackled during labor, actions that are difficult to reconcile with advancing prenatal health and infant health outcomes. Dorothy Roberts, *Unshackling Black Motherhood*, 95 MICH. L. REV. 938, 943 (1997). Women who give birth in prison are unlikely to be able to raise their newborns and may even lose custody of their children; the policy does not seem to consider how this will affect the health of the woman and child.

The task force also failed to consider the ample research on what creates success-ful rehabilitation programs for this population and did not consider the evidence that distinctive treatment approaches are often necessary. Brief for the Am. Pub.

Health Ass'n et al., at 12–16. Three decades of research of drug-dependent pregnant women has demonstrated that not only must treatment consider the distinct concerns of every drug dependent individual but that drug dependent pregnant women raise unique concerns that must be considered. *See id.* Everyone's addiction may be dependent on more than one substance, and many have medical conditions that must be treated alongside their drug dependency, such as trauma, depression, or HIV. *See id.* In many cases, treating substance abuse is far more likely to be successful if programs address nonmedical issues that contribute to the abuse, such as lack of adequate education, job skills, employment opportunities, familial support, public assistance, and shelter. Drug dependent pregnant women face unique treatment obstacles because they are more likely to be the victims of sexual abuse and to have child care responsibilities that cannot simply be dropped to enter a program; outpatient programs rarely have child care, and residential programs rarely accept children. *See id*; Dorothy Roberts, *Punishing Drug Addicts Who Have Babies: Women of Color, Equality, and the Right of Privacy*, 104 HARV. L. REV. 1419, 1449 (1991).[36] Studies have shown that treatment outcomes improve substantially when treatment programs consider patients' needs for transportation to appointments, job training, primary medical care, education, child care, and medical care for infants and children. *See* Brief for the Am. Pub. Health Ass'n et al., at 16–25.

Rather than creating a program that bridged pregnant women to such treatment and increased prenatal health care, the task force formulated a policy that further deterred them from it. A drug dependent pregnant woman has less incentive to use a hospital's resources when she knows she might be forced into a treatment program that will not meet her needs or face prosecution. MUSC's resident bioethicist noted that the policy "alienated" the patient population of pregnant substance using women rather than promoting their health outcomes. Marshall *et al.*, *supra*; *see also* Brief for the Am. Pub. Health Ass'n et al., at 16–25. Moreover, prosecution of drug dependent pregnant women in general deters them from using health and counseling services for fear that they will be reported to government authorities and charged with a crime. *See* Roberts, *Punishing Drug Addicts Who Have Babies*, at 1422.

Respondents' policy pursues law enforcement goals to the detriment of the very health interests the state uses to justify the search. It therefore cannot fall within our "special needs" line of cases.

Even if we are to apply the balancing test to these facts, we are underwhelmed by the state's argument that governmental interests outweigh the infringement on the patients' privacy interests. The Court of Appeals underestimated the privacy interests involved in the diagnostic testing when it dismissed these interests as minimal. Although not invasive, the taking of bodily fluids and testing them for sensitive

---

[36] Yet this may be a moot point, as it may even be difficult for pregnant women to find drug treatment centers that will accept them, as many consider a pregnant woman too high a risk. *See* Roberts, *supra*, at 1447.

medical information involves a breach of a patient's bodily integrity and autonomy. It deprives a patient of the ability to make intimate decisions in the medical setting – a circumstance in which one is perhaps most vulnerable and in which autonomy is decidedly vital.

The state's purported interests here are comparably weak. While there is certainly an important state interest in protecting public health, there is little evidence that the state's policy furthers that interest. On the contrary, the policy contradicts the advice of leading public health authorities such as the American Medical Association, the American Public Health Association, the American Academy of Pediatrics, and the Institute of Medicine. These and other public health authorities caution against punitive measures against substance using pregnant women, warning that these women will likely avoid prenatal care if they fear that it could lead to arrest. *See* Brief for the Am. Pub. Health Ass'n et al., at 16–25; Board of Trustees Report, *Legal Interventions during Pregnancy*, 264 JAMA 2663, 2667 (1990) (cautioning that pregnant women who use illegal drugs will avoid seeking care if it could result in a jail sentence); Am. Pub. Health Ass'n, Policy Statement No. 9020, *Illicit Drug Use by Pregnant Women* (reprinted in 81(2) *Am. J. Pub. Health* 253 (1991)) (recommending against punitive measures against drug-abusing pregnant women); Am. Soc'y of Pediatrics Committee on Substance Abuse, *supra*, at 642 (advocating for "non-punitive access" to prenatal care); INSTITUTE OF MEDICINE, PRENATAL CARE: REACHING MOTHERS, REACHING INFANTS, at 79 (Sarah S. Brown, ed., 1988) (pregnant women who abuse drugs may avoid seeking medical care because they fear that, if their drug use is discovered, they will be arrested and their other children will be taken into custody); *see also* Am. Nurses Ass'n Task Force on Drugs and Alcohol Abuse/Addictions Position Statement (Apr. 5, 1991) ("The threat of criminal prosecution is counterproductive in that it prevents many women from seeking prenatal care and treatment for their alcohol and other drug problems."); Marilyn L. Poland, Mitchell P. Dombrowski, Joel W. Ager, & Robert J. Sokol, *Punishing Pregnant Drug Users: Enhancing the Flight from Care*, 31 DRUG AND ALCOHOL DEPENDENCE 199 (1993); CTR. FOR HEALTH POL'Y RES., GEORGE WASHINGTON UNIV., AN ANALYSIS OF RESOURCES TO AID DRUG-EXPOSED INFANTS AND THEIR FAMILIES, at 78 (1993); *see also* CTR. FOR REPRODUCTIVE RIGHTS, PUNISHING WOMEN FOR THEIR BEHAVIOR DURING PREGNANCY at 6, 8–10 (2000). Given that the Respondents' policy identified lack of prenatal care as more common among pregnant women who use cocaine, driving this population further from health care is counterintuitive. Moreover, as discussed above, there is little evidence that the policy is effective in achieving its goal of improving the health outcomes for those who test positive and must choose between incarceration or treatment.

We also note with deep concern the disproportionate impact this policy has on African American women. It was implemented only at MUSC, a hospital that serves a disproportionate African American population (70%) compared to

Charleston's African American population (30%) – no other public or private hospitals in the area employed such a program. Brief for Ctr. For Const. Rights, as Amicus Curiae Supporting Plaintiffs-Appellants, *Ferguson v. Charleston*, 186 F.3d 469 (1999) (No. 97-2512), 1998 WL 34309576 at 14–15. Its criteria for identifying indicia of cocaine use also focused on lack of prenatal care, which correlates with race and income. *See* Roberts, *Unshackling Black Motherhood*, at 947. MUSC reported only African American women to the authorities. *See id.*, at 943.

Of all illicit drug use, MUSC's targeted only cocaine dependency, though scientific research does not support cocaine use as a significant risk to fetal health, particularly when compared to health issues such as lack of prenatal care, tobacco, and alcohol use. Brief for Ctr. For Const. Rights, at 16–21. Data on the extent and severity of the effects of maternal cocaine use are controversial because of the multiple variables that cloud the outcome, such as the pregnant woman's use of additional drugs, cigarettes, alcohol, and her socioeconomic status. *See* Roberts, *Punishing Drug Addicts Who Have Babies*, at 1429–30. The policy's focus on cocaine use augments its disproportionate effect on African American women because the cheapest and most accessible form of cocaine tends of be concentrated in urban and African American communities. Brief for Ctr. For Const. Rights, at 16.

Given that the policy disproportionately affects African American women, it would be thoroughly commendable if it improved health outcomes for this population. The African American community has a far higher infant death rate than the white community, particularly when class is factored in. *See* Roberts , *Punishing Drug Addicts Who Have Babies*, at 1446.[37] The primary reason for this discrepancy is a difference in prenatal care. *Id.* This is not to say that poor African American women simply neglect to receive prenatal care; rather, the disparity is the result of substantial barriers to care, such as financial barriers, institutional barriers, cultural barriers, and lack of social support. *Id.* at 1446–47 & n.144. As a result, poor African American women receive vastly inadequate prenatal care compared to white women, and the care they do receive is often later in their pregnancy than white women. *Id.* at 1446–47; Brief for Ctr. For Const. Rights, at 13. Similarly, pregnant drug dependent women often receive little or no prenatal care and may be malnourished. *Id.* at 1430.

A policy truly focused on patient health would focus on patient needs and use methods that public health experts support as effective. Such a program might provide evidence-based support services to help patients achieve and maintain sobriety and address other causes of prenatal and pregnancy-related health problems among this at-risk group. It might realize and address Dorothy Roberts's concerns

---

[37] In 1987, the black infant mortality rate was twice that of white children. *Id.* at 1446. In New York City, infant mortality rates in poor African American communities of Central Harlem were three times that of upper- and middle-income areas in the city. *See* Roberts, *Punishing Drug Addicts Who Have Babies*, at 1446.

that "When a society has always closed its eyes to the inadequacy of prenatal care available to poor Black women, its expression of interest in the health of unborn Black children must be viewed with suspicion." *Id.* at 1446.

It is therefore even more profoundly troubling that the Respondents' policy instead focuses on using coercive and punitive measures to pursue law enforcement goals. Such coercive and punitive measures fall disproportionately on African American pregnant women, further alienating them from receiving appropriate prenatal care. It also disproportionately requires this population to shoulder a coercive and punitive burden. This disparate effect is deeply disturbing and undermines any argument that the policy serves legitimate public health and criminal justice goals.

III

The case before us also concerns a state actor's power to compel medical treatment without a patient's informed consent.[38] We hold that our decision in *Cruzan* inadequately captured the constitutional dimension of informed consent. Individuals have a fundamental right to informed consent and to refuse medical treatment grounded in the right to privacy. We also hold that pregnancy cannot be a factor in determining when the state can override an individual's right to refuse medical treatment; to do so would violate the equal protection clause by providing women a weaker standard of protection, one already visible in many state laws.

III.I

Most cases concerning the right to refuse medical treatment have arisen in the context of state common law, where the right to refuse medical treatment is well settled. *See Cruzan v. Director, Missouri Department of Health*, 497 U.S. 261, 271 (1990).[39] Under common law, the right to refuse medical treatment is the logical corollary of informed consent – one cannot exercise true consent without the opportunity to withhold it. *See id.* at 270. Courts often balance this right against four countervailing state interests: (1) the prevention of suicide; (2) the preservation of life; (3) the protection of third parties; and (4) the preservation of the ethical integrity of the medical profession. *See id.* at 271; *see also* Susan Goldberg, *Medical*

---

[38] While there is no one accepted definition of "medical treatment," we are satisfied that the actions taken by MUSC constitute medical treatment. MUSC's health care providers required patients to provide urine samples in a health care setting for diagnostic purposes. *See* Ferguson, 184 F.3d at 474. They chose patients based on what they maintain were diagnostic criteria – in particular pregnancy and pregnancy-related conditions such as separation of the placenta from the interuterine wall. *See id.* They then tested these samples for the presence or absence of chemicals that they were concerned could contribute to pregnancy-related complications. *See id.*

[39] Prior to *Cruzan*, several courts also referenced constitutional law. *See Cruzan*, 497 U.S. at 278.

Choices during Pregnancy: Whose Decision Is It Anyway?, 41 RUTGERS L. REV. 591, 597 (1989).

Just a decade ago, we considered the constitutional dimension of this common law right in *Cruzan*. The case raised the question of whether there was a constitutional right to refuse medical treatment and concomitant "right to die." We declined to resolve this issue, maintaining that "in deciding a question of such magnitude and importance it is the better part of wisdom not to attempt, by any general statement, to cover every possible phase of the subject." *Cruzan*, 497 U.S. at 277–78 (*quoting Twin City Bank v. Nebeker*, 167 U.S. 196, 202 (1897)). *Cruzan* therefore recognized only a "constitutionally protected liberty interest" in the right to refuse unwanted medical treatment. *Cruzan*, 497 U.S. at 278.

The constitution, however, affords far more robust protections to informed consent. For the right to privacy to be meaningful, it must include the right to be free from unwanted and unwarranted bodily intrusions by the government, including medical treatment performed without informed consent. It seems uncontroversial that such a right could exist without protecting an individual from compelled tissue donation or surgery. *See, e.g., McFall v. Shimp*, 10 Pa. D. & C. 3d 90 (1978) (refusing to require the defendant to donate life-saving bone marrow to the plaintiff, his cousin, even though the plaintiff's prognosis for survival was "otherwise very dim"); *In re AC*, 573 A.2d 1235 (1990) (trial court erred in forcing a pregnant woman to undergo a cesarean surgery). Justice O'Connor's concurrence in *Cruzan* detailed the intrusiveness of nasogastric feeding, which often requires patients to be physically restrained, and declared that "[r]equiring a competent adult to endure such procedures against her will burdens the patient's liberty, dignity, and freedom to determine the course of her own treatment." *Cruzan*, 497 U.S. at 288-89 (Justice O'Connor concurring) (quoting MAJOR, *The Medical Procedures for Providing Food and Water: Indications and Effects*, in BY NO EXTRAORDINARY MEANS: THE CHOICE TO FORGO LIFE-SUSTAINING FOOD AND WATER at 25 (J. Lynn ed., 1986)). Such intrusions are abhorrent to the right to bodily integrity intrinsic to the right to privacy.

A violation of the right to privacy's protection of informed consent, however, requires no threshold of invasiveness. Overriding informed consent and the right to refuse medical treatment involves both an intrusion on bodily integrity as well as an individual's ability to make intimate choices concerning her body. As with the decision of whether to bear or beget a child, the decision of whether to undergo medical testing or treatment is profoundly personal by nature. It may involve the decision to expose one's body to testing that can yield distressing or sensitive results; to provide one's bodily fluids or tissues to strangers; to submit to painful or debilitating treatment. The state's infringement on an individual's ability to reject medical treatment encroaches on her fundamental autonomy, regardless of the invasiveness of the procedure.

We therefore hold that the right to informed consent and the corresponding right to refuse medical treatment are encompassed within the right to privacy and that infringements on this right are subject to strict scrutiny.

Our holding does not create an insurmountable burden for state action. Nor do we intend to overrule existing case law securing the state's police power to protect the public health in *Jacobson v. Massachusetts*. It seems uncontroversial to us that, in rare circumstances, such police power must be used to override the right to refuse medical treatment to secure public health, a compelling state interest. In such circumstances, a narrowly tailored state action would survive strict scrutiny.

Our holding that individuals have a right to refuse medical treatment similarly does not overrule our previous holdings concerning whether compelled medical treatment constitutes an unlawful search and seizure in violation of the Fourth Amendment. *See, e.g., Skinner v. Railway Labor Executives Association*, 489 U.S. 602 (1989); *Winston v. Lee*, 470 U.S. 753 (1985); *Schmerber v. California*, 384 U.S. 757 (1966). We do hold, however, that the right to privacy creates a separate, high burden that the state must overcome if it seeks to compel medical treatment in order to gather evidence. The Fourth Amendment protects only against unreasonable searches and seizures, and we have approved even warrantless compelled medical treatment for the purposes of gathering evidence, depending on the invasiveness and risk of the procedure and the necessity of the compelled treatment in fairly determining the guilt or innocence of a party. *See, e.g., Schmerber*, 384 U.S. at 766–72. Our holding today – which requires strict scrutiny for infringements on the right to refuse medical treatment – sets forth a higher burden than these cases.

We are unconvinced, however, that this poses an unreasonable burden on the state. It is well-settled, for example, that the state has a compelling interest in protecting the public against criminal activity and fairly establishing guilt or innocence. *See Winston*, 470 U.S. at 762; *Schall v. Martin*, 467 U.S. 253, 264 (1984) ("The 'legitimate and compelling state interest' in protecting the community from crime cannot be doubted").

In such cases, the state will face a higher burden in that it must now prove that the compelled treatment was necessary and narrowly tailored to achieve its goal. When the state seeks to infringe the medical autonomy and invade the bodily integrity of its people, this burden is a reasonable one. The right to privacy prohibits, for example, the state from compelling treatment where the individual at issue would be willing to consent to a different treatment that would serve the state's interests, compelling medical treatment would violate her right to privacy. Compare *Schmerber*, 384 U.S. at 771 (declining to determine whether the Fourth Amendment would have required the state to grant the defendant's request for a breathalyzer test instead of a blood test, as the defendant refused both tests).

III.II

It is insufficient to recognize the right to informed consent and to refuse medical treatment without specifically protecting pregnant women's right to exercise them. As the facts of this case demonstrate, pregnancy often prompts unique levels of intervention in treatment decisions (welcome or not) by health care workers, law enforcement, and policymakers. The policy formulated by the task force and implemented by MUSC specifically targeted pregnant women because of concerns about the effects of cocaine use on the fetus. *Ferguson*, 186, F.3d at 474. We therefore turn to the question of what weight, if any, pregnancy should be given in determining whether the state can override a woman's right to informed consent and to refuse medical treatment.

Under common law, courts considering the compelled medical treatment of pregnant women have weighed the woman's right to refuse treatment against the state's countervailing interest in protecting fetal life. This interest does not fall neatly into any of the four more established common law categories of countervailing state interests – it might be viewed as protection of life, protection of third parties, some combination of the two, or perhaps a separate, fifth category. Courts have also shown a justifiable reluctance – at least in reported cases – to order treatment that would be jeopardous to the pregnant woman yet benefit the fetus. *See, e.g., Jefferson v. Griffin Spalding County Hospital*, 274 S.E. 457 (Ga. 1981) (per curiam) (cesarean surgery ordered that improved chances of survival for pregnant woman); *In re Jamaica Hospital*, 491 N.Y.S. 2d 898, 899 (1985) (blood transfusion ordered that would save the life of both the pregnant woman and the fetus); *Raleigh Fitkin-Paul Morgan Memorial Hospital v. Anderson*, 201 A.2d 537 (N.J. 1964) (per curiam) (ordering a blood transfusion "to preserve the lives" of the pregnant woman and the child); *Taft v. Taft*, 446 N.E. 2d 395 (Mass. 1983) (reversing family court order that pregnant woman submit to an operation intended to increase the chances that she would carry the pregnancy term).

We could not – and do not – predict the protection that the common law right to refuse medical treatment would give the petitioners. We only note that their cases would be analyzed quite differently than if they were not pregnant. The weight of the state's interest in protecting the fetus would be balanced against their own interest in determining their course of medical treatment and their bodily integrity.

We reject the common law approach and hold that a woman's pregnancy – and any purported state interest in the fetus she carries – may not limit or in any way affect her right to informed consent or to refuse medical treatment.

We first distinguish our declaration in *Casey* and its progeny that the state has an interest in fetal life that becomes even stronger at the point of viability. *Planned Parenthood of Southeastern Pa. v. Casey*, 505 U.S. 833, 869–79 (1992); *Voinovich v. Women's Medical Professional Corp.*, 523 U.S. 1036 (1998). Without reconsidering the validity of this rule considering our holding today, we note that they were limited to the question of when and how a state could regulate a woman's ability to terminate a pregnancy. Our holding today is limited to the issue of when the state may deprive a pregnant woman of informed consent and compel unwanted treatment upon her.

While many may argue that a pregnant woman has a moral duty to make sacrifices for the benefit of the fetus, we do not impose every moral duty as a legal duty. We reject the notion that the state can compel medical treatment of pregnant women because it has an interest in fetal life that is equal to its interest in the life of a born individual. Even if such an interest were to exist, however, this would not justify depriving women of their right to informed consent and the right to refuse medical treatment. We do not force individuals – even parents – to undergo medical treatment such as organ or tissue donation for the good of other living individuals.

We see no reason to distinguish a pregnant woman forced to endure unwanted treatment from a non-pregnant person. We therefore disagree with Judge Belson's dissent in *In re A.C.*, opining that,

> [A] woman who carries a child to viability is in fact a member of a unique category of persons. Her circumstances differ fundamentally from those of other potential patients for medical procedures that will aid another person, for example, a potential donor of bone marrow for transplant. This is because she has undertaken to bear another human being, and has carried an unborn child to viability. *In re A.C.*, 573 A.2d 1235, 1256 (1990) (Belson, J., concurring in part and dissenting in part)

We reject the notion that by becoming pregnant and agreeing to carry a pregnancy, women submit to a separate legal status that allows heightened state oversight, diminished autonomy, and an inferior right to bodily integrity. To deny a woman informed consent over her health care choices simply because she is pregnant denies her not only her autonomy but also her right to be valued as a human being. *See* Roberts, *Punishing Drug Addicts Who Have Babies*, at 1463–64.

It is also vital to recognize and protect against the disproportionate burden that pregnant women of color bear when the state intrudes on the right of pregnant women to make informed health care decisions. The state and health care community have a horrific history of discriminatory, coerced, exploitive, or forced treatment of the African American community – and particularly of African American pregnant women – that continues into the present. We note only a few examples, as such a history is too prolific to give full consideration here. A *New England Journal of Medicine* survey found that women of color represented eighty-one percent of cases in which courts ordered women to undergo cesarean surgery against their wishes. Veronika E. B. Kolder, Janet Gallagher, & Michael T. Parsons, *Court-Ordered Obstetrical Interventions*, 316 NEW ENG. J. MED. 1192, 1193 (1987). In the context of drug screening policies such as the one at issue, African American pregnant women are more likely to be reported for drug use than white women, even where likelihood of drug use remains the same, in part due to health care professionals' racist attitudes. Ira J. Chasnoff, Harvey J. Landress, & Mark E. Barrett, *The Prevalence of Illicit-Drug or Alcohol Use during Pregnancy and Discrepancies in Mandatory Reporting in Pincellas County, Florida*, 322 NEW

ENG. J. MED. 1202, 1205 (1990); *see also* Roberts, *Punishing Drug Addicts Who Have Babies*, at 1432.

These reports often result in coercive measures such as threats of arrest if individuals do not consent to drug treatment that, as discussed above, may not be appropriate to their needs.

The health care community and state also have a troubling history of forcing or coercing African American women to undergo sterilization. *See* Roberts, *Punishing Drug Addicts Who Have Babies*, at 1443. For example, in a 1974 case brought by poor teenage African American women in Alabama, a federal district court found that federally funded programs sterilized an estimated 100,000–150,000 poor women annually. *See Relf v. Weinberger*, 372 F. Supp. 1196, 1199 (D.D.C. 1974) on remand sub nom. *Relf v. Mathews*, 403 F. Supp. 1235 (D.D.C. 1975), vacated sub nom. *Relf v. Weinberger*, 565 F.2d 722 (D.C. Cir 1977). In some such cases, the state coerced women to undergo sterilization by threatening to withhold welfare benefits. Roberts, *Punishing Drug Addicts Who Have Babies*, at 1443. This is not merely history; health care providers continue to pressure African American women to undergo sterilization because of their beliefs about the number of children they should have or because they believe African American women are incapable of effectively using other birth control methods. *Id.*

In this case, as discussed above, the task force policy also made the screening of African American women without their informed consent more likely through its selection of MUSC and its criteria for screening. But the attitudes of the task force and health care staff demonstrate the obstacles African American pregnant women face in obtaining health care that respects their dignity. Nurse Brown, who was a founding member of the task force that created the policy and its primary enforcer, frequently expressed racist views about her African American patients to drug counselors and social workers, including her belief that most African American women should undergo sterilization procedures and that hormonal birth control should be put in the drinking water in African American communities. *See* Roberts, *Unshackling Black Motherhood*, at 947

An African American woman's right to informed consent – and thus her right to privacy – is therefore often violated both because of her pregnancy and her race. When pregnant women are denied informed consent over their health care choices, they are denied both autonomy and their right to be valued as a human being – when this is done because of race, this denial reaches a new dimension. Roberts, *Punishing Drug Addicts Who Have Babies*, at 1463–64, 1471–80. In the context of African American women, this denial of their personhood is particularly meaningful because both the state and private entities (with the support of the state) have historically denied African American women their full humanity and identity.

While it may be morally commendable for a woman to undergo specific medical treatment that the state prefers, her pregnancy does not give the state reason to curtail her rights to refuse these treatments. The state may not create in pregnant women a unique class of individuals with limited rights and exceptional burdens. Putting aside the fact that many women hardly choose to become pregnant or to continue their pregnancy,[40] pregnancy itself simply does not render a woman a less autonomous human being. To hold otherwise would reaffirm harmful and constraining stereotypes about women's social roles and capacities.

The state is not prohibited from pursuing its goals in ways that do not curtail a pregnant woman's rights to informed consent and to refuse medical treatment. States may, for example, mandate health insurance coverage for certain testing and treatment; offer public health outreach and information; incentivize testing and treatment; and take additional steps to ensure that women have access to quality prenatal care. In the context of substance use disorder, states may invest in evidence-based treatment programs for all women, offer programs that address issues that impede addiction treatment (such as homelessness, economic opportunity, and mental health issues), and look to underlying social and economic issues that cause drug use. But the state may not presume that its preferences for the care of pregnant women deserve more deference than the ability of pregnant women to make their own medical decisions.

IV

We therefore reverse the judgment of the Court of Appeals. Because the Court of Appeals did not decide the issue of consent, we remand for further proceedings consistent with this decision.

---

[40] Forty-nine percent of pregnancies in the United States are unintended. *Achievements in Public Health 1990–1999: Family Planning*, 48 MMWR 1073 (1999). A woman's choice of whether to terminate or continue her pregnancy may also be severely constrained. There are significant obstacles to choosing to terminate a pregnancy, most notably financial constraints and the ability to find a health care provider to perform the procedure.

8

State v. Oakley, 629 N.W.2d 200 (Wis. 2001)

Commentary by Aziza Ahmed

On its face, *State v. Oakley* is a simple but egregious case about child support and reproductive rights. David Oakley, a father of nine, failed to pay the entire amount of child support he owed his children, and the State of Wisconsin charged Oakley with nine counts of intentionally refusing to provide child support under Wisconsin Statute 948.22(2).[1] At the sentencing hearing in the Circuit Court, the Judge sentenced Oakley to prison on the first count, imposed and stayed an eight-year term on two other counts, and imposed a five-year term of probation consecutive to his incarceration.[2] This was a reduced sentence because Oakley's lawyer convinced the judge that Oakley would not be able to support his family from prison. Most controversially, the Judge conditioned Oakley's probation on not having any additional children, unless, the court stated, it could be shown that "he is meeting the needs of his other children and can meet the needs of this one."[3] On appeal, Oakley argued that the condition of probation ordering him not to father additional children violated the Fourteenth Amendment and the Constitution of the State of Wisconsin. Deciding against Oakley, the appeals court found the ban on Oakley's reproduction "entirely related to his fathering of children he is not inclined to support."[4] The court held that a condition of probation may impinge on a fundamental constitutional right as long as "the condition is not overly broad and is reasonably related to the defendant's rehabilitation."[5]

---

[1] Wis. Stat. § 948.22 (1997–1998).

[2] *State v. Oakley*, 239 Wis. 2d 235 (2000) citing *Krebs v. Schwartz*, 212 Wis. 2d 127, 131, 568 N.W.2d 26 (Ct. App. 1997).

[3] *State v. Oakley*, 245 Wis.2d 447 (2001) (citing Judgement of Conviction and Sentencing).

[4] *State v. Oakley*, 239 Wis.2d 235 (2001) (citing to the Circuit Court decision).

[5] *State v. Oakley*, 239 Wis.2d 235 (2000) citing *Krebs v. Schwartz*, 212 Wis.2d 127, 131, 568 N.W.2d 26 (Ct. App. 1997).

Unlike the actual decision, Solangel Maldonado's rewritten opinion considers the context of Oakley's life and the broader history of child support, bringing a reproductive justice lens to bear on the terms of probation and punishment. Maldonado finds the reproductive ban unconstitutional because it violates Oakley's fundamental right to procreate.[6] Placing the decision in its historical context, as Maldonado does, demonstrates how the *Oakley* decision emerges from the convergence of political, economic, and social forces, including the decline of the welfare state, the rise of a personal responsibility narrative, and an increasing reliance on criminal law as a means of addressing perceived social problems.

Importantly, as described below, the case also demonstrates that often disparate legal frameworks shape reproductive decision making. In Oakley's case, welfare law, criminal, and family law converge, resulting in a decision that would limit his right to procreate. Contextualizing the original decision identifies the case as an outcome of a regulatory landscape in which single men, often black and Latino, became ensnared in overlapping legal regimes that disenfranchise and punish instead of offering support to poor families. Fathers characterized as "deadbeat dads," a pejorative term popularized in the 1990s, bore the punitive load of these overlapping legal regimes in the context of child custody. As represented by the *Oakley* decision, the criminal law also became a way to regulate the family. And, as discussed in detail below, and evident in the rewritten opinion, the punishment of fathers helped the state to justify its own neglect of poor families – instead displacing responsibility onto individuals.

THE REWRITTEN OPINION

Maldonado's rewritten opinion delves into the nature of the child support system in the United States and how its structure impacts poor men of color in distinctly negative ways. Oakley's case is the product of welfare reforms impacting child support that took place in the latter half of the twentieth century that disenfranchised poor families. His prison sentence, one faced by many poor fathers who cannot pay child support, is the product of the state's growing reliance on the criminal justice system to address social welfare issues.[7]

Maldonado emphasizes that the negative consequences of child support laws are experienced disproportionately by black and Latino men.[8] And those negative

---

[6] Solangel Moldanado, *State v. Oakley* Rewritten in this volume.

[7] JONATHAN SIMON, GOVERNING THROUGH CRIME: HOW THE WAR ON CRIME TRANSFORMED AMERICAN DEMOCRACY AND CREATED A CULTURE OF FEAR at 17 (2007). For a description of the welfare state see, generally, DAVID GARLAND, THE WELFARE STATE: A VERY SHORT INTRODUCTION (2016).

[8] While Maldonado emphasizes the reality of these laws on the lives of men of color – particularly black and Latino – it is worth noting that Oakley is white. It is unclear how his race may have impacted the decision but it is likely that the appeals court did not know his race, making it possible that their decision relied on racialized tropes of "deadbeat dads." Solangel Maldonado. *E-mail Communication with Timothy Kay Oakley's Lawyer* (July 6, 2017).

consequences of the American child support system rest on a series of assumptions built into the laws at the intersection of welfare and family law. America's child support system expects that children have two parents, each capable of being fiscally responsible for their children. The state controls and regulates parental responsibilities for a child's financial wellbeing through state mandated child-support. Since at least the 1960s, conservative politicians, often supported by their liberal counterparts, have shifted American welfare institutions away from social and economic support to a system purportedly emphasizing personal responsibility by limiting benefits and creating work requirements. Rather than lift people out of poverty, the American welfare system's regulatory framework, which emphasizes work and responsibility rather than addressing the systemic causes of poverty, undermines its capacity to achieve broad scale poverty reduction.[9]

Maldonado carefully describes how the welfare system in the United States has disenfranchised poor men.[10] The erosion of the welfare state came hand-in-hand with the growth of a racialized criminal law response to perceived social problems – including child support. In her article *Fathers Behind Bars: Rethinking Child Support Policy toward Low-Income Noncustodial Fathers and Their Families*, Tonya Brito argues that the nexus between welfare institutions and the penal state began with a series of reforms in the 1970s and lasting through the 1990s.[11] The 1974 passage of the Child Support Enforcement Act established the Office of Child Support Enforcement and the creation of state-level compliance agencies. The Act required that custodial parents accessing Aid to Families with Dependent Children (AFDC) give the state rights to collect child support payments, which were then utilized to reimburse the government for welfare benefits. Amendments in 1984 and 1988 allowed families not otherwise receiving public benefits to use state child support offices' services and required states to "strengthen paternity establishment, create and utilize child support guidelines in setting orders, and implement wage withholding to increase collections."[12] As Maldonado details in her opinion, the strengthening of child support enforcement was propelled forward by politicians across the political spectrum, including Bill Clinton, who blamed "deadbeat dads" for poverty.[13]

---

[9] *Id.*

[10] For more discussion on the role of race in shaping welfare law and impacting racial minorities *see generally,* Ann Cammett, *Deadbeat Dads and Welfare Queens: How Metaphor Shapes Poverty Law,* 34 B.C. J.L. & SOC. JUST. 233 (2014); Sanford Schram, *Contextualizing Racial Disparities in American Welfare Reform: Towards a New Poverty Research,* 3 PERS. POL. 253–68 (2005).

[11] Tonya Brito, *Fathers Behind Bars: Rethinking Child Support Policy toward Low-Income Noncustodial Fathers and Their Families,* 15 IOWA J. GENDER, RACE & JUST. 417 (2012).

[12] *Id.*

[13] Richard Casey Hoffman, *Bill's List, Crack Down on Deadbeat Dads,* N.Y. TIMES (Dec. 5, 1992), www.nytimes.com/1992/12/05/opinion/bill-s-list-crack-down-on-deadbeat-dads.html.

In 1992, Congress passed the Child Support Recovery Act (CSRA) which allowed federal prosecution of individuals who willfully failed to provide child support to a child living in another state when they had the capacity to pay.[14] As Maldonado highlights in the rewritten decision, many fathers were doomed from the moment a court determined their child support payments because the court utilized statutory guidelines to calculate payment amounts that did not necessarily factor in the father's actual earnings. More specifically, the court may, at its discretion, impute an income when the judge determines that the father is able to pay but has chosen not to do so. The ability to pay, and thus an imputed income, can be demonstrated by evidence that lacking the financial resources to pay ordered support results from a father's voluntary and intentional act. Child Support Recovery Act of 1992 (CSRA) Pub. L. No. 1-2-521. The leeway this provided to judges meant that more courts found men liable for not paying child support. This was a catch-22 for poor men: judges determined that those with no capacity to pay their child support were voluntarily unemployed, guaranteeing that they could not keep up with court ordered payments and placing them at risk for incarceration. This began a vicious cycle for many – being in jail rendered men unable to work and having been recently incarcerated made it difficult to find work – all while child support went unpaid and arrears accrued.[15]

In 1996, President Clinton initiated a major overhaul of welfare with the Personal Responsibility and Work Opportunity Reconciliation Act (PRWORA).[16] As detailed in the rewritten opinion, PRWORA specifically sought to "prevent and reduce the incidence of out-of-wedlock pregnancies ... and encourage the formation and maintenance of two-parent families." In doing so, PRWORA aimed to encourage "responsible motherhood and fatherhood."[17] With the passage of PRWORA, Congress did away with AFDC and replaced it with Temporary Assistance for Needy Families (TANF), which required that recipients work in exchange for government assistance and sanctioned individuals who did not engage in work.[18] In 1998, President Clinton signed the Deadbeat Parents Punishment Act which, amongst other transformations, demands mandatory restitution and prohibits parents from traveling out of state for the purpose of evading child support.[19] In his speech accompanying the signing of the legislation Clinton reinforced the idea that poverty is the product of fathers rather than larger structural issues facing poor people

---

[14] Child Support Recovery Act of 1992 (CRSA) Pub. L. No. 1-2-521.

[15] For a discussion of the relationship between labor, poverty, race, and welfare see Loic Waquant, *From Slavery to Mass Incarceration: Rethinking the "Race Question" in the US*, 13 NEW LEFT REV. 41(2002).

[16] Brito, at 417.

[17] Pub. L. No. 104-193, § 101(3) (1996).

[18] Brito, at 417.

[19] Deadbeat Parents Punishment Act of 1998, Pub. L. 105–87 (1998).

including, for example, difficulty finding employment, affordable housing, or low levels of education. He stated:

> One of the main reasons single mothers go on welfare is that fathers have failed to meet their responsibilities to the children. Even when a family manages to stay out of poverty a father's failure to pay child support puts mothers who are raising children by themselves under terrible pressure ... we have waged an unprecedented campaign to make deadbeat parents live up to their obligations. Thanks to tougher laws, more sophisticated tracking, and powerful new collection tools we've increased child support collections by 68 percent in the last five years.[20]

As argued by Brito, and demonstrated by the Clinton quote, over time the tracking of fathers became more automated and more punitive. States began to prosecute fathers for failure to pay child support and, by the time of David Oakley's arrest, the punitive approach to child support was in full effect. Oakley's six-year prison sentence reflects this punishment-oriented approach. To the court, despite his inability to pay, Oakley represented the "deadbeat parents" – with an emphasis on fathers – who lay at the heart of childhood poverty. In doing so, the court avoids highlighting the structural issues that keep families poor. As the court articulates:

> Refusal to pay child support by so-called "deadbeat parents" has fostered a crisis with devastating implications for our children ... The effects of the nonpayment of child support on our children are particularly troubling ... Child support – when paid – on average amounts to over one-quarter of a poor child's family income. There is little doubt that the payment of child support benefits poverty-stricken children the most. Enforcing child support orders thus has surfaced as a major policy directive in our society.[21]

The court conceptualizes child support orders as central to lifting children out of poverty. This frame allows the judge to lay the blame for child poverty entirely on the parent and elides the state's responsibility in addressing economic inequality.

The idea of a deadbeat dad not only served as an effective rhetorical device to displace state responsibility, it furthered ideas of who deserved to be a parent. For reproductive justice advocates this raises an extensive history of coercive state involvement in reproduction. Maldonado's clear assertion that the probation condition in *Oakley* fully implicates the fundamental right to procreate is a critical intervention in the narrative of the case. The idea that only some people are fit to be parents is at the center of a long line of cases that articulate concerns about who is and should be reproducing. One of the most often cited of these cases is *Buck v. Bell*, a 1927 Supreme Court decision authored by Oliver Wendell Holmes,

---

[20] White House, Remarks by the President at the Signing of the Deadbeat Parents Punishment Act of 1998, available at https://clintonwhitehouse4.archives.gov/WH/New/html/19980624-13821.html.

[21] *State v. Oakley*, 248 Wis.2d 654 (2001).

upholding Virginia's eugenic sterilization law. The case involved a young woman, Carrie Buck, who was to be sterilized under the Virginia Sterilization Act. At the time, physicians diagnosed many young poor women as "feebleminded." The infamous line from this decision, "three generations of imbeciles are enough" draws on the mainstream eugenics thinking of the time. The Court has never overturned *Buck v. Bell* but has used the case to support its assertion that the right to privacy, and in turn the right to do what one wants with one's own body, is not absolute.[22] The legacy of *Buck* persists. As recently as the 2010s, the State of North Carolina compensated African American women and their families for sterilizations they experienced in the mid-1900s (over 7,000 people were sterilized, not all were compensated).[23] In California, women in prison were sterilized without their consent through the 2000s.[24]

In the context of welfare, the idea that federal and state government should limit the fertility of some – particularly the poor – continues to animate lawmaking. PRWORA, for example, had the explicit goal of preventing teen pregnancies and births outside of marriage and to encourage the formation and maintenance of two-parent families. In turn, many states adopted policies to regulate the ability of individuals to have children. These efforts included family caps (preventing an increase in public benefits for a child born to a family already receiving these benefits)[25] and conditioning additional funds on utilizing family planning.[26] Legislators touted these welfare provisions as a way to curtail dependency.[27]

As demonstrated by *Oakley*, the belief that only some parents should have additional children spills over into the context of child support. With reference to a prohibition on reproduction, the court reasons that, given the "suffering" endured by children, "it is not surprising that the legislature has attached severe sanctions to this crime."[28] In turn, rejecting Oakley's argument that the prohibition on his fathering more children violates his fundamental rights, the court holds that as a convicted individual he does not "enjoy the same degree of liberty as citizens who have not violated the law" and that the lower court's ruling that Oakley not reproduce while on probation is constitutional.[29] The State's focus on preventing

---

[22] *Roe v. Wade*, 410 U.S. 113, 154 (1973).

[23] All Things Considered, *Payments Start for N.C. Eugenics Victims, But Many Won't Qualify*, National Public Radio (Oct. 31, 2014), www.npr.org/sections/health-shots/2014/10/31/360355784/payments-start-for-n-c-eugenics-victims-but-many-wont-qualify.

[24] CALIFORNIA STATE AUDITOR, STERILIZATION OF FEMALE INMATES: SOME INMATES WERE STERILIZED UNLAWFULLY, AND SAFEGUARDS DESIGNED TO LIMIT OCCURRENCES OF THE PROCEDURE FAILED (2013).

[25] Rebekah Smith, *Family Caps in Welfare Reform: Their Coercive Effects and Damaging Consequences*, 29 HARV. J.L. & GENDER 151 (2006).

[26] Tamar Lewin, A Plan to Pay Welfare Mothers for Birth Control, N.Y. TIMES (Feb. 9, 1991), www.nytimes.com/1991/02/09/us/a-plan-to-pay-welfare-mothers-for-birth-control.html.

[27] *Id.*

[28] *State v. Oakley*, 248 Wis.2d 654 (2001).

[29] *Id.*

Oakley from procreating is particularly pronounced when placed against the other options available to the State of Wisconsin. As argued by Oakley's lawyers, the State could utilize other measures to ensure enforcement, including placing a lien on personal property. Instead, the court unnecessarily impinges on Oakley's right to reproduce.

Making this point to the court, the Center on Fathers, Families, and Public Policy wrote in their brief to the Supreme Court in support of the Writ of Certiorari that welfare and child support laws exhibit "a trend of the government to place limits on the fundamental rights of poor persons to procreate."[30] The court's use of a reproductive ban over other options seems to belie the State of Wisconsin's claim that its primary interest is concern for economic stability and care for children. Rather, the State of Wisconsin insists on its authority to determine who is fit to parent and procreate. Instead of simply trusting the State of Wisconsin to determine who should and should not reproduce, Maldonado's holding provides a limiting principle to guide the actions of the State.

In recent years, the Supreme Court addressed procedural issues arising with the carceral responses to child support. In 2011, in *Turner v. Rogers*, the Court held that when poor people face incarceration in the context of civil contempt, they do not have a right to counsel. The Supreme Court also stated, however, that there must be fair procedures in place to determine "ability to pay." While few quantitative assessments have been done, at least one study has shown that the modification provided by *Turner* produced little change in the incarceration of men due to failure to pay child support.[31] While *Turner* received some attention, in 2015, the issue of incarcerating men received some public reckoning when a police officer shot and killed Walter Scott, a young African American man, as he ran away after being pulled over.[32] According to reports after his death, Scott was fleeing the police out of fear that unpaid child support payments would result in his imprisonment. While Scott's case added to a growing critique of the carceral state, the confluence of laws that would lead to a young man fleeing the police out of fear of incarceration have yet to be systematically addressed. Instead, child support laws continue to fail the families who need additional resources while incarceration debilitates the capacity of the parent who owes child support from working.

---

[30] Brief of Fathers, Families, and Public Policy as Amicus Supporting Oakley, *State v. Oakley*, No 01-1573 (2002).

[31] Elizabeth Patterson, *Turner in the Trenches: A Study of How Turner v. Rogers Affected Child Support Contempt Proceedings* 25 GEO. J. ON POVERTY L. POL'Y (2017) (study found that while there was a decrease in incarceration due to a pre-screening process that had been put in place once a defendant appeared in hearings rates of incarceration stayed the same or increased).

[32] Alan Blinder, *Ex-Officer Who Shot Scott Pleads Guilty*, N.Y. TIMES (May 2, 2017), www.nytimes.com/2017/05/02/us/michael-slager-walter-scott-north-charleston-shooting.html.

CONCLUSION: REGULATING THE FAMILY

Increased reliance on criminal law to address social challenges, alongside the erosion of the welfare state, results in a carceral, and, now sometimes deadly, mode of regulating the family. The case of David Oakley represents the convergence of these troubling trends that continue to govern the lives of poor families, especially African American and Latino, today. In her rewritten decision which speaks from a reproductive justice perspective, Maldonado acknowledges the role of structural inequality in producing fathers who cannot financially support their children and reclaims the place of reproductive rights in the context of the possibility of parenthood. As she concludes in her decision:

> Given that the majority of poor fathers who do not pay child support are African-American or Latino, conditions of probation restricting the right to procreate would disparately impact poor and minority men and by extension, poor and minority communities. These communities would be forced to choose between having fewer children or sending more of their men to prison.

In turn, for reproductive justice scholars and practitioners, Oakley's case is a manifestation of the punitive welfare schemes purportedly designed to raise families out of poverty but that repeatedly fail to do so. Instead, these laws further entrench economic, racial, and social inequality.

State v. Oakley, 629 N.W.2d 200 (Wis. 2001)

Justice Solangel Maldonado delivered the opinion of the court

This case presents important questions about the State's power to restrict the reproductive rights of its citizens. We must decide whether the State may, as a condition of probation, prohibit a defendant convicted of intentionally refusing to pay child support from having another child unless he shows that he can support that child and his current children. We hold that this condition of probation infringes upon the fundamental right to procreate guaranteed by the Due Process Clause of the Fourteenth Amendment of the U.S. Constitution. Thus, we conclude that the trial court order prohibiting the defendant from having another child during the period of probation unless he first establishes his ability to support all of his children is unconstitutional.[33]

I FACTS

David Oakley (Oakley), the petitioner, has nine children – four children with his first wife, a daughter with his second wife, a son with a woman he never married,

---

[33] Editor's note. In the published opinion, the Supreme Court of Wisconsin addressed a second issue involving the State's withdrawal of a prior plea agreement. This version of the opinion does not address that issue.

and three children with his current partner. Although Oakley has paid seventy percent of his court-ordered child support obligations, he has nevertheless accumulated arrears of $25,000. In addition, during a period of unemployment after his release from prison in an unrelated offense, Oakley did not make any child support payments for a consecutive 120-day period in 1998, in violation of Wis. Stat. § 948.22 (2) (1997–1998).[34] Consequently, the State charged him with nine counts of nonsupport. After dismissal of two counts, and an initial plea agreement that was later withdrawn, Oakley agreed to plead no contest to three counts of intentionally refusing to support his children. The State agreed to cap its sentencing recommendation to a total of six years.

At sentencing, Judge Fred H. Hazlewood informed Oakley that by pleading no contest he waived his right to have the State prove that he intentionally refused to support his children for at least 120 days contrary to Wis. Stat. § 948.22(2). In accordance with the terms of the plea agreement, the State recommended that Oakley be sentenced to six years in prison. Oakley, in turn, asked for the opportunity to maintain full-time employment, provide for his children, and make serious payment towards his arrears.

After observing that "if Mr. Oakley goes to prison, he's not going to be in a position to pay any meaningful support for these children," Judge Hazlewood rejected the State's recommendation to sentence Oakley to six years in prison. Instead, he sentenced Oakley to three years in prison on the first count, imposed and stayed an eight-year term on the two other counts, and imposed a five-year term of probation consecutive to his incarceration. As a condition of probation, Judge Hazlewood ordered that Oakley "be employed full-time." In addition, while noting that Oakley "couldn't pay what had been ordered even when he was employed" and would always "struggle to support these children," Judge Hazlewood imposed the condition of probation at issue in this case. The judge barred Oakley from having any additional children "while on probation unless it can be shown to the Court that he is meeting the needs of his other children and can meet the needs of this one." After sentencing, Oakley filed for post-conviction relief.

In a per curiam opinion, the court of appeals affirmed Judge Hazlewood's rulings. *State v. Oakley*, No. 99–3328–CR, 2000 WL 1285478, at *1 (Wis. Ct. App. Sept. 13, 2000). The court of appeals found that the condition of probation "merely prohibits Oakley from having additional children whom he cannot support" and "is narrowly drawn and is reasonably related to Oakley's rehabilitation and protection of the public." *Id.* at *3. Oakley petitioned this court for review, which we granted.

---

[34] All subsequent references to the Wisconsin Statutes will be to the 1997–1998 version, unless otherwise indicated.

II HISTORICAL, LEGAL, AND SOCIAL CONTEXT

Before turning to the legal issues in this case, it is important to understand the historical, legal, and social context of our current child support system and its enforcement mechanisms.

Parents have primary responsibility for the care and maintenance of their children. When a parent does not reside with a child, a court may order the parent to pay an amount determined by the court as necessary to fulfill the parental duty of support. Federal law requires each state to establish guidelines to be used in determining child support award amounts.[35] In Wisconsin, child support is determined as a percentage of the noncustodial parent's monthly income.[36] For example, a noncustodial parent with five children may be obligated under the guidelines to pay thirty-four percent of his monthly income as support.[37] In theory, because child support awards in this state are based on the nonresident parent's monthly income, a child support award should never exceed a parent's ability to pay the amount ordered. In practice, however, many indigent parents cannot afford to pay the amount ordered by the court for a variety of reasons.

First, a parent may be unable to fulfill a child support requirement because child support awards are not always based on actual income but rather imputed income.[38] Courts impute income when a parent fails to appear in court or fails to provide credible evidence documenting her full income – for example, if the court does not believe that the parent has reported all of her income.[39] A court may also impute income if the court determines that a parent is voluntarily unemployed or underemployed.[40] To illustrate, a court may order a nonresident parent of five children, whom the court believes is voluntarily unemployed or underemployed, to pay $700 per month in child support based on the court's determination that given the parent's skills, he should be able to secure a job earning $25,000 per year. However, if the court does not consider barriers to employment such as a criminal record or lack of employment experience, the child support award will not accurately reflect a nonresident parent's income earning capacity and may lead to the accrual of arrears.[41]

---

[35] Family Support Act of 1988, P.L. 100–485 (HR 1720), P.L. 100–485, Oct. 13, 1988, 102 Stat 2343.

[36] Wis. Admin. Code DCF § 150.03(1) (1999).

[37] Wis. Admin. Code DCF § 150.03(11) (1999) (providing that the court may deviate from the child support guidelines if the guideline amount is shown to be unfair to the child or the parties).

[38] Wis. Admin. Code DCF § 150.03(1), (3–4) (1999).

[39] See, e.g., Daniel R.C. v. Waukesha Cty. (In the Interest of Kevin C.), 510 N.W.2d 746 (Wis. Ct. App. 1993) (holding that evidence that the noncustodial father's income was higher than reported supported the trial court's imputation of income at a higher amount for the purposes of entering a support order).

[40] Wis. Admin. Code DCF § 150.03(3) (1999).

[41] Elaine Sorensen & Chava Zibman, A Look at Poor Dads Who Don't Pay Child Support, in Assessing the New Federalism, at 3 (2000), www.urban.org/sites/default/files/publication/62536/409646-A-Look-at-Poor-Dads-Who-Don-t-Pay-Child-Support.PDF [hereinafter Sorensen & Zibman, Poor Dads].

Second, even when the child support award accurately reflects the parent's ability to pay at the time of the award, the parent may lose his job and no longer be able to comply with the order. While a parent may petition the court to modify the order based on a change in circumstances, some obligors, the majority of whom lack access to legal counsel, are not aware of this remedy or lack the wherewithal to file a petition for modification without legal assistance.[42] Additionally, courts are hesitant to lower the amount awarded because of its impact on the child who would now be receiving less support.

Third, some states backdate child support orders for nonmarital children to the date of the child's birth even if the parents were living together.[43] As a result, a parent may find that he owes months or years of back child support at the time the order is issued.

Fourth, many states charge nonresident fathers for the medical costs of the child's birth if Medicaid paid for these expenses.[44] States also seek reimbursement if the child received welfare benefits.[45] In fact, a substantial portion of Oakley's arrears, including thousands of dollars in interest, were owed to the State.

Many noncustodial parents fail to comply with their court-ordered child support obligations. Approximately one-third of single parent households with established child support orders do not receive any payment while another one-third receive only partial payment.[46] In 1997, out of $26.4 billion awarded by a court order, only $15.8 billion was actually paid, amounting to a deficit of $10.6 billion.[47] While a portion of these arrears were owed to the state because the children were receiving public assistance while the arrears accrued, mothers, who are the custodial parent in approximately 85 percent of cases,[48] disproportionately bear the burden of nonpayment.[49] In fact, 32.1 percent of custodial mothers were below the poverty

---

[42] Many child support obligors, many of whom did not complete high school, *see id.* at 4, would find the process of locating the necessary forms, familiarizing themselves with the legal standard for modification, and submitting evidence in support of their motion quite daunting.

[43] *E.g., Johns v. Richards* 717 So. 2d 1103 (Fla. Dist. Ct. App. 1998) (holding that Florida's retroactive child support statute authorizes backdating child support to child's birth date).

[44] EARL S. JOHNSON, ANN LEVINE, & FRED DOOLITTLE, FATHER'S FAIR SHARE: HELPING POOR MEN MANAGE CHILD SUPPORT AND FATHERHOOD at 10 (1999).

[45] Elaine Sorensen & Chava Zibman, *To What Extent Do Children Benefit from Child Support?*, in Assessing the New Federalism, at 6 (2000), www.urban.org/sites/default/files/publication/62036/309299-To-What-Extent-Do-Children-Benefit-from-Child-Support-.PDF [hereinafter Sorensen & Zibman, *To What Extent*].

[46] Timothy Grail, *Child Support for Custodial Mothers and Fathers*, Current Population Reports, United States Census Bureau, 4 (Oct. 2000).

[47] United States Census Bureau, U.S. Dep't of Commerce, Current Population Survey, *Child Support 1997*, table 1 (1998).

[48] Sorensen & Zibman, *To What Extent*, *supra* note 45, at table 1.

[49] *Child Support 1997*, table 1; DANIEL R. MEYER, *Fathers and the Child Support System*, in CHILD SUPPORT: THE NEXT FRONTIER at 88 (J. Thomas Oldham & Marygold S. Melli eds., 2000).

line in 1997[50] and African American and Latina custodial mothers are even more likely to be poor.[51]

The negative effects on children of inadequate child support are significant and troubling. In addition to engendering long-term consequences such as poor health and low educational attainment, inadequate child support contributes to childhood poverty.[52] One out of six children in the United States, over twelve million children, lives in poverty.[53] Poverty rates are almost three times higher for African American and Latino children.[54] In Wisconsin, poverty strikes approximately 200,000 children, with 437,000 at or below 200 percent of the poverty level in 1999.[55] Child support is particularly important to poor children. When paid, child support amounts, on average, to over one-quarter of a poor child's family income.[56] However, poor children are unlikely to receive child support because their nonresident parent is often poor as well.[57] The majority of the 2.6 million nonresident fathers with incomes below the poverty level do not pay court-ordered child support.[58] Indeed, only three percent of poor, nonresident fathers pay court-ordered child support.[59]

---

[50] Grail, *supra* note 46, at 2.

[51] See Theresa J. Feeley, Issue Brief, *Low-Income Noncustodial Fathers: A Child Advocate's Guide to Helping Them Contribute to the Support of Their Children*, Nat'l Ass'n of Child Advocates (Feb. 2000), at 2 (noting that low-income custodial mothers are disproportionately African American); Grail, *supra* note 46, at 7 (showing the average monthly income for black and Latina custodial mothers is less than that of white, non-Latina custodial mothers).

[52] MARSHA GARRISON, *The Goals and Limits of Child Support Policy*, in CHILD SUPPORT: THE NEXT FRONTIER, at 16 (J. Thomas Oldham & Marygold S. Melli eds., 2000).

[53] JOSEPH DALAKER & BERNADETTE D. PROCTOR, *Poverty in the United States*, in CURRENT POPULATION REPORTS, at vi (United States Census Bureau, 2000).

[54] Daniel T. Lichter, *Poverty and Inequality among Children*, 121 ANN. REV. SOC. 130 (1997) (citing 1996 U.S. Bureau of the Census study showing that in 1994, 43.8 percent of all African American children were poor, as compared to 16.9 percent of white children and 41.5 percent of Latino children).

[55] Children's Defense Fund, *Child Poverty by State 1997* (2000); U.S. Census Bureau, *Low Income Uninsured Children by State: 1997, 1998, and 1999*, Current Population Survey (1998–2000).

[56] Sorensen & Zibman, *To What Extent, supra* note 45, at 6.

[57] Sorensen & Zibman, *Poor Dads, supra* note 41, at 13 (citing 1997 *National Survey of America's Families*) (2.6 million nonresident fathers have incomes below poverty line); *see also* Elaine Sorensen & Robert Lerman, *Welfare Reform and Low-Income Noncustodial Fathers*, CHAL-LENGE (July–Aug. 1998), at 101, 102 (3.1 million noncustodial fathers were low-income, mean-ing that they earned 130 percent or less of poverty line); Sorensen & Zibman, *Poor Dads, supra* note 41, at 5 (dead broke fathers earned on average $5,570 in 1996).

[58] *See* Johnson *et al., supra* note 44, at xii (finding that poverty is "a cause of lack of child support"); ELAINE SORENSEN & MARK TURNER, BARRIERS IN CHILD SUPPORT POLICY: A LITERATURE REVIEW at 11 (1996), www.ncoff.gse.upenn.edu/litrev/sb-litrev.pdf (studies have found that the ability to pay child support is a strong predictor of payment rate). Nearly all nonresident fathers who pay court-ordered child support have incomes above the poverty level. Sorensen & Zibman, *Poor Dads, supra* note 41, at 3.

[59] Sorensen & Zibman, *Poor Dads, supra* note 41, at 4 & figure 1 (citing 1997 *National Survey of America's Families*). These figures only address court-ordered child support payments. How-ever, some nonresident parents make informal cash and noncash contributions. When a

It is worth noting that most poor children will continue to need public support even if all nonresident parents paid the full amount of child support ordered. One study concluded that even if all of the child support owed were paid, it would lift only five percent of children out of poverty.[60] Thus, while child support is a crucial component in the fight to end childhood poverty, child support alone will not lift the majority of poor children out of poverty. Nevertheless, child support remains an important parental obligation that the courts must enforce.

Lawmakers have aggressively pursued parents who do not meet their court-ordered child support obligations. These parents face criminal penalties under federal[61] and state law,[62] suspension of drivers, professional, occupational, and recreational licenses,[63] wage garnishment,[64] seizure of tax refunds,[65] liens on property,[66] denial of a passport,[67] and even booting of vehicles.[68] Similar to other states, Wisconsin imposes severe criminal sanctions on parents who intentionally refuse to pay child support. It makes it a Class E felony for any person "who intentionally fails for 120 or more consecutive days to provide spousal, grandchild or child support which the person knows or reasonably should know the person is legally obligated to provide . . ." Wis. Stat. §948.22(2). Failure to pay support in accordance with a child

---

custodial parent is receiving public assistance for a child, she must assign her right to collect child support from the other parent to the state. Consequently, some or most of the payments made through the formal child support system are used to reimburse the state for the support it has provided to the child. Not surprisingly, many custodial mothers receiving public assistance and their children's nonresident fathers prefer informal contributions. *See* Sorensen & Lerman, *supra* note 57, at 103–4. In addition to, or in lieu of, informal cash contributions, some nonresident parents make noncash contributions to their children. They provide diapers, baby formula, and other essentials such as cribs, strollers, groceries, and clothing, as well as toys. Courts do not take these contributions into account when setting the child support amount and child support enforcement officials do not count them when determining whether a nonresident parent has complied with the court-ordered obligation. *Id.* at 104–5.

[60] ELAINE SORENSEN & CHAVA ZIBMAN, *Child Support Offers Some Protection against Poverty*, in NATIONAL SURVEY OF AMERICA'S FAMILIES, at 2 (Urb. Inst., D.C., Mar. 2000).

[61] Child Support Recovery Act ("CSRA"), 18 U.S.C. § 228(a) (2000) (providing for federal criminal prosecution of parents who owe $5,000 or more in child support obligations or have arrears dating one year or longer).

[62] Wis. Stat. § 948.22 (providing for state criminal prosecution of parents who intentionally fail to pay child support for a period of 120 or more consecutive days).

[63] Wis. Admin. Code DCF § 152.10 (setting out procedures for suspension of licenses when a lien against a payer of support exceeds 300 percent of the support order).

[64] 42 U.S.C. § 666(a)(8), (b)(3) (2000) (providing that income may be withheld in the amount of a state child support order); Wis Stat § 767.265 (providing for the assignment of wages to comply with support orders).

[65] 42 U.S.C. § 664 (2000) (authorizing collection of past due support from federal tax refunds).

[66] Wis. Stat. § 767.30 (providing that liens may be attached to personal property to comply with support orders).

[67] 42 U.S.C. § 652(k) (2000) (directing the Secretary of State to refuse a passport to an individual with arrearages on a support order over $5,000).

[68] Elizabeth S. Scott, *The Legal Construction of Norms: Social Norms and the Legal Regulation of Marriage*, 86 VA. L. REV. 1901, 1926 (2000).

support order "is prima facie evidence of intentional failure to provide child ... support." Wis. Stat. § 948.22(4). The legislature recently increased the penalty for a Class E felony so that intentionally refusing to pay child support is now punishable by up to five years in prison. See Wis. Stat. § 939.50(3)(e)(1999–2000).

Efforts to ensure that nonresident parents pay court-ordered child support have intensified in recent years. Congress passed the Child Support Recovery Act of 1992 (CSRA) which makes it a federal crime to "willfully fail[] to pay a past due support obligation with respect to a child who resides in another State" if the obligation "has remained unpaid for a period longer than one year, or is greater than $5,000." 18 U.S.C. § 228 (1992). In addition, when Congress enacted the Personal Responsibility and Work Opportunity Reconciliation Act (PRWORA) in 1996, it expressly sought to "prevent and reduce the incidence of out-of-wedlock pregnancies ...," "[pro-mote] responsible fatherhood and motherhood," and "end the dependence of needy parents on government benefits ..." Pub. L. No. 104-193, § 401(a), 100 Stat. 2105, 2113 (1996). To achieve these goals, PRWORA made dozens of changes to child support laws to facilitate establishment of paternity and enforcement of support orders. It also imposed time limits on welfare benefits, see 42 USC § 608(a)(7), and allowed states to deny welfare benefits to children born to families that were already receiving benefits for other family members before the child's birth.[69] As a result of these time limits and family caps on welfare benefits, child support is more important to children in poor families than ever before.[70]

Parents who do not meet their child support obligations are often labelled "deadbeat parents."[71] This term suggests that obligor parents are able to pay the amount ordered but refuse to do so. Indeed, the federal Deadbeat Parents Punishment Act of 1998, Pub. L. 105–187, amending the CSRA, expressly includes a presumption that a parent is able to pay the amount ordered.[72] Undoubtedly, many

---

[69] Before PRWORA was enacted, states seeking to impose a family cap on welfare benefits were required to obtain a waiver from the federal government. PRWORA is silent on family caps which means that states have complete discretion over whether to adopt a family cap. Almost half the states have adopted family caps. See SHIRENE HANSOTIA & CARMEN SOLOMON-FEARS, Welfare Reform: Family Caps in the Temporary Assistance for Needy Families Program, in CRS REPORT FOR CONGRESS (Congressional Research Service, D.C., July 23, 1998).

[70] Daniel R. Meyer & Maria Cancian, Child Support and Economic Well-Being Following an Exit from AFDC (1996) (report submitted to the Wisconsin Department of Workforce Development); Elaine Sorensen & Chava Zibman, To What Extent Do Children Benefit from Child Support? New Information from the National Survey of America's Families, 1997, FOCUS 36–37 (Spring 2000).

[71] Deadbeat Parents Punishment Act of 1998, Pub. L. 105–87.

[72] The Deadbeat Parents Punishment Act of 1998 provides: "Presumption. – The existence of a support obligation that was in effect for the time period charged in the indictment or information creates a rebuttable presumption that the obligor has the ability to pay the support obligation for that time period." 18 U.S.C. § 228(b). At least one federal court has held that the presumption of ability to pay violates the Fifth Amendment's Due Process Clause because it relieves the state of its obligation to prove that a parent has willfully refused to comply with the support order. See United States v. Grigsby, 85 F. Supp.2d 100 (D. R.I. 2000). The Grigsby

parents who are able to support their children refuse to do so. In fact, one study found that forty-three percent of fathers who do not comply with their court-ordered child support obligations can afford to pay the amount awarded.[73] However, many nonresident parents cannot afford to pay the amount ordered. The majority of these parents, who are disproportionately African American (41%) or Latino (17%), are unemployed and poor themselves.[74] Those who are employed rarely work year-round and earn, on average, $5,570 per year.[75] Poor nonresident fathers who do not pay child support face multiple barriers to employment. Over forty percent do not have a high school diploma, twenty-six percent are incarcerated, and many more have criminal records that make them unattractive to potential employers.[76] These parents are not necessarily deadbeat, rather they are dead broke.

Since nonresident parents are presumed to have the ability to comply with their court-ordered child support obligations, antipathy toward parents who fail to meet these obligations is substantial even when undeserved. Lawmakers and society stigmatize these parents as uncaring and neglectful. The title of the Deadbeat Parents Punishment Act and President Clinton's assertion that "single mothers go on welfare [because] fathers have failed to meet their responsibilities to the children" have further served to perpetuate these stereotypes. Public Remarks of Bill Clinton on Deadbeat Parents Punishment Act (June 24, 1998). The portrayal of parents who do not comply with a child support order as selfish and irresponsible is reminiscent of lawmakers' sentiments towards mothers who need public assistance to support their children.[77] Lawmakers, politicians, and the media have labelled indigent mothers as lazy "welfare queens" who refuse to work and who bear

---

court reasoned that the presumption is unconstitutional because: "[T]he issuance of a support order by a Court does not establish beyond a reasonable doubt that the parent involved will have the ability to pay that obligation ... In many cases, the parent is not even before the Court to contest the order and his or her ability to make the payments is thus the result of an ex parte proceeding with little or no evidence presented on the issue. Therefore, in the run of cases, it is unreasonable to conclude that a parent has the ability to pay solely based on the issuance of a court order and to command a jury to make that inference is arbitrary." *Id.* at 107. *See also* 144 Cong. Rec. H3044–45 (Daily ed. May 12, 1998) (Statement of Rep. Paul) (opposing the mandatory presumption provision because it shifts the burden of proof to the defendant).

[73] Sorensen & Zibman, *Poor Dads, supra* note 41, at 3.

[74] *Id.* at 3–4 & table 1.

[75] *Id.* at 4–5 & table 1.

[76] *Id.*

[77] As Professor Tonya Brito of the University of Wisconsin Law School has noted, "deadbeat dads," are a "group whose negative image rivals that of 'welfare queens'." Tonya Brito, *The Welfarization of Family Law*, 48 U. KAN. L. REV. 229, 251 (2000). *Id.* at 264 (describing the demonization of nonresident fathers and arguing that "the public perception that all nonsupporting fathers are 'deadbeats' (fathers 'who can afford to pay child support but choose not to, depriving their former families of desperately needed income') is never challenged by the competing reality that some of these men are 'turnips' (fathers who have insufficient income to pay child support because they are young, uneducated, and lack significant work experience") (internal citations omitted).

additional children in order to increase their welfare benefits.[78] PRWORA allows states to require family planning counseling for families receiving public assistance,[79] and states have tried to persuade women receiving public assistance to use long-acting forms of birth control precisely because they believe these women are procreating recklessly.[80]

Apparently, our State shares this view as well. At oral argument, the State's attorney remarked that a woman who is on notice that Oakley has nine children whom he does not support might still choose to have children with him because "we've got welfare."[81] The suggestion that the poor intentionally have children they cannot support because they expect the State will support them is ridiculous and deeply offensive. It also perfectly illustrates the misconceptions and attitudes that pervade our national consciousness and conversations about "deadbeat dads" and "welfare queens."

It is against this backdrop that we examine the constitutionality of the condition of probation in this case. The constitutionality of a condition of probation raises a question of law, which this court reviews independently without deference to the decisions of the circuit court or the court of appeals. *See State v. Griffin*, 388 N.W.2d 535 (Wis. 1986); *Edwards v. State*, 246 N.W.2d 109 (Wis. 1976). It is to this question that we now turn.

III CONSTITUTIONALITY OF THE PROBATION CONDITION

At its core, this case is about procreative liberty. The U.S. Supreme Court and this court have long recognized that the right to procreate is a fundamental right that is protected under the due process clause of the Fourteenth Amendment. *See Meyer*

---

[78] See Dorothy Roberts, *Welfare and the Problem of Black Citizenship*, 105 YALE L.J. 1563, 1563 (1996) (reviewing LINDA GORDON, PITIED BUT NOT ENTITLED: SINGLE MOTHERS AND THE HISTORY OF WELFARE (1994) and JILL QUADAGNO, THE COLOR OF WELFARE: HOW RACISM UNDERMINED THE WAR ON POVERTY (1994)) (noting that "[w]hen Americans discuss welfare, many have in mind the mythical Black 'welfare queen' or profligate teenager who becomes pregnant at taxpayers' expense to fatten her welfare check."); Catherine R. Albiston & Laura Beth Nielsen, *Welfare Queens and Other Fairy Tales: Welfare Reform and Unconstitutional Reproductive Controls*, 38 HOW. L.J. 473, 484–86 (1995) (describing stereotypes of welfare recipients as presumably black, sexually promiscuous, lazy, and unwilling to work).

[79] See Wendy Chavkin, Tammy A. Draut, Diana Romero, & Paul H. Wise, *Sex Reproduction and Welfare Reform*, 7 GEO. J. POVERTY L. & POL'Y. 379, 384 (2000).

[80] Cf. Darci Elaine Burrell, *The Norplant Solution: Norplant and the Control of African-Americans Motherhood*, 5 UCLA WOMEN'S L.J. 401, 404 (1995) (arguing that proposals to offer or require the five-year contraceptive Norplant, targeted poor, African American women who are perceived as "'deviant' and thus less deserving of motherhood than white women"); Albiston & Nielsen, *supra* note 78, at 490–92 (discussing welfare reform proposals to reward welfare recipients who agree to use Norplant with a bonus payment and mandatory Norplant proposals making welfare benefits contingent on the recipient's agreement to use Norplant).

[81] Oral Argument at 30:13, *State v. Oakley*, 629 N.W.2d 200 (2001), www.wicourts.gov/supreme/scoa.jsp?docket_number=1999AP003328&begin_date=&end_date=&party_name=&sortBy=date.

v. Nebraska, 262 U.S. 390, 399 (1923) (recognizing that the right "to marry, establish a home and bring up children" is an essential part of the liberty protected by the due process clause); *Skinner v. Oklahoma ex rel. Williamson*, 316 U.S. 535, 541 (1942) (recognizing the right to procreate as "one of the basic civil rights of man"); *Zablocki v. Redhail*, 434 U.S. 374 (1978) ("it is clear that among the decisions that an individual may make without unjustified government interference are personal decisions 'relating to marriage, procreation' . . .") (internal citations omitted); *Carey v. Population Servs. Int'l*, 431 U.S. 678, 685 (1977) ("The decision whether or not to beget or bear a child is at the very heart of this cluster of constitutionally protected choices"). This court, in a case involving involuntary sterilization, has emphasized that the right of a citizen to procreate is central to the zone of privacy protected by the Constitution:

> If the right of privacy means anything, it is the right of the individual, married or single, to be free from unwarranted governmental intrusion into matters so fundamentally affecting a person as the decision whether to bear or beget a child. *In re Guardianship of Eberhardy*, 307 N.W.2d 881, 891 (Wis. 1981) (quoting *Eisenstadt v. Baird*, 405 U.S. 438, 453 (U.S. 1972), at 453)

The liberty interest at stake is the fundamental right to procreate, therefore, Oakley argues that the condition of probation must satisfy strict scrutiny – that it must be narrowly tailored to serve a compelling state interest. *See Carey*, 431 U.S. at 686 ("where a decision as fundamental as that whether to bear or beget a child is involved, regulations imposing a burden on it may be justified only by compelling state interests, and must be narrowly drawn to express only those interests"). Oakley does not dispute the State's substantial interest in requiring parents to financially support their children but argues that the means employed here – the probation condition prohibiting procreation – is not narrowly tailored to serve that interest. According to Oakley, the condition of probation eliminates his right to procreate because he "probably never will have the ability to support" his children. Therefore, if he exercises his fundamental right to procreate while on probation, his probation will be revoked, and he will face the stayed term of eight years in prison.

The State does not dispute that the condition of probation impinges on Oakley's fundamental right to procreate. The State disagrees, however, with the position that the condition must satisfy strict scrutiny. In the State's view, because a probationer does not have the same constitutional rights as an individual who has not been convicted of a crime, the trial court may impose conditions that impinge on the probationer's constitutional rights so long as they are reasonable and not overly broad.

Although a court may "impose any conditions [of probation] which appear to be reasonable and appropriate," Wisconsin Stat. § 973.09(1)(a), the validity and reasonableness of a condition is measured by how well it serves to effectuate the dual objectives of probation – the rehabilitation of those convicted of crime and the protection of the state and community interest. *See State v. Heyn*, 456 N.W.2d 157,

161 (Wis. 1990); *Huggett v. State*, 266 N.W.2d 403, 407 (Wis. 1978). However, "there are constitutional limitations on conditions of probation." *Edwards v. State*, 249 N.W.2d 109, 111 (Wis. 1976). *See also People v. Pointer*, 199 Cal. Rptr. 357, 363 (Cal. Ct. App. 1984) ("the discretion to impose conditions of probation ... is further circumscribed by constitutional safeguards" and "[a] probationer has the right to enjoy a significant degree of privacy, or liberty, under the Fourth, Fifth and Fourteenth Amendments to the federal Constitution"); *State v. Mosburg*, 768 P.2d 313, 314 (Kan. Ct. App. 1989) (noting that although courts have significant discretion in imposing probation conditions, "[t]here are ... limitations on probation conditions that infringe on constitutionally protected rights"). This court has held that "conditions of probation may impinge upon constitutional rights as long as they are not overly broad and are reasonably related to the person's rehabilitation." *Edwards*, 249 N.W.2d, at 111. Given the heightened importance of the liberty interest at stake – the right to procreate – whether one chooses to frame the means-end inquiry as "not overly broad" or as "narrowly tailored," the essence of the inquiry is the same. As the California Court of Appeals has recognized, when a condition of probation infringes on a fundamental right, it "must be subjected to special scrutiny to determine whether the restriction is entirely necessary to serve the dual purposes of rehabilitation and public safety." *See Pointer*, 199 Cal. Rptr. at 365. As that court held:

> Where a condition of probation requires a waiver of precious constitutional rights, the condition must be narrowly drawn; to the extent it is overbroad it is not reasonably related to the compelling state interest in reformation and rehabilitation and is an unconstitutional restriction on the exercise of fundamental constitutional rights. *Id.* at 365 (internal quotations and citations omitted).

Like the California Court of Appeals, we now hold that a condition of probation that infringes on the fundamental right to procreate is overly broad and thus, invalid, unless the State demonstrates that such condition is necessary to serve the State's interests in rehabilitating the defendant and protecting the public and is narrowly tailored to effectuate those interests. If alternative means exist that would further the State's interests without infringing on the defendant's right to procreate, the condition is unconstitutional. *See id.* (concluding "that the condition of probation prohibiting conception is overbroad, as less restrictive alternatives are available").

We conclude that the order prohibiting Oakley from having another child during the period of probation unless he can show that he has supported his existing children and can meet the needs of another child is overly broad. Although the State's interest in ensuring that parents support their children is of great magnitude, especially now that the State has significantly curtailed its assistance to needy families, there are other less intrusive mechanisms for exacting compliance with child support obligations. As such, the State has failed to show that the condition of probation is necessary to achieve the State's interest in ensuring that Oakley's children are supported.

The United States Supreme Court has previously rejected a State's efforts to advance its interest in ensuring that parents support their children by imposing conditions that interfere with the exercise of a fundamental right. In *Zablocki v. Redhail*, the Court struck a Wisconsin statute that prohibited an individual from exercising the fundamental right to marry unless she first established that she had met her child support obligations and that the child was unlikely to become a public charge in the future. 434 U.S. 374, 388–90 (1978). The Court, applying strict scrutiny, held the statute unconstitutional and explained that prohibiting child support obligors and nonresident parents whose children might need public assistance from marrying would not provide their children with support. The Court further noted that Wisconsin had other means of advancing the State's interest in ensuring that children were supported that did not infringe upon the fundamental right to marry:

> First, with respect to individuals who are unable to meet the statutory requirements, the statute merely prevents the applicant from getting married, without delivering any money at all into the hands of the applicant's prior children. More importantly, regardless of the applicant's ability or willingness to meet the statutory requirements, the State already has numerous other means for exacting compliance with support obligations, means that are at least as effective as the instant statute's and yet do not impinge upon the right to marry. Under Wisconsin law, whether the children are from a prior marriage or were born out of wedlock, court-determined support obligations may be enforced directly via wage assignments, civil contempt proceedings, and criminal penalties. *Id.* at 389–90 (footnote omitted) (emphasis added).

The restriction on marriage at issue in *Zablocki* applied to all child support obligors in arrears and those whose children were at risk of becoming public charges. In contrast, the restriction on procreation in this case applies to an individual who has been convicted of a crime. This distinction does not diminish the import of *Zablocki*'s holding. The right to procreate, like the right to marry, is fundamental. Indeed, when reaffirming the fundamental nature of the right to marry, the Court stressed that the "decision to marry has been placed on the same level of importance as decisions relating to procreation, childbirth, child rearing, and family relationships." *Zablocki*, 434 U.S. at 386. Consequently, under *Zablocki*, any restriction on these fundamental rights, regardless of whether it is imposed on a probationer or on an individual who has not been convicted of a crime, is unconstitutional if the State has other means available to further its interests that do not infringe on such rights.

The "means for exacting compliance with support obligations" described by the Court in *Zablocki* still exist today. 434 U.S. at 389. As described above, Wisconsin has extensive means at its disposal to compel parents to comply with their child support obligations. These means further the state's interest but do not impair the fundamental right to procreate. *See, e.g.,* Wis. Stat. § 767.265 (garnishment/wage assignment); § 767.30 (lien on personal property); § 785.03 (civil contempt); Wis. Admin. Code DCF § 152.10 (suspension of licenses). These means, as well as other conditions of probation or criminal penalties,[82] are available in the present case. For example, the trial court could have imposed as a condition of probation that Oakley work a minimum of 60 hours per week, pay a fixed amount towards his arrears each month, and attend money management and parenting classes. The court could also have required Oakley to make significant in-kind contributions to his children, such as groceries, clothing, diapers, and school supplies, or to provide child care as an offset to cash payments.[83] Parental support is not only financial and includes in-kind contributions and caregiving. When faced with a parent who has accumulated substantial arrears that the parent is unlikely to ever be able to pay, a trial court should consider creative enforcement mechanisms that include not just cash but other necessary services such as child care. These non-cash contributions are oftentimes highly valued in poor communities[84] and could serve a rehabilitative purpose. Specifically, these contributions may lead nonresident parents to spend more time with their children and address the emotional distance between non-resident parents and their children that the State suggested at oral argument and in its written submissions makes nonresident parents less likely to pay support.

Whether it would be appropriate to order a probationer, as a condition of probation, to provide non-cash contributions to his children is a decision for a trial court to make on a case-by-case basis. The wisdom of such an order depends on the needs of the child, the needs of the custodial parent, the relationship between the nonresident parent and the custodial parent, the relationship between the nonresident parent and the child, and the parenting skills of the nonresident parent. Such an order would not be appropriate in cases where the nonresident parent has abused the custodial parent or child. To be clear, we are not suggesting that such an order would be appropriate in Oakley's case. That is a determination for a trial court to make based on the specific circumstances of each case. However, the potential availability of alternative means of enforcing the parental duty of support that do not

---

[82] We recognize that the trial court could have sentenced Oakley to prison instead of granting him probation and that Oakley would be unable to exercise his right to procreate if imprisoned. Imprisonment is accompanied by incidental restrictions on constitutional rights. *Cf. Turner v. Safley*, 482 U.S. 78, 95 (1987) (recognizing that the "right to marry, like many other rights, is subject to substantial restrictions as a result of incarceration" but that "a prison inmate 'retains those [constitutional] rights that are not inconsistent with his status as a prisoner or with the legitimate penological objectives of the corrections system'"). However, Oakley has not been imprisoned and, as a probationer, he retains "a significant degree of privacy under the Fourth, Fifth and Fourteenth Amendments." *People v. Pointer*, 199 Cal. Rptr. at 363. Probation is not an "act of grace," *Gagnon v. Scarpelli*, 411 U.S. 778, 782 n.4 (1973), and thus the State may not place unnecessary restrictions on a probationer's fundamental rights merely because these restrictions are incidental consequences of incarceration.

[83] *Cf.* Sorensen & Lerman, *supra* note 57, at 104–5 (noting that many low-income nonresident parents make in-kind contributions to their children or provide child care).

[84] *Id.* at 105.

impair a fundamental right demonstrates that a condition of probation prohibiting procreation is not necessary to serve the State's interest in the child's support and is, therefore, overly broad. We recognize that these means may ultimately not be completely successful in achieving the State's objective of collecting child support. But the same was true in *Zablocki*, and the Supreme Court nevertheless found the statute that impinged on a fundamental right in that case unconstitutional. More importantly, the State has failed to show that the restriction on procreation would be any more effective than less restrictive means.

Moreover, the condition is overly broad because it does not merely restrict but rather abolishes Oakley's ability to exercise his constitutional right to procreate during the period of probation. Although the trial court's order permits Oakley to have another child if he shows "that he is meeting the needs of his other children and can meet the needs of this one," as a practical matter, the order is essentially a blanket prohibition on the right to procreate. The trial court was aware that Oakley was unlikely to ever be able to satisfy the order's financial requirement. In fact, Judge Hazlewood remarked that "it would always be a struggle to support these children and in truth [Oakley] could not reasonably be expected to fully support them." He noted that Oakley "couldn't pay what had been ordered even when he was employed." The trial court's recognition of Oakley's inability to meet the condition of probation demonstrates that the prohibition is not narrowly drawn to serve the state's interest in enforcing Oakley's support obligations. It also suggests that the condition of probation is a compulsory, state-sponsored, court-enforced financial test for future parenthood, and not a condition to exact compliance from obligors who have the financial means to support their children but refuse to do so.

The State cites the court of appeals' decision in *Krebs v. Schwartz* in support of its argument that the condition of procreation in this case is not overly broad. 568 N.W.2d 26 (Wis. Ct. App. 1997). In *Krebs*, the court of appeals upheld a probation condition that required a defendant convicted of sexually assaulting his daughter to obtain permission from his probation officer prior to engaging in a sexual relationship. *Krebs* is distinguishable from this case. In *Krebs*, the probationer's right to engage in sexual activity was not eliminated but merely restricted. In the instant case, it is very clear that Oakley will probably never be able to fully support his children. Therefore, his right to procreate is not restricted but is in fact eliminated. Moreover, Krebs was convicted of sexual assault and requiring him to obtain permission from his probation officer before engaging in a sexual relationship may be the only way for the State to protect potential sexual assault victims. There is nothing that the State can do to protect a potential victim of sexual assault after the assault has occurred. In contrast, the State can protect Oakley's existing and future children from nonsupport through the numerous means discussed above, including charging with him felony nonsupport and incarceration if he fails to comply with his current child support obligations.

Although a condition of probation that unnecessarily infringes on a probation-er's fundamental right to procreate when the State has other means available to further its interests is invalid, we feel compelled to address the State's flawed argument that the condition of probation is reasonably related to Oakley's rehabili-tation. A condition of probation is reasonably related to the goal of rehabilitation if it assists the convicted individual in conforming his or her conduct to the law. *See State v. Miller*, 499 N.W.2d 215, 217 (Wis. Ct. App. 1993). The State asserts that additional children could enlarge the emotional distance between Oakley and his older children, thereby shrinking his "already-questionable resolve" to support them. Thus, by prohibiting him from having additional children, the State argues, the condition of probation prevents Oakley from taking on additional support obligations and increases the likelihood that he will support his current children.

The State's argument suffers from the same logical flaw that the Supreme Court flagged in the Wisconsin statute at issue in *Zablocki*, which prevented a child support obligor from marrying but did nothing to bring any money to the obligor's children. *See* 434 U.S. at 389. Just as the statute in *Zablocki* was "grossly under-inclusive" to the extent that it was intended to prevent marriage applicants from incurring additional financial obligations because it did "not limit in any way new financial commitments by the applicant other than those arising out of the contem-plated marriage," *id.* at 390, so too is the probation condition in this case. The condition of probation does not prevent Oakley from assuming additional financial obligations generally. The order does not prevent Oakley from purchasing costly items on a credit card, thereby incurring additional financial obligations. It also does not prohibit Oakley from marrying and assuming the legal obligation of supporting a spouse. Indeed, the State indicated during oral argument that it would applaud Oakley if he married one of the mothers of his children.[85] Spouses have a reciprocal duty of support so, by marrying, Oakley would legally assume additional support obligations.

More important, preventing Oakley from fathering additional children will not increase the likelihood that he will support his current children. The condition of probation simply prohibits the birth of additional children but does nothing to address the underlying cause of Oakley's crime – nonsupport. It is doubtful that prohibiting Oakley from having another child will deliver any money to his current children or help him acquire the employment and parenting skills that may lead him to support his children financially and emotionally. To the contrary, the condition decreases the likelihood that Oakley will be able to support any of his children. If Oakley violates the condition of probation (either intentionally or accidentally because no contraceptive is foolproof) and has another child, he would most likely be incarcerated, leaving him with no way to support any of his children.

---

[85] Oakley was married to two of the mothers of his children. Both marriages ended in divorce.

Consequently, it is not at all clear how the condition of probation serves a rehabilitative purpose.

The State argues that the condition of probation protects future children from nonsupport and protects the public from having to support children that Oakley is unlikely to support. We find this argument both confusing and troubling. A child who does not exist will never be a victim of nonsupport because there will never be a support obligation where there is no child. We do not believe that the State is suggesting that not being born at all is preferable to being born to a parent who fails to provide support or that the State is advocating abortion based on parents' financial status. A child is no less deserving of life because her parents are unable or unwilling to provide for her support. We are similarly troubled by the State's suggestion that the public needs to be protected from having to support children who are not fully supported by their parents. The State has a parens patriae duty to protect its most vulnerable citizens – children. This is an obligation that we all share.

Today we join the many courts that have invalidated conditions of probation that prohibit a defendant from exercising his or her fundamental right to procreate. See U.S. v. Smith, 972 F.2d 960 (8th Cir. 1992) (invaliding condition prohibiting probationer from fathering additional children outside of marriage unless he could demonstrate that he was fully supporting his existing children); People v. Zaring, 10 Cal. Rptr. 2d 263 (Cal. Ct. App. 1992) (condition of probation prohibiting defendant from getting pregnant is impermissibly broad); Pointer, 199 Cal. Rptr. at 357 (condition of probation prohibiting mother convicted of child endangerment from having a child infringes on fundamental right and is overly broad); People v. Dominguez, 64 Cal. Rptr. 290 (Cal. Ct. App. 1967) (condition prohibiting defendant from becoming pregnant outside of marriage is invalid); Thomas v. State, 519 So.2d 1113 (Fla. Dist. Ct. App. 1988) (condition prohibiting probationer from becoming pregnant unless she was married is grossly erroneous); Howland v. State, 420 So.2d 918, 919–20 (Fla. Dist. Ct. App. 1982) (holding "that the condition of probation prohibiting appellant from fathering a child does not reasonably relate to the crime of child abuse and relates to noncriminal conduct"); Burchell v. State, 419 So.2d 358 (Fla. Dist. Ct. App. 1982) (per curiam) (condition prohibiting defendant from fathering any children is invalid); Rodriguez v. State, 378 So.2d 7 (Fla. Dist. Ct. App. 1979) (conditions of probation prohibiting probationer convicted of child abuse from marrying and having additional children are invalid because they have no relationship to the crime of child abuse, and relate to noncriminal conduct); People v. Ferrell, 659 N.E.2d 992, 995 (Ill. App. Ct. 1995) (invalidating the condition that prohibited a female probationer from engaging in any activity that could cause pregnancy because it violated state statute precluding courts from mandating the use of birth control), pet. for leave to appeal denied, 664 N.E.2d 644 (Ill. 1996); Trammell v. State, 751 N.E.2d 283, 290–91 (Ind. Ct. App. 2001) (condition of probation prohibiting defendant from becoming pregnant "excessively impinges upon her privacy right of procreation and serves no discernible rehabilitative purpose"); *State v. Mosburg*, 768 P.2d 313 (Kan. Ct. App. 1989) (invalidating probation condition prohibiting pregnancy by a mother who pled no contest to endangering her child because it unduly intruded upon her constitutional right to privacy); *State v. Norman*, 484 So.2d 952 (La. Ct. App. 1986) (striking condition prohibiting female defendant from having children out of wedlock); *State v. Richard*, 690 N.E.2d 667 (Ohio Ct. App. 1996) (striking condition requiring defendant either to use birth control or have a tubal ligation); *State v. Livingston*, 372 N.E.2d 1335 (Ohio Ct. App. 1976) (condition prohibiting defendant from having another child during the five-year probationary period was unconstitutional).[86]

We hold that the condition of probation prohibiting Oakley from having another child during the period of probation unless he first establishes his ability to support all his children violates his fundamental right to procreate and is, therefore, unconstitutional and invalid.

Our decision today is not blind to the grave harms caused by inadequate child support. However, prohibiting a probationer from procreating is unlikely to provide support to the children and is likely to have unintended consequences that will harm children, women, and economically vulnerable communities. First, we can only imagine the psychological harm that will befall a child who learns that his or her birth sent a parent to prison. In effect, the condition of probation criminalizes the birth of a child to a probationer who is unlikely to adequately provide for his children. If Oakley violates the condition of probation (either intentionally or as a result of contraceptive failure) and has another child, that child may be regarded by siblings and their mothers as directly responsible for the father's incarceration. The child may also blame herself. We are unwilling to impose such a heavy burden on an innocent child.

Second, the condition of probation imposes a substantial burden on all of Oakley's children and their mothers. If Oakley has another child, he will be incarcerated, thereby automatically depriving all his children of financial and

---

[86] The Oregon Court of Appeals is the only court that has upheld a condition of probation prohibiting a defendant from having any future children. In *State v. Kline*, 963 P.2d 697 (Or. App. 1998) the father was convicted of viciously abusing his children. In revoking the father's probation on the mistreatment charge, the court imposed a further condition that he not father additional children until he first demonstrated that he had completed drug treatment and anger management programs, as well as counseling. The court of appeals upheld the condition. Kline is distinguishable from this case. As the court of appeals noted in Kline, the trial court did not eliminate Kline's right to procreate but simply required Kline to complete drug treatment and anger management before he could exercise such right. *Id.* at 699. In contrast, Oakley will not be able to exercise his right to procreate during the period of probation because, as conceded by Judge Hazlewood, Oakley will most likely never be able to support his existing children.

emotional support. The custodial mothers would also lose a potential source of income and emotional support, requiring them to bear sole responsibility for their children's well-being.

Although the probationer in this case is a man, conditions restricting the procreative liberty of probationers are often imposed on women. Trial judges have repeatedly prohibited female probationers convicted of child abuse or drug crimes from exercising their fundamental right to procreate.[87] The FDA's approval of Norplant, the surgically implanted five-year contraceptive, in 1990, facilitated trial judges' ability to enforce such conditions.[88] Although no appellate court in the country has upheld conditions of probation prohibiting a female probationer from having a child, the majority of probationers do not appeal these conditions. Were we to uphold the condition of probation in this case, we fear that more trial judges would impose such restrictions with the imprimatur of a state supreme court.

While the majority of parents who owe child support are fathers, mothers who do not reside with their children are even less likely than nonresident fathers to pay child support.[89] If we uphold this condition today, we can be assured that it will be imposed on female probationers convicted of felony nonsupport who, if they become pregnant, will feel compelled to terminate the pregnancy to avoid going to prison. As other courts have recognized, in those cases the woman's constitutionally-protected decision to terminate a pregnancy would not be truly voluntary. For this reason, the court in *Pointer* struck a condition of probation that prohibited a woman convicted of felony child endangerment from becoming pregnant while on probation. 199 Cal. Rptr. 357. The court explained that if the woman: "became pregnant during the period of probation the surreptitious procuring of an abortion might be the only practical way to avoid going to prison. A condition of probation that might place a defendant in this position, and if so, be coercive of abortion, is in our view improper." *Id.* at 366. *See also Mosburg*, 768 P.2d at 315 (striking condition of probation prohibiting a woman who had been

---

[87] Andrew Horwitz, *Coercion, Pop-Psychology, and Judicial Moralizing: Some Proposals for Curbing Judicial Abuse of Probation Conditions*, 57 WASH. & LEE L. REV. 75 (2000).

[88] Melissa Burke, *The Constitutionality of the Use of the Norplant Contraceptive Device as a Condition of Probation*, 20 HASTINGS CONST. L.Q. 207 (1992) (discussing cases in which judges required Norplant as a mandatory condition of probation for mothers convicted of child abuse); Kristy M. Walker, *Judicial Control of Reproductive Freedom: The Use of Norplant as a Condition of Probation*, 78 IOWA L. REV. 779, 790 (1993) (discussing the condition of probation requiring a female probationer convicted of child abuse to submit to the surgical implantation of Norplant); Stephanie B. Goldberg, *No Baby, No Jail: Creative Sentencing Has Gone Overboard, A California Court Rules*, 78 A.B.A. J. 90–92 (Oct. 1992) (discussing cases in which court ordered the defendant to submit to implantation of Norplant). See also DOROTHY ROBERTS, *From Norplant to the Contraceptive Vaccine*, in KILLING THE BLACK BODY, at 104 (1997) (arguing that long-acting contraceptives such as Norplant and Depo-Provera have been used to limit black women's reproductive liberty).

[89] Sorensen & Zibman, *To What Extent, supra* note 45, at 3.

convicted of endangering her child from getting pregnant because it "unduly intrudes on [her] right to privacy" and if she were to become pregnant, the condition would "forc[e] her to choose among concealing her pregnancy (thus denying her child adequate medical care), abortion, or incarceration").

The risk of coercive abortion is also present when the probationer is a man. Because the condition of probation is triggered only upon the birth of a child, the risk of imprisonment creates a strong incentive for a man in Oakley's position to demand that any woman that he impregnates (either intentionally or accidentally) have an abortion. It also places the woman in an unenviable position – she can either have an abortion that she may not want or be responsible for Oakley going to prison for eight years.

Relatedly, the condition of probation may lead to or exacerbate family violence. If a man under this condition of probation impregnates his partner and she refuses to have an abortion, the likelihood of imprisonment upon the birth of the child may create an incentive for the probationer to use whatever means necessary, including violence, to force the woman to have an abortion or to forcibly cause a miscarriage. Battering during pregnancy is a "serious public health problem."[90] We cannot uphold a condition of probation that may increase the likelihood of violence against pregnant women.

This court cannot ignore the potential impact of these conditions of probation on racial minorities and indigent defendants. One small study of cases in which judges imposed mandatory implantation of Norplant as a condition of probation on mothers convicted of child abuse found that "courts have imposed the condition exclusively on lower income and minority women."[91] Other commentators have expressed concern about the race and class biases that influence judges' decisions to impose these conditions on certain defendants.[92] Given that the majority of poor fathers who do not pay child support are African American or Latino, conditions of probation restricting the right to procreate would disparately impact poor and minority men and, by extension, poor and minority communities. These communities would be forced to choose between having fewer children or sending more of their men to prison. As the Supreme Court has warned, the power to restrict procreation "can cause races or types which are inimical to the dominant group to wither and disappear." *Skinner*, 316 U.S. at 541. Moreover, our sordid history of forced sterilization of individuals deemed unworthy of reproduction, *see Buck v. Bell*, 274 U.S. 200, 207 (1927) (endorsing

---

[90] Julie A. Gazmararian *et al.*, *Prevalence of Violence against Pregnant Women*, 275 JAMA 1915, 1919 (1996). *See also* ELIZABETH M. SCHNEIDER, BATTERED WOMEN AND FEMINIST LAWMAKING at 150 (2000) (noting that "the correlation between pregnancy and battering is astonishingly high").

[91] Burke, *supra* note 88, at 242.

[92] *See* Goldberg, *supra* note 88, at 90–91 (citing the staff attorney at the Center for Reproductive Law and Policy).

forced sterilization of the developmentally disabled on the view that "[t]hree generations of imbeciles are enough"),[93] serves as a constant reminder of the dangers of allowing the government to decide who among us should be allowed to exercise our fundamental right to have children.

The decision of the court of appeals is reversed.

---

[93] It was later discovered that the petitioner was not developmentally disabled, only indigent. *See* Paul A. Lombardo, *Three Generations, No Imbeciles: New Light on Buck v. Bell*, 60 N.Y.U. L. Rev. 30 (1985).

9

Sojourner A. v. N.J. Dep't of Human Servs., 177 N.J. 318 (2003)

Commentary by Ann Cammett

INTRODUCTION

Since the Johnson Administration's "War on Poverty" in the 1960s,[1] the merging of race and welfare in the public imagination has eroded support for the social safety net.[2] Metaphorical constructs such as the "Welfare Queen" and other racialized tropes have served as cultural signposts to structure our understanding of which families should be deserving of public aid. These narratives historically have been deployed to reduce empathy and trigger resentment toward low-income mothers, who many presume to be African American. State legislators target these mothers by weaponizing racial biases under the pretext of promoting personal responsibility and protecting financial resources from so-called undeserving recipients of state aid. "Family caps" emerged in the 1990s as one approach to achieving these purported cost reduction and self-sufficiency goals. Welfare grants are typically allocated according to family size but states impose family caps in order to deny additional financial assistance to children born into families already receiving benefits. Advocates quickly initiated legal challenges to family caps because they represent a constitutionally suspect government intrusion on women's reproductive rights and create severe penalties for already poor families,

In *Sojourner A. v. New Jersey Department of Human Services*,[3] the Supreme Court of New Jersey held that the state's family cap on welfare benefits did not violate the equal protection or due process guarantees of the state constitution. Consequently, New Jersey families are eligible for Medicaid and food stamp benefits but are

---

[1] Economic Opportunity Act of 1964, Pub. L. No. 88-452, 78 Stat. 508 (1964).
[2] *See* Ann Cammett, *Deadbeat Dads & Welfare Queens: How Metaphor Shapes Poverty Law*, 34 B.C. J.L. & Soc. Just. 233 (2014).
[3] *Sojourner A. v. N.J. Dep't of Human Servs.*, 177 N.J. 318, 828 A.2d 306 (2003).

prohibited from obtaining an increase in cash assistance for any child born more than ten months after the family initially applies for and obtains benefits.[4] New Jersey was in the vanguard in the effort to cap payments and became, in 1992, the first state in the country to put such a restriction in place. Despite litigation and numerous legislative efforts to repeal New Jersey's family cap provision (referred to as the "child exclusion") the law remains intact.[5] This commentary contextualizes the Family Cap phenomenon within the larger discourse of poverty, race, and family engineering that dominated the welfare discussions of the 1990s.

THE BACKGROUND AND IMPACT OF FAMILY CAPS

Many states that implemented family cap policies did so after passage of the Personal Responsibility and Work Opportunity Reconciliation Act (PRWORA) of 1996,[6] also known as "welfare reform." PRWORA effectively eliminated the Aid to Families with Dependent Children program, replacing it with stingier, more discretionary state block grants called Temporary Assistance for Needy Families (TANF). TANF authorized states to write family caps into their benefit programs but the Department of Human Services in New Jersey had already done so. Prior to the enactment of PRWORA, state officials sought a waiver in order to prevent automatic incremental increases to families upon the birth of children born after the family began to receive welfare benefits. Thus, after TANF authorized family caps as part of the program's implementation, the legislature responded by seamlessly replacing its earlier program with Work First New Jersey (WFNJ), a welfare-to-work program featuring child exclusion. WFNJ's stated purpose was to "encourage employment, self-sufficiency and family stability."[7] The underlying assumption of the program was that it would discourage childbearing, incentivize work, and minimize welfare dependency, thereby reducing welfare costs borne by the public.

The highest number of states with family caps was twenty-four but, since 2002, seven states repealed their caps.[8] Repeal came because of evidence that caps failed to reduce the number of children born into families already receiving assistance but

---

[4] N.J. Stat. Ann. § 44:10–61a, b, e (West 2018).

[5] In 2016, both houses of the New Jersey legislature voted for repeal, only to be vetoed by then-Governor Chris Christie, who said that the Child Exclusion provides for equal treatment of welfare recipients and other residents, "who do not automatically receive higher incomes following the birth of a child." See Bryce Covert, *Chris Christie Rejects Effort to Repeal Racist, Sexist Rule That Punishes Poor Children*, THINK PROGRESS (July 5, 2016), https://thinkprogress.org/chris-christie-rejects-effort-to-repeal-racist-sexist-rule-that-punishes-poor-children-f831bc51f40e/.

[6] Personal Responsibility and Work Opportunity Reconciliation Act of 1996 (PRWORA), Pub. L. No. 104–193, 110 Stat. 2105 (1996).

[7] See generally N.J. Stat. Ann. 44:10-56 (West 2018).

[8] See CTR. ON REPROD. RIGHTS & JUSTICE, BERKELEY LAW, BRINGING FAMILIES OUT OF 'CAP'TIVITY: THE PATH TOWARD ABOLISHING WELFARE FAMILY CAPS 1 (2016), www.law .berkeley.edu/wp-content/uploads/2015/04/2016-Caps_FA2.pdf.

still may improperly influence how low-income women make decisions about pregnancy. Moreover, capping benefits pushes people deeper into poverty and has deleterious effects on families by increasing food and housing insecurity and worsening health and social outcomes for children.[9]

Family caps were and are predicated on an unproven causal link – that the promise of increased public assistance influences a woman's decision to have children. Researchers have been unable to demonstrate, even retrospectively, such a nexus.[10] The Center on Reproductive Rights and Justice at Berkeley Law decries the notion that money motivates low-income women when making childrearing decisions – a connection that arises from the "rational actor" economic theory. Voluminous social science research demonstrates that welfare recipients do not actually have additional children in order to receive very modest increases in their families' basic needs grant.[11] Further, many pregnancies are unintended, a fact that calls into question the rational actor theory. Nor is there any evidence that welfare recipients have more children than other families or base their childbearing on the existence or lack of family caps.[12]

On the other hand, family cap policies burden women of reproductive age and influence decisions without creating self-sufficiency. A study commissioned by New Jersey State officials determined that New Jersey's "Family Development Program [FDP] and the [Child Exclusion] did have a statistically significant impact on birth, abortion, and family planning decisions," but also found that "women do not move off welfare more quickly, stay off welfare longer, or earn more money when they leave welfare … [n]or does FDP 'significantly' improve employment prospects, employment stability, and earnings among program participants."[13] Moreover, while the State's policies create pressure for WFNJ recipients to terminate pregnancies, the State's Medicaid program does not cover abortion due to financial indigence, creating additional economic burdens on poor women who choose to terminate pregnancies.[14] Further, family caps do not promote self-sufficiency because welfare benefits are subsistence level to begin with so that a reduction makes the financial situation in the family more precarious. Therefore, the efficacy of these programs – and the underlying justifications for adopting them – is called into question.

Family Caps – and other welfare-related laws – are predicated on persistent noxious stereotypes about low-income mothers, who policymakers presume to be African American. Stigmatizing tropes such as the Welfare Queen were built on

---

[9] *Id.* at 7.

[10] *Id.* at 5. The report notes that "various personal values, familial conditions, and structural factors influence women experiencing both intended and unintended pregnancy."

[11] *Id.* at 3.

[12] *Id.* at 5.

[13] *Sojourner A. ex rel. Y.A. v. N.J. Dep't of Human Servs.*, 350 N.J. Super. 152, 161, 794 A.2d 822, 827 (App. Div. 2002).

[14] *See Harris v. McRae,* 448 U.S. 297 (1980); *Right to Choose v. Byrne,* 91 N.J. 281, 319, 450 A.2d 925, 941 (1982) (Pashman, J., concurring in part and dissenting in part).

longstanding white supremacist and sexist stereotypes that inform widely held beliefs about black women – who are perceived as living off the public dole while having children who the state supports. Many scholars have explored the history and construction of welfare reform and the use of the Welfare Queen trope as race code to identify so-called undeserving beneficiaries of welfare. Ange-Marie Hancock, Dorothy Roberts, Kaaryn Gustafson,[15] and others have all explored the history and law that give voice to racial anxieties about black mothers, which have provided the basis for punitive legislation and social policy. As further proof of stereotypes enabling a flawed discourse, political scientist Martin Gilens posits that exhaustive studies examining Americans' attitudes on race and their views on welfare spending have demonstrated that "perceptions of [B]lacks continue to play the dominant role in shaping the public's attitudes toward welfare."[16] Therefore, although the majority of public assistance recipients nationally are white, welfare's association with black people in the public imagination continues to drive policy on poverty issues as a whole. As such, the rhetorical discourse about self-sufficiency, personal responsibility, and the pattern of women's childbearing has laid the groundwork for the evisceration of the social safety net, including the rush to adopt family caps.

Other social engineering incentives, such as marriage promotion, favored by proponents of family caps drove changes to welfare law. Although stereotypes of mothers fuel the negative perceptions of low-income families – portraying them as inherently dysfunctional and in need of legislative correction – public stigmatization also extends to low-income fathers.[17] The political backlash over expanded access to public assistance for mothers evolved in tandem with the identification of "Deadbeat Dads" (who failed to pay child support) as the engines of child poverty. While it is generally understood that welfare reform altered the national landscape of entitlements, it is less commonly known that it simultaneously restructured the national child support system.[18] By concretizing legislative findings about the importance of marriage, responsible fatherhood, and the negative consequences of raising children in single parent homes, Congress put into place a clear rationale for disincentivizing childrearing outside of marriage.[19] PRWORA contained punitive,

---

[15] *See, e.g.,* Ange-Marie Hancock, The Politics of Disgust: The Public Identity of the Welfare Queen 3 (2004) (analyzing the "politics of disgust" arising in the discourse of welfare reform); Dorothy E. Roberts, Shattered Bonds: The Color of Child Welfare 66–67 (2002) (discussing the child welfare system's devaluation of black motherhood); Kaaryn Gustafson, *Degradation Ceremonies and the Criminalization of Low-Income Women,* 3 U.C. Irvine L. Rev. 297, 342–43 (2013) (describing the subordination of black women as connected to purported deficient mothering).

[16] *See* Martin Gilens, Why Americans Hate Welfare: Race Media and the Politics of Antipoverty Policy at 71 (2000).

[17] *See generally* Cammett, *supra* note 2.

[18] *Id.; see also* Tonya Brito, *The Welfarization of Family Law,* 48 U. Kan. L. Rev. 229 (1999).

[19] *See* Angela Onwuachi-Willig, *Return of the Ring: Welfare Reform's Marriage Cure as the Revival of Post-Bellum Control,* 93 Cal. L. Rev. 1647 (2005)(noting that post civil-war states' primary interests in sanctioning marriages between former slaves stemmed from the need to

mandatory child support enforcement mechanisms, triggered universally against fathers or non-custodial mothers, regardless of their ability to pay. These child support provisions were intended to transfer the financial support of low-income children receiving public assistance away from the state to unmarried fathers, despite mitigating economic factors, such as extreme poverty. In this social context, the rush to enact family caps is better understood as arising from ascendant reactionary social policies with a focus on normative family structure incentives, rather than a more nuanced analysis of economic factors that contribute to poverty in marginalized communities. The taint of racism, and its attendant resentments, licensed policy-makers to focus on policing and punishing the childbearing decisions of disfavored parents. As such, they failed to provide critical benefits to poor children.

OPINION OF THE SUPREME COURT OF NEW JERSEY

The Supreme Court of New Jersey's 2003 decision, with no dissenting opinions, rejected the plaintiffs' claims that child exclusion violated their equal protection and fundamental privacy rights under the state constitution, even while acknowledging that there are circumstances in which the New Jersey Constitution provides greater protection than the U.S. Constitution.[20] With respect to the due process claims, the New Jersey Supreme Court rejected the notion that the child exclusion provision of the WFNJ impermissibly infringed woman's reproductive rights, casually noting that it was not the effect of the statute on reproductive choice but rather the "nature of the burden or the extent of the governmental intrusion" that the Court must consider.[21] It characterized the governmental intrusion as "indirect and insignificant,"[22] finding that it "does not present a direct obstacle to bearing children."[23] The Court found that withholding an incremental increase in cash assistance to influence reproductive decision making was not an "undue" burden, nor does it create a "new burden" on reproductive autonomy.[24] Rather, just as "working families do not receive automatic increases when additional children are born," the family cap does no more than place "welfare families on par with working families."[25] Moreover, the Court concluded that there was ample justification for the child exclusion because, "[t]he goals of promoting self-sufficiency and decreased dependency on welfare are laudable; the focus on education, job training and child care should advance those goals and, ultimately, result in improving the lives of children born into welfare families."[26]

---

minimize the states' economic responsibility, especially for children born during slavery; note also PRWORA findings, including 42 U.S.C. § 601(a)).

[20] *Sojourner A. v. N.J. Dep't of Human Servs.*, 177 N.J. 318, 325, 828 A.2d 306, 310 (2003).

[21] *Id.* at 333.

[22] *Id.* at 325.

[23] *Id.*

[24] *Id.* at 315.

[25] *Id.* at 335.

[26] *Id.*

Ultimately, the Supreme Court summed up its analysis with one observation: "[t]his case is not about a woman's right to choose whether and when to bear children but, rather, about whether the State must subsidize that choice."[27]

On the equal protection question, the court gave relatively short shrift to the claim that the state denies children equal protection of the law because of their birth status when the children are ineligible for benefits as a result of the Child Exclusion. Noting that the families do continue to receive additional food stamps and Medicaid benefits under the provision, the Court dismissed the equal protection claim by asserting that it is the family that does not receive additional cash assistance when a new child is born. Rather than recognize a child-based distinction, the Court opined that, "[a]ll of the children in the family unit share presumably in the total amount of cash assistance available, as is the case in other similarly situated family units."[28]

While admitting that the test for state constitutional claims requires a more flexible analytical framework, including a sufficient public need for denial when evaluating equal protection and due process claims, the Court defaulted to the rational basis analysis undertaken by the federal court. The Court concluded that, "the family cap was 'rationally related to the legitimate state interests of altering the cycle of welfare dependency ... [and] promoting individual responsibility and family stability'."[29] On this basis the Supreme Court of New Jersey summarily dismissed the plaintiffs' claims.

THE FEMINIST REWRITE

Professor Cynthia Soohoo, writing as Chief Justice Soohoo, offers a detailed road-map of how the Court might have reached a contrary conclusion by adhering to a more robust state-based rights paradigm in order to render a decision that honors the lived experience of the litigants. She provides a deep analysis of the issues at play, acknowledging the suffering of the plaintiffs and exposing the Court's tendency to dwell in the abstractions of law that favor deference to state policy. Most notably, she reaches her conclusions by applying not only a more nuanced analysis under the state constitution but also an honest appraisal of history in the reproductive rights context and a thoughtful application of international law norms. Taken together, she provides a potent reimagining of an expanded framework for thinking about client-centered rights. Her feminist judgment differs from the original in several significant ways.

Soohoo finds, unsurprisingly, that the state's Child Exclusion law impermissibly violates the reproductive and procreative rights of women receiving WFNJ benefits. In doing so she discerns the real purpose of the statute, which is to penalize the

[27] *Id.* at 337.
[28] *Id.* at 336.
[29] *Id.* at 330.

plaintiffs for their reproductive choices while receiving public benefits. Under U.S. Supreme Court jurisprudence, statutes that impose indirect interference on fundamental rights need only satisfy rational basis review but Soohoo exposes the New Jersey Supreme Court's unwillingness to honor its own expanded state law precedents to fully engage in the balancing test that it has developed.

The Supreme Court acknowledges that it adopted the more nuanced test because "the inflexibility of the tiered framework prevents a full understanding of the clash between individual and governmental interests."[30] Notably, this requires that when government action affects an important personal right – like the right to privacy – it obligates the state to establish a "greater public need" than is traditionally required under the federal constitution, and show a "real and significant" relationship between the statutory classification and the State's asserted interest. Soohoo takes this mandate at face value and surfaces the Court's failure to do so by finding that, "[a]lthough the Appellate Division purported to apply a balancing test, it erred by applying the test in a manner that was functionally equivalent to the federal rational basis test." Indeed, she demonstrates how the Court "failed to take into account the full extent" of the State's intrusion on a woman's right to have a child by introducing a significant financial burden and failed to closely scrutinize the government's objectives and the relationship between the objective and the child exclusion. While the original decision makes light of the impact of the child exclusion's effect on procreative freedom, Chief Justice Soohoo places it squarely at the center, forcing the State to grapple with its obligation to honor the fundamental nature of that right, not to mention the impact of that abrogation on the lives of very poor litigants. In doing so, she makes clear that while "decreased dependency and promotion of work"[31] may be legitimate state goals in the welfare context, the State is not free to adopt unconstitutional means to achieving them.

Soohoo also subtly addresses the failure of the original decision to grapple with the racist impact of Family Caps and other welfare "reform" initiatives. By incorporating a robust discussion of historical population control incentives, Soohoo brings the specter of the Welfare Queen to its logical conclusion by linking the State's normative intent with a history of using racist measures to target disfavored populations. Reminding us that, "the United States . . . [has] a long history of states trying to use public benefit programs to modify poor people's behavior to impose 'morality' and encourage certain family structures," she notes that the government has long engaged in a range of activities, from embracing eugenics to coercive "population control policies targeting certain populations deemed unfit."[32] This shameful history reminds us that, as author William Faulkner so aptly notes, "the past is not dead, it's

---

[30] *Id.*
[31] *Id.* at 335.
[32] Cynthia Soohoo in this volume at 215.

not even past,"[33] especially when confronting attempts to use the law in the service of social engineering. These racist stereotypes and the politics of resentment have long informed national policy. Moreover, Soohoo reminds us that these approaches to population control have been disfavored by more enlightened thinkers, and under international law. While not directly scrutinizing the motivations of the drafters of widely enacted welfare legislation, Soohoo reminds us that that policymaking is rarely neutral, and that unexamined legislation serves as a cautionary tale exposing the implicit biases of lawmakers and jurists alike.

Finally, Chief Justice Soohoo finds that the child exclusion violates the equal protection rights of children denied subsistence level benefits, rendering them a separate and unequal class among similarly situated children. She starkly reframes the Court's rejection of their equal protection claim. While the original Supreme Court decision curtly dismisses them by subsuming their financial interests into that of their families' interests, Soohoo elevates the significance of their injury by situating their harm in a rights-based framework, which is justified by prior decisions in both the state and federal constitutions. Naming birth status discrimination against children born outside of marriage on equal protection grounds, she notes that, "[e]ven if the State has a legitimate interest . . ., such as promoting marriage, it is illogical and unjust to pursue that interest in a manner that penalizes children."[34] Moreover, she points out that discrimination against children based on their social origin or birth status would run afoul of our treaty obligations under the International Covenant on Civil and Political Rights, to which the United States is a signatory. Despite U.S. treaty obligations, conforming to international law conventions would represent a big departure from existing U.S. jurisprudence.[35] Notwithstanding the reluctance of the Courts, under general international law principles the child exclusion provision in New Jersey's welfare program would be considered to be in violation of international human rights norms.[36] For added measure, Soohoo invokes the Convention on the Rights of the Child,[37] ratified in nearly every country in the world, except the United States and Somalia. While not ratified by the U.S., the Convention articulates

---

[33] WILLIAM FAULKNER, REQUIEM FOR A NUN (1950).

[34] Soohoo, *supra* note 32 at 228.

[35] *See, e.g.*, Jenny S. Martinez, *Enforcing the Decisions of International Tribunals in the U.S. Legal System*, 45 SANTA CLARA L. REV. 877, 887 (2005) ("[T]he United States has demonstrated neither a consistent pattern of obedience and respect for international law and decisions of international courts and tribunals, nor a consistent pattern of defiance and disregard."); Steven Arrigg Koh, *"Respectful Consideration" after Sanchez-Llamas v. Oregon: Why the Supreme Court Owes More to the International Court of Justice*, 93 CORNELL L. REV. 243, 247 (2007) ("United States courts have long seemed to view treaties as both fundamental and antithetical to American jurisprudence").

[36] *See* Amicus Curiae Brief for The Center for Economic and Social Rights, The International Women's Human Rights Law Clinic, and The Center for Constitutional Rights in Support of Plaintiffs-Appellants at 1, *Sojourner A. v. N.J. Dep't of Human Servs.*, 177 N.J. 318, 828 A.2d 306 (2003) (Appeal No. A-160-01), available at 2002 WL 34565338.

[37] Convention on the Rights of the Child, Nov. 20, 1989, 155 U.N.T.S. 3.

internationally accepted standards for the protection of children's rights, including that children should not be discriminated against because of their birth status and that they should not be discriminated against or punished because of the "status, activities, expressed opinions or beliefs of the child's parents."

CONCLUSION

In deciding *Sojourner A.*, the Supreme Court of New Jersey rationalizes family caps as constitutional in that they place "welfare families on par with working families" because "working families do not receive automatic increases when additional children are born."[38] In doing so the Court isolates differently situated families from their social, political, and historical contexts and sets forth a false equivalency regarding access to opportunity. Families on welfare subsist on marginal benefits that define the contours of their economic lives, which lead to coerced decisions around reproductive choice. Families with employed parents receive automatic tax benefits that privilege the choice to have children and confer social status that mothers receiving public assistance are denied. In framing this and most welfare policies around this false distinction the courts provided cover for lawmakers that sowed the politics of division that dominate our current political environment. Specifically, the *Sojourner A.* Court lends its imprimatur to and normalizes the flawed discourse about welfare that arises from race, class, and gender biases and then ensconces them in law. This approach focuses on fairness in the abstract sense, rather than a searching inquiry that forces legislatures to analyze the conditions that create the vast need for public assistance in the first place and set its sights on providing effective remedies.

Soohoo's vision of progress in this case represents the road not taken. She gives voice to the litigants and their real struggles by embracing, rather than ignoring, a more protective state law; an option that was readily available to the New Jersey Supreme Court. She offers a different vision: a foundation for a reproductive jurisprudence that acknowledges the government's historical efforts to control the procreation of disfavored groups and clarifies the role of the State as a protector of rights for the most vulnerable. One of the implications of Soohoo's work is that it sheds light on the short-sighted goals of welfare policy, borne of the long-nurtured American bootstrap mythology. This reactionary posture obscures the importance of child wellbeing as a very important goal, as well as the long-term economic and social gains for poor families – and our nation. And she goes further. By embracing and applying international law norms, she provides us with insight into the ways in which U.S. jurisprudence can fit within the aspirational positive rights goals of a community of nations, especially when foregrounding our disgraceful treatment of poor children.

[38] *Sojourner A.*, 177 N.J. at 335 (citing *C.K. v. Shalala*, 883 F. Supp. 991, 1013 (D.N.J. 1995)).

Sojourner A. v. N.J. Dep't of Human Servs., 177 N.J. 318 (2003)

The opinion of the Court was delivered by Chief Justice Cynthia Soohoo. This case involves a challenge to the constitutionality of a provision of the Work First New Jersey Act ("WFNJ") that prohibits increased cash assistance for families upon the birth of a child when the family is receiving WFNJ benefits, N.J.S.A. 440:10-61 (the "Child Exclusion"). Although the State typically bases cash assistance grants on need and family size, the Child Exclusion prohibits the increase of cash assistance benefits if an additional child is born more than ten months after the family applies for and obtains benefits. N.J.S.A. 44:10-61a, b, and e. By departing from the general rule of calculating benefits based on family size and need in order to discourage or penalize child-bearing, the Child Exclusion impermissibly violates the reproductive and procreative rights of women who receive WFNJ benefits. The provision also violates the equal protection rights of children impacted by the Child Exclusion by punishing them for the procreative decisions of their parents.

I

A

WFNJ is the state's welfare program, which provides cash assistance to poor families who do not have any other means of support. N.J.S.A. 44:10-59(a) ("[B]enefits shall be provided . . . when other means of support and maintenance are not present"). In general, the state calculates the amount of cash assistance benefit that an eligible family receives based on family size. N.J.A.C. 10:90-3.3, Schedule II. However, even before the Child Exclusion is factored in, the cash benefit is calculated to be at most 45 percent of the state's standard of need, making it insufficient to meet the subsistence needs of the family unit. N.J.S.A. 44:10-42; N.J.AC. 10:69-10.2(a); 10:90-3.3.[39]

The Child Exclusion alters WFNJ's benefit calculation by adding another factor besides need and family size. It provides:

> The level of cash assistance benefits payable to an assistance unit with dependent children shall not increase as a result of the birth of a child during the period in which the assistance unit is eligible for benefits. N.J.S.A. 44:10-61(a)

The Child Exclusion only applies to WFNJ cash assistance, and does not affect other benefits the family may be eligible to receive under programs such as

---

[39] For example, according to the Plaintiffs, "while New Jersey's standard of need recognizes that a family of three requires at least $985 per month to meet its subsistence needs, that family will not receive more than $424 in public assistance." Supplemental Brief of Plaintiffs-Appellants, p. 9, n 5.

Medicaid and food stamps. N.J.S.A. 44:10-61b; N.J.A.C. 10:90-2.18. In addition, in order to offset the impact of the Child Exclusion, a family unit affected by the Child Exclusion "is entitled to retain a larger amount of earned income." *C.K. v. N.J. Dep't of Health & Human Servs.*, 92 F.3d 171, 179 (3d Cir. 1996) (citing N.J.S.A. 44:10-3.5 & 3.6).

B

New Jersey's Child Exclusion, which went into effect in 1992, precedes recent federal welfare legislation reform. In 1996 Congress passed the Personal Responsibility and Work Opportunity Reconciliation Act ("PRWORA"). 42 U.S.C.A. § 601 et seq. PRWORA replaced the Aid to Families with Dependent Children ("AFDC") program with Temporary Assistance for Needy Families ("TANF"), a block grant program that gives increased discretion to states. *Id.*

TANF continued AFDC's purpose of providing support for children so that they can be raised in their family home but it also added the additional statutory purpose of ending dependence on government benefits. Specifically, PRWORA states that TANF's purpose is to:

(1) provide assistance to needy families so that children can be cared for in their own homes or in the homes of relatives;
(2) end the dependence of needy parents on government benefits by promoting job preparation, work, and marriage;
(3) prevent and reduce the incidence of out-of-wedlock pregnancies and establish annual numerical goals for preventing and reducing the incidence of these pregnancies; and
(4) encourage the formation and maintenance of two-parent families. 42 U.S.C. § 601(a).

In 1992 when the AFDC program remained in effect, New Jersey became the first state to adopt a Child Exclusion provision as a method of welfare reform. In order to adopt the provision, the state sought an AFDC waiver because the exclusion violated existing federal requirements prohibiting denial of benefits to otherwise eligible needy children. *Sojourner A. v. N.J. Dep't of Human Servs.*, 350 N.J. Super. 152, 159, 794 A.2d 822 (App. Div. 2002). Although the waiver request articulated three primary goals: "(1) breaking the cycle of poverty; (2) enhancing the role of individual responsibility; and (3) strengthening and reuniting families," *id.* at 159, the State's waiver application made clear that the Child Exclusion sought to achieve these goals by dissuading women receiving benefits from having additional children. The State described the choice to have a child while receiving AFDC benefits as "irresponsible and not socially desirable" and justified the Child Exclusion as a means of encouraging women to "be responsible" in "their decisions to have another child while receiving welfare." Pa104–06. Similarly, the legislative sponsor of the Child Exclusion stated that the provision was "intended to discourage AFDC recipients from having additional children during the period of their welfare dependence." Pa872.

The federal government granted the state's waiver request as a five-year research experiment. As part of the research experiment waiver, the Department of Health and Human Services required New Jersey to evaluate the impact of the Child Exclusion on "marital status and birth rates." Pa126. These results are discussed in more detail below. According to a 1999 study, after New Jersey adopted the Child Exclusion, eighteen other states obtained AFDC waivers to implement similar provisions. Shelly Stark & Jodie Levin-Epstein, EXCLUDED CHILDREN: FAMILY CAP IN A NEW ERA at 18, n.2 (Ctr. for Law & Soc. Policy, February 1999).

In 1997, in response to the federal government's replacement of the AFDC program with TANF, New Jersey adopted WFNJ to replace its prior welfare system. Among WFNJ's stated aims are breaking the cycle of welfare dependency and encouraging employment and individual responsibility and family stability. N.J.S.A. 44:10-56. WFNJ added new job training and search assistance services, remedial education, GED classes, and support services such as day care and transportation to job or school. N.J.S.A. 44:10-57. WFNJ also retained the Child Exclusion using statutory language that "was nearly identical to the cap under AFDC." *Sojourner A.*, 350 N.J. Super. at 160; N.J.S.A, 44:10-61; N.J.A.C. 10:90-2.18. Following the passage of TANF, an additional three states enacted Child Exclusion provisions. Stark & Levin-Epstein, EXCLUDED CHILDREN, at 18, n.2.

Between May 1993 and June 1998, twenty-eight thousand newborns in New Jersey were subject to the Child Exclusion resulting in a per capita decrease in cash benefits for their families. Jodie Levin-Epstein, OPEN QUESTIONS: NEW JERSEY'S FAMILY CAP EVALUATION at 1 (Ctr. for Law & Soc. Policy, February 1999). Since 1993, the percentage of cases subject to the Child Exclusion has grown to twelve percent of the State's caseload. *Id.* African American families are disproportionately impacted by the Child Exclusion because they comprise approximately fifty percent of the families in the welfare program even though they are only fourteen percent of the State population. DP-1 Profile of General Demographic Characteristics: 2000 Data Set: Census 2000 Summary File 1 (SF 1) 100-Percent Data Geographic Area: New Jersey.

C

While the state characterizes the Child Exclusion provision as a welfare reform initiative, it is important to view the provision in the broader context of population control policies, both in the United States and internationally. In the 1950s and 1960s, many countries around the world concerned about the economic and environmental impacts of large populations adopted policies designed to decrease births. In recent years, population control policies have come under increasing criticism for adopting coercive methods and forcing women to have abortions, undergo sterilization, or use inappropriate contraceptive measures. Betsy Hartmann, REPRO-DUCTIVE RIGHTS AND WRONGS at 163–68, 206, 251–54 (Boston: South End Press, 1995), Dorothy Roberts, KILLING THE BLACK BODY at 139–43 (Vintage Books, 1997). By focusing solely on the state goal of reducing births, coercive population policies violate women's right to bodily autonomy and to make their own procreative decisions about whether to continue a pregnancy, become steril-ized, or use contraception. Hartmann, REPRODUCTIVE RIGHTS AND WRONGS at 70; Roberts, KILLING THE BLACK BODY at 140.

In 1994, 179 nations, including the United States, condemned the use of coercive population incentives and penalties at the U.N. International Conference on Population and Development ("ICPD"). The ICPD Program of Action emphasized that "[t]he principle of informed free choice is essential to the long-term success of family planning programmes" and that "[a]ny form of coercion has no part to play." Int'l Conference on Population & Dev., Cairo, Egypt, September 5–13, 1994, Programme of Action, ¶7.12, U.N. Doc. A/CONF.171/13/Rev.1 (1995). Both the ICPD Program of Action and the Declaration and Platform of Action of the 1995 Beijing Conference recognized that women have the "right to make decisions concerning reproduction free from discrimination and coercion." Id.; Fourth World Conference on Women, Beijing, P.R.C., September 4–15, 1995, Beijing Declar-ation and Platform for Action, ¶95, U.N. Doc. A/CONF.177/20 (Oct. 17, 1995). The ICPD also emphasized that, rather than adopting coercive measures, state family planning goals "should be defined in terms of unmet needs for information and services," recognizing that government actions should help facilitate women's ability to realize their reproductive choices rather than coercing those choices. Id.

Although the United States has not faced the same population pressures as countries like China or India, there is a long history of population control policies targeting certain populations deemed unfit. In 1927, the Supreme Court upheld Virginia's compelled sterilization of an eighteen-year old under a sterilization statute, prohibiting reproduction by "potential parents of socially inadequate off-spring." Buck v. Bell, 274 U.S. 200, 207, 47 S. Ct. 584 (1927). By 1931, thirty states had enacted eugenic sterilization laws. Paul A. Lombardo, Medicine, Eugenics and the Supreme Court: From Coercive Sterilization to Reproductive Freedom, 13 J. CON-TEMP. HEALTH L. & POL'Y 1, n.2 (1996). In 1942, in Skinner v. Oklahoma, the Supreme Court struck down an Oklahoma statute providing for involuntary steriliza-tion of "habitual criminals" on equal protection grounds. 316 U.S. 535 (1942),[40] but it has never explicitly overruled Buck v. Bell.[41]

---

[40] The Supreme Court recognized procreation as "one of the basic civil rights of man" and applied strict scrutiny in reviewing the Oklahoma statute. Id. at 542.

[41] The Supreme Court has stated that the fundamental liberty interest protecting a woman's decision whether to bear a child protects a woman's right to carry a pregnancy to term against state interests motivated by population control or eugenic purposes. Planned Parenthood of Southeastern Pennsylvania v. Casey, 505 U.S. 833, 859, 112 S.Ct. 2791 (1992). However, in 1995,

Efforts to control the racial make-up of the U.S. population and, in particular, to perpetuate a "pure" white majority have been reflected in other areas of the law, including bans on inter-racial marriage[42] and immigration restrictions.[43] In the 1920s, the U.S. introduced an immigration quota system that limited the number of immigrants who could be admitted to the U.S. from other countries and allocated each country a quota based upon the national origins of people living in the U.S. recorded in the census.[44] The government designed the quota system to maintain the racial mix of the population and the system continued until the 1960s.[45] Further, restrictions on naturalization prevented Asians who immigrated to the United States from becoming citizens until the 1940s and 1950s.[46]

the Supreme Court denied a petition for certiorari of a woman with intellectual disabilities challenging a Pennsylvania involuntary sterilization statute. *Estate of C.W.*, 640 A.2d 427 (Pa. Super. Ct. 1994), *cert. denied* 115 S.Ct. 1175 (1995).

[42] In 1940, thirty states had laws barring interracial marriage. Roberts, KILLING THE BLACK BODY at 71. In 1967, when the Supreme Court struck down prohibitions on interracial marriages in *Loving v. Virginia*, sixteen states prohibited marriages on the basis of racial classifications. 388 U.S. 1, 6, 87 S.Ct. 1817, 1821,18 L. Ed.2d 1010 (1967). Other laws prohibited interracial cohabit- ation. *See e.g. McLaughlin v. Florida*, 379 U.S. 184, 85. S.Ct.283, 13 L.Ed2d 222 (1964) (holding that criminal statute prohibiting an unmarried black man and a white woman or an unmarried white woman and a black man from "habitually liv[ing] in and occupy[ing] in the nighttime the same room" violated equal protection).

[43] In the United States, there is a history of immigration laws designed to restrict immigration from certain countries. For instance, the Chinese Exclusion Act of 1882 prohibited the immigration of Chinese Laborers. Act of May 6, 1882 (Chinese Exclusion Act), ch. 126, § 1, 22 Stat. 58 (repealed 1943). The Page Act, an earlier immigration law, sought to decrease the Chinese population in the United States by prohibiting the immigration of women for "lewd and immoral" purposes. While the Act did not prohibit the immigration of all Chinese women, it included specific enforcement mechanisms targeting Chinese immigration. The Page Act resulted in virtual complete exclusion of Chinese women from the United States because government officials "demonstrated a consistent unwillingness, or inability, to recognize women who were not prostitutes among all but wealthy applicants for immigration." George Anthony Peffer, IF THEY DON'T BRING THEIR WOMEN HERE: CHINESE FEMALE IMMIGRATION BEFORE EXCLUSION at 9 (Urbana: University of Illinois Press, 1999).

[44] The first Quota Act was passed in 1921. Act of May 19, 1921, ch. 8, 42 Stat. 5 (repealed 1952). It continued a 1917 bar on immigration from countries in the Asiatic Barred Zone and allocated an annual quota to other countries (outside of the Western Hemisphere) of three percent of the number of residents from each country living in the U.S. recorded in the census of 1910. *Id.* In 1924, the National Origins Act imposed a quota system which remained in effect until 1965. Johnson Act, ch., 190 § 1, 43 Stat. 153 (1924) (repealed 1965).

[45] ***Patrick Weil, *Races at the Gate: A Century of Racial Distinctions in American Immigration Policy (1865–1965)*, 15 GEO. IMMIGR. L.J. 625, 626 (2001) (stating that a "racialist" approach to immigration dominated American policy from the 1920s until 1965 which based selection on national or ethnic origin).

[46] Natsu Taylor Saito, *Alien and Non-Alien Alike; Citizenship, "Foreignness," and Racial Hier- archy in American Law*, 76 OR. L. REV. 261, 271 (1997). The Naturalization Act of 1790 required that people seeking naturalization be a "free white person." Naturalization Act of 1790, 1 Stat. 103 (repealed by the Act of Jan. 19, 1795 which re-enacted its racial restrictions). This language was later modified to include "aliens of African nativity" and "persons of African descent." Act of July 14, 1870, ch. 255, §7, 16 Stat. 254. The racial limitations on naturalization were not removed until 1952. Immigration and Nationality Act, ch. 477, 66 Stat. 163 (1952). *See*

In the U.S., state legislators have proposed population control measures to decrease the cost to the public of supporting the children of poor families. In the 1960s, several states considered bills imposing compulsory sterilization on mothers receiving welfare benefits who continued to conceive children outside of marriage. Roberts, KILLING THE BLACK BODY at 94. Although these measures did not pass, in the 1970s, there were widespread reports of non-consensual sterilization imposed by government doctors and public health facilities in order to reduce population growth among poor, minority populations.[47] As a result of sterilization abuse, in 1973 the Department of Health, Education and Welfare issued rules restricting sterilizations performed under programs receiving federal funds, including requiring informed consent and 30-day waiting periods. Roberts, KILLING THE BLACK BODY at 96–97.

In the United States, there is also a long history of states using public benefit programs to modify poor people's behavior to impose "morality" and encourage certain family structures.[48] The Supreme Court has struck down state provisions restricting benefits to children because of the behavior of their parents, holding that such provisions violate children's equal protection rights.[49] At the same time, the

---

Ozawa v. United States, 260 U.S. 178, 43 S.Ct. 65 (1922) (holding that Ozawa, a person of Japanese descent born in Japan who resided in the U.S. for twenty years was ineligible for citizenship because naturalization provision only applied to "free white persons and to aliens of African nativity and to persons of African descent").

[47] Research conducted by Gena Correa in the 1970s indicated that doctors performed sterilization procedures on women without informed consent based on a belief that it was the best way to reduce undesirable population growth among the poor. Roberts, KILLING THE BLACK BODY at 92. *See Relf v. Weinberger*, 372 F. Supp. 1196 (D.D.C. 1974), order vacated by 565 F.2d 722 (D.C. Cir. 1977) (describing "uncontroverted evidence . . . that minors and other incompetents have been sterilized with federal funds and that an indefinite number of poor people have been improperly coerced into accepting a sterilization operation under the threat that various federally supported welfare benefits would be withdrawn . . ."); Sally J. Torpy, *Native American Women and Coerced Sterilization: On the Trail of Tears in the 1970s*, 24 AM. INDIAN CULTURE & RESEARCH J. 2 (2000) (describing sterilization of Native American women who were threatened with the loss of benefits or removal of their children if they had additional children and asked to consent to sterilization during labor); HEALTH RESEARCH GROUP, A HEALTH RESEARCH GROUP STUDY ON SURGICAL STERILIZATION: PRESENT ABUSES AND PROPOSED REGULATIONS at 7 (Washington, D.C., 1973) (describing sterilization of Mexican American women in a California county hospital where residents were instructed to strong arm vulnerable patients to accept sterilization); Hartmann, REPRODUCTIVE RIGHTS AND WRONGS at 247–48 (describing how the Puerto Rican government encouraged sterilization without providing adequate information about the permanency of the procedure or meaningful access to alternative forms of contraceptives).

[48] Roberts, KILLING THE BLACK BODY at 202. Going back to the initial creation of the Aid to Dependent Children program, the predecessor program to the AFDC, the Social Security Act of 1935 explicitly allowed states to impose eligibility requirements based on sexual morality, including "man-in-the-house" and "suitable home" rules. Lucy A. Williams, *The Ideology of Division: Behavior Modification Welfare Reform Proposals*, 102 YALE L.J. 719, 723 (1992).

[49] *New Jersey Welfare Rights Organization v. Cahill*, 411 U.S. 619, 620, 93 S.Ct. 1700 (1973) (holding that limiting benefits to households composed of two married adults of the opposite sex violates equal protection); *King v. Smith*, 392 U.S. 309, 336 88 S.Ct. 2128 (1968) (Douglas,

Supreme Court recognized that when a state administers benefit programs it must "reconcile the demands of its needy citizens with finite resources to meet those demands." *Dandridge v. Williams*, 397 U.S. 471, 472, 90 S. Ct. 1153 (1970). State decisions setting benefit eligibility and levels may indirectly impact constitutionally protected rights. In cases where states seek to further legitimate state interests, the Supreme Court has applied a rational basis review, deferring to the state in determining how to allocate limited benefits among myriad possible recipients.[50] However, the state may not use its benefit allocation to accomplish an improper purpose. Cf. *Dandridge*, 397 U.S. at 484, 90 S. Ct. 1153 ("Although a State may adopt a maximum grant system in allocating its funds ... it may not, of course, impose a regime of invidious discrimination in violation of the Equal Protection Clause of the Fourteenth Amendment").

D

We now turn to consider evidence of the impact of the Child Exclusion. Both survey data and the Plaintiffs' experience show that the Child Exclusion did affect the child-bearing decisions of AFDC recipients. When the State introduced the Child Exclusion, under the AFDC waiver, it hired Rutgers School of Social Work to evaluate the program. The Rutgers study found that New Jersey's "Family Development Program and the [Child Exclusion] did have a statistically significant impact on birth, abortion, and family planning decisions." Pa754; *Sojourner*, 350 N.J. Super. at 161, 794 A.2d at 827. According to the study, between October 1992 and the end of 1996, "there were 1,429 more abortions and 14,057 fewer births among AFDC recipients than would have occurred in the absence of the FDP." *Id.* at 162, 794 A.2d at 827.

The Rutgers study was consistent with the experience of Plaintiffs Angela B. and Sojourner A. In 1995 when Sojourner A. became pregnant with her second child, she considered ending the pregnancy because of financial hardship imposed by the

---

J., concurring) (holding that denying AFDC benefits to children whose mother "cohabits" with an able bodied man violates equal protection because "the immorality of the mother has no rational connection to the need of her children under any welfare program").

[50] In *Dandridge*, the Supreme Court applied a rational basis standard of review in an equal protection challenge to Maryland's AFDC scheme that capped the total amount of benefits families received based on the minimum wage a steadily employed head of the household received. *Id.* at 485, 486. The State cited its interest in "allocating available public resources in such a way as fully to meet the needs of the largest possible number of families" as well as interests in encouraging employment, maintaining equity between families receiving welfare and those supported by a wage earner, and "providing incentives for family planning." *Id.* at 483. *Dandridge* was decided before the Supreme Court recognized a woman's fundamental right to decide whether or not to have a child in *Roe v. Wade* and, in analyzing the equal protection challenge, the Court did not explore whether the State's classification impacted a fundamental right. *Id.* at 484 ("[H]ere we deal with state regulation ... not affecting freedoms guaranteed by the Bill of Rights, and claimed to violate the Fourteenth Amendment ...").

Child Exclusion but in the end decided to have the child. Pa545; Pa551–52. When she became pregnant again in 1997 and 1998, after having faced the hardship of trying to support two children on diminished benefits, she terminated the pregnancies. Pa55; Pa556–57. In 1995, Plaintiff Angela B., a mother of three, also considered having an abortion when she was pregnant with a fourth child because of the Child Exclusion but ultimately decided to continue the pregnancy. Pa545; Pa551–52.

The Child Exclusion also imposes significant hardship on women receiving WFNJ benefits who choose to have an additional child or continue a pregnancy. Even when supplemented by Food Stamps, WFNJ benefits do not provide enough income for most families with children. Pa509–10. As a result, the reduction of benefits caused by the Child Exclusion can have a big impact on women and their families. Angela B. was forced to support herself and four children on diminished WFNJ benefits. Pa540–42, Pa 574. She described running out of Food Stamps in the middle of every month and relying on food pantries and charities to feed her children. Pa541, Pa570. Angela B also testified that she lacks funds for diapers, medicine, and public transportation to doctors' appointments. Pa544–45; Pa574–75. Sojourner A. supports two children on a cash assistance benefit calculated for one child and testified that she lacks adequate money for diapers, milk, and clothes for her baby. Pa558–59. Both plaintiffs lack stable housing. They live with friends and family and would be unable to afford an apartment on their own. Pa561, Pa571, Pa549–50.

Plaintiffs' experience is supported by expert opinions establishing that per capita reductions of benefits, like the Child Exclusion, have a devastating impact on families that struggle to meet basic needs such as food, clothing, and housing. Pa577. Plaintiffs' expert John Cook, an expert in food insecurity and hunger, testified that when a poor family adds a family member without any additional resources, the family copes by reducing the quality and quantity of food available. Psa9. Dr. Deborah Frank, the Director of the Growth and Development Program at Boston Medical Center, opined that families that experience a per capita reduction in public assistance benefits suffer extreme hardship and deprivation including increased risk of nutritional deficit as well as long-term effects including increased vulnerability to infection, decreased learning capacity, and increased vulnerability to lead poisoning. Pa637.

Although the named Plaintiffs currently have housing, most families receiving welfare pay more than thirty percent of their income for housing, with some paying nearly half their income for rent. Pa606–7. Under these circumstances, adding an additional child and expenses without additional benefits increases the risk of homelessness or inadequate or unsafe housing. Pa580; Pa 608–9.

Although the Child Exclusion significantly impacted the reproductive decision-making of women receiving WFNJ benefits, there is no evidence that it furthered the State's stated purpose of reducing welfare dependency or increasing employment levels. The Rutgers study found that the Child Exclusion was not "effective in reducing recipiency and moving welfare recipients from welfare and into employment." *Sojourner*, 350 N.J. Super. at 162, 794 A.2d at 828.

II

On September 5, 1997, Plaintiffs filed a class action lawsuit against the New Jersey Department of Human Services and its Commissioner challenging the constitutionality of N.J.S.A. 44:10-61 and N.J.A.C. 10-90-2.18. The Plaintiffs argue that the Child Exclusion seeks to impermissibly coerce their procreative decisions, violating their fundamental right to privacy and personal autonomy. In addition, Plaintiffs argue that the Child Exclusion violates the equal protection rights of poor children "based on their parents' reproductive choices and the timing of [their] birth."

The trial court denied an initial request for a preliminary injunction and declaratory relief and granted class certification on July 17, 2000. On December 18, 2000, the trial court granted the Defendants' cross-motion for summary judgment. In rejecting the Plaintiffs' privacy claim, the court purported to apply the balancing test established by this Court. The trial court accepted the Defendants' assertion that the Child Exclusion was enacted to further the State's interest in "promoting self-sufficient citizens, diminishing dependency upon welfare and creating [parity] between welfare recipients and working people ..." *Sojourner A.*, 350 N.J. Super. at 158. The court found that Defendants demonstrated "a legitimate and substantial relationship between the statutory classification and the ends asserted" and that the cap only imposed a "slight imposition or mere burden" on the Plaintiffs' right to privacy. *Id.* The Appellate Division affirmed the trial court decision, holding that the statute "does not substantially intrude upon a woman's right to bear children, and the statute is reasonably related to legitimate government objectives [of] breaking the cycle of poverty, promoting responsibility and self-reliance, and decreasing welfare dependency and strengthening families." *Sojourner A.*, 350 N.J. Super. at 157.

As noted by the Appellate Division, a federal challenge was brought against the Child Exclusion under the former N.J. benefit scheme under the AFDC program, and the district court and Third Circuit held that the cap did not violate Due Process or the Equal Protection clause of the Constitution. *C.K.*, 92 F.3d at 194–95. Thus, we limit our decision to claims under the N.J. Constitution.

III

A

The Plaintiffs have alleged that the Child Exclusion impermissibly infringes on their right to privacy, raising equal protection and substantive due process claims under the New Jersey Constitution. *See Greenberg v. Kimmelman*, 99 N.J. 552, 569, 494 A.2d 294 (1985) (noting that in cases involving fundamental rights "due process and equal protection analyses, while proceeding along parallel lines, may overlap"). Specifically, the Child Exclusion discriminates between two groups of women who receive WFNJ benefits based on their decision about whether to have a child. WFNJ recipients who do not have a child after they begin receiving benefits – either because they do not become pregnant or because they terminate a pregnancy – will receive the full benefit allocation based on family size. Women who become pregnant and choose to continue the pregnancy receive a diminished benefit allocation. The Child Exclusion also unconstitutionally infringes on Plaintiffs' procreative decision making by penalizing them for choosing to bear a child.

This Court has adopted a different approach for equal protection and due process claims under the New Jersey Constitution than the U.S. Supreme Court uses in cases brought under the federal Constitution. Rather than employing the "mechanical approach" of tiered levels of scrutiny, we have adopted a balancing test. *Robinson v. Cahill*, 62 N.J. 473, 491, 303 A.2d 273 (1973). The balancing test is particularly appropriate in cases that involve a classification that "indirectly infringes on a fundamental right" because "the inflexibility of the tiered framework prevents a full understanding of the clash between individual and governmental interests." *Planned Parenthood of Cent. N.J. v. Farmer*, 165 N.J. 609, 630, 762 A.2d 620 (2000).

Our balancing test considers the nature of the affected right, the extent to which the government's restriction intrudes upon the right, and the public need for the restriction. *Greenberg*, 99 N.J. at 567, 494 A.2d 294. Further, when government action affects an important personal right, like the right to privacy, we require that the government establish a "greater public need" than is traditionally required under the federal constitution. *Right to Choose v. Byrne*, 91 N.J. 287, 309, 450 A.2d 925 (1982). The State must also establish a "real and significant" relationship between the statutory classification and the State's asserted interest. *Planned Parenthood*, 165 N.J. at 612–13, 762 A.2d 620.

B

Although the Appellate Division purported to apply a balancing test, it erred by applying the test in a manner that was functionally equivalent to the federal rational basis test.[51] In reaching its holding, the Appellate Division found that "the legislative enactment does not substantially intrude upon a woman's right to bear children, and the statute is reasonably related to legitimate governmental objectives [of] breaking the cycle of poverty, promoting responsibility and self-reliance, and decreasing welfare dependency and strengthening families." *Sojourner A.*, 350 N.J. Super. 152, 157, 794 A.2d 822 (2002). The Appellate Division failed to take account of the full

---

[51] The Supreme Court has held that statutes that impose an indirect interference with fundamental rights need only satisfy rational basis review. *Harris v. McRae*, 448 U.S. 297, 325, 100 S.Ct. 2671 (1980); *Maher v. Roe*, 432 U.S. 464, 478-79, 97 S.Ct. 2376 (1977).

extent of the intrusion on a woman's right to have a child and failed to closely scrutinize the government's objectives and the relationship between the objective and the Child Exclusion.

The Appellate Division characterized the governmental intrusion as indirect and insignificant, *id*. at 169, finding that it "does not present a direct obstacle to bearing children," *id*. at 171. Its conclusion seems to solely rest on the fact that the government accomplished its intrusion through the allocation of benefits. The Appellate Division failed to consider the impact that the Child Exclusion has on the Plaintiff class, which by definition consists of poor women, whose subsistence level benefits were cut below the level the state calculated as appropriate for their family size.

The Appellate Division cited to federal cases for the proposition that the State has not imposed a burden on the plaintiffs' procreative rights because the State has no obligation to fund any benefit and "it is not obligated to remove obstacles that it did not create, including a lack of financial resources." *Id*. at 174. On this issue, the New Jersey Constitution requires that we depart from the federal standard. We have emphasized that, although the State does not have an obligation to fund any benefit program, once it undertakes to do so it must proceed in a neutral manner. *See e.g., Right to Choose*, 91 N.J. at 306–7, 307, n.5, 450 A.2d 925 (holding that once the state "undertakes to fund medically necessary care attendant upon pregnancy, . . . government must proceed in a neutral manner" and that in the "constitutionally protected zone, the State may be an umpire, but not a contestant"). Cf. *Planned Parenthood*, 165 N.J. at 613, 762 A.2d 620 (holding that the state must maintain neutrality with respect to a minor's childbearing decisions and "the State may not affirmatively tip the scale"). *See Moe v. Sec'y Admin. & Fin.*, 417 N.E.2d 387, 401 (Mass. 1981) ("While the State retains wide latitude to decide the manner in which it will allocate benefits, it may not use criteria which discriminatorily burden the exercise of a fundamental right"); *State Dep't of Health & Soc. Servs. v. Planned Parenthood of Alaska*, 28 P.3d 904, 910 (Alaska 2001) (holding that the state "may legitimately attempt to limit its expenditures . . . a State may not accomplish such a purpose by invidious distinctions between classes of its citizens").

We view this neutrality principle as essential to ensure that all residents of New Jersey, rich and poor, can fully enjoy the protections of our constitution. We have criticized statutes that "can be understood only as an attempt to achieve with carrots what government is forbidden to do with sticks." *Right to Choose*, 91 N.J. at 308, 450 A.2d 925 (*citing* Laurence Tribe, AMERICAN CONSTITUTIONAL LAW, § 15–10 at 933 n.77 (1978)). Failure to impose a neutrality requirement would create a situation in which the government could interfere with the constitutional rights of persons who rely on government benefits for their basic subsistence in ways that would be impermissible for wealthy individuals. *See* Cass Sunstein, *Why the Unconstitutional Conditions Doctrine is an Anachronism (with Particular Reference to Religion, Speech, and Abortion)*, 70 B.U. L. REV. 593, 604–5 (1990) (arguing that the distinction between penalties and non-subsidies cannot be sustained given the rise of the regulatory state and the level of influence that modern government spending and funding have on people's lives); Dorothy Roberts, *The Only Good Poor Woman: Unconstitutional Conditions and Welfare*, 72 DENV. U. L. REV. 931 (1995) (criticizing the distinction between direct interference with a protected activity and refusal to subsidize a protected activity because it reflects "a constitutional framework designed to protect only property owners" that fails to preserve poor women's liberty).

We now proceed to consider the nature of the affected right, the extent to which the government's restriction intrudes upon the right, and the public need for the restriction.

IV

A

The decision whether to bear a child goes to the heart of a woman's right to control her body and determine her future. *Planned Parenthood*, 165 N.J. at 631–32, 762 A.2d 620 (recognizing "the importance of a woman's right to control her body and her future, a right we as a society consider fundamental"); *Right to Choose*, 91 N.J. at 306, 450 A.2d 925.

Whether described as a right to privacy or liberty, this Court has repeatedly recognized that our constitution protects women's fundamental choices about procreation and reproduction.[52] *Right to Choose*, 91 N.J. at 303–4, 450 A.2d 925, *Planned Parenthood*, 165 N.J. at 629, 762 A.2d 620. We have recognized that "a [woman's] right to control her reproductive decisions is among the most fundamental rights she possesses . . ." *Id.* at 613. Indeed, personal dignity and autonomy lie at the heart of a woman's right to make reproductive decisions and this is imbedded in liberty protected by the New Jersey constitution. *Id.* at 613, 632. While most cases involving reproductive rights have involved the decision not to procreate, it is well established that the right to have a child is equally protected as fundamental to individual liberty and autonomy. *See J.B. v. M.B.*, 109 N.J. 396, 537 A.2d 1227 (1988) (recognizing that the rights to personal intimacy, marriage, sex, family, and procreation are fundamental rights protected both by the state and federal constitutions); Cf., *Eisenstadt v. Baird*, 405 U.S. 438, 453, 92 S. Ct. 1029 (1972) ("[i]f the right of privacy means anything, it is the right of the individual, married or single, to be free from unwarranted governmental intrusion into matters so fundamentally affecting a person as the decision whether to bear or beget a child").

---

[52] Art. 1, par. 1 of the New Jersey Constitution provides "All persons . . . have certain natural and inalienable rights, among which are those of enjoying and defending life and liberty . . . and of pursuing and obtaining safety and happiness."

Because of our constitutional commitment to this right, in the appropriate case involving intrusions into women's reproductive rights, we have not hesitated to interpret our Constitution "to provide greater rights than its federal counterpart." *Planned Parenthood*, 165 N.J. at 632, 762 A.2d 620; *In re Grady*, 85 N.J. 235, 249, 426 A.2d 467, 474 (1981) (noting governmental intrusion in a case involving sterilization "may require more persuasive showing of a public interest under our State constitution than under the federal constitution"). Indeed, we have struck down intrusions into women's reproductive decision-making that have been upheld under the federal constitution including holding that private, non-profit hospitals cannot prohibit the use of facilities for elective abortions, *Doe v. Bridgeton Hospital Ass'n, Inc.*, 71 N.J. 478, 366 A.2d 641 (1976) and requiring that state Medicaid funds cover abortions necessary to preserve a woman's health, *Right to Choose*, 91 N.J. at 293, 450 A.2d 925. We have also struck down a statute that conditioned a minor's ability to obtain an abortion on parental notification or judicial waiver but did not impose the same requirements on a minor's ability to access pregnancy related medical or surgical care. *Planned Parenthood*, 165 N.J. at 612, 762 A.2d 620.

Having established the nature of the affected right, we now consider the extent of the governmental intrusion.

B

In determining the extent of the State's intrusion on the Plaintiffs' fundamental rights, the Appellate Division improperly relied on the distinction between "direct" and "indirect" interference rather than looking at the intent and actual impact of the Child Exclusion. *Sojourner A.*, 350 N.J. Super. at 171, 794 A.2d 822. Based solely on the characterization of the Child Exclusion as an "indirect" interference, the Appellate Division concluded that the Child Exclusion does not "substantially interfere with a woman's right to have children." *Id.* at 169.[53] Our balancing test

---

[53] Although we reject the Appellate Division's reliance on federal cases distinguishing between "direct" and "indirect" interference, we note that the nature of state interference in those cases is qualitatively different. In *Bowen v. Gilliard*, 483 U.S. 587, 107 S.Ct. 3008 (1987) and *Califano v. Jobst*, 434 U.S. 47, 98 S.Ct. 95 (1977) plaintiffs challenged benefit rules that impacted plaintiffs' decisions to marry and to live as a family unit. In both cases, there was no argument or evidence that the rules were adopted to discourage marriage or break up family units. At most, the cases establish that when the State makes benefit allocation decisions, motivated by neutral factors such as decreasing costs and effectively allocating resources that indirectly influence private decision-making, rational basis review will be applied. However, the cases do not establish that all government decisions involving benefit allocations are subject to rational basis review because the purpose motivating benefit allocations matter. Where the State adopts a benefit scheme specifically to pressure a constitutionally protected choice, rational basis review is inappropriate. *Cf. Bowen*, 483 U.S. at 601–2, 107 S.Ct. 3008 (1987) ("That some families may decide to modify their living arrangements in order to avoid the effect of the amendment, does not transform the amendment into an act *whose design* and direct effect are to 'intrud[e] on choices concerning family living arrangements'") (emphasis

explicitly rejects the Appellate Division's approach and instead requires a fact specific inquiry to determine the extent to which a governmental restriction actually intrudes upon a right in practice. *Planned Parenthood*, 165 N.J. at 633–36, 762 A.2d 620 (looking at actual effects of a parental notification requirement on a minor's ability to terminate a pregnancy based on certifications describing the actual experience of minors).

In *Planned Parenthood*, we considered a challenge to a statute that conditioned a minor's right to obtain an abortion on parental notification or judicial waiver but did not place a corresponding requirement for medical and surgical care related to pregnancy. In considering the nature of the government restriction, we looked at the impact the provision had on the exercise of the fundamental right for the population at issue. Because the State imposed the restriction on minors, we looked at how the restriction interacted with and exacerbated challenges that pregnant minors already face in accessing abortion. *Id.* at 638. We considered that it takes minors longer to recognize they are pregnant and decide to have an abortion and that they must overcome a lack of financial resources and familiarity with the medical system. *Id.* at 633. We recognized that burdens that may not be significant for adults, such as making a phone call to the court or an attorney to commence a judicial waiver proceeding, would pose great difficulties for minors. *Id.* at 636.

Similarly, when assessing the impact of the Child Exclusion, we must consider the situation of women receiving WFNJ benefits and recognize that reducing the benefit level of a family that relies on public assistance to meet basic subsistence needs imposes a severe penalty on poor women and their families. According to the states' own expert, welfare benefits, even when coupled with Food Stamps, do not provide enough income for most families with children. Pa509–10. By decreasing the family benefit below this level, the Child Exclusion provision imposes severe hardship on women who decide to continue pregnancies and have an additional child.

Further, both the Plaintiffs' experience and the Rutgers study show that the Child Exclusion does in fact pressure WJNJ recipient's decision as to whether to have an additional child. Both plaintiffs considered abortions after discovering they were pregnant. Pa543; Pa551–52. Sojourner A. terminated two pregnancies when faced with giving birth to additional children subject to the Child Exclusion given the difficulties she already faced in trying to provide for two children at a benefit level set for one child. Pa552, Pa556–57. In addition to the experience of the named Plaintiffs, the Rutgers study showed that the Child Exclusion did affect the

added and citations omitted); *Califano*, 434 U.S. at 54, n.11, 98 S.Ct. 95 ("This is not a case in which government seeks to foist orthodoxy on the unwilling"); *Dandridge*, 397 U.S. at 484, 90 S. Ct. 1153 ("[H]ere we deal with state regulation … not affecting freedoms guaranteed by the Bill of Rights, and claimed to violate the Fourteenth Amendment …").

reproductive choices of WFNJ recipients, resulting both in an increased rate of abortion and a decrease in births.[54]

While there is substantial evidence that the Child Exclusion influenced the child bearing decisions of WFNJ recipients, we note that the harm inflicted on Plaintiffs for choosing to have a child alone constitutes a constitutionally suspect government intrusion, irrespective of whether the provision actually caused them to forego having a child or have an abortion because the Child Exclusion inflicts a penalty on Plaintiffs for having a child.[55] See Yvette Marie Barksdale, *And the Poor Have Children: A Harm-Based Analysis of Family Caps and the Hollow Procreative Rights of Welfare Beneficiaries*, 14 LAW & INEQUALITY 1, 70 (1995) (arguing that when determining whether the government has impermissibly interfered with constitutionally protected choices, courts should focus on whether the government inflicts harm because of the exercise of a constitutional right). In *Sanchez v. Department of Social Services*, 314 N.J. Super. 11, 713 A.2d 1056 (App. Div. 1998), the Appellate Division considered the constitutionality of a WFNJ provision that reduced the benefits of individuals who moved to New Jersey from states with a lower benefit levels. The Appellate Division struck down the provision because it found that it unconstitutionally penalized the exercise of the right to travel without serving any compelling state interest. *Id.* at 23.

Based on the undisputed evidence, we find that the Child Exclusion constitutes a significant intrusion on Plaintiffs' fundamental right to choose to have a child. The New Jersey Legislature adopted the provision with the specific purpose of dissuading WFNJ recipients from having more children and, in fact, births among the WFNJ population have decreased and abortions have increased among the same population. The Child Exclusion also constitutes a constitutionally significant intrusion because it penalizes Plaintiffs' exercise of a fundamental right because the State disfavors the choice of WFNJ recipients to have additional children.

---

[54] We emphasize that the Court does not take the position that an increase in the abortion rate is inherently problematic. The New Jersey Constitution protects women's ability to make their own decisions about whether to continue or terminate a pregnancy, which includes the right to choose an abortion. What is troubling is that the State purposefully adopted the Child Exclusion to discourage WFNJ recipients from having children by imposing a financial burden on their choice, and the Rutgers study showed that the provision "did have a statistically significant impact on birth, abortion, and family planning decisions." Pa754. Ironically, while the State's policies create financial pressure for WFNJ recipients to terminate a pregnancy, the State's Medicaid program does not cover the medical costs for an abortion for poor women who terminate a pregnancy for financial reasons. *Right to Choose*, 91 N.J. at 319, 450 A.2d 925 (Pashman, J., concurring in part and dissenting in part).

[55] The State argues that the Child Exclusion does not harm WFNJ recipients because the provision does no more than place them on "par with working families." *C.K.*, 883 F. Supp. at 1013. In fact, working families receive government assistance when they have additional children in the form of tax deductions and credits which are worth more than the incremental WFNJ benefit for additional children.

Having found that the Child Exclusion constitutes a significant intrusion on Plaintiffs' child-bearing decisions, we proceed to consider the State's purported interest in the provision and the relationship between the interest and the provision.

C

The State has articulated various state interests for its Child Exclusion. The motion judge considered the state interest in "diminishing the dependency upon welfare and creating parity between welfare recipients and working people." *Sojourner A.*, 350 N.J. Super. at 172, 794 A.2d 822. In *C.K.*, the federal district court considered a challenge to the Child Exclusion under the AFDC program and recognized a state interest in putting WFNJ recipients on par with "working people." *C.K.* 883 F. Supp. at 1013 (discussing state interest in giving "AFDC recipients the same structure and incentives as working people"). The district court also identified a state interest in "promot[ing] individual responsibility and stabiliz[ing] the family unit." *Id.*

Applying a rational basis standard, the Appellate Division focused on the state's interests in (1) diminishing dependency on welfare, (2) promoting individual responsibility, and (3) strengthening the family unit.[56] Applying this deferential standard, the Appellate Division found that these state goals were reasonable "and reflect a legislative decision that a ceiling on welfare benefits provides incentives for persons to enter the workforce." *Sojourner A.*, 350 N.J. Super. at 172–73, 794 A.2d 822.

When legislation impinges on a constitutionally protected right, we must look more closely at the State's purported justification. *Planned Parenthood* 165 N.J. at 619–20, 762 A.2d 620. Given N.J.'s heightened protection for privacy rights, we "demand stronger and more persuasive showings of a public interest," *State v. Saunders*, 75 N.J. 200, 217, 381 A.2d 333 (1977) and a "real and significant" relationship between the statutory classification and the State's asserted interest, *Planned Parenthood*, 165 N.J. at 612-13, 762 A.2d 620.

The Appellate Division improperly applied a highly deferential standard, stating that courts should not second guess public officials in their decision to allocate public welfare funds. *Id.* at 172. After finding that the state had articulated legitimate state interests, it failed to consider whether the Child Exclusion furthers the State's interests. In fact, the State has not provided any evidence that the Child Exclusion

---

[56] Both *C.K.* and the motion judge discussed placing WFNJ recipients in the same position as "working people." It is unclear whether creating "parity" is presented as a separate interest justifying the Child Exclusion or whether the State's position is that by creating similar incentives for WFNJ recipients and "working people" it will diminish dependency, promote responsibility, and strengthen the family unit. We do not consider creating "parity" as a separate state interest. However, we note that in fact the Child Exclusion does not create the same system of incentives for WFNJ recipients and other families.

strengthens the family unit or promotes individual responsibility.[57] As for diminishing dependency on welfare, the evidence supports the opposite conclusion. The defendant's expert conceded that while other aspects of the WFNJ program such as work participation requirements, time limits, and child support requirements may have furthered the State's interest in decreasing dependency, the Child Exclusion has not led to declines in welfare rolls or increased work participation. Pa856–57, Pa860.[58]

Further, the State must establish a "real and significant relationship" between the statutory classification that treats women who have children while receiving WFNJ benefits differently than other WFNJ recipients and the state's asserted interests. In *Sanchez*, the Appellate Division required that the State do more than articulate the goal of promoting work among new WFNJ recipients to justify reduced benefits to a class of recipients who had exercised their right to travel and considered how the specific classification furthered the State's interest. 314 N.J. Super. at 26–28, 713 A.2d 1056. *Sanchez* involved both federal and state equal protection claims, and the Appellate Division concluded that the two-tiered benefit scheme resulting from the provision reducing the benefit amount received by individuals who moved to New Jersey from states with lower benefit levels did not even satisfy the federal rational relationship standard. *Id.* at 26. ("However salutary the goals, we disagree that the statute is a rational means to reach them"). The court emphasized that although the State can pursue its goal to encourage new residents to work "It cannot be accomplished in an irrationally discriminatory manner." *Id.* at 27.

As in *Sanchez*, the State's creation of different benefit levels for women receiving WFNJ benefits who have the same number of children based solely on whether the children were born ten months after a woman enrolled in WFNJ discriminates against women for exercising a fundamental right. This classification and penalty on the exercise of a constitutionally protected right does not further the State's interest

---

[57] The State argues that the Child Exclusion is justified because working families do not receive additional salary when they have another child but, as discussed, *supra* note 2, in fact they receive additional "benefits" in the form of tax deductions and credits. As for parity, even before the Child Exclusion is applied, families receiving WFNJ $424 a month, and an individual earning minimum wage ($5.15 an hour) for a 40 hour a week job earns $206 a week or approximately $824 a month. Both the family living on a minimum wage income and the family receiving WFNJ benefits must live on less than N.J.'s standard of need for a family of three, which is $985, but the family receiving WFNJ benefits is receiving less than half of N.J.'s standard of need. By diminishing benefit levels that are already below the standard of need, the Child Exclusion undermines rather than strengthens the family unit. The State does not articulate what promoting individual responsibility means and to the extent the State's purpose is to discourage women receiving WFNJ benefits from having additional children as a "responsible" decision, it is not a legitimate state interest.

[58] Perhaps recognizing that the Child Exclusion does not decrease dependency, the State argues that the money it has saved as a result of the Child Exclusion has been diverted to programs like job training and childcare. However, the State's burden is to show its differential treatment of women who have children while receiving WFNJ benefits decreases dependency. The fact that the State has adopted other programs that may further its goals does not satisfy its burden.

in decreasing dependency. If, as the Appellate Division suggests, the State intended to create a ceiling on benefits to incentivize work because of financial pressures parents feel to support their children, there is no rational reason to only impose the incentive on WFNJ recipients who have additional children[59] rather than imposing a cap on benefits that applies to all families receiving benefits.

Even more troubling, the only possible reason for the State to decrease the benefits of women who have a child ten months after enrolling in WFNJ is to discourage their child-bearing or to impose a hardship on them for choosing to have a child. Both outcomes arguably could decrease dependency by resulting in smaller families or creating greater incentives to work because of the increased financial pressures of a larger family. However, while decreased dependency and promotion of work are legitimate states goals, the State is not free to adopt unconstitutional means to achieve its goals.

Our Constitution does not permit the State to impose unjustifiable burdens on the child-bearing decisions of all women within the state, including WFNJ recipients. The State has failed to demonstrate that the Child Exclusion furthers its interests in diminishing welfare dependency and has failed to provide adequate justification for setting lower benefit allocations for WFNJ recipients because they give birth within ten months of enrolling in WFNJ. Indeed, the evidence strongly suggests that the State adopted the Child Exclusion for the impermissible purpose of influencing Plaintiffs' child-bearing decisions and penalizing them for having a child.

D

The Plaintiffs raise an additional equal protection challenge on behalf of their minor children because the Child Exclusion improperly penalizes poor children by diminishing their benefits based on the circumstances of their conception and birth and the behavior of their parents, circumstances over which they have no control and cannot change.

The Child Exclusion creates two classes of children, those impacted by the Child Exclusion and those who are not.[60] The former class receives a diminished per

---

[59] Indeed, if the State's goal is to encourage work through the reduction of benefits to WFNJ recipients, it does not make sense to focus on the Plaintiff class because the Child Exclusion will impact them immediately after the birth of a child, a time at which it is most difficult for women to obtain work outside of the home given the time needed to physically recover from child-birth, the childcare demands of newborn infants, and the low availability of childcare for infants.

[60] The State improperly describes the classification challenged by Plaintiffs as the distinction between children born before a family receives WFNJ benefits and children born ten months after the family receives benefits within the same family unit. While the State is correct that all children within a family unit share their family's WFNJ benefit, the relevant distinction is not between children within the same family unit but between family units that are impacted by the Child Exclusion and those that are not impacted by it.

capita benefit because the State denies an increase in their family benefit upon the birth of a child subject to the Child Exclusion. The Child Exclusion does not impact the latter class of children who receive a larger per capita benefit. In drawing these distinctions, the Child Exclusion penalizes children because of their mothers' decision to have a child or continue a pregnancy while receiving WFNJ benefits.

Our Court and the Supreme Court have prohibited birth status discrimination against children born out of wedlock on equal protection grounds. *Schmoll v. Creecy*, 54 N.J. 194, 202, 254 A.2d 194 (1969), overruled on other grounds by *Lafage v. Jani*, 166 N.J. 412, 766 A.2d 1066 (2001) (holding that children born out of wedlock can recover damages for the wrongful death of their father); *Trimble v. Gordon*, 430 U.S. 762, 97 S. Ct. 1459 (1977) (prohibiting discrimination on the ability to inherit intestate between kids born in and out of wedlock); *Weber v. Aetna Casualty & Surety Co.*, 406 U.S. 164, 175–76, 92 S. Ct. 1400 (1972) (holding workers compensation scheme that discriminates against unacknowledged illegitimate children violates Equal Protection).

These cases recognize that the law should not penalize children because of their parents' behavior. *State v. Clark*, 58 N.J. 72, 88, 275 A.2d 137 (1971); *Weber*, 406 U.S. at 175–76, 92 S. Ct. 1400 ("[N]o child is responsible for his birth and penalizing an illegitimate child is an ineffectual – as well as an unjust-way of deterring the parent"). Even if the State has a legitimate interest, such as promoting marriage, it is illogical and unjust to pursue that interest in a manner that penalizes children. *New Jersey Welfare Rights Organization*, 411 U.S. 619, 93 S. Ct. 1700 (striking down a N.J. welfare provision that restricted benefits to families with two married parents).

In *Plyler v. Doe*, 457 U.S. 202, 102 S. Ct. 2382 (1982), the Supreme Court recognized that the principle that children should not be penalized for the actions of their parents also applies outside of the illegitimacy context. The Court struck down a Texas law that excluded undocumented children from public school on equal protection grounds. Because of the importance of education and the unfairness of disadvantaging children because of the actions of their parents, the Court reasoned that the law could not be rational unless the state could show that it furthers a "substantial state interest." It stated "[e]ven if the State found it expedient to control the conduct of adults by acting against their children, legislation directing the onus of a parent's misconduct against his children does not comport with fundamental conceptions of justice." *Id.* at 2396.

Here, the Child Exclusion similarly punishes children because of their mother's stigmatized and disfavored behavior – the choice to have a child or continue a pregnancy while receiving cash assistance benefits. Because the children have no control over their birth status or their mother's child-bearing decisions, it is irrational and unjust for the State to penalize them by withholding subsistence level benefits.

Our holding that it is improper to discriminate or punish children for their birth status or the actions of their parents is supported by international human rights law. The International Covenant on Civil and Political Rights, ratified by the U.S. in

1992, prohibits discrimination against children based on their social origin or birth. International Covenant on Civil and Political Rights, opened for signature Dec. 16, 1966, art. 24 & 26, 999 U.N.T.S. 171 (entered into force Mar. 23, 1976).[61] Although not ratified by the U.S., the Convention on the Rights of the Child ("CRC") has been ratified by almost all the countries in the world and is recognized as articulating internationally accepted standards for the protection of children's rights.[62] The CRC also emphasizes that children should not be discriminated against because of their birth and that they should not be discriminated against or punished because of the "status, activities, expressed opinions or beliefs of the child's parents." Convention on the Rights of the Child, opened for signature, Nov. 20, 1989, art. 2, 1577 U.N.T.S. 3 (entered into force September 2, 1990).

V

We hold that the Child Exclusion violates the privacy and equal protection rights of the Plaintiffs and the equal protection rights of their minor children impacted by the Child Exclusion. The decision of the Appellate Division is reversed, and the State is enjoined from enforcing the Child Exclusion.

---

[61] Article 26 states that "the law shall prohibit discrimination and guarantee to all persons equal and effective protection against discrimination on any such grounds such as ... social origin, ... birth or other status." Art. 24 provides that "[e]very child shall have, without any discrimination as to ... social origin ... birth, the right to such measures of protection as are required by his status as minor, on the part of ... the State."

[62] Somalia is the only country other than the U.S. that has not ratified the CRC.

10

K.M. v. E.G., 37 Cal. 4th 130 (2005)

Commentary by Nancy Polikoff

K.M. v. E.G. is a second-generation lesbian mother custody dispute.[1] The women involved in these cases became parents through assisted conception, when one partner used semen from a known or unknown donor; through one partner's sexual intercourse; or through adoption, when one woman became the legal adoptive parent because two women could not adopt together. The legally salient fact about these families was that only the woman who gave birth to or adopted the child was a legal parent. Some of the disputes that emerged in the 1980s occurred after the legal parent died, when her relatives filed for custody.[2] Most disputes arose when the couple split, and the legally recognized parent denied her former partner all contact with their child.[3]

The small group of lawyers focusing on these planned lesbian families sought to remedy the vulnerability of the legally unrecognized parent and her child. They persuaded trial judges in some states to interpret existing adoption statutes to allow second-parent adoption, thereby creating parentage in a birth mother's partner without terminating the birth mother's parental rights.[4]

---

[1] The first generation of disputes pitted recently-out lesbian mothers against their former husbands, fighting to keep custody of the children they bore in different-sex marriages. Those mothers, emerging in significant numbers in the 1970s, were inspired by both the women's liberation movement and the gay liberation movement. For a review of some of the early case law, *see* Nan D. Hunter & Nancy D. Polikoff, *Custody Rights of Lesbian Mothers: Legal Theory and Litigation Strategy*, 25 BUFF. L. REV. 691 (1976); Rhonda R. Rivera, *Our Straight-Laced Judges: The Legal Position of Homosexual Persons in the United States*, 30 HASTINGS L.J. 799, 883–904 (1979).

[2] E.g. *In re Hatzopoulos*, 4 FAM. L. REP. (BNA) 2075 (Dec. 6, 1977).

[3] Some of the earlier cases are summarized in Nancy D. Polikoff, *This Child Does Have Two Mothers: Redefining Parenthood to Meet the Needs of Children in Lesbian-Mother and Other Nontraditional Families*, 78 GEO. L.J. 459 (1990).

[4] *See* David L. Chambers & Nancy D. Polikoff, *Family Law and Gay and Lesbian Family Issues in the Twentieth Century*, 33 FAM. L.Q. 523, 540 (1999).

Unfortunately, most lesbian couples did not have access to second-parent adoption. Some states did not permit it. And only those with the money and connections to hire a specialized lawyer and pay for a home study, and with no blemishes to impede the adoption process, could benefit from this practice. For example, low income women and those with any criminal justice system involvement – disproportionately women of color – were unlikely to seek second-parent adoption. Therefore, advocates argued, state by state, that a legally unrecognized intended and functional parent should be able to maintain a relationship with the child she raised. The first big win came in 1995, when the Wisconsin Supreme Court in *Holtzman v. Knott (In re H.S.H-K)* established a multi-part test which, when satisfied, gave visitation rights to the legally unrecognized parent.[5]

Gaining visitation rights was an incomplete victory because it did not fully recognize that the child had two parents. California, the site of *K.M. v. E.G.*, was not even one of the states that adopted the Wisconsin test. Rather, California courts stood by a 1991 appellate court ruling in *Nancy S. v. Michele G.* that denied all rights to a non-biological mother who had functioned as an equal parent for seven years.

K.M. V. E.G. AND *ELISA B. V. SUPERIOR COURT*

The turning point in parentage law for same-sex couples came on August 22, 2005, when the California Supreme Court ruled in three cases brought by the same-sex partners of women who had given birth to children. The most consequential case decided that day for the future of LGBT parentage law was *Elisa B. v. Superior Court*, and it figures decisively in the feminist concurrence.[6] Emily and Elisa were together for four years when they decided to raise children. Both women became pregnant using donor semen. Elisa bore one child and Emily gave birth to twins. Elisa was the family breadwinner and Emily was a stay-at-home mother. After the couple separated, Elisa provided financial support for a short time but then stopped. Emily went on public assistance, and the state filed an action for child support against Elisa, arguing that she was a legal parent of Emily's biological children.

The court held that under California's Uniform Parentage Act (UPA) Elisa was the children's parent. The court applied the statutory presumption of parentage that attaches to a man who receives a child into his home and holds the child out as his natural child. This provision from the original Uniform Parentage Act (1973) sought to equalize the status of children born to married and unmarried women.

When *Nancy S. v. Michele G.* was decided, it was assumed that the UPA applied only to a person holding out a child as his biological child and that it would be

---

[5] 533 N.W.2d 419 (Wis. 1995). Over the subsequent decade, numerous states followed suit. See NATIONAL CENTER FOR LESBIAN RIGHTS, LEGAL RECOGNITION OF LGBT FAMILIES at 5–6 (2016), www.nclrights.org/wpcontent/uploads/2013/07/Legal_Recognition_of_LGBT_Families .pdf.

[6] 117 P.3d 360 (Cal. 2005).

rebutted by lack of biological tie.[7] But in the intervening years, the California Supreme Court applied the presumption to a man who entered a relationship with a woman who was already pregnant and who raised the resulting child as his own.[8]

The UPA also contained a provision permitting its standards for determining paternity to be applied to determinations of maternity.[9] The California courts twice applied the "holding out" presumption to a woman who raised a child as her own but was not the child's biological mother.[10] Using those precedents, *Elisa B.* held that a child could have two mothers, a biological mother and a mother who received the child into her home and held out the child as her own. *Elisa B.* overturned the holding in *Nancy S.* and leapfrogged California over the states that had followed *In re H.S.H-K* because it gave a child two equal legal parents.

Elisa B. had a greater impact on LGBT family law than *K.M.* because its facts were more common. Given the cost and invasiveness, few lesbian couples have become parents when one woman was impregnated by an embryo formed by the egg of her partner and donor semen.

The *K.M.* Court considered the case to be the equivalent of a dispute between a birth mother and a known donor. The birth mother, E.G., argued that K.M. was the counterpart of a sperm donor whose genetic material was provided to a physician to conceive a pregnancy. Under Cal. Fam. Code 7613(b), that donor was not the resulting child's legal parent. The court ruled instead that K.M.'s genetic material did make her a legal parent, because it read 7613(b) as inapplicable to a woman's donation of ova to her partner "to produce children who would be raised in their joint home." Therefore, because K.M. and E.G. intended to raise the children together in their home, the court found it unnecessary to decide the case based on the couple's intent concerning legal parentage at the time of the ova transfer.

THE FEMINIST CONCURRENCE

The feminist concurrence by Justice Murray vigorously disagrees with the majority's refusal to apply the plain language of Cal. Family Code 7613(b) denying parentage to a donor of semen to a doctor for insemination of a woman not his wife. Justice Murray would apply this statute to ovum donation by operation of Cal. Family Code 7650, the same provision that the *Elisa B.* court used to apply the "holding out" test for paternity to determinations of maternity. Justice Murray would hold that K.M. cannot assert parentage based on her biological tie. Instead, the feminist

---

[7] Nancy D. Polikoff, *From Third Parties to Parents: The Case of Lesbian Couples and Their Children*, 77 LAW AND CONTEMP. PROBS. 195, 212 (2014).

[8] *In re Nicholas H.*, 46 P.3d 932 (Cal. 2002).

[9] CAL. FAM. CODE § 7650 (West 2005). This provision originated in the 1973 Uniform Parentage Act Section 21.

[10] *In re Karen C.*, 124 Cal. Rptr. 2d 677 (Cal. Ct. App. 2002); *In re Salvador M.*, 4 Cal. Rptr. 3d 705 (Cal. Ct. App. 2003).

concurrence applies the reasoning of *Elisa B.* to the *K.M. v. E.G.* dispute and finds that K.M. is a parent because she received the children into her home and, with E.G.'s assent, held the children out as her own.

The feminist concurrence objects to the majority's focus on the marriage-like relationship between K.M. and E.G. and Justice Murray aligns herself with con-temporaneous critique proffered by some LGBT rights advocates of the movement's emphasis on achieving same-sex marriage. Shortly after *K.M.*, many activists, scholars, and lawyers published a statement entitled *Beyond Same-Sex Marriage: A New Strategic Vision for All Our Families and Relationships.*[11]

The statement echoed the feminist values of the concurrence: respect for families that do not fit the two-parent marital norm and insistence on a public obligation to support the well-being of children through a robust social and economic safety net. It presented "a new vision for securing governmental and private institutional recognition of diverse kinds of partners, households, kinship relationships and families." It expressly advocated alliance with single parents – LGBT and non-LGBT. It called for a separation of benefits from marital status and for access for all to government programs providing health care, housing, welfare, and enhanced Social Security. Like Justice Murray, it disdained the privatization of dependency.[12]

As much as *K.M.* saw the two women as the equivalent of a married couple, however, they were not married. It was remarkable that the court extended parental status to two unmarried women. To this day, in other states, only marriage entitles women in a same-sex couple to recognition as the parents of the child they are raising.[13] Justice Murray understates the importance to a feminist agenda of breaking down the rigid legal barrier between marriage and nonmarital relationships, even those relationships that have traits most associated with marriage. It is not a sufficient step but it is necessary to achieving the reconsideration of "fixed notion of family" that Justice Murray urges.

As Justice Murray points out, the California legislature extended to unmarried women the ability to bear a child as a single parent using donor insemination. This

---

[11] *Beyond Same-Sex Marriage: A New Strategic Vision for All Our Families & Relationships,* MONTHLY REVIEW (Aug. 8, 2006), https://mronline.org/2006/08/08/beyond-same-sex-marriage-a-new-strategic-vision-for-all-our-families-relationships/.

[12] The numerous critiques of marriage by LGBT advocates include Paula Ettelbrick, *Since When Is Marriage a Path to Liberation?*, OUT/LOOK (Fall 1989); Nancy D. Polikoff, *We Will Get What We Ask For: Why Legalizing Gay and Lesbian Marriage Will Not "Dismantle the Legal Structure of Gender in Every Marriage,"* 79 VA. L. REV. 1535 (1993); NANCY D. POLIKOFF, BEYOND (STRAIGHT AND GAY) MARRIAGE: VALUING ALL FAMILIES UNDER THE LAW (2008); Katherine Franke, *The Politics of Same-Sex Marriage Politics,* 15 COLUM. J. GENDER & L. 236 (2006).

[13] Married same-sex couples can use stepparent adoption procedures everywhere but a number of states prohibit second parent adoption by unmarried couples. A state's marital presumption must apply equally to the spouse of a woman who gives birth, *see Pavan v. Smith,* 137 S.Ct. 2075 (2017), but many states lack any statutory or equitable basis for finding parentage for a mother's unmarried partner who is not the child's biological parent.

was a definitive endorsement of childrearing outside of marriage, something the Beyond Same-Sex Marriage statement also supported. The reasoning of *K.M.* back-pedals that endorsement. But assigning parentage under a "holding out" statute can also place single motherhood at risk, as a subsequent California case, *Jason P. v. Danielle S.*, bears out.

Jason P. v. Danielle S. was a dispute over the parentage of a two and a half year-old child, Gus, born through IVF to Danielle using sperm donated by Jason, a man with whom she had previously lived in a romantic relationship. After their split, Danielle purchased sperm from a sperm bank to have a child on her own. When she told Jason of her plan, he offered his semen as an alternative but made clear in a letter that he was not ready to be a father and did not want Danielle to tell others.

Under *K.M.*, as originally decided, Jason would not be Gus's father because Jason and Danielle did not intend to conceive a child they would raise in their joint home, and never raised Gus in a joint home. They did resume their romantic relationship when Gus was a year old, and after that Danielle and Gus visited Jason four or five times during a five-month period when he lived in New York.

The trial court dismissed Jason's parentage action because he was a sperm donor. The California appeals court reversed, holding that Jason was entitled to an oppor-tunity to demonstrate under 7611 that he qualified as a presumed parent because he "receive[d] the child into his ... home and openly [held] out the child as his ... natural child."[14]

On remand, the trial court found that Jason satisfied the "received into his home" test based on Danielle and Gus's visits to Jason in New York. It further found that by the time Gus was two years old, less than six months before Jason and Danielle broke up, Jason was openly holding him out as his child and that Danielle supported Jason's parental relationship with Gus. The appellate court affirmed.[15] It found irrelevant that Jason initially rejected being a parent and credited instead that, with Danielle's permission, "he slowly developed a *father–son* relationship with Gus."[16]

Jason P. is a story of the "holding out" test gone wrong. Neither Danielle nor Jason wanted Jason to be a father, and they behaved consistently with that intent after Gus was born. Jason never changed a diaper and never spent a night alone with Gus. The amount and type of contact between Jason and Gus, which the court found "slowly" became a father–child relationship, arose in the context of Danielle resuming a romantic relationship with Jason a year after Gus's birth, which she subsequently terminated, prompting Jason to follow through on a threat to file for full custody if she broke up with him.

The viability of the known donor option for single women and lesbian couples depends upon legal certainty that the donor cannot disrupt the child's family. *Jason*

---

[14] *Jason P. v. Danielle S.*, 226 Cal. App. 4th 167, 179 (Cal. Ct. App. 2014).
[15] *Jason P. v. Danielle S.*, 9 Cal. App. 5th 1000, 1023 (Cal. Ct. App. 2017).
[16] *Id.* at 1024 (emphasis added).

P. eliminated that certainty by giving known sperm donors a unilateral right to claim parentage based on post-birth conduct. That rule makes it prudent for women to restrict contact between a known donor and his offspring to avoid an ensuing parentage action – an outcome that creates fewer choices for women.

In a subsequent California case, a single mother conceived using unknown donor semen, expecting that she would be the child's only legal parent. After the child's birth, she renewed a relationship with a former boyfriend, and when that relationship ended the court deemed the boyfriend a "holding out" parent.[17] What initially looked like the answer to establishing parentage for both mothers in a lesbian couple who planned for and raised a child together turned into exactly what Justice Murray sought to avoid: a framework facilitating the imposition of a two-parent norm on unmarried women.

MODERN DEVELOPMENTS

The decade after *K.M.* and *Elisa B.* brought changes that made the law more inclusive of families formed by lesbian couples.[18] Over a dozen states allowed the legally unrecognized parent to obtain custody upon dissolution of the couple's relationship.[19] Others went further and granted equal rights to the legally unrecognized parent.[20] A handful of states with "holding out" provisions similar to California's followed the holding of *Elisa B.*[21] Two state courts considering the type of family K.M. and E.G. formed with IVF agreed that both women were legal parents.[22] As same-sex marriage spread and ultimately became universal in 2015, courts extended the marital presumption of parentage to a birth mother's wife, although questions remain on a state-by-state basis about when and with what evidence the presumption is rebutted.[23]

A few state legislatures wrote laws assigning parentage, on a gender-neutral and marital status-neutral basis, to any person who consented to a woman's insemination with donor semen with the intent to parent the resulting child.[24] Two states codified parentage for those who met the statutory definition of a de facto parent.[25]

---

[17] *R.M. v. T.A.*, 233 Cal. App. 4th 760 (Cal. Ct. App. 2015).
[18] For a summary of these changes, see Courtney G. Joslin, *Leaving No (Nonmarital) Child Behind*, 48 Fam. L.Q. 495 (2014).
[19] *Id.* at 500–1.
[20] *Id.* at 501–2.
[21] *See* Courtney Joslin, Shannon Minter, & Catherine Sakimura, Lesbian, Gay, Bisexual, and Transgender Family Law § 5.22 (2018 ed.) (citing Colorado, Kansas, Massachusetts, New Hampshire, and New Mexico) (hereinafter LGBT Family Law).
[22] *D.M.T. v. T. M.H.*, 129 So. 3d 320 (Fla. 2013); *St. Mary v. Damon*, 309 P.3d 1027 (Nev. 2013).
[23] LGBT Family Law, *supra*.
[24] *Id.* at § 3:3.
[25] Del. Code Ann. tit 13, § 8-201(c) (2004); Me. Rev. Stat. Ann. tit 19-A § 1851 (2016).

UNIFORM PARENTAGE ACT (2017)

Piecemeal reforms, and the advent of nationwide marriage equality after *Obergefell v. Hodges* in 2015,[26] caused the Uniform Laws Commission to revisit its Uniform Parentage Act.[27] The revised UPA recognizes non-biological parentage where appropriate while protecting the ability of a single woman to bear and raise a child on her own, finding a compromise that satisfies Justice Murray's call to protect at least some non-normative families.

Under Section 702, a person who provides gametes for use in assisted reproduction is a donor and "is not a parent of a child conceived through assisted reproduction."[28] This definition categorically excludes K.M. and Jason P. from asserting parentage based on their genetic connection.

The UPA's assisted reproduction article also provides a way for someone other than the woman giving birth – including the person who provided gametes – to become a parent. The person must consent to the assisted reproduction with the intent to parent the resulting child. Without written consent, or an oral agreement proven by clear and convincing evidence, consent can be shown only if "the woman and the individual for the first two years of the child's life ... resided together in the same household with the child and openly held out the child as the individual's child ..."[29]

Under this test, K.M. is a parent and Jason P. is not. Neither could prove the required agreement. But K.M. could show that she lived with E.G. and the children for the first two years of the children's lives and that both women held the children out as K.M.'s children. Jason P. could not meet this test.

This scheme for parentage when a woman conceives using donor gametes is obviously more protective of single motherhood than *Jason P*. But it is also more protective than the court's ruling in *K.M.*, which deprives a woman of sole parentage after conceiving with gametes from her cohabiting partner if she and the partner planned to continue living together. The 2017 UPA, in the absence of an agreement to parent together, permits a finding of parentage only after the birth mother raises the child with her partner as two parents for the child's first two years.

The 2017 UPA contains two other provisions relevant to these fact patterns. A narrower "holding out" provision remains. Under section 204(a)(2), a person is a presumed parent if "the individual resided in the same household with the child for the first two years of the life of the child, including any period of temporary absence,

---

[26] 135 S. Ct. 2584 (2015).

[27] NATIONAL CONFERENCE OF COMMISSIONERS ON UNIFORM STATE LAWS, UNIFORM PARENTAGE ACT (2017). The Uniform Law Commission drafts and promulgates model statutes written by committees of lawyers, law professors, and judges. The model statutes become law only if enacted on a state-by-state basis by state legislatures.

[28] *Id.* at §702.

[29] *Id.* at §704(b)(2).

and openly held out the child as the individual's child." For the reasons discussed above, K.M. meets this test but Jason P. does not. Only a person who lives with the child as a parental figure from the moment of birth can become a "holding out" parent.

For a person not married to the woman who gives birth; who does not live with the child for the child's first two years; and who does not intend to be the parent of a child conceived through assisted reproduction, one additional path remains. The 2017 UPA recognizes de facto parentage under narrow circumstances; a person must show the following by clear and convincing evidence:

(1) the individual resided with the child as a regular member of the child's household for a significant period;
(2) the individual engaged in consistent caretaking of the child;
(3) the individual undertook full and permanent responsibilities of a parent of the child without expectation of financial compensation;
(4) the individual held out the child as the individual's child;
(5) the individual established a bonded and dependent relationship with the child which is parental in nature;
(6) another parent of the child fostered or supported the bonded and dependent relationship required under paragraph (5); and
(7) continuing the relationship between the individual and the child is in the best interest of the child.[30]

K.M. meets all of these criteria. Jason P. fails at subsection (1); he was never a "regular member of the child's household." His behavior also did not amount to "consistent caretaking" or undertaking the "full and permanent responsibilities of a parent."

CONCLUSION

Operating with a decades-old statute, Justice Murray did not have the freedom to recraft all of parentage law. She might, however, applaud the new UPA as a step in the right direction. It presents states with the option to recognize as parents more than two people who satisfy the parentage criteria, thereby rejecting the impulse to "try to force all families into the narrow contours of marriage and the nuclear family form." It also protects single-mother families, thereby giving courts less leeway to implement the privatization of dependency

No legal test can fully do justice to the complex ways that people come together to raise children. Requiring parents to live together, as do both the *K.M.* holding and the "holding out" provision of the UPA, excludes those committed to fully coparenting in separate homes. Law professor Angela Kupenda wrote more than twenty

---

[30] *Id.* at §609.

years ago of the importance to African American children of allowing two single African American adults, not in a romantic relationship and not necessarily living in one home, to coparent through adoption.[31] She noted that "the preference for the traditional nuclear family does not adequately fit the realities and traditions of many black adults and children."[32] Given the barriers to adoption by two unmarried persons, the law that establishes parentage in the absence of adoption will fall short if it always requires the parents and child to form a unit resembling the traditional nuclear family. On the other hand, the living together requirement allows an often-stigmatized single mother to rely on the help of relatives, friends, and current or former romantic partners without opening herself to litigation challenging her parental rights.

When a married man and woman want a child, conceive a child through sexual intercourse, and raise that child together, the elements of marriage, gestation, genetics, intent, and function converge in the assignment of legal parentage to each of them. Change any one of those elements and the law must decide who is a parent. Although the decision is not always easy, Justice Murray and the new UPA both remind us that it should never turn on privileging marriage over all other family forms.

K.M. v. E.G., 37 Cal. 4th 130 (2005)

Justice Melissa Murray, concurring in the judgment

The question presented in this case is whether a woman who provided ova to her lesbian partner so that the partner could bear children by means of in vitro fertilization ("IVF") is a legal parent of those children. A majority of this court has concluded that Family Code section 7613, subdivision (b), which provides that a man is not a father if he provides semen to a physician to inseminate a woman who is not his wife, does not apply when a woman provides her ova to impregnate her partner in a lesbian relationship in order to produce children who will be raised in their joint home. Accordingly, when partners in a lesbian relationship decide to produce children in this manner, both the woman who provides her ova and her partner who bears the children are the children's legal parents. See K.M. v. E.G., 117 P.3d 673, 675 (2005).

While I agree with the majority's conclusion in this case – that both K.M. and E.G. are legal parents of the twins – I write separately to emphasize my concerns with the majority's reasoning. To reach its outcome, the majority rejects the

---

[31] Angela Mae Kupenda, *Two Parents Are Better than None: Whether Two Single, African American Adults – Who Are Not in a Traditional Marriage or a Romantic or Sexual Relationship with Each Other – Should Be Allowed to Jointly Adopt and Co-parent African American Children*, 35 U. LOUISVILLE J. FAM. L. 703 (1996).

[32] *Id.* at 707.

application of section 7613(b), concluding that it is inapt in these circumstances. In doing so, the majority undermines the legislature's efforts to empower men and women to pursue parenthood via assisted reproductive technology ("ART") without fear that a sperm or ovum donor will later assert claims to parenthood. Moreover, in concluding that section 7613(b) is inapplicable to the facts of this case, the majority focuses unduly on the fact of the partners' romantic relationship – a relationship, which the majority equates, fairly or not, with marriage – and on the biological connection between the ovum donor partner and the resulting children. Above all, the majority is guided by its desire, whether conscious or unconscious, to privatize the dependency of children within the traditional two-parent dyad. These impulses, I posit, go beyond the four corners of this dispute, further entrenching our society's prioritization of marriage, marriage-like relationships, and the nuclear family.

What is perhaps most troubling is that all of this is completely avoidable. That is, we might recognize K.M.'s rights as a parent without unduly crediting biology, romantic relationships, or the privatization of dependency that marriage and parent-hood have traditionally served. As I explain, section 7611(d) of the Uniform Parent-age Act ("UPA") provides ample grounds upon which to recognize K.M. as a legal parent of the twins. As importantly, deciding this case based on the application of section 7611(d) does not require us to fetishize biology or the normative assumptions that attend marriage and the traditional two-parent dyad.

I

Certain facts in this case are disputed. K.M. and E.G. met in October 1992 and became romantically involved in June 1993. The couple began living together in March 1994 and registered as municipal domestic partners in San Francisco at that time.

E.G. maintains that, prior to their meeting and subsequent relationship, she was seriously considering becoming a single mother. She had begun visiting fertility clinics to investigate ART options and had applied to be an adoptive parent. E.G. further maintains that she apprised K.M. of these plans and her desire to be a single mother. Indeed, when E.G. began pursuing artificial insemination ("AI"), K.M. attended most of the appointments with her. K.M. maintains that she did so because she and E.G. had discussed and planned to raise a child together. E.G. claims that she was also forthright with K.M. about her desire to become a single parent.

From July 1993 through November 1994, E.G. attempted artificial insemination 13 times. These attempts were unsuccessful. In December 1994, E.G. consulted with Dr. Mary Martin, a fertility specialist at the University of California, San Francisco about IVF. When E.G.'s initial attempts at IVF failed because she was unable to produce sufficient ova, Dr. Martin suggested using K.M.'s ova. E.G. recounts that she asked K.M. to donate her ova but insisted that she would only accept the ova if K.M. "would really be a donor" and E.G. would "be the mother of any child." E.G.

further explained that she "had seen too many lesbian relationships end quickly, and [she] did not want to be in a custody battle." Accordingly, not only would she be the child's single parent, she would not consider allowing K.M. to adopt the child "for at least five years," until she was confident that their relationship as a couple "was stable and would endure." E.M. and K.G. agreed that K.M. would not disclose to others that she was biologically related to the resulting children.

K.M. objects to this account. Although she agreed not to disclose her status as the ova donor, she maintains that she and E.G. planned to raise a child together as a couple – and, indeed, that she only agreed to provide her ova in reliance on this plan. K.M. maintains that E.G. did not express a desire to be a single parent and, indeed, that she would not have donated her ova if she had known E.G. wished to raise the child alone.

E.G. notes that, in March 1995, prior to donating her ova, K.M. signed the fertility clinic's standard ovum donation form, agreeing to provide E.G. with ova for IVF and surrendering all parental rights and responsibilities upon donation.[33] K.M. concedes that she signed this paperwork, relinquishing all parental rights, but claims that she did so without full recognition of the consequences. As she explains, she understood the paperwork to apply to anonymous gamete dona- tions, not situations in which the gamete donor and the recipient were in a committed relationship, as she and E.G. were. E.G. maintains that the clinic paperwork represented binding contractual terms to which K.M. fully and know- ingly assented.

The ova donation and implantation resulted in a successful pregnancy for E.G. On December 7, 1995, E.G. gave birth to twin girls. The twins' birth certificates listed E.G. as their mother and did not provide a father's name. Soon after the twins' arrival, K.M. asked E.G. to marry her,[34] and on Christmas Day 1995, the couple exchanged rings. Although they did not disclose K.M.'s genetic connection to the children, the couple raised the children together in their home until their relation- ship ended in March 2001. K.M. then filed the present action to be recognized as a legal parent of the twins.

Though the couple contest the circumstances preceding the twins' birth, what is not in dispute are K.M. and E.G.'s actions throughout the pregnancy and after the birth of the twins. Although K.M. never revealed her biological connection to the twins, as E.G. concedes, she was a constant and supportive presence throughout E.G.'s pregnancy. Further, once the twins were born, K.M., with E.G.'s assent, assumed a parental role in their lives. K.M. held the twins out as her own children, providing financial support and care both throughout the couple's relationship and after its conclusion. K.M.'s extended family were a regular presence in the twins' lives and were recognized as members of the twins' extended family. Indeed, E.G.

---

[33] E.G. also signed a consent form, as the recipient of the ovum, on the same date.
[34] K.M. v. E.G., 117 P.3d 675, 676 (Cal. 2005).

referred to both her mother and K.M.'s parents as the twins' grandparents. She also referred to K.M.'s siblings as the twins' aunt and uncle and to K.M.'s nieces as their cousins. Two school forms listed both K.M. and E.G. as the twins' parents, and members of their community, including the couple's nanny, recognized E.G. and K.M. as the twins' mothers.

II

In March 2001, K.M. and E.G. ended their relationship, and K.M. filed the present action. California has adopted various provisions of the UPA, and these statutory terms govern the determination of legal parentage. Of particular import is section 7613(b), which provides: "The donor of semen provided to a licensed physician and surgeon or to a licensed sperm bank for use in assisted reproduction by a woman other than the donor's spouse is treated in law as if he were not the natural parent of a child thereby conceived, unless otherwise agreed to in a writing signed by the donor and the woman prior to the conception of the child."

Applying the plain language of section 7613(b), the trial court below granted E.G.'s motion to dismiss, finding that K.M. voluntarily signed the ovum donation form, thereby donating her genetic material to E.G. and relinquishing and waiving all rights to claim legal parentage of any resulting children. The Court of Appeal affirmed the judgment on the ground that K.M. did not qualify as a parent "because substantial evidence supports the trial court's finding that only E.G. intended to bring about the birth of a child whom she intended to raise as her own." The appellate court concluded that K.M.'s status was "consistent with the status of a sperm donor ... i.e., 'treated in law as if he were not the natural father of a child thereby conceived'."[35]

The majority of this court, however, takes a different view. Focusing on the biological connection between the children and the ovum donor partner, as well as the marriage-like relationship between the partners at the time the children were conceived and born, the majority concludes that section 7613(b) of the UPA is inapplicable in circumstances where one partner in a committed relationship provides her ova to impregnate the other partner so that they might produce children to be raised jointly within their relationship. Accordingly, when partners in a lesbian relationship decide to produce children in this manner, both the woman who provides her ova and her partner who bears the children are the children's legal parents, regardless of whether the genetic parent waived her rights to parentage in writing.

While I agree with the outcome, which vests K.M. with the rights and responsibilities of legal parentage, the majority's reasoning gives me pause. In the sections that follow, I elaborate my concerns.

---

[35] See Cal. Fam. Code § 7613(b).

III

The majority's consideration of this case focuses on the applicability of section 7613 (b). This, of course, is unsurprising, as section 7613(b) deals explicitly with situations involving parental claims made in the context of ART. Section 7613(b) provides that a man is not a legal father if he provides semen to a physician to inseminate a woman who is not his wife. This provision of the UPA was intended to relieve sperm donors of the rights and obligations of legal fatherhood.[36]

In 1975, when the California legislature originally proposed adopting the model UPA, the reach of the UPA's predecessor provision to section 7613(b) was limited to "married" women.[37] The legislature later amended the section to omit the term "married,"[38] thereby allowing single women to accept sperm donations without vesting the sperm donor with the obligations and rights of paternity. Under section 7650, the terms of section 7613(b) also apply equally to ovum donors.[39] On this account, the terms of section 7613(b) should apply to allow single women to pursue sperm and ovum donation secure in the knowledge that they – and they alone – will be the legal parent of any resulting children.

In concluding that section 7613(b) is inapplicable here, the majority seems to have disregarded the legislature's intent that undergirded this provision and its subsequent amendment. A straightforward application of the statutory terms would have yielded the result that both the legislature and E.G. intended – the confirmation of her status as the sole legal parent and the dismissal of K.M.'s claims to legal parentage.

Instead, the majority's conclusion that section 7613(b) is inapplicable here depends on its broad interpretation of the facts of this case. As both sides acknowledge, California does not recognize marriages between persons of the same sex. This is a grave injustice, and one that I hope will be remedied, whether by the legislature or by judicial fiat, in the future. But for the purposes of this case, the facts are clear: although they may have been a couple in a committed relationship, K.M. and E.G. were not married. As such, the plain terms of section 7613(b) credit E.G.'s

---

[36] See *Jhordan C. v. Mary K.*, 179 Cal. App. 3d 386, 392 (1986) (noting after analyzing the legislative history of the provision that it was meant to "provide [] men with a statutory vehicle for donating semen ... without fear of liability for child support").

[37] Section 7613(b) was originally enacted as section 7005(b) of the Civil Code, almost entirely adopting the language of the model UPA. The UPA was later moved to the state's Family Code. Cal. Fam. Code §§ 7600–750 (West 2004).

[38] The legislative history indicates that this omission was intentional. The original version of the legislation, Senate Bill 347, 1975–1976 Leg., Reg. Sess. § 11, introduced Feb. 4, 1975, proposed adopting the model UPA in full. To limit distinctions between marital and non-marital children, the legislature amended the bill three months later to delete the term "married." S.B. 347, 1975–1976 Leg., Reg. Sess. (Ca. 1975).

[39] Although section 7613(b) concerns sperm donation, Family Code section 7650(a) provides that "[i]nsofar as practicable, the provisions of this part applicable to the father and child relationship apply" to claims seeking to establish a mother–child relationship. Cal. Fam. Code § 7650 (West 2005).

professed desire to be a single parent and render K.M. akin to a sperm donor – an individual without legal rights and obligations to the resulting children.

Nevertheless, despite the plain language of section 7613(b), the unavailability of marriage seems to have weighed heavily on the majority in its decision. Indeed, the majority's view of the factual circumstances here appears to have been colored by an intuition that, had the option been available, K.M. and E.G. would have married;[40] and, as importantly, that even in the absence of a formal marriage license, K.M. and E.G. were essentially like a married couple, raising the twins in a traditional nuclear family setting. Relying on these intuitions, the majority concludes that applying the plain language of section 7613(b) is inapt in these circumstances because K.M. is no mere anonymous sperm donor but a partner in a committed, marriage-like relationship. In this way, the majority's translation of the couple's relationship into a marriage renders K.M. akin to a spouse, for whom the marital presumption of parentage trumps the application of section 7613(b).

To further bolster its conclusion that section 7613(b) should not apply, the majority pairs the fact of K.M.'s genetic connection to the twins with the fact of the couple's romantic relationship, distinguishing this situation from the traditional anonymous sperm donor scenario that section 7613(b) contemplated.

Under the majority's logic, section 7613(b) could never apply in a situation where a woman in a committed relationship used ART for the purpose of becoming a single mother. Indeed, any situation in which a romantic partner provided genetic material to her lesbian partner would result in shared parentage, whether that was the parties' intention or not. The majority's reasoning seems driven by a desire to compensate for the injustices wrought by same-sex couples' exclusion from civil marriage. But the court seems completely unconscious of the other injustices and inequities that its dismissal of 7613(b) would inevitably engender. Not only does the inapplicability of section 7613(b) likely preclude intentional single motherhood in certain circumstances, it further entrenches the normative assumption that committed, two-parent households, rather than single-parent households, are the appropriate setting in which to raise children.

The court's lack of attention to these other concerns is likely due to its – and family law's – general preoccupation with the privatization of dependency within the family. The facts of *Elisa B. v. Superior Court*,[41] a companion case to this action, are instructive on this point. *Elisa B.*, like the instant case, concerns parentage in the

---

[40] This intuition is informed by the fact, which neither K.M. nor E.G. dispute, that after the twins' birth, E.G. asked K.M. to marry her and the couple subsequently participated in a commitment ceremony in which they exchanged wedding rings. The couple also registered as municipal domestic partners, a fact noted in the majority's opinion. *See K.M. v. E.G.*, 117 P.3d 675, 684 n.3 (Cal. 2005). It is worth noting that section 297.5 (d) of the California Family Code, which went into effect on Jan. 1, 2005, and which provides that registered domestic partners have the same "rights and obligations" to "a child of either of them" as do spouses, is inapplicable to the facts of this case.

[41] 117 P.3d 660 (Cal. 2005).

context of a committed lesbian partnership in which the couple successfully used ART to have children. Unlike this case, however, the conflict between the former partners resulted in one partner disclaiming parentage and its attendant financial responsibilities, compelling the other partner to seek public assistance in order to provide for the children.[42]

Elisa B. surfaces many of the anxieties that single motherhood inevitably prompts in our society. Many fear that at the conclusion of a non-marital relationship, one partner will disappear, leaving the other to shoulder the emotional and financial burdens of parenthood alone. When the weight of this burden becomes too great, the state must step in to provide public assistance for the single mother and her children. In this regard, the looming threat with which single mother-headed families is associated is one that is inextricably linked to dependence on the state.[43]

Obviously, this case differs substantially from *Elisa B.* in many respects. As an initial matter, there is no indication that E.G.'s desire to be a single mother would result in her dependence on the state.[44] And unlike *Elisa B.*, where one partner disavowed legal parentage and its responsibilities, K.M. ardently seeks recognition as a parent and has continued to support E.G. and the twins, even after the demise of the couple's romantic relationship.

Despite these differences, one cannot help but glimpse the shadow of *Elisa B.* – and the specter of single motherhood – haunting the majority's disposition of this case. At bottom, this court's disposition of *Elisa B.* is one that credits, whether consciously or not, the two-parent family as the preferred form for raising children because this family form optimizes the privatization of dependency within the family. As the saying goes, "two heads are better than one," and, in this instance, it appears that the majority believes that two parents are better than one. On this account, refusing to apply section 7613(b) to defeat K.M.'s claim of parenthood serves this end. It prioritizes the two-parent dyad over single parenthood, thereby assuring that two parents are available to provide for the twins both emotionally and financially. The court's crediting of the couple's relationship as marriage-like further underscores this impulse. The fact that K.M. has provided financial and emotional support to E.G. and the twins in the context of a committed relationship further

[42] Both Elisa and her partner, Emily, gave birth to children using ART – Elisa to a son and Emily to twins, one of whom had Down syndrome and required heart surgery after birth. All three children were conceived using the same sperm donor. After the couple's separation, Elisa, the only working partner, briefly provided for Emily and the twins but eventually withdrew financial support. *Id.* at 663–64.

[43] In earlier cases, this court acknowledged this discomfort with family dependence on the state. *See In re Marriage of Buzzanca*, 61 Cal. App. 4th 1410, 1424 (1998) (internal citations omitted) ("Very plainly, the Legislature has declared its preference for assigning individual responsibility for the care and maintenance of children; not leaving the task to the taxpayers. That is why it has gone to considerable lengths to ensure that parents will live up to their support obligations").

[44] In fact, the record shows that both K.M. and E.G. had insurance and retirement plans, and E.G. added the twins soon after their birth as beneficiaries to her health insurance coverage.

embeds the notion that she can, and should, continue to play this breadwinner/caregiver role – as estranged spouses do – even if the relationship has ended.

The court's desire to ensure that both K.M. and E.G. will be responsible for the care and support of the twins is understandable. But, meaningfully, it also serves the purpose of absolving the state of any obligation – beyond denominating K.M. a legal parent with all the responsibilities of that status – to ensure that families have the resources that they need to provide the conditions under which children can flourish. Though the majority may not recognize it as such, its vision of LGBT equality and parental rights is undergirded by a neoliberal impulse that insists on relieving the state of any obligation to assist families in the care and rearing of children.

As importantly, this is a vision of LGBT equality that is underwritten, ironically, by the perceived inequality of alternative family forms. It is a vision of LGBT rights that is laced with a profound skepticism, whether acknowledged or not, that a single woman can support a family without the financial and emotional assistance of a partner. We live in an age when marriage is not a foregone conclusion. This is especially true among minority communities and the working and lower-middle classes. In these enclaves, single parenthood is common, and single parents are frequently supported by networks of extended family, friends, and paid caregivers. Further, as LGBT persons explore ART as a conduit to parenthood, the idea of the two-parent dyad as the predominant familial structure becomes even more remote. As IVF, AI, adoption, and surrogacy become tried and true means for LGBT persons to have children, the traditional family configuration becomes far less common and other configurations emerge. Open adoption arrangements, for example, may bring birth parents into the lives of adoptive parents and their offspring on a regular basis. Those who rely on surrogacy may too wish to maintain a relationship with their gestational surrogate as their child grows and develops. Likewise, some may prefer to include sperm and ova donors as "secondary" parents in their child's life. At a time when so many Americans are actively questioning marriage as a conduit to family formation and embracing a broader vision of how families are created and constituted, it is odd that the majority would go to such lengths to prioritize this narrow vision of the two-parent nuclear family over alternative family forms.

IV

As the foregoing sections make clear, while I agree with the outcome here, I am deeply troubled by the majority's refusal to apply 7613(b) – a decision that will impact other scenarios involving lesbian couples using ovum donation as part of the IVF process. As importantly, I am deeply concerned that the assumptions and intuitions upon which the majority relies translate all committed relationships into "marriage-like" unions reify the normative priority of marriage and the two-parent dyad, and in so doing, further entrench the notion of the two-parent nuclear family as a principal vehicle for the privatization of dependency.

What is most troubling about the majority's interpretation of these facts to preclude section 7613(b)'s application and denominate K.M. a legal parent is that it is utterly unnecessary. In *Elisa B.*, the court reached its decision that *Elisa B.* was a legal parent, with the legal rights and obligations of that status, by applying the terms of section 7611(d) to the facts of that dispute. Here, the facts make clear that section 7611 (d) similarly provides ample grounds for perfecting K.M.'s status as a legal parent.

Section 7611(d) provides that "A person is presumed to be the natural parent of a child if the person ... receives the child into his or her home and openly holds out the child as his or her natural child."[45] This provision was designed to recognize as parents unmarried, biological fathers. Focusing on the claim that K.M. and E.G. agreed to keep confidential K.M.'s genetic relationship to the children, the trial court refused to apply section 7611(d) to recognize K.M. as a presumed parent. As the lower court explained, because "the children were received into the parties' home as [E.G.]'s children and, up until late 1999, both parties scrupulously held confidential [petitioner]'s 'natural,' i.e., in this case, her genetic relationship to the children," K.M. cannot be said to have openly held the twins out as her own, as required under section 7611(d).[46]

This, in my view, is a crabbed and utterly wrongheaded interpretation of section 7611(d). Section 7611(d) cares not for whether a party acknowledges a formal, genetic relationship with a child. As this court acknowledged in *In re Nicholas H.*,[47] section 7611(d) is not preoccupied with formal, genetic relationships but, rather, asks whether a party has functioned as a parent.[48] That is, section 7611(d) takes seriously not the genetic fact of parenthood but rather whether the child and the presumed parent have developed a parent–child relationship in the absence of formal ties. In *Nicholas H.*, of paramount importance was the fact that the person claiming status as a legal parent had functioned as a parent for much of the child's life. Likewise, in *Elisa B.*, this court relied on similar indicia of functional parenthood to determine that Elisa B. was a presumed – and therefore, legal – parent for the purposes of section 7611(d).[49]

Here, the facts, as related by the majority, make clear that K.M. has formed a parent–child relationship with the twins. Upon the twins' birth, K.M. received them into her home and openly held them out as her children, even if she did not disclose – per E.G.'s request – the fact of her genetic relationship. Throughout the

---

[45] *See* Cal. Fam. Code § 7611(d).

[46] *See K.M. v. E.G.*, 117 P.3d 675, 677 (Cal. 2005).

[47] 45 P.3d 932 (Cal. 2002).

[48] Critically, the presumed father in Nicholas H., like Elisa B., was not the biological parent of the child – he began his relationship with the child's biological mother during her pregnancy. *Id.* at 934.

[49] The indicia highlighted by the court included the fact that Elisa breast-fed all three children, gave all three children the same surname, claimed all of the children as dependents on her tax returns, and referred to the children publicly as her triplets. *Elisa B. v. Superior Court*, 117 P.3d 660, 669 (Cal. 2005).

twins' lives, she and E.G. shared caregiving responsibilities – caring for them in babyhood and beyond. On school forms and medical forms, K.M. was listed as a parent or coparent. K.M.'s family were openly regarded as members of the twins' extended family. And, most importantly, the twins regarded K.M. as their parent.

Given these facts, it is surprising that the majority did not pursue K.M.'s claim to parenthood as a presumed parent under section 7611(d).[50] I suspect that the fact of K.M.'s genetic relationship likely colored the majority's view of whether section 7611 (d) was applicable – in both *Elisa B.* and *Nicholas H.* the presumed parent lacked a genetic relationship to the child. But, regardless of whether K.M. is a genetic parent, the facts all make clear that she has functioned as a parent.

Accordingly, there is no need to strain the facts of this case to invalidate the application of section 7613(b) in order to vest K.M. with the rights and obligations of legal parenthood. We can easily credit K.M.'s claim to legal parenthood by simply crediting the facts before us: K.M. has served as a parent to these children, and she wishes to do so in the future as a legal parent.

In writing separately and raising this alternative basis for decision, I do not mean to denigrate the important work the majority has done here. As this case and its companion, *Elisa B.*, suggest, law has been a critical factor in ensuring the family rights of LGBT persons. Law's interventions to protect the rights of LGBT parents is especially important when viewed against the backdrop of the long history of discrimination and denigration to which LGBT persons have been subjected – particularly those who have sought to build families and raise children. With this context in mind, although I lament its conservative underpinnings, I recognize the majority opinion important work in articulating and protecting the parental rights of LGBT persons.

But it is also worth remembering that LGBT families, like the families of other marginalized groups, have the potential to prompt the law to reconsider fixed notions of family and gain a better understanding of how family life is lived on the ground. This process of reflection and reconsideration is vital to ensuring that law keeps pace with the dynamism of modern family life. This kind of reflection and reconsideration cannot happen if courts reflexively try to force all families into the narrow contours of marriage and the nuclear family form.

For these reasons, although I concur in the judgment, I would rest this decision on different statutory grounds.

---

[50] Appellant's Opening Brief at 24–29, K.M. v. E.G., 13 Cal. Rptr. 136 (Ct. App. 2004) (No. A101754).

11

Reber v. Reiss, 42 A.3d 1131 (2012)

Commentary by Kevin Maillard

INTRODUCTION

In 2015, over 200,000 in vitro fertilization ("IVF") cycles treatment were recorded in the United States,[1] resulting in approximately 75,000 pregnancies.[2] In just under four decades since the first successful transfer in 1981,[3] "test tube babies"[4] went from rarefied headline fodder to a viable and plentiful option for many people living with infertility. Despite this growth, the legal landscape remains a jurisprudential frontier. With the opening of reproduction to scientific intervention, precedents of domestic relations fail to encompass the myriad outcomes of having children apart from sex. Couples experiencing infertility may endure extreme emotional stress in the struggle to have children, and the pursuit of this end goal oftentimes obscures contingencies for future conflicts. In the haze of the elusiveness of infertility and the satisfaction of pregnancy, couples may not foresee complicated breakups,

---

[1] Ctrs. for Disease Control and Prevention, Assisted Reproductive Technology (ART) Data, http://nccd.cdc.gov/drh_art/rdPage.aspx?rdReport=DRH_ART.ClinicInfo&rdRequestForward=True&ClinicId=9999&ShowNational=1 (last visited Aug. 30, 2018).

[2] *Id.*

[3] Victor Cohn, *First U.S. Test-Tube Baby Is Born*, WASH. POST (Dec. 29, 1981), https://www.washingtonpost.com/archive/politics/1981/12/29/first-us-test-tube-baby-is-born/a6f3de2f-422f-43bd-9b45-0d798ed18e8e/?utm_term=.b0a0fb30c9bd ("America's first test-tube baby was born in Norfolk yesterday, 3½ years after two British scientists showed the world how to start the miracle of human conception in a laboratory dish").

[4] *See* Ciara Nugent, *What It Was Like to Grow Up as the World's First "Test-Tube Baby,"* TIME (July 25, 2018), http://time.com/5344145/louise-brown-test-tube-baby/; Joe Sommerlad, *World's First Test Tube Baby at 40: How the Public Reacted to the IVF Breakthrough of the Century*, INDEP. (July 24, 2018, 11:00 PM), www.independent.co.uk/news/health/test-tube-baby-40th-anniversary-world-first-reaction-ivf-louise-brown-a8454021.html; Jane Warren, *Miracle Baby Who Started the IVF Revolution*, EXPRESS (July 24, 2018, 7:28 AM), www.express.co.uk/life-style/life/993326/ivf-revolution-first-test-tube-miracle-baby-fertility.

divorce, and disagreement, resulting in many difficult cases for state courts in the last decades. Assisted reproduction is a largely unregulated[5] field of legal inquiry, and many of these cases are of first impression in the individual states in which they take place.

In *Reber v. Reiss*,[6] a divorcing couple were conflicted over entitlement to possession and use of pre-embryos they had created together. This conflict of interests presents a challenge to reproductive justice. Who gets to keep the embryos: the wife, who wanted the experience of gestating her biological children from her own fertilized eggs, or the husband, who did not consent to their use and did not want to share parentage with his ex-wife?

When faced with this dilemma, the Superior Court of Pennsylvania, choosing from multiple models of dispute resolution from other jurisdictions, opted for a balancing test,[7] favoring Andrea's interest in reproduction over Bret's objection to unwanted reproduction. Dara Purvis has rewritten this opinion, taking a different outcome than the Superior Court. In the Purvis opinion, courts should decide conflicts over the use of embryos through mutual contemporaneous consent rather than an adversarial process. The outcome is a predictable result: when one party objects, there is no overruling of that interest. This approach rejects forced reproduction and forced parenthood in the event of disagreement.[8] In *Reber*, then, Andrea's proprietary claim on embryos that the Superior Court favored failed to properly acknowledge and protect Bret's coequal interest in the outcome.[9] Purvis's sharply different view – one rooted in feminist principles – refuses to "underscore gender stereotypes by giving them the force of law." She dispenses with the assumption that men have a lesser interest in reproductive freedom when in conflict with (in her words) the "ticking biological clock and ... the so-called natural maternal tendencies" of women.

REBER V. REISS FACTS

In anticipation of infertility after cancer treatment, Bret Reber and Andrea Reiss cryopreserved embryos created from his sperm and her ova.[10] At the time of retrieval

---

[5] The American Society of Reproductive Medicine (ASRM), unsurprisingly, rejects the characterization of an unregulated field. ASRM, Oversight of Assisted Reproductive Technology, www.asrm.org/globalassets/asrm/asrm-content/about-us/pdfs/oversiteofart.pdf.

[6] 42 A.3d 1131 (Pa. Super. Ct. 2012).

[7] *Id.* at 1136.

[8] Purvis in this volume at 264. ("If the parties failed to anticipate the circumstances they now find themselves in, and did not give one person control over the embryos in that context, a court cannot impose parenthood on an unwilling participant").

[9] *Id.* at 259. ("The law weighs interests of the parties in advance, judging that the harm of being forced to become a parent against your will outweighs the harm of losing what may be your last chance to have biological children").

[10] Reber, 42 A.3d at 1132–33. A footnote in the original case notes a low survival rate for unfertilized frozen eggs, so the couple chose early stage fertilization through IVF. *Id.* at 1133 n.4.

and storage, the couple entered an agreement for storage of the embryos but left the section of the agreement blank regarding the fate of the embryos in the event of a divorce.[11]

A divorce did, in fact, eventually occur. Even in the absence of any agreement about post-divorce embryo disposition, the Pennsylvania trial court granted Andrea's petition for possession of all 13 embryos.[12] This balancing of interests favored Andrea's interest in becoming a parent based on her age, health, and divorce status – factors which she presented as incompatible with adoption or gestation.[13] Most notably, the Superior Court asserted an experiential difference in childbirth for women, holding that "there is no question that [adoption] occupies a different place for a woman than the opportunity to be pregnant and/or have a biological child."[14] The court rooted its decision in a finding that the embryos were Andrea's last chance at parenting and procreation.[15]

Bret contended that the decision to undergo IVF was a "safeguard"[16] to the possibility of post-cancer treatment infertility. From this view, he agreed to create pre-embryos – not children – as an option for reproduction at a future date. Andrea took the opposite view of IVF as implicit, open-ended consent to procreation.[17] As stated by the Superior Court, "[Bret] knew the potential result of his participation in IVF was going to be a child at some point in the future."[18] And in this view, the circumstances that led to IVF as a "safeguard" indeed occurred, which justifies awarding the pre-embryos to Andrea.

Reber was the first case in the United States to allow a party who desired to procreate with disputed embryos (Andrea) to override the interests of the non-consenting party (Bret).[19] The Pennsylvania judge who decided *Reber* did so at a point in the developing legal history of assisted reproduction when there was no

---

[11] *Id.* at 1136.

[12] *Id.* at 1134.

[13] *Id.* at 1137, 1137–40 ("[Andrea] has no ability to procreate biologically without the use of the disputed pre-embryos").

[14] *Id.* at 1138.

[15] *Id.* at 1142.

[16] *Id.* at 1140.

[17] *Id.* at 1138 ("She stated, 'I always wanted to have children. I wouldn't have gone through ... the whole IVF thing if I hadn't wanted children'").

[18] *Id.*

[19] *See* Meagan R. Marold, *Ice, Ice, Baby! The Division of Frozen Embryos at the Time of Divorce*, 25 Hastings Women's L.J. 179, 193 (2014) ("While [other courts] found in favor of the party seeking to avoid procreation, they did leave the door open for the possibility of an infertile party to prevail over the party not wishing to be a parent. However, a court did not seize this opportunity until Reber v. Reiss in 2012"); Mark Strasser, *The New Frontier? IVF's Challenges for State Courts and Legislatures*, 17 SMU Sci. & Tech. L. Rev. 125 (2014) (categorizing cases based on those that resulted in "no involuntary parenthood" and those that displayed a "new trend" by allowing involuntary parenthood); *see also* Michael T. Flannery, *"Rethinking" Embryo Disposition Upon Divorce*, 29 J. Contemp. Health L. & Pol'y 233 (2013) (discussing various cases dealing with the disposition of embryos upon divorce).

clear statutory resolution of the conflict over possession of pre-embryos.[20] The lack of statutes[21] or strong precedent forced courts to re-examine longstanding assumptions about reproduction and parentage. Reproductive technology creates unprecedented and unusual points on the way to procreation that involve consent (for instance, signing contracts prior to conception and conceiving with the assistance of third parties) and conflict that were previously irrelevant because sexual intercourse was the only way to conceive. With sperm and egg harvesting, fertilization outside of the body, and implantation occurring separately in the reproductive timeline, more points of conflict now exist between progenitors than ever before. Purvis accounts for this difference in her analysis, which finds ground in the presence (and absence) of an agreement between the parties.

THE RE-WRITTEN OPINION

In her rewritten opinion, Purvis sharply rejects the reasoning of the Superior Court. In balancing Andrea's procreative desires with Bret's avoidant ones, she shows how "emotional arguments may obscure ambiguous facts and replace them with problematic stereotypes."[22] With Andrea's primary argument resting on her desire for pregnancy, the *Reber* Court presents her "natural maternal tendencies" – as characterized by Purvis – as a compelling argument for negating Bret's desire to avoid parenthood.[23] From this viewpoint, the Superior Court's recognition of women's interests in reproduction, parenthood, and pregnancy underscores gendered assumptions about "biological clocks."[24] that transform maternal urgency into the force of law.

Purvis deeply considers Andrea and Bret's specific and influential life circumstances, though many questions are left unanswered about how Andrea and Bret found themselves in this predicament.[25] Why did they leave the most crucial section on the consent form completely blank? Why did they make their decision in such haste – had they not considered the idea of parenthood at some earlier point? Did knowledge of Bret's new relationship and pregnant girlfriend have any impact on the conflict after the marriage ended?[26] These crushing realities have

---

[20] Reber, 42 A.3d at 1134.

[21] *See* Cynthia E. Fruchtman, *Withdrawal of Cryopreserved Sperm, Eggs, and Embryos*, 48 FAM. L.Q. 197, 204 (2014) ("The preprinted deposit agreement forms that address disposition in the case of death or divorce or that anticipate changes in consent often fail to take into account the developing law concerning whether or not a progenitor can be forced to procreate against his or her will").

[22] Purvis in this volume, at 261.

[23] Reber, 42 A.3d at 1139 ("Thus, simply because adoption or foster parenting may be available to [Andrea], it does not mean that such options should be given equal weight in a balancing test").

[24] Purvis this volume at 262.

[25] *Id.* ("We acknowledge at the outset that Andrea is in an immensely sympathetic position").

[26] Bret developed a relationship with another woman approximately 18 months after he and Andrea separated. Bret and the other woman had a biological son together, and Bret testified that "this child was conceived intentionally and that he intends to have more children." Reber, 42 A.3d at 1133.

drastically different consequences: if Andrea "wins," she forces Bret to reproduce against his will, and if Bret "wins," Andrea's options for biological pregnancy and motherhood disappear.

Purvis prefers a contemporaneous mutual consent model to escape the forced urgency of a previously decided contract. This framing of the conflict allows Bret and Andrea to make reproductive decisions at the time of embryo use rather than at the time of retrieval and storage. Purvis asserts several benefits to this test, including that it reduces the risk of a court using gendered stereotypes to break the tie between progenitors who have conflicting desires for the future of their frozen embryos. In the event of a dispute, Purvis decides that a court must side with the party refusing consent to avoid imposing parenthood on an unwilling party. Neither party has a superior right to use the disputed embryos. Under this analysis, Bret, as the refusing party, would block use of the embryos and Andrea could not force "involuntary conception" upon him.

CONSIDERING CONSENT

Questioning a woman's attempt to impose parenthood on an unwilling father may appear to sympathize with misogynist men's rights discourses[27] of aggression towards "vindictive women"[28] seeking financial support. It may also appear to de-gender motherhood to "the legal generic category of 'Parent'."[29] It may even destabilize pregnancy as the normative and singular expression of true motherhood.[30]

It is quite apparent that Andrea desires motherhood, and the Superior Court viewed pregnancy as the only option to satisfy that goal. Andrea wishes "to procreate

---

[27] See Deborah Dinner, The Divorce Bargain: The Fathers' Rights Movement and Family Inequalities, 102 Va. L. Rev. 79 (2016); see also A Voice for Men, About, Mission Statement, www.avoiceformen.com/policies/ (stating their mission as "to lift [men and boys] above the din of misandry, to reject the unhealthy demands of gynocentrism in all its forms, and to promote their mental, physical and financial well-being without compromise or apology").

[28] Kelly Alison Behre, Digging Beneath the Equality Language: The Influence of the Fathers' Rights Movement on Intimate Partner Violence Public Policy Debates and Family Law Reform, 21 Wm. & Mary J. Women & L. 525, 570 (2015) (noting that the fathers' rights movement relies on narratives of "the old archetype of the vindictive and dishonest nature of women" as well as "reverse sexism, identifying men ... as victims of systematic oppression"); Kelly Behre, The Fathers' Rights Movement Undermines Victims of Domestic Violence, N.Y. Times (June 13, 2014, 3:33 PM), www.nytimes.com/roomfordebate/2014/06/13/fathers-rights-and-womens-equal ity/the-fathers-rights-movement-undermines-victims-of-domestic-violence.

[29] Martha Albertson Fineman, The Neutered Mother, 46 U. Miami L. Rev. 653, 660 (1992).

[30] See Kevin Maillard, Other Mothers, 85 Fordham L. Rev. 2629 (2017); see also Mary Becker, Maternal Feelings: Myth, Taboo, and Child Custody, 1 S. Cal. Rev. L. & Women's Stud. 133, 159 (1992) ("At its most extreme, recognition of reproductive labor done only by women (pregnancy, childbirth, and nursing) reinforces the notion that biology is both destiny and the key link between parent and child ... To give too much weight to biology is to deny the many kinds of intense relationships between children and the people who parent them."); Fineman, supra note 29; Rena K. Uviller, Fathers' Rights and Feminism: The Maternal Presumption Revisited, 1 Harv. Women's L.J. 107 (1978).

biologically"[31] and the court sympathizes with her limited options for parenthood. The court states that Andrea agreed to "do her best to assure that [Bret] never has to pay to support the child or children,"[32] without foreclosing his optional responsibility.

Purvis has a vastly different opinion about how to view this conflict. She rightfully notes that the original *Reber* opinion reifies gendered stereotypes by insisting on genetic pregnancy as the singular manifestation of reproduction and maternal care. Even if Andrea desires a biological pregnancy, it is a gross misapplication of some feminist principles to focus singularly on her maternal interests and needs without fair consideration of Bret's objection. The pre-embryos are not a product of a sexual act between the parties, and their formation cannot be given personhood. It is banked and shared genetic material that provides possibilities. When those possibilities are fraught with conflict, the mutual agreement cannot continue.

Reproductive justice is not a one-sided issue. It is necessary to consider the interests of men and women, and such a consideration of fairness is not antithetical to feminist concerns. The fate of the embryos invokes issues of consent to the use of one's genetic material that was provided for a postponed decision. A decision – which it is crucial to recognize – that did not occur with mutual consent. This is not about being "tricked" into parentage or male remorse over parental responsibility. It is also not about evading fatherhood after a casual sexual encounter. Traditional assignations of paternity resulting from intercourse and its propagative modifications do not apply here.[33] As described in *In re C.K.G.*,[34] the "technological fragmentation of the reproductive process" forces reconsideration of traditional definitions of parentage and the consequences of reproduction. Andrea's justification for possession of the embryos in *Reber* is unauthorized, unintended, and forced – the very definition of nonconsensual that should trigger a reasonable person's concern for justice. Bret and Andrea's contract simply lacked the language that would authorize proceeding with implantation. Silence, then, cannot justifiably manifest as consent to assisted reproduction.

A requirement of affirmative consent of both parties to parenthood facilitates predictability and avoids unilateralism, as Purvis argues in her support of

---

[31] *Reber v. Reiss*, 42 A.3d 1131, 1139 (Pa. Super. Ct. 2012).

[32] *Id.* at 1141.

[33] The law considers genetic fathers – not including sperm donors or extramarital fathers – to be legal fathers of children, even in cases of unintentional pregnancy or misrepresentation of use of birth control. The biological tie is enough to trigger parental status, even in cases where the father refused, failed, or neglected to consent. Jill E. Evans, *In Search of Paternal Equity: A Father's Right to Pursue a Claim of Misrepresentation of Fertility*, 36 LOY. U. CHI. L.J. 1045, 1047 (2005) ("Child support obligations attach immediately upon birth, without regard to whether fatherhood was desired or conception occurred through the mother's deceit as to her fertility or use of birth control"); *see generally*, Donald C. Hubin, *Daddy Dilemmas: Untangling the Puzzles of Paternity*, 13 CORNELL J.L. & PUB. POL'Y 29 (2003).

[34] 173 S.W.3d 714 (Tenn. 2005).

contemporaneous consent. In *Woodward v. Commissioner of Social Security*,[35] a surviving spouse sought to collect Social Security survivor benefits for her posthumously born children. The twins were born two years after the husband died, conceived from sperm collected before he underwent treatment for leukemia.[36] The District Court in Massachusetts held that affirmative consent to conceive and support children was required in order to declare paternity.[37] In the absence of such an agreement, the twins could not be considered legal "children" of the decedent.

Woodward provides a lesson in caution and scope. Presumably, that husband banked his sperm as a "safeguard," like Bret, perhaps without anticipating its use beyond the duration of his life. True to most conflicts between couples in assisted reproduction, there are limited expectations of the use of the embryos, and one of the parties can push their claim beyond the immediate vision of the original intended use. In both *Reber* and *Woodward*, the former wives wanted use of their (ex and deceased) husbands' genetic material to conceive children. For posthumously conceived children, uncertainty arises because the deceased father left no clear record of his intentions. Dead, the husband has no channel to express his wishes. In *Reber*, however, it is painfully clear that Bret, alive, made his wishes clear, and subjective intent should matter.

Purvis focuses her attention on the timing and evidence of consent but there is also the issue of reproductive outcomes to which she offers less discussion. Missing in the *Reber* discussion is a close examination of Andrea's functional interests – her whys and hows of becoming a parent – in addition to the formalistic interests – her what (pregnancy) – that could still be achieved without disturbing the reproductive refusals of Bret. It is assumed without question that she wants the pre-embryos for a specific, personal reason but it should be entirely fair to ask whether Bret should have an equal claim to the material, why Andrea is justified in denying his interests, and whether that goal is a compelling one. Andrea claims that the pre-embryos are her last chance to "become a parent," but does that mean pregnancy, or genetic parentage, or the action of caregiving?

Purvis's attention on Bret's interests seems to work against women's concerns. Her approach declines to recognize gestation and motherhood as the most deserving parental claims, in efforts to take both men's and women's interests seriously. By saying that Andrea's interest in pregnancy is not a unilateral exercise of maternity but a mutual conflict of unresolved contract, Purvis tacitly asserts that Reber is less a case about reproduction than a case about consent to reproduction. Without the contemporaneous consent of both parties, neither can circumvent and overcome the objection of the other. This approach refreshingly acknowledges reproduction in

---

[35] 760 N.E.2d 257 (Mass. 2002).
[36] *Id.* at 260.
[37] *Id.* at 259 ("The survivor or representative must then establish both that the decedent affirmatively consented to posthumous conception and to the support of any resulting child").

this context as a deliberate, interpersonal discourse, and not an adversarial sweepstake. Purvis reveals an underexamined fact of reproductive technology: the affirmative consent of men and women must be taken in equal measure, without consideration of shoulds and oughts. Although technological advancements now make it possible for reproduction to occur outside of the mutuality of sex, it should not facilitate the circumvention of affirmative consent.

Reber v. Reiss, 42 A.3d 1131 (2012)

Judge Dara Purvis

This case presents a novel problem: how to resolve a dispute over stored embryos that were created years previously when the litigants were still in an intact marriage. Not anticipating the end of their relationship, the parties did not specify who would have control over the embryos, or in what circumstances the embryos could be implanted, if they were to divorce or otherwise disagree.

FACTS

Bret Howard Reber (Husband) and Andrea Lynn Reiss (Wife) married on October 12, 2002. After only one year of marriage, Andrea was diagnosed with breast cancer, in November 2003. Because the medical treatment for breast cancer could affect her fertility, Andrea's doctors advised her to investigate using IVF[38] to keep open the possibility of having biological children in the future. At the time, it was not feasible to freeze unfertilized eggs for future use but it was possible to freeze early stage embryos created through IVF. Bret and Andrea had apparently not discussed whether or when they wanted to become parents but Andrea's cancer diagnosis effectively forced them into a quick decision. Bret agreed that doctors could use his sperm to fertilize his then wife's eggs and store the embryos.

Bret and Andrea entered into an agreement with the Reproductive Science Institute of Suburban Philadelphia (RSI) to store the embryos. The agreement specified that RSI would store the embryos for three years and then destroy them but RSI apparently failed to do so, and the embryos remain in frozen storage today. The agreement also had a standard clause asking married couples storing embryos to specify who would hold "legal ownership of the embryos and the right to consent to

---

[38] In vitro fertilization refers to a process in which a medical professional removes ova from a woman's ovaries and subsequently fertilizes them with sperm. Typically, multiple ova are removed and fertilized at the same time. One or more of the resulting embryos is then transferred to a woman's uterus, and the fertility clinic freezes and stores any additional embryos. See Davis v. Davis, 842 S.W.2d 588, 597 (Tenn. 1992), on reh'g in part, No. 34, 1992 WL 341632 (Tenn. Nov. 23, 1992).

their release for any purpose" if the spouses divorced while the embryos were still in storage but Bret and Andrea did not fill in the clause to provide an answer.

After successful retrieval of eggs for IVF and storage of embryos, Andrea went through extensive treatment for her breast cancer, including surgery, chemotherapy, and radiation treatment. Approximately three years after Andrea's initial diagnosis, in December 2006, Bret filed for divorce.

Despite the demise of their marriage, Andrea believes that the stored embryos are her only chance to become a mother, both because she is otherwise unable to become a biological mother due to the effects of the cancer treatments and because she, as a single cancer survivor in her forties, is unlikely to be successful in pursuing adoption. After Bret refused to grant permission for her to use the stored embryos, she sued.

ANALYSIS

We acknowledge at the outset that Andrea is in an immensely sympathetic position. A sudden, life-threatening medical condition forced her and Bret to make a quick decision regarding her future reproductive possibilities. In a perfect world, Andrea and Bret would have made the decision whether to try to have biological children without any time pressure beyond the general pressure of time faced by any other married couple in their thirties. Had the two more time to consider the ramifications of the IVF and storage process, perhaps they might have paid attention to the issues raised by the clause in the agreement that they neglected, asking what should happen if they divorced while embryos were still in storage. Andrea and Bret faced an extreme circumstance pressuring a swift decision that many couples agonize over for years, so it is understandable why the process did not generate an agreement considering all contingencies.

Furthermore, Andrea's sense of frustration with her current situation is entirely understandable to anyone who has wanted to become a parent.[39] Since their divorce, Bret began dating another woman and has had a child with her. He apparently intends to have more children with his new partner. Andrea, however, does not have any other paths to biological parenthood readily available, and has rational concerns about the possibility of successfully becoming an adoptive parent.

Our sympathy for Andrea's unfulfilled desire, however, cannot provide an answer to the legal issue presented by this unusual circumstance: Who should control stored embryos when the intended parents no longer agree, and did not previously agree about how to resolve such a conflict? The interests of the intended parents are squarely in conflict. Andrea seeks to become a genetic and biological parent using

---

[39] Not everyone wants to become a parent, of course, and the choice to remain childless warrants respect. And it is worth noting that wanting to become a parent yet facing difficulty doing so is an issue shared by lots of people, for lots of different reasons. As such, Andrea's story is not unique. What is unique is that she had access to treatment that could help offset the infertility that resulted from her cancer care and had the financial wherewithal to pay for that treatment.

the stored embryos, and Bret does not want to become a parent to any genetic children conceived with Andrea.

Courts in Pennsylvania have not yet addressed this type of dispute, so we look to other jurisdictions to assess a range of possible solutions. There are three general models used: the contractual model, the contemporaneous mutual consent model, and the balancing test model. In all three, a trend quickly emerges that the right of the party wishing not to use stored embryos generally prevails over the asserted right of the party wishing to use the stored embryos. Courts justify this by comparing ordering a fertility clinic to allow one party to use stored embryos to other types of unwanted familial relationships, such as now-historical lawsuits seeking injunctions as a remedy for the breach of promise to marry someone.[40] No court today would order a man to marry a woman if he changed his mind regarding their engagement – along similar lines, courts conclude that the public policy against compelling people to enter into familial relationships should prohibit ordering a man to father a child with a woman if he changed his mind regarding parenthood.[41] The only arguable exception is if a man (or other partner) does not want to become a parent after a female partner (or surrogate) is already pregnant, because the decision to terminate an ongoing pregnancy would interfere with the pregnant woman's rights.[42] Where, as here, no existing pregnancy is implicated, courts have generally refused to compel the creation of a new pregnancy.

Fertility clinics universally require parties creating and storing embryos to sign a legal agreement at the outset of the process. Such agreements generally answer at least some questions regarding how long additional embryos will be stored and who has control over the stored embryos. Even in the face of such agreements, some participants have later challenged the agreements, often arguing that the subject matter means that the agreements are unenforceable due to conflicts with public policy.[43]

The contractual model rejects such challenges and enforces the provisions agreed to by the parties before the embryos were created. In many cases, this means enforcing a contractual term saying that in specified circumstances – often if the intended parents divorce or the embryos were still in storage after a certain period of time – the clinic would destroy the embryos.[44] In other cases, the contract specified

[40] See In re Marriage of Witten, 672 N.W.2d 768, 781 (Iowa 2003).

[41] J.B. v. M.B., 783 A.2d 707, 717–20 (2001); A.Z. v. B.Z., 725 N.E.2d 1051, 1057–59 (2000).

[42] See Planned Parenthood of Cent. Mo. v. Danforth, 428 U.S. 52, 71 (1976).

[43] For example, one woman seeking to use stored embryos argued that participation in the initial IVF procedure indicated her ex-husband's consent to have children with her, and to allow him to back out after the embryos were created would itself violate public policy. In re Marriage of Witten, 672 N.W.2d at 773.

[44] See, e.g., Roman v. Roman, 193 S.W.3d 40, 50 (Tex. App. 2006), rev. den. (2007), cert. den., 552 U.S. 1258 (2008) (enforcing contract term that embryos would be destroyed if parties divorced); Litowitz v. Litowitz, 48 P.3d 261, 271 (2002), cert. den., 537 U.S. 1191 (2003) (enforcing contract term to destroy if embryos were held in storage for five years).

that decision making control over the embryos would be given to one of the two intended parents[45] or to the fertility clinic itself,[46] or that the embryos could only be used if both intended parents agreed at the time of usage.[47]

The merits of the contractual model are obvious: the interested parties explicitly memorialized their intention at a prior point in time, so that rather than substitute a court's judgment in a personal and emotional dispute, courts merely enforce the agreed-upon disposition that the parties drafted themselves. This is not perfect, of course. The mere fact that the participants in the agreement have come to court to resolve a dispute indicates that one of the parties has changed his or her mind and presumably regrets his or her previous decision.

Disputes over stored embryos generally arise when the circumstances of the family have changed dramatically from the time in which they made the agreement, and in many, if not most cases, years have passed between signing the contract and seeking to enforce it. It is understandable why people's preferences may have changed during that time. Moreover, a contractual frame may not be the most accurate indication of a person's actual preferences. Contractual doctrines that often assume parties negotiating at arm's length over business propositions may not reflect the reality of two people in a romantic relationship with emotion and informal power dynamics in play.

The second model, contemporaneous mutual consent, rejects the decisions made at the time that an agreement was executed, and instead asks the wishes of the parties at the time that the stored embryo might be used. This model considers the changing preferences of parties to such agreements. As the Iowa Supreme Court acknowledged in a case adopting the rule of contemporaneous mutual consent, "[o]ne's erroneous prediction of how she or he will feel about the matter at some point in the future can have grave repercussions."[48] A party to an agreement regarding the disposition of stored embryos might regret granting consent to use the embryos even in the event of major life changes such as divorce, or, as in this case, a party might view the stored embryos as her last chance to become a biological parent and wish she had established a right to use the embryos.

The contemporaneous mutual consent model chooses between such changes of heart, and sides with the person who regrets granting consent to use embryos and now does not want the embryos implanted. Under this logic, compelling someone to become a biological parent is worse than not facilitating someone's desire to

---

[45] *Cwik v. Cwik*, 2011-Ohio-463 (Ct. App.); *Dahl v. Angle*, 194 P.3d 834 (2008).

[46] *Dodson v. Univ. of Ark. for Med. Scis.*, 601 F.3d 750 (8th Cir. 2010); *Karmasu v. Karmasu*, 2009-Ohio-5252; *Cahill v. Cahill*, 757 So.2d 465, 468 (Ala. Civ. App. 2000) (enforcing contract term that control of embryos given to fertility clinic if couple divorced).

[47] *Kass v. Kass*, 696 N.E.2d 174 (N.Y. 1998) (enforcing contract term that only if both parties agreed at the time could embryos be used).

[48] *In re Marriage of Witten*, 672 N.W.2d 768, 778 (Iowa 2003).

become a parent.[49] The state does not otherwise compel people to stay in relationships or create relationships they no longer wish to be in, and at least in theory the party seeking to become a parent can do so without the other party's involvement. By contrast, forcing someone to become a parent "irrevocably extinguishe[s]" their wish not to be a parent.[50] Both parties to an agreement governing the use of stored embryos thus hold a veto: regardless of the terms of the agreement itself, embryos may only be used if both people agree to the use of the embryos at that time. If either person changes his mind and wishes to prevent use of the embryos, the IVF process cannot proceed to the stage of trying to create a pregnancy.

This model is obviously efficient: as soon as a party objects, the dispute is over. And the rule is predictable, even if the potential changed minds of the parties may not be. The law weighs the interests of the parties in advance, judging that the harm of being forced to become a parent against your will outweighs the harm of losing what may be your last chance to have biological children. But the drawbacks are just as obvious: there is no way to preserve the right to use stored embryos, as even the most formalized, informed, and memorialized intent at the time of their creation is overcome by a contemporaneous change.

The third model is a balancing test, weighing the interests of the two parties arguing over disposition of the embryos. The Tennessee Supreme Court articulated this model in *Davis v. Davis*, although the court first specified that, if possible, disputes should be resolved by enforcing an agreement between the parties.[51] In the Tennessee case, however, the agreement did not contemplate the parties divorcing before disposition of the embryos was decided, so the court was left to resolve the dispute without contractual guidance. In the absence of a contractual indication of the parties' intent, the court instead simply identified the interests of each party and compared them.[52] Under this balancing test, the court would grant control over the embryos to whichever party had a stronger interest that would not impose unacceptable hardships on the other party. In the *Davis* case, balancing of a husband and wife's interests, the husband, who wanted the embryos disposed of, would face "unwanted parenthood," with both "financial and psychological consequences."[53] By contrast, the wife had experienced burdensome medical procedures in order to create the stored embryos which she hoped to use.[54]

---

[49] *See, e.g.,* A.Z. v. B.Z., 725 N.E.2d 1051, 1059 (2000) ("We derive from existing State laws and judicial precedent a public policy in this Commonwealth that individuals shall not be compelled to enter into intimate family relationships, and that the law shall not be used as a mechanism for forcing such relationships when they are not desired").

[50] *J.B. v. M.B.,* 783 A.2d 707, 717 (2001).

[51] *Davis v. Davis,* 842 S.W.2d 588, 597 (Tenn. 1992), on reh'g in part, No. 34, 1992 WL 341632 (Tenn. Nov. 23, 1992).

[52] *Id.* at 603.

[53] *Id.*

[54] *Id.* at 604.

The court's comparison was made easier due to the wife's desire not to implant and develop the embryos to be children that she would raise herself but instead to donate the embryos to another couple.[55] As a result, the court found for the husband, and directed the fertility clinic to dispose of the embryos.[56] In passing, however, the court noted that "[t]he case would be closer if [the wife] were seeking to use the preembryos herself, but only if she could not achieve parenthood by any other reasonable means."[57]

The balancing test has the advantage of being sensitive to the unique equities of each individual case. Comparing the facts of *Davis* and the facts presented here demonstrate how circumstances affect the arguments and sympathies of each litigant: Mary Sue Davis sought use of the embryos in the abstract, hoping to donate them to another couple to help them become parents, perhaps a laudable goal but one that demonstrated the lack of personal urgency and lowered stakes for Mary Sue individually. By contrast, here Andrea argues that the stored embryos are her last chance to become a parent, something that she deeply wants to do.[58] Unlike the contractual and contemporaneous mutual consent models, the balancing test allows a court to take the varying equities into account, providing individualized results for individualized circumstances.

The downsides to the balancing test are just as clear: considering the specific facts of each case means a much less efficient and less predictable rule. Moreover, assessing the equities of litigants one by one invites courts to make decisions based on which party crafts the most emotionally engaging narrative. Asking courts and judges to assess interests one by one also allows, if not invites, application of problematic cultural and social norms regarding whose desires to become or not become a parent are more understandable and appropriate. Gendered stereotypes about parenting are arguably already reflected in the law. The Supreme Court has repeatedly held that statutes recognizing women as legal parents in contexts where men would be denied parental status are constitutional.[59] Differential treatment of men and women's desire to become parents would be a natural extension of the stereotype. Parents who are LGBTQ have been described as dangerous or even predatory towards their own children.[60] Such baseless accusations long affected custody determinations, and it is easy to imagine similar prejudices underlying choices about whose desire to be a parent is compelling enough to convince a

---

[55] *Id.*

[56] *Id.* at 605.

[57] *Id.* at 604.

[58] As noted above, Andrea argues both that the embryos are her only chance to become a biological parent and that she is unlikely to have the opportunity to become a parent through adoption.

[59] *See Nguyen v. INS,* 533 U.S. 53, 59 (2001); *Lehr v. Robertson,* 463 U.S. 248 (1983); *Caban v. Mohammed,* 441 U.S. 380 (1979).

[60] *See* Clifford J. Rosky, *Like Father, Like Son: Homosexuality, Parenthood, and the Gender of Homophobia,* 20 YALE J.L. & FEMINISM 257 (2009).

court.[61] Assisted reproductive technologies are already available inconsistently, and used more by white people than people of color, even though people of color, especially black women, people are more likely to face issues of infertility.[62] One reason is the bias of medical professionals using counseling and diagnoses in ways that channel white patients towards paths like IVF more often than patients who are people of color.[63] Explicitly asking courts to award embryos based on sympathy invites reproducing such bias in court.

Turning to the case at hand, the difficult facts illustrate deeper problems with the balancing test. First, there is the concern for diminished fertility. The *Davis* court noted that when applying a balancing test that weighs the desire to become a parent against the desire not to become a parent, the diminished fertility of one the party wishing to use the embryos would shift the balance into her favor. In the abstract, this is understandable: who would not be responsive to the emotional plea of someone who believes this is her last chance to become a parent?

The facts presented here, however, demonstrate how emotional arguments may obscure ambiguous facts and replace them with problematic stereotypes. First, it is extremely difficult to accurately assess an individual's fertility, absent true black and white circumstances such as a woman having undergone a hysterectomy. Even with the dramatic history of the litigants before this court, Andrea having been advised to undergo egg retrieval before her cancer treatment began, Bret and Andrea disagree as to whether she is incapable of having biological children. What if Andrea had not undergone cancer treatment but instead had a medical condition such as polycystic ovary syndrome (PCOS) that would make it more difficult to conceive? What if she based her argument on the fact that she was forty-four years old and thus the chances of carrying a pregnancy to term were statistically tiny? What if she was forty years old, or thirty-five? Attempting to incorporate such an indeterminate factor into a balancing test would all but force judges to supplement their analysis of fertility with how personally sympathetic they found the litigants.

Second, Andrea argues that the embryos are also her last chance at becoming a parent to any children, as she argues that adoption as an older, single cancer survivor is unlikely to occur. This is even more difficult to show, as it depends upon the decisions of individuals and entities completely uninvolved in this case. Is it possibly fair to impose parenthood upon Bret based on our assumptions regarding adoption? On the other hand, how could Andrea prove a negative, that she will be unable to adopt?

Obviously, it is possible to imagine testimony by experts and physicians that would attempt to establish whether Andrea could have biological children and whether she would be likely to successfully adopt. Courts are often called upon to evaluate

[61] *See* Mark Strasser, *Fit to Be Tied: On Custody, Discretion, and Sexual Orientation*, 46 Am. U. L. Rev. 841 (1997).
[62] *See* Dorothy E. Roberts, *Race and the New Reproduction*, 47 Hastings L.J. 935, 939 (1996).
[63] *Id.* at 940–41.

competing evidence. The danger, however, is that because the factual determinations are already murky, stereotypes based on gender, race, sexual orientation, and
so on can more easily affect the court's decision.

Third, by the nature of retrieving eggs and sperm for IVF, women seeking to use
stored embryos created from their own genetic material will always have a stronger
argument than will men. The process of collecting eggs is a more physically invasive
and demanding process than the process of collecting sperm.[64] The *Davis* trial court
recognized this, noting the "many painful, physically tiring, emotionally and mentally taxing procedures" undergone by the wife in that case.[65]

Fourth, gendered stereotypes about parenting will come into play in assessing
how deeply an individual person wishes to become (or wishes not to become) a
parent. As one professor has summarized the Supreme Court's application of such
stereotypes, the perception of the desire to become a parent is "grounded in gender
assumptions that women naturally parent, while men, outside of marriage, choose to
parent or not, and nearly always choose not to do so."[66] For all of the reasons
outlined above, the balancing test invites courts to apply such stereotypes to litigants,
crediting the desire of women to become mothers as justified by a ticking biological
clock and their own so-called natural maternal tendencies, whereas men are more
often presumed to have no particularly strong desire to become fathers and, in any
case, can blithely father children well into their dotage.[67] From one perspective, this
could help women, as it strengthens the position of women such as Andrea in asking
to control a specialized circumstance of their own fertility. It is this court's belief,
however, that facilitating application of such stereotypes will merely strengthen the
gendered stereotypes in family law more broadly. Although it may frustrate some
individual women to rebuff a model that would help their case, courts must question
any circumstance in which gendered stereotypes might affect the judgment and
refuse to underscore gender stereotypes by giving them the force of law. For all these
reasons, this court rejects the balancing test.

---

[64] In order to retrieve eggs for use in IVF, the woman whose eggs will be used must take a series of
injections of hormones (typically administered at home) that stimulate her body to develop
many eggs to the point that they would be released in a standard menstrual cycle, rather than
just one. The eggs are then removed by a physician in an outpatient procedure. *See J.B.
v. M.B.*, 783 A.2d 707, 709 (2001). Risks of the egg retrieval process include ovarian hyper-
stimulation syndrome as a result of the fertility drugs, infections caused by the needle used to
aspirate eggs, and the risks of general anesthesia. Mayo Clinic, *In Vitro Fertilization (IVF)*,
www.mayoclinic.org/tests-procedures/in-vitro-fertilization/about/pac-20384716.

[65] *Davis v. Davis*, No. E-14496, 1989 WL 140495, at *2 (Tenn. Cir. Ct. Sept. 21, 1989), rev'd,
No. 180, 1990 WL 130807 (Tenn. Ct. App. Sept. 13, 1990), aff'd, 842 S.W.2d 588 (Tenn. 1992),
on reh'g in part, No. 34, 1992 WL 341632 (Tenn. Nov. 23, 1992).

[66] Nancy E. Dowd, *Fathers and the Supreme Court: Founding Fathers and Nurturing Fathers*, 54
EMORY L.J. 1271, 1310 (2005).

[67] We focus here upon gender but, as discussed above, these concerns are reproduced and
magnified in the context of other characteristics such as sexual orientation, race, class, and
so on.

Bret argues that this court should adopt the contemporaneous mutual consent model, under which a party asserting a right not to procreate always prevails against a party seeking use of the embryos to become a parent. This, however, goes too far in the opposite direction as the balancing test. Rather than the indeterminacy of the battling sympathies of the balancing test, the contemporaneous mutual consent model introduces an indeterminacy over time. No matter how strongly they promise or agree to use embryos later, the second one party changes his or her mind, the storage facility will keep the embryos indefinitely or destroy them.

Instead, this court adopts as a first-line rule the contractual model: so long as the parties voluntarily entered into an agreement that addresses disposition of embryos in the circumstances at hand, the court will enforce that agreement, even if one of the parties changes his or her mind in the interim. This gives agency and decision-making power to the parties to the agreement, rather than leaving disposition of the embryos entirely to a court applying a balancing test. It credits the (hopefully) thoughtful decision at the time of the agreement, emphasizing the importance of the agreement and the need for parties to consider the long-term implications of the creation of the embryos.[68] Should the parties subsequently both change their minds, they may amend the initial agreement to specify different plans for disposition of the embryos, as long as the modifications are similarly made voluntarily and mutually.[69] Such agreements will be evaluated using typical contractual principles, meaning that one party could challenge an agreement on the grounds that her assent was only secured through duress, or her partner misrepresented the agreement to her. We decline to affirmatively require any additional protections in the process of forming the agreement but, given the stakes of the decision, the legislature could statutorily demand protections such as requiring each party to receive independent legal advice and counseling regarding their reproductive future from the fertility clinic. Moreover, fertility clinics presenting clients with such agreements should take care that each client reads and completes the agreement in full.

Andrea argued before this court that because the only medical or biological contribution to the IVF process that a man makes is to donate his sperm, the court should interpret Bret's voluntary contribution as indicating his consent to the entire IVF process, including implantation of embryos at any later date. We reject this reading of assent: Bret consented some time ago to creating embryos in preparation for his wife's cancer treatment, and not to any specific timetable of use, much less open-ended permission for use at any time that Andrea chose in the future. To be clear, Bret could grant such open-ended permission but only if he does so explicitly and in writing, memorialized in the agreement between Bret and Andrea. In the absence of specific direction in the agreement, this court will not interpret consent to creation of embryos as consent to use of those embryos at any point.

---

[68] See *Kass v. Kass*, 696 N.E.2d 174, 180 (1998).
[69] See *Davis v. Davis*, 842 S.W.2d 588, 597 (Tenn. 1992).

In the absence of a provision in the agreement directing disposition of the embryos in the circumstances at hand, courts should apply the contemporaneous mutual consent model. If the parties failed to anticipate the circumstances they now find themselves in and did not give one person control over the embryos in that context, a court cannot impose parenthood on an unwilling participant.

For obvious reasons, the resolution of this case will disappoint Andrea. In any circumstance, fights over the disposition of embryos will be deeply personal and emotionally staggering. In this specific context, this result is the gloomy coda to a devastating set of burdens faced by Andrea. We believe that this is the fairest resolution of the disagreement between Andrea and Bret but know that our decision extinguishes a fervent and entirely understandable hope to become a mother through use of the stored embryos.

We stress, therefore, to persons considering IVF in the future, think carefully about how you would feel if you were in Andrea's position today. If you would want the ability to use stored embryos even if your current relationship ends, make that explicit in your agreement. If your partner will not grant such open-ended permission, explore the possibility of freezing gametes rather than embryos, or consider whether to create embryos using donor gametes instead of or in addition to embryos using your partner's gametes.[70] Understandably, these alternative options may create insurmountable financial or other barriers, demand extremely difficult conversations with a partner, and may be less attractive to the parties but the intertwining of law and procreation creates possibilities and challenges. There are no perfect solutions in this context, nor can courts distill a perfect resolution from such intractable conflict.

Lacking a contractual grant of control over the embryos to Andrea, Bret's current refusal to consent to implantation of the embryos means that she may not direct implantation of the embryos. The embryos will remain in storage at the fertility clinic subject to the clinic's standard policies regarding how long to keep embryos in storage and, if standard policies direct it, the clinic may destroy the embryos.

---

[70] Such decisions are possible today due to advances in medical technology, although they were not available to Andrea. Even cutting-edge medical technology is not infallible, however, and freezing eggs and embryos does not guarantee success in later bringing a pregnancy to term.

12

Adoptive Couple v. Baby Girl, 570 U.S. 637 (2013)

Commentary by Rose Cuison Villazor

INTRODUCTION

Adoptive Couple v. Baby Girl raises difficult tensions and issues that animate many reproductive justice cases – the rights of non-marital fathers versus non-marital mothers, the rights of biological parents versus adoptive parents, whether to privilege biological or genetic ties over non-biological ties to the child, and expectations regarding parenthood that reflect gender biases and stereotypes. But the case adds one other dimension that distinguishes it from conventional reproductive justice cases: it presents a conflict between the rights of an American Indian[1] parent and/or Indian tribe versus non-Indian adoptive parents to raise an Indian child. Central to the resolution of this Indian versus non-Indian parent conflict is an understanding of the purpose of the Indian Child Welfare Act (ICWA), which created substantive and procedural protections to prevent the break-up of the Indian family.

In seeking to address these issues, the majority and the dissents in *Adoptive Couple* issued opposing views about the scope of the ICWA. But Nancy Dowd's re-written opinion raises larger concerns about the Supreme Court's determination that ICWA does not protect biological Indian fathers if they did not have custody of the child in the first place. In so doing, Dowd argues that the Court created more stringent requirements for biological fathers that are tied to societal gender stereotypes about fatherhood and motherhood. The re-written judgment intervenes by highlighting the need to protect the constitutional rights of biological fathers both within and outside the context of ICWA. A critical contribution, the re-written judgment challenges the normative expectations about parenthood on gender lines. However, the re-written judgment's privileging of biological ties might have the unintended

---

[1] Author's note: I use the term "American Indian" instead of Native American, or Indigenous people, because many American Indian tribes and members prefer to use that term.

legacy of limiting the reproductive rights of non-biological parents, thus highlighting the tightrope that courts and advocates must walk when seeking justice in the reproductive realm.

This commentary places *Adoptive Couple* within the broader social, political, and legal context of the passage of ICWA and Congress's simultaneous goals of protecting Indian tribal sovereignty and the Indian family and explains the majority and dissenting opinions in *Adoptive Couple*, both of which addressed primarily the rights (or lack thereof) of the father and said very little about the rights of the Indian tribes to the child. This discussion creates a foundation to understand Dowd's dissenting opinion and her critique of the majority's establishment of a "biological plus custody" standard for biological fathers. The commentary ends by considering the legacy of the re-written opinion, including its important challenge to legal narratives about fatherhood. Dowd's analysis is consistent with the trend in other areas of law, including citizenship law, in which the Supreme Court has struck down rules that made it more difficult for fathers but not mothers to pass down their citizenship. However, this approach has the dangerous potential to undermine some of the increasing legal protections for non-biological parents.

ADOPTIVE COUPLE V. BABY GIRL

In *Adoptive Couple*, a biological father challenged the termination of his parental rights during the adoption of his daughter. Unlike in typical termination of parental rights cases, in which the issues traditionally concern whether a biological parent's connection to his or her child may legally cease, *Adoptive Couple* raised the added issue of whether the father, a member of the Cherokee Nation, may invoke protections under the Indian Child Welfare Act (ICWA).[2] ICWA provides substantive and procedural protections before Indian children may be separated from their families. To understand the legal issues surrounding *Adoptive Couple*, it is important to place the case within the broader historical, political, and legal context of ICWA.

Congress passed ICWA to protect "the continued existence and integrity of Indian tribes."[3] That is, Congress saw the connection between keeping Indian children with their families and the sovereignty of Indian tribes. Conducting several hearings over the span of four years, Congress found that "abusive child welfare practices" had "resulted in the separation of large numbers of Indian children from their families and tribes through adoption or foster care placement, usually in non-Indian homes."[4] Thus, in passing ICWA, Congress sought to address at least two harms that resulted from these state adoption practices: the separation of Indian children from their families, and loss to Indian tribes of future members. In other

[2]   25 U.S.C. 1901(3).
[3]   *Id.*
[4]   *Id.*

words, ICWA had dual policy goals: protecting the Indian family and ensuring tribal sovereignty.

Notably, the Supreme Court in *Mississippi Band of Choctaw Indians v. Holyfield*[5] emphasized these mutual goals, stating that when Congress passed ICWA, it did so to "protect the rights of the Indian child as an Indian and the rights of the Indian community and tribe in retaining its children in its society."[6] Accordingly, in cases that implicate ICWA, it is not only the rights of the father that are at stake; it is also the rights of federally recognized tribes to keep their future citizens.

At the outset, the Court in *Adoptive Couple*[7] addressed the issue of who should ultimately have custody of a toddler, named Veronica, her biological father, Dusten Brown, who is a member of the Cherokee Nation, or her adoptive parents, Matt and Melanie Capobianco.[8] Veronica's biological parents were engaged in December 2008 and her birth mother, Christine Maldonado, got pregnant in January 2009. The couple, however, broke off their engagement in May 2009. Prior to the break-up, Mr. Brown did not provide financial assistance to Ms. Maldonado. In June 2009, Ms. Maldonado sent a text to Mr. Brown asking him whether he would prefer to pay child support or give up his parental rights. Mr. Brown chose the latter.[9]

Ms. Maldonado decided to put Veronica up for adoption and chose the Capobiancos to adopt Veronica. On September 15, 2009, Veronica was born. The next day, Ms. Maldonado signed adoption forms terminating her parental rights and consenting to the adoption. Four months after Veronica's birth, the Capobiancos served Mr. Brown with notice regarding Veronica's adoption. Mr. Brown initially signed the papers, believing that he was relinquishing parental rights to Ms. Maldonado. When Mr. Brown discovered that Veronica was going to be adopted by the Capobiancos, however, he sought to stay the adoption proceedings. He took a paternity test to demonstrate that he is indeed the biological father.[10]

Mr. Brown prevailed at the trial level, resulting in the Family Court awarding custody of Veronica to him. The Capobiancos appealed the decision but the South Carolina Supreme Court affirmed the lower court's decision on two grounds. First, the court held that because the case involved an American Indian child, the Indian Child Welfare Act (ICWA) of 1978 applied to the case. The court also held that under ICWA, Mr. Brown is a "parent." As such, two provisions of ICWA prohibited the termination of Mr. Brown's parental rights. First, the Capobiancos failed to establish that "active efforts ha[d] been made to provide remedial services and rehabilitative

---

[5] 486 U.S. 1021 (1988).
[6] 490 U.S. 30, 32 (1989).
[7] *Adoptive Couple v. Baby Girl*, 570 U.S. 637 (2013).
[8] For discussion of the parties in the case, *see* Dan Frosch and Timothy Williams, *Justices Say Law Doesn't Require Child to Be Returned to Her Indian Father*, N.Y. TIMES A17 (June 25, 2013).
[9] *See Adoptive Couple*, *supra* note 7, at 643.
[10] *See id.* at 643–45.

programs" that were required to prevent the breakup of the Indian family. Second, the Capobiancos did not demonstrate that Mr. Brown's "custody of [Veronica] would result in serious emotional or physical harm to her beyond a reasonable doubt." Lastly, the court held that even if it had decided to terminate Mr. Brown's parental rights, it would have had to comply with ICWA's adoption-placement preferences. Under section 1915(a) of ICWA, preferences for the adoption of American Indian children would be given to a member of the child's extended family, other members of the Indian child's tribe, or other Indian families.[11]

The Supreme Court decided 5–4 in favor of the Capobiancos. Writing for the majority, Justice Alito held that certain provisions of ICWA did not apply. Specifically, the Court held that neither sections 1912(f) nor 1912(d) of ICA bars termination of Mr. Brown's parental rights. First, Justice Alito wrote that section 1912(f), which bars involuntary termination of parental rights with respect to an Indian child, was inapplicable. That provision states that parental termination may not be ordered in the "absence of a determination ... that the continued custody of the child by the parent or Indian custodian is likely to result in serious emotional or physical damage to the child." However, the facts indicate that Mr. Brown never had legal or physical custody of Veronica. As such, there was no "continued custody" of the child, making section 1912(f) inapplicable.[12]

Further, section 1912(d) provides that those seeking to terminate parental rights to an Indian child must provide "remedial services and rehabilitative programs designed to prevent the break-up of the Indian family and that efforts have been unsuccessful." The Court held, however, that the statute does not apply because there was no break-up of the Indian family in the first instance. Mr. Brown abandoned the child. Accordingly, there was no separation or break-up of the Indian family.[13]

Lastly, the court found ICWA's section 1915(e) in applicable. The majority explained that this provision provides that preferences should be given to (1) members of extended family, (2) other members of the Indian child's tribe, or (3) other Indian families. In the case at hand, however, the Capobiancos were the only party that sought to adopt Veronica. Mr. Brown did not seek to adopt the child (but argued instead against termination of parental rights). No one in his family or the Cherokee Nation sought to adopt the child.[14]

CONCURRING AND DISSENTING OPINIONS

Justice Breyer concurred with the majority and offered three "observations." First, he explained the absence of statutory language regarding how "absentee" Indian fathers who had little involvement with their infant children might be treated by ICWA.

[11] See id. at 645–46.
[12] See id., at 646–51.
[13] See id., at 651–52.
[14] See id., at 655–56.

From his perspective, the majority's reading of ICWA as inapplicable to those absentee fathers may be a "better reading" of the statute but also risks excluding too many fathers. Further, he explained that the majority's opinion is a narrow one and does not address the situations that concerned Justice Sotomayor's dissenting opinion. Lastly, Justice Breyer noted that other provisions of ICWA, particularly those that gave preferences to the Indian child's tribe, may be relevant in similar cases.[15]

Justice Sotomayor, joined by Justices Ginsburg, Kagan, and Scalia, dissented. She first disagreed with the majority's conclusion that section 1912(f) did not apply to any parent who has not had physical or legal custody of the child. She further rejected the majority's opinion that a father who has not had "continued custody" cannot invoke section 1912(d)'s protection against the break-up of the Indian family. Justice Sotomayor pointed out the broader implications of the majority's holding on other fathers whom she thought may be unfairly excluded from ICWA's protections. Emphasizing that the purpose of ICWA is to protect the "stability and security of Indian ... families," she explained that the majority's holding that sought to prevent the "dissolution of 'intact' Indian families" missed the overall congressional concern about the removal of Indian children from their homes and Indian tribes. Lastly, Justice Sotomayor opined that the majority's concerns about potential equal protection issues regarding racial preferences were irrelevant in a case involving statutory analysis. Nevertheless, she emphasized that classifications that were grounded on Indian tribal membership were not "impermissible racial classifications."[16]

WHAT THE COURT MISSED

Both the majority and dissenting opinions in *Adoptive Couple* framed the issue in this case as one that questioned the ability of the biological father to gain protection from ICWA. In so doing, the Court missed the opportunity to address a race-based concern lurking in the ICWA's background – whether ICWA's preferential treatment of American Indian parents and tribes violate equal protection principles.

Justice Alito, writing for the majority, used language to "racialize" Mr. Brown. He began the opinion, for example, by noting that Veronica, whose biological father is an enrolled member of the Cherokee Nation, was 3/256 Cherokee (or 1.2% Cherokee). Hinting at unfair racial preferences, Justice Alito notes that had Veronica not been Cherokee – and by extension, had Mr. Brown not been Cherokee – he would not have had the right to contest the adoption in the first instance. Finally, he notes that the birth father was seeking to use the "ICWA trump card" when he tried to override the adoption. His deployment of these texts demonstrates a simplistic and anxious view of race, equating blood quantum with racial identity and "preferential" use of race at the cost of white families.

[15] *See id.* at 666–67.
[16] *See id.* at 690.

Justice Sotomayor critiqued the "racing" of Mr. Brown by noting the political dimension of American Indian tribal membership. She explained that federally recognized tribes, as independent political entities, have the right to decide membership requirements, which a Court should not second-guess.[17] Although she was headed in the right direction of emphasizing that classifications based on tribal membership are not race-based, Justice Sotomayor could have taken another step by explicitly stating that such classifications are political in nature.

In particular, in *Morton v. Mancari*,[18] the Supreme Court held that the preferential employment of members of American Indian tribes by either Indian tribal employers or other employers on or near an Indian reservation did not constitute race discrimination.[19] In rejecting the race discrimination claim brought by a white applicant against the employer, the Supreme Court explained that the employer did not even engage in "'racial' preference [but rather utilized] an employment criterion reasonably designed to further the cause of Indian self-government."[20] The Supreme Court later held in *Rice v. Cayetano*[21] that *Mancari*'s discussion of the political nature of American Indian tribes was limited to federally recognized tribes and did not apply to Native Hawaiians, who are not federally recognized as American Indian tribes.

To be sure, *Mancari* addressed preferential hiring in the employment context and not "placement preferences for the adoption of Indian children,"[22] which was the issue in *Adoptive Couple*. Nevertheless, the analysis is apt because at the heart of both cases is an examination of Congress's intent to protect the rights of American Indian tribes.[23] That is, both laws seek to promote the self-determination rights of American Indian tribes. Far from a race-based classification, preferences towards members of American Indian tribes seek to achieve such congressional policy.

The Court's failure to address the race versus political dichotomy was not only a missed opportunity but also left open claims that ICWA is racially discriminatory. Indeed, in a recent case, *Brackeen v. Zinke*,[24] a district court held that ICWA's American Indian preferences constitutes race-based discrimination.[25] In so doing, the court distinguished *Brackeen* from *Mancari* by explaining that, unlike the latter Supreme Court case in which preferences are given to members of American Indian tribes, ICWA includes preferences to children whose parents are not only members

---

[17] *See id.*
[18] 417 U.S. 535 (1974).
[19] *See id.* at 551.
[20] *Id.* at 553.
[21] 528 U.S. 495, 515 (2000) (stating that ancestry can be a proxy for race).
[22] *Adoptive Couple*, 570 U.S. at 638.
[23] *See Morton*, 417 U.S. at 554–55 (discussing Congress's obligation to promote the self-governing rights of American Indian tribes); Indian Child Welfare Act, 25 U.S.C. § 1901 (stating that Congress has the responsibility to protect and preserve Indian tribes and resources).
[24] 2018 WL 4927908 (N.D. Tex., Oct. 4, 2018).
[25] *See id.* at *12.

of American Indian tribes but also those who are biologically American Indian.[26] Notably, this case could eventually undermine the congressional goal embedded within ICWA of preserving the American Indian family and the self-determination rights of American Indian tribes.

DOWD'S REWRITTEN OPINION AND LEGACY

Dowd's re-written opinion highlights two points about *Adoptive Couple* that warrant scrutiny. First, her opinion debunks the good versus bad framing of Dusten Brown. In so doing, she gestures towards the unfair treatment that unwed fathers experience when addressing their parental rights of their non-marital children. Second, Dowd critiques the majority's position that "biological plus custody" is needed to gain protection under ICWA. Instead, she contends that, "biology alone should trigger presumptive parental rights." I address each of these below.

To begin, from a feminist principle perspective, Dowd correctly highlights that the majority's holding and reasoning are grounded on gender stereotypes about fatherhood. The majority's discussion of Dusten Brown, as Dowd notes, focuses on him as the "uncaring father who gave up his rights in a text message." Dowd complicates this narrative by pointing out facts that suggest that Brown did in fact desire not only fatherhood but also the "traditional" family by proposing to marry Ms. Maldonado, Veronica's birth mother. Further, after the relationship had gone awry and he later discovered that he risked losing his parental rights, Brown sought counsel to protect his rights as a father. Here too, Dowd negates the majority's framing of Brown as a disengaged father and shows that far from being a disinterested parent, he wanted to be a father to his daughter. By recasting the Court's framing of Brown, Dowd draws attention to the ways in which both law and society rely on stereotypes to make determinations about a father's fitness to be a parent.

Dowd's focus on calling out gender stereotyping has support in recent Supreme Court cases, including *Sessions v. Morales-Santana*,[27] in which the Court struck down a derivative citizenship law that imposed more stringent physical residency requirements for unwed US citizen fathers than US citizen mothers, which made it more difficult for fathers to pass down their citizenship to their non-marital child who was born abroad.[28] As the Court explained, the derivative citizenship statute "date[s] from an era when the lawbooks of our Nation were rife with overbroad generalizations about the way men and women are."[29]

Next, Dowd contends that biology should trigger presumptive parental rights. She rejects the "biology plus" line of argument that the Court seemed to have adopted. Instead, she argues for a presumptive constitutional protection for biological fathers.

[26] *See id.* at *12.
[27] 198 L. Ed. 2d 150 (2017).
[28] 137 U.S. at 1689.
[29] 137 S. Ct. at 1689.

Such an argument is consistent with the earlier point about the need to protect the rights of fathers. However, privileging biological over non-biological ties might have the unintended consequence of impacting the rights of other parents who are considered non-traditional in that they lack the biological tie to their children. Such parents may include those who are medically unable to have children and either adopt or use another person's egg or sperm to have children. It also includes same-sex or opposite-sex couples, where one partner may not have a biological connection to a child who is being jointly parented, who lack a biological connection. Notably, a presumptive rule that favors biological ties could create a hierarchy among parents and alienate "non-traditional" parents. Although Dowd's opinion certainly does not intend to create such a hierarchy, it seems a probable outcome given the privileging of certain parents.

Adoptive Couple v. Baby Girl, 570 U.S. 637(2013)

Justice Nancy Dowd, dissenting

Gender, race, and class intersect in this contested adoption case but the majority opinion fails to address those identities and engage in the analysis essential to insure the protection of fundamental liberties. The tragic, inexplicable outcome is that the child at the heart of this controversy will be removed from her fit parent's loving care and custody.

A brief summary of the case in this closely-divided decision is in order. The prospective adoptive parents challenged the decision of the South Carolina Supreme Court that their requested adoption violated the protections for Native American children and families under the Indian Child Welfare Act (ICWA), 92 Stat. 3069, 25 U.S.C. sections 1901–63. Congress enacted ICWA in response to sustained and widespread abuses that separated Native American children from their families and their tribes. The Act establishes robust protections before termination of parental rights in a variety of legal proceedings, including adoption, and also creates clear adoption placement preferences for Native American children to be placed with Native American parents.

The Oklahoma biological father, a registered member of the Cherokee Nation, objected to the proposed adoption of his infant daughter as soon as he was given notice of it. The prospective adoptive couple waited four months after the birth and temporary placement with them of the child to initiate the process to obtain the father's consent to adoption. The father mistakenly signed the papers presented to him by the process server, assuming that they constituted a surrender of his custody rights to the biological mother days before he was to deploy overseas. When he realized his error, the process server refused to allow him to reverse his signature and threatened to have him arrested. The father immediately sought legal counsel to establish paternity, object to the adoption, and seek custody. The adoptive parents at this critical juncture made the decision to contest the father's declared desire to raise his biological daughter.

The father's objection to the adoption and claim for custody was consolidated with the South Carolina prospective adoptive parents' petition for finalization. Less than a week after he first learned of the prospective adoption, the father was deployed. The trial took place upon his return to the United States, when the child was two years old. The trial court found for the father under ICWA and ordered his daughter to be transferred to his custody. She was immediately transferred to her father's care on December 31, 2011, at 27 months of age.

The adoptive couple chose to appeal. The South Carolina Supreme Court affirmed the decision in favor of the father. 398 S.C. 625, 731 S.E. 2d 550 (2012). According to the court, three separate provisions of ICWA precluded the adoption. First, the father's parental rights could not be involuntarily terminated because the adoptive parents had failed to show the father's custody of the child would result in "serious emotional or physical harm to her beyond a reasonable doubt" as required by the statute. § 1912(f). Second, they also failed to comply with ICWA requirement that efforts be made to prevent the breakup of an Indian family. Section 1912(d). Third, even if termination of the father's rights were permissible, the trial court would have been required to consider adoption placement preferences in the statute, which would disfavor the prospective adoptive couple as compared to members of the Cherokee Nation willing to adopt the child. Section 1915 (a).

The Court granted certiorari and now reverses, by a 5–4 vote, the decision of the South Carolina Supreme Court. Justice Alito, writing for the majority, holds that the trial court and the South Carolina Supreme Court misinterpreted ICWA, and the father could not claim the protection of parental rights provided by the statute. Justice Alito distills the essence of the decision in his summary early in the opinion:

> [W]e hold that 25 U.S.C. § 1912(f) – which bars involuntary termination of a parent's rights in the absence of a heightened showing that serious harm to the Indian child is likely to result from the parent's "continued custody" of the child – does not apply when, as here, the relevant parent never had custody of the child. We further hold that § 1912(d) – which conditions involuntary termination of parental rights with respect to an Indian child on a showing that remedial efforts have been made to prevent the "breakup of the Indian family" – is inapplicable when, as here, the parent abandoned the Indian child before birth and never had custody of the child. Finally, we clarify that § 1915(a), which provides placement preferences for the adoption of Indian children, does not bar a non-Indian family like Adoptive Couple from adopting an Indian child when no other eligible candidates have sought to adopt the child. We accordingly reverse the South Carolina Supreme Court's judgment and remand for further proceedings. *Id.* at 2557.

Although the Court assumes the biological father was a "parent," the majority construes ICWA to permit termination of his parental rights because he never had "custody" of his infant daughter.[30] Based on this statutory interpretation of ICWA, the majority orders the case remanded to the South Carolina Supreme Court for further proceedings with no further instructions to the courts below to hold a best interests hearing for the child.[31] At the time the Court issued the decision in this case on June 25, 2013, the child had been living with her father for over 18 months, and was about to turn 4. Thus, roughly half of her life she had lived with the prospective adoptive parents, and half of her life she had lived with her father.[32]

Justice Sotomayor, joined by Justices Ginsberg, Kagan, and Scalia, dissented. Justice Sotomayor disputes the statutory interpretation of the majority as inconsistent with the plain meaning of the statute and with Congress' intent to preserve Indian families by maximum statutory protection of parental and familial rights. She writes,

> When it excludes noncustodial biological fathers from the Act's substantive protections, this textually backward reading misapprehends ICWA's structure and scope. Moreover, notwithstanding the majority's focus on the perceived parental shortcomings of Birth Father, its reasoning necessarily extends to all Indian parents who have never had custody of their children, no matter how fully those parents have embraced the financial and emotional responsibilities of parenting. The majority thereby transforms a statute that was intended to provide uniform federal standards for child custody proceedings involving Indian children and their biological parents into an illogical piecemeal scheme. *Id.* at 2573.

While Justice Sotomayor critiques the majority's interpretation of "continued custody" as "literalness strangling meaning," Justice Scalia in his dissent concludes that evaluation of the feasibility of "continued custody" under the statute was a forward-looking standard, to determine if there was any reason to deny custody going forward, rather than a backward-looking requirement that only a parent with physical or legal custody was entitled to claim rights. In addition, Justice Scalia notes the failure of the majority to accord the high constitutional respect ordinarily given to biological parenthood:

> The Court's opinion ... needlessly demeans the rights of parenthood. It has been the constant practice of the common law to respect the entitlement of those who bring a child into the world to raise that child ... This father wants to raise his daughter, and the statute amply protects his right to do so. There is no reason in law or policy to dilute that protection. *Id.* at 2572.

---

[30] Furthermore, if ICWA did not prohibit the adoption over his objection, the Court notes, under both Oklahoma and South Carolina statutes, his consent would not be required for the adoption because he had not provided financial support to the biological mother during the pregnancy. S.C. section 63-9-310 (A)(5)(b); Oklahoma 10-7505-4.2 (C)(1).

[31] Justices Breyer and Thomas concurred in the majority opinion.

[32] [Author's note: After last ditch efforts failed, the father surrendered his daughter to the prospective adoptive couple on Sept. 23, 2013, when she was four years old.]

I

This case is about the rights of fathers at the birth of their biological children; and, conversely, about the rights of children at birth to a relationship with their willing and able biological fathers. The ICWA, 92 Stat. 3069, 25. U.S.C. sections 1901–63, plainly confers full parental rights on the biological father at birth based on his undisputed status as a biological parent. Those rights include the right to be included in any adoption decision and would require his consent for an adoption to go forward. Under the tortured reading of the majority, the father, although a parent, has no rights under ICWA because he never had "custody" of his daughter, nor does he have any rights under state law, because state law demands more than biology to recognize him as a parent at the child's birth. S.C. 63-9-310 (A)(5)(b); S.C. 63-17-20(B) (2010); *see* also Okla. Stat., Tit. 10, section 7800 (2013). Both the majority's interpretation of ICWA and its unblinking acceptance of state standards for recognizing parental rights implicate constitutional parental and familial rights with deep roots in our jurisprudence. *Meyer v. Nebraska*, 262 U.S. 390 (1923); *Pierce v. Society of Sisters*, 268 U.S. 510 (1925); *Troxel v. Granville*, 530 U.S. 57 (2000).

Moreover, as Justice Scalia notes in his dissent, biological parenthood is significant. *Id.* at 2572. Although not the sole basis to recognize parenthood, it is nevertheless important because, among other things, it links a child to her ancestry and extended family as well as to parents who have a presumed interest in her care and growth. The deeply rooted common law standard cited by Justice Scalia is present as well in our constitutional recognition of the power and importance of biology. *Santosky v. Kramer*, 455 U.S. 745, 758–59 (1982). At the birth of a child, when biological differences do not justify differential treatment of parents by sex, applying a unique standard of parenthood solely to fathers implicates the constitutional prohibition against sex discrimination in addition to the fundamental rights of parents. Because this is a Native American father and child, race[33] also is present in this case, and indeed ICWA is designed to be protective of racial identity. The majority treated both Native American identity and ICWA's protections of Native American families with disrespect and disparagement.[34]

The majority opinion and the dissent of Justice Sotomayor address the statutory interpretation issues raised by this case. The majority criticizes the very purpose and

---

[33] Race is a powerful social construct and the category is used here to denote that Native ancestry and tribal membership are important identities that create community and belonging and are worth protecting.

[34] Alito begins his opinion for the majority as follows: "This case is about a little girl (Baby Girl) who is classified as an Indian because she is 1.2% (3/256) Cherokee. Because Baby Girl is classified in this way, the South Carolina Supreme Court ... required her to be taken, at the age of 27 months, from the only parents she had ever known and handed over to her biological father, who had attempted to relinquish his parental rights and who had no prior contact with the child." *Id.* at 2556. The opinion further on refers to the father's invocation of ICWA's protections as an "ICWA trump card" played "at the eleventh hour to override the mother's decision and the child's best interests." *Id.* at 2565.

legitimacy of ICWA, and then proceeds to interpret Congress' protection of parental rights as triggered only when a biological parent has "custody" of a child. Justice Sotomayor in her dissenting opinion ably and persuasively articulates the purpose and meaning of ICWA: to honor and protect Native American parental rights and family integrity from all unjustified interventions, not solely those of removal. *Id.* at 2574. Consistent with this clear intent, ICWA confers robust parental rights on fathers. As she notes, those rights meet and exceed the Court's "current constitutional baseline" of the rights of non-marital fathers. Under ICWA they include the necessity of the father's consent for an adoption to proceed, his right to withdraw that consent until finalization, and involuntary termination of his rights only upon a showing of harm to the child or unfitness.[35] Under Justice Sotomayor's analysis, ICWA resolves the issues raised in this case unequivocally in favor of the father's full parental rights.

I write separately to address constitutional issues embedded in this case. Upholding the father's rights within the framework of the parental rights of fit parents is constitutionally required. Biological parenthood should trigger constitutional protection for fundamental parental rights for both fathers and mothers. Requiring something more from fathers, whether by interpreting ICWA to add a custody requirement or using state statutes if ICWA were inapplicable to require demonstration of more than a biological relationship ("biology plus") for one's consent to be mandatory is not constitutionally defensible. We should take this opportunity to address our current standard of unique constitutional requirements for fathers as compared to mothers. There has never been a case under that standard where the evaluation of father's rights comes literally at birth. This case suggests that, rather than parsing a bad standard to distinguish rights at birth when no "plus" is yet possible, we should revisit and revise our standard.

In addition, the rights of the father are not all that should command our attention. The rights of the child at the center of this controversy are constitutionally protected, and merit respect and attention. The rights of this child require intensified scrutiny because she is a non-marital child of color. Resolving the difficult custodial issues raised by the tangled litigation of this case must be subject to the paramount rights of the child to determine her best interests, defined from her perspective.

I respectfully dissent.

---

[35] "These protections [for the parent] are numerous. Had Birth Father petitioned to remove this proceeding to tribal court, for example, the state court would have been obligated to transfer it absent an objection from Birth Mother or good cause to the contrary. *See* section 1911 (b). Any voluntary consent Birth Father gave to Baby Girl's adoption would have been invalid unless written and executed before a judge and would have been revocable up to the time a final decree of adoption was entered. *See* sections 1913(a)(c). And section 1912, the center of the dispute here, sets forth procedural and substantive standards applicable in "involuntary proceedings[s] in a State court," including foster care placements of Indian children and termination of parental rights proceedings. Section 1912(a)." *Id.* at 2574.

II

An implicit gender lens pervades this case but not a gender analysis as commanded by our cases. On the one hand, standards of presumed gender roles inappropriately influence the analysis of the facts. On the other hand, the majority ignores the influence of social expectations that impact significantly and differentially on the decision-making of both the mother and the father. These gender issues are further affected by intersections with critical identity factors: (1) the racial identities of the Native American father and Latina mother, and the racial identity of their child; and (2) the parents' non-marital status, which subjects them to different legal rules but also to a different set of social expectations and judgments. Moreover, (3) their class status, which translates into limited economic resources, is a key factor that triggers the mother's pursuit of adoption as a way to care for her third child.

Two entirely different pictures of the father emerge in this case. The majority presents him as an uncaring father who gave up his rights in a text message, a selfish man who uses the "race card" among other abuses of power to try to prevent a reasonable choice by a low-income Latina mother with few other good options to support her new child, having already two children to care for, and no race card of her own to play. Justice Sotomayor's dissent presents a caring but flawed father, one who makes mistakes but who should not lose his parental rights. These two different retellings of the story of this case are not insignificant, as they underpin the legal analysis. Wrapped up in these different pictures are gendered expectations of the good father. Missing is an understanding of the gender expectations and context within which both the father and mother functioned.

Additional facts bring this context into sharper focus. The father and mother in this case had been in a relationship off and on since they were 16. Both had married and then divorced their spouses. Both had children from their prior marriages. Although the statutes governing custody and support are gender neutral, their circumstances at the time this pregnancy occurred reflected common gender patterns post-divorce. The mother had primary custody of her two children and was struggling financially. The father sustained a relationship with his previously born child from his first marriage and paid child support but was not a coequal parent. Formally, he had agreed to sole custody for the mother, a common pattern for military personnel to insure clarity and simplicity during deployment.

At the time of the renewed relationship between the father and the mother, the father was living on a military base four hours from the mother, and knew he was subject to future deployment. They were engaged to be married when they learned she was pregnant. His response was to suggest that they move up their wedding. His action traditionally would be viewed as "doing the right thing." It also was consistent with their plan before the pregnancy. Furthermore, if they were married, he could provide financially for the mother and his child because he would be entitled to additional dependent benefits.

For reasons not reflected in the record, the mother not only refused to move up the wedding date but also six months later broke off the relationship with the father. She viewed the relationship as over; he viewed it as one in a series of ups and downs and hoped they would reconcile. The parties did not communicate much, or well. Much has been made by the litigants and the majority of an exchange of text messages between the mother and father a month after the breakup. The mother asked him if he would pay child support or would rather give up his rights. The father responded he would give up his rights. Nothing in the prior experience of either prospective parent would have suggested a text message would establish legal rights or could be a legal basis to relinquish rights. Moreover, their divorce experience would suggest knowledge that the father would have financial responsibility as well as custodial rights.

The mother functioned within social norms placing the expectation of care on mothers. In the scenario of a broken relationship before the birth, the mother would still be expected to care for the child and might be raising the child with little or no care from the father (or possibly might not want to coparent with him). She faced the challenge of pursuing child support from a partner she was no longer speaking to, who might be even more difficult to pursue if deployed overseas, and who already had another child to support from his previous marriage. Even though the father would be legally obligated to pay support, her texted question asking if he would pay support suggests her reality was that in fact child support could not be counted on. Moreover, even if he willingly paid support, the amount of support the law would obligate him to pay might be insufficient to meet the burden of raising another child. She would know that he would be entitled to custodial rights, and therefore she would be required to coparent with him. Taking matters into her own hands, his texted answer, in her view, left her as the sole decision-making parent for the child that she was carrying because she would bear the burden of raising that child.

While the mother might have viewed herself as the sole parent, the adoption agency would have known otherwise, and would have been obligated to inform the prospective adoptive parents. Nevertheless, the mother, adoption agency, and adoptive parents created a plan without consulting the known father. Only the most minimal effort (and an incorrect one) was made to determine his tribal status; no effort was made to communicate directly with him. After taking temporary custody of the child days after the birth and removing the child from Oklahoma to South Carolina, the adoptive couple delayed four months before they attempted to reach the father to seek his consent to the adoption. The father was viewed through a familiar lens: the uncaring, uninvolved non-marital father. Because he was a father, that perhaps triggered a legal strategy to preclude his assertion of rights that would derail the adoption. Indeed, it has been the position of the prospective adoptive parents in this litigation that he is not a "parent" at all.

When the father's consent was finally sought, the father made clear that he did not want to relinquish his parental rights. Misapprehending the legal papers as sole custody papers, he realized his mistake immediately. When the process server threatened him that he could not intervene to tear up the papers or indicate his signature was in error, he filed a legal action without delay, the next day. Despite his communication of his desire not to sacrifice his parental rights, the adoptive parents refused to accept his position. While the actions of the prospective adoptive parents might, on the one hand, be understandable, on the other hand they are hardly defensible, given their failure to timely include the father in the adoption process when there was no reason to exclude him. If he was as they assumed, an uncaring, uninvolved father, he would have had every reason to welcome the opportunity to surrender his rights.

The scope of the father's constitutional protection must focus on the time frame of this case. The child in this case was transferred to the temporary custody of the adoptive parents days after her birth, after the mother signed papers relinquishing her rights. The father was known before the birth but his relinquishment of rights was not requested at birth. The father's scope of constitutional protection should be measured at the time custody was transferred to the prospective adoptive parents.

The rights of known fathers at birth is a context of fatherhood previously unaddressed by this court. This case, then, is different in a constitutionally significant way from other "fathers' rights" cases that have previously come before us. At the same time, it provides an opportunity to revisit the broader issue of whether parental rights can be subject to gender-specific standards without violating the Constitution.

III

A

We begin with the recognition in this case that we are evaluating parental rights, rights typically accorded the greatest respect by this Court. "The liberty interest ... of parents in the care, custody, and control of their children – is perhaps the oldest of the fundamental liberty interests recognized by this Court." *Troxel v. Granville*, 530 U.S 57, 65 (2000). This standard treats nonmarital parents as equal to marital parents. *Id.*; *Stanley v. Illinois*, 405 U.S. 645 (1972). The Court has also recognized the unique and powerful bond of biology and accordingly has given that parental connection great respect. *Smith v. Organization of Foster Families*, 431 U.S. 816 (1977); *Quilloin v. Walcott*, 434 U.S. 246, 255 (1978), although biological parenthood is neither the only nor always preferred construction of parenthood depending upon the context. *Michael H. v. Gerald D.* 491 U.S. 110 (1989) (recognizing marital non-biological father); *Moore v. City of East Cleveland*, 431 U.S. 494 (1977) (recognizing grandmother's functional parent status and the family as constitutionally protected).

In this case the parent who does not want to surrender his rights and consent to the adoption is an unmarried father. Our cases have permitted differentiation between non-marital fathers and non-marital mothers but that differentiation must meet our standard for non-discrimination on the basis of sex under Equal Protection.

The standard for evaluating sex discrimination remains that articulated so clearly by Justice Ginsberg in *United States v. Virginia*, 518 U.S. 515 (1996): "Parties who seek to defend gender-based government action must demonstrate an 'exceedingly persuasive' justification for that action ... [such classifications will be subject to] skeptical scrutiny of official action denying rights or opportunities." *Id.* at 531. The burden of justification is demanding, and it rests entirely on the State. The State must show "at least that the [challenged] classification serves 'important governmental objectives and that the discriminatory means employed' are 'substantially related to the achievement of those objectives'." *Mississippi Univ. for Women v. Hogan*, 458 U. S. 718, 724 (1982). The standard must be applied "free of fixed notions concerning the roles and abilities of males and females. Care must be taken in ascertaining whether the state's objective itself reflects archaic and stereotypic notions. Thus, if the statutory objective is to exclude or 'protect, members of one gender because they are presumed to suffer from an inherent handicap or to be innately inferior, the objective itself is illegitimate." *Id.* at 725. It must not rely on "overbroad generalizations about the different talents, capacities, or preferences of males and females." *United States v. Virginia, supra*, at 533.

The law may recognize biological differences where they are relevant. *Id.* But those differences may not be used to justify discriminating between men and women where differences are irrelevant to capabilities.[36] For too long, flawed views of men's and women's physical differences justified broad discrimination and sex subordination. The temptation to do so at the birth of a child extends the real difference of pregnancy to presumed differences and capabilities to parent. "Indeed, the idea that mother's presence at birth supplies adequate assurance of an opportunity to develop a relationship while a father's presence at birth does not would appear to rest on an overbroad sex-based generalization ... There is no reason, other than stereotype, to say that fathers who are present at birth lack an opportunity for a relationship on similar terms." *Nguyen v. Immigration & Naturalization Service*, 533 U.S. 53, 86–87 (2001) (Justice O'Connor, dissenting). As Justice Ginsberg noted in *Sessions v. Morales-Santana*, our analysis of outmoded stereotypes continues to evolve, and therefore requires that the classification "must substantially serve an important governmental interest today, for 'in interpreting the [e]qual [p]rotection

---

[36] "Physical differences between men and women, however, are enduring ... Inherent differences between men and women, we have come to appreciate, remain cause for celebration, but not for denigration of the members of either sex or for artificial constraints on an individual's opportunity ... such classifications may not be used, as they once were, to create or perpetuate the legal, social, and economic inferiority of women [or men]." *United States v. Virginia*, at 533–34 (emphasis added).

[guarantee], [we have] recognized that new insights and societal understandings can reveal unjustified inequality ... that once passed unnoticed and unchallenged'." *Sessions v. Morales Santana*, 198 L. Ed. 2d 150, 163 (2017) (slip opinion at 9), citing to *Obergefell v. Hodges*, 135 S. Ct 2584 (2015) (slip op., at 20). Our evolving knowledge of men, masculinities, and fatherhood should lead us to re-examine our standard with "new insights and societal understandings."

Our standards expressly prohibit the use of physical differences to sustain gender stereotypes. When a non-discriminatory, gender-neutral standard just as effectively achieves the state's interest, it is to be preferred over sex differentiation that rests on stereotypic assumptions of capabilities as parents, or even true generalizations. As this Court very recently noted:

> Even if stereotypes frozen into legislation have "statistical support," our decisions reject measures that classify unnecessarily and overbroadly by gender when more accurate and impartial lines can be drawn. *J. E. B. v. Alabama ex rel. T. B.*, 511 U. S. 127, 139, n. 11 (1994); *see, e.g., Craig v. Boren*, 429 U. S. 190, 198–99 (1976); *Weinberger v. Wiesenfeld*, 420 U. S. 636, 645 (1975). In fact, unwed fathers assume responsibility for their children in numbers already large and notably increasing. *See* Brief for Population and Family Scholars as Amici Curiae 3, 5–13 (documenting that nonmarital fathers "are [often] in a parental role at the time of their child's birth," and "most ... formally acknowledge their paternity either at the hospital or in the birthing center just after the child is born"); Brief for American Civil Liberties Union *et al.* as Amici Curiae 22 (observing, inter alia, that "[i]n 2015, fathers made up 16 percent of single parents with minor children in the United States"). *Sessions v. Morales Santana, supra*, at 166, fn 13

Vigilance regarding limitations and stereotypes ensures equality for women and men, as wrongful restrictions on one typically affect both. "Stereotypes about women's domestic roles are reinforced by parallel stereotypes presuming a lack of domestic responsibilities for men ... These mutually reinforcing stereotypes created a self-fulfilling cycle of discrimination that forced women to continue to assume the role of primary family caregiver and fostered employers' stereotypical views about women's commitment to work and their value as employees." *Nevada Department of Human Resources v. Hibbs*, 538 U.S. 721, 736 (2003).

No "inherent differences" differentiate mothers and fathers at the birth of the child. They begin at birth equally capable of the care of their children. The key is to acknowledge that differences exist (including pregnancy, childbirth, and lactation) but those differences are not relevant to recognizing the capability or status at birth of a biological father to parent as compared to a biological mother. Actual differences of capability and capacity are not determined by sex but by individual character and personality in relation to care. Those differences might be relevant if at all to a determination of custody but not to a determination of who is a constitutionally recognized parent, and they would be objectively determined, not stereotypically assumed.

In this case the majority's interpretation of ICWA rejects the rights of the biological father written into ICWA and required by our sex discrimination standard. Without ICWA's protection, the father is subject to a state law analysis that similarly would not recognize his parental rights on the basis of biological parenthood, as the state would do so for the biological mother. Unmarried fathers under state law must meet a different constitutional standard in order to have rights. This standard deserves and requires re-examination. The gendered lens of this case should lead us to reconsider our prior holdings leading to the "biology plus" standard. In the alternative, this case presents a distinctive issue unaddressed in those opinions.

B

Unmarried fathers' parental rights have not been treated as constitutionally coequal with those of unmarried mothers, in a series of cases beginning with *Stanley v. Illinois*, 405 U.S. 645 (1972). In those cases, decided in the 1970s and 1980s, culminating in *Lehr v. Robertson*, 463 U.S. 248 (1983), mostly involving stepparent adoption, the Court moved from an initial recognition of the strong parental rights of fathers as parents to a gender-specific standard that required biology plus something more to trigger constitutional parental rights for unmarried fathers.

In *Stanley*, the state of Illinois removed a man's biological children from his custody after the death of their mother, with no hearing provided to the father, on the basis that he, like all nonmarital fathers, was presumed unfit to parent under state law. We held that an unmarried father could not be treated any differently than an unmarried mother or married father, and therefore could not lose his children without a hearing proving his unfitness. A presumption that all unmarried fathers were unfit was unconstitutional. "The private interest here, that of a man in the children he has sired and raised, undeniably warrants deference and, absent a powerful countervailing interest, protection. It is plain that the interest of a parent in the companionship, care, custody, and management of his or her children 'come[s] to this Court with a momentum for respect lacking when appeal is made to liberties which derive merely from shifting economic arrangements'." *Stanley* at 651 (citations omitted). We emphasized the fundamental importance of parental rights, and that those rights are unaffected by the absence of marriage. "To say that the test of equal protection should be the 'legal', rather than the biological, relationship is to avoid the issue. For the Equal Protection Clause necessarily limits the authority of a State to draw such 'legal' lines as it chooses." *Id.* at 652.

At the same time, *Stanley* rested on a negative view of unmarried fathers. The Court did not entirely disagree with the Illinois presumption that all or virtually all unmarried fathers were unfit (in other words, the presumption was treated as most likely true) but rather noted that the chance that a father might be fit defeated its constitutionality. "It may be, as the State insists, that most unmarried fathers are unsuitable and neglectful parents. It may also be that Stanley is such a parent, and that his children should be placed in other hands. But all unmarried fathers are not in this category; some are wholly suited to have custody of their children." *Stanley*, at 653–54, fn 6 and 7.[37]

Following *Stanley*, in a trilogy of stepparent adoption cases the Court refined its analysis. In *Quilloin v. Walcott*, 434 U.S. 246 (1978), the Court found no Due Process or Equal Protection violation in a Georgia adoption proceeding that utilized a best interests standard to approve an adoption by a stepparent of an 11-year-old child who had only sporadic and minimal contact with his biological father since birth and his whose father had not legally solidified his parental relationship. Three years after the child's birth, the mother married. She had never shared a household with the biological father, and he was uninvolved with his son's care. The child requested that the adoption be granted, although the child also indicated he still wanted to have visitation with his biological father, a possibility that would be foreclosed if the adoptive father refused visitation because the biological father would no longer have any rights.[38]

Rather than a conflict between asserted state interests and the unwed father in *Stanley*, in *Quilloin* the Court juxtaposed the interests of the unmarried father against the interests of the mother, the child, the functional father (the stepfather), and a marital family unit. The Court distinguished *Stanley* because *Quilloin* did not involve breaking up a family unit, as the father never had custody and even in this proceeding was not seeking custody. The Court deemed the best interests standard constitutionally sufficient in this situation, and easily found that the situation of married and unmarried fathers differed, so that treating them differently did not violate Equal Protection.

This analysis reflected the then-current lack of consistent, uniform laws for imposing financial support of children on non-marital fathers. As at least some commentators have noted, the analysis also reflects a strong preference for a two-parent marital or marital-type family. Janet Dolgin, *Just A Gene: Judicial Assumptions about Parenthood*, 40 U.C.L.A. L. Rev. 637, 649–50 (1993). Stepparent adoption accomplished this goal. Finally, the opinion reflects then-current social

---

[37] *See also Stanley*, at 656: "it may be argued that unmarried fathers are so seldom fit that Illinois need not undergo the administrative inconvenience of inquiry in any case, including Stanley's. The establishment of prompt efficacious procedures to achieve legitimate state ends is a proper state interest worthy of cognizance in constitutional adjudication. But the Constitution recognizes higher values than speed and efficiency."

[38] "The child also expressed a desire to continue to visit with appellant on occasion after the adoption. The child's desire to be adopted, however, could not be given effect under Georgia law without divesting appellant of any parental rights he might otherwise have or acquire, including visitation rights." *Quilloin, supra*, at 251.

norms condemning unmarried parenthood and a father's failure to marry the mother once a non-marital pregnancy existed.[39]

A year later, despite this strong endorsement of marital family in *Quilloin*, in *Caban v. Mohammed*, 441 U.S. 380 (1979), the Court upheld the biological father's objection to a stepparent adoption. The father in *Caban* shared a household with the mother and during that time two children were born. After they split up, the mother married another man, and the biological father continued his relationship with his children. The father married as well, so at the time of the proceeding both biological parents were in marital family units. The Court was strongly impressed by the conduct of the biological father and held that the granting of an adoption (to the stepfather) without the consent of the father violated his constitutional rights. *Caban* appears to step away from the preference for the marital family; at the same time, however, it was the functional replication of the marital family in the relationship of the biological parents that was persuasive to the Court in recognizing the equal rights of the father and the mother with respect to adoption. In *Caban*, in contrast to *Quilloin*, the relationship between the father and his children was significant and sustained.

The *Caban* Court specifically rejected the idea that mothers and fathers are different as parents:

> [M]aternal and paternal roles are not invariably different in importance ... The present case demonstrates that an unwed father may have a relationship with his children fully comparable to that of the mother. Appellant Caban, appellee Maria Mohammed, and their two children lived together as a natural family for several years. As members of this family, both mother and father participated in the care and support of their children. There is no reason to believe that the Caban children – aged 4 and 6 at the time of the adoption proceedings – had a relationship with their mother unrivaled by the affection and concern of their father. We reject, therefore, the claim that the broad, gender-based distinction of § 111 is required by any universal difference between maternal and paternal relations at every phase of a child's development. *Id.* at 389.

The Court similarly rejected the idea that fathers more than mothers would fail to give consent to an adoption. In the adoption context, the Court viewed mothers and fathers as equals, so there was no need to view mothers as dominant in parental rights regarding adoption. "It may be that, given the opportunity, some unwed fathers would prevent the adoption of their illegitimate children. This impediment to adoption usually is the result of a natural parental interest shared by both genders

---

[39] *See also Michael H v. Gerald D.*, 491 U.S. 110, 118 (1989), asserting as a truism that, in law as in life, a child can have only one father. Not only is this assumption challenged by our recognition of same sex marriage but it also elevates form over function, as not only are there children of same sex parents who have two fathers or two mothers but also many children who have multiple parental figures due to patterns of cohabitation and divorce.

alike; it is not a manifestation of any profound difference between the affection and concern of mothers and fathers for their children. Neither the State nor the appellees have argued that unwed fathers are more likely to object to the adoption of their children than are unwed mothers; nor is there any self-evident reason why, as a class, they would be." *Id.* at 391–92.

Caban represents an evolving understanding about fathers, the view that their interests and abilities are coequal with mothers. There, the Court wrote:

> The effect of New York's classification is to discriminate against unwed fathers even when their identity is known, and they have manifested a significant paternal interest in the child. The facts of this case illustrate the harshness of classifying unwed fathers as being invariably less qualified and entitled than mothers to exercise a concerned judgment as to the fate of their children. Section 111 both excludes some loving fathers from full participation in the decision whether their children will be adopted and, at the same time, enables some alienated mothers arbitrarily to cut off the paternal rights of fathers. We conclude that this undifferentiated distinction between unwed mothers and unwed fathers, applicable in all circumstances where adoption of a child of theirs is at issue, does not bear a substantial relationship to the State's asserted interests. *Id.* at 394.

Our exploration of fatherhood culminated in *Lehr v. Robertson*, 463 U.S. 248 (1983). *Lehr*, like this case, is one in which the majority and dissenting opinions offer starkly contrasting stories about the case. In *Lehr*, the unmarried parents lived together and sustained a relationship before their daughter was born but not after her birth. Eight months after their child was born, the mother married someone other than the biological father. After the child was two, the mother and her husband petitioned for him to adopt the child, and a court granted the adoption without notice and an opportunity to be heard by the biological father. In this case, the Court announced that biology alone was not enough to trigger notice and an opportunity to be heard. While biology was not irrelevant, the Court found biology alone insufficient to trigger constitutional protection equivalent to that provided to mothers at the birth of children. Biology,

> offers the natural father an opportunity that no other male possesses to develop a relationship with his offspring. If he grasps that opportunity and accepts some measure of responsibility for the child's future, he may enjoy the blessings of the parent–child relationship ... and make uniquely valuable contributions to the child's development. If he fails to do so, the Federal Constitution will not automatically compel a State to listen to his opinion of where the child's best interests lie. *Id.* at 262.

Lehr reasoned that the most important aspect of parental relationships is functional family bonds and ties. In *Lehr*, then, a biological father could be entirely excluded from an adoption proceeding without offending due process or fundamental rights if he had not engaged in conduct sufficient to attain constitutional parenthood status. Lehr's pre-birth conduct was irrelevant; his post birth conduct in the two years after the birth and prior to the initiation of the adoption proceeding excluded him from Constitutional fatherhood. The Court adopted a standard that did not apply to all parents who fail to care for their children. It was a standard applied solely to fathers.

Ironically, the facts in *Lehr* challenge the application of its standard to the father in that case. There, the father had acted. According to the dissent, the father's allegations in his complaint, taken as true given the procedural posture of the case, were that he diligently attempted to establish contact with his daughter but the mother hid herself from him despite his persistent efforts to find her. The majority focused on the lack of a father–child relationship but did not consider the alleged efforts of the father to establish a relationship, efforts that the mother blocked at every turn.

Justice White's dissent would accord constitutional recognition based on biology alone. He argues that the importance of the biological link is enough to honor it; the nature of the functional relationship goes to the weight of parental interests when the parents are engaged in legal disputes but not to the presence of a constitutional interest subject to protection. He explains that "The 'biological connection' is itself a relationship that creates a protected interest . . . Whether Lehr's interest is entitled to constitutional protection does not entail a searching inquiry into the quality of the relationship, but a simple determination of the fact that the relationship exists . . ." *Lehr, supra,* at 271–72.

It is precisely this point that this case raises. Because this case presents the standing of the respective biological parents at birth, the biological link should trigger constitutional protection. The substance of parental rights (e.g., conferring custodial rights, for example) would require further proceedings to determine the best interests of the child. But there is simply no need to insert biological differences into the evaluation of father's rights as compared to mother's rights.

It is to this issue that I now turn. Certainly, our expectations and understanding of men as parents has evolved from the negative perspective of *Stanley*. At the moment of childbirth traditional expectations may be the strongest; we must separate those embedded stereotypes for the benefit of both mothers and fathers as they begin their lifetime of parenting that particular child. Our standard of biology plus represents a standard that stands in sharp contradiction to our understanding of gender equality. Just as our social understanding of fatherhood has changed, so too should our recognition that our view of fathers as different from mothers is a vestige of deep stereotypes, not a recognition of inherent difference.

C

Biology alone should trigger presumptive parental rights as well as responsibilities to the coparent. Both rights and responsibilities are and should be robust. "Biology plus" asks for both too much and too little. It asks more from fathers than mothers, to prove themselves but it does not ask for very much, only that they "seize" an opportunity by showing "some" responsibility for the child. *Lehr, supra*, at 262. We should recognize fathers as coequal parents with the expectation that they will be fully engaged in the care of their children as constructive coparents with mothers. To construct mothers as different from fathers by virtue of pregnancy is to engage in stereotyping of both mothers and fathers. To see fathers as lesser, as having to "make up" or equalize the contribution of mothers in pregnancy is an inherently unworkable standard as well as one that assumes the gender stereotypes that separate fathers from mothers. Mothers as a group may, more often, be fully responsible for care. That disproportionate reality, however, should not translate into automatic singular rights.

Rights at birth are not the same as women's rights and choices during pregnancy, and to control their reproductive lives. *Roe v. Wade*, 410 U.S. 113 (1973); *Planned Parenthood v. Casey*, 505 U.S. 833 (1992). The physical differences of pregnancy do not translate into different capabilities to parent based on sex any more than a child's parents must necessarily be one man and one woman. *Obergefell v. Hodges*, 135 S. Ct. 2584 (2015). Present and future conduct matter most at birth.

The fathers' rights cases stand out as creating a nebulous framework where equal rights do not begin until fathers have "acted" like a father. But we have no such standard for mothers. They are presumed to have full parental rights from birth. If we look backward at mothers' pregnancy work and try to create an equal contribution for fathers, then we search for an equivalent which is not possible, or we allow something unequal to suffice. We then do not value the distinctive role of women and pregnancy, and we are tempted to fall back on traditional norms of economic fatherhood as the way to measure men's parenting. Alternatively, if we carry women's significant contribution during pregnancy forward, then either men never catch up to become parenting equals, or if we deem that they do, then women's care is undervalued. The better course, one substantiated by parenting research, is to treat men and women as equally capable (not actually but potentially) at birth.

The biology plus standard functions similarly to the presumed unfitness standard of *Stanley*, and that is why it is wrong; it assumes too much. We should take this opportunity to hold that *Lehr* was wrongly decided by adopting a constitutionally infirm standard that conflicts with our sex discrimination standard. Biological parenthood should trigger constitutional parenthood. It would not be the exclusive means to accomplish constitutional parenthood. Other non-biologically based definitions of parenthood would be equally constitutionally protected, such as marital and adoptive parenthood, or the construction of parental ties through assisted reproductive technologies. Moreover, our jurisprudence on families suggests we might recognize a broad definition of parenthood that includes functional parenthood. *Moore v. City of East Cleveland*, 431 U.S. 494 (1977).

To recognize biological fathers as constitutional parents is consistent with our precedents regarding the importance of biological bonds; our rejection of marriage as the sole constitutionally significant definition of parenthood; and our rejection of differentiating between marital and non-marital children. It does not elevate this form of parenthood above all others but, on the other hand, it recognizes its value and equal status for men as well as women. The biological standard recognizes the importance of heritage in addition to the opportunity that a biological link creates to connect parental status with parental function. It permits children's identity, typically derived from both of their parents, to be honored.

In this case, denying constitutional protection by reading ICWA, or the alternative relevant state statutes, to require more than biological connection violates this standard. Reaching a substantive judgment based on the conclusion that fathers must "prove" or demonstrate something more to gain constitutional protection violates the rights of biological parents because it means we reinforce old stereotypes about men and fatherhood, and undermine the equality of parents. The parental conduct relevant to privileges or rights should be the same for mothers and fathers and should not be grounded in physical differences that do not relate to the capability and quality of an individual's care for children.

The idea that mothers and fathers are different and distinctive is a powerful one. But it is an idea grounded in stereotypes and gender roles, not in fact. The harm in sustaining this differentiation is not just in cases involving adoption or custody but in other areas as well.

The "biology plus" standard not only unjustifiably demands more of fathers but also it demands too little. While constitutional parenthood creates the opportunity to exercise rights, expectations of parents without regard to sex should justifiably be strong. Parental rights carry significant responsibilities; those should be equally shouldered by fathers and mothers, responsibilities not just of economic support but of the care of children. Indeed, it might be argued that the father in this case did not do enough, during the pregnancy, at the birth, and immediately post birth. Assuming the mother will do all care is hardly coequal parenting. But his actions should not be seen as hard-wired by gender. He operated in a gendered framework of expectations of fatherhood but our role is not to validate or reinforce those biases. *Palmore v. Sidoti*, 466 U.S. 429 (1984). Rather, it is to sustain equality, and the gender-neutral responsibilities that equality brings.

IV

Even if we are not prepared to abandon the biology plus standard, we are faced in this case with a scenario not addressed in our prior cases: what rights do fathers have at birth? The facts here present a constitutionally distinguishable situation where biology triggers constitutional protection in order to preserve the father's ability to establish and sustain his social and functional relationship with his child.

The adoptive parents in this case, and the agency that represented them, knew of the identity of the father in this case. Their knowledge of his paternity should trigger their obligation to respect his constitutionally protected parental rights. Their delay of four months to attempt formal service to terminate his parental rights should be viewed skeptically; debating his actions or inactions during this time frame therefore should be estopped. What is relevant are his actions when presented with papers, and his immediate actions to protect his rights when he realized that he was mistaken as to the rights that he had signed away.

This case requires evaluation of the father's rights at birth. Unlike any of the prior father's rights cases, there is no record of parenting because there is no time frame in which that could have occurred. One simply cannot apply a standard of "biology plus" because there has been no opportunity for any "plus" to occur.

To treat men and women differently at this stage is to extend the biological differences of pregnancy into a "plus" for women which men can never match or equal. If you assume women's capability to parent, that reflects stereotypes about their "natural" mothering and predominance as parents. The emotional and physical care that both fathers and mothers can provide suggests that their equality going forward from the birth should be assumed.

One cannot defend a standard that looks backward for mothers (pregnancy and giving birth) while focusing forward for fathers, to say that mothers and fathers are different. The gender equality cases demand that we exercise skeptical scrutiny to determine whether stereotypes are at work, to ensure that we treat men and women equally. Assuming women's parenting capability and actual care is fraught with some of the most deeply rooted sex stereotypes. Discounting men's capability to care for children perpetuates gender stereotypes that undermine equality as well. Certainly, much is arguably needed to make parenting truly equally supported for both mothers and fathers. Equal protection and fundamental rights require that any differentiation between the two as parents is constitutionally unsupportable.

V

Finally, equal treatment of fathers and mothers also necessitates grappling with differentiations and hierarchies among fathers. Although the gendered nature of fatherhood is universal, the experience of fatherhood is nevertheless raced and classed. Gender clearly intersects with race in this case. It is not solely the father's identity as a man that matters, it is also his identity as a Native American father. The disparagement of his tribal identity is evident in the first sentence of the majority opinion, by the Court's dismay that this child has what is deemed a small amount of Cherokee blood. Furthermore, her father's assertion of tribal rights under ICWA is viewed as an unfair and unmerited identity trump card that derails the adoption. This characterization of the father plays into stereotypes disparaging the fatherhood of Native American men, and men of color generally (just as related stereotypes disparage mothers of color, especially black women). NANCY E. DOWD, REDEFINING FATHERHOOD 58–80 (NYU Press 2000). The Court also uses what it characterizes as the "dominantly Hispanic" identity of the biological mother to play its own racial trump game, as if these opposing identities raise the issue of whether one should prevail over the other in a racial hierarchy. Thus, lurking in the gendered constitutional standard of fatherhood applied in this case is the possibility that such analysis is more likely to be used to the detriment of fathers when the fathers are not white. A reformed constitutional standard must include sensitivity to and inclusion within the analysis of the potential for particular parental norms to incorporate or apply racial, ethnic, or tribal stereotypes that violate equal protection and fundamental rights regarding race and parenthood, as is the case here with respect to race and fatherhood. *Cf. Palmore v. Sidoti* 466 U.S. 429.

VI

The majority opinion directs that this case be remanded to the Supreme Court of South Carolina but without any further instructions on how the lower courts should proceed. This raises one final constitutional issue: whether remand without further instructions violates the rights of the child by failing to consider her best interests in the pragmatic steps that the lower courts will be faced with resolving on remand. The analysis of the case, by focusing on the rights of the biological father and the prospective adoptive parents, thus far has not considered her separable rights at all.

This case most importantly is about her. After a brief period of time with her birth mother, she was separated from her mother and placed in the temporary custody of her prospective adoptive parents while also being denied any relationship with her father. Months after her birth, her adoptive parents and her father began litigation over her custody. She, of course, knew nothing of this, and continued to be cared for by her prospective adoptive family. There is every indication that they provided loving care. When she was two, she was transferred to the care of her biological father. She bonded with her father, and there is no question that he has provided loving care. At the time of this decision, she is about to turn four years old. Developmentally she has benefitted from the care of multiple parental figures. The challenge for the Court is to recognize and honor her liberty interests, including how to sustain to adulthood her positive development, functional relationships, and long term familial and cultural identities.

This Court has hinted at but not fully fleshed out a concept of children's rights. *Troxel v. Granville*, 530 U.S. 57, 88–91 (2000), dissenting opinion of Justice

Stevens;[40] *see generally* U.N. Convention on the Rights of the Child, UN General Assembly, Convention on the Rights of the Child, 20 November 1989, United Nations, Treaty Series, vol. 1577, p. 3. A necessary corollary of the strong recognition of parental rights are the rights of the child. Without defining the child's interests in detail, surely it includes the child's developmental and familial rights. Those rights do not vary based on the marital status of her parents, nor their racial identities. To the contrary, those children whose identities have historically triggered stigma and inequality should require greater protection and scrutiny.

Here the child's right in the posture of this case requires a close examination of her best interests regarding custody and her concept of "family." At a minimum that means remand for a full best interests hearing. In that hearing it should include consideration of the child's relational and long-term developmental interests to determine whether sustaining all existing relational ties must be supported.

In determining best interests, the courts below should view this from her perspective and her established family relationships. In its prior jurisprudence the Court has suggested that a child cannot have two fathers. *Michael H. v. Gerald D.*, 491 U.S. 110, 118 (2001). Yet our evolving understanding of family suggests that many children in fact have more than one father. A numerical limitation tied to a gender allocation is yet another instance of being wedded to traditional gendered family norms that fly in the face of equal protection and fundamental family rights. The content of the child's relationships in this case should be considered in devising a custodial order that serves those interests either by affording contact and parenting by all of her functional parents or, at the very least, insuring a supported custodial transition that sustains her developmental best interests.

---

[40] "[T]his Court has not yet had occasion to elucidate the nature of a child's liberty interests in preserving established familial or family-like bonds . . ., it seems to me extremely likely that, to the extent parents and families have fundamental liberty interests in preserving such intimate relationships, so, too, do children have these interests, and so, too, must their interests be balanced in the equation. At a minimum, our prior cases recognizing that children are, generally speaking, constitutionally protected actors require that this Court reject any suggestion that when it comes to parental rights, children are so much chattel. *See ante*, at 64–65 (opinion of O'CONNOR, J.)" (describing States' recognition of "an independent third-party interest in a child"). The constitutional protection against arbitrary state interference with parental rights should not be extended to prevent the States from protecting children against the arbitrary exercise of parental authority that is not in fact motivated by an interest in the welfare of the child. *Troxel*, at 88–89.

13

Burwell v. Hobby Lobby Stores, Inc., 573 U.S. 682 (2014)

Commentary by Suzanne A. Kim

INTRODUCTION

Burwell v. Hobby Lobby Stores, Inc.,[1] decided in 2014, broke ground in its unprecedented articulation of religious personhood rights for commercial entities, posing challenges to reproductive justice and the foundations of antidiscrimination law. The case addressed whether the Affordable Care Act's (ACA) contraceptive mandate should yield to a Religious Freedom Restoration Act (RFRA) claim by for-profit corporations objecting on religious belief grounds to providing health insurance coverage for contraception[2] to employees. Concluding that the corporations seeking exemptions were "persons" for free exercise purposes under RFRA, the Court held that US Department of Health and Human Services (HHS) regulations interpreting the ACA contraceptive coverage requirement violated RFRA by substantially burdening the exercise of religion.[3]

The *Hobby Lobby* re-write by Anthony Kreis underscores the far-reaching implications of the original decision by connecting the reproductive health access questions at stake to the day to day conditions in women's lives and broadly systemic effects of the *Hobby Lobby* decision for marginalized communities. In so doing, the rewritten opinion sets the stage for deeper consideration of *Hobby Lobby*'s challenge to the health and well-being of women, communities of color, lower-income communities, and other marginalized groups.

---

[1] *Burwell v. Hobby Lobby Stores, Inc.*, 573 U.S. 682 (2014).
[2] *Id.* at 688. The four types of contraceptives at issue involve emergency contraception and intrauterine devices ("IUD"). *Id.* at 701.
[3] *Id.* at 729–30 (also determining that mandate did not qualify as the least restrictive means available to further the compelling governmental interest in providing access to the challenged contraceptive methods).

BURWELL V. HOBBY LOBBY

In *Hobby Lobby*, three for-profit corporations (collectively "Hobby Lobby and Conestoga")[4] challenged HHS regulations requiring employers to provide the full range of Federal Drug Administration-approved contraceptives through ACA-covered health plans.[5] Hobby Lobby and Conestoga argued that their exercise of religion was burdened by paying for contraception that they described as "abortifacients," which operate by terminating pregnancy, based on their religious belief that pregnancy begins at fertilization.[6] This contrasted with scientific and medical consensus that pregnancy begins at implantation of a fertilized egg and that the challenged contraceptive methods, thus, were not abortifacients.[7]

HHS provided exemptions from the "contraceptive mandate" for religious non-profits, religious organizations like churches, and employers with fewer than fifty employees.[8] None of the companies challenging the mandate's application qualified for the exemption.[9] Accordingly, the corporations and their owners[10] argued that the HHS regulations mandating coverage of the challenged contraception violated their rights under the Free Exercise Clause of the First Amendment[11] and under the Religious Freedom Restoration Act of 1993.[12]

---

[4] *Hobby Lobby Stores, Inc., v. Sebelius*, 723 F.3d 1114, 1120 (2013); *Conestoga Wood Specialties Corp. v. Sec'y of U.S. Dep't of Health and Human Servs.*, 724 F.3d 377, 381 (3rd Cir. 2013).

[5] *Hobby Lobby, supra* note 1. ACA generally requires employers with fifty or more full-time employees to offer "a group health plan or group health insurance coverage" that provides minimum essential coverage. HHS defined "minimum essential coverage," under the ACA, to include all FDA-approved contraceptives, provided without cost-sharing to employees. Hobby Lobby and Conestoga objected specifically to four products that may have the effect of preventing an already fertilized egg from developing any further by inhibiting its attachment to the uterus.

[6] *Hobby Lobby, supra* note 1, at 701.

[7] Notwithstanding the plaintiffs' nomenclature to describe the contraception, the medical and scientific community and federal law define pregnancy as beginning upon implantation of a fertilized egg in the uterine wall. *See* Rachel Benson Gold, *The Implications of Defining When a Woman Is Pregnant*, GUTTMACHER REP. ON PUB. POL'Y (May 2005), at 7, [www .guttmacher.org/pubs/tgr/08/2/gr080207.html [http://perma.cc/NA27-ARWD]. Accordingly, the contraceptives at issue in *Hobby Lobby* do not cause abortion based on scientific agreement, as they do not operate after implantation. *See, e.g.*, Brief of Physicians for Reproductive Health et al. as Amici Curiae Supporting Defendants-Appellees at 10-12, *Conestoga Wood Specialties Corp. v. Sebelius*, 724 F.3d 377 (2013) (No. 13-1144), 2013 WL 1792349 (citations omitted).

[8] Under this accommodation, "the insurance issuer must then exclude contraceptive coverage from the employer's plan" and provide plan participants with separate payments for contraceptive services "without imposing any cost-sharing requirements on the [employer], its insurance plan, or its employee beneficiaries." *Hobby Lobby, supra* note 1, at 698 (2014).

[9] *See id.* at 698–99.

[10] These parties are collectively referred to as "Hobby Lobby and Conestoga" hereinafter.

[11] U.S. CONST. AMEND. I.

[12] *Hobby Lobby, supra* note 1, at 688. RFRA, in pertinent part, prohibits the "Federal Government from taking any action that substantially burdens the exercise of religion unless that action constitutes the least restrictive means of serving a compelling government interest." *Id.* at 705.

The Court held, in Justice Alito's majority opinion, that the ACA contraceptive mandate regulations violated RFRA.[13] First, the Court concluded that RFRA permits for-profit corporations like Hobby Lobby and Conestoga to challenge regulations like HHS's contraceptive mandate for violation of Free Exercise Clause rights.

Second, in applying RFRA to Petitioners' challenges, the Court determined that the contraceptive mandate substantially burdened the exercise of religion by requiring them to engage in conduct that "seriously violates their sincere religious belief that life begins at conception" or face "severe economic consequences."[14] While the Court assumed that the "interest in guaranteeing cost-free access to the four challenged contraceptive methods is a compelling governmental interest," it reasoned that the Government had failed to show that the contraceptive mandate is the least restrictive means of furthering that interest.[15]

The Court determined that, as an alternative, the government could assume the cost of providing contraceptives to women unable to obtain coverage due to their employers' religious objections. Further, the government could extend the accommodation that HHS had already established for religious nonprofit organizations to for-profit employers with religious objections to the contraceptive mandate.[16]

RE-WRITTEN OPINION IN *BURWELL V. HOBBY LOBBY*

Anti-choice and many religious freedom advocates welcomed the majority decision in *Burwell v. Hobby Lobby*, while others roundly criticized the decision for how it struck the balance between contraceptive healthcare access and corporate religious rights.[17] Commentary focused on the implications of this balance for women's

---

[13] *Id.* at 689. Justice Alito was joined by Chief Justice Roberts and by Justices Scalia, Kennedy, and Thomas. Justice Ginsburg dissented, joined by Justice Sotomayor and almost entirely by Justices Breyer and Kagan.

[14] *Id.* at 720.

[15] *Id.* at 728.

[16] *Id.* Limiting its holding, the Court stated that it was not intended to invalidate all insurance coverage mandates, like those for "vaccinations or blood transfusions," if they conflicted with an "employer's religious beliefs." *Id.* at 733 ("In any event, our decision in these cases is concerned solely with the contraceptive mandate").

[17] The scope of corporate personhood rights, as articulated in *Citizens United v. FEC.*, 558 U.S. 310 (2010), took on particular resonance in the unique context of their application in the religious accommodation context. While for profit entities had not previously obtained religious accommodation rights under common law or statutory law, Hobby Lobby and Conestoga argued that they were entitled to the same protections as non-profit religious entities, Brief for Petitioner's at 25–28, *Conestoga Wood Specialties Corp. v. Sebelius*, 2014 WL 173487, No. 13-356 (Jan. 10, 2014), regardless of the longstanding approach to religious accommodation for commercial entities. CARLOS A. BALL, THE FIRST AMENDMENT AND LGBT EQUALITY: A CONTENTIOUS HISTORY (2017).

health, equal health care access, reproductive and sexual rights, gender equality, racial equality, antidiscrimination law, and corporate rights more broadly.[18] Numerous health care and women's rights organizations submitted amicus briefs in the case, highlighting the importance of the ACA Women's Health Amendment and the contraceptive coverage for a range of health concerns for women across the socioeconomic spectrum and from communities of color.[19] *Hobby Lobby* also attracted sharp criticism for its implications for gender equality and for sexual minorities.[20] Such concerns echoed those raised by Justice Ginsburg in dissent about the slippery slope of religious accommodation and its sweeping potential outcomes.[21]

The *Hobby Lobby* re-write responds to these many concerns by engaging reproductive justice substantively and methodologically, illuminating the issues at stake and their intersecting impacts on gender equality, health, sexual rights, and economic and racial justice. Justice Kreis centers women in his opinion and contextualizes the day-to-day and broader societal consequences of the contraception coverage requirement.[22] This focus on lived experience invites closer inspection of the multi-dimensionally subordinating influences of lack of access to low-cost reproductive health care and of encroachments on reproductive decisional autonomy, especially when viewed through an integrated, intersectional lens.

The rewritten opinion narrows the decisional field by focusing on key, dispositive questions within the free exercise and RFRA analyses. Pursuant to this vision, the revision explores the broad effects on women and other communities of commercial actors who enter the marketplace and use religious claims as a "sword" against their covered employees.

The majority and re-written *Hobby Lobby* opinions differ in their approach to the existence of a burden on free exercise. In the original opinion, "A law that 'operates so as to make the practice of religious beliefs more expensive in the context of

[18] Such concerns echoed those raised by Justice Ginsburg in dissent about the slippery slope of religious accommodation and its sweeping potential impacts. Hobby Lobby, *supra* note 1, at 769 (2014) (Ginsburg, J. dissenting).

[19] *See, e.g.,* Brief of the Center for Reproductive Rights as Amici Curiae in Support of Defendants-Appellees and Affirmance. *Id.*; Brief of the Guttmacher Institute and Professor Sara Rosenbaum as Amici Curiae in Support of the Government. *Id.*

[20] Neil S. Siegel & Reva B. Siegel, *Compelling Interests and Contraception*, 47 CONN. L. REV. 1025, 1042 (2015); Terri R. Day & Danielle Weatherby, *LGBT Rights and the Mini RFRA: A Return to Separate but Equal*, 65 DEPAUL L. REV. 907 (2016); Alex J. Luchenitser, *A New Era of Inequality:* Hobby Lobby *and Religious Exemptions from Anti-discrimination Laws*, 9 HARV. L. & POL'Y REV. 63 (2015).

[21] Hobby Lobby, *supra* note 1, at 770–71 (Ginsburg, J. dissenting) ("Would the exemption ... extend to employers with religiously grounded objections to blood transfusions ... antidepressants, ... and vaccinations?"). *See also Id.* at 770 (Ginsburg, J. dissenting) (discussing the historical relationship between threats to antidiscrimination law as applied in the race and gender context through claims for religious exemptions).

[22] *See, e.g.,* Mari J. Matsuda, *Looking to the Bottom: Critical Legal Studies and Reparations*, 22 HARV. C.R.-C.L. L. REV. 323 (1987) (for a critical race feminist approach).

business activities' imposes a burden on the exercise of religion."[23] In contrast, Justice Kreis characterizes "a substantial burden" as existing "only when individuals are forced to choose between following the tenets of their religion and receiving a governmental benefit, or coerced to act contrary to their religious beliefs by the threat of civil or criminal sanctions."[24] Applying this standard, the revised opinion characterizes the claimed outcomes as "far too attenuated" to amount to a substantial burden.[25]

Within its more streamlined doctrinal frame, the Kreis opinion communicates a substantially narrower conception of RFRA's influence on free exercise analysis than that conveyed in the original opinion, which viewed the statute as providing "very broad protection for religious liberty."[26] While the majority viewed Congress as going "far beyond what this Court ha[d] held [was] constitutionally required" in RFRA, the revised opinion portrays RFRA's aims as significantly more modest, merely restoring free exercise analysis to the same form of heightened scrutiny for free exercise claims used prior to *Employment Div. Dept. of Human Resources of Ore. v. Smith*, in which the Court held that neutral laws of general applicability cannot violate the Free Exercise Clause.[27]

Having narrowed the field of inquiry, the Kreis opinion illuminates the far-reaching social justice implications of the contraceptive mandate by embracing as compelling the government's interest in "enhancing the agency of female employees to make personal health care decisions."[28] This dramatically contrasts with the

---

[23] *Hobby Lobby, supra* note 1, at 710.

[24] Anthony Michael Kreis, *Burwell v. Hobby Lobby*, in this volume at 306 (quoting *Navajo Nation v. U.S. Forest Serv.*, 535 F.3d 1058, 1070 (9th Cir. 2008)). This question turns on whether the challenged governmental action places "substantial pressure on an adherent to modify his behavior and to violate his beliefs." *Id.* at 24 (quoting *Thomas v. Review Bd. Of Indiana Employment Security Div.* at 718)).

[25] *Id.* at 27. In dissent, Justice Ginsburg asserted that, even assuming RFRA's applicability, the contraceptive coverage regulations did not "substantially burden[]" Hobby Lobby's and Conestoga's exercise of religion. *Id.* at 760–61. The requirement "calls on the companies covered by the requirement to direct money into undifferentiated funds that finance a wide variety of benefits under comprehensive health plans [...], which must offer contraceptive coverage without cost sharing, just as they must cover an array of other preventative services." *Id.* Moreover, the dissenters challenged the suggestion that the employee's decision, in consultation with her physician, to pursue a course of health care treatment, including use of contraception, is attributable to her employer. *Id.*

[26] *Hobby Lobby, supra* note 1, at 694.

[27] *Employment Div. Dept. of Human Resources of Ore. v. Smith*, 494 U.S. 872 (1990) (rejecting free exercise claim of employees dismissed from jobs and denied unemployment benefits because they had ingested peyote, an essential element of a religious ceremony but in violation of state law generally forbidding consumption of peyote). Justice Ginsburg contended that, per the Court's analysis in Smith, the free exercise claim was invalid because "prohibiting the exercise of religion ... is not the object of [the relevant governmental regulation," which was "aimed at women's well being, not the exercise of religion ... any effect it has on such [free] exercise is incidental." *Hobby Lobby, supra* note 1, at 745 (Ginsberg, J., dissenting) (quoting *Smith*, 494 U.S. at 878).

[28] Kreis, *supra* note 24, at 300.

majority's articulation of the state's compelling interest in "guaranteeing cost-free access to the four challenged contraceptive methods."[29] The rewrite's wider framing of the state interest underscores the importance of making available the full range of FDA-approved contraceptive options in enabling women to make better medical decisions,[30] and connects the contraceptive mandate squarely to its role as part of a comprehensive legislative effort to support women's health.[31]

This more capacious understanding of the government's interest also signals the impact of women's control over their reproductive decisions, recognized through the rewrite's focus on the impermissible gender-based burden religious accommodation would impose.[32] The contraceptive mandate's role in mitigating gender inequality renders salient these externalities: "We must be especially sensitive to the reality that excusing Hobby Lobby from their obligations not only imposes costs on third parties who derive no benefit from the accommodation, but those costs fall squarely on the shoulders of a protected class and would implicate this Court in sanctioning sex discrimination."[33] Those encroachments on low-cost access, reproductive decision-making, and bodily control impede women's ability to participate fully in society and achieve economic and employment opportunity.[34] Effects are especially pronounced for women of color and lower-income communities, taking into account the disparate burden on women of contraceptive costs, gender-based wage gaps (wider for women of color),[35] and the entanglement of gender, race, and poverty.[36] Reproductive control is critical to rebutting

---

[29] *Hobby Lobby*, *supra* note 1, at 728.

[30] Kreis, *supra* note 24, at 302 ("Importantly, women's need to access the full range of FDA-approved contraception is crucial because 'women's contraceptive method choices are influenced by concerns about side effects and drug interactions, how frequently they expect to have sex, their perceived risk of sexually transmitted infections, and the nature of their intimate relationship(s)'.") (quoting Brief of the Guttmacher Institute and Professor Sara Rosenbaum as Amici Curiae 14).

[31] *Id.*

[32] The Kreis opinion identifies the "negative externalities for persons who derive no benefit from the accommodation." *Id.* at 30.

[33] *Id.* at 309. The Kreis opinion furthers Justice Ginsburg's articulation of third-party harm to the corporations' employees and covered dependents, women not holding their employers' beliefs and denied access to contraceptive coverage that would otherwise be covered under the ACA. *Hobby Lobby*, *supra* note 1, at 745–46 (Ginsberg, J. dissenting).

[34] Brief of National Women's Law Center *et al.*, as Amici Curiae 22.

[35] "Women who work full time, year-round in the United States were paid only eighty cents for every dollar paid to their male counterparts in 2016." National Women's Law Ctr., *FAQs about the Wage Gap*, NATIONAL WOMEN'S LAW CENTER, at 2 (Sept. 2017), https://nwlc-ciw49tixgw5l bab.stackpathdns.com/wp-content/uploads/2017/09/FAQ-About-the-Wage-Gap-2017.pdf. "For every dollar earned by white, non-Hispanic men, African American women earn just 64 cents, while Hispanic women earn just 54 cents." Brief of National Women's Law Center et al., as Amici Curiae 22 (citing Nat'l Women's Law Ctr., FAQ About the Wage Gap, at 2 (2013), www .nwlc.org/sites/default/files/pdfs/wage_gap_faqs_sept_2013.pdf.

[36] "[W]omen, particularly women of color, are more likely to be poor than men." Brief of National Women's Law Center et al., as Amici Curiae 22. (citing Nat'l Women's Law Ctr.,

the longstanding legally-entrenched narrative of women's and men's "separate spheres" in society.[37]

Lastly, and crucially, the revised opinion focuses attention on the intersecting and widespread implications of the religious exemption argument for health care access, for reproductive rights, and for antidiscrimination law more broadly. First, concern about the boundaries of exemption extend to the provision of health care more generally: If granted in this context, what principle limits against exemptions for other forms of medical care?[38] Moreover, the revised opinion's focus on the indeterminacy of the proposed religious exemption illuminates the slippery slope down which religious exemptions regarding reproductive health access have gone since *Hobby Lobby*. For instance, in *Zubik v. Burwell*, the Supreme Court considered a religious non-profit's argument that the administrative requirement of giving notice of a religious objection imposes a "substantial burden" on religious exercise.[39] The ongoing legal push to broaden the scope of religious exemption to include "moral conviction" objections of for-profit entities to providing contraceptive coverage similarly reveals the continuing contest over religious exemption's boundaries.[40]

Without such a limit on RFRA's application, antidiscrimination law itself remains equally vulnerable to religious exemption claims. "If Hobby Lobby and Conestoga are correct about RFRA's applications, what anti-discrimination provision in federal employment, housing, or public accommodations law would remain safe from attack by individuals claiming a religious right to discrimination?"[41] This question underscores the historical relationship between threats to antidiscrimination law as applied in the race and gender context through claims for religious exemptions.[42]

INSECURE AND UNEQUAL: POVERTY AND INCOME AMONG WOMEN AND FAMILIES 2000–2011, at 3 (2012), www.nwlc.org/sites/default/files/pdfs/nwlc_2012_povertyreport.pdf). "In 2011, the poverty rate for women in the U.S. was 14.6%, compared with 10.9% for men. For African American women, the rate was 25.9% and 23.9% for Hispanic women." Nat'l Women's Law Ctr., INSECURE AND UNEQUAL, at 3. "In addition to wage gaps within occupations, Asian women are overrepresented in the most poorly paid jobs in the nation." Nat'l Women's Law Ctr., THE WAGE GAP AND ASIAN WOMEN, at 4 (2017), www.nwlc.org/wp-content/uploads/2017/03/Asian-Women-Equal-Pay-2.pdf.

[37] *Bradwell v. Illinois*, 83 U.S. 130 (1872). In addition to emphasizing the gendered implications of reproductive control, the rewrite addresses the ideological choices about religion animating the majority approach. Religious liberty comes in various forms such that an accommodation for the companies based on certain beliefs runs the risk of establishing one religion over another. *Id.* at 12.

[38] Kreis, *supra* note 24, at 310.

[39] *Zubik v. Burwell*, 136 S. Ct. 1557 (2016) (skirting "substantial burden" imposed by accommodation and remanding to appellate courts to determine how to provide contraception without requiring notice).

[40] *See* Complaint, *ACLU v. Wright*, No. 3:17-CV-05772 (N.D. Cal. Oct. 6, 2017) (challenging HHS and other agency final interim rules permitting employer denial of contraceptive coverage on grounds of religious or moral conviction).

[41] *Id.* at 15.

[42] *See Hobby Lobby*, *supra* note 1, at 769 (Ginsburg, J. dissenting).

Importantly, the revision also draws a connection between the instant exemption claims concerning reproductive care and those concerning "human sexuality more broadly," thus threatening antidiscrimination measures protecting the rights of lesbian, gay, bisexual, and transgender persons.[43] The opinion, thus, brings Hobby Lobby to bear on current legal debates about religious exemption in the intersecting domains of sexuality, gender identity, and family form.[44]

CONCLUSION

The Kreis rewrite of *Hobby Lobby* bring significantly different implications for health care and reproductive justice than the original opinion. It thoughtfully illuminates the centrality of reproductive care for justice and the interlocking impacts of *Hobby Lobby* for a wide cross-section of communities, including those marginalized because of gender, sexuality, race, and economic status. The broader understanding of the government interest advanced by the contraceptive mandate denotes its importance for health, gender equality, and racial and economic justice. The rewrite invites consideration of how barriers to low-cost access and incursions on reproductive decision-making subordinate based on gender, race, and class. In keeping with reproductive justice's intersectional approach, the revised opinion focuses attention on the broader impacts for marginalized communities of decisions that affect reproductive health and autonomy.

Had the Kreis approach prevailed, we would likely find ourselves in a different place today. The rewrite provides firmer footing for access to reproductive health services for women across the socioeconomic spectrum. Additionally, the current landscape of law and policy debates concerning the scope of protection for religious objection to government actions and the relationship between religious accommodation and antidiscrimination law might be more level. Justice Kreis would not likely have brooked an argument that administrative requirements to give notice of religious objections are religious burdens.[45] A narrower boundary for understanding religious exemption might also have similarly curbed the ongoing

---

[43] Kreis, *supra* note 24, at 311 ("No principled distinction could be drawn between granting exemptions to accommodate religious beliefs about the nature of human reproduction here and not also bless discrimination rooted in religious beliefs about human sexuality more broadly that harms lesbian, gay, bisexual, and transgender persons").

[44] *Masterpiece Cakeshop, Ltd. v. Colo. Civil Rights Comm'n*, 138 S.Ct. 1719 (2018) (considering First Amendment Free Exercise and Free Speech claims of commercial business owner for religious exemption from state antidiscrimination provision on grounds of religious objection to same-sex marriage); *Barber v. Bryant*, 860 F.3d 345 (5th Cir. 2017) (challenging constitutionality of Mississippi H.B. 1523, allowing religious moral belief exemptions for commercial and other actors on the basis of beliefs about same-sex marriage, nonmarital sexual relations, and gender identity).

[45] *Zubik v. Burwell*, 136 S.Ct. 1557 (2016) (skirting "substantial burden" imposed by accommodation and remanding to appellate courts to determine how to provide contraception without requiring notice).

legal push to broaden the scope of religious exemption to include "moral conviction" objections of for-profit entities.[46] Indeed, while not arising in the RFRA or reproductive health care context, the claim by Masterpiece Cakeshop, another commercial entity, for religious exemption from generally applicable public accommodation law on free exercise grounds might have been weaker.[47] The Kreis opinion also highlights the far-reaching impacts of the majority decision on sexuality and gender identity-based rights of LGBTQ communities, which continue to be contested in connection with religious freedom claims, even in the commercial sphere.[48]

In short, the Kreis opinion would possible have slowed the progression of corporate personhood rights in the free exercise domain and weakened claims to exemption from generally applicable law. The contests between religious accommodation on one hand and rights to health, reproductive care, bodily autonomy, and anti-discrimination on the other might look much wider than they are today. In other words, if the Kreis opinion had prevailed, Justice Ginsburg would probably not have warned of the majority walking into an ensuing "minefield."[49]

Burwell v. Hobby Lobby, 573 U.S. 682 (2014)

Justice Anthony Michael Kreis delivered the opinion of the Court

Today, Petitioners ask this Court to allow for-profit corporations to raise religious objections for the purpose of escaping a United States Department of Health and Human Services (HHS) mandate that corporate employers provide health-insurance coverage for Food and Drug Administration (FDA) approved contraceptive methods. The exemption that the Petitioners seek under the Religious Freedom Restoration Act of 1993 (RFRA), 107 Stat. 1488, 42 U.S.C. § 2000bb et seq., would undermine "[t]he ability of women to participate equally in the economic and social life of the Nation" because equal participation is "facilitated by their ability to control their reproductive lives." *Planned Parenthood of Southeastern Pa. v. Casey*, 505 U.S. 833, 856, 112 S. Ct. 2791, 120 L.Ed.2d 674 (1992). We hold that, because the Government's policy has the purpose and effect of enhancing the agency of female employees to make personal health care decisions to benefit their families, careers, and quality of life, the HHS mandate to simply offer compliant health insurance plans does not impose a substantial burden on for-profit employers. Further, any claim to an accommodation under RFRA in this

---

[46] *See* Complaint, *ACLU v. Wright*.

[47] *Masterpiece Cakeshop, Ltd. v. Colo. Civil Rights Comm'n*, 138 S.Ct. 1719 (2018).

[48] *Barber v. Bryant*, 860 F.3d 345 (5th Cir. 2017) (challenging constitutionality of Mississippi H.B. 1523, allowing religious moral belief exemptions for commercial and other actors on the basis of beliefs about same-sex marriage, nonmarital sexual relations, and gender identity).

[49] 134 S. Ct. 2751, at 35 (2014) (Ginsburg, J. dissenting).

context must fail because it would constitute an impermissible burden on women in contravention of this Court's tradition to reject religious free exercise claims that impose costs on unwilling, identifiable third parties. The employers ask this Court for a remedy that raises a serious Establishment Clause problem, which we must avoid. As such, we decline to extend RFRA to grant for-profit corporations the right to discriminate against women.

I

In 2009, Congress enacted the Affordable Care Act (ACA), a major piece of legislation intended to improve health care access and reduce the uninsured population. To further Congress' goal to better the quality of care Americans receive, the ACA mandated that health plans cover certain types of preventive care without cost to the employer participant or beneficiary. 42 U.S.C. § 300gg–13(a)(4). To that end, Senator Barbara Mikulski introduced the Women's Health Amendment to these minimum coverage requirements that pertained specifically to women.

Senator Mikulski and the backers of her amendment argued that it was necessary because the costs of preventative care for women exceeded the amount paid by men. American women who are of "childbearing age spend 68 percent more in out-of-pocket health care costs than men." 155 Cong. Rec. 29070 (2009) (statement of Sen. Feinstein). Because "women have different health needs than men, and these needs often generate additional costs," women tend to avoid preventative care altogether, including obtaining contraception. *Id.* at 29302 (statement of Sen. Mikulski). The amendment's supporters suggested expanding access to contraception would reduce unintended pregnancies. See *id.* at 29768 (statement of Sen. Durbin) ("This expanded access will reduce unintended pregnancies"). Improved access to contraception is especially important for women who have health conditions that pregnancies can exacerbate, sometimes to the point of becoming life threatening. *See* Brief for American College of Obstetricians and Gynecologists et al. as Amici Curiae 14–15. Additionally, unintended pregnancies are associated with increased rates of depression and anxiety among expecting mothers, premature births, and low birth weights. Institute of Medicine, Clinical Prevention Services for Women: Closing the Gaps 103 (2011) ("IOM Report"). The record is abundant with evidence that cost of healthcare disparately impacts women, triggering a cascade of consequences that impacts their welfare and the welfare of their children.

With the amendment's adoption, the ACA required new insurance plans to include coverage without added costs of "such additional preventive care and screenings . . . as provided for in comprehensive guidelines supported by the Health Resources and Services Administration [(HRSA)]," a unit of HHS. 42 U.S.C. § 300gg–13(a)(4). Working with medical professionals at the Institute of Medicine

(IOM),[50] HRSA drafted recommendations for what preventative treatments should fall under the mandatory coverage requirements. IOM Report (2011), iv. IOM defined the scope of preventive care as services "shown to improve well-being, and/or decrease the likelihood or delay the onset of a targeted disease or condition." Id. at 3.

The IOM reported that covered plans should make available the "full range" of FDA-approved contraceptives.[51] The negative health consequences experienced by women carrying unintended pregnancies, which account for almost half of pregnancies in the United States, IOM Report 102–3, justified the IOM's recommendation. The IOM further proffered that contraceptive use lengthens the time between pregnancies, helping to combat the "increased risk of adverse pregnancy outcomes for pregnancies that are too closely spaced." Id. at 103. IOM explained that the cost of subsidizing contraception was significantly less than the cost of adverse medical consequences of unplanned pregnancies, which totals nearly $5 billion annually. Id. at 107. Improving low-cost access to contraception was particularly important for unmarried women, women between 18 and 24 years old, and women of lesser economic means, who disproportionately account for the number of unintended pregnancies in the United States. Id. at 2. Importantly, women's need to access the full range of FDA-approved contraception is crucial because "women's contraceptive method choices are influenced by concerns about side effects and drug interactions, how frequently they expect to have sex, their perceived risk of sexually transmitted infections, and the nature of their intimate relationship(s)." See Brief of the Guttmacher Institute and Professor Sara Rosenbaum as Amici Curiae 14. Consistent with the IOM's expert advice, HHS, the Department of Labor, and the Department of Treasury promulgated regulations requiring health plans to include contraceptive coverage. 77 Fed.Reg. 8725–26 (2012).

Since August 2012, the contraception regulations require all group health plans and health insurance issuers to offer compliant contraceptive coverage, barring any exemption granted to an employer or plan. Id. The costs of bucking the government's mandates are steep. Failure to comply with the contraception mandate results in a $100 fine each day per employee. 26 U.S.C. § 4980D(b)(1). An employer with more than fifty employees that fails to provide health insurance at all is penalized substantially in an amount that can total millions for a large corporation.

---

[50] The National Academy of Sciences established the IOM in 1970 "to secure the services of eminent members of appropriate professions in the examination of policy matters pertaining to the health of the public." INSTITUTE OF MEDICINE OF THE NATIONAL ACADEMIES, NEW FRONTIERS IN CONTRACEPTIVE RESEARCH: A BLUEPRINT FOR ACTION IV (2004).

[51] FDA-approved contraceptive methods offer women a wide variety of options, including oral contraceptive pills, diaphragms, injections, implants, emergency drugs, and intrauterine devices. FDA, Birth Control: Medicines to Help You, www.fda.gov/ForConsumers/ByAudience/ForWomen/ FreePublications/ucm313215.htm.

See 26 U.S.C. § 4980H. Noncompliant employers also face the risk of litigation from the Department of Labor and plan participants. 29 U.S.C. § 1132.

Non-profit employers whose mission is primarily the inculcation of religious values and who primarily serve coreligionists are exempt from the contraception mandate. 45 C.F.R. § 147.130(a)(1)(iv)(B); 77 FR 8725-01 (Feb. 15, 2012). Smaller employers with fewer than fifty employees that hold religious objections to the contraception mandate cannot escape the HHS requirements but may, without penalty, opt not to offer insurance at all. 26 U.S.C. § 4980H(c)(2)(A).

Respondent Hobby Lobby, Inc. ("Hobby Lobby"), is a closely-held, for-profit corporation that sells arts and crafts products. Hobby Lobby has 514 brick-and-mortar stores in 41 states with over 13,000 employees. Hobby Lobby is owned by the Green Family, who are devout Christians. The Greens contend that they operate Hobby Lobby in accordance with their Christian faith. According to the Greens, one tenet of their religious beliefs is that it is sinful to terminate a pregnancy. Thus, while Hobby Lobby provides insurance for its employees, the company objects to offering a plan that includes coverage for contraceptive devices that might terminate a pregnancy.

The Greens argue that compliance with the HHS mandate would render them complicit in the commission of a sin, violating the dictates of the family members' consciences.

Petitioner Conestoga Wood Specialties Corporation ("Conestoga"), is a closely-held, for-profit corporation that sells a variety of wood products. Conestoga is principally owned by the Hahn Family, who are practicing Mennonite Christians. Conestoga's mission statement includes a declaration that the company will embrace the Hahns' "Christian principles reflecting respect, support, and trust for our customers, our suppliers, our employees and their families."

Conestoga provides health insurance to its employees. However, the plan excludes coverage for contraception or abortifacients. Because the Mennonite Church deems the termination of fertilized embryos sinful, the Hahns object to some types of contraception required by the HHS regulations, specifically "Plan B" (the "morning after pill") and "Ella" (the "week after pill").[52]

Hobby Lobby and Conestoga Wood are both large for-profit corporations with a substantial workforce far in excess of fifty employees. As such, neither party can escape the government's requirement to provide employees health insurance

---

[52] Plan B is an emergency contraceptive pill that blocks the ovaries from releasing an egg and can also inhibit a fertilized egg from implanting in the uterus. Plan B is effective within a seventy-two-hour window after unprotected sex. FDA-approved label for Plan B (levonorgestrel) tablets, 0.75mg, 4 (July 10, 2009), www.accessdata.fda.gov/drugsatfda_docs/label/2009/021045s015lbl .pdf. Ella is an emergency contraception pill that delays ovulation and can alter the endometrium to prevent the implantation of a fertilized egg in the uterus. Ella is effective within a five-day window after unprotected sex. FDA-approved label for Ella (ulipristal acetate) tablet § 12.1 (May 2, 2012), www.accessdata.fda.gov/drugsatfda_docs/label/2012/022474s002lbl.pdf.

consistent with the Women's Preventive health care regulations without substantial monetary liability.

II

Hobby Lobby and Conestoga seek relief from the contraception mandate under the Religious Freedom Restoration Act of 1993 (RFRA). However, it is a useful exercise to review the law of religious exemptions prior to 1993 to illustrate why this case is brought under RFRA rather than the First Amendment and why First Amendment doctrine before 1990 informs our decision here today.

Prior to the 1960s, religious objectors secured accommodations from government mandates that impinged on their religious beliefs through legislation and common law doctrine. A well-known example of the latter is the priest-penitent confessional privilege, which emerged in 1813 as a common law exception to compelled testimony. *People v. Philips*, Court of General Sessions, City of New York (June 14, 1813), excerpted in Privileged Communications to Clergymen, 1 Cath. Lawyer 199 (1955). Pre-1960s jurisprudence did not embrace the position that the Constitution mandated religious exemptions from civil law. Justice Felix Frankfurter reflected this thinking in a later repudiated decision, writing "Conscientious scruples have not, in the course of the long struggle for religious toleration, relieved the individual from obedience to a general law not aimed at the promotion or restriction of religious beliefs." *Minersville Sch. Dist. v. Gobitis*, 310 U.S. 586, 594 (1940) overruled by *W. Virginia State Bd. of Educ. v. Barnette*, 319 U.S. 624 (1943).

In *Braunfeld v. Brown*, 366 U.S. 599 (1961), this Court first articulated that a more exacting analysis might apply to religious objectors' religious liberty claims and that the Free Exercise Clause may, at times, demand an accommodation. In 1963, in *Sherbert v. Verner*, 374 U.S. 398 (1963), we applied heightened scrutiny to a constitutional free exercise claim. In doing so, we rejected the theory that religious exemptions could only be conferred by statute or common law rule. We reaffirmed the constitutional exemption model in which a claimant could secure an accommodation as a matter of right without legislative action in *Wisconsin v. Yoder*, 406 U.S. 205 (1972).

The *Sherbert–Yoder* era ended in 1990 when this Court abandoned the constitutional exemption model in favor of the traditional legislative exemption model in *Employment Div., Dept. of Human Resources of Ore. v. Smith*, 494 U.S. 872 (1990). Rejecting decisions like *Sherbert* and *Yoder*, this Court held that neutral laws of general applicability would satisfy the Free Exercise Clause, leaving religious objectors in the cold and at the mercy of legislators and the common law. This would be particularly problematic for religious minorities who might not have the political clout or favorability to motivate legislators to exempt them from statutory mandates. The decision fomented opposition from both sides of the political spectrum.

In 1993, Congress near-unanimously passed the Religious Freedom Restoration Act to repudiate Smith, restore the *Sherbert–Yoder* doctrine's heightened scrutiny, and preserve pre-*Smith* decisions. The Act prohibits the federal "Government [from] substantially burden[ing] a person's exercise of religion even if the burden results from a rule of general applicability" unless the Government "demonstrates that application of the burden to the person – (1) is in furtherance of a compelling governmental interest; and (2) is the least restrictive means of furthering that compelling governmental interest." 42 U.S.C. §§ 2000bb–1(a), (b). RFRA was subsequently amended in 2000 by the Religious Land Use and Institutionalized Persons Act (RLUIPA), to protect "any exercise of religion, whether or not compelled by, or central to, a system of religious belief." § 2000cc–5(7)(A). While the law of religious accommodations has been restored as a legislative prerogative consistent with earlier American practices, the required analysis under federal law reflects more modern jurisprudence. Though true that free exercise jurisprudence has been upended by *Sherbert–Yoder*, *Smith*, RFRA, and RLUIPA, the rule of construction we must apply today to free exercise claims is the product of a relatively stable law developed over the last five decades. Under RFRA, the doctrines that govern our analysis today are *Sherbert*, *Yoder*, and their progeny.

The Greens and the Hahns assert that the HHS mandate substantially burdens their free exercise and that the Government's rationale for the regulatory scheme cannot withstand RFRA's strict scrutiny test.

The Greens and Hobby Lobby were denied a preliminary injunction against HHS but the Tenth Circuit reversed. The Tenth Circuit held that Hobby Lobby is a "person" under RFRA, and an injunction was appropriate because the Greens established a likelihood of success on their RFRA claim. The Tenth Circuit determined the mandate substantially burdened the Greens' religious exercise and the Government was unlikely to prevail because HHS failed to demonstrate a compelling interest in mandating the Greens offer insurance plans covering the full range of FDA approved contraception.

In Conestoga's suit, the District Court rejected the Hahns' request for a preliminary injunction. The Third Circuit affirmed. The Circuit Court of Appeals held that a for-profit corporation, like Conestoga, could not "engage in religious exercise" for the purposes of RFRA. The panel further reasoned that HHS' mandate did not personally require the Hahns to take action or bear the risk civil penalties but rather HHS only imposed obligations on Conestoga as a corporation.

Like the courts below, this Court has been asked to answer whether a for-profit corporation can avail itself of RFRA's protections as a "person." However, these instant claims can be decided on other narrower grounds, avoiding an interpretation of the statute that would have considerably broader implications. In the interest of judicial restraint, we will not address it today.

III

As a threshold matter under RFRA, this Court must determine whether the contraception mandate constitutes a substantial burden on religious exercise. Under RFRA, a substantial burden exists "only when individuals are forced to choose between following the tenets of their religion and receiving a governmental benefit or coerced to act contrary to their religious beliefs by the threat of civil or criminal sanctions." *Navajo Nation v. U.S. Forest Serv.*, 535 F.3d 1058, 1070 (9th Cir. 2008) (en banc) (internal citations omitted). The touchstone of the substantial burden requirement is that the challenged government action must place "substantial pressure on an adherent to modify his behavior and to violate his beliefs." *Thomas v. Review Bd. of Indiana Employment Security Div.*, 450 U.S. 707, 718 (1981). In enacting RFRA, Congress intended to protect citizens from the type of difficult choices where this Court granted relief before deciding *Employment Division v. Smith*. For this reason, *Sherbert* and *Yoder* appropriately illustrate the kind of restrictions on religious practice that meet the substantial burden requirement under RFRA.

In *Sherbert*, we held the denial of unemployment benefits to an applicant because her religious objection to working on Saturdays – her Sabbath Day as a practicing Seventh Day Adventist – burdened her exercise of religion. The state "force[d] her to choose between following the precepts of her religion and forfeiting benefits, on the one hand, and abandoning one of the precepts of her religion in order to accept work, on the other hand. Governmental imposition of such a choice puts the same kind of burden upon the free exercise of religion as would a fine imposed against appellant for her Saturday worship." *Sherbert* at 404.

In *Wisconsin v. Yoder*, we granted relief from a state compulsory school attendance law, which criminalized parents' failure to send children to public or private school until the age of 16. In *Yoder*, Amish families objected to sending their children to school after the eighth grade and raised a free exercise claim. The compulsory education law burdened the Amish's religious practice because it required families to send their children away from Amish communities to schools hostile to their cultural and religious values. The school attendance law "carrie[d] with it a very real threat of undermining the Amish community and religious practice as they exist today; they [were faced with the difficult choice to] either abandon belief and be assimilated into society at large or be forced to migrate to some other and more tolerant region." *Yoder* at 218.

In both *Sherbert* and *Yoder*, a burden imposed by a government regulation fell squarely on the shoulders of the objecting parties, forcing the objectors themselves to decide between compliance with a governmental command and giving up a religious practice.

In contrast to *Sherbert* and *Yoder*, this Court recognized, in *Bowen v. Roy*, 476 U.S. 693, 707–8, (1986), that mere administrative requirements fall short of a substantial burden. There, Roy asserted his daughter's Social Security number substantially burdened his religious practice because the use of a unique identifier harmed her spirit. We declined to extend Roy an accommodation because "Roy may no more prevail on his religious objection to the Government's use of a Social Security number for his daughter than he could on a sincere religious objection to the size or color of the Government's filing cabinets." *Id.* at 700. In rejecting Roy's claim, we emphasized that "wholly neutral" mandates from the government that do not "create any danger of censorship," "intrude on the organization of a religious institution or school," or "affirmatively compel [persons] by threat of sanctions, to refrain from religiously motivated conduct or to engage in conduct that they find objectionable," are the types of substantial burdens on religious practices that warrant heightened judicial scrutiny. The contraception mandate makes no such demand of Hobby Lobby or Conestoga and, consequently, the companies' RFRA claim is without merit.

It is true that these corporations face steep fines if they refuse to provide compliant insurance plans because of their owners' objection to abortion and the use of drugs they deem abortifacients. However, the claims of complicity in sin because of third party conduct are far too attenuated to deem the financial consequences of non-compliance with the contraception mandate a substantial burden on the owners of closely-held corporations' religious practice. The mandate's ultimate end is the empowerment of women – to guarantee a fuller range of decision-making so that they can better their lives. Female employees are not around-the-clock agents of the corporations that employ them. In that vein, employees' personal health care choices cannot be imputed as a difficult choice for their employer. No reasonable observer would assign responsibility to an employer for the private health care decisions made by a woman in consultation with her doctor. Compliance with the HHS mandate cannot possibly constitute a burden on employers' religion because it does not place contraception objectors in an untenable position to use them or risk of government penalty akin to the challenged state laws in *Sherbert* and *Yoder.*

That their female employees are free to control their own destinies is not a substantial burden on the entrepreneurs who founded Hobby Lobby and Conestoga Wood, though it undeniably offends the religious sensibilities of the family owners. Moral offense to government policy a burden does not make. In *Lyng v. Nw. Indian Cemetery Protective Ass'n*, 485 U.S. 439, 441–42 (1988), this Court rejected a religious free exercise claim to block the government from timber harvesting in, or constructing a road through, federally owned lands considered sacred by Native American tribes. In declining to recognize the free exercise claim, we acknowledged that government policies that offend religious sensibilities absent some coercion to act in contravention of one's religious beliefs could not sustain a constitutional free exercise claim. As we noted in *Lyng*, permitting objections of this kind would inevitably render government ineffective:

A broad range of government activities – from social welfare programs to foreign aid to conservation projects – will always be considered essential to the spiritual well-being of some citizens, often on the basis of sincerely held religious beliefs. Others will find the very same activities deeply offensive, and perhaps incompatible with their own search for spiritual fulfillment and with the tenets of their religion. The First Amendment must apply to all citizens alike, and it can give to none of them a veto over public programs that do not prohibit the free exercise of religion. *Lyng v. Nw. Indian Cemetery Protective Ass'n*, 485 U.S. 439, 452 (1988).

The HHS mandate does not force any member of the Green or Hahn families to take advantage of its benefits or use contraception. Members of the families remain free to not use some or all methods of birth control covered under the mandate. They retain their right to proselytize to the general public about their views on family planning. The relationship between the families and their corporate employees' most private, intimate decisions made in consultation with medical professionals of their choice, however, is far too attenuated to constitute a substantial burden. We cannot faithfully interpret RFRA as a tool to bestow upon religious objectors who elect to create businesses and employ individuals a veto power over their female subordinates' health care.

Today we are called to address employers' objection to contraception, however if Hobby Lobby and Conestoga prevailed, what limiting principle would hedge against religious employers requesting opt-outs for other forms of medical care? Religious objectors could raise challenges to insurance coverage of blood transfusions, vaccinations, pills with gelatin coating, antidepressants, HIV prevention, or mental health-care. It is inconceivable that any court would conclude providing insurance coverage for these types of care would substantially burden third party employers' religious practice. Women's reproductive healthcare choices do not burden employers' religious exercise any more than any other employee healthcare decision. Absent a substantial burden, the companies' attack on the mandate necessarily fails under RFRA.

IV

Hobby Lobby and Conestoga cannot prevail on their claims for want of a substantial burden, nonetheless, even if the corporations could demonstrate a substantial burden, we are mindful that relief under RFRA cannot result in negative externalities for persons who derive no benefit from the accommodation. When persons choose to enter the public marketplace and create businesses on their own volition, they must accept the basic rules and regulations regarding the treatment of customers and employees. Any exemptions or accommodations secured by objectors to laws regulating the commercial sector cannot unreasonably assign the cost of the objectors' faith practices to third parties. Here again, our pre-*Smith*, *Sherbert–Yoder* era First Amendment doctrine is instructive.

Our decision in *United States v. Lee*, 455 U.S. 252 (1982) is particularly analogous to the instant case. Lee, a member of the Old Order Amish, owned a small carpentry business. As a sole proprietor, Lee had several employees but held a sincere religious belief against withholding Social Security taxes from his employees or paying the employer Social Security taxes. In the Amish tradition, Lee proffered, there is an affirmative obligation to care for the aged. Consequently, Lee reasoned that contributing to Social Security conflicts with the Amish religious mandate because it shifts the fulfillment of the duty from the individual to the government. That tension notwithstanding, this Court held that Lee's civil obligation to pay into Social Security passed constitutional muster. *Id.* at 260–61.

This Court emphasized in *Lee* that "[w]hen followers of a particular sect enter into commercial activity as a matter of choice the limits they accept on their own conduct as a matter of conscience and faith are not to be superimposed on statutory schemes which are binding on others in that activity. Granting an exemption from social security taxes to an employer operates to impose the employer's religious faith on the employees." *Id.* at 261.

Here, the Green and Hahn families are no different than Mr. Lee in that each of these parties voluntarily entered the commercial sector to create companies and hire employees. It must then follow, they also agreed to obey the rules and regulations governing employment relationships that protect the rights of their less powerful employees. Considering our decision in *Lee*, we think it is worth emphasizing that Hobby Lobby and Conestoga ask this Court for relief from government policy that would create a burden on third parties and force their employees to bear the cost of their religion. Allowing the Greens and the Hahns to crack the door open for exemptions here raises the specter of a flood of litigation attacking how businesses treat their employees and customers in an untold number of ways – exemptions that would require non-adherents to bear the costs of business owners' religious beliefs.

This Court granted constitutionally-based religious exemptions under conditions where the claimants were coerced to engage in conduct against the tenets of their faith and where granting an exemption would not produce negative externalities. *See W. Virginia State Bd. of Educ. v. Barnette*, 319 U.S. 624, 642 (1943) (religious exemption from mandatory flag salute); *Thomas v. Review Bd. of Indiana Employment Security Div.*, 450 U.S. 707 (1981) (religious exemption to collect unemployment benefits); *Hobbie v. Unemployment Appeals Comm'n*, 480 U.S. 136, 146 (1987) (same). This Court later acknowledged this principle in RFRA litigation. *See Gonzales v. O Centro Espirita Beneficente Uniao do Vegetal*, 546 U.S. 418, 435–37 (2006) (granting a 130-member religious sect an exemption to federal drug laws, noting the government failed to identify burdens imposed on non-adherents).

We have admonished that a request for a permissive religious accommodation, like RFRA, "demands careful scrutiny to ensure that it does not so burden non-adherents or so discriminate against other religions as to become an establishment."

Bd. of Educ. of Kiryas Joel Vill Sch. Dist. v. Grumet, 512 U.S. 687 (1994) (Kennedy, J., concurring) and thus "courts must take adequate account of the burdens a requested accommodation may impose on non-beneficiaries." *Cutter v. Wilkinson*, 544 U.S. 709 (2005).

While this Court has been unafraid to accommodate religious objectors under the pre-Smith constitutional exemption regime, it rejected those claims which would result in harmful spillovers to third parties. *See Estate of Thornton v. Caldor*, Inc., 472 U.S. 703, 709–10 (1985) (holding a state law that mandated employers accommodate employees requests for time off to observe the Sabbath unconstitutional because it forced coworkers to work weekend hours); *Trans World Airlines, Inc. v. Hardison*, 432 U.S. 63, 84–85 (1977) (interpreting Title VII's religious accommodation requirement as limited to situations when the burden on the employer or fellow employees is de minimis); *Prince v. Massachusetts*, 321 U.S. 158, 166–67 (1944) ("[t]he right to practice religion freely does not include liberty to expose" a child to harm in contravention of labor law).

The appropriate balance in judicially crafted religious accommodations is illustrated exceptionally well by *State v. Miller*, 549 N.W.2d 235 (Wis. 1996). In *Miller*, members of the Old Order Amish faith were fined for failing to display bright orange triangles on their horse-drawn buggies. They objected on religious grounds. The Amish asserted, among other things, the colors were too "loud and bright" and that they could achieve the state's traffic safety concerns with lanterns and duller reflecting tape. The Wisconsin Supreme Court, using the same test codified by the federal RFRA, ruled in the Amish's favor. Ultimately, safety needs were satisfied, and individual religious liberty preserved without any detriment to non-adherent third parties. This example illustrates a fundamental point about the nature and boundaries of religious liberty: religious liberty is a shield from government, not a sword to injure others.

Like the HHS mandate, civil rights protections against invidious discrimination ultimately guarantee that vulnerable citizens will not be kept out of the public square, saddled with undue economic burdens, or suffer the indignity of limited agency. If Hobby Lobby and Conestoga are correct about RFRA's application, what anti-discrimination provision in federal employment, housing, or public accommodations law would remain safe from attack by individuals claiming a religious right to discrimination? Again, we should heed the lessons of pre-*Smith* doctrine, which rejected such claims. *See, e.g., Newman v. Piggie Park Enterprises, Inc.*, 256 F. Supp. 941, 945 (D.S.C. 1966) (denying owner of restaurant's asserted religious right to not comply with Title II of the Civil Rights Act), aff'd in relevant part and rev'd in part on other grounds, 377 F. 2d 433 (4th Cir. 1967), aff'd and modified on other grounds, 390 U. S. 400 (1968); *Dole v. Shenandoah Baptist Church*, 899 F.2d 1389, 1397 (4th Cir. 1990) (rejecting a religious school's free exercise claim to pay men higher salaries notwithstanding the Equal Pay Act); *United States v. Columbus Country Club*, 915 F.2d 877, 885 (3d Cir. 1990) (country club raised a free exercise claim exempting it from the Fair Housing Act's prohibition of sex and religious discrimination) (decided on other grounds); *E.E.O.C. v. Tree of Life Christian Sch.*, 751 F. Supp. 700 (S.D. Ohio 1990) (rejecting an accommodation for a school objecting to the Equal Pay Act on religious grounds for the purpose of providing a head of household allowance to faculty members). *See also State by McClure v. Sports & Health Club, Inc.*, 370 N. W. 2d 844, 847 (Minn. 1985) (declining to recognize health club owners' claim to a federal constitutional exemption to state anti-discrimination law citing religious objections to persons cohabiting outside of marriage and same-sex couples denied).

To permit these companies to discriminate against women in such a fashion could well render female employees who do not conform to sex-based expectations susceptible to religiously motivated discrimination in the workplace despite Title VII's prohibition against sex discrimination. The uniform rejection of free exercise challenges to civil rights protections pre-*Smith* instruct us that this simply cannot be. In order to remain faithful to RFRA's intent to preserve the *Sherbert–Yoder* era doctrine, we should not interpret RFRA in such a way that will deviate from this Court's longstanding tradition to reject accommodations causing third party harms.

While courts pre-*Smith* routinely refused to recognize a religious right to avoid liability for civil rights violations targeting racial minorities and women, the real civil rights danger in a Hobby Lobby and Conestoga victory may well lie in wait for those vulnerable groups that have yet to receive the full benefit of federal anti-discrimination protections in public life. While federal law does not expressly protect lesbian, gay, bisexual, and transgender persons from discrimination in employment, should Congress adopt statutes delineating these persons as a protected class or this Court interpret existing law banning sex discrimination to shield individuals against sexual orientation and gender identity discrimination, for-profit actors might object to workplace fairness requirements. No principled distinction can be drawn between granting exemptions to accommodate religious beliefs about the nature of human reproduction here and not also bless discrimination rooted in religious beliefs about human sexuality more broadly that harms lesbian, gay, bisexual, and transgender persons.

We must be especially sensitive to the reality that excusing Hobby Lobby and Conestoga from their obligations not only imposes costs on third parties who derive no benefit from the accommodation but those costs fall squarely on the shoulders of a protected class and would implicate this Court in sanctioning sex discrimination. This specter raises a thicket of thorny constitutional concerns that this Court is wise to avoid.

This Court has long worked to dismantle forms of sex discrimination. *Reed v. Reed*, 404 U.S. 71, 74, 76–77 (1971) (administration of estates); *Frontiero v. Richardson*, 411 U.S. 677, 688–91 (1973) (housing allowances and medical benefits); *Stanton v. Stanton*, 421 U.S. 7, 14, (1975) (sex-differentiated ages of majority);

Craig v. Boren, 429 U.S. 190, 197 (1976) (liquor sales); *Califano v. Goldfarb*, 430 U.S. 199, 206–7 (1977) (social security benefits); *Weinberger v. Wiesenfeld*, 420 U.S. 636, 648–53 (1975) (same); *Califano v. Westcott*, 443 U.S. 76, 84, (same) (1979); *United States v. Virginia*, 518 U.S. 515, 531 (1996) (equal educational programs). Relatedly, this Court has protected the rights of women to make reproductive health care choices and seek contraception without the interference of government. *See Griswold v. Connecticut*, 381 U.S. 479, 485 (1965) (protecting the right of married couples to use contraception); *Eisenstadt v. Baird*, 405 U.S. 438, 438 (1972) (striking down a law making it a felony for a person to provide conception to unwed persons).

Regrettably, this was not always true. We are mindful, too, that religious justifications for restricting women's equal participation in civic life and society at large were cited by this Court to condone sexist laws. When this Court upheld Illinois' proscription of women practitioners of law, Justice Bradley concurred, writing:

> The constitution of the family organization, which is founded in the divine ordinance, as well as in the nature of things, indicates the domestic sphere as that which properly belongs to the domain and functions of womanhood ... The paramount destiny and mission of woman are to fulfill the noble and benign offices of wife and mother. This is the law of the Creator. *Bradwell v. State*, 83 U.S. 130, 141 (1872) (Bradley, J., concurring)

In more recent memory, this Court condoned the exclusion of women from an entire profession, citing the State of Michigan's "moral and social" concerns. *Goesaert v. Cleary*, 335 U.S. 464, 466 (1948). These conventions should be left to the past. Outmoded sex-based stereotypes, sometimes rooted in religious and moral understandings of the "proper" roles for men and women, should find no refuge in our interpretation of federal law.

Denying contraception access to women restricts their ability to make decisions that are in the best interest of their families, their health, and their careers. Liberty is not advanced where the law substitutes a woman's well-reasoned judgment that takes account of her needs, her hopes, and her endeavors, for her employer's. Importantly, this impact is exponentially more harsh on women of color, who are at greater risk to suffer from chronic conditions that pregnancies can exacerbate, including diabetes, heart disease, and obesity. *See generally*, KAISER FAMILY FOUND., PUTTING WOMEN'S HEALTH CARE DISPARITIES ON THE MAP: EXAMINING RACIAL AND ETHNIC DISPARITIES AT THE STATE LEVEL (2009). We are also mindful of the disparate impact that denying contraception access would have on women of lesser means. Choking off access to reproductive health care would be too high a price for those women, who are disproportionately women of color, in exchange for exempting their employers from a non-intrusive healthcare policy. *See* NAT'L WOMEN'S LAW CTR., INSECURE AND UNEQUAL: POVERTY

AND INCOME AMONG WOMEN AND FAMILIES 2000–2011 at 3 (2012), www.nwlc .org/sites/defavdt/files/pdfs/nwlc_2012_ povertyreport.pdf. This Court is not in the business of reinforcing structural inequalities in the name of corporate religion.

A permissive accommodation under RFRA that restricts the autonomy of women cannot square with this Court's warnings against third-party burdens or this Court's refusal to perpetuate government policies that restrict the right of women to control their destinies. Thus, though the lack of a substantial burden relieves us of the need to proceed to the remainder of RFRA's compelling interest test, we could not construe RFRA in a way that would subordinate women to the whims of their employer's religious beliefs without running head-on into a morass of serious constitutional questions.

VI

While we have been asked to answer whether the Religious Freedom Restoration Act covers for-profit corporations, we need not resolve that question today. Even if this Court held that the owners of closely-held, for-profit corporations like Hobby Lobby and Conestoga can avail themselves of RFRA's protections, their claims would necessarily fail for want of a substantial burden on their religious free exercise.

The judgment of the Court of Appeals for the Third Circuit is affirmed. The judgment of the Court of Appeals for the Tenth Circuit is reversed.

It is so ordered.

14

Young v. UPS, 135 S. Ct. 1338 (2015)

Commentary by Mary Ziegler

The Pregnancy Discrimination Act (PDA), the law at the heart of *Young v. United Parcel Service, Inc.*, may have the most untapped potential of any federal law governing sex discrimination. First passed in 1978, the PDA amended Title VII of the Civil Rights Act of 1964 to prohibit discrimination based on pregnancy, childbirth, or related medical conditions. The PDA mattered because it undercut employer policies that excluded women and provided a potent check on pregnancy-based stereotyping.[1]

But the PDA, at least as the courts have interpreted it, also made a difference because of the discrimination that the law may not have addressed: what protection will women have if their capacity to work diminishes because of pregnancy? While pregnancy-related complications can affect any woman, the gap in protections has been particularly painful for the women most vulnerable to discrimination. Because women of color are more likely to suffer from poor outcomes during pregnancy,[2] these vulnerable women more often need accommodation. And women of color and immigrant women do a disproportionate share of low-wage work and find themselves in workplaces where anti-pregnancy hostility is common. By allowing employers to deny women accommodations, the courts before *Young* ensured that the PDA worked much better for some women than it did for others.[3]

---

[1] For the text of the PDA, *see* 2 U.S.C. §§ 2000e et seq. For the Court's decision in *Young*, see Young v. UPS, 135 S.Ct. 1338, 575 U.S. 135 S. Ct. 1338 (2015).

[2] *See Why America's Mothers Are in a Life-and-Death Crisis*, N.Y. TIMES (Apr. 11, 2018), www .nytimes.com/2018/04/11/magazine/black-mothers-babies-death-maternal-mortality.html (accessed June 21, 2018); Nina Martin, *Nothing Protects Black Women from Dying in Pregnancy and Childbirth*, PROPUBLICA (Dec. 17, 2017), www.propublica.org/article/nothing-protects-black-women-from-dying-in-pregnancy-and-childbirth (accessed June 21, 2018).

[3] See Vicki Schultz, *Taking Pregnancy Discrimination Seriously*, 91 DENVER U. L. REV. 995, 1095–96 (2015); National Partnership for Women and Families, *The Pregnancy Discrimination*

At first glance, the Court's *Young* decision seems to be a victory for pregnant workers. After all, before *Young*, employers could exclude pregnant women without making much of an effort. If a policy did not expressly discriminate against pregnant women, most courts ignored a policy's exclusionary effects. The women litigating *Young* set out to change that, arguing that the PDA required employers to accommodate pregnant women any time protections were available to workers with a similar incapacity to work. *Young* fashioned a new test that made it somewhat easier for pregnant women to demand accommodations.[4]

But Meredith Harbach's opinion shows us that *Young*, too, left some of the PDA's promise unfulfilled. By not requiring that employers accommodate any pregnant workers, *Young* ensures that more pregnant women, particularly poor women of color and those in low wage work, will face involuntary exits from the workplace. And, as Harbach's opinion shows, when it comes to the PDA, *Young* may have also missed part of the point of prohibiting pregnancy discrimination in the first place.

BACKGROUND

For many, the story of *Young* begins with another pair of Supreme Court cases, *Geduldig v. Aiello* (1974) and *General Elec. Co. v. Gilbert* (1976), but the beginning came much earlier. At the time that *Geduldig* and *Gilbert* came down, pregnancy discrimination was a serious problem. In the 1960s, only forty-four percent of women continued working full-time during pregnancy, and some states passed laws preventing pregnant women from working or prohibiting their hiring.[5] Many feminists focused on the stereotypes plaguing women who could afford to stay home. As pioneering feminists recognized, employers often assumed that women would stay at home with their children after giving birth, forcing women to leave a position during pregnancy. Other hirers worried that the presence of pregnant women sent the wrong moral message to children, especially if a working woman was not married.[6]

At first blush, it seemed that employers relied on stereotypes that would apply to white, relatively wealthy women who could afford not to work while raising

---

Act at 35 (Oct. 2015), 1–2, www.nationalpartnership.org/research-library/workplace-fairness/preg nancy-discrimination/the-pregnancy-discrimination-act-at-35.pdf (accessed Feb. 19, 2018).

[4] *See Young*, 135 S. Ct. at 1353–56.

[5] On women's workforce participation in the 1960s, *see* George Gao and Gretchen Livingston, *Working during Pregnancy Is Much More Common than It Used to Be*, PEW RESEARCH FACT TANK (Mar. 23, 2015), www.pewresearch.org/fact-tank/2015/03/31/working-while-pregnant-is-much-more-common-than-it-used-to-be/ (accessed May 14, 2018). On the spread of pregnancy-dismissal policies, *see* Deborah Dinner, *The Costs of Reproduction: History and Legal Construction of Sex Equality*, 46 HARVARD C.R.-C.L. L. REV. 415, 447 (2011).

[6] On feminist challenges to pregnancy discrimination in the 1960s and early 1970s, see Dinner, *supra* note 5, at 442–64; Deborah Dinner, *Recovering the LaFleur Doctrine*, 22 YALE J. L. FEMINISM 343, 372–87 (2010).

children. In practice, however, starting in the 1960s, minority women – especially those with fewer skills, less education, and less prior job experience – more often found themselves forced out of work. Pregnant women of color more often struggled to keep their jobs: according to the US Census Bureau, between thirty-two and thirty-eight percent of African American women worked during their first pregnancy. This number was strikingly low given that women of color, especially single mothers, were generally much more likely to work than white women. By the late 1960s, forty-seven percent of women of color had joined the workforce compared to only 39.8 percent of white women. Nearly sixty percent of single mothers worked.[7]

At the same time, between the New Deal and the 1970s, more employers responded to market forces and political pressures by creating voluntary health, disability, or temporary leave programs. When crafting temporary leave policies, however, employers rarely treated pregnancy as a disability, and pregnant women often learned that they were not eligible to receive workmen's compensation or unemployment insurance.[8]

By the early 1970s, for many women, the status quo had become unsustainable. Rising inflation and a spike in the number of single mothers encouraged more women to enter the workforce, and women in their childbearing years experienced soaring rates of labor-market participation. Pregnancy discrimination remained particularly painful for women of color. In the 1970s, the wage gap between white and nonwhite women again began to grow, and rates of workforce participation for pregnant African American women stayed stubbornly lower than those of their white counterparts. It was no surprise that many saw pregnancy discrimination as one of the biggest obstacles for working women.[9]

Feminist attorneys, including future Supreme Court Justice Ruth Bader Ginsburg, argued that pregnancy discrimination violated the Fourteenth Amendment and Title VII of the 1964 Civil Rights Act. As Ginsburg reasoned, only women got pregnant, and discriminating based on pregnancy necessarily involved sex discrimination. Moreover, feminist attorneys reasoned that pregnancy discrimination reflected "stereotyped notions that women belong in the home with their children, that women are not serious members of the work force, and that women generally have a male breadwinner in their families to support them."[10] Those

---

[7] On the workforce participation of women of color and single mothers, *see* Deborah Dinner, *Strange Bedfellows at Work: Neomaternalism in the Making of Sex Discrimination Law*, 91 WASHINGTON U. L. REV. 453, 471 (2014). On the workforce participation of pregnant women by race, *see* Kristin Smith, Barbara Downs, and Martin O'Connell, *Maternity Leave and Employment Patterns, 1961–1995*, CURRENT POP. REP. 6 (2001), www.census.gov/prod/2001pubs/p70-79.pdf (accessed June 27, 2018).

[8] *See* Dinner, *Strange Bedfellows*, *supra* note 7, at 468–70.

[9] *See id.* at 471–73. On the ongoing disparity between white and nonwhite pregnant working women, *see* Smith et al., *supra* note 7, at 6.

[10] As transgender and nonbinary individuals have become more politically organized and visible, it has become increasingly problematic to equate pregnancy and womanhood. *See The World*

litigating *Geduldig* further recognized that, for some women, particularly poor women who faced sexual violence or who lacked access to contraceptive services and abortion, pregnancy could be involuntary. But *Geduldig* rejected an argument that pregnancy discrimination violated the Equal Protection Clause's prohibition on sex discrimination and, two years later, *Gilbert* reached the same result when it came to Title VII.[11]

By the time *Gilbert* came down, employers' treatment of pregnant women had begun to change. In 1960, sixty percent of employers surveyed fired pregnant women rather than providing them with even unpaid leave, and only one-fifth of those who permitted leave let women set the parameters based on their own needs. By 1973, three-quarters of the companies surveyed by Prentice-Hall allowed for maternity leave, and sixty percent let women determine the length and timing of their own leaves. But *Gilbert* discouraged employers from accommodating pregnant women, and many African American women remained concentrated in low-wage industries that offered no parental leave at all. A coalition of feminists, union leaders, and abortion foes mobilized to outlaw pregnancy discrimination.[12]

By July 1978, the PDA had sailed through both houses of Congress. But what protections did the law provide? The question turned on the second clause of the PDA, which required employers not to discriminate against "women affected by pregnancy . . . the same for all employment-related purposes . . . as other persons not so affected but similar in their ability or inability to work." In 1974, in *Cleveland Board of Education v. LaFleur*, the Court struck down mandatory unpaid maternity leave policies for pregnant women. Together with *LaFleur*, the PDA required employers to individually assess women's capacity to work rather than resorting to stereotypes about pregnant women. And women who are fully capable of working had the right to do so.[13]

But from the beginning, the benefits available under the PDA were not equally available. In some ways, African American gained from the PDA because they were more likely to work during pregnancy. However, these women more often worked in

---

of *Pregnant Trans Men*, The Advocate (July 19, 2017), www.advocate.com/arts-entertainment/2017/7/19/world-pregnant-trans-men (accessed June 21, 2018); S. E. Smith, *For Nonbinary Parents, Giving Birth Can Be Especially Fraught*, Rewire (Jan. 25, 2018), https://rewire.news/article/2018/01/25/nonbinary-parents-giving-birth-can-especially-fraught/ (accessed Jan. 21, 2018).

[11] For the arguments made by feminists in *Geduldig*, see Brief for Appellant at 19, 24, 66–69, Geduldig v. Aiello, 417 U.S. 484 (1974) (No. 73-640). For the decision in *Geduldig*, see Geduldig v. Aiello, 417 U.S. 484 (1974). For the decision in *Gilbert*, see General Electric Company v. Gilbert, 429 U.S. 125 (1976).

[12] On the increasing availability of maternity leave, see Dinner, *Strange Bedfellows*, supra note 7, at 493. On the ongoing gap between white and nonwhite women's workforce participation during pregnancy, see Smith et al., supra note 7, at 6.

[13] For the text of the PDA, see 2 U.S.C. §§ 2000e et seq. For the Court's decision in *LaFleur*, see *Cleveland Board of Education v. LaFleur*, 414 U.S. 632, 643–50 (1974). On the interpretation of the PDA before *Young*, see Joanna L. Grossman, *Pregnancy, Work, and the Promise of Equal Citizenship*, 98 Georgetown L.J. 567 (2010).

small firms and low-wage jobs that were less likely to offer the kind of fringe benefits that triggered PDA protections.[14]

And what about women who have some incapacity? This question hit home for many, especially African American who were more likely to suffer complications during pregnancy. Most lower courts reasoned that the PDA did not require employers to accommodate women who had some physical limitations. Many employers responded with so-called pregnancy-blind policies, superficially-neutral policies that left pregnant women out.[15]

Peggy Young ran up against one such policy. A part-time driver at UPS, Young's job required her to lift and deliver packages. But after she became pregnant, Young faced an elevated risk of miscarriage. Her doctor advised her to avoid lifting packages weighing more than a certain amount. UPS had a disability policy that accommodated workers injured on the job, those who had lost their driving certification from the Department of Transportation, and workers with disabilities recognized under the Americans with Disabilities Act. By contrast, UPS did not accommodate pregnant workers. As Young realized, UPS had created a perfect pregnancy-blind policy.[16]

When the case came to court, Young argued that the PDA disallowed the exclusion that UPS had in place. She looked at the second clause of the statute, arguing that if employers chose to accommodate any "other workers," pregnant women who were similarly capable of working had to receive the same accommodation. UPS took a dramatically different position, reasoning that the PDA only required employers to create superficially neutral policies.[17]

In a six-to-three decision, the Supreme Court's decision in *Young* split the difference. Justice Stephen Breyer's majority rejected Young's position because the majority believed that it would require employers to favor pregnant women over other workers. Moreover, *Young* reasoned that a contrary interpretation would mark a major departure from previous congressional approaches to discrimination: Congress had allowed an employer to inadvertently harm workers if the employer had a legitimate, authentic, and non-discriminatory reason for acting.[18]

The *Young* Court found UPS's reading of the law equally unconvincing. UPS argued that the second clause of the PDA simply defined sex discrimination as including pregnancy discrimination. As the Court explained, such a reading would make the second clause superfluous. Moreover, *Young* concluded that UPS's

---

[14] See Dinner, *Strange Bedfellows*, *supra* note 7 at 508.

[15] On the higher rate of complications for African American during pregnancy, *see* Nina Martin and Renee Montagne, *Nothing Protects Black Women from Dying in Pregnancy and Childbirth*, PROPUBLICA (Dec. 7, 2017), www.propublica.org/article/nothing-protects-black-women-from-dying-in-pregnancy-and-childbirth (accessed Feb. 19, 2018). On the spread of pregnancy-blind policies and their treatment by the lower courts, *see* Grossman, *supra* note 13 at 610–15.

[16] For the facts of *Young*, *see* Young, 135 S. Ct. at 1344–45.

[17] *See id.* at 1348.

[18] *See id.* at 1349–50.

reading would allow employers "to treat pregnancy less favorably than diseases or disabilities resulting in a similar inability to work."[19]

As a middle-ground position, the Court looked to the *McDonnell Douglas* burden-shifting framework, a procedure used at the summary-judgment stage of individual disparate treatment, or intentional discrimination, claims under Title VII.[20] After *Young*, when establishing a prima facie case, a plaintiff had to prove that "she belongs to the protected class, that she sought accommodation, that the employer did not accommodate her, and that the employer did accommodate others similar in their ability or inability to work." According to *Young*, a worker could create an inference of discrimination by showing that an employer's policies imposed a "significant burden" on pregnant workers and that the employer had not offered a "sufficiently strong" reason for doing so.[21]

Employees like Young could demonstrate a significant burden by showing that an employer accommodated a large percentage of non-pregnant workers while not according pregnant workers the same treatment. And *Young* made it seem that employers might struggle to find a sufficiently strong justification for such a burden as expense and inconvenience did not suffice. As Justice Breyer wrote: "why, when the employer accommodated so many, could it not accommodate pregnant women as well?"[22]

Rewriting Young

Young struck a compromise between the positions taken by Peggy Young and her employer. Harbach's opinion illuminates how much the Court's opinion left undone. In Harbach's reasoning, the second clause of the original PDA did more for women than many might have believed. Harbach begins with the plain text of the statute. As she demonstrates, there is little ambiguity in the text of the PDA's second clause. Congress mandated that pregnant women be treated like others similar in their ability or inability to work. Harbach cuts through the supposed ambiguities identified by the *Young* Court. What difference does it make if Congress did not compare pregnant employees to "any other workers" rather than "other workers?" Harbach reminds us that Congress knew what it was doing when adding the PDA's second clause.

Nor, as Harbach reasons, does the purpose of the PDA offer a reason to deviate from the plain language of the statute. Congress, Harbach writes, responded directly to the *Gilbert* decision by establishing that pregnancy was like other conditions that

[19] *See id.*
[20] For the burden-shifting framework, *see McDonnell Douglas Corp. v. Green*, 411 U.S. 792, 802 (1973).
[21] *Young*, 135 S. Ct. at 1353–55.
[22] *Id.*

undermined employees' ability to work. Congress set out to eliminate pregnancy discrimination, encouraging employers to evaluate workers based on their actual abilities rather than their pregnancy alone. Allowing employers to refuse accommodations only to pregnant workers while favoring others who are similarly unable to work would frustrate Congress's purpose.

Young narrowly defined lawmakers' aims: Congress wanted to eliminate some pregnancy discrimination but not require employers to treat pregnant workers better than their colleagues. Harbach sees a broader purpose at work in the PDA: recognition that Title VII's prohibition of sex discrimination would be meaningless unless the law outlawed pregnancy discrimination. Harbach reminds us that pregnancy discrimination has effectively relegated many women, especially poor women and women of color, to a permanent second-class status at work.

Harbach also provides a searing critique of the most frequent argument against reading the PDA to require some accommodation of pregnant workers. UPS reiterated that if the Court sided with Young, pregnant women would receive special treatment. Specifically, as UPS saw it, pregnant women could select any comparator they liked and then demand identical accommodations, regardless of the surrounding circumstances. Harbach responds that the harms that UPS envisioned are far from inevitable. The PDA, she writes, requires employers to compare pregnant women to those who are like others in their ability to work. This analysis, in turn, requires information about the nature of a woman's physical limitation and the details of her job responsibilities.

We need not worry, Harbach writes, that pregnant workers performing janitorial services will compare themselves to the CEO of a company. Moreover, employers will not have to dismantle seniority policies, merit raises, or other systems involving promotion and pay. The PDA does nothing to stop employers from treating pregnant women differently so long as pregnant women have the same chance accorded to workers who are equally able (or unable) to work.

Most important, Harbach reminds the reader not to be so afraid of recognizing that pregnant women might need special accommodation. Pregnant workers have long labored under the burden of societal assumptions about women's potential, future intentions, and limitations. Poor African American felt the sting of these policies even more than their colleagues. Congress intended the PDA to help uproot the entrenched discrimination facing women in the workplace. This effort would inevitably fail if the PDA did nothing to address past subordination and merely mandated formally equal treatment.

Pregnant workers, Harbach writes, are different from others to whom they are compared, including those injured on the job. These employees "have not been subject to longstanding, systematic, class-wide discrimination and thus do not require the PDA's class-based, comparative remedy in order to receive equal employment opportunities." If we take the PDA's purpose seriously, as Harbach shows, we must be willing to treat pregnant workers differently on some occasions.

Harbach further illuminates some of the gaps in the protections that *Young* created. First, *Young* requires pregnant workers to satisfy the complex rules of *McDonnell-Douglas*'s burden-shifting framework. The intricacies of burden shifting will create uncertainty for pregnant litigants and make it harder for some to find counsel. As important, *Young* does not clarify to whom pregnant workers must compare themselves. Is it workers who are similar in their inability to work? Others with a similar source of injury? The Court has not clearly answered this question and, if the lower courts choose some comparators, more pregnant workers will lack protection.

Young tries to get around this problem by suggesting that pregnant workers can prove pretext by demonstrating a significant burden on pregnant employees. In the case at bar, the Court emphasized that the policy excluded all pregnant workers while accommodating many others who were similarly unable to work. But what will happen to those working in smaller businesses? What if employers accommodate only a handful of employees who are similarly incapacitated? Women's ability to prove a significant burden will likely depend on factors that bear little relationship to the extent of the pregnancy discrimination they face.

If the Supreme Court adopted the approach that Harbach proposes, employers could no longer accommodate some workers while leaving out pregnant employees with a similar inability to work. Such an opinion would likely make the biggest difference for low-wage workers who are rarely able to negotiate with their employers. And, symbolically, Harbach's opinion would recognize that remedying past and present pregnancy discrimination can require more than formally equal treatment. Harbach's opinion reminds us that Peggy Young and women like her were not asking for much. Far from asking for "most favored nation status," Young simply wanted the Court to recognize what Congress intended the PDA to accomplish – and to put an end to the second-class status foisted upon so many pregnant workers.

Peggy Young v. United Parcel Service, Inc. 135 S. Ct. 1338 (2015)

Justice Meredith Harbach delivered the opinion of the Court

Petitioner Peggy Young is one of countless women in the United States who have sought to combine pregnancy, motherhood, and work outside the home. To support her family, Ms. Young worked as a driver for Respondent United Parcel Service, Inc. (UPS). After she became pregnant, her doctor cautioned against lifting packages weighing more than ten-to-twenty pounds for the duration of her pregnancy. Young informed UPS of her restrictions and asked to continue working. Although UPS had a policy of accommodating workers with similar physical limitations, the company refused to accommodate Young's lifting restrictions. Instead, UPS prohibited Young from continuing to work in her prior position, and further determined she was not eligible for a temporary reassignment. Young had no choice but to take an extended, unpaid leave, during which she lost her health insurance as well as her salary. She returned to work at UPS shortly after she gave birth.

In practical terms, UPS's decision forced Young to choose between continuing a healthy pregnancy and providing financially for her family, depriving her of the agency to determine when and how to create and support a family. This decision relegated her to the "marginalized worker" status the Pregnancy Discrimination Act (PDA) was intended to eradicate. Because UPS's decision failed to treat Young "the same for all employment-related purposes ... as other [non-pregnant] persons ... similar [to Young] in their ability or inability to work," 42 U.S.C. § 2000e(k) (2012), we vacate the Fourth Circuit's opinion below, and remand Young's case for further proceedings consistent with our holding today.

I

A

Young's experience is all too common, even as women – including pregnant women and mothers – have participated in the paid workforce in sizeable numbers for many years. Indeed, women of color, especially African American women, immigrants, and low-income women have always had high levels of workforce participation. *See* Sarah Jane Glynn, The New Breadwinners: 2010 Update, Ctr. for American Progress, 2 (Apr. 2012), https://cdn.americanprogress.org/wp-content/uploads/issues/2012/04/pdf/breadwinners.pdf.

In today's economy, women represent close to half of the American workforce – just under forty-seven percent. *See* UNITED STATES DEP'T OF LABOR: WOMEN'S BUREAU, WOMEN IN THE LABOR FORCE: CIVILIAN LABOR FORCE BY SEX, www.dol.gov/wb/stats/NEWSTATS/facts/women_lf.htm. Among all women as a class, fifty-seven percent work. African American women work at an even higher rate of fifty-nine percent, while white, Latina, and Asian women participate at slightly less than the overall average. *See* UNITED STATES DEP'T OF LABOR: WOMEN'S BUREAU, WOMEN IN THE LABOR FORCE: LABOR PARTICIPATION RATE BY SEX, RACE AND HISPANIC ETHNICITY, www.dol.gov/wb/stats/NEWSTATS/facts/women_lf.htm.

As a reflection of women's – including pregnant women's – increasingly indispensable role as workers and breadwinners, the number of pregnant women who work has risen dramatically over time. In the early 1960s, fewer than half of first-time pregnant women worked during pregnancy, and even fewer worked fulltime. See Maternity Leave and Employment Patterns of First-Time Mothers: 1961–2008, U.S. Census Bureau, 4 tbl.1 (2011). But by the turn of the new century, more than two-thirds of women worked during their first pregnancy, and well over fifty percent worked full-time. *See id.* What is more, women in the workforce today work later into their pregnancies. *See id.* at 7 tbl.3 (in 2006–2008, 81.6 percent of pregnant women worked until one month or less before birth). The number of women working while parenting minor children is even higher. Recent figures estimate that, among mothers of children under eighteen years old, roughly seventy-one percent work outside the home. *See* D'Vera Cohn, Gretchen Livingston, & Wendy Wang, *After Decades of Decline, a Rise in Stay-at-Home Mothers*, Pew Research Ctr. (Apr. 8, 2014), www.pewsocialtrends.org/2014/04/08/after-decades-of-decline-a-rise-in-stay-at-home-mothers/.

Increasingly, women's income is essential to their families' economic well-being and financial security. As of 2010, women were either breadwinners or cobreadwinners in nearly two-thirds (63.9 percent) of American families with children. *See* Glynn, *supra*, at 2. In lower-income families, almost seventy percent of working wives earn as much or more than their husbands, and almost half of middle-income wives are breadwinners. *See id.* at 3. African American women are by far the most likely to be breadwinners and have experienced the largest increases in breadwinner status over time. By 2010, more than half of married African American women earned as much or more than their husbands, an almost twenty-five percent increase from 1975. *Id.*[23]

Overall, by 2013, in a "record" forty percent of all households with children under 18 years old, mothers were either the sole or primary breadwinners in their family. *See* Wendy Wang, Alison Aughinbaugh, Omar Robles, & Hugette Sun, Breadwinner Moms: Mothers are the Sole or Primary Provider in Four-in-Ten Households with Children; Public Conflicted about the Growing Trend, Pew Research Ctr., 1 (May 29, 2013), http://assets.pewre search.org/wp-content/uploads/sites/3/2013/05/Breadwinner_moms_final.pdf. Of these "breadwinner moms," sixty-three percent were single mothers, while thirty-seven percent were married mothers out-earning their husbands. *Id.* Single working mothers are younger, more likely to be women of color, less likely to have a college degree, and more likely to never have been married. *Id.* at 1, 4–5. Their average income is less than half of that earned by married breadwinner mothers. *Id.* at 1 ($23,000 for single mothers; $57,100 for married mothers). Although single mothers as a class have the lowest median income among all families with children, never-married mothers are the most disadvantaged, with a median income hovering around the poverty threshold. *Id.* at 19.

Thus, women's income is especially important for low-income and single-parent households, and single breadwinner mothers and their children are especially vulnerable. Of all households with children under eighteen years old, roughly a quarter of them are led by single mothers. *See id.* at 17 tbl. More broadly, the

---

[23] What is more, African Americans are significantly less likely than other cohorts to marry, and more likely to divorce, meaning that they are less likely to have access to the double income that marriage can provide, although they may nevertheless seek child support. *See Marriage and Divorce: Patterns by Gender, Race, and Educational Attainment* (Oct. 2013), U.S. Dep't of Labor: Bureau of Labor Statistics, www.bls.gov/opub/mlr/2013/article/marriage-and-divorce-pat terns-by-gender-race-and-educational-attainment.htm.

significance of women's wages manifests during an era in which women and children continue to represent a disproportionate percentage of the poor in our country, especially female-headed households with children, and women and children of color. *See* JOAN ENTHMACHER, KATHERINE GALLAGHER ROBBINS, JULIE VOGTMAN, & ANNE MORRISON, INSECURE & UNEQUAL: POVERTY AND INCOME AMONG WOMEN AND FAMILIES 2000–2013, Nat'l Women's L. Ctr., 3 (2014), https://nwlc.org/resources/insecure-unequal-poverty-and-income-among-women-and-families-2000-2013/. In 2013, almost forty percent of female-headed families with children lived in poverty; among those living in poverty, more than half (51.9 percent) of poor, female-headed families with children lived in extreme poverty. *See id.* at 4.

Low-income workers are particularly susceptible to a combination of high caregiving demands at home – including single parenthood, children with disabilities, and elder care – while simultaneously having far less flexibility or time off than middle-class or professional workers. They frequently shoulder these responsibilities with very little in the way of social support. These workers often confront employment discrimination because of their family responsibilities. *See* Stephanie Bornstein, *Work, Family, and Discrimination at the Bottom of the Ladder*, 19 GEO. J. POVERTY L. & POL'Y 1, 4–5 (2012).

Given these statistics, the ability of women to combine pregnancy, motherhood, and wage-work is essential, and the intersection of gender, race, and class make this especially so for families of color, low-income, and single-parent families. Yet as the facts of Young's case demonstrate, pregnant women[24] continue to face discriminatory barriers in their efforts to build and maintain families while also working to support their families.

B

In interpreting the PDA, we begin by situating the statute within historical context and its legislative history. *Cf. California Fed. Sav. & Loan Ass'n v. Guerra*, 479 U.S. 272, 284 (1987).

Women in the United States have always worked, although their relationship to that work – particularly waged work and work outside the home – has always been

---

[24] While, consistent with the PDA's own language, we use the term "women" in our discussion of the statute, we observe that self-identified women are not the only persons who can become pregnant and face discrimination in the workplace and beyond. Instead, trans and non-binary persons also can become pregnant yet not find themselves represented in the traditional language of "pregnant women." As the class of recognized individuals who can become pregnant expands, continued focus on pregnancy discrimination exclusively as *sex* discrimination will no longer be adequate to protect all who have or will face the discrimination historically experienced by pregnant women. *See, e.g.*, Lara Karaian, *Pregnant Men: Repronormativity, Critical Trans Theory, and the (Re)conceive(ing) of Sex and Pregnant in Law*, SOC. & LEG. STUDIES 1 (2013).

fraught. Importantly, women's experiences with work have been far from monolithic across race and class divisions.

Early in our nation's history, most women lacked the agency to determine whether, where, and how they worked. The law of coverture prevented married, white women from working for pay outside the home, and generally deprived them of autonomy. See HENDRIK HARTOG, MAN & WIFE IN AMERICA, A HISTORY at 105–9 (2000). African American women, too, lacked agency and autonomy but the positive law and institution of slavery compelled their uncompensated work for others outside the home. Even after emancipation, people of color served as a source of inexpensive, "unfree labor." Once they could work for pay, women of color's economic contributions became crucial for family support. See Evelyn Nakano Glenn, *Cleaning Up/Kept Down: A Historical Perspective on Racial Inequality in "Women's Work,"* 43 STAN. L. REV. 1333, 1336–44 (1991). Thus, women of color, especially African American women, of necessity worked outside the home even as "separate spheres" ideology channeled white, middle- and upper-class women toward the home. *See id.*

Societal attitudes about pregnancy, childbirth, and motherhood, intersecting with race and class, frequently have affected the ways in which women have (or have not) engaged in market work. For white, middle-class women, the "cult of domesticity" loomed large. Even as these women gradually acquired rights to own property, participate in paid labor, enter into contracts, and, finally, vote, pregnancy and motherhood lingered as disqualifying or disabling statuses for women's employment opportunities. As Congress has recognized "[h]istorically, denial or curtailment of women's employment opportunities has been traceable directly to the pervasive presumption that women are mothers first, and workers second. This prevailing ideology about women's roles has in turn justified discrimination against women when they are mothers or mothers to be." The Parental and Medical Leave Act of 1986: J. Hearing before the Subcomm. on Labor-Mgmt. Relations and the Subcomm. on Labor Standards of the H. Comm. on Educ. and Labor, 99th Cong. 2d Sess. 100 (1986). Even today, public attitudes about working mothers remain ambivalent, on the one hand recognizing the important economic benefits maternal employment provides but also voicing concerns about impacts on children and marriages. *See* Wang *et al., supra,* at 2–3.

Different realities and dynamics have impacted the participation of women of color in the paid workforce. Even as white women remained confined primarily to the home well into the twentieth century, women of color were working outside the home in significant numbers. Often they performed heavy labor and worked in dangerous industries, while receiving lower pay than did the relatively few white women who worked outside the home. Glenn, *supra,* at 1337–39. Women of color also frequently worked in domestic service, performing social reproduction in the home for white, middle-class households. Yet women of color, too, were wives and mothers. They performed house- and care work in other households, often to the detriment of their ability to care for their own families. *Id.* at 1339–43. Consequently, as measured by the hegemonic code of domesticity, society judged women of color as deficient when compared to white middle-class women working in the home. *Id.* at 1343.

Women of color made significant gains in the workplace during the second half of the twentieth century, particularly after the mid-1960s. The civil rights movement and the enactment of the Civil Rights Act of 1964,[25] which prevents employment discrimination because of race, color, religion, sex, or national origin, enabled workers of color to enter new sectors of the workforce, and wage gaps between white women and women of color began to narrow. *Id.* at 1344–47.

Despite the gains achieved by the mid-twentieth century, it could hardly be said that any women worked or participated in society on equal terms with men. Even after passage of the Civil Rights Act of 1964, sex discrimination, again frequently intersecting with race and class, continued to disadvantage women in the workplace and beyond.

Until the barrier-breaking sex discrimination litigation that began in the 1970s, women routinely confronted sex discrimination and barriers to equality across multiple aspects of their lives. But beginning with our decision in *Reed v. Reed,*[26] this Court came to recognize that "traditional sex-based classifications confined or depressed women's opportunities." *AT & T Corp. v. Hulteen,* 556 U.S. 701, 725–26 (2009). Through a series of opinions in the 1970s and beyond, barriers to women's equal participation in work and civic life based on sex began to fall.

Thus, over time, sex-based classifications had less power to subvert women's equal opportunities in the workplace. Yet racial and class-based differences persisted. Women's work outside the home continued to be segregated by race and class, with women of color continuing to perform lower-status work. Wage inequality between white women and women of color remained. And women of color were prominently represented in the service sector, a marketized version of the domestic service work they had performed in previous generations. Glenn, *supra,* at 1344–47.

Beyond this broader discrimination based on sex, race, and class, attitudes about pregnancy and motherhood have long been drivers of disadvantage for all women in the workforce. For much of our country's history, it was both legal and standard to deny pregnant women equal employment opportunities. *See* Joanna L. Grossman, *Pregnancy, Work, and the Promise of Equal Citizenship,* 98 GEO. L.J. 567, 595–98 (2010). Pregnant women and mothers worked under distinct disadvantages as compared to their male colleagues because of overtly discriminatory treatment, employment policies that disproportionately and negatively affected their work opportunities, and stubborn, persistent stereotypes about their competence and ability to work.

---

[25] 42 U.S.C. § 2000e-2(a)(1) (2012).
[26] 404 U.S. 71 (1971).

These attitudes have justified the exclusion and differential treatment of women across a range of occupations and professions,[27] including blanket bans from certain occupations and professions; refusals to hire married women or mothers of young children,[28] and termination of employment once women were married or became pregnant.[29] Employers routinely placed women on pregnancy leave "often while still ready, willing, and able to work, with no secure right to return to their jobs after childbirth." *Hulteen*, 556 U.S. at 719 (Ginsburg, J., dissenting).[30] Once forced to leave work, women frequently suffered further economic disadvantage by losing benefits, including paid sick leave, health insurance, and seniority accrual. *See, e.g., Nashville Gas Co. v. Satty*, 434 U.S. 136, 137 (1977).

Thus, when put into practice, these stereotypes have operated to discriminate against women, denying them workplace stability and advancement over the course of their careers. The cumulative effects of this discrimination have led to economic disadvantage and exclusion from public life during and after pregnancy, contributing to widespread gender inequality in the workforce and society. By virtue of these policies and practices, pregnant women and mothers were hindered in their efforts to combine market work and motherhood, even as their male colleagues were able to do so. By the mid-1970s, government studies into the efficacy of Title VII in the workplace confirmed that pregnancy-based exclusions and limitations continued to "financially burden women workers and act to break down the continuity of the employment relationship, thereby exacerbating women's comparatively transient role in the labor force." *General Elec. Co. v. Gilbert*, 429 U.S. 125, 158 (1976) (Brennan, J., dissenting). Pregnant women and mothers continued to be marginalized in the workforce.

C

We confronted a clear example of this phenomenon in *General Electric Company v. Gilbert*, 429 U.S. 125 (1976), in which the Court upheld an employer's decision to deny pregnant workers employment benefits available to other employees who were

---

[27] Historically, our own decisions accepted this reasoning. Women were not fit for the practice of law, for example, because "[t]he paramount destiny and mission of woman [were] to fulfil [sic] the noble and benign offices of wife and mother. This is the law of the Creator." *Bradwell v. State*, 83 U.S. 130, 141 (1872). Labor laws limiting hours for women only were necessary "to preserve the strength and vigor of the race." *Muller v. Oregon*, 208 U.S. 412, 421 (1908).

[28] *See, e.g., Phillips v. Martin Marietta Corp.*, 400 U.S. 542 (1971).

[29] Women were pushed out of employment upon becoming pregnant across a range of occupations. *See, e.g., Condit v. United Air Lines, Inc.* 631 F.2d 1136, 1137 (4th Cir. 1980) (requiring that stewardesses "shall, upon knowledge of pregnancy, discontinue flying"); *Cleveland Bd. of Educ. v. LaFleur*, 414 U.S. 632, 634–35 (1974) (forcing pregnant teachers to take unpaid leave for five months before due date); *Narragansett Elec. Co. v. R.I. Comm'n for Human Rights*, 374 A.2d 1022, 1023 (R.I. 1977) (public utilities company required women to take leave after the fifth month of pregnancy); *EEOC v. Chrysler Corp.*, 683 F.2d 146, 147 (6th Cir. 1982) (requiring auto workers to take leave in fifth month of pregnancy).

[30] For examples, *see Hulteen*, 556 U.S. at 719 n.4 (Ginsburg, J., dissenting).

not pregnant but otherwise similar in their inability to work. In *Gilbert*, the employer provided a disability plan covering nonoccupational sickness and accidents but excluding disabilities arising from pregnancy. *Id.* at 128–29. When women employees presented claims for coverage of pregnancy leave, their employer denied them because the plan did not extend to absences related to pregnancy. *Id.* Startlingly, the *Gilbert* Court concluded that G.E.'s policy was "facially evenhanded" because it did not expressly single out either men or women for differential protection. *Id.* at 138–39. Thus, the Court concluded, exclusion of pregnancy from an employee benefits policy was "not a gender-based discrimination." *Id.* at 136.

In a "swift and strong repudiation," of the *Gilbert* decision, *Hulteen*, 556 U.S. at 728 (Ginsburg, J., dissenting), Congress stepped in to correct the majority's judgment and reasoning in *Gilbert*, amending Title VII in 1978 with the Pregnancy Discrimination Act (PDA) to make "clear that it is discriminatory to treat pregnancy-related conditions less favorably than other medical conditions." *Newport News Shipbuilding & Dry Dock Co. v. EEOC*, 462 U.S. 669, 684 (1983). As we have previously observed, the text of the PDA "unambiguously expressed [Congress's] disapproval of both the holding and the reasoning of the Court in ... *Gilbert*." *Id.* at 678.

In passing the PDA, Congress recognized that "discrimination against pregnant women is one of the chief ways in which women's careers have been impeded and women employees treated like second-class employees." 123 Cong. Rec. 10,582 (1977) (statement of Rep. Hawkins). They enacted the PDA to "guarantee women the basic right to participate fully and equally in the work force, without denying them the fundamental right to full participation in family life." 123 Cong. Rec. 29,658 (1977) (statement of Sen. Williams). Pregnancy could no longer justify women's marginalization in the workplace.[31]

The PDA makes plain that discrimination based on pregnancy is, in fact, sex discrimination. § 2000e(k). Beyond correcting that central fallacy in *Gilbert's* holding, the Act also created a comparative remedy to ensure that pregnant women, as a class, would not be treated less-favorably than other employees: "women affected by pregnancy, childbirth, or related medical conditions shall be treated the same for all employment related purposes ... as other persons not so affected *but similar in their ability or inability to work* ..." *Id.* (emphasis added).

D

The PDA's passage represented a significant step forward for pregnant women and working mothers in the workplace, especially in cases of overtly discriminatory

---

[31] While members of Congress were motivated by equality for pregnant women in the workplace, it is also clear that they were motivated by a desire to continue to privatize dependency and avoid reliance on public assistance. *See* 123 Cong. Rec. 29,387 (1977) (statement of Sen. Javits) ("Losing a substantial portion of their income will mean that many families will ... go on welfare").

treatment based on pregnancy. But it would be a mistake to conclude that in the wake of the PDA, pregnant women and working mothers have enjoyed the same employment opportunities as their male counterparts.

Instead, research demonstrates that pregnant women and mothers continue to suffer disadvantages because of the same stereotypes and biases that pre-dated passage of the PDA. Employers often rate pregnant women as less-competent and less-deserving of promotion; they are also less likely to be recommended for hiring and are awarded lower salary recommendations than other workers. *See, e.g.,* Stephen Benard, In Paik, & Shelley J. Correll, *Cognitive Bias and the Motherhood Penalty,* 59 HASTINGS L.J. 1359, 1372, 1386–87 (2008). Recent cases confirm that employers have continued to discriminate against pregnant women and mothers based on these stereotypes and biases.[32]

The effects of this discrimination continue to be stratified across racial and class-based lines. Pregnancy discrimination is especially significant for African American women and other women of color, as well as working-class and lower-income women. *See generally* Brief of Amicus Curiae Black Women's Health Imperative, Joined by Other Black Women's Health Organizations, in Support of Petitioner, *Young v. United Parcel Serv., Inc.* (2015) (No. 12-1226).

Racial bias affects the manner and extent to which pregnancy discrimination manifests. In contrast to white working mothers, whom society views more positively if they stay at home to care for children, African American mothers are viewed more positively if they work outside the home. Yet once they become pregnant, African American women are more likely to be stereotyped as bad or unreliable workers. This intersection of bias around gender, race, class, and market work ultimately leads to working African American mothers being treated even worse than white, or other preferred-race, female coworkers. *See* Bornstein, *supra,* at 39.

Class also intersects with pregnancy discrimination in significant ways. Low-wage workers face extreme hostility to pregnancy, including immediate dismissal or being banned from positions, and a refusal to make even modest accommodations for pregnancy. *See id.* at 16–24. These women also have suffered mistreatment and harassment about their pregnancies, with employers sometimes urging them to use birth control or get abortions. *Id.* at 29–31.

Much of the physical work that most frequently requires accommodation is lower-wage work. *See* IT SHOULDN'T BE A HEAVY LIFT: FAIR TREATMENT FOR PREGNANT WORKERS, Nat'l Women's Law Ctr., 1, 5–7 (2013), https://nwlc.org/resources/it-shouldnt-be-heavy-lift-fair-treatment-of-pregnant-workers/ [hereinafter HEAVY LIFT] (examples include retail, food service, health care, stocking/package

---

[32] *See, e.g., Taylor v. Bigelow Mgmt.,* 242 F. App'x 178, 180 (5th Cir. 2007) (supervisor commented on non-suitability of women for management positions because they become pregnant and miss work); *Back v. Hastings on Hudson Union Free Sch. Dist.,* 365 F.3d 107 (2d Cir. 2004) (alleging discriminatory comments after return from maternity leave and tenure denial based on stereotypes about the compatibility of motherhood and work).

handling, cashiers, cleaners, police officers, corrections officers, mail carriers, office clerks, and truck drivers). It is in these environments that anti-pregnancy hostility is most likely to manifest, and women of color and immigrant women make up a disproportionate share of low-wage work. *See* ACCOMMODATING PREGNANCY ON THE JOB: THE STAKES FOR WOMEN OF COLOR AND IMMIGRANT WOMEN, Nat'l Women's Law Ctr., 1–2 (May 2014), https://nwlc.org/resources/accommodating-preg nancy-job-stakes-women-color-and-immigrant-women/ [hereinafter ACCOMMO-DATING PREGNANCY ON THE JOB]; HEAVY LIFT, *supra*, at 1. Indeed, a recent survey of pregnancy-discrimination cases documented "an extreme hostility to pregnancy in low-wage workplaces." Bornstein, *supra*, at 5.

As the facts of this case illustrate, women in jobs involving physical labor are especially vulnerable to pregnancy discrimination because their job duties may conflict with physical limitations or restrictions during some stages of pregnancy. These women will more frequently require temporary work accommodations – lifting restrictions, refraining from climbing ladders, sitting during shift work – so that they can continue their work during pregnancy. *See* generally HEAVY LIFT, *supra* (collecting pregnant workers' stories). Pregnancy accommodations are especially important for women of color, who are already at increased risk of pregnancy complications and poor outcomes, and already struggle with barriers to adequate healthcare. *See* ACCOMMODATING PREGNANCY ON THE JOB, *supra*, at 3–4.

When employers refuse to make these accommodations, even as they provide similar or even identical accommodations to others, they force pregnant women to choose between continuing to provide for themselves and their families and protecting their health and pregnancies. *See, e.g.*, *Arizanovska v. Wal-Mart Stores, Inc.*, 682 F.3d 698 (7th Cir. 2012) (pregnant stocker denied light-duty exception from lifting requirement despite availability of light-duty for ADA-eligible employees); *Serednyj v. Beverly Healthcare, LLC*, 656 F.3d 540 (7th Cir. 2011) (nursing home activity director denied accommodations for physical tasks despite accommodations for ADA disabilities and on-the-job injuries); *Wiseman v. Wal-Mart Stores, Inc.*, 2009 U.S. Dist. LEXIS 48020, at *1–2 (D. Kan. June 9, 2009) (store policy barred pregnant employee from carrying water bottle at work). Forced leave by way of failure to accommodate leads to a cascade of negative consequences for pregnant women, including unpaid leave, lost benefits, financial insecurity, and job loss. *See* HEAVY LIFT, *supra*, at 9–12. The instability, prolonged absence from work, and the economic harms that result ultimately lead to pregnant women's continued marginalization in the workplace, along with the economic consequences that accompany that marginalization.

But not all women leave. Some women facing the choice between a healthy pregnancy and continued income remain at work despite medical advice because of their precarious financial situation. *See* HEAVY LIFT, *supra*, at 12; ACCOMMODAT-ING PREGNANCY ON THE JOB, *supra*, at 2–3. Those who persevere in working without accommodations then face complications that threaten their health and that of their pregnancies. *See* HEAVY LIFT, *supra*, at 12; ACCOMMODATING PREGNANCY ON THE JOB, *supra*, at 3–4.

Failure to accommodate pregnancy perpetuates the sex discrimination the PDA expressly intends to prohibit. And importantly, the burdens imposed by this continued discrimination are not distributed equally across all demographics. Instead, they are disproportionately borne by the women in our society who are least equipped to shoulder them. Women of color and immigrant women are more likely than white women to be family breadwinners and single parents. *See* ACCOMMODATING PREGNANCY ON THE JOB, *supra*, at 1–2; HEAVY LIFT, *supra*, at 3. They are more likely to live in poverty. See ACCOMMODATING PREGNANCY ON THE JOB, *supra*, at 2. And they are more likely to perform the low-wage, physical labor that most frequently requires pregnancy accommodation. Thus, the women most likely to suffer from a lack of accommodation are those who already are more likely to face discrimination because of their sex and race, in addition to pregnancy, and simultaneously can least afford to forego a paycheck during pregnancy.

Ultimately, then, the marginalization and economic inequality Congress intended the PDA to address persists, even as we approach forty years since the statute's passage.[33] In fact, pregnancy discrimination claims have been increasing. *See, e.g.,* Vickie Elmer, *Workplace Pregnancy Discrimination Cases on the Rise,* WASH. POST (Apr. 8, 2012). Employers continue to deny pregnant women equal employment opportunities, effectively depriving them of the resources and opportunities to decide when and how to create and sustain their families. And the intersection of sex, race, and class continues to disproportionately burden families of color, immigrant families, and low-income families. Pregnant women remain relegated to second-class, marginal worker status.

II

A

Having provided the broader context in which Young's case arises, we turn now to a summary of the facts. Peggy Young worked part-time for Respondent UPS as an "air driver" – a worker who would pick up letters and packages arriving from the airport for delivery by 8:30 that morning. Although her job responsibilities formally included the ability to lift packages weighing up to seventy pounds and move packages weighing up to 150 pounds, her day-to-day work almost never involved

---

[33] For scholarly critique of the PDA's current interpretation and implementation, *see, e.g.,* Deborah Dinner, *The Costs of Reproduction: History and the Legal Construction of Sex Equality,* 46 HARV. C.R.-C.L. L. REV. 415 (2011); Grossman, *supra*; Deborah A. Widiss, *Gilbert Redux: The Interaction of the Pregnancy Discrimination Act and the Amended Americans with Disabilities Act,* 46 U.C. DAVIS L. REV. 961 (2013).

such heavy lifting. Young typically finished her work with UPS by mid-morning, at which time she would proceed to her second job at a flower delivery company.

After suffering several miscarriages, in July 2006 Young sought and received a leave of absence from UPS to undergo in vitro fertilization treatment. The treatment was successful, and she became pregnant. Her doctor recommended that she not lift more than twenty pounds during the first twenty weeks of her pregnancy, and no more than ten pounds thereafter. Young delivered a doctor's note to her supervisor and UPS's occupational health manager and asked to return to work.

UPS's occupational health manager later told Young that company policy foreclosed the possibility of her continued work as an air driver while under a twenty-pound lift restriction. The manager likewise refused to temporarily reassign her to another position, reporting that such reassignments were provided only to those employees injured on the job. The company rebuffed Young's offers to perform either light duty or her regular job with assistance from willing coworkers for heavier packages. When she later spoke with UPS's division manager, he told her that she was "too much of a liability" while pregnant and could not return to work until she was no longer pregnant. Consequently, Young had no choice but to take an extended, unpaid leave from UPS, during which she lost her medical coverage. She returned to work just short of two months after giving birth.

Young filed this lawsuit, arguing that UPS discriminated against her in violation of Title VII and the PDA by refusing to accommodate her pregnancy-related lifting restrictions and failing to treat her the same as the other, accommodated drivers who were similar in their inability to work. UPS responded that the "other persons" it accommodated differed from Young in that they had either (1) been injured on the job; (2) had lost their Department of Transportation (DOT) certification; or (3) suffered from a disability contemplated by the Americans with Disabilities Act of 1990 (ADA), Pub. L. No. 101-336, 104 Stat. 327, codified at 42 U.S.C. § 12102 (2012). Consequently, UPS argued that it had not discriminated against Young because of sex or pregnancy but instead treated her the same as all other workers who did not fall within one of those three categories. *See* Br. for Resp't 34.

B

Title VII of the Civil Rights Act of 1964 forbids an employer like UPS to "discriminate against any individual with respect to terms, conditions, or privileges of employment because of such individual's … sex." 78 Stat. 253, 42 U.S.C. § 2000e-2(a)(1) (2012). As explained above, Congress clarified and amended Title VII's prohibition on sex discrimination in 1978. In its entirety, the PDA's statutory amendment states:

> The terms "because of sex" or "on the basis of sex" include, but are not limited to, because of or on the basis of pregnancy, childbirth, or related medical conditions; and women affected by pregnancy, childbirth, or related medical conditions shall

be treated the same for all employment-related purposes, including receipt of benefits under fringe benefit programs, as other persons not so affected by similar in their ability or inability to work. *Id.* § 2000e(k) (2012).

In this case, Young is raising a "disparate-treatment" claim that UPS intentionally treated her less favorably than others who were not pregnant but otherwise were similar in their inability to work. *See McDonnell Douglas Corp. v. Green*, 411 U.S. 792, 802 (1973).

C

Young filed a pregnancy discrimination complaint with the Equal Employment Opportunity Commission (EEOC) in July 2007 and received her right-to-sue letter a little over a year later. She subsequently filed this complaint in district court, arguing that she could show by direct evidence that UPS had intentionally discriminated against her because of sex, or that alternatively she could establish a prima facie case of discrimination under *McDonnell Douglas*. *See* App. 60–62.

After discovery, UPS moved for summary judgment. *See* Fed. R. Civ. P. 56(a). In response, Young pointed to evidence corroborating her claims of pregnancy discrimination. Viewed in the light most favorable to Young, the summary judgment evidence established the following: Upon learning of Young's pregnancy-related lifting restrictions, UPS's occupational health manager determined that Young could not return to work because of her lifting restriction, and further that she did not qualify for a temporary alternative work assignment. Mem. 17–20. When Young later asked UPS's Capital Division Manager for an accommodation, he replied that, while pregnant, she was "too much of a liability" and therefore could not return until she "was no longer pregnant." Mem. 20.

Young's summary-judgment evidence further established that UPS had a light-duty-for-injury policy for several employees but not for pregnant workers. UPS did not dispute that, at the time it denied her request, it did provide temporary accommodations to other workers who were similarly unable to work: those injured on the job, those whose disabilities qualified as such under the ADA, and those who had lost their DOT certification.

Indeed, in the same period during which UPS denied Young's request, UPS accommodated several individuals with disabilities that rendered them "similar in their inability to work" to Young. *See* J.A. 400–1 (ten-pound lifting restriction); *id.* at 635 (foot injury); *id.* at 637 (arm injury); *id.* at 381 (recurring knee injury); *id.* at 655 (ankle injury); id. at 655 (knee injury); *id.* at 425, 636–37 (leg injury); *id.* at 446 (ankle injury). This included accommodations for employees who had been injured off the job. *See id.* at 446 (ankle injury); *id.* at 433, 635–36 (cancer). The summary judgment record also included evidence that the only time light duty requests "became an issue" was "with women who were pregnant." *Id.* at 504.

The District Court granted summary judgment for UPS, and the Fourth Circuit affirmed. Agreeing with the District Court, the Fourth Circuit concluded that "UPS has crafted a pregnancy-blind policy" that was "at least facially a 'neutral and legitimate business practice'." 784 F.3d 192, 201 (4th Cir. 2013). Further, UPS had not run afoul of the PDA because Young was not sufficiently like those accommodated by virtue of on-the-job injuries, ADA disabilities, or loss of DOT certification.

Young filed a petition for certiorari asking us to determine "[w]hether, and in what circumstances, an employer that provides work accommodations to nonpregnant employees with work limitations must provide work accommodations to pregnant employees who are 'similar in their ability or inability to work'." Pet. for Cert. 1. We granted the petition to clarify the purpose and effect of the PDA, and particularly its requirement that pregnant women must be treated "the same" as other workers "similar in their ability or inability to work."

III

The crux of the parties' disagreement centers around the meaning of the PDA's second clause and, indeed, whether that clause creates any substantive rights or obligations at all.

Young's argument rests on the statute's plain language and purpose. She maintains that the statute requires UPS to treat her pregnancy-related "inability to work" the same as it treats other, non-pregnant employees who are "similar in their . . . inability to work." Br. for Pet'r 15–16. Because UPS accommodated several classes of similarly situated drivers with work restrictions but failed to accommodate her lifting restrictions, she argues UPS violated the express terms of the PDA. Id. at 16–17.

UPS's (as well as the lower courts and our dissenting colleagues) view is the opposite. Indeed, under their reading of the second clause, it has virtually no meaning at all, much less a plain one. UPS argues that the PDA simply clarifies that sex discrimination includes discrimination based on pregnancy – nothing more. See Br. for Resp't, at 25. On this view, the two clauses of the PDA prohibit singling out pregnant employees but nevertheless permit employers to apply the same "neutral terms and conditions" to pregnant employees as to some other, similarly situated employees. Id. at 28. Thus, analysis of alleged discrimination under the PDA would involve comparing any accommodations for pregnant women to those provided to other employees within a facially neutral group (such as off-the-job-injuries) to determine whether an employer engaged in sex discrimination. Id. at 28. The Fourth Circuit agreed, observing that to do otherwise would "grant pregnant employees a 'most favored nation' status with others based on their ability to work, regardless of whether such status was available to the universe – male and female – of nonpregnant employees." Young v. United Parcel Serv., Inc., 784 F.3d 192, 202 (4th Cir. 2013).

IV

A

We have no difficulty concluding that clause two of the PDA means exactly what it says. The statute's unambiguous language, the statutory purpose, and Congressional intent make clear that the second clause creates a substantive requirement of equal treatment. When a woman is pregnant, she must be treated the same as other, non-pregnant workers who are similarly able to work. The simple fact of pregnancy cannot disqualify a woman who is otherwise capable of working. And conversely, if a woman's pregnancy results in some restriction or limitation, she must be treated the same as other, non-pregnant workers who are similar in their inability to work.

The starting point for this conclusion is the plain language of the statute itself. *See Desert Palace, Inc. v. Costa*, 539 U.S. 90, 98 (2003). Our "cardinal canon" of statutory construction is that "a legislature says in a statute what it means and means in a statute what it says there." *Conn. Nat'l Bank v. Germain*, 503 U.S. 249, 253–54 (1992) (citation omitted).

The first clause of the PDA has the clear effect of explicitly adding pregnancy to the list of protected traits under Title VII. The Second Clause, which begins with "and," suggests that it adds something more beyond the language in the First Clause. We are mindful of our earlier admonition not to "read the second clause out of the Act," and our prior ruling that "the PDA means what it says." *Int'l Union v. Johnson Controls*, 499 U.S. 187, 205, 211 (1991). We find no ambiguity in Congress's statutory directive that women affected by pregnancy "shall be treated the same ... as others similar in their ability or inability to work." Indeed, the Court of Appeals below acknowledged as much. *See* Pet'r App. 20a ("standing alone," language is "unambiguous"). This clause adds a requirement of equal treatment for pregnant workers, regardless of intent or the cause of any inability to work. Where the statutory text is unambiguous, our interpretive work is done. *Costa*, 539 U.S. at 98–99.

B

Even so, the PDA's purpose supports our interpretation. The overarching purpose of both Title VII and the PDA is to "achieve equality of employment opportunities and remove barriers that have operated in the past to favor an identifiable group of ... employees over other employees." *Guerra*, 479 U.S. at 288 (quoting *Griggs v. Duke Power Co.*, 401 U.S. 424, 429–30 (1971)) (alteration in original).

In crafting the Second Clause, Congress set out the standard by which employers are to ensure that pregnant workers receive equal employment opportunities. Congress wrote the Second Clause "to specifically define the standards which require that pregnant workers be treated the same as other employees on the basis of their ability or inability to work." S. Comm. On Labor and Human Resources, 96th Cong., Legislative History of the Pregnancy Discrimination Act of 1978, 206 (Comm. Print 1980) (statement of Rep. Hawkins). We have previously recognized that the effect of the PDA's second clause is to create a legal remedy for pregnancy discrimination. *Guerra*, 479 U.S. at 285 ("[T]he second clause was intended to ... illustrate how discrimination against pregnancy is to be remedied").

To achieve equality of employment opportunities, the second clause operates to ensure that "[w]omen who are either pregnant or potentially pregnant [are] treated like others similar in their ability to work." *Johnson Controls*, 499 U.S. at 204 (internal quotations and citation omitted). The clause manifests that purpose by creating a comparative right of accommodation, requiring that when considering what benefits or accommodations to provide pregnant women affected in their ability to work, employers must compare those pregnant workers to other employees who are similar vis-à-vis their ability to work, and treat pregnant and non-pregnant workers the same. *See Newport News Shipbuilding*, 462 U.S. at 684 & n.24 ("The [PDA] makes clear that it is discriminatory to treat pregnancy-related conditions less favorably than other medical conditions").

In crafting this remedial standard, Congress made clear that the relative ability or inability to work, rather than the condition of pregnancy, was the pertinent consideration when making employment decisions, including accommodations, concerning pregnant workers. The Senate Report stated that "[p]regnant women who are able to work must be permitted to work on the same conditions as other employees; and when they are not able to work for medical reasons, they must be accorded the same rights, leave privileges and other benefits, as other workers who are disabled from working." S. Rep. No. 95-331, at 4 (1977). Thus, the PDA "requires equal treatment when disability due to pregnancy is compared to other disabling conditions ... [T]he bill adopts as its standard equality of treatment and thereby permits the personnel and fringe benefit programs already in existence for other similar conditions to be the measure of an employer's duty toward pregnant employees." S. Comm. on Labor and Human Resources: Legislative History of the Pregnancy Discrimination Act of 1978 67 (statement of Sen. Javits); S. Rep. No. 95-331, at 4 ("[W]hen [pregnant women] are not able to work for medical reasons, they must be accorded the same rights, leave privileges and other benefits, as other workers who are disabled from working").

C

Finally, Congress's intent in passing the PDA further confirms our interpretation of the statute's plain meaning.

Congress's narrow goal was to abrogate *Gilbert*. Specifically, in writing Clause 2, Congress was responding to the *Gilbert* Court's curious reasoning that pregnancy was not "comparable ... to covered diseases or disabilities" because "it ... is often a voluntarily undertaken and desired condition." *Gilbert*, 429 U.S. at 136; *see Newport News Shipbuilding*, 462 U.S. at 669, 678 (PDA "unambiguously expressed" Congressional disapproval of both holding and reasoning in *Gilbert*). To make clear that pregnancy is, in fact, comparable to other diseases and disabilities in its potential to affect ability to work, the Second Clause makes this comparability explicit. And the requirement that pregnant women be treated "the same" as others similar in their ability to work was intended to overrule *Gilbert* and to act as an antidote to pregnancy discrimination. *See Guerra*, 479 U.S. at 285.

Congress's more overarching goal was to end the subjugation of women as a class and promote equal opportunity and the ability for women to work outside the home and simultaneously have a family. As legislative sponsor Senator Williams explained during its passage, "[t]he entire thrust ... behind this legislation is to guarantee women the basic right to participate fully and equally in the work force, without denying them the fundamental right to full participation in family life." *See* 123 Cong. Rec. 29,658 (1977) (statement of Sen. Williams). Congress recognized this could only be accomplished if pregnant women were compared to and "treated the same" as other employees similar in their ability or inability to work. Our plain language interpretation of Clause 2 effectuates Congress's intent.

One of the primary concerns animating the PDA's passage was lost income and financial instability for pregnant women and their families. Congress was particularly concerned about the plight of low-income women who were forced out of work while pregnant. *See* 123 Cong. Rec. 10,581 (1977) (opening statement of Rep. Hawkins) (exclusion of protections would have "a particularly severe impact on low-income workers who may be forced to go on leave without pay for childbirth or pregnancy related disabilities"). As detailed, failure to vindicate Congress's intent would have especially stark consequences for women of color and low-income women, who are most likely to require pregnancy accommodations, and least likely to be able to afford unpaid leave during pregnancy.

In sum, the plain language of the PDA requires that employers treat pregnant women, as a class, the same as other, non-pregnant employees who are similar in their ability or inability to work. This comparative remedy is substantiated by the statute's purpose and Congressional intent.

V

UPS's arguments as to the proper interpretation of the PDA, and the purportedly "absurd" results that Young's interpretation would bring, are unavailing.

A

Acknowledging that we must read statutes to avoid rendering any clause "superfluous, void, or insignificant," the dissent imagines an exceedingly modest role for

Clause: a "clarifying function." But read as interpreted by UPS and the dissent, Clause 2 would add nothing of substance to the statute at all.

According to our dissenting colleagues, the second clause adds clarity by making plain that unlawful sex discrimination "includes disfavoring pregnant women relative to other workers of similar inability to work." But Title VII case law already makes clear that analyzing discrimination claims frequently involves comparing how a plaintiff was treated relative to other "persons of [the plaintiff's] qualifications." *McDonnell Douglas*, 411 U.S. at 802; *see also Bazemore v. Friday*, 478 U.S. 385, 395–96 (1986) (lower pay to black employee as opposed to similarly-situated white employee was a "wrong actionable under Title VII"). If the Second Clause in the PDA did not exist, our established precedent would nevertheless find pregnancy discrimination if an employer disfavored pregnant women relative to other, non-pregnant workers who were similar in their ability or inability to work. There was no need for Congress to include any "clarification" of our already-existing Title VII case law in this regard.[34]

What is more, to follow UPS's argument here would be to undercut Congress's objective to overturn not only the holding but also the reasoning of *Gilbert. Newport News Shipbuilding*, 462 U.S. at 678. Like UPS's argument here, there, the *Gilbert* Court concluded that the defendant did not violate Title VII because its disability plan did not discriminate "based upon gender as such." *Gilbert*, 429 U.S. at 134. Narrowly reading the PDA in this way would not accomplish Congress's goal of overturning *Gilbert* in full. Certainly, the first clause made explicit Congress's rejection of the Court's earlier conclusion that discrimination against pregnancy was not sex discrimination. But Congress intended the second clause to go further: to make clear that pregnancy is comparable to other conditions affecting the ability to work, and to remedy pregnancy discrimination by treating pregnant workers the same as other workers affected in their ability to work. *Guerra*, 479 U.S. at 285. UPS and the dissent disregard this precedent.

B

Beyond their apparent concern about reading too much into the language of the PDA, UPS and the dissent worry that Young's plain meaning argument would lead to pregnant women receiving "most-favored-nation" status as compared to other employees.[35] Cue the parade of horribles.

---

[34] The dissent's interpretation is especially curious given those Justices' usual commitment to textualist interpretation. How, then, does the dissent arrive at its cramped read of the PDA? It seems to us it is via ideological preferences posing as principles, which subvert the clear text, purpose, and intent of the statute.

[35] Given the history of discrimination against women in employment, the context in which the PDA was enacted, and current working conditions of pregnant women and mothers, discussed *ante*, it is apocryphal, if not ironic, that UPS argues that Young's plain meaning interpretation of the second clause would confer on pregnant women "most favored nation" status.

UPS argues (and the dissent agrees) that Young's interpretation would "mandate special treatment for pregnancy, requiring an employer to provide an accommodation to a pregnant employee if the same accommodation has ever been provided to any other employee *for any reason*." Br. for Resp't 12, 28 (emphasis added). Indeed, UPS continues: "Under petitioner's approach, pregnant employees could choose their own comparators and select from a smorgasbord of options provided to any non-pregnant employees, regardless of circumstances (e.g., light-duty work, additional leave, technological or ergonomic adjustments to the workplace). That would be absurd." Br. for Resp't 45.

The statute need not be read in the austere way espoused by UPS and the dissent. First, to state the most obvious reason, the PDA in fact specifies (and thus limits, in some sense) the comparators for PDA plaintiffs: "others similar in their . . . inability to work." 42 USC 2000e(k) (2012).

Second, as the concurrence observes, the requirement of "same" treatment may be fixed. But, the determination of when another employee is "similar" to a pregnant woman in her inability to work is contextual. For it depends both on the scope of the pregnant woman's limitation and its relationship to her job responsibilities. So, to take one of Petitioner's examples, an employer's provision of transportation to a CEO as an accommodation for a back injury would not require the same treatment for a pregnant mailroom clerk. It is not at all clear that a back injury would significantly limit the CEO in completing her work responsibilities, although her mobility might be compromised. Any connection between her injury and her ability to work would be attenuated, at best. Were a mail clerk to suffer a back injury, on the other hand, her ability to perform job responsibilities would be significantly compromised. Thus, even if both a CEO and a pregnant clerk suffered identical back injuries, the two workers would not be "similar in their ability or inability to work," notwithstanding the similarity of their injuries, because of the divergent nature of their work responsibilities.

Third, and relatedly, if an employer's provision of a particular benefit or accommodation to a non-pregnant employee is based on rank, status, or tenure with the company, the PDA would not require that pregnant workers be treated the same, because the employer would not be providing such benefit or accommodation based on an "ability or inability to work." Title VII makes clear that "it shall not be an unlawful employment practice for an employer to apply . . . different terms, conditions, or privileges of employment pursuant to a bona fide seniority or merit system, or a system which measures earnings by quantity or quality of production, or to employees who work in different locations . . ." 42 U.S.C. § 2000e-2(h) (2012). The PDA therefore does not require employers to provide pregnant workers with the same benefits and accommodations extended to other employees when they are granted not based on their ability or inability to work but instead on some other factor, such as tenure or rank. See Reply Br. 15–18. Thus, continuing with Respondent's examples, employers might provide differential benefits to "a CEO [who] receives company-provided transportation as an accommodation for a back injury," or paid leave provided to "full-time management employees who have been employed for at least 15 years," without running afoul of the PDA.

Fourth and finally, even if a plain reading of the PDA's second clause were to lead to more favorable treatment for pregnant women as compared to some of their coworkers in some situations, such an effect would hardly be inconsistent with the aims of the PDA. We have already held that workplace policies providing benefits to pregnant workers but not disabled workers more broadly, do not violate Title VII or otherwise undercut the purposes of the PDA. *See Guerra*, 479 U.S. at 292. To the contrary, we found such practices to be consistent with Title VII and the PDA's common purpose of achieving equal employment opportunity. *Id.* at 288–89. Indeed, as Justice Brennan observed in his *Gilbert* dissent:

> [D]iscrimination is a social phenomenon encased in a social context and, therefore, unavoidably takes its meaning from the desired end products of the relevant legislative enactment, end products that may demand due consideration to the uniqueness of "disadvantaged" individuals. A realistic understanding of conditions found in today's labor environment warrants taking pregnancy into account in fashioning disability policies.

Gilbert, 429 U.S. at 159 (Brennan, J., dissenting). Thus, favorable treatment for pregnant workers further the Congressional purpose of the PDA: by "taking pregnancy into account," such policies allow "women, as well as men, to have families without losing their jobs." *Guerra*, 479 U.S. at 285, 289 (Congress intended PDA to be "a floor beneath which pregnancy disability benefits may not drop – not a ceiling above which they may not rise") (internal quotations and citation omitted).

Congress's intent in passing the PDA was to eradicate employment practices that relegated and reinforced pregnant women's status as marginal, second-class workers. Those class-based harms could only be rectified by requiring that employers accommodate pregnant women when they accommodate other, temporarily injured workers. To provide this class-based, comparative remedy is not to elevate pregnant workers to "most favored nation" status but rather to end the second-class status pregnant women and mothers suffered by virtue of discrimination in the workplace.

Consistent with that intention, Congress could enact a statute that might, in some limited contexts, lead to more favorable treatment for pregnant workers as compared to some other workers, such as those who suffer injury off the job. Cf. 42 U.S.C. § 2000e(j) (2012) (requiring employers' accommodation of religious observance and practice). Considering the uniqueness of pregnant women's disadvantages, this class-based remedy is necessary to provide them with equal employment opportunities. And given the context discussed in Part I, *supra*, such could hardly be said to be an "absurd" result.[36]

---

[36] Certainly, if Congress disagrees with our interpretation of the PDA, they can amend the statute or enact legislation. After all, correcting an earlier misunderstanding of Title VII was the impetus for the PDA in the first place. *See Newport News Shipbuilding & Dry Dock Co.*

C

Finally, UPS's arguments about the application of the PDA to so-called neutral, pregnancy-blind policies also fail.

It may be true that as a general matter, employers "can limit benefits to ... employees on the same neutral terms and conditions as to other employees," Br. for Resp't 25. But it is no answer to say that policies are "pregnancy-neutral" if they result in pregnant employees being treated less-favorably than others similar in their ability to work. The PDA, after all, is not pregnancy blind. It is pregnancy conscious. As such, the statute precludes the implementation of so-called "neutral, pregnancy blind" policies if, in application, they fail to treat pregnant workers the same as comparable employees.

Consistent with its pregnancy blind argument, UPS argues that even if the PDA requires identical treatment between pregnant workers and others similar in their inability to work, Young has no cause to complain in this case. This is so because while Young did not receive the accommodation available to one subset of employees (those injured on the job), she was treated the same as yet another subset (those with an off-the-job lifting restriction). Nothing in the PDA, Respondent claims, "requires UPS to align pregnant employees with one group or the other." Br. for Resp't 28. And Young, Petitioner argues, provided "no basis (let alone a principled one) for why she should be treated the same as one group, but not the other." Br. for Resp't 34–35.

But this argument completely disregards the Congressional purpose and function of the PDA: to require that pregnant women, as a class, be treated the same as others who are similarly limited in their ability to work. Comparing women to those injured off-the-job is inapposite. Unlike pregnant women, those other workers have not been subject to longstanding, systematic, class-wide discrimination as a group and thus do not require the PDA's class-based, comparative remedy in order to obtain equal employment opportunities.

What is more, if the Respondent's argument were an accurate reading of the PDA, employers could refuse to accommodate pregnant workers even while accommodating nearly all others, provided they could identify at least one, non-pregnant worker they also failed to accommodate. Far from promoting pregnant workers to "most favored" status, that interpretation would create a race to the bottom, consigning pregnancy to "least favored nation" status. Under this approach, employers could use "discriminatory criteria as long as they were careful to draw their discriminatory lines broadly enough to include members of a non-protected class." *E.E.O.C. v. Bd. of Governors of State Colls. & Univs.*, 957 F.2d 424, 431 (7th Cir. 1992). Such an

---

v. E.E.O.C., 462 U.S. 669, 686 (Rehnquist, J., dissenting) ("Congress ... was free to legislatively overrule *Gilbert* in whole or in part, and there is no question but what the Pregnant Discrimination Act manifests congressional dissatisfaction with the result we reached in *Gilbert*").

interpretation would be utterly at odds with Congress's intent to remedy the treatment of pregnant women as marginal, second class workers.

In sum, Respondent's and the dissent's analysis miss the mark as a matter of
statutory construction, intent, and purpose. The correct reading of the statute gives
effect to its plain meaning and requires that if employers accommodate non-
pregnant workers who, like pregnant workers, suffer from a work restriction
impacting their ability to work, those employers must treat pregnant workers
the same.

VI

A party is entitled to summary judgment if there is "no genuine dispute as to any
material fact and the movant is entitled to judgment as a matter of law." Fed. R. Civ.
P. 56(a). Under our interpretation of the PDA, we must vacate the judgment of the
Fourth Circuit. Viewing the summary judgment record in the light most favorable
to Young, there exist genuine issues of material fact with respect to both clauses of
the PDA.

Under the First Clause, Young has adduced summary judgment evidence that,
at a minimum, creates a fact question concerning whether UPS's refusal to
accommodate her lifting restriction while accommodating others was a facial
violation of the statute. Moreover, UPS's Capital Division Manager statement that
he could not accommodate her because she was "too much of a liability" and
could "not come back" until she was "no longer pregnant" created a genuine
dispute as to whether UPS discriminated against her with respect to the terms,
conditions, or privileges of her employment because of her pregnancy. 42 U.S.C.
§ 2000e-2(a)(1) (2012); § 2000e(k).

Young also produced direct evidence that UPS had a light-work policy that, by its
written terms, excluded pregnant women from accommodations that were available
to other employees who were similar in their inability to work.

The evidence suggests that rather than treating her the same, UPS treated
Young differently from at least several other UPS employees who were
"similar ... in their inability to work," 42 U.S.C § 2000e(k) (2012), including
employees injured both on and off the job. Indeed, according to the deposition
of one UPS employee, "the only light duty requested [due to physical] restrictions
that became an issue" at UPS "were with women who were pregnant." J.A. 504.
Thus, there exists a genuine dispute as to whether UPS provided more favorable
treatment to at least some employees whose work limitations cannot reasonably be
distinguished from Young's.

The intersection of sex, race, and class have long impaired women's ability to
combine pregnancy, motherhood, and work outside the home to support their
families. With the PDA, Congress responded to provide pregnant women with
equal opportunities to participate in the workforce while also creating and

supporting families. To ensure pregnant women's equal status in the workplace, the PDA requires employers to treat pregnant women the same as other workers similar in their ability or inability to work. Failure to accommodate pregnant workers while accommodating other, similarly limited workers is pregnancy discrimination, full stop.

For the reasons explained above, we vacate the judgment of the Fourth Circuit and remand the case for further proceedings consistent with this opinion.

It is so ordered.

15

Whole Woman's Health v. Hellerstedt, 136 S. Ct. 2292 (2016)

Commentary by Myrisha Lewis

INTRODUCTION

In 2016, *Whole Woman's Health v. Hellerstedt* entered the post–*Roe v. Wade* canon of cases related to a pregnant person's right to have a legal abortion in the United States.[1] After the erosion of the abortion right in the Supreme Court's 1992 decision in *Planned Parenthood v. Casey*, many abortion rights proponents feared that the Supreme Court's decision in *Whole Woman's Health* would severely curtail a woman's right to terminate a pregnancy and perhaps even overrule *Roe*.[2] In *Casey*, the Court adjudicated the constitutionality of a number of restrictions on abortion access posed by the Pennsylvania Abortion Control Act of 1982 (as amended).[3] The *Casey* plurality articulated the "undue burden" standard, which allowed a court to invalidate an abortion restriction that "has the purpose or effect of placing a substantial obstacle in the path of a woman seeking an abortion of a nonviable fetus."[4] Under this new test, the Court upheld a twenty-four-hour waiting period, parental notification, and a biased informed consent requirement, while rejecting spousal notification.[5]

When the Court released its decision in *Whole Woman's Health*, scholars and advocates deemed it the most important Supreme Court decision related to abortion

---

[1] *Roe v. Wade*, 410 U.S. 113 (1973); *Whole Woman's Health v. Hellerstedt*, 136 S. Ct. 2292 (2016). *See* CAROL SANGER, ABOUT ABORTION: TERMINATING PREGNANCY IN TWENTY-FIRST CENTURY AMERICA at xi–xii (2017). *See id.* at 25.

[2] *Planned Parenthood of Southeastern Pennsylvania v. Casey*, 505 U.S. 833, 877 (1992); Mary Ziegler, *Substantial Uncertainty: Whole Woman's Health and the Future of Abortion Law*, 2016 SUP. CT. REV. 77, 105 (2016); *Fourteenth Amendment-Due Process Clause-Undue Burden– Whole Woman's Health v. Hellerstedt*, 130 HARV. L. REV. 397, 403–4 (2016).

[3] *Casey*, 505 U.S. at 843.

[4] *Id.* at 877.

[5] *Id.* at 844, 879.

in decades.[6] Ostensibly, the decision in *Whole Woman's Health*, which found certain provisions of a Texas abortion statue, H.B. 2, to be unconstitutional, "put[] teeth" into *Casey*'s undue burden standard.[7] Despite the victorious story that many abortion rights proponents tell about *Whole Woman's Health*, David Cohen's rewritten opinion reveals that many women, especially women of color and low-income women, remain unable to actually exercise the right to an abortion due to laws that restrict the availability of funding for abortions and others that target abortion providers for onerous legal requirements that often result in the closure of their facilities.[8]

THE SUPREME COURT'S DECISION IN *WHOLE WOMAN'S HEALTH*

Amy Hagstrom Miller founded Whole Woman's Health in 2003 in Austin, Texas as "a privately-owned, feminist organization committed to providing holistic care for women."[9] That holistic care includes abortion and comprehensive gynecological care provided in multiple clinics across the United States.[10] Annually, Whole Woman's Health serves over 30,000 patients.[11]

Whole Woman's Health is aware of the political and legal environment in which it operates. The Whole Woman's Health Alliance Stigma Relief Fund website observes that "[a]ccess to quality abortion care is under threat due to increasing numbers of restrictive laws being enacted by state legislatures."[12] Instead of directly prohibiting patient access to abortion services, "restrictive laws" such as "TRAP ('Targeted Regulation of Abortion Providers) laws" impose onerous legal require-ments on facilities and health care professionals that provide abortions with the ultimate aim to reduce or eliminate access to abortion.[13] Examples of TRAP laws include "regulations requiring certain building structures for facilities in

---

[6]   John A. Robertson, *Whole Woman's Health v. Hellerstedt and the Future of Abortion Regula-tion*, 7 U.C. IRVINE L. REV. 623 (2017).

[7]   Ziegler, *supra* note 2, at 78.

[8]   *See* discussion *infra* of "TRAP" laws, including H.B. 2. *See generally* Laurence H. Tribe, *The Abortion Funding Conundrum: Inalienable Rights, Affirmative Duties, and the Dilemma of Dependence*, 99 HARV. L. REV. 330 (1985) (discussing the impact of funding restrictions on the ability to exercise the right to an abortion). *See e.g.*, Alexa Garcia-Ditta, *Inside San Antonio's New $3 Million Abortion Facility*, TEXAS OBSERVER (Aug. 19, 2015), www.texasobserver.org/inside-san-antonios-new-3-million-abortion-facility/ (discussing the costs and changes required to comply with H.B. 2).

[9]   *About Us*, WHOLE WOMAN'S HEALTH, https://wholewomanshealth.com/about-us/ (last visited July 19, 2018).

[10] *See id.*

[11] *Id.*

[12] *The Stigma Relief Fund*, WHOLE WOMAN'S HEALTH ALLIANCE STIGMA RELIEF FUND, www.wholewomanshealthalliance.org/the-stigma-relief-fund/ (last visited July 19, 2018). *See also* discussion *infra* of TRAP laws.

[13] MELISSA MURRAY & KRISTEN LUKER, CASES ON REPRODUCTIVE RIGHTS AND JUSTICE at 789 (2015).

which abortions are performed, to onerous recordkeeping and reporting requirements, to requiring doctors who perform abortions to have admitting privileges at
local hospitals."[14]

One such TRAP law, enacted in 2013, was H.B. (House Bill) 2, which regulated
many Texas abortion providers, like Whole Woman's Health, to the point of
closure.[15] H.B. 2 required facilities providing abortions to conform to the same
minimum standards required of ambulatory surgical centers although many of those
ambulatory surgical centers were exempted from the law's requirements.[16] The law
also required any physician providing abortions to have "active admitting privileges
at a hospital that . . . is located not further than 30 miles from the location at which
the abortion is performed or induced."[17]

Rather than accept closure at the hands of the Texas legislature, Whole Woman's
Health and other health care providers litigated the constitutionality of H.B. 2 both
before and after the statute's effective date.[18] The litigation commenced after
H.B. 2's effective date ultimately reached the United States Supreme Court.[19] The
constitutional issues in Whole Woman's Health were whether the provisions of
H.B. 2 constituted an undue burden on a woman's right to an abortion in the state
of Texas, with a focus on the statute's "surgical-center" and "admitting privileges"
requirements.[20] Given the number of statutes in existence across the United States
that mirrored those at issue in the case, the Court's decision in Whole Woman's
Health would have far-reaching consequences.[21]

The Supreme Court rejected the surgical-center requirement because evidence
indicated that this requirement did not provide any health-related benefit to
patients.[22] Over time, the number of medication abortions as opposed to surgical
abortions in the United States has increased.[23] Medication abortions terminate a
pregnancy using pharmaceuticals instead of surgery.[24] In a world where medication
abortions are becoming increasingly prevalent, a surgical-center requirement would

---

[14] Id.

[15] Id. See also Whole Woman's Health v. Hellerstedt, supra note 1, at 2303, 2312.

[16] Id. at 2314–15 (citing Tex. Health & Safety Code Ann. § 245.010(a) (2015)).

[17] Id. at 2299 (citing Tex. Health & Safety Code § 171.0031(a) (2015)).

[18] Whole Woman's Health, supra note 1, at 2304–10 (discussing claim preclusion and litigation
    related to H.B. 2 both before and after the statute's effective date).

[19] Id.

[20] Id.

[21] Marcia Coyle, Whole Woman's Health v. Hellerstedt: What the Supreme Court Is Deciding in
    the Most Important Abortion Ruling in Decades (Updated), PBS (June 9, 2016), www.pbs
    .org/independentlens/blog/whole-womans-health-vs-hellerstedt-what-the-supreme-court-is-decid
    ing-in-most-important-abortion-ruling-in-decades/.

[22] Whole Woman's Health, supra note 1, at 2315.

[23] Karen Pazol, Andreea A. Creanga, and Suzanne B. Zane, Trends in Use of Medical Abortion in
    the United States: Reanalysis of Surveillance Data from the Centers for Disease Control and
    Prevention, 2001–2008, 86 CONTRACEPTION 746, 746 (2012).

[24] Medical Abortion, MAYO CLINIC (July 7, 2018), www.mayoclinic.org/tests-procedures/medical-
    abortion/about/pac-20394687.

be particularly inapplicable as complications resulting from a medication-induced abortion would typically occur after a patient left the facility.[25]

Moreover, the Court noted, H.B. 2 exempted from the surgical-center requirement other centers providing medical services with higher rates of risk and complications, like liposuction and colonoscopies.[26] Texas grandfathered in or granted waivers to "[t]wo-thirds of the facilities to which the surgical-center standards appl[ied]," but did not provide any exemptions to abortion providers, even though abortions are safer than other surgical procedures that occur outside of hospitals.[27] As a result, the Court concluded that the surgical-center requirement "provide[d] few, if any, health benefits for women, pose[d] a substantial obstacle to women seeking abortions, and constitute[d] an 'undue burden' on their constitutional right to do so."[28]

The Court's analysis of the admitting-privileges requirement led to a similar conclusion. Evidence indicated that the admitting-privileges requirement led to the closure of about half of the approximately forty facilities providing abortions in Texas, with eight of these clinics closing before the effective date of the admitting-privileges requirement.[29] Additionally, half of the clinics closed within seven months of the enforcement of H.B. 2's requirements.[30] Like the surgical center requirements, the admitting-privileges requirement provided no benefit to a woman's health.[31] Post-abortion complications present very similarly to miscarriages and can be managed by emergency room physicians, with specialist consultations as needed.[32] Therefore, both contested provisions of H.B. 2 were unconstitutional.[33]

The Court's ruling in favor of Whole Woman's Health and the other petitioners has been used to strike down or modify other statutes and regulations targeting abortion providers in other states.[34] Yet, the scope of a woman's right to an abortion in the United States is far from settled. Not only do anti-abortion activists continue to

[25] *Whole Woman's Health, supra* note 1, at 2315.

[26] *Id.*

[27] *Id.*

[28] *Id.* at 2318.

[29] *Id.* at 2312. *See generally* Daniel Grossman, *The Use of Public Health Evidence in Whole Woman's Health v. Hellerstedt*, 177 J. AM. MED. ASS'N I. MED. 155 (2016) (documenting the rates and impacts of clinic closures related to H.B. 2 in Texas).

[30] Sarah E. Baum, Kari White, Kristine Hopkins, Joseph E. Potter, and Daniel Grossman, *Women's Experience Obtaining Abortion Care in Texas after Implementation of Restrictive Abortion Laws: A Qualitative Study*, PLOS ONE (Oct. 26, 2016), http://journals.plos.org/plosone/article?id=10.1371/journal.pone.0165048.

[31] *Whole Woman's Health, supra* note 1, at 2311.

[32] John A. Robertson, *Science Disputes in Abortion Law*, 93 TEX. L. REV. 1849, 1873 (2015) (citing *Planned Parenthood of Greater Tex. Surgical Health Servs. v. Abbott*, 748 F.3d 583, 590 (5th Cir. 2014)).

[33] *Whole Woman's Health, supra* note 1, at 2318.

[34] *See e.g.*, Amy Hagstrom Miller, *A Year After Landmark SCOTUS Ruling Abortion Rights Are Still under Attack*, TIME INC. (June 27, 2017), http://time.com/4835000/whole-womans-health-abortion-rights-supreme-court-anniversary/.

create new statutes that target abortion providers in an effort to restrict the right to an abortion but, as noted by David Cohen, many hurdles continue to hinder women's exercise of their constitutional right.[35]

THE FEMINIST JUDGMENT

In his rewritten opinion, Cohen addresses numerous issues to which the Court gives short shrift in its abortion jurisprudence, in general, and in *Whole Woman's Health*, in particular. In keeping with the tenets of reproductive justice, Cohen expands the undue burden analysis of *Planned Parenthood v. Casey* by centering on the racial and economic aspects of the burdens imposed by H.B. 2 on women in Texas. The rewritten opinion brings the concerns of low-income women and women of color to the forefront of abortion jurisprudence. While the majority opinion referred to specific geographic areas such as Rio Grande, El Paso, and West Texas, the opinion did not consider the racial composition of those areas nor the economic character-istics of the women of reproductive age in those areas.[36] Further, insofar as *Whole Woman's Health* "put[] teeth" into the undue burden standard, *Cohen*'s opinion does the same to the Court's "independent constitutional duty to review factual findings where constitutional rights are at stake."[37]

Cohen's opinion is consistent with the Court's often-cited reliance upon "factual findings and research-based submissions" in its abortion jurisprudence.[38] Yet, as indicated by an analysis of both the underlying motivations for TRAP laws like H.B. 2 and the effects of TRAP laws on women of reproductive age, the Court's statement is not as strong in practice as it is on paper. The *Casey* undue burden test purportedly invalidates statutes that have the "purpose" of "plac[ing] a substantial obstacle in the path of a woman seeking an abortion before the fetus attains viability," but analyzing challenged legal restrictions reveals that many state legisla-tures enact TRAP laws with the explicit purpose of placing a substantial obstacle in the path of a woman seeking an abortion.[39] Nevertheless, the Court has upheld

---

[35] *Id.*

[36] *Whole Woman's Health, supra* note 1, at 2303.

[37] Ziegler, *supra* note 2, at 78; *Gonzales v. Carhart*, 550 U.S. 124, 165 (2007).

[38] *Whole Woman's Health, supra* note 1, at 2310 (citing *Planned Parenthood of Se. Pa. v. Casey*, 505 U.S. 833, 888–94 (1992)).

[39] *Casey*, 505 U.S. at 877. *See also* Richard H. Fallon, Jr., *Constitutionally Forbidden Legislative Intent*, 130 HARV. L. REV. 523 (2016) (discussing the role of intent in constitutional jurispru-dence); R. Alta Charo, *Whole Women's Victory – or Not?*, 375 N. ENG. J. MED. 809, 810 (2016); Linda Greenhouse and Reva Siegel, *The Difference a Whole Woman Makes*, 126 YALE L.J. FOR. 149, 153 (2016) ("Some of the laws that states enacted sought, like the measures in *Casey*, to dissuade women from acting on a decision to end a pregnancy). *Id.* ("The day after the Texas Senate approved the bill requiring providers to obtain admitting privileges and to outfit themselves as ambulatory surgical centers, then-Lieutenant Governor David Dewhurst tweeted a photo of a map that showed all of the abortion clinics that would close as a result of the bill. 'We fought to pass S.B. 5 thru the Senate last night, & this is why!'").

many of these post-*Roe* restrictions on the right to an abortion even though they are certainly substantial obstacles in effect (and purpose).[40] This is especially true, as Cohen illustrates, when combined with state efforts to reduce funding for family planning in general.

Cohen skillfully draws a complete picture of the interplay between TRAP laws and abortion funding restrictions, like the Hyde Amendment, which has restricted the use of Medicaid funds for abortion as part of every federal budget passed since 1976.[41] Representative Henry Hyde, remembered mostly for the amendment that bears his name, was clear that his goal was to end access to abortion.[42] He said, "I would certainly like to prevent, if I could legally, anybody having an abortion, a rich woman, a middle class woman, or a poor woman. Unfortunately, the only vehicle available is the [Medicaid] bill."[43] In *Harris v. McRae*, the Court upheld the constitutionality of this funding restriction.[44]

Unlike the majority opinion in *Whole Woman's Health*, Cohen's opinion recognizes the impact of the Hyde Amendment on low-income women, even though the Hyde Amendment was not at issue in Whole Woman's Health. As Cohen's opinion makes clear, the Hyde Amendment "places an extreme burden on low-income women and women of color" because it impedes access to the financial assistance that might be necessary for them to exercise their right to an abortion. Thus, the rewritten opinion shows that that H.B. 2, was part of a trend in which "states often pair [. . . anti-abortion laws] with other laws that impact women's reproductive and family lives."

Within the broader context of health law, Cohen's analysis focuses on several issues that experts emphasize when analyzing the U.S. health care system as a whole: the cost of health care, the quality of the services provided, access to health care, and choice.[45] Access and cost often combine in the reproductive justice sphere.[46] In the abortion context, access is a multifaceted concept and includes factors such as "accessibility (distance to clinics), availability (wait times for services, type of procedures offered), and affordability (out-of-pocket costs)."[47] As indicated by

---

[40] *See generally Casey*, 505 U.S. at 877 (providing the undue burden test). *See also* discussion *supra* and *infra* on the impacts of TRAP laws on the exercise of the right to an abortion.

[41] Cynthia Soohoo, *Hyde-Care for All: The Expansion of Abortion-Funding Restrictions under Health Care Reform*, 15 CUNY L. REV. 391, 392 (2012).

[42] Adam Clymer, *Former Rep. Henry Hyde Is Dead at 83*, N.Y. TIMES (Nov. 30, 2007), www.nytimes.com/2007/11/30/washington/29cnd-hyde.html.

[43] Soohoo, *supra* note 41, at 391.

[44] *See id.* at 392. *See also Harris v. McRae*, 448 U.S. 297, 318 (1980).

[45] BARRY R. FURROW, THOMAS GREANEY, SANDRA JOHNSON, TIMOTHY JOST, AND ROBERT SCHWARTZ, HEALTH LAW: CASES, MATERIALS AND PROBLEMS at 1–2 (7th ed. 2013).

[46] *Id.* at 1 ("Cost, quality, access, and choice are the chief concerns of the health care system . . ."). *See, e.g.*, n 47 *infra*.

[47] Caitlin Gerdts *et al.*, *Impact of Clinic Closures on Women Obtaining Abortion Services after Implementation of a Restrictive Law in Texas*, 106 AM. J. PUB. HEALTH 857, 858 (2016).

the rewritten opinion, these out-of-pocket costs are especially burdensome for indigent women due to the Hyde Amendment, even when they receive Medicaid.

Cohen foregrounds how laws like H.B.2 deprive low-income women of abortion access in ways that may not be readily apparent. For instance, as the record in *Whole Woman's Health* revealed, in the nineteen-month period before and after the enforcement of the admitting-privileges requirement of H.B. 2, the number of women of reproductive age living over 50, 150, and 200 miles from a clinic in Texas increased by 150 percent, over 350 percent, and 2,800 percent, respectively.[48] The Fifth Circuit Court of Appeals, which decided the case in 2015 before it reached the U.S. Supreme Court, found no undue burden in the face of this evidence that women would have to drive long distances and across state lines to obtain an abortion, thus approving Texas' argument that women whose local abortion providers closed could go to "nearby New Mexico" for services.[49]

The rewritten opinion emphasizes the arduous financial and logistical nature of a drive of over 100 miles for a woman seeking an abortion. Though Justice Ginsburg noted at oral argument that New Mexico did not have the same stringent admitting-privileges and surgical-center requirements for abortion providers as Texas did, Cohen's analysis is particularly poignant as it addresses the many challenges of seeking an abortion outside of one's geographic area.[50] Moreover, increased wait times correspond with later gestation periods in pregnancy. Waiting longer to have an abortion can ultimately cause some women who initially preferred a medication abortion to require a surgical abortion as the pharmaceuticals used for a medication abortion can usually only be taken up until the tenth week of a pregnancy.[51] For some women who face delays due to distance or financial need, it may be too late for a medication abortion by the time of their appointments, thus restricting patient choice.

FUTURE IMPLICATIONS

In an ideal world, Cohen's opinion would reduce future Supreme Court litigation related to TRAP laws as many existing TRAP laws, like H.B. 2, offer no benefits to women's health.[52] While *Whole Woman's Health* is seen as a victory for proponents of the right to an abortion in the United States, a favorable court decision is just the beginning as litigation has significant costs. For example, the Whole Woman's

---

[48] *Whole Woman's Health, supra* note 1, 2292, 2302 (2016).

[49] *Id.* at 2304.

[50] Transcript of Oral Argument at 37, *Whole Woman's Health*, 136 S. Ct. 2292 (No. 15-274).

[51] UC Davis Health Dep't of Obstetrics and Gynecology, Division of Family Planning, www.ucdmc.ucdavis.edu/obgyn/pdfs/Pt%20ed%20AB%20info%202014%2008-22.pdf (last visited June 18, 2018); *The Abortion Pill*, Planned Parenthood, www.plannedparenthood.org/learn/abortion/the-abortion-pill (last visited June 18, 2018).

[52] *See* discussion *supra* of H.B. 2's impacts on women's health.

Health Clinic in Austin that closed in 2014 as a result of H.B. 2 did not reopen again until April 2017 – approximately ten months after the U.S. Supreme Court's decision holding the contested provisions of H.B. 2 unconstitutional.[53] The first clinic to reopen in Texas reopened in Dallas in February 2017 – approximately eight months after the U.S. Supreme Court's June 2016 decision.[54] In spite of the legal victory, many women in Texas continued to face the restrictions caused by the closure of reproductive health care facilities even after the Supreme Court's decision.

The Cohen opinion lays the groundwork for an evolution in abortion jurisprudence. His opinion recognizes and incorporates the reality that since the 1970s, anti-abortion activists have targeted low-income women and women of color who are most impacted by laws that remove financial access to abortion and add legal restrictions that increase the financial and logistical costs of abortion. Also, for many years, amici in abortion cases have offered concrete evidence of the differential impacts of abortion restrictions on women based on their race and economic status; these differential impacts indicate that many women are essentially precluded from exercising their right to an abortion. Other rights, such as the right to counsel and the right to vote do not exist with similar financial restrictions, and Justice Cohen moves the impacts of this differential treatment of the right to an abortion to the forefront of the legal analysis of abortion regulation.[55]

By acknowledging that cost and access-based restrictions have a differential impact on low-income women of color, especially black women and Latinas, Cohen's evidence-based analysis lays the groundwork for overturning decisions like *Maher v. Roe* and *Harris v. McRae*, which is a possibility that he foreshadows in the second-to-last paragraph of the rewritten opinion.[56] Similarly, the role of cost in access to contraceptive care continues to resurface in Supreme Court decisions and analyses of the American health care system, with far less attention than that provided by Cohen.[57] Even in a post-Affordable Care Act America in which the government has sought to widen access to health care,[58] cost and access continue to

---

[53] Alexandra Sifferlin, *Texas Abortion Clinic at Center of Historic Supreme Court Decision Reopens*, Health, TIME INC. (Apr. 28, 2017), http://time.com/4759278/texas-abortion-clinic-whole-womans-health-supreme-court/.

[54] *Id.*

[55] Tribe, *supra* note 8, at 334 (1985).

[56] MARY ZIEGLER, AFTER ROE at 132 (2015) ("In *Maher v. Roe*, the Court upheld a Connecticut law authorizing Medicaid funding only for first-trimester abortions that were deemed 'medically necessary'").

[57] INST. OF MED., CLINICAL PREVENTIVE SERVICES FOR WOMEN: CLOSING THE GAPS 53 (2011) ("[s]tudies have demonstrated that even moderate copayments for preventive services such as mammograms and Pap smears deter patients from receiving those services"). This Institute of Medicine Report was also cited in the Brief for U.S. Department of Health and Human Services in *Burwell v. Hobby Lobby Stores*, 134 S. Ct. 2751, 2780 (citing Brief of Petitioner at 50).

[58] *See* HEALTHCARE.GOV, *Patient Protection and Affordable Care Act*, www.healthcare.gov/gloss ary/patient-protection-and-affordable-care-act/ (last visited June 18, 2018) (observing that the Patient Protection and Affordable Care Act is "[t]he first part of the comprehensive health care

be barriers for comprehensive health care, especially in the context of reproductive rights.[59]

In sum, Cohen's approach, in contrast to the majority of the U.S. Supreme Court, furthers the goals of reproductive justice by allowing women, regardless of race or income, to exert increased control over their reproductive lives and, in turn, to exert more control over the multiple other aspects of their lives directly impacted by their ability to make reproductive decisions.[60] Cohen provides the example of a woman identified as Ida, who "has ... a risk factor for cervical cancer ...," but "cannot afford to get a Pap test that doctors told her she needed every six months to check on her condition." Ida faced the following choices: "It's $60 for a checkup ... [e]ither I pay $60 or I buy food for my children ... Either I pay the rent and give my children a place to live, or I have a mammogram, a Pap test, or contraceptives. It's one or the other but not both." Ultimately, Cohen's approach would create a future in which women like Ida no longer face decisions such as deciding among housing, food, childcare, and preventive medical services such as a Pap test or face financial obstacles to their ability to exercise their constitutional right to an abortion.

Whole Woman's Health v. Hellerstedt, 136 S. Ct. 2292 (2016)

Justice David Cohen, concurring

I join the Court's opinion that the Texas abortion restrictions at issue in this case create an undue burden that violates the Due Process Clause of the Fourteenth Amendment. The admitting privileges and ambulatory surgical center requirements have no medical benefit; instead, they burden the women of Texas by making, for many women, access to their constitutionally protected right to choose to terminate their pregnancies almost non-existent. If this law does not violate the Constitution, then it is hard to imagine any law that does.

I write separately to highlight two important aspects of this case that we have almost completely ignored. First, anti-abortion laws have a differential impact on

reform law enacted on March 23, 2010 ... The law provides numerous rights and protections that make health coverage more fair and easy to understand, along with subsidies ... to make it more affordable"). *See also* 42 U.S.C. § 300gg-13 (2018).

[59] *See also* Haeyoun Park and Margot Sanger-Katz, *4 Ways Trump is Weakening Obamacare, Even After Repeal Plan's Failure*, N.Y. TIMES (Sept. 27, 2017), www.nytimes.com/interactive/2017/07/19/us/what-trump-can-do-to-let-obamacare-fail.html; Ariane de Vogue and Tami Luhby, *Trump Administration Tells Court it Won't Defend Key Provisions of the Affordable Care Act*, CNN (June 9, 2018, 6:03 AM), www.cnn.com/2018/06/07/politics/trump-admin-aca/index.html; Ashley Parker and Amy Goldstein, *Trump Signs Executive Order that Could Effectively Gut the Affordable Care Act's Individual Mandate*, WASH. POST (Jan. 20, 2017), www.washingtonpost.com/politics/trump-signs-executive-order-that-could-lift-affordable-care-acts-individual-mandate/2017/01/20/8c99e35e-df70-11e6-b2cf-b67fe3285cbc_story.html?noredirect=on&utm_term=.a794c895d30d.

[60] Kimberly M. Mutcherson, *Transformative Reproduction*, 16 J. GENDER, RACE, & JUST. 187, 194 (2013).

particular groups of women based on race, ethnicity, and class. In Texas, as in much of this country, the burden of anti-abortion restrictions falls disproportionately on women of color and indigent women. Today's opinion from the Court mandates that we focus on the burden of anti-abortion restrictions; however, we do a disservice to these women by ignoring how anti-abortion restrictions burden women in particular ways because of these identity characteristics.

Second, anti-abortion laws do not exist in a vacuum, as states often pair these restrictions with other laws that impact women's reproductive and family lives. Texas exemplifies this practice. The state tried to restrict abortion access, while simultaneously drastically cutting family planning funding. These cuts have a disproportionate effect on the same women affected by the abortion restrictions. In combination with the abortion restrictions they are even more insidious, as the combined effect of these two actions is a bald denial of all facets of the constitutional right of reproductive autonomy.

Only by highlighting the real impact of anti-abortion restrictions can we tell a complete story of the burdens at issue in this case. Future courts applying the doctrine derived from today's opinion should do the same.

I

The Court's opinion interprets the undue burden test from *Planned Parenthood v. Casey*, 505 U.S. 833 (1992), to require that "courts consider the burdens a law imposes on abortion access together with the benefits those laws confer." *Whole Woman's Health v. Hellerstedt*, 136 S. Ct. 2292, 2309 (2016). Though I would prefer we return to the days of strict scrutiny from *Roe v. Wade*, 410 U.S. 113 (1973), in a world in which *Casey* provides the governing legal standard, I fully endorse this clarification. When a law burdens a fundamental right without conferring the most serious of benefits to the state, the constitution requires us to strike the law down, as we do today.

In doing so, the section of the majority opinion focusing on the burdens imposed by H.B. 2, Texas's anti-abortion law at issue here, tells an important story. In the first part of the analysis, regarding the requirement that doctors performing abortions have admitting privileges at a local hospital, the opinion rightly explains that abortion providers have a difficult time obtaining admitting privileges, mainly because the procedure is so safe that abortion doctors do not send enough patients to hospitals each year. *Id*. at 2312–13. In Texas, this difficulty translates to almost half of the state's forty abortion clinics being unable to meet this requirement and thus having to close. *Id*. at 2313. With only about twenty clinics remaining in the state, women seeking an abortion are burdened by having fewer doctors, longer waiting times, increased crowding, and longer driving distances. *Id*. The opinion rightly concluded that, without any corresponding health benefit, these problems combine to create an unconstitutional undue burden. *Id*.

The imposition of the second part of H.B. 2 – that abortion clinics meet the rigorous but medically-unnecessary (for abortion) requirements of ambulatory surgical centers – would make things even worse. If implemented, this requirement would result in the entire state having only seven or eight abortion clinics (from forty before H.B. 2). *Id*. at 2316. With so few clinics for such a large state (both population-wise and geographically), the effects noted above would be amplified. Patients would have to travel even longer distances, clinics would struggle even harder to provide high quality of care, women's health would suffer, and the surviving clinics would have to spend large sums of money if they wanted to try to expand to meet demand. *Id*. at 2316–18. Without any health benefit to abortion patients, this part of H.B. 2 also fails the *Casey* test because of the extreme burdens on women's health. *Id*. at 2318.

There is nothing wrong with this analysis, and I join it in its entirety. H.B. 2 burdens too many people's constitutional rights without any medical justification whatsoever. This Court has no choice but to strike it down.

II

A

Nonetheless, I write separately because the majority opinion is incomplete and ignores important aspects of how we have framed this analysis in the past. It paints a picture of H.B. 2's burdens by describing how this law harms a generic Texas woman but stops there. While the overall impact of the law is important, it is equally – if not more – important to understand exactly which segments of Texas's population will suffer the most under H.B. 2. Only by doing so can we truly appreciate how unduly burdensome these abortion restrictions are.

H.B. 2 affects the state's different populations of women in distinct ways. For instance, African American women in Texas bear a disproportionate share of H.B. 2's burden because they use abortion services more than other populations. In 2013, the year before H.B. 2 took effect, African American women comprised just over thirteen percent of the population of Texas women of reproductive age but obtained just over twenty-five percent of the abortions in the state. Compare March of Dimes, Peristats, Population of Women 15–44 Years by Race/Ethnicity: Texas, 2013 with Texas Dep't of State Health Services, Induced Terminations of Pregnancy by County of Residence and Race Ethnicity Texas (2013) (15,719 out of 61,912 total abortions). There are many reasons for this disparity but one of the main reasons is that African American women in Texas disproportionately lack adequate access to sex education, contraception, and quality prenatal care. *See* Br. of Twelve Organizations Dedicated to the Fight for Reproductive Justice as Amici Curiae at 8–14 [hereinafter RJ Brief]. Because of this disparity, as a matter of simple numbers, the burdens described in the majority opinion fall heavier on African American women than others in Texas.

Some of the burdens discussed by the Court's opinion have more salience than others for African American women in Texas. African Americans are more likely to live in Texas's big cities, with sixty-five percent of the black population living in Houston or the Dallas/Fort Worth area. See Black Demographics, Texas, available at http://blackdemographics.com/states/texas/. Significant numbers of African Americans live in Austin and San Antonio as well. Id. These cities are locations where abortion providers have been able to continue operating despite H.B. 2, which means that, for most African American women in Texas, the problems related to travel are not going to be their biggest issue. Rather, because of the reduced number of clinics in those cities as well as the increased demand they will face because of closed clinics elsewhere in the state, African American women will struggle with the increased wait times and potential reduced quality of care at the clinics that remain in these urban centers. See Whole Woman's Health, 136 S. Ct. at 2313, 2318.

The burden this law places on African American women runs deeper than just limiting their ability to access safe quality abortion care but also extends to the entirety of reproductive health care. Many of the clinics that would be closed if this law were to take full effect provide other health services along with abortion care, such as care related to sexually transmitted diseases, contraception, pregnancy tests, abnormal Pap smear treatment, and education. RJ Brief, supra, at 23. For African American women, who are more likely to be uninsured in Texas than women generally, id. at 23–24, the closure of these clinics which offered low-cost or even free reproductive health services would be devastating beyond abortion care. In the words of Amici, H.B. 2 would, if allowed to take effect, "exacerbate African-American women's inferior access to reproductive health services and compound the myriad harms they already suffer as a result." Id. at 24.

Latinas in Texas face these problems as well, as many also live in urban areas and are uninsured but H.B. 2 presents Latinas with their own unique issues. Latinas live throughout Texas but are heavily concentrated in the Rio Grande Valley and El Paso areas. Pew Research Center, Mapping the Latino Population, by State, County and City, Appendix A1 (August 29, 2013). In fact, in the Rio Grande Valley, ninety percent of women of reproductive age are Latina. Br. of National Latina Institute for Reproductive Health et al. as Amici Curiae at 6 [hereinafter NLIRH Brief].

With this geographic distribution, Latinas in particular bear the brunt of H.B. 2's burdens as they affect women further away from the major metropolitan areas. The Rio Grande Valley and El Paso are isolated from the urban centers of Texas by hundreds of miles of barren land. It is these urban centers where abortion facilities would remain after H.B. 2's full implementation. As the district court in this case found, "women in the border communities of the Rio Grande Valley and El Paso will be affected most heavily due to longer travel distances (in some cases exceeding

500 miles), higher than-average poverty levels, and other issues uniquely associated with minority and immigrant populations." *Whole Woman's Health v. Lakey*, 46 F. Supp. 3d 673, 683 (W. D. Tex. 2014). Although the district court did not specifically connect this finding with race, given the population density of Latinas in the areas the court mentioned, it is impossible to deny that these burdens will fall heavily on the Latina population.

The issue of transportation deserves further attention. In the Fifth Circuit oral argument for this case, Judge Edith Jones belittled the notion that the long drive from the Rio Grande Valley would be a difficult one. She condescendingly asked the lawyers for the clinics, "Do you know how long that takes in Texas at 75 miles an hour? This is a peculiarly flat and not congested highway." Tara Culp-Ressler, *Judge to Texas Women: Living 150 Miles from an Abortion Clinic Is No Big Deal if You Drive Fast*, THINK PROGRESS (Jan. 7, 2014). This question shows a blatant disregard for the reality facing Latinas living in the Rio Grande Valley. As was documented extensively in the trial record, many parts of the Rio Grande Valley lack public transportation or other private transportation options (such as taxis or Uber), making it extremely difficult for the many Latinas in the Valley who do not own cars or have drivers' licenses to get to the cities to the north. NLIRH Brief at 8. For Latinas in the Valley who have cars, the price of gasoline for such a long trip can be prohibitive, or the fear of immigration checkpoints can prevent them from traveling. *Id.* at 9. Finally, even if a Latina in the Valley has a car, the money to pay for gasoline, and no fear of immigration agents, such a long trip poses problems with respect to taking time off work and finding childcare. *Id.* at 9–10.

In other words, Judge Jones' implication that all that separates the women of the Valley and El Paso from an abortion is a brief road trip is far from the truth. The closure of more than three-quarters of Texas's clinics would result in abortion becoming all but out of reach for Latinas in the Rio Grande Valley and Western Texas.

Without access to abortions in clinics, more Latinas will turn to self-induced abortions. Even before the law was implemented, Texas generally and Latinas in the state in particular had a higher rate of self-induced abortion than the rest of the country, partly because of easier access to abortion drugs across the Mexican border. Daniel Grossman, Kari White, Kristine Hopkins, and Joseph E. Potter, *The Public Health Threat of Anti-abortion Legislation*, 89 CONTRACEPTION 73 (2014). Forecasting what would happen if H.B. 2 were implemented, experts predicted that "[t]he confluence of extremely limited access to abortion in the context of poverty, access to misoprostol from Mexico, as well as familiarity with the practice of self-induction in Latin America, makes it particularly likely that self-induction will become more commonplace in Texas." *Id.* Evidence from this case indicates that these experts were correct, as the last remaining clinic in the Rio Grande Valley reported a significant increase in the number of women post-H.B. 2 who called the clinic looking for help after self-induction. NLIRH Brief at 14, 37–38.

Self-induced abortion is often safe and empowering for women, especially for those far from abortion clinics who want to control their reproductive lives on their own. However, safety usually requires sufficient support, including accurate information. Without this kind of support, women "may use ineffective dosages and may not realize the abortion failed until much later in pregnancy, forcing them to seek a second-trimester abortion or continue the pregnancy and have a child they do not want or feel they cannot care for." Grossman et al., *Public Health Threat*, supra, at 73–74. Even worse, women may try to use unsafe methods to self-induce. "One woman who called the McAllen clinic [when it had temporarily closed because of H.B. 2] said 'If you can't see me [for an appointment] then I can tell you what is underneath my kitchen and bathroom sinks, and you can tell me what I can take to abort'." NLIRH Brief at 38.

Intimately connected to the issues facing African American women and Latinas are the issues facing low-income women if H.B. 2 were to be fully implemented. While a first trimester abortion is not expensive compared to many medical procedures, for women living below or near the poverty level, the procedure is almost completely out of reach. An amicus brief submitted to us by the National Network of Abortion Funds does the math:

> A single woman earning 100 percent of the poverty line earns $980.83 per month. An average first-trimester abortion, without any ancillary costs, would consume nearly half a month of earnings. The average second-trimester abortion would consume a month and a half of earnings or more. Adding costs of travel, lodging, childcare and lost earnings, an abortion can easily consume a large percentage of the patient's earnings. Br. of Amici Curiae National Network of Abortion Funds et al. at 19 [hereinafter NNAF Brief]

For almost all other medical procedures that are financially out of reach, low-income women can use Medicaid to cover the cost of the procedure. However, in most states, including Texas, the Hyde Amendment prohibits low-income women from using Medicaid to pay for an abortion. *Bell v. Low Income Women of Tex.*, 95 S.W.3d 253, 266 (Tex. 2002) (approving the Hyde Amendment under the state constitution); *Harris v. McRae*, 448 U.S. 297 (1980) (approving the Hyde Amendment under the federal constitution). Thus, a low-income woman who wants to exercise her constitutional right to terminate her pregnancy is faced with a dilemma – pay for the procedure using funds that would have otherwise been used for shelter, clothing, food, and childcare or go without the abortion. Notably, this is exactly the reason Medicaid was enacted in the first place, to prevent low-income people from having to make this impossible choice between life necessities and health care

Yet, because of the Hyde Amendment, low-income women in Texas make this choice every day when it comes to abortion, something that places an extreme burden on low-income women and women of color. Heather D. Boonstra, *Abortion in the Lives of Women Struggling Financially: Why Insurance Coverage Matters*, 19 GUTTMACHER POLICY REV. 46 (2016); *Harris*, 448 U.S. at 344 (Marshall, J., dissenting) (concluding that the Hyde Amendment was "designed to deprive poor and minority women of the constitutional right to choose abortion"). If H.B. 2 were to be fully implemented and thus close more than three-quarters of the clinics in the state, low-income women in Texas would have an even more difficult time access-ing abortion. Increased travel distances will make obtaining the procedure even more expensive, putting it further out of reach financially; delays at the clinics because of the increased number of patients will make the cost of the abortion procedure itself go up; and ancillary costs such as childcare, lodging, and days off from work will increase. NNAF Brief, *supra*, at 8–17.

As the district court recognized, "[a] woman with means, the freedom and ability to travel, and the desire to obtain an abortion, will always be able to obtain one, in Texas or elsewhere." *Whole Woman's Health*, 46 F. Supp. 3d at 683. However, for women without these resources, H.B. 2 will make obtaining an abortion and exercising their constitutional right almost impossible.

There are other groups of women for whom H.B. 2 would make obtaining an abortion more difficult – undocumented immigrants, women experiencing domes-tic violence, women living in rural areas, and others – but the discussion here suffices to demonstrate the point of this concurrence. As powerful as the majority opinion is with respect to explaining how the undue burden test incorporates a weighing of the benefits against the burdens of any abortion restriction, it is incomplete in its assessment of the burdens because it fails to explain how the law impacts particular groups of women more severely than women as an undifferentiated whole.

B

This kind of detailed analysis about the people actually affected by an abortion restriction is not unprecedented in our abortion jurisprudence; however, we have more often ignored this evidence when brought to our attention.

Our best showing in this regard came in *Casey*, 505 U.S. 833 (1992). In that case, one of the provisions at issue required married women seeking an abortion to notify their spouse before doing so. *Id.* at 887. Instead of speaking broadly about how this law would affect all women, or even a bit more narrowly about how it would affect all married women, the joint opinion explained in detail how the law would impact a particular subset of women – those who are in a marriage plagued by domestic violence. *Id.* at 888–98.

This section of the opinion demonstrated a keen understanding of the plight of women dealing with domestic violence. The opinion quoted extensively from the district court findings in the case and told the story of how, for a particular group of women, this requirement was an immense burden. It included detailed information about the number of women and families affected by domestic violence, the forms that domestic violence can take, the reasons a woman might not want to inform her husband about her intention to have an abortion, the increased risk a woman faces when informing an abusive husband about her pregnancy, how common it is for women to engage in non-consensual sex with their abusive husbands in order to avoid being harmed, and the difficulties an abused woman would face in meeting any of the exceptions under the law. *Id.* at 888–91. The opinion then cited journal articles about the incidence of domestic violence, the forms it takes, and specific research about abortion and domestic violence. *Id.* at 891–93.

Taken together, this information convinced the authors of the joint opinion that, because of its effect on a particular segment of the population, the spousal notification provision was unconstitutional. The opinion concluded:

> In well-functioning marriages, spouses discuss important intimate decisions such as whether to bear a child. But there are millions of women in this country who are the victims of regular physical and psychological abuse at the hands of their husbands. Should these women become pregnant, they may have very good reasons for not wishing to inform their husbands of their decision to obtain an abortion ... The spousal notification requirement is thus likely to prevent a significant number of women from obtaining an abortion ... We must not blind ourselves to the fact that the significant number of women who fear for their safety and the safety of their children are likely to be deterred from procuring an abortion as surely as if the Commonwealth had outlawed abortion in all cases. *Id.* at 892–93.

As this analysis proves, this kind of detailed explanation of how abortion restrictions impact particular groups of people is essential to understanding the full scope of a constitutional violation. Had the *Casey* joint opinion not considered the specific problems associated with domestic violence and abortion, it might have allowed its general perception – that most married women discuss these issues with their husbands – to control its decision. If it had, it would likely have concluded that the spousal notification was an obstacle but not a substantial one.

Unfortunately, we failed to take this kind of a deep dive in our other major decisions about abortion over the past few decades, including in other sections of the *Casey* joint opinion itself. Making matters worse, we failed even though we had the relevant information directly in front of us. For instance, in *Casey*, though we struck down the spousal notification provision based on this kind of information, we upheld a Pennsylvania provision requiring every woman to wait twenty-four hours between initial counseling and having her abortion and a separate provision mandating that minors obtain the consent of a parent or appear before a judge to approve the abortion. *Id.* at 885–87.

Despite the detailed look at the specifics of how particular women would be affected by the spousal notice provision, the joint opinion barely scratched the surface of how these two provisions would affect particular groups of women in

Pennsylvania. In discussing the twenty-four-hour waiting period, the opinion explained that the district court had found that "for those women who have the fewest financial resources, those who must travel long distances, and those who have difficulty explaining their whereabouts to husbands, employers, or others, the 24–hour waiting period will be 'particularly burdensome'." *Id.* at 886. Nonetheless, the opinion noted that "[a] particular burden is not of necessity a substantial obstacle. Whether a burden falls on a particular group is a distinct inquiry from whether it is a substantial obstacle even as to the women in that group." *Id.* at 887. It concluded that "we are not convinced that the 24-hour waiting period constitutes an undue burden." *Id.* The opinion's analysis of the parental consent provision did not discuss any of these issues at all, instead relying completely on precedent. *Id.* at 899–900.

We missed a golden opportunity in those parts of the decision, an opportunity that had been spoon-fed to us. An amici curiae brief filed on behalf of some of the nation's leading civil rights organizations – such as the NAACP Legal Defense and Education Fund, Inc., the Asian American Legal Defense and Educational Fund, the Mexican American Legal Defense and Educational Fund, the National Black Women's Health Project, the Southern Poverty Law Center, and others – explained in detail how these restrictions would have a particularly devastating impact on poor women and women of color. Brief of Amici Curiae of the NAACP Legal Defense and Educational Fund, Inc., *et al.*, *Casey*, 505 U.S. 833 (1992). Generally, the brief explained in detail how "restrictions on the right to abortion fall most heavily on poor women because they are in a worse position to overcome barriers of cost, availability, or delay imposed or generated by the regulation of abortion." *Id.* at 18.

For the provisions the Court ultimately approved, the brief went into even more detail. It explained how long distances to travel to an abortion provider impact poor woman, especially if they must make multiple trips because of a twenty-four-hour waiting period. For instance, Amici wrote that the "24-hour delay may require duplicate journeys, overnight stays away from home, and two or more absences from work, often without pay, as well as added transportation expenses. For many poor women, the additional expense caused by the waiting period will be prohibitive." *Id.* at 22–23. The delay could lead to increased health risks, which would impact women of color in particular, as Amici note that they "disproportionately suffer from illnesses exacerbated by pregnancy, [and thus] will be most affected by significant delays in obtaining abortion services." *Id.* at 24.

The brief contained similar information about the parental consent provision. The brief told stories of young women who were harmed by parental consent requirements, including one young woman who died of an illegal abortion rather than telling her parents and another who was killed by her father when she told him about her pregnancy. *Id.* at 26. It also explained that, because adolescent women of color under 15 are almost twice as likely to have an abortion as white women adolescents of the same age, the requirement will hit them the hardest. *Id.* at 27.

Nonetheless, despite this information being presented to the Court, the joint opinion ignored how the Pennsylvania provisions fall much harder on poor women and women of color. Without considering this perspective, the Court blithely concluded that there was no substantial obstacle, a mistake that continues to harm women in Pennsylvania – and elsewhere – to this day.

Just three years before *Casey*, the Court made the same mistake in *Webster v. Reproductive Health Services*, 492 U.S. 490 (1989). That case involved several Missouri abortion restrictions, including a prohibition on the use of public employees and facilities in the performance of abortions and a definition of viability that required extensive medical testing on fetuses past 20 weeks. The Court upheld all of the provisions, *id.* at 522, but the bigger issue in the case was whether it would overrule *Roe v. Wade*. Only Justice Scalia wrote in favor of doing so, *id.* at 532 (Scalia, J., concurring), but the fact that *Roe*'s survival was at stake attracted almost eighty different amicus briefs.

One of the briefs, filed on behalf of over 100 civil rights, women's rights, labor rights, and religious organizations, squarely presented the Court with the issue of how overturning *Roe* generally and approving Missouri's regulations specifically would impact poor women and women of color. Referencing the harms from the pre-*Roe* period, the opening paragraph of the brief made this entirely clear:

> While women of all classes and colors will be endangered by any dismantling of the constitutional framework of *Roe v. Wade*, the burden will fall most heavily and inexorably on poor women, a vastly disproportionate number of whom are women of color – African-American, Latina, Native American and Asian. Women of color were over-represented among the women who died, were left sterile or suffered other serious medical complications as a result of illegal abortions prior to this Court's decision in *Roe v. Wade*, and would be similarly effected by its reversal. Brief Amici Curiae of the National Council of Negro Women, Inc., *et al.*, Webster, 492 U.S. 490 (1989), at 3–4 (footnotes and citations omitted)

The rest of the brief cataloged this impact in depth. First, the brief presented statistics about the number of poor women and women of color who died from illegal abortion before *Roe v. Wade*. *Id.* at 9–19. Then, the brief explained in detail how a more relaxed standard of review would impact poor women and women of color. The central position of the brief was that rejecting *Roe* and adopting a rational basis review standard would allow states to enact laws that would disproportionately affect already-disfavored groups of women, such as poor women and women of color. *Id.* at 23–61. As the brief summed up, these restrictions "would not save potential human life, but rather would force poor women and women of color to resort to illegal abortion with its resultant risks of death, maiming, trauma, and familial, social and economic disintegration." *Id.* at 36.

Nonetheless, the Court completely ignored this information. The various opinions from the Court failed to mention this particular consequence of overturning *Roe* and approving Missouri's regulations. Poor women and women of color were, as with the *Casey* opinion, completely ignored.

The same pattern surfaced in both of the cases that we decided about so-called "partial birth abortion" bans. *Stenberg v. Carhart*, 530 U.S. 914 (2000) (striking down Nebraska's ban); *Gonzales v. Carhart*, 550 U.S. 124 (2007) (reversing course and upholding the federal ban).

In neither case did the majority opinion mention anything about the impact that this type of procedure ban would have on poor women or women of color. Moreover, as with *Webster* and *Casey*, this oversight did not happen because the Court did not have the information before it. Rather, in both cases, advocates presented the Court with the relevant information only to be, once again, ignored. *See* Brief Amici Curiae of Seventy-Five Organizations Committed to Women's Equality, *Stenberg*, 530 U.S. 914 (2000), at 10–11 [hereinafter Stenberg Brief]; Brief Amici Curiae for the National Women's Law Center et al. Supporting Respondent, *Gonzales v. Carhart*, 550 U.S. 124 (2007), at 13–19. Both briefs forcefully state the central point of this concurring opinion: "Because the loss of access to legal abortion will most directly affect the most vulnerable women, this Court should look particularly searchingly at the statute in question." Stenberg Brief at 12.

The pattern here is clear. Other than this Court's one foray into explaining in detail how the spousal notification in *Casey* would affect women in an abusive relationship, we have, despite having clear evidence presented to us, ignored the stark reality of anti-abortion restrictions – that they affect poor women and women of color in disproportionate ways. My hope is that this concurring opinion is a small step in the direction of correcting these past wrongs.

III

Looking even deeper into Texas' actions, the Court should have also addressed the effect of the state's cuts to family planning services that pre-dated H.B. 2. These cuts have had a devastating impact on Texas women's overall reproductive health, including contraceptive care, cancer screening and treatment, sexually-transmitted disease care, and other care. Coupled with the abortion restrictions at issue here, Texas is showing a flagrant disregard for not just women's access to abortion but also for women's ability to control the entirety of their reproductive health and well-being.

It all started in 2011, when Texas severely cut its family planning budget. Over the course of two years, the state legislature cut a $111 million budget by two-thirds, to a total of $37.9 million. Kari White, Daniel Grossman, Kristine Hopkins, and Joseph E. Potter, *Cutting Family Planning in Texas*, 367 N. ENGLAND J. MED. 1179 (2012). These cuts were accompanied by a new disbursement system that prioritized giving funds to clinics that provided comprehensive primary care over clinics that provided only family planning services. *Id.*

At the same time, the state began on its path of prohibiting abortion providers from receiving state family planning funds. That year, the state prohibited organizations associated with abortion clinics, mainly Planned Parenthood clinics, from participating in one of the state's Medicaid programs designed to further women's health. Amanda J. Stevenson, Imelda M. Flores-Vazquez, Richard L. Allgeyer, Pete Schenkkan, and Joseph E. Potter, *Effect of Removal of Planned Parenthood from the Texas Women's Health Program*, 374 N. ENGLAND J. MED. 853, 854 (2016). After a legal challenge, this rule was ultimately implemented in 2013. *Id.* Because the state was now excluding an otherwise-qualified provider from its Medicaid program, the federal government ceased its payments to that program, which amounted to ninety percent of the reimbursements. *Id.*

The results of these cuts and restrictions were dramatic. As a result of the 2011 changes, eighty-two family planning clinics closed, which amounted to twenty-five percent of the entire state's clinics. Kari White *et al.*, *The Impact of Reproductive Health Legislation on Family Planning Clinic Services in Texas*, 105 AM. J. PUB. HEALTH 851, 853 (2015). At many of the clinics that remained open, service hours were cut drastically, with some reducing hours to just one or two days per week. *Id.* Many clinics reported long lines and wait times. *Id.* Clinic clients were forced to pay more for services because clinics could no longer offer reduced-rate or sliding-scale services. *Id.* at 854. Because of the financial hit the clinics took, they were no longer able to offer female sterilization or long-acting reversible contraception as widely as they had done before. In fact, the number of clinics in Texas offering this type of contraception decreased by twenty-five percent. *Id.* at 855. Overall, after these 2011 changes, these clinics saw a fifty-four percent decrease in clients served. *Id.*

When the Planned Parenthood restriction went into effect in 2013, the women of Texas felt the effects even more broadly. After this took effect, the number of women receiving long-acting reversible contraception declined even further in the state. Stevenson, *Effect of Removal, supra*, at 858. Even more concerning, it appears that women who are covered by Medicaid had more unintended pregnancies because they did not have the tools that would have allowed them to autonomously choose whether to get pregnant or not. The state saw a twenty-seven percent increase in the number of women covered by Medicaid who had children. *Id.* It is impossible to know whether the pregnancies were intended or not but as the researchers who studied the issue concluded, "it is likely that many of these pregnancies were unintended, since the rates of childbirth among these women increased in the counties that were affected by the exclusion and decreased in the rest of the state." *Id.*

Feeling the effect of both the 2011 and 2013 changes in Texas' funding for family planning, women in the state reported that they faced a large number of barriers to accessing this type of care. Among the barriers reported were not being able to pay for services, not feeling comfortable with the health care provider, being unable to get time off work or school, issues with their insurance company, lack of services where they live, difficulty finding childcare or transportation, being unable to speak the language of the service provider, and not having family support. Texas Policy Evaluation Project, Research Brief: Barriers to Family Planning Access in Texas: Evidence From a Statewide Representative Survey (2015), http://liberalarts.utexas .edu/txpep/_files/pdf/TxPEP-ResearchBrief_Barriers-to-Family-Planning-Access-in-Texas_May2015.pdf. Women also reported using less effective methods of contraception and missing return appointments for the continued effectiveness of other methods of contraception. C. Junda Woo, Hasanat Alamgir, and Joseph E. Potter, *Women's Experiences after Planned Parenthood's Exclusion from a Family Planning Program in Texas*, 93 CONTRACEPTION 298 (2016). These barriers were felt most acutely by Texas's indigent and Spanish-speaking populations. Texas Policy Evaluation Project, *supra*. This same population also reported that they were less likely to be using their preferred method of birth control because of these barriers. *Id.*

A 2013 report from the Center for Reproductive Rights and the National Latina Institute for Reproductive Health shines the spotlight on how these cuts affected the state's Latina population in particular. Center for Reproductive Rights & National Latina Institute for Reproductive Health, Nuestra Voz, Nuestra Salud, Nuestro Texas: The Fight for Women's Reproductive Health in the Rio Grande Valley (2013) [hereinafter Nuestra Voz]. The report focuses on the Lower Rio Grande Valley, one of the poorest regions of the country. The region's 1.3 million people are overwhelmingly Latino, with one-third of the people there living in poverty. *Id.* at 14.

Even before the cuts, health care access was difficult for Latinas in this region of Texas. Texan Latinas had worse health measures than other Texan women on a range of outcomes – diabetes, cardiovascular disease, obesity, and cancer. *Id.* However, reproductive health care was one of the areas where Latinas in the region were faring better. As the report explains:

> The Valley's women – rural, Latina, immigrant, uninsured, and poor – are largely unable to afford private health care. Consequently, they tend to forgo preventive care and seek medical attention only in emergencies. Until recent policy changes, a notable exception was family planning services; this population did access women's preventive care such as Pap tests, breast exams, contraceptive services and counseling, and testing for sexually transmitted infections from clinics providing such care at low or no cost. *Id.* at 15.

Nonetheless, reproductive health outcomes for Latinas in Texas were not perfect. Unintended pregnancy rates were high, cervical cancer was more prevalent than among other populations, and contraception use was low. *Id.* at 15–16.

With Latinas in this region already struggling, Texas made the situation much worse with its cuts in 2011 and 2013. As a result of the cuts, twenty-eight percent of the family planning clinics in the region closed, and many others reduced their services.

Id. at 6. For Latinas in the region, the closures and reduction in services crippled access to care. "[T]hey have lost care from providers they had long trusted to serve the needs of a largely immigrant, Spanish-speaking community." *Id.* at 7. With this loss came an increase in waiting times at clinics, delays in care, and longer travel to access care. *Id.* at 7–8. Costs increased at the clinics that remained, and free services that previously existed were replaced by higher priced private care. *Id.* at 7. Latinas in the region were forced to go without contraception, ultrasounds, mammograms, Pap tests, breast exams, and follow-up care. *Id.* Undocumented Latinas were hit particularly hard, as they lost trusted providers and now faced the difficult choice between traveling to an unfamiliar clinic, at risk of their status being exposed by unsympathetic health care workers or immigration patrols outside their home town or foregoing medical care altogether. *Id.* Some Latinas even resorted to the black market, purchasing supplies from across the border in Mexico. *Id.* at 8. For some, this helped fill the gap created by Texas' slashing of family planning funds but, for others, it meant women using goods that were "ineffective, inappropriate to women's individual health care needs, more likely to be used incorrectly because women do not receive proper instructions, and, in some case, dangerous to women's health." *Id.*

One of the women profiled in the report exemplifies the situation for Latinas in the region trying to access reproductive health care. Identified only by her first name, Ida's story is repeated in full here:

> Ida from Donna described her situation as "desperate" because her supply of contraception was about to run out in one week's time. She was given a year's supply from a Planned Parenthood health center before it closed, but once her current supplies ran out, she knew she would not be able to afford more. Ida supports her two children on her own. "Right now I'm not prepared for another child … my financial situation is rough, pretty rough … I don't know how to get more pills because they charge for them now, they have no funds for that, no one does now." Ida also has human papillomavirus (HPV), a risk factor for cervical cancer, and has had surgery to remove cervical cysts in the past. Now, she cannot afford to get a Pap test that doctors told her she needed every six months to check on her condition. "It's $60 for a checkup. I thought, either I pay $60 or I buy food for my children … Sometimes I don't have money for milk, food, other things … Either I pay the rent and give my children a place to live, or I have a mammogram, a Pap test, or contraceptives. It's one or the other, but not both." She would like to go to Mexico for health care but is not legally permitted to cross the border on her temporary permit. "Being unable to see a doctor has me worried sick. I'm so afraid of the virus coming back. Last time it wasn't cancerous, but I'm afraid that if it does come back it will be worse, because I'm not having regular checkups." *Id.* at 25.

Ida's story illustrates just how seriously Texas, both in passing the abortion restrictions at issue here and in almost simultaneously and drastically cutting family planning funding, has infringed upon constitutional rights. The right identified in

Roe and *Casey* and given depth by the majority opinion in this case can be called, in its specific form, the right to terminate a pregnancy. *See Roe*, 410 U.S. at 715 (protecting the right "to choose to terminate her pregnancy"); *Casey*, 505 U.S. at 871 (protecting the right "to terminate her pregnancy before viability"). However, that right is not an isolated one, as it stems from a more general right of procreative autonomy – the right to determine when and if you are going to have a child – that we recognized in *Skinner v. Oklahoma*, 316 U.S. 535, 541 (1942) (stating that "procreation [is] fundamental to the very existence and survival of the race"), *Griswold v. Connecticut*, 381 U.S. 479, 484–86 (1965) (protecting the right of married couples to use contraception), and *Eisenstadt v. Baird*, 405 U.S. 438, 453 (1972) (protecting "the decision whether to bear or beget a child"). But even this broader right is part of a more general constitutionally protected right of familial autonomy and privacy – the right to be in control of your family and not to have the government interfere with your decisions to that effect. We recognized this general right in, among others, *Meyer v. Nebraska*, 262 U.S. 390, 400 (1923) (recognizing the right to control a child's education), *Pierce v. Society of Sisters*, 268 U.S. 510, 534–35 (1925) (protecting the "liberty of parents and guardians to direct the upbringing and education of children under their control"), *Moore v. East Cleveland*, 431 U.S. 494, 499 (1977) (protecting decisions about "family living arrangements"), and *Troxel v. Granville*, 530 U.S. 57, 65 (2000) (plurality decision recognizing liberty interest in "the interest of parents in the care, custody, and control of their children").

Ida's situation implicates all of these rights. She is trying to parent the two children she already has but the family planning cuts place her in the difficult position of choosing between rent and food for her family and her Pap test. She wants to keep the size of her family at three for the time being but the state of Texas is trying to force abstinence on her because she cannot afford contraception now that the Planned Parenthood near her has closed. If she chooses to be sexually active and becomes pregnant as a result of not having access to contraception, she will have a hard time accessing an abortion clinic because of the few that would remain in her region as well as the entire state.

In other words, through its actions in cutting family planning funding and closing abortion clinics, the state of Texas is telling Ida, and everyone like her, that she is no longer in control of her reproduction and family. She cannot control whether to have a child nor is she in control of parenting the children she already has. Only by recognizing Texas's two-prong attack – on abortion and family planning – can we truly appreciate the extent to which the state has denied Texas women their constitutional rights.

Today's majority opinion forcefully and correctly concludes that H.B. 2 is unconstitutional, and I join that decision in full. However, without noting the particular ways in which Texas's law targets women of color and poor women, as well as how it works in conjunction with the state's attacks on family planning funding to limit women's ability to choose how and when to parent, the opinion is incomplete.

The kind of analysis undertaken in this separate opinion is essential to fully assess the burden part of the balancing test the Court applies today. With this more complete assessment of a law's effects, this Court should in the future re-consider many of the abortion restrictions it has previously approved. Waiting periods, bans on specific procedures, special processes for minors, excessive and biased informed consent protocols, public and private insurance bans on funding abortions, and all other abortion restrictions share the reality elucidated here – they burden all women but particularly burden certain groups of women, almost always women of color and poor women. When we conduct this kind of detailed analysis in the future, I expect these restrictions will be struck down as unconstitutional, like H.B. 2 today.

But those are issues for another day. For now, I hope merely that future opinions from this Court and others take heed of these matters in assessing other states' actions that implicate these important constitutional rights.

Index